RAILWAYS ON THE SCREEN

John Huntley

IAN ALLAN Publishing

First published 1993

ISBN 0 7110 2059 0

© John Huntley 1993

Published by Ian Allan Ltd, Shepperton, Surrey; and printed in
Great Britain by Ian Allan Printing Ltd, Coombelands House,
Addlestone, Surrey KT15 1HY

Front cover:

Overall: **A camera and cameraman
literally 'tied' to the front of a
locomotive.**

Inset: **Scenes from two
programmes shot on the Bluebell
Railway.** *Both: M. T. Blackburn*

Back cover:

Left: **John Huntley amongst the
archives.**

Right, top to bottom: **Poster from
'Brief Encounter'. Still from
'Murder on the Orient Express'.
'Steam and the Dragon' video
cover from Railfilms.**

 Each entry in the index of films has a number of
symbols to indicate the proportion of railway
content in the programme.

Availability

The various items may be available
in film form as indicated (35mm or
16mm or 8mm).

Some films are available in silent
or sound versions.

Many films are available on video
and the number is increasing all the
time. Films available in this form are
marked VID.

Some films are available as reference prints only for study purposes
and do not imply copyright ownership. This applies to many films
from the British Film Institute; specialist archive collections are
marked to the appropriate source,
eg. HA (Huntley Archives), TUA,
IOW (Isle of Wight Film Archive),
etc.

Film and Video Abbreviations

125	Video 125 (Peter Middleton)
ABP	Associated British Picture Corporation
AFI	American Film Institute
AG	Allan Garraway
ARPS	Assocation of Railway Preservation Socieites
AW	Alan Willmott (Windjammer Films)
BFI	British Film Institute
BG	Bob Godfrey
BJ	A. Barrett Jenkins
BLV	Branch Line Video
BRV	B&R Video Productions
BTF	British Transport Films Video
CFF	Children's Film Foundation
CJB	CJ Barnard, Folkestone
COI	Central Office of Information
CCV	C&C Video
CV	Colour Views, Birmingham (Patrick Whitehouse and John Adams)
DC	David Cleveland
DH	Derek Henderson
DSB	German Railways
DSR	Danish Railways
EAR	East African and Harbours Board
ELV	Electra Films Video
ETV	Educational and Television Films
FEST	Festiniog Railway Society
FSE	Flying Scotsman Enterprises
GHV	Goodheart Video
GWP	Graham Whistler Photography
HA	Huntley Archive
HB	Harold Bain
IOW	Isle of Wight Film Archive
IV	Ivor Gotheridge
IWM	Imperial War Museum
JCV	John Cocking Video
JMC	Jumpcut Video
JP	John Payne
MFB	Monthly Film Bulletin
MFS	Meteor Film Service (Geoff Holyoake)
NFA	National Film Archive
NLV	Nick Lera Film and Video
NRM	National Railway Museum
ONL	OnLine Video
PFB	Petroleum Film Bureau
PJ	Philip Jenkinson Collection
P&S	Pictures and Sounds
PSO	Preserved Steam on Video
RDV	Rands Video
RFV	Railfilms Video
RFW	Ray Freeman Video
RSV	Railscene Video
RVO	Rail Video
RVV	RV Television Video
SCTS	Southern Counties Touring Society
SFC	Scottish Film Council
SFR	Swiss Railways
SFV	Salford Films Video
SLV	Sight Lines Video
SNCB	Belgian Railways
SNCF	French Railways
SPV	Steam Powered Video
SRV	Steam Reflections Video
STV	Sutcliffe TV Steam Video
TCF	20th Century Fox Films
TH	Tim Hall
TM	Tom Martin Collection
TUA	Tua films (Rob Foxon)
TVP	Transport Video Publishing
TW	Trevor White
UIC	International Railway Film Bureau
VLV	Videolines Video
VT	Vic Thompson
WW	Wilf Watters
NA	Not Available. This may indicate that the film has been lost, the negative destroyed or the company which made the film is no longer in business.

Introduction

When *Railways in the Cinema* was first published by Ian Allan over twenty years ago, life was relatively simple. Films were available only in the cinema or on television. They were transient things viewed once or twice and then existing only in the memory. Film shows based on archive footage were a rarity, seen only at the National Film Theatre, the Royal Festival Hall or on club evenings with such as Ivo Peters or Cam Camwell. In order to view railway films at home it was necessary to set up a screen, pull down the blinds and thread up a rather complicated projector.

The introduction of home video equipment, both to record and play back, transformed the entire situation. Films and TV programmes can now be viewed at an instant's notice; a vast new industry has sprung up and dominates page after page of railway magazine advertising. Enthusiasts document events on their own video cameras and play back the results that night. We are in a world of audio visual production of a scale never before dreamed possible. Things progress so rapidly that no book – and not many magazines – can hope to keep up to date. So this record comprises the material originally assembled in 1969, with the addition of newly-researched archive films, a cross-section of the more important feature films since then that have involved railway scenes, and extensive coverage of the first era of the Video.

I think you will be surprised at the number of VID symbols in the listings. Even relatively obscure feature films are now freely available almost hourly on TV. Video has enjoyed its first great boom and is now settling down to become no longer a novelty, but a standard part of the railway scene. It is time to take stock.

There is no doubt that the index section was the most prized part of the original book, so this edition devotes most of its content to a detailed listing of both feature films and videos, incorporating some of the original text into the listings in alphabetical order. In some cases, video availability may have come about since this book was published; it's always worth a check on your favourite item. Equally, all the specialist video companies regularly make additions to and deletions from their lists. Every effort has been made to include accurate information but once again it is important to check with the producers.

Many people have helped with this book; amongst them are Ian Allan, Simon Forty, Alan Butcher and Peter Waller (Ian Allan Ltd); Geoffrey Kitchenside; Trevor Bailey; R. C. Riley; Dennis Bentley; Edgar Anstey; Charles Potter; Don Saunders; Alan Willmott; Patrick Whitehouse; John Adams; Bob Ennis; Amanda Huntley; Tom Martin; and all those lovely people who used to ring up and say 'Did you see that "Schools" class shot in that old 1930s film on TV this morning at 9.50am!'

I have drawn on various sources, notably the articles 'Railways on the Screen' and 'Railways and Photography' by David Gunston; the notes for the Channel Four series 'Going Loco'; individual books on the history of many an obscure railway as well as documentation by such folk as Jim Palm ('Titfield Thunderbolt') and others who are credited under the individual entries. Thanks to the publishers for permission to reproduce quotations from the 'Night Mail' verse by W. H. Auden; Fawcett Books for the notes on American railroad history and other publications as recorded. All photographs in the book are taken from my own or the publisher's collection with additional credits as shown in the captions. The publishers and myself will be pleased to correct any errors or omissions in the credits and apologize for any that may exist.

As I am principally a film man with railway interests, there may be items of railway history (or, alas, corrections!) which those with specialist interests may be able to add to this book. If so, I shall always be glad to hear from you through the publishers at Shepperton.

John Huntley

An Outline History of Railways on Film

It is now generally accepted that the world's first railway scene was taken, in July 1895, at La Ciotat, a small seaside country station on a branch line from Marseilles on the old PLM Railway. Other attempts had been made beforehand, like the Edison Kinetoscope film 'Black Diamond Express' but this was not a true film for it was not intended for projection to an audience in the modern sense. 'The Arrival of a Train at La Ciotat Station' was first shown in the salon of the Grand Café on the Boulevard de Capucines in Paris on 28 December 1895. It was an immediate success and went round the world, often under the false title 'Arrival of the Paris Express'. It was made by the Lumière Brothers of Lyons and features a nice three-quarter view of a PLM Bourbonnais class. It set the scene for many imitations. In May 1896, George Albert Smith, portrait photographer of Brighton, filmed the arrival of the London Express hauled by a Gladstone class locomotive at Hove station on the LBSCR. That same month Robert Paul, of Muswell Hill, filmed 'GNR Trains at Wood Green', featuring locomotives of the Great Northern Railway hauling five and six coach expresses, ending with a nice view of a North London 4-4-0 Tank on a local suburban train of 4-wheel coaches on its way to High Barnet. Other scenes of this type in the early days of the cinema include 'Train Entering East Berlin Station' (1896); 'Train Leaving Jerusalem Station' (1896); 'Train on a Level Crossing at Joinville-le-Pont' (1896) and a later cinema version of 'Black Diamond Express' (1897).

The next stage was the short-lived series of 'Phantom Rides', an idea taken up in the video era as 'Cab Rides'. One of the most important was 'Railway Ride Over the Tay Bridge' (1897), giving two views of Wheatley NBR 'P' class 2-4-0 locomotives passing on the up track. We glide across the whole bridge span, from Wormit to Dundee, and we are even provided with a fine view of the locomotive sheds north of Tay Bridge station. Other survivors include a 'Phantom Ride taken from the Buffers of an Engine' from Ilfracombe to Barnstaple on the LSWR with a view of the single line bridge over the River Taw, the abandoned Barnstaple Town Station, the then new Barnstaple Town Station some hundred yards further on and a fine collection of Adams locomotives and stock in the yard at Ilfracombe (1898); 'Down Exeter Incline' showing the LSWR from Queen Street Station, through Exeter Tunnel and on to the GWR Station at Exeter St. Davids (1896); 'View From an Engine Front' with Shilla Mill Tunnel on the LSWR main line (1900).

Foreign items include 'Panorama Pris D'Une Train en Marche' (1896) and 'Phantom Ride: Chamonix' (1898). There was also 'Hale's Tours' a railway carriage on springs surrounded by a giant cinema screen of passing scenery from a train ('Trip Through the Rocky Mountains' was typical) which came from America.

Below:
A scene from the first ever railway film - the 'Arrival of a Train at La Ciotat' - as shot by Lumière in July 1895.

The following era was that of the story film, starting with 'Romance of a Railway' (1902) on the Delaware, Lackawanna & Western Railroad, a publicity film for smokeless fuels on railways and featuring Phoebe Snow. It was made by Edwin S. Porter for the Edison Company and was immediately followed by 'The Great Train Robbery' (1903) also made on the DL&WR, both featuring a number of typical American 4-4-0s of the turn of the century. They spawned literally hundreds of short story films featuring railways including 'The Lonedale Operator' (1911) on the AT&SF, directed by D. W. Griffith; 'The Switch Tower' (1913); 'The Attempt on the Special' (1911); 'Between Orton Junction and Fallonville' (1913); and 119 episodes of 'The Hazards of Helen' (1914-1917) nearly all on the AT&SF at locations like Cajon Pass, San Bernadino and Silverton, all in California.

British examples of the story film started early with 'Kiss in the Tunnel' (1898), one version on the LSWR made by George Albert Smith and another featuring Queensberry Tunnel on the GNR and the arrival of a Midland Johnson locomotive and train at Monsal Dale station, made by the Banforth Company of Holmfirth. 'When the Devil Drives' (1907) made by Robert Paul for Charles Urban has scenes on the LNWR at Llandudno, including rare shots of a 2-2-2-2 and some early Bassett-Lowke gauge O models. 'Lieutenant Daring and the Plans of the Minefield' (1913) has good scenes of SE&CR 'F1' 4-4-0 at Charing Cross and Wainwright

Class D 4-4-0 No 729 on the run to Folkestone. In America, 'The Wreck' (1914) used a specially-staged railway crash between two old 4-4-0s as part of the story. Many more followed.

Next came the 'Industrials', a series of films featuring many manufacturing processes that fascinated audiences in pre-TV days, many of them made by Charles Urban and his company 'Kineto'. Two classic examples are 'Building a Locomotive at Crewe' (1911) featuring a Webb compound, LNWR 0-6-0s and the first appearance of Crewe's locomotive No 5000 *Coronation*, a 'George' class 4-4-0; and 'Building a Locomotive at Swindon' (1912) showing all the stages on the construction of Churchward GWR Starclass 4-6-0 No 4041 *Prince of Wales*.

All the films described above were short, the longest being 30 minutes, with many only 10 minutes long. As we move forward to the Twenties, full-length feature films began to appear. First came the John Ford classic 'The Iron Horse' (1924), the story of the building of the Intercontinental line across America featuring the Union Pacific and Santa Fe in particular and using some superb preserved Union Pacific locomotives. The last spike was driven on 10 May 1869 with two grand old locomotives (Union Pacific coal-burning No 119 and

Left:
Buster Keaton in a characteristically graceful and melancholic pose taken from 'Go West' (1925).

Left, below:
A photo taken during the filming of a 1920s melodrama. Note the crowds at the far end of the bridge watching the stunt from out of shot.

Central Pacific wood-burning *Jupiter)* very accurately reproduced. The success of 'The Iron Horse' led to a whole series of railroad melodramas including 'The Overland Limited' (1925), and 'The Block Signal' (1926).

It was a tradition in American cinema of the Twenties that successful feature films always inspired comedy imitations, First of many to follow 'The Iron Horse' was 'The Iron Mule' (1925) featuring an amazingly accurate reproduction of the De Witt Clinton 0-2-2 locomotive and train of pioneer American days named *The Twenty Cent Limited* running on the 1830 Likskillet and Sassatras line; all this for a one-reel short film featuring Al St John. In 1927 came a feature-length masterpiece, Buster Keaton's classic 'The General'. This was a comedy version of a real incident in the American Civil War, later to be made into a straight drama as 'The Great Locomotive Chase' (1956), in which a group of Federal spies stole a complete train from the Confederates and were chased for many miles before being forced to abandon their engine and flee to the woods. For his film, Buster Keaton acquired 46 miles of lumbercamp railroad, six locomotives of virtually the same vintage as the original Western and Atlantic Railroad's *The General* (now preserved at Chattanooga) and a great collection of vintage stock. In the making of the film two of the locomotives were destroyed, one by design and the other by accident!

In France, Abel Gance produced another railway classic of the silent screen 'La Roue' (1919-1923) made in the Nice railway yards with extensive assistance from PLM. Scenes in the snow were recorded at Chamonix and on a funicular railway of the Grand Moulais area. In Germany there was the magnificent railway opening sequence in 'Berlin' (1927), and also a spectacular crash in the 'Nord Express' in Fritz Lang's feature 'Spione' (1927). Russia produced 'Turksib', a dramatised account of the building of the Turkestan-Siberian railway (Victor Turin, 1929).

Two main films mark the end of the silent railway film in Britain. The first was the very detailed recording of the Darlington Centenary Celebrations of 1925, produced by Debenhams of York and running in its original form for 30 minutes. The first part covers the visit to the area by the Duke and Duchess of York (later King George VI and Queen Elizabeth) including the opening of a hospital extension and a tour of the Centenary Exhibition. The second part features the Grand Parade of 23 July 1925 including such locomotives as 'Derwent' (Stockton Darlington Railway, 1847), 'Aerolite' (NER, 1869), Gresley Pacific 'Tagalie' (1925), Gresley-Garratt double engine 2395 (1925) and George Stephenson's 'Locomotion' of 1825. These were the early days of the 'Big Four' and the parade ended with a representative train from each of the new companies.

The feature film was represented by 'The Wrecker' (1929), based on a stage play by Arnold Ridley and featuring a spectacular real crash in which a Stirling SECR 4-4-0 No 148 and a set of eight-wheel coaches collided at speed with a Foden steam lorry full of ballast at Spains Crossing near Herriard on the now abandoned LSWR Basingstoke-Alton light railway.

As 'The Wrecker' was being completed in 1929, the 'Talkies' arrived and the silent film era came to an end. 'The Wrecker' was issued in a half-sound version and another railway film then being made at Elstree was hastily switched to a talkie. In the case of 'The Flying Scotsman' (1930), the first thirty minutes are silent with music and titles to explain the dialogue; after which, for no apparent reason, everyone suddenly starts to talk! Starring a then unknown Ray Milland as the fireman, and Moore Marriott as the engine driver, the film features LNER Gresley Pacific class 4472 *Flying Scotsman* throughout. There are no models, no trick effects or back projection scenes, every single shot used the 1922-1933 *Flying Scotsman* in its original form with right-hand drive. Castleton Knight, the producer, managed to get exclusive use of 4472 for six weeks to make the film, with excellent coverage of the whole run from Kings Cross to Edinburgh non-stop (a service that started in 1928 and partly inspired the film). The detailed scenes of the corridor through the tender and the near-crash as the train divides from the locomotive were filmed on four Sunday mornings on the Hertford Loop in the area of Cuffley, Stapleford Signal box and Hertford North. A classic and very real stunt scene in which Alec Harley and Pauline Johnson go out on the running boards of the *Flying Scotsman* train was also filmed on the Hertford Loop. A mis-calculation over tunnel clearances in Ponsbourne Tunnel nearly killed the cameraman and the director; a similar mistake over a platform clearance at Crews Hill could easily have killed or seriously injured Ray Milland and cut short a brilliant Hollywood career.

'The Ghost Train', also from a play by Arnold Ridley is one of the great 'lost' films. Originally made as a silent film in 1927, it was remade as a talkie in 1931 with Jack Hulbert and Cicely Courtneidge with material shot at Paddington, on Barmouth Viaduct and the Limpley Stoke – Camerton branch of the GWR. Only a few photographs survive of these two important productions, although the third film version with Arthur Askey, made in 1941, is often shown on television. Unfortunately, it contains hardly any authentic railway scenes and was almost entirely shot in the Gainsborough Studios at Shepherds Bush. Real railway stations were not available to film companies during World War 2!

There were two great railway enthusiasts in the film world who helped to produce many transport-orientated pictures in Britain. One was the producer Michael Balcon, responsible for 'The Wrecker' (1929), 'The Ghost Train' (1931), 'Rome Express' (1932) and 'Seven Sisters' (1936) which used a lot of material from 'The Wrecker'. He also produced 'Bulldog Jack' (1935), 'Oh! Mr Porter' (1937), 'Train of Events' (1949) and 'The Titfield Thunderbolt' (1952). Alfred Hitchcock, the other keen railway man, used a Greenline coach and the LNER run to the Night Train Ferry as a theme for the finale of 'Number Seventeen' (1932); a scene with the

Flying Scotsman on the Forth Bridge in 'The Thirty Nine Steps' (1935); a railway crash in 'Secret Agent' (1936); a journey across Europe by train in 'The Lady Vanishes' (1938); an American journey in 'Strangers on a Train' (1951) and countless other railway scenes in many of his Hollywood feature films like 'Shadow of a Doubt' (1943) and the famous symbolic 'Train into a Tunnel'.

The inspiration of Balcon and Hitchcock spread far and wide in the Thirties. 'The Last Journey' (1936), directed by Bernard Vorhaus and shot extensively on the GWR has become a classic. Available on video, it is often seen at railway film shows as the train makes its way from Paddington (via the Reading-Basingstoke line!) to Millbay Docks Station at Plymouth, packed with Kings, Castles, Stars and Pannier Tanks. 'Kate Plus Ten' (1937) with Jack Hulbert also used extensive facilities provided by the GWR. The railway action starts at night at Brentford Docks (freight only) and uses Churchward's own personal saloon car as support coach to a gold bullion sealed freight wagon. The action then moves to the Westbury-Bath line where the train smashes through some realistic looking 'studio' level crossing gates at Freshford. Finally the scene moves to that old faithful, the Limpley Stoke – Camerton branch including an abandoned coal mine at Dunkerton and the round-up of the crooks at Camerton station.

'The Silent Passenger' (1935) directed by Reginald Denham was unusual in having the Great Eastern as a background. This story by Dorothy Sayers of a villain tracked down by Lord Peter Wimsey was shot mainly at Liverpool Street and Stratford Works with GER 4-4-0 'Claud Hamilton' Class 8788 featured as well as a great moment for an 'N7' class 0-6-2T No 2616 on the Chingford run which smashes through some big double doors in Stratford Works that needed demolishing for some rebuilding anyway!

Underground scenes are more unusual in feature films but good use was made of the Central Line and the theme of the abandoned British Museum Station in 'Bulldog Jack' (1935) directed by Walter Forde with Jack Hulbert as Bulldog Drummond. The finale includes a lovely mixture of actuality filming and a giant gauge 1 model layout.

Models are always a temptation for film makers, but they can nearly always be spotted. Hitchcock used an enormous O gauge layout of the LNER and the Harwich Train Ferry in 'Number Seventeen', built by Bassett-Lowke and Bing at Elstree. Cecil B. De Mille used rather obvious models for train crashes in 'Union Pacific' and 'The Greatest Show on Earth', whilst some very good night train scenes in Temple Mills Yard, Stratford for 'It Always Rains on Sunday' (1947) were nearly ruined by just one clumsy model shot of a shunting goods train.

That other great giveaway that spoils many otherwise good railway films is back projection i.e. scenes done in the studio with a mock-up footplate and passing scenery projected onto a ground glass screen of shots previously taken from a moving train. They do spoil some scenes in 'The Last Journey', but the cab is so well reproduced that it almost works, More damaging were the process (American name for background projection) shots in 'La Bête Humaine' (France 1938), a wonderful film directed by Jean Renoir from the novel

by Emile Zola, with Jean Gabin most convincing as the engine driver. Excellent real shots of a run on SNCF to Le Havre and scenes of an SNCF Pacific feature in the last reel, but back projection shots nearly spoil the ending.

Hundreds of railway scenes abound in American feature films of the Thirties but only a few were about railways as such. 'The Phantom Express' (USA 1932), about railway crashes, was mostly done with models. 'Streamline Express' (USA 1936) was about a train of the future – a vast model of an imaginary 150mph double deck diesel train was built, complete with barber's shop, beauty parlour, dance floor, pool room and – just imagine – a telephone link with relay stations along the line!

'Union Pacific' (1939) was a De Mille remake of the old 'Iron Horse' story. It used six locomotives of 'about 1860' vintage although in fact the oldest seems to have been *J W Bowker* (Virginia and Truckee Railroad, 1875). The last shot was a spectacular 1939 Union Pacific aluminium-bodied diesel racing into the distance. The old 'La Roue' story was the subject of a very poor 1956 remake; it is interesting only because of its archive scenes of SNCF electric locomotive BB9004, then the fastest railway engine in the world, on the Paris-Lyons run.

The first feature film ever made with what we would recognise as a modern story line was 'The Great Train Robbery' in 1903. Since then this theme has fascinated many film makers. Filmed mainly using facilities in Southern Ireland, including preserved steam and a re-vamped Victorian-looking station, 'The First Great Train Robbery' was based on real events in 1855 on the SER and starred Sean Connery. The second 'Great Train Robbery' near Cheddington on the old LNWR London to Birmingham Railway took place in August 1963 and was the basis for a German film initially called 'Gentlemen Prefer Cash' made in 1967, which was shot partly on BR in the Folkestone area (although BR had no idea what the film was all about!). But the actual train robbers who were in gaol (not all were caught as we know) sued the film makers for blackening their characters and the picture was shown only briefly in Germany under the title 'The Great British Train Robbery', and has never been heard of again.

At about the same time a British film called 'Robbery', directed by Peter Yates, with Stanley Baker and Frank Finlay was going into production. Immediately, twenty lawyers were put to work on the script to make sure that this time there would be no libel or other actions to stop the film being shown. The film was clearly an accurate representation of the actual robbery, but now all the people involved were turned into totally

With the scrapping of hundreds of branches and the total concentration on establishing a modern image, major rail operators soon had nothing to offer film companies. Nor were the film makers particularly interested. It is significant that the first two versions of 'The Thirty Nine Steps' were made on the Forth Bridge itself. Hitchcock used it in 1935 and Rank used it in 1959. The 1978 version had to go elsewhere. So now it was the era of the preservation societies. The third 'Thirty Nine Steps' was made on the Severn Valley.

Initially the specialised and preserved railways were only used when the action was beyond what British Rail could provide. And the relationship could be a rough one in the early days. Longmoor Military Railway smashed up a fine collection of old SECR bogie stock for the train wreck in 'Bhowani Junction' (Britain 1956); they turned Gordon into an Indian locomotive and toppled it on its side. Ealing Studios broke up a lovely old Wisbech and Upwell Tramway saloon (at one time used on the Tollesbury branch) at the end of 'Titfield Thunderbolt' (1952); and they nearly wrecked a priceless railway relic – *Lion*. Columbia Pictures smashed a 'Black Five' up beyond recovery (it went to the scrap metal dealers) in the making of 'The Virgin Soldiers' (1969). Rumour had it at the time that Columbia had bought up three more 'Black Fives' 'just in case we might need them one day'. However they eventually came back onto the market and were found safe homes. The same thing happened in America. For 'Denver and Rio Grande' (1952) Paramount bought two superb narrow gauge Silverton branch six-coupled locomotives, filled them with dynamite and set them on a head-on collision course on the D&RG tracks near Canyon Creek. There was practically nothing left of them after the smash. Meanwhile in France, SNCF provided no less than four good old engines to be smashed to pieces for the making of 'The Train' (1964).

By the end of the 1960s, it began to dawn on people that perhaps breaking up into tiny fragments excellent and fully operational old steam engines was not, on the whole, a good thing. The preservation movement was beginning to gain ground and they were certainly not in the business of destroying the world's railway heritage. By the 1970s, even the ever helpful American railroad companies were no longer interested. When 20th Century Fox asked Southern Pacific for railway facilities for the making of 'The Silver Streak' in 1976, they didn't want to know. In the end, Fox had to use part of the Canadian system to make the film; and now, for the big crash at the end of the film, they had to mock the whole thing up in a Boeing aircraft hangar with a dummy streamlined diesel. You couldn't even wreck some old diesel by then!

By now, it was time for the preservation societies to take over. The enormous success of that classic of them all 'The Railway Children' made entirely on the Keighley and Worth Valley Railway, proved two things: that people still loved films with steam engines; and that the preservation societies had the technical expertise to achieve such magnificent results. When the early discussions about this production were in hand, a startled technician at a meeting said 'but, for God's sake, they are just a bunch of amateurs'. When the film was finished he said: 'If that's what working with amateurs is

fictitious characters, to make sure the disclaimer on the front of the film really meant what it said. Nevertheless the robbery itself was well reproduced.

The actual robbery took place near Cheddington in Buckinghamshire; it lasted 22 minutes and involved a well-organised assault on the overnight Glasgow-London Mail Train, including giving a false red signal with the real signal covered over. It is said that some of the robbers had worked out the plan after seeing a feature film called 'The League of Gentlemen' at a prison film show whilst they were serving time for previous offences! The film version was staged at Husbards Bosworth near Market Harborough, Leicestershire; it took 29 hours to film and used an identical class of diesel hauled train, complete with a 54ft long, maroon Royal Mail coach as at Cheddington. Incidentally the robbers stole £3 million, and the film cost just under £3 million to make!

Railway scenes continued to abound, especially as steam began to be phased out all over Europe. Notable in the twilight of the steam era were 'Night Train' (Poland 1959), 'Closely Observed Trains' (Czechoslovakia 1966) and 'The Flying Scot' (Britain 1957).

With the end of steam the appeal of the old railway and railroad films undoubtedly took a nosedive. As David Shepherd has said, 'I've tried to come to terms with the brave new railways but there seems to be no romance in the scene'. Nonetheless, the steam train still supplied the background for films like 'Julia' (USA 1977) or 'Murder on the Orient Express' (Britain 1974).

like, Heaven protect me in future from professionals'. That was in 1970. Over the next 20 years, hundreds of TV commercials, documentaries, newsreels and feature films have been made on preserved railways. You will find them listed in this book.

Just as British Rail very slowly caught on to the fact that the steam engine might just still have a place in their affairs, so they also realised that there was money to be had from film companies, as the preservationists had found out. As far back as 1964 Marylebone station had been used for the Beatles' first film (indeed for the opening scene). It was periodically loaned out to film companies thereafter for such films as 'The Ipcress File' (1965) and British Rail continued to give various assistance such as the use of Guildford station for the TV remake of 'Brief Encounter' (1982) or the use of Bingham Road station on the now-abandoned Woodside Line for Tony Hancock's 'The Rebel' (1960). In recent years, all this activity has led to the formation of a British Rail Film Facilities Unit and now, if you've got the right money, you can turn part of St Pancras 1991 into Zurich 1943. And still people like 20th Century Fox (as for 'Shining Through') want railways in their movies, just as it has been since the very first story film back in 1903.

John Huntley

Below:
Scene shot on location with Austrian Railways during the making of the 1979 version of 'The Lady Vanishes'. Despite fine rail scenes like this it never captured the magic of the original version.

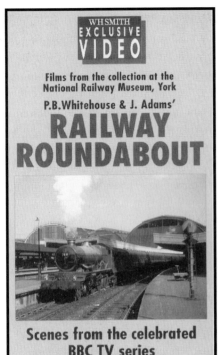

INDEX OF FILMS

49TH PARALLEL (Britain 1941)

Produced and directed by Michael Powell. With Laurence Olivier, Leslie Howard, Eric Portman and Raymond Massey. War-time melodrama set in Canada. Includes finale on a freight train on the Canadian-American border.

35mm, Sound, 123mins Rank

100 RIFLES (USA 1969)

Directed by Tom Gries. With Jim Brown, Raquel Welch and Burt Reynolds. Vicious tale of vengeance in war-torn Mexico. Includes a spectacular train wreck, staged on the 20th Century lot in Hollywood.

35mm, Sound, Colour, 109mins, TCF

125 YEARS AFTERWARDS (Belgium 1961)

Produced by SNCB. After a short history, the film underlines the modern characteristics of the Belgian network and its use of modern techniques.

35/16mm, Sound, Colour, 27mins, SNCB

150 YEARS OF AUSTRIAN RAILWAYS (Britain 1987)

RV Television. Scenes of Strasshof Locomotive Depot, Vienna, for the Grand Parade of 150 Years of Austrian locomotives and railways.

VID, Sound, Colour, 60mins, RVV

150 YEARS OF GERMAN RAILWAYS (Britain, 1985)

RV Television. History of German railways from the import of the British locomotive *Adler* ('Eagle') to modern Intercity trains. Grand Parade of trains in September 1985 in Nürnberg for the Anniversary. Commentary by Paul Brown.

VID, Sound, Colour, 60mins, RVV

2D2 (France 1947)

SNCF. Produced in association with Les Amis des Chemins de Fer. The development of the first major electrification project for the Paris-Lyons-Marseilles line after World War 2; the start of a highly successful scheme that was to produce record-breaking electric services for France and put it out in front as a railway-orientated country. The new electric service is contrasted with the start of railways in France, with an elaborate reconstruction of the first Paris-Orleans line, using Thomas Russel Crampton's British built, long-boilered locomotives, made more famous in France than in Britain. Old No 80 is still preserved in France and was steamed for this film, complete with replica 1840s carriages.

35/16mm, Sound, 24mins, SNCF

3.10 TO YUMA (USA 1957)

Columbia picture. Directed by Delmer Daves. With Glenn Ford, Van Heflin and Felicia Farr. Western about a contest between a farmer and a local bandit. Includes spectacular train arrival and departure scene at Yuma.

35/16mm, Sound, 92mins, Columbia\HA (rail; ref only)

602 MUST GO THROUGH (Norway 1958)

Railway operation through snow in Norway.

16mm, Sound, 13mins, BTF

1066 DC (Britain 1986)

Video 125. Produced by Peter Middleton. Commentary by Peter Egan. A driver's eye view of the line from Hastings to Charing Cross, with the East Sussex scenery at one end and the complexity of the approach across the River Thames to Charing Cross. The singling of many lines through the old tunnels is explained, along with a historical outline of the building of the route to the sea.

VID, Sound, Colour, 90mins, 125

1990 GRAND STEAM GALA (Britain 1990)

RV Television. Detailed coverage of the 1990 Ffestiniog Grand Steam Gala, with gravity slate trains, models, motive power etc.

VID, Sound, Colour, 60mins, RTV

3985 CHALLENGER (USA 1987)

Steam Powered Video. Produced by Video Rails. The largest preserved operating locomotive in the United States is seen from Cheyenne to Pocatello. Servicing, cab scenes, run-pasts and aerial shots.

VID, Sound, Colour, 60mins, SPV

4472 (Britain 1963-4)

Made by G S Holyoake. Shots of former LNER 'A3' No 4472 *Flying Scotsman* at King's Cross, Southampton, Eastleigh, Basingstoke and High Wycombe.

16/9.5/8mm, Silent, Colour, 4mins, MFS

4472: FLYING SCOTSMAN (Britain 1968)

Produced by Rowan Ayers. A documentary on the fortieth anniversary of the non-stop run of the 10 am King's Cross – Edinburgh *Flying Scotsman* on 1 May 1968. First transmission: BBC2 colour 9pm Sunday 11 August 1968. Second transmission: BBC1 6.20-7pm 8 October.

16mm, Sound, Colour, 52mins, BBCTV/HA (ref)

1

45XX TANKS (Britain 1960)

Made by P B Whitehouse and John Adams. Film shows these engines working from Brent Junction via Gara Bridge to Kingsbridge and back. Former LMS and LNER carriages. GWR 'Manor' on mainline train at Brent. Features '45XX' class and '4575' class.

16mm/VID, Silent, Colour, 6mins, HA/NRM/Stirling

6200 THE PRINCESS ROYAL (Britain 1933)

Brand new at Crewe Works on 27 June 1933, LMS Pacific locomotive, which had been built at a cost of £12,657. A move to Camden Shed finds No 6200 backing off shed, and then a fine assault up Camden Bank with Crab 2-6-0 13193 (2893) giving rear-end banking assistance. Further north, 6200 passing on a very long train. Back at Euston 6209 *Princess Beatrice* departs on the 'Royal Scot' to Glasgow. 6131 *The Royal Warwickshire Regiment*, 6166 *London Rifle Brigade*, and Jubilee 5594 *Bhopal* on an express. Finally a Stanier 2-6-2T pulls out.

35mm, Sound, 8mins, NA (lost)

6207: A STUDY IN STEEL (Britain 1937)

LMS film Made by Commerical and Educational Films Department, Topical Press Agency. A very detailed record of the design and construction of LMS Princess Royal 4-6-2 No 62-07 with the slightly unlikely name of *Princess Arthur of Connaught*.

35/16mm, Silent, 18mins, NFA/HA

A

A4 TO WEYMOUTH (Britain 1967)

Made by G S Holyoake. Shots of preserved LNER Class 'A4' No 4498 *Sir Nigel Gresley* on excursion runs from Waterloo to Bournemouth and Weymouth. Rebuilt 'Battle of Britain' class No 34089 *602 Squadron* is seen as a banker on Upwey Bank.

16/9.5/8mm/VID, Silent, Colour, 4mins, MFS

A4s IN ACTION (Britain, 1938)

Amateur record of streamlined A4 Pacifics of the LNER in action at Durham and Newcastle some with the 'Silver Jubilee' and 'Coronation' trains.

16mm (from 9.5mm original), Silent, 8mins, HA

ABANDONED STATIONS

With all the closures of the 1950s and 1960s, the country is littered with abandoned stations in various states of preservation or decay; many have disappeared under housing developments or motorways. Films include a detailed record of the abandoned Southampton Docks station, Lavenham, Ashey, Leiston and stations on the old M&GN.

16mm, Silent, 12mins, HA

ABC MURDERS (Britain 1992)

London Weekend Television. With David Suchet as Inspector Poirot. Much of the plot hinged on the murderer's knowledge of the railway timetable, so there was extensive use of stock shots of various parts of the system.

TV, Sound, Colour, 90mins, LWT TV

ABERMULE CRASH (Britain 1921)

Topical Budget. Newsreel of the results of the head-on collision between Abermule and Montgomery on the Cambrian Railway on January 26, 1921. Both locomotives

were old Cambrian 4-4-0s; Abermule station was closed in 1965.

16mm, Silent, 3mins, HA

ABOUT BRITAIN: STEAM ON THE SETTLE AND CARLISLE (Britain 1983)

Border Television. Produced and directed by William Cartner. Written and presented by Allan Carter. A great assembly of motive power on the Settle and Carlisle, many filmed from the air, including outings with a Duchess, the 'A4' *Sir Nigel Gresley* and other 'run pasts'.

16mm, Sound, Colour, 26mins, Border

ABSOLUTE BLOCK CONTROL (Britain 1938)

An LNER film. A film explaining the practices of semaphore signalling, using diagrams, signalbox scenes and trackside views on the LNER.

35mm/VID, Sound, 14mins, BTF/TVP

AC ELECTRIC LOCOMOTIVE DRIVERS' PROCEDURE (Britain 1964)

Produced by British Transport Films. Part 1. Vacuum Brake Faults. Ways of detecting and correcting vacuum brake faults in mainline locomotives of British Railways. Part 2. Air Brake Faults. How to detect and correct air brake faults in mainline locomotives of British Railways.

35/16mm, Sound, 21mins, BTF

ACCIDENT ON THE CHEMIN DE FER DE L'OUEST, PARIS (France 1899)

Maker unknown. Brief shot of the locomotive that ended up in the street after crashing the buffer at the terminus.

35mm, Silent, 3mins, Pathe

THE ACE OF SPADES (Britain 1935)

Real Art Production. Produced by Julius Hagen. Directed by George

Pearson. With Michael Hogan, Sebastian Shaw and Felix Aylmer. A political candidate is advocating the building of a railway through land belonging to a peer, who is killed in a car accident, resulting in a suspicion of murder. There is much talk about a railway but we never see it!

35mm, Sound, 66mins, Real Art

ACROSS THE ANDES (Britain, 1933)

Amateur record of a train journey across the Andes, with steam-hauled trains, including a unique scene of the passengers, some of them in elegant clothes, clearing a large rock fall by hand.

16mm, Silent, 4mins, HA

ADAMS TANK ON THE LYME REGIS BRANCH (Britain 1960)

Made by P B Whitehouse and John Adams. A day's work on the Axminster to Lyme Regis branch of a 4-4-2T, designed by William Adams for the LSWR in 1882. They were the only class suitable for the sharp curves of the Lyme Regis line; one example (No 30583), withdrawn in 1961, has been preserved on the Bluebell Railway. (See: *Locomotive Preserved: Adams Radial*).

16/8mm/VID, Silent, Colour, 7mins, CV/NRM

ADVANCED PASSENGER TRAIN (Britain 1970-82)

The best material on the ill-fated APT is to be found in official British Transport Films (test, etc) at the Rainhill Parade (1980) and in the National Railway Museum scenes in *Mallard* (qv).

See individual film titles.

AGAINST THE WIND (Britain 1947)

Ealing Studios. Produced by Michael Balcon. Directed by Charles Crichton. With Simone Signoret, Robert Beatty, Jack Warner, Gordon Jackson and John Slater. Training and activities of spies from London operating on the Continent during World War 2. Includes detailed scene of attack on train, filmed on a Belgian freight-only line in the Mons area.

35mm, Sound, 96mins, Weintraub The Alan Willmott Collection

AGATHA (Britain 1978) Warner

Directed by Michael Apted. With Vanessa Redgrave, Dustin Hoffman, Timothy West and Alan Badel. The story of the disappearance of the author Agatha Christie to a secret hide-out in a Harrogate hotel in 1926. Includes scenes of 'Harrogate' station, filmed at York station with LNER 'A1' 4-6-2 No 4472 *Flying Scotsman* playing a double role with nameplates as for No 4474 *Victor Wild* on one side and No 4480 *Enterprise* on the other side! Special false 'Harrogate' totems were put up by the film company and caused at least six passengers to panic when they assumed they had got to their destination without a change at York!.

35mm, Sound, Colour, 105mins, Warner

THE ALAN WILLMOTT COLLECTION

Alan Willmott has worked in the documentary and travel film world for over 35 years, many of them on the distribution and presentation side of British Rail's film and audio-visual department. Alan, although not actually involved on the production side, learned much on film-making techniques through his involvement with this unit, and was able to study camera-work, picture and sound-editing and commentary writing, etc. British Rail's audio-visual department finally closed in 1987, and Alan made the decision to leave full-time service with BR and set up his own 16mm film production activities, including film presentations for clubs, societies, etc under the trade name of 'WIND-JAMMER FILMS'. For many years Alan's main interest has been in steam operated railways in Britain, especially the many branch and secondary lines which existed before the 'Beeching era', as well as the narrow-gauge lines which still abound mainly in Wales. He started to make 16mm colour sound films on such railways on a limited budget whilst still engaged with BR, and his first effort, on one of his favourite lines, the Vale of Rheidol (Aberystwyth to Devil's Bridge) in Wales, was *Train Ride to Devil's Bridge* (1962). This led to a publicity film for the Ffestiniog Railway in 1965 — *Ffestiniog Summer* — which was later revised in 1977 because of the many improvements and extensions to that railway. Other films Alan has completed to date include: *Land of The Little Trains* (1973), *Steam Train to Stonehenge* (1974), *Fathew Flyer* (1978) and *Turn to the Wind* (1978), Alan's tribute to the English Windmill, narrated by actor Peter Barkworth. A more detailed and ambitious film *Railway of the Rheidol Valley* followed in 1982, and then one on the Isle of Man Railways — *Tracks Around the Island* in 1986, narrated by John Huntley. Alan's other film achievements *Ffestiniog Holiday* (1984) and *Return to Bewdley* (1987) (A Day on the Severn Valley Railway) have both been screened on Channel Four Television. May 1991 saw the completion of a new 22min film *Talyllyn 1-2-5*; to promote and to mark the 40th year of preservation of the Talyllyn Railway, at Tywyn in Wales. Another film, being made in two parts, will tell the story and progress of many of the privately operated steam passenger-carrying railways around Britain. *Railway Recreation* is due for completion early in 1993.

ALL ABOUT FREIGHT TRAINS (Canada c1950)

A study of the freight service trying to compete with the ever-advancing road traffic, a story by then being repeated in many parts of the world. Early diesel age.

16mm, Sound, 9mins, RFV

ALL CHANGE (Britain 1964)

Made by F A Sussmann. A study of the impending end of the steam locomotive in Britain.

16mm, Sound, Colour, 8mins, HA

ALL IN ONE PIECE (Britain 1960)

Produced by British Transport Films. Weight...Impact...Vibration, three sources of damage to badly packed goods. This short film demonstrates the correct method of loading and handling the various types of freight carried daily on British Railways.

35/16mm, Sound, 18mins, BTF

ALL MY CHOO CHOOS (USA 1926)

A Mack Sennett-style high speed comedy with Monty Banks. Very spectacular stunts staged with almost unbelievable vigour and the active co-operation of the good old Atchison, Topeka and Santa Fe notably using the freight branches around the Los Angeles Yard. Musical accompaniment assembled by Philip Jenkinson.

16mm, Silent, 19mins, PJ/HA

ALL THAT MIGHTY HEART (Britain 1963)

Produced by British Transport Films. This is a film about London as seen by London Transport. Starting at dawn we see the slow build-up to rush hour and afterwards the mid-morning lull. The scenes change to Saturday afternoon, the hurly-burly of sport and pastime, then on to the evening gaiety of the West End, while below the surface men are tunnelling the new tube line from Victoria to Walthamstow.

35/16mm, Sound, Colour, 24mins, BTF

ALMA'S CHAMPION (USA 1912)

A Vitagraph production. With Lillian Walker, William Dunn and Willis Claire. Melodrama. Alma runs away from her guardian, the manager of a railroad company. On the train she is helped by the President's son who is training as a railway engineer and she afterwards accepts his proposal of marriage, rejecting that of her guardian.

35mm, Silent, 11mins, NFA

ALONG THE LINE (Britain 1947)

Crown Film Unit. Railwaymen and their jobs, including a group of LMS drivers and a shed foreman at Willesden.

35mm/16mm, Sound, 15mins, COI

ALONG THESE LINES (Britain 1966)

Dumar Production for R&ER. A detailed account of the Ravenglas & Eskdale narrow gauge railway.

16/8mm, Sound, Colour, 22mins, HA

ALPINE ROUNDABOUT (Britain, 1956)

Astral Films. Journey on railway through the Grison Canton and the Engadine Valley in Switzerland.

35mm, Sound, Colour, 17mins, Astral

AMERICAN STEAM IN ACTION (USA 1920-40)

Assembly of basic American steam scenes, including the Union Pacific, the Pennsylvania, the Baltimore & Ohio and typical old Western Railroads.

35/16mm, Silent, 14mins, HA

AMONG THE HARDWOODS (Australia 1936)

Produced by the Department of Commerce, Melbourne. About a lumber camp, it includes steam-hauled 4-4-0 locomotives and lumber trains.

16mm, Sound, 11mins, HA

ANBRICO VIDEO TRANSPORT FILMS

This company operates from Pudsey and issues films on a wide range of transport subjects. It has issued a series on Continental railways:

Swiss Mountain Railways Miscellany

Swiss Locomotive Propelled Rack Railways

Mainline Operations Around Innsbruck

Glacier Express of Switzerland

The Cornergrant Mountain Rack Railway

Swiss Electric Traction Miscellany

It has also issued tapes on British railways:

The Scarborough Express (1984)

The Permanent Way Centenary Steam Special (1984)

The North Yorkshire Moors Railway (1984)

Preserved Steam Locomotive Miscellany

A Class 50 Miscellany

The Class 50 at Work on The Western

Other tapes available include:

Rhatische Bahn (Six Videos)

Bernese Oberland Narrow Gauge Miscellany

From Bern to Jungfrau

Railways in the Republic of Ireland

ANDOVER STEAM (Britain 1987)

Made by Tom Martin. A record of a visit by LNER Class 'A1' Pacific No 4472 *Flying Scotsman* and SR 'Merchant Navy' Class Pacific No 35028 *Clan Line* to Andover station.

16mm, Silent, Colour, 6mins, TM/HA

ANIMAL, VEGETABLE AND MINERAL (Britain 1947)

An LMS film. The loose-coupled freight services of the LMS, much dependent on shunting yards at almost every single station and the use made of such facilities for farm products, small engineering parts etc.

35mm/VID, Sound, Colour, 11mins, BTF/TVP

ANNA KARENINA (USA 1935)

MGM. Produced by David O Selznick. Directed by Clarence Brown. With Greta Garbo, Frederic March, Basil Rathbone, Maureen O'Sullivan and Freddie Bartholomew. Original screen version of the Tolstoy novel of a tragic woman in Russian society of the 19th century. She throws herself under a train in the final reel. The railway and the locomotive were all put together by MGM, with an old revamped 4-4-0; and all shot in the studio, except for a few vague 'atmosphere' images.

35mm, Sound, 95mins, MGM

ANNA KARENINA (Britain 1947)

London Films. Directed by Julien Duvivier. With Vivien Leigh and Ralph Richardson. Tolstoy drama. The heroine is struck down by a train in the final episode. The locomotive is strictly 'studio'.

35mm, Sound, 139mins, London Films

ANNUAL FILM MAGAZINE (East Africa 1959)

East African Railways and Harbours. Events of 1959, including a Royal train used by the Queen Mother on a tour and general railway construction scenes.

16mm, Sound, Colour, 22mins, EAR

ANTOINE ET ANTOINETTE (France 1947)

Gaumont Cinema. Directed by Jacques Becker. With Roger Pigaut and Clair Maffei. A young married couple find they have won a lottery but lost the ticket. Includes scenes on the Paris Metro.

35mm, Sound, 87mins, Gaumont

ANY TOWN (Britain, 1935)

Produced by Commercial and Educational Films (Topical Press Agency) for the London, Midland & Scottish Railway. A detailed record of a year in the life of the LMS, cov-

ering scenes all over the system. There is a sequence devoted to 'Wakes Week' in 'Any Town', which is actually Rochdale, Lancs. In addition to shots of 'Royal Scots' in action, there are glimpses of the old pre-grouping locomotives and stock, including LNWR Bowen-Cooke 'G2' class 0-8-0 No 9428 and L&Y Aspinall 0-6-0 No 12400; the LNWR class dates from 1921 and the L&Y locomotive is of 1889 vintage. There is a very rare shot of an LMS Railway Air Services De Havilland DH84 Dragon Rapide G-ACPX, registered in 1934.

16mm/VID, Sound, 14mins, BTF/HA:ref/RFV

ARCH AT EUSTON (Britain 1966)

BBC Television News. Scenes of the famous arch and columns at Euston station after the announcement that they could not be salvaged during the rebuilding of Euston Station. Interview with John Betjeman.

16mm, Sound, 3mins, HA

ARCHIVE STEAM CAB RIDE (Britain 1988)

Rail Video. Bournemouth to Weymouth and return. This is the first tape to be released entirely based on a 1960s steam cab ride. The journey starts at Bournemouth Central in the cab of a BR Standard Class 4 2-6-0 on a local train for Weymouth. Edited views show the loco and the crew in action, followed by arrival at Weymouth and views of Weymouth shed. The return journey is made on the footplate of a rebuilt Bulleid Pacific.

VID, Sound, Colour, 30mins, RVO

ARISTOCRATS OF STEAM (Britain 1991)

Transport Video Publishing. Four classic locomotives still preserved:- *Duchess of Hamilton*, *Duke of Gloucester*, *Princess Margaret Rose* and *The Great Marquess*.

VID, Sound, Colour, 30mins, TVP

THE ARLBERG RAILWAY (Britain 1906)

Charles Urban Trading Company. Views from a train travelling between Langen and Bruden.

35mm, Silent, 6mins, NFA

ARMSTRONG WHITWORTH LOCOMOTIVE FOR AUSTRALIA (Britain 1922)

Topical Budget newsreel. A massive 4-6-2 locomotive bound for Australia emerges from the Armstrong Whitworth works at Scotswood, Newcastle upon Tyne.

35/16mm, Silent, 3mins, HA

THE ARMY LAYS THE RAILS (Britain 1941)

An Army Film Unit production for the Ministry of Information. The work of the Royal Engineers as wartime railwaymen, including scenes at Longmoor.

35/16mm, Sound, 7mins, IWM

AROUND SNOWDONIA (Britain 1932)

An Alba production. From the *Our Island* series. Directed by Duncan Robbins. Primitive early sound travelogue. Includes scene of Snowdon Mountain Railway.

16mm, Sound, 11mins, HA

AROUND THE WORLD IN EIGHTY DAYS (Britain 1956)

United Artists. Produced by Michael Todd. Directed by Michael Anderson. With David Niven, Cantinflas, Robert Newton, Shirley MacLaine, Charles Boyer, Ronald Colman, Noel Coward and just about every movie star of the day and the day-before-yesterday. Jules Verne's tale of a Victorian man-about-town who decides to go round the world in 80 days to win a bet. There are two major railway sequences. The first is done with massive co-operation from Indian Railways, featuring big 4-6-2 North British locomotives, a journey simulated from Bombay to Calcutta via Colby and Allahabad which ends with a break in the line when the single-line track runs out!

There's an elephant on the line (makes a change from a cow) and fine driver's eye views of the rural countryside, castellated bridges and spectacular river crossings. The second main railway scene takes place on the Durango-Silverton preserved railway, featuring old locomotive No 60 *Jupiter* during the attack by Red Indians), Buster Keaton as a train guard and superb exploitation of the narrow gauge railroad including yellow and brown liveried stock, one of the large wooden trestle bridges, clerestory roofs and a great performance by the classic six-coupled locomotive.

70mm Todd-AO, Sound, Colour, 178mins, United Artists

AROUND THE WORLD IN EIGHTY DAYS (Britain 1990)

BBC Television. Written and presented by Michael Palin. A land trip around the world in the steps of Philleas Fogg. Includes a start on the Venice-Orient Express from Victoria, through Switzerland but comes to a stop in Innsbruck because of industrial action! There are a number of interesting railway sections, notably across America.

AROUND THE WORLD IN SEARCH OF STEAM (Britain 1989)

Railfilms. Produced and directed by Nick Dodson. The work of Colin Garratt in search of mainly British steam, like a Manchester built Sharp Stewart 0-6-0T from Bridgewater Street in Spain; a Stanier '8F' from the LMS in Turkey; plus steam scenes on the Isle of Man and in China. There is an outline of Colin Garratt's life, his home in Leicestershire and the special quality of his photographs – smoky shed scenes, locomotives in full cry, industrial dramas, rusted giants languishing in graveyards festooned with wild flowers, scrapyard scenes cutting up old engines and those twilight and night shed scenes so characteristic of this photographer's work.

VID, Sound, Colour, 55mins, RFV

ARRIVAL OF A TRAIN AT LA CIOTAT STATION (France 1895)

This item had been filmed by the Lumière Brothers during their family holidays in July 1895; today there is a commemorative plaque on La Ciotat station recording how the inventors set up their camera and made one of the earliest films ever shown to the public showing the entry of the train into the station. Fortunately this remarkable film still survives in the Cinémathèque Française and the National Film Archive.

The scene (which consists of a single continuous shot) starts with a three-quarter view from the platform as the train is seen approaching some way off. The sturdy little Bourbonais class 2-4-2 locomotive thunders towards the camera gradually filling the screen; for such an early film, the detail is excellent. When the film was first shown audiences who had never before experienced the motion picture leapt back from their seats lest they be mown down by what appeared to them such a startlingly realistic impression, particularly as the shot was sometimes accompanied by the release of loud sshhes of air from a cylinder operated by a man below the screen and out of view of the audience. The delightful mixture of first, second and third class carriages follows, all gleaming with polished wood and shining brass. The carriages come to a stop in front of the camera and the scene ends with bustling activity on the platform as whole families step from the train and others board the waiting carriages. Members of the Lumière family are seen on the platform as part of the general 'crowd' scene.

35/16/8mm/VID, Silent, 52secs, NFA/HA/125

ASHOVER LIGHT RAILWAY (Britain 1928)

I Gotheridge. A fragment, including a limestone train going over Stretton crossing; views of the USA Baldwin 4-6-0T ex-US War Department 10-12-D locomotives, the tramcar-type coaches; and a passenger train at Clay Cross station.

16/8mm, Silent, 2mins, Gotheridge/HA

AT BERTRAM'S HOTEL (Britain 1987)

Television. *Miss Marple* episode, with Joan Hickson. Includes scenes made at Marylebone station.

TV, Sound, Colour, 54mins, LWT TV

ATTIC ARCHIVES (Britain 1983-90)

BBC Television. Produced and directed by Dennis Dick. Presented by John Huntley. A series of archive film programmes made over the years in Bristol and later in Aberdeen. In each series there was usually a whole programme devoted to railways or at least to transport of the past. Typical of the series was 'On The Move' in Part One with trams, trains and railway inserts (Leeds and Glasgow), plus a classic scene from a then rediscovered film 'Let's Imagine a Branch Line', recording a journey by John Betjeman on the Somerset & Dorset Railway before it closed. Later programmes had scenes of Scottish steam at Connel Ferry, Achnasheen, Kyle of Localsh and Ballachulish. For a programme called 'Steaming Away', there was film of the Tay Bridge, the Forth Bridge, snowed-up trains at Newmachar in the winter of 1962-63 just north of Aberdeen on the old Great North of Scotland Railway; items from the collection of Allan Garraway, whose father recorded many scenes on the LNER in the 1930s, including the LNER Royal Train bound for Wolverton (station for Sandringham on the now abandoned Kings Lynn-Hunstanton line). In the same programme, there were views of the 'Coronation Scot' train in colour in 1938, archive film of building locomotives at Crewe in 1911 and Swindon in 1912 and film from the Garraway of the breakdown train in operation as well as newsreel of a crash in 1928 at Carlisle and Castle Cary in 1937.

Yet another programme made in Aberdeen was called 'Gateway to Scotland', which included the 'Royal Scot' train from Euston to Glasgow in 1932; a journey towards the end of steam in 1955; the Kings Cross to Edinburgh East Coast Main Line to Scotland; and steam scenes in the two capital cities. A programme called 'Steam Scotland' was a complete show devoted to an amazing collection of films taken by Stuart Sellar which covered virtually the whole of Scotland in the final days of steam, with many scenes taken on lines that have long since closed. The material was so rich that it was used in a second half-hour called 'Days of Steam', introduced on this occasion by George Hume of BBC Scotland.

VID, Sound, Colour, 28mins each episode, BBC TV

THE ATTEMPT ON THE SPECIAL (USA 1911)

A Pathe release. Nell, the point-man's daughter, and Jack train a greyhound to carry messages between them. A gang plan the destruction of the 'Special', a train carrying a million dollars. They attack the cabin and tie Nell up, but the greyhound appears with a note and bites through her ropes. She sends the dog back with a request for help and tries to escape only to be struck down and left lying across the railway track. Jack gathers help together and one party goes to warn the train while the other sets off to stop the gang. Nell is sighted on the track and as the train rushes past one of the men on the cowcatcher stoops down and picks her up. Meanwhile the gang have been routed and the 'Special' can continue on its way.

35mm, Silent, 7mins, NFA

AUSTRALIAN STEAM RAILWAYS (Britain 1970-75)

Nick Lera Production. Nick Lera recorded various aspects of the Australian scene, including a coast-to-coast run in 1970, an Australian vintage train, the Tait electrics in Melbourne, the world's last working steam crane locomotives in Sydney, the Great Lithgow zig-zag on the scenic Blue Mountains railway and New Zealand's Ferrymead Museum with working tram and live steam exhibits.

16mm, Silent, Approx 15mins, NL/HA

AUSTRIAN CAB RIDES (Britain 1987)

SF. Austrian Federal Railways: Arlberg Pass. Cab ride in a Class 1042 electric locomotive from Bludenz to Landeck. Cab ride in a Class 1044 electric locomotive on the Semmering Bahn at a basic 1 in 40 over the Alps.

VID, Sound, Colour, 55mins, SFV

AUSTRIAN NARROW GAUGE (Britain 1960)

Made by P B Whitehouse and John Adams. A film study of Austrian narrow gauge, including preserved railways.

16/8mm, Silent, 12mins, CV/NRM

AUSTRIAN RACK (Britain 1962)

Made by P B Whitehouse and John Adams. A film made of the Achensee Bahn, a partly rack operated railway running between Jenbach to Achensee.

16/8mm, Silent, Colour, 4mins, CV/NRM

AUSTRIAN RAILWAY SPECTACULAR (Britain, 1985)

Salford Films. Arlberg Pass, Innsbruck, Salzburg, Linz and Vienna. Private lines and narrow gauge railways. Steam, diesel and electric.

VID, Sound, Colour, 60mins, SFV

AUSTRIAN RAILWAY VIDEO SPECTACULAR (Britain 1987)

RV Television. Directed and produced by John Cocking. Research and script by Alan Pike, OBE. Through trains include the 'Wiener Walzer', Zürichsee, Transalpin, Arlberg Express, Orient Express, Akropolis, Gondoliere etc. Arlberg, Karwendel and Semmering lines. Innsbruck-Salzburg-Vienna-Graz line. Pinzgauerbahn, Zillertalbahn, Murtalbahn, Feistritztalbahn, Graz-Köflachbahn, Schneebergbahn, Mariazellerbahn, Ybsstalbahn, Atterseebahn, Stiermärkische Lan-

desbahnen, Salzburg Lokalbahn etc. Rack steam trains to Achensee and Schafberg. Narrow gauge steam trains from Gros Gerungs to Gmund.

VID, Sound, Colour, 60mins, RVV

THE AVENGERS (British Television Series)

British television series featuring agent Steed and a variety of girl assistants; one episode Something Happened on the Way to the Railway Station included scenes on the diesel hauled and dmu traffic from St Albans to St Pancras. An episode called Death at Noon included scenes at the abandoned LMS Stanbridgeford station on the Leighton Buzzard to Dunstable line, closed to passengers on 2 July 1962. The dusty old station was renamed 'Lang's Halt' for the use of the 40-strong Elstree Studios TV unit who shot the scenes in two days in October 1968.

One episode with Patrick Macnee and Diana Rigg incorporated scenes shot on Lord Gretton's 10.25in gauge miniature railway at Stapleford Park, Melton Mowbray, using locomotive No 750 Freelance 4-4-2 *Blanche of Lancaster* built in 1948. Shown on ITV Television 1967-69.

35mm, Sound, 28mins each episode, EMI

AWAYDAY (Britain 1989)

BBC Television. Procuded by Ken Stephenson for Falkman TV. A much more personal look than most TV railway films, this series took people like Katharine Whitehorn to look at the Strathspey Preserved Railway from Aviemore to Boat of Garten; or Peter McEnery and David Shepherd on the Severn Valley. An excellent and very individual look at preserved railways; one of the best was to hear George Hinchcliffe talking about *Flying Scotsman* BBC Television: July and August 1989.

VID, Sound, Colour, 29mins per episode, BBC Television

B

B&R VIDEO PRODUCTIONS

A wide variety of videos are issued by this company including an *Archive Newsreel*, *Dieselelectric Power* and a complete set of steam railway compilations under such titles as *Steam Heritage, Steam Northbound, Yesterday's Steam, Steam Nostalgia, Steam Remembrance, Steam South and West* and *Steam Survival*. The company has drawn extensively on amateur private collections and brought to light much that would probably have remained unseen except for their efforts.

BACK TO THE FUTURE 3 (USA 1989)

Universal/Stephen Spielberg. Directed by Robert Zemeckis. With Michael J. Fox, Christopher Lloyd and Lea Thompson. The third in the classic Spielberg time-travel trilogy. The return from 1885 is achieved with a steam engine pushing the DeLorean time-travel car up to the vital 88 miles per hour. With the help of the Sierra Railroad, a special 2-6-0 mock-up steam time machine and a section of track was built in Sonora and Jamestown, California, the same Sierra Railroad location as used in *High Noon* and many other films.

35mm, Sound, Colour, 116min, Universal

BAD DAY AT BLACK ROCK (USA, 1954)

MGM. Produced by Dore Schary. Directed by John Sturges. With Spencer Tracy, Robert Ryan, Dean Jagger and Walter Brennan. A one-armed stranger arrives by train at a quiet desert town. His enquiries meet with hostility from the townsfolk, who have something to hide.
  'The train in this film is a temperamental guest star. Having made her entrance and exit, she leaves us and Spencer Tracy cooling our heels, waiting desperately for her return. There is no other way out of town. At the end, it sweeps him

away to...where? What an exit!' (Tony Bilbow). The railway scene was done on the Sierra Railroad, which was used so effectively for *High Noon*, to which this film may be compared.

35mm, Sound, Colour, 81mins, MGM

BAHNLAND SCHWEIZ VOLUMES I AND II (Britain 1987)

Magazine assemblies of material recorded for various sections of the Swiss Railway System, plus extra material for Volume II on the South-West area including Re 4/4 IV electric locomotives and trains at Domodossola, Lausanne, Montreux, Locarno, Interlaken. There is also a steam section on the Emmental-Burgdorf-Thun Bahn.

VID, Sound, Colour, 55mins, JC

THE BALA LAKE RAILWAY (Britain 1976)

HTV Television. Produced and directed by John Mead. Presented by Wynford Vaughan-Thomas. A narrow gauge built on the track bed of the old standard branch line to Bala from Llanuwchllyn. Includes scenes of Hunslet 0-4-0ST *Maid Marian* in action. (From the *Great Little Trains of Wales* series)

16mm/VID, Sound, Colour, 26mins, HTV/Castle

THE BALLYBUNION RAILWAY (Britain 1988)

Anglia Television. A short history of the Listowel & Ballybunion Lartique monorail in Ireland with archive film.

16mm, Sound, Colour, 4mins, Anglia

BALTIC COAST EXPRESS (Britain 1991)

Railfilms. Produced and filmed by Nick Dodson. Taking advantage of relaxed conditions and no Iron Curtain, this is a journey, mainly behind steam, from Berlin, across Poland and on to Brest thence, following the Baltic Coast through Vilnius, Riga, Tallinn and on to Leningrad.

Steam action includes Polish classes TKT48, OL49, TY2, OK1, OK22 and PT47. In the Western CIS, classes P36, L and E of Russian State Railways. There are scenes of an old 'O' 0-8-0 and a visit to the remnants of the Estonian narrow gauge system.

VID, Sound, Colour, 60mins, RFV

BANK HOLIDAY (Britain 1938)

Gainsborough Picture. Directed by Carol Reed. With Margaret Lockwood, Hugh Williams, Kathleen Harrison, Rene Ray and Garry Marsh. The story of a day out at Brighton and the lives of the people who meet en route. 'Still quite refreshing' said Leslie Halliwell. There is a very large studio reconstruction of Waterloo station, intercut with a few genuine shots. After extensive coverage of the real Waterloo, with concourse, platforms and glimpses of Southern 4-6-0s, the train promptly leaves from King's Cross!

35mm, Sound, 86mins, Rank

BANK HOLIDAY AT BEWDLEY (Britain 1961)

Made by P B Whitehouse and John Adams. The comings and goings of trains and people on August Bank Holiday on a station that later became part of the Severn Valley preserved railway.

16/8mm, Silent, Colour, 7mins, CV/NRM

BARGING THROUGH LONDON (Britain 1924 and 1979)

Harry Parkinson (1924). J Huntley and Michael Essex-Lopresti (1979). A record of the Regents Canal in London made first in 1924 and then the identical locations re-shot in 1979, includes scenes of the London, Tilbury and Southend railway passing over the canal; Kings Cross station; St Pancras station; and the canal being crossed by the railway outside Euston and St Pancras stations.

16mm, Silent, 18mins, HA

BARNEY OLDFIELD'S RACE FOR LIFE (USA 1914)

Directed by Mack Sennett. With Mabel Normand, Mack Sennett, Ford Sterling, Barney Oldfield and the Keystone Cops.

Boy and girl are going steady but the villain turns up on the scene. At first ousted by the hero, he seeks revenge by capturing the girl. His gang tie her to the railroad track, go off in search of a locomotive to run down the heroine. As the villain races to the heroine's doom, the Keystone Cops go to the rescue on a hand trolley and the hero roars alongside the railroad truck in a requisitioned sports car. The girl is rescued at the last minute and the villain vanquished.

That stand-by of the early Hollywood films the Atchison, Topeka & Santa Fe, features in the first railroad scene when the villain and his gang steal AT&SF hand trolley No 5568. Next they grab a 4-4-0 locomotive No 492 and set off down the track, pursued in some good travelling shots, by Barney Oldfield in his Benz 7 car No 26. The final rescue as Mabel Normand is carried from the track in front of No 492 looks terrifyingly close, even by Mack Sennett standards.

16mm, Silent, 16mins, HA
🚂🚂🚂

BARNSTAPLE: TORRINGTON (Britain 1964-70)

Made by Vic Thompson. A record of the latter days of the LSWR diesel-hauled traffic between Barnstaple Junction station (still in use) and the line to Bideford and Torrington (freight only after 1965 and now closed).

16mm, Silent, 12mins, VT/HA
🚂🚂🚂🚂🚂

BATAILLE DU RAIL (France, 1947)

Produced by Co-operative Generalé du Cinema Française for the Railway Resistance Movement and Ciné Union. Directed by Rene Clement. Script by Rene Clement. Photography by Henri Alekan. Music by Yves Baudrier. With Salina Daurend and Lozach. An account of the Railway Resistance Movement in France and the effective sabotaging of a German convoy. The film was almost a documentary, being based on many of the tricks carried out by the Resistance. The German tank train was filmed at Lannion and Chagny with SNCF locomotive 240-D-234; details of the derailment were done in the yard at Caen (already wrecked by Allied bombing) whilst the spectacular derailment of an old World War 1 2-6-0 (SNCF 140-D-57) and a complete goods train was staged near Rennes.

35mm, Sound, 87mins, SNCF
🚂🚂🚂🚂

BATTERSEA FUN FAIR (Britain 1951)

Amateur film. Shots of the Emmett comic train built for the Festival of Britain.

16mm, Silent, 3mins, HA
🚂

BATTLE OF THE BULGE (USA 1965)

Warner Bros. Directed by Ken Annakin. With Henry Fonda, Robert Shaw, Robert Ryan and Telly Savalas. The battle of the Ardennes in December 1944. Includes a train crash staged by Dutch Railways.

35mm, Sound, Colour, 167mins, Warner
🚂

BBC VIDEO

A number of television programmes are available direct from the BBC including their own Great Railway Journeys of the World, Steam Days, Train now Departing and Metroland.

🚂🚂🚂🚂🚂🚂

BEHOLD A PALE HORSE (USA 1964)

Columbia. Directed by Fred Zinneman. With Gregory Peck, Omar Sharif and Anthony Quinn. Includes steam scenes on Spanish State Railways near Madrid to represent the 1950s era.

35mm, Sound, 121mins, Columbia
🚂

BELLEROPHON (Britain 1989)

Video 125. A record of Haydock Foundry 0-6-0WT Bellerophon, built in 1874, owned and operated by the Vintage Carriages Trust on the Keighley & Worth Valley Railway. It was filmed at Oakworth as part of an historic video session.

VID, Sound, Colour, 8mins, VID125
🚂🚂🚂🚂🚂

THE BENGUELA RAILWAY (Britain 1928)

Produced by British Instructional Films. 'A milestone in African civilisation', a detailed account of the Benguela Railway running from Lobito to Elizabethville.

35mm, Silent, 37mins, NFA
🚂🚂🚂🚂

BERLIN (Germany 1927)

A Fox Europa Film. Directed by Walter Ruttman. Script by Karl Mayer. A documentary film on Berlin as it was in 1927; the material involves many shots of all forms of transport in the city, including the railways, underground system, surburban steam routes and the automobiles of the day.

35/16mm, Silent, 78mins, BFI/HA
🚂🚂

BERLIN AIR LIFT (Britain 1948)

The newsreels include scenes of East and West German steam-hauled freight trains resuming service after the blockade of Berlin by the Russians.

16mm, Sound, 4mins, HA
🚂

BERLIN EXPRESS (Britain 1948)

RKO Radio. Directed by Jacques Tourneur. With Merle Oberon and Robert Ryan. Drama of occupied Germany. Railway scenes between Frankfurt and Berlin.

35mm, Sound, 87mins, RKO
🚂🚂

THE BERN LÖTSCHBERG (Britain, 1985)

Salford Films. BLS Railway through the Swiss Alps. BLS to Interlaken, Zweisimmen, Belp, Schwarzenberg

Right:
In this scene from 'Against the Wind' (1947) Gordon Jackson and John Slater are seen on a Belgian freight line as saboteurs in the occupied Europe of World War 2.

Below:
No 4472 *Flying Scotsman* played two roles in the film 'Agatha' (1978), No 4474 *Victor Wild* and No 4480 *Enterprise* with different nameplates on each side of the locomotive. This particular scene was shot at York. Note the Harrogate nameboards.

Below right:
Having been captured by the villain, Mabel Normand is tied to the railroad track - will the Keystone Cops arrive in time to save her? Scene from 'Barney Oldfield's Race for Life '(1914).

Facing page, top:
'La Bête Humaine' (1938) was based on a novel by Emile Zola. An exciting melodrama full of passion and murder, directed by Jean Renoir, it has numerous railway scenes, including a final thrilling sequence.

Facing page, left:
Jean Gabin as Jacques Lantier, the engine-driver with murderous tendencies in 'La Bête Humaine' (1938).

Facing page, right:
Simone Simon starred as Severigne Robaud in 'La Bête Humaine' (1938). The railway scenes were all filmed on the French railway system.

and Neuchatel. Also Alpine route connecting the Rhone and Kander valleys.

VID, Sound, Colour, 60mins, SFV

🚂 🚂 🚂 🚂 🚂

BERN-LÖTSCHBERG-SIMPLON CAB RIDE (Britain 1988)

RV Television. Complete ride from Thun to Brig from the front of a Eurocity Express in the cab of an Re 4/4. There are maps of the route.

VID, Sound, Colour, 57mins, RVV

🚂 🚂 🚂 🚂 🚂

BERN-LÖTSCHBERG-SIMPLON RAILWAY: 75TH ANNIVERSARY (Britain, 1988)

RV Television. August 1988. Events included a parade of electric locomotives at Frutigen; steam parade at Darligen; historic electric locomotives from all over Europe.

VID, Sound, Colour, 60mins, RVV

🚂 🚂 🚂 🚂 🚂

LA BÊTE HUMAINE (France 1938)

A Paris Film production. Directed by Jean Renoir. Script by Jean Renoir, from the novel by Emile Zola. Photography by Curt Courant. Music by Joseph Kosma. With Jean Gabin, Simone Simon, Fernand Ledoux, Carette, Blanchette Brunoy, Gerard Landry, Berlioz and Jean Renoir.

Jacques Lantier, an engine-driver who is subject to murderous brainstorms, nearly kills a young girl and swears to renounce women, but when he meets Severigne Robaud he is irresistibly attracted. The latter's husband, in a fit of jealousy, has already killed a man in his wife's presence but, during the subsequent enquiry, Jacques, who realises this, is silent. Consequently, with the hold he possesses over the pair, he is able to continue a clandestine love affair with Severigne. She slowly insinuates into his mind the idea of killing Robaud but, after making one abortive attempt, Lantier's mind snaps as he is about to try for the second time and he murders Severigne instead.

The narrative ends with a final thrilling sequence in which Lantier, on the footplate of the Paris express, confesses to his fireman, overpowers him, and finally plunges to death off the tender, leaving the train to meet what might be a disastrous fate but what actually turns out to be a rapid tracking shot into 'The End'.

In the New Statesman of 29 April 1939, Peter Galway reviewed the film thus: 'The railway sequences in *La Bête Humaine* are a knockout. The camera is mounted in front of the engine, the sound, instead of being dubbed in afterwards, recorded on the spot. On the wide screen of London's handsome new Continental cinema the result is a superlatively exciting and beautiful spectacle enriched by the entire gamut of sounds that make up the life of the permanent way; trains tearing and screaming through the sunny countryside, trains burrowing through tunnels towards the pinprick of light with a muffled but redoubled roar, trains clanking and wheezing in the temporary repose of the junction. In basing a film on Emile Zola's famous novel, Jean Renoir has almost produced a documentary of the French railway system – a fact which would certainly have delighted that scrupulously accurate author.'

35/16mm, Sound, 85-90mins (Various versions), Paris/NFA/HA (rly only)

🚂 🚂 🚂

BETWEEN ORTON JUNCTION AND FALLONVILLE (USA 1913)

An Edison film. A tale of a railroad disaster. A station agent and an engineer are rivals. The latter appeals mostly to Edna. Edward starts on his engine, and is passing a station when Jim hears a call for assistance down the line. The agent has allowed a train to pass the block, and Jim realises that Edward Burke may be going to his death. He wires to Edna, and she gallops across country to try to intercept the train. Edna arrives in the nick of time to avoid the crash, and she and Burke return to thank Jim for his timely aid.

35/16mm, Silent, 7mins, NFA

🚂 🚂 🚂

BETWEEN THE TIDES (Britain 1958)

British Transport Films. The secret world of rock pools and seashore life when the tide has gone out. This BTF film won no less than 15 international awards, including first prize at Venice, Bologna and Cork. There is not a single shot of transport in the entire film!

35/16mm, Sound, Colour, 19mins, BTF

BEWDLEY-TENBURY BRANCH (Britain 1961)

Made by P B Whitehouse and John Adams. Train working between Bewdley, Tenbury Wells and Wooferton Junction in the last season of full service.

16/8mm, Silent, 7mins, CV/NRM

🚂 🚂 🚂 🚂 🚂

BEYER GARRATT LOCOMOTIVES ON SUDAN RAILWAYS (Britain 1948)

A record of the GEA Beyer-Garratt locomotives starting at Atbara sheds, Sudan Railways and covering various parts of the system.

16mm, Silent, 23mins, NFA/HA

🚂 🚂 🚂 🚂 🚂

BEYER-GARRATT LOCOMOTIVES ROUND THE WORLD: NEW SOUTH WALES (Britain 1952-53)

Produced for Beyer Peacock by Kinocrat Films. Produced by Gerald Cookson. Directed by M A Crane. Photography by Robert Dovey and Reg Perier. The construction, shipment, testing and operation of Beyer-Garratt GEA locomotives in New South Wales, Australia.

16mm, Sound, Colour, 38mins, NFA/HA

🚂 🚂 🚂 🚂 🚂

BEYER-GARRATT LOCOMOTIVES ROUND THE WORLD: QUEENSLAND (Britain, 1948)

Produced for Beyer Peacock by Kinocrat Films. Directed by M A Crane. Photography by Reg Perier. The Queensland countryside and industrial sites served by Queensland Railways using Beyer Garratt GEA locomotives.

16mm, Sound, Colour, 17mins, NFA/HA

🚂 🚂 🚂 🚂 🚂

BHOWANI JUNCTION (USA 1956)

MGM. Produced by Pandro S Berman. Directed by George Cukor. With Ava Gardner, Stewart Granger and Bill Travers. Anglo-Indian drama at the time of independence. Includes a number of authentic railway scenes and a spectacular accident, staged on the Longmoor Military Railway, using as extras members of the British Army who had recently been on active service in Egypt and looked suitably tanned. The subject matter was too sensitive for India, so the railway scenes and the main location had to be moved to Lahore in Pakistan. Pakistan Railways provided the railway station and the steam locomotives including Beyer Peacock 4-6-0 No 3008.

35mm, Sound, Colour, 109mins, MGM

🚂 🚂

THE BIG LAND (USA 1957)

Warner. Directed by Gordon Douglas. With Alan Ladd and Virginia Mayo. The building of a rail link for cattlemen in Texas in the pioneer days. Includes extensive scenes on the Sierra Railroad, a preserved line 100 miles east of San Francisco and part of the 'Mother Lode' gold mining region. Locomotive No 3 in the stock list, it was originally Rogers 4-6-0 No 4493, built in 1891. Stock included the SR coach No 6 and Combine No 5 (in Britain, a brake composite), as well as shots of old No 3.

35mm, Sound, 92mins, Warner

🚂 🚂

THE BIG SHOT (USA 1942)

Warner Brothers. Directed by Lewis Seiler. With Humphrey Bogart and Irene Manning. Gangster melodrama. Includes race between car and steam train to beat a level crossing by inches; done by Warner Brothers stunt man and used in a number of films.

35mm, Sound, 82mins, Warner

🚂 🚂

BINGHAM, UTAH, MINES (USA 1912)

Edison. Record of a mining operation including small steam industrial locomotives.

16mm, Silent, 6mins, HA

🚂

BIOSCOPE BYGONES: RAILWAYS (Britain 1963)

Anglia Television. Directed by Len Caynes. Research by Geoffrey Weaver. Presented by Dick Joice and John Huntley. A lot of old film about railways, including the Darlington Centenary Celebrations of 1925, spectacular crash scenes from *The Wreck* and *The Wrecker*, 1937 scenes of 'Coronation Scot' and the delivery of LMS '7P' 4-6-0 No 6100 *Royal Scot* to Bressingham Museum in Norfolk.

16mm, Kinescope, Sound, 18mins, Anglia/HA

🚂 🚂 🚂 🚂

BIRMINGHAM RAILWAYS (1931-62)

Assembly of various Birmingham steam railway scenes including New Street (1931); SLS tour: Birmingham New Street to Halesowen (1962); Birmingham Snow Hill in 1941, 1945 and scenes of the abandoned station after closure.

16mm, Silent, 14mins, CV/NRM/HA

🚂 🚂 🚂 🚂 🚂

BIRTH OF A CUNEO (Britain 1962)

Made by P B Whitehouse and John Adams. An account of the making of a railway painting by Terence Cuneo.

16/8mm, Silent, 9min, CV/NRM

🚂 🚂 🚂

THE BIRTH OF A LOCOMOTIVE (USA 1989)

Steam Powered Video. A detailed record of the design, construction, testing and initial runs of General Motors locomotive DDGM F59PH.

VID, Sound, Colour, 38mins, SPV

🚂 🚂 🚂 🚂 🚂

BLACK FIVE (Britain 1968)

Produced and directed by Paul Barnes. Made for the British Film Institute Production Board. A detailed study of BR Class 5 Locomotives during the last days of steam in Britain.

16mm, Sound, Colour, 23mins, BFI

🚂 🚂 🚂 🚂 🚂

BLACK FIVES ARE BEAUTIFUL (Britain 1960-90)

A film by Tom Martin. An assembly of material showing the famous Black Fives in action in many different locations. A detailed study of a classic class of locomotive.

16mm, Silent, Colour, 14mins, TM/HA

🚂 🚂 🚂 🚂 🚂

BLACK FIVES ON THE GREAT CENTRAL (Britain 1966)

A film by Tom Martin. The last days of the Great Central Railway, with scenes of 'Black Fives' at Marylebone, Stoke Mandeville, Aylesbury, Brackley and Woodford Halse. There are scenes of the last day of steam on 3 September 1966.

16mm, Silent, Colour, 14mins, TM/HA

🚂 🚂 🚂 🚂 🚂

BLACK DIAMOND EXPRESS (USA 1927)

Warner Bros. Directed by Howard Bretherton. With Monte Blue and Edna Murphy. An engine driver wins the girl and stops a robbery. The climax includes a runaway coach careering down a steep, winding gradient.

35mm, Silent, 95mins, Warner

🚂 🚂 🚂 🚂 🚂

BLACK DIAMOND EXPRESS (USA 1896)

Thomas Edison Kinetoscope Film. The Black Diamond Express is seen approaching in the distance; it moves towards and past the camera, watched by workmen in the foreground who wave their handkerchiefs.

35/16mm/VID, Silent, 40sec, NFA/HA/125

🚂 🚂 🚂 🚂 🚂

THE BLACK SHEEP OF WHITEHALL (Britain 1942)

Ealing Studios. Directed by Basil Dearden and Will Hay. With Will Hay and John Mills. Comedy, including a railway sequence, filmed on the Southern Railway.

35mm, Sound, 80mins, Rank

BLACKMORE VALE AND THE BLUEBELL (Britain 1987)

Online. Sheffield Park in 1965. 'P' class in action in 1969; *Blackmore Vale* returned to steam in 1976; GWR *Earl of Berkeley* named in 1982; Metropolitan *Chesham* set; Trackwork; Locomotive sheds; Rapier Steam crane; Kingscote station.

VID, Sound, Colour, 55mins, Online

THE BLOCK SIGNAL (also known as Tragic Railway) (USA 1926)

With Ralph Lewis, Jean Arthur and Hugh Allen. Melodrama. A tale of an old engine driver, his involvement in a crash and subsequent clearing of his name. It was released in Britain in 1927; The *Bioscope* of 3 February 1927 said:

'Though there is nothing out of the ordinary in this picture, the vicissitudes of humble folk, pleasing character studies, and swiftly-moving trains, keep the interest alive and provide satisfactory entertainment. The plot is simple and the continuity excellent. Ralph Lewis makes a splendid old engine-driver, one of those impersonations which stands out with touching human appeal. Sidney Franklin introduces much humour as the facetious friend. The rival lovers are well contrasted, and Jean Arthur is a pleasing Grace. The picture is presented in an admirable manner, with swiftly moving trains, engine sheds and platforms all finely photographed. The accident is quite a good thrill.'

The Block Signal contains an extensive amount of Santa Fe motive power as it was in the mid-1920s; it is still shown in America to railway historical societies.

35/16/8mm, Silent, 87mins, Blackhawk/HA

THE BLUE EXPRESS (USSR 1929)

Produced by Sovkino. Directed by Ilya Trauberg. Music by Edmund Meisel. With Sergei Minin, I Chernyak, Gudkin and Savaliev. Made at the Leningrad studios. A political tale in which all the action takes place on a train. Motive power from Leningrad is used for some spectacular shots of locomotives in action at speed.

35mm, Sound (musical accompaniment only), 85mins, Sovfilm

BLUE PULLMAN (Britain 1960)

Produced by British Transport Films for the British Transport Commission. The story of Britain's new luxury express trains – the diesel Pullmans. The film shows something of the construction of these locomotives, their tests and trials and their high-speed capacity. Sequences follow the first public run of the Manchester to London diesel Pullman service. Awarded Gold Plaque in the Category of Technical Industrial Information at the Third International Festival of Films for TV, International Congress and Exhibition of Electronics and Atomic Energy, Rome, 1961; A Certificate of Merit, Institutional Public Relations Category of documentary films, Fourth International Film Festival, Vancouver, 1961; and a Certificate of Merit, International Film Week, Mannheim, 1961.

(Many other British Transport Films have won International awards; this list is presented as a typical example).

35/16mm, Sound, Colour, 24mins, BTF

BLUE SCAR (Britain 1948)

Outlook Productions. Directed by Jill Craigie. With Emrys Jones and Gwyneth Vaughan. Welsh coal-mining melodrama. Includes shots of GWR South Wales local trains.

35mm, Sound, 102mins, NFA

THE BLUEBELL LINE (Britain, 1961)

Made by G S Holyoake. A detailed survey of the motive power of the Bluebell Line, including the first Bluebell passenger train on 29th October 1961.

16/9.5/8mm, Sound and Silent, Colour, 4mins, MFS

THE BLUEBELL LINE (Britain 1962)

Made by P B Whitehouse and John Adams. The first part of the film shows the activity at Sheffield Park on a Saturday afternoon and the second part shows a Bluebell Special arriving at Horsted Keynes with GNR 0-6-0ST No 1247.

16/8mm, Silent, 9mins, CV/NRM

BLUEBELL LINE VISIT (Britain 1965)

SCTS. Arriving in a Valiant 1931 Gilford coach, the Society saw LBSCR 'E4' No 473 *Birch Grove* and LBSCR 'A1X' 0-6-0T No 55 *Stepney* as well as the old LNWR inspection saloon.

16mm, Silent, 4mins, HA/SCTS

BLUEBELL ON PARADE (Britain 1988)

Online. Produced by Wilf Watters. Commentary by Jim Palm. A detailed record of the Bluebell Preserved Railway, featuring the Standard Class 4 Tank, the 'Q1', Pullman Car No 64, the Adams Radial, the 'Terriers' and visiting locomotives such as the replica *Rocket* and 'Merchant Navy' class *Port Line*. Archive film shows the railway in 1960 when the first steps to re-open the line were being taken.

VID, Sound, Mostly colour, 55mins, Online

BLUEBELL RAILWAY VISIT (Britain 1960)

SCTS. Arrival at Sheffield Park station to see SECR 'P' 0-6-0T *Bluebell*, LBSCR 'A1X' 0-6-0T No 55 *Stepney* and ex-Dorking Graystone Betchworth Limestone works *Townsend Hook*.

16mm, Silent, 6mins, HA/SCTS

BLUEBELL RAILWAY (Britain 1960-61)

A film by Tom Martin. A diary of some activities in the early days of the Bluebell. (Presented with 'live' commentary by Klaus Marx at Fairfield Hall, Croydon, 1989)

16mm, Silent, Colour, 12mins, TM/HA

THE BLUEBELL RAILWAY (Britain 1959)

Julian Pettifer visits the Bluebell Railway shortly before it opened to the public in 1960. He talks to the then Chairman, a volunteer engine driver and Capt Peter Manisty of the ARPS. The locomotive seen is LBSCR 'A1X' 0-6-0T No 55 *Stepney*.

16mm, Sound, 6mins, TM/HA

THE BOB AINSWORTH COLLECTION

Bob Ainsworth from Plymouth has been recording the railway scene in the South West for many years. His films include a detailed account of the GWR branch line from Yelverton to Princetown ('Shadows Across the Moor'), a record of a special steam outing from Plymouth to Bristol ('Steam Far West'), details of many Cornish Railways (including the miniature lines) and much else. The films are all professionally made on 16mm and have enjoyed a short release at one time on video. For details, see under 'Steam in the Far West'.

BOCHE BUSTER RAILWAY GUN ON THE ELHAM VALLEY LINE (Britain 1941)

A detailed account of the 18-inch gun used between Bishopsbourne Tunnel and Barham on the Elham Valley line from Canterbury to Folkestone and built by the SER in 1889. The line closed to passengers in 1940, re-opened in 1946 but finally closed in 1947. The gun unit was assembled at LNER Darlington Road works; the motive power is SR English Electric diesel 0-6-0 No 3.

16mm, Silent, 9mins, IWM

BOER WAR (Britain 1899-1900)

The building of a temporary military railway in South Africa (1899); a troop train crossing the Modder River (1899); LSWR Class 'T9' 4-4-0 No 703 with a troop train bringing soldiers back from the Boer War and a decorated train hauled by LSWR Class 'T9' 4-4-0 No 773 taking Lord Kitchener from Southampton Docks station on his way back to London (1900).

16mm, Silent, 4mins, HA

BOURNE END CRASH (Britain 1945)

Gaumont British News. Newsreel record of LMS accident at Bourne End on 30 September 1945. LMS Royal Scot 4-6-0 No 6157 *The Royal Artilleryman*, hauling the Perth express, derailed down an embankment between Boxmoor and Watford, killing 43 people.

16mm, Sound, 4mins, Visnews/HA

BOURNEMOUTH BELLE (Britain 1945-1948)

An assembly of news clips and amateur film showing the SR 'Bournemouth Belle' hauled by 'Merchant Navy' class locomotives including 21C12 *United States Line*. There is also a shot of the earlier Bournemouth Limited, hauled by a 'King Arthur' class locomotive and filmed in 1929.

16mm, Silent, 6mins, HA

BOURNEMOUTH LINE: STEAM AND DIESEL (Britain 1983)

Rail Video. This was the first tape issued by Rail Video of Bournemouth and appears in their catalogue as RV1. Filmed between 1959 and 1968, it set the pattern for much of the later output of Rail Video, using 16mm but also quite extensively amateur 8mm film, much of it devoted to the last decade of steam. This tape covers Bulleid Pacifics, followed by the earliest of the diesels used in the Southern Region.

VID, Sound, Colour, 60mins, RVO

BOXCAR BERTHA (USA 1972)

AIP. Produced by Roger Corman. Directed by Martin Scorsese. With Barbara Hershey, David Carradine, John Carradine and Barry Primus. In the early 1930s, an unhappy girl falls in with gangsters and train robbers. 'A kind of *Bonnie and Clyde* but Roger Corman uses trains instead of motor cars. Set in Arkansas at the time of Depression, this film is exciting and stylish' (Tony Bilbow). The railroad was provided by a combination of Southern Pacific and a logging camp railroad in Arkansas.

35mm, Sound, Colour, 88mins, AIP

BRAKE SYSTEMS OF A C ELECTRIC LOCOMOTIVE (Britain 1967)

Produced by British Transport Films.
Part 1. The Compressed Air Supply and the straight Air Brake System. The brakes on the locomotive are operated by compressed air. The function and working of every component in the system is explained in detail by animated diagrams.
Part 2. The Proportional Air Vacuum System. Application of the train's vacuum-operated brakes automatically applies the locomotives air brakes to a controlled degree. The same animation techniques describes and explains this system.

35/16mm, Sound, 27mins, BTF

BRANCH LINES (Britain 1983)

Anglia Television. The fight for survival on the remaining branch lines, including the Norwich to Sherringham line (saved) and the Kings Lynn to Hunstanton line (lost).

16mm, Sound, Colour, 11mins, Anglia

BRANCH LINE EXCURSION NO 1 (Britain 1963-65)

Made by G S Holyoake. Survey of tank engines including GWR 0-4-2T No 1450, BR Class 3

2-6-2T No 82036 and GWR 0-6-0 PT No 9773.

16/9.5/8mm, Silent, Colour, 4mins, MFS

🚂 🚂 🚂 🚂 🚂

BRANCH LINE EXCURSIONS NO 2 (Britain 1964)

Made by G S Holyoake. LSWR class 'M7' 0-4-4T No 30053, BR class 2 2-6-0 No 78038 and BR class 3 2-6-2T.

16/9.5/8mm, Silent, Colour, 4mins, MFS

🚂 🚂 🚂 🚂

BRANCH LINE VIDEO

Based at Leighton Buzzard, this video company specialises in making a vast range of railway journeys not covered by most companies. Its catalogue includes *Branch Line to Whitby*, *Branch Line to Uckfield*, *Branch Line to Shanklin*, and many others. They have also produced a series on Cross Country routes, notably *Brighton to Eastbourne*, *Carlisle to Hexham* and *Newcastle to Carlisle*. The technique is to use photographs supplemented by a cab ride, lineside shots and railway architecture. A series of cross-country routes includes *Brighton to Eastbourne* and *Newcastle to Carlisle* as well as main line routes such as *Waverley Route*, plus *Memories of the Isle of Wight*, *Rails Around Exeter* and *Rails Around Salisbury*.

🚂 🚂 🚂 🚂 🚂

BRANCH LINES IN THE SOUTH EAST (Britain 1989)

Transport Video Publishing. The Chesham, Ongar and Newport Pagnell branches (Alan Willmott, 1950s); Westerham and North Woolwich branches (1960s); Hemel Hempstead branches, Staines West to Uxbridge at Colnbrook, etc.

VID, Sound, 50mins, TVP

🚂 🚂 🚂 🚂

BRANCH RIDE TO SHANKLIN (Britain 1989)

Branch Line Video. Written and produced by Ian Heys and Garry Price. A cab ride from Ryde Pier to Shanklin, with details of the seven stations on route, including

Sandown, Brading, Ryde St Johns and Lake station opened in 1987. There is also a visit to Ryde Works.

U-Matic, Sound, Colour, 55mins, BLV

🚂 🚂 🚂 🚂 🚂

BRANCH RIDE TO UCKFIELD (Britain, 1987)

Written and produced by Ian Heys and Garry Price. A cab ride from Oxted to Uckfield, with visits to stations, signalboxes and lineside installations. (Branch Line Video No 2)

VID, Sound, Colour, 60mins, BLV

🚂 🚂 🚂 🚂 🚂

BRANCH RIDE TO WHITBY (Britain 1989)

Branch Line Video. Written and produced by Ian Heys and Garry Price. A journey from Middlesborough to Whitby, with a close look at the semaphore signalling and the historical background of each of the stations, all linked by means of a cab ride.

U-Matic, Sound, Colour, 110mins, BLV

🚂 🚂 🚂 🚂 🚂

BRASS TACKS REPORT: BACK DOOR BEECHING (Britain 1982)

BBC Television. Produced by Alan Dobson. Editor; Colin Adams. Written and presented by Tony Wilkinson. The demise of uneconomical and rundown lines; railways under threat. Examples come from East Anglia, the Mid Wales line, the Worcester to Oxford line, the Cambrian Coast Line and the Settle and Carlisle. A reminder that railways don't just happen anymore; they have to be fought for.

16mm, Sound, Colour, 38mins, BBC TV

🚂 🚂

BREAKHEART PASS (USA 1975)

United Artists. Produced by Jerry Gershwin. Directed by Tom Gries. With Charles Bronson, Ben Johnson, Richard Crenna and Jill Ireland. A motley group of passengers on a winter train across the American west in 1873 are involved in smuggling and murder. 'Botched

murder mystery on wheels' (Leslie Halliwell). 'The train is the only star worth looking at in this plotty Alistair MacLean adventure yarn.' (Tony Bilbow). The railway scenes were done with the help of Southern Pacific (USA) and Canadian Pacific, with a bit of ATSF thrown in. Yet another section was shot on the Cumbries & Toltic Railroad located on the Colorado-New Mexico border.

35mm, Sound, Colour, 94mins, United Artists

🚂 🚂 🚂

BREAKTHROUGH: ROBERT STEPHENSON (Britain 1981)

BBC Television. Written and produced by Molly Cox. Directed by Barbara Kindred. Presented by John Craven. The life of Robert Stephenson, covering his famous father's work at Rainhill (using the replica of *Locomotion*) and then Stephenson's extraordinary life, building the London to Birmingham Railway, Kilsby Tunnel and major engineering all over the world.

16mm, Sound, Colour, 25mins, BBC TV

🚂 🚂

BRIDGE 114 (Britain 1960)

Produced by British Transport Films. Replacing an old railway bridge is no easy matter, especially when rail services cannot be interrupted. So when modernisation at Amersham meant a new track layout and a new bridge, careful preparations had to be made. Between last train Saturday and the first through on Sunday morning, the operation was complete only one half hour over schedule.

35/16mm, Sound, Colour, 9mins, BTF

🚂 🚂 🚂 🚂 🚂

BRIDGE OF A SONG (Britain 1955)

Produced by British Transport Films. The latest developments in British Transport – whether it be in London buses or in railway sidings at Margam steelworks, in the construction of a canal lock between Nottingham and the Humber ports or in the use of modern equipment at BRB laundries or continuous foundries – all such new things bring an echo from the past. The work songs and popular ballads of yesterday serve to bridge time and remind us that the history of transport is continuous – that history is being made today just as certainly it was made a century ago.

35/16mm, Sound, 15mins, BTF

THE BRIDGE ON THE RIVER KWAI (Britain 1957)

Columbia Pictures. Produced by Sam Speigel. Directed by David Lean. With Alec Guinness, William Holden, Jack Hawkins, Sessue Hayakawa, James Donald and André Morrell. British POWs in Burma are employed by the Japanese to build a bridge as part of the Burma railway development; there is a major clash of personality between the British Colonel Nicholson and the Japanese Commander of the camp, involving the issue of whether officers should work alongside the men. At the same time as the prisoners are building the bridge, a British special force is approaching with instructions to destroy it. The end is disaster for all. The bridge itself was built by Dorman Long of Middlesbrough at Kituyala, some 20 miles from Colombo in what was then Ceylon. 500 workmen, and 35 elephants were employed to meet the deadline; the finished bridge was 425ft long and 50ft high above the river. Before it was blown up, a 2ft single line narrow gauge railway was laid across the bridge. When it collapsed, it carried with it an ex-Ceylon Railways Beyer Peacock 4-4-0T locomotive, four vestibule coaches and a small diesel banker – the latter there to make sure that the coaches really all went into the river! This one shot cost Columbia Pictures £85,000.

35mm, Sound, Colour, 161mins, Columbia (HA: railway only)

BRIEF ENCOUNTER (Britain 1946)

Cineguild Production. Produced by Anthony Havelock-Allan. Directed by David Lean. From the play by Noel Coward (part of the 'Tonight at 8.30' set). Photography by Ronald Neame. With Celia Johnson, Trevor Howard, Stanley Holloway and Joyce Carey. An affair between two middle-aged married people. Much of the action takes place in a railway buffet (old-fashioned style, with bath buns) and around the station. There are one or two shots of fast run-throughs taken at Watford Junction but most of the railway action was shot on Carnforth station on the North West main line. David Lean needed a very specific location. A station where mainline trains raced through at speed; a station where there was also a local service. It had to have an elderly buffet to match the studio set of the interior which, like many sections of the station and the surrounding streets, was built at Denham Studios. He also wanted a station with slopes connecting platforms and not steps. The expresses were provided by the mainline, steam-hauled trains to Scotland (not many stopped at Carnforth) and the local service came from the trains on the line to Arnside and Barrow-in-Furness. No station name ever appears in the film but the sharp-eyed may spot a destination board for a train to Clapham, Giggleswick and Hellifield. It must be stressed that most of the film is made in the studio but the railway shots certainly added atmosphere. Vast arrays of arc lights were needed in those days for a night location of this kind and loco men on the expresses were suddenly confronted with a station bathed in a mass of brilliant lights. Their instinct was to slow up; thus spoiling David Lean's shots time and time again. So the LMS Operating Department had to issue a special notice asking drivers not to slow up at Carnforth but if anything to go even faster!

'This film has long been widely considered as a classic. One of the main reasons for its success was the completely authentic atmosphere of the railway station sequences, filmed at Carnforth. The sandwiches and penny sponge cakes, under a glass dome in the refreshment room, the smoke, the steam and sounds of the trains were all an inherent part of the situation of the two leading characters. The whole of that atmosphere was essential to the story which was firmly of that period.' (Peter Handford)

35/16mm, Sound, 86mins, Rank (Carnforth only:HA)

BRIEF ENCOUNTER (Britain 1975)

ITC production for television. Directed by Alan Bridges. With Richard Burton and Sophia Loren. Remake of the David Lean film; an unmitigated disaster. Peter Handford could hardly believe it: 'The decision to remake the film and update the story into the 1970s would have seemed incredible, but for the fact that such unimaginative insensitivity is not rare in the film industry. The resulting remake was a disaster from every point of view, from the casting of the delectable Italian Sophia Loren to play the part of the housewife, originally played by the essentially English and wholly believable Celia Johnson, to the choice of a new location, on the electrified Southern Region at Winchester. What possible atmosphere was supposed to be created, in sight and sound, by the occasional comings and goings of multiple-unit electric trains, at a plasticised and sunlit station, is impossible to understand. Anyone who saw the original film and then had the misfortune to see the modern version, must have been amazed that any producer could be so insensitive as not to realise that the steam age atmosphere was essential to the story.'

16mm, Sound, Colour, 72mins, ITC

BRIEF ENCOUNTERS WITH THE THIRD RAIL (Britain 1991)

A film by Tom Martin. A special assembly made for a celebration of the Southern Electric Group and Brighton 150, including the 'Brighton Belle' (1969), the last 'Brighton Belle' (1972), the 'Nelson' stock farewell tour (1972), preserved 2 BIL/4 SUB units of Southern Electric, the remains of Bulleid's Double Decker at Ashford, the last diesel propelled train on the Merton

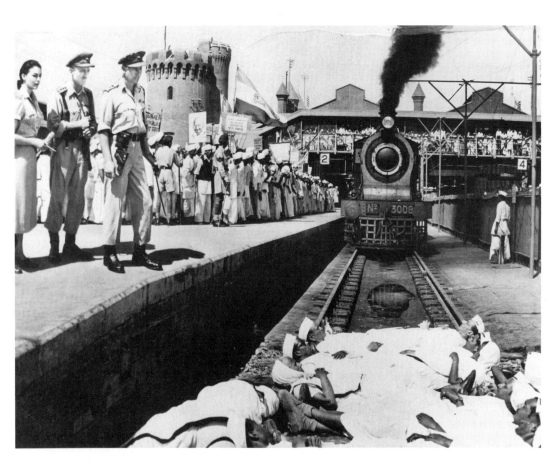

Left:
Beyer Peacock 4-6-0 No 3008 had a part in 'Bhowani Junction' (1956). Although the film was based in India, because of the sensitivity of the film's content the railway scenes were filmed in Pakistan. *National Film Archive*

Below left:
This 425ft long, 50ft high bridge was blown up with a six coach train to make only 15 seconds of the climax of 'The Bridge Over The River Kwai' (1957).
Columbia Pictures Corporation

Right:
Alec Guinness as Colonel Nicholson in David Lean's 'The Bridge Over the River Kwai' (1957).

Below:
In 'Broadway Limited' (1941), a freight train enters a tunnel on the South Pacific Railroad.

Abbey branch (1974) and two versions of the Royal Train on Southern Electric.

16mm, Silent, Colour, TM/HA

🚂 🚂 🚂 🚂 🚂

THE BRIENZ-ROTHORN-BAHN (Britain 1961)

Made by P B Whitehouse and John Adams. A colour film of the sole remaining steam operated mountain railway in Switzerland.

16/8mm, Silent, Colour, 6mins, CV/NRM

🚂 🚂 🚂 🚂 🚂

BRIGHTON BELLE (Britain 1933)

The run of the Brighton Belle from Victoria station to Brighton, during its first weeks of operation.

35mm, Silent, 5mins, NFA/HA

🚂 🚂 🚂 🚂 🚂

THE BRIGHTON BELLE (Britain 1959)

Made by P B Whitehouse and John Adams. A record of the Brighton Belle Pullman train on a run from Victoria to Brighton.

16/8mm, Silent, Colour, 7mins, CV/NRM

🚂 🚂 🚂 🚂 🚂

BRIGHTON ROCK (Britain 1947)

Associated British Picture Corporation. Directed by John Boulting. With Richard Attenborough, William Hartnell and Hermione Baddeley. Crime drama set against the Brighton holiday scene. Includes scenes at Brighton station as well as Brighton trolleybuses.

35mm, Sound, 92mins, Weintraub

🚂

BRIGHTON TO EASTBOURNE (Britain 1989)

Written and produced by Ian Heys and Gary Price. A journey from Brighton to Eastbourne, with details of stations, signalboxes, etc (Cross Country Series No 1)

VID, Sound, Colour, 60mins, BLV

🚂 🚂 🚂 🚂

BRILL BRANCH (Britain 1935)

A short silent newsreel of the last days of the line from Quainton Road and Westcott to Brill on the Metropolitan Railway which was closed in 1935. Metropolitan Beyer Peacock 4-4-0T No 41 is featured.

35/16mm, Silent, 3mins, HA

🚂 🚂 🚂 🚂 🚂

BRILL TO BAKER STREET (Britain 1986)

Transport Video Publishing. London Transport film looking at 120 years of the Metropolitan Railway, including the Chesham branch and material from Quainton Road to Brill in 1935

VID, Sound, 54mins, TVP

🚂 🚂 🚂 🚂 🚂

BRISTOL TEMPLE MEADS IN STEAM DAYS (Britain 1938)

Originally an amateur 9.5mm record of scenes at Bristol, including GWR 4-6-0 No 5015 *Kingswear Castle*, LMS 4-6-0 No 6129 *The Scottish Horse*, GWR '4800' class 0-4-2T No 4855 with an auto-train, and GWR '5700' class 0-6-0T No 7755.

16mm, Silent, 7mins, HA

🚂 🚂 🚂 🚂

THE BRISTOLIAN IN THE DAYS OF STEAM (Britain 1958)

The story of No 7018 *Drysllwyn Castle* working this crack express on 12 May 1958, when steam still reigned supreme. The preparation at Bristol, of both locomotive and train is well covered with typical Adams and Whitehouse thoroughness. The work of not only enginemen, but also, guard, catering staff and traffic operatives are all depicted. Once the preparations are over, and we have left Bristol Temple Meads the story of the journey is covered both from the passenger's view , and on the footplate. No 7018, the subject of experimental development work in the 1950s was considered an exceptional member of the class, as she goes on to show us while we stand with Driver Rowsell as an authenticated 100mph plus is achieved.

16mm/VID, Silent, 7mins, CV/NRM/HA/RSV

🚂 🚂 🚂 🚂 🚂

BRITAIN CAN MAKE IT NO 14 (Britain 1946)

Produced by Film of Fact Ltd. Conversion of steam locomotives from coal to oil burning on the Great Western Railway.

16mm, Sound, 10mins, HA

🚂 🚂 🚂 🚂

BRITANNIAS IN EAST ANGLIA (Britain 1965)

A detailed record of runs by steam-hauled trains in the last days before electrification from Liverpool Street to Norwich. Features BR Britannia class 4-6-2 Nos 70000 *Britannia*, 70001 *Lord Hurcomb*, 70006 *Robert Burns*, 70010 *Owen Glendower* and 70014 *Iron Duke*. The film was originally on 8mm.

16mm, Silent, Colour, 6mins, HA

🚂 🚂 🚂 🚂 🚂

BRITANNIAS: THE FIRST OF THE LAST (Britain 1979)

First Picture production. Produced by John Samson. An account of the design, building, running and ultimate preservation of BR 'Britannia' 4-6-2 locomotives including early scenes of No 70000 *Britannia* and a loan example of the class running on the Severn Valley Railway. 'Britannias' were introduced in 1951, were designed at Derby Works and 55 were eventually built.

16mm, Sound, Colour, 25mins, First Picture

🚂 🚂 🚂 🚂 🚂

BRITISH LOCOMOTIVES (Britain 1959)

Produced by Greenpark Productions for the Locomotive and Allied Manufacturers' Association, the Central Office of Information, the Foreign, Commonwealth Relations and Colonial Offices and the Board of Trade.

A colour film on the development of the British locomotive to the latest and most powerful types of diesel and electric locomotives. Briefly reviewing railway progress since the opening of the Stockton and Darlington railway in 1825, the film surveys the British Railways' modernisation plan; and sequences show many different categories of locomotive and rolling-stock, specially designed and manufactured for overseas markets, in operation in different parts of the world. (Including the Union of South Africa and East Africa, India, Australia and Latin America).

35/16mm, Sound, Colour, 20mins, COI/LAMA/HA

BRITISH RAIL FILM CLASSICS (Britain 1985)

Geoffrey Jones Films. Three British Transport films issued on one tape by the original producer and director: 'Locomotion', 'Rail', and 'Snow'.

VID, Sound, Colour, 32mins, G Jones Films

BRITISH RAILWAYS (Britain 1947-53)

Made by P B Whitehouse. A collection of the earliest shots taken by Pat Whitehouse, prior to the 'Railway Roundabout' days.

16/8mm/VID, Silent, Colour, 9mins, CV/NRM/RSV

BRITISH STEAM CAVALCADE (Britain 1983) Volume 1

Nick Lera Collection. An assembly of individual films including 'Longmoor Military Railway', 'Twilight of Southern Steam', 'King George V at Paddington' and a sequence from 'From Manchester to Java'.

VID, Sound, Colour, 60mins, NLV

BRITISH STEAM CAVALCADE (Britain 1984) Volume 2

Nick Lera Video. A video in three parts. The 1980 Rainhill Parade, the Settle and Carlisle line from 1978 to 1981 and the 75th Anniversary of Tyseley in 1983. Locomotives range widely from *Lion, Maude, Green Arrow, Flying Scotsman* to *Sir Nigel Gresley, Sir Lamiel* and *Evening Star*. There is a classic shot of *Green Arrow* crossing Ribblehead in a howling gale.

VID, Sound, Colour, 47mins, NLV/Locomotion

BRITISH STEAM IN ACTION (Britain 1990)

Rail Video 1927-50. Film by C R L Coles this tape contains very rare archive film. Many locations are featured such as the LMS/LNWR main line, Nine Elms, Isle of Wight (SR days), Paddington, Ruislip, Waterloo, Winchester, LNER Exhibition at New Barnet, Potters Bar and Kings Cross. Classes shown include Claughtons, Precursors, Compounds, unrebuilt 'Royal Scots', 'George Vs', 'O2s', 'N15s', 'Castles', 'Kings', 'Counties', 'County Tank', GC 'A5', 'T9', Adams Jubilee, 'A3s', 'A4s', GN Atlantics, Turbomotive 6202 and many more.

VID, Sound, 30mins, RVO

BRITISH STEAM IN ACTION (Britain 1989)

Rail video. Volume Two.
This is the second tape made from the films of John Shaw. It starts with film of the Somerset & Dorset Railway at Midsomer Norton, Masbury, Chilcompton and the Highbridge branch. Two railtours over the S&D are also shown. The Settle & Carlisle railway is featured including Ribblehead, Settle, Blea Moor and Dent. Some of the last West Coast steam is seen at Shap and Oxenholme. Loco classes shown include Bulleids, Standard 3s, 4s, 5s, 'Clans', 'Britannias', '9Fs', Collett Goods, 'Black 5s', 'Jubilees', '8Fs', Fairburn 2-6-4Ts and a few early diesels.

VID, Sound, Colour, 30mins, RVO

BRITISH STEAM IN THE FIFTIES (Britain 1989)

Rail Video. Volume One.
Film of steam in action on British Rail from all big four companies. Locations such as Paddington, Derby, Ramsgate, York, Birmingham New Street and Snow Hill are featured. Locomotives include Kings, Britannias, Unrebuilt Patriots, 'Schools', 'A1s' and '9Fs'.

VID, Sound, 30mins, RVO

BRITISH STEAM IN THE FIFTIES (Britain 1989)

Rail Video. Volume Two
Made from film shot by Max Lock in the 50s this tape comprises both black and white and colour film. Locations shown include Stoke on Trent, Great Barr, North Wales, LM main line, Lickey Incline, Swindon, 'Last train to Ross-on-Wye', Birmingham New Street and Doncaster. Loco classes include 'Duchesses', 'Royal Scots', 'Patriots', 'Crabs', LMS Stanier tanks, Panniers, Standard classes, Midland Compound, GW 4-6-0s and 0-6-2T, 'Black 5s' and 'Jubilees'.

VID, Sound, Colour, 30mins, RVO

BRITISH STEAM LOCOMOTIVES

1896-1900. British Film Institute. Produced by John Huntley. Wheatley NBR 2-4-0 locomotives and trains on Tay Bridge (1897); 4-4-0 Drummond locomotive and Royal Train, Portsmouth (1897); 4-4-0 Drummond 'T9' class locomotive No 706 of the London & South Western Railway at Southampton with decorated City Imperial Volunteers train (1900); Lord Kitchener special train, Southampton (1900).

16mm, Silent, 12mins, BFI/HA

BRITISH STEAM RAILWAYS (Britain 1983)

Perry's Movies. An assembly of 8mm films which were quickly put together to make a 60mins video in the early pioneering days. Contains some quite rare but largely unexplained material.

8mm/VID, Sound, 60mins, Perrys

BRITISH TRAINS REMEMBERED (Britain 1983)

Pelly's Movies. A motley assembly of steam railway scenes from many sources (and without much reason), including brief bits of 'Coronation Scot', the Bassett-Lowke films of 1929, travelogues of the 1940s etc

VID, Sound, 45mins, Pelly's

BRITISH TRANSPORT FILMS

From 1949 to 1986 British Transport had its own film unit. The unit was originally set up by the British Transport Commission and its films were still released under the name 'British Transport Films'.

The idea of an official railway film unit in this country goes back to the LMS in 1933. The press and public relations office of the day already made available photographs and lantern slides but had not up to then considered films. During the American and Canadian tour of the 'Royal Scot' train, a large amount of local film poured into Euston from grateful film units who had been given facilities at various points on the tour. Encouraged by Brundenell, writer and then editor of the *LMS Magazine*, A J Potter and Aldwinckle, with the blessing of the publicity-minded Chairman of the LMS Sir Joshua Stamp (later Lord Stamp), put all the silent film material together into a 30min film. With the help of Frank Brockliss, the projector importers and manufacturers, a horse-drawn dray for transport and George Marks, projectionist, a 35mm show, using a portable 'ironhouse' projection box (it was inflammable film) was given one Sunday morning to LMS staff at St Pancras town hall. The screening was so successful that other shows were arranged all over the country.

A J Potter takes up the story:
'By early autumn we were ready. For transport to each centre we had an old 1st class LNWR compo brake vehicle which had been converted to give us a toilet, a day compartment, a sleeping compartment, a small workshop and storage space for our gear. This consisted of a 35mm Simplex sound portable arc projector, complete with a transformer, rotary converter, resistances and a Westinghouse metal rectifier (it took four men to lift it). We also had an ironhouse (in those days we were projecting inflammable nitrate film), non-synchroniser and screens of varying sizes. A projectionist, Joe Hall, was hired from J Frank Brockliss of Wardour Street (he is still with the firm but is now their chief engineer) and we were off, equipped to cope with any voltage and current we were likely to meet.

'Making all the contacts, speaking to the press, and being responsible for the success of each screening was my mission in life. Our tour began at Abergavenny, and one evening in mid-September 1936 we slipped out of Euston attached to the end of a main-line train for South Wales. We always arrived at the place of showing during the morning of the day of the screening. I shall always remember waking up in a siding in Abergavenny station, looking out of the window and seeing the station master (with Sugar Loaf Mountain behind him) inspecting our coach with unconcealed astonishment.

'At 2pm, a flat horse-drawn dray arrived and we unloaded and made for the town hall. We set up during the afternoon, had an early tea and went back to the hall at 5.30pm. Television was more or less non-existent in those days, and there was already a long queue for the 6pm show. The great moment came — 6pm, 15 September 1936. From the stage, before a full house (about 600 people complete with the Mayor and other civic personages), I introduced the films. The lights went down and we hit the screen with a picture 8ft wide. The railways' first-ever non-theatrical show with sound films had begun.

'At 7.30pm it was all over. We had a few drinks in the Mayor's parlour, interviews with the local press and then got on with the 8pm screening, which — again with a full house — was an equal success. At 9.30pm a hurried dismantle, and at 10pm a horse and cart arrived for the gear; then back to the coach at the station — equipment safely loaded, and for us some supper and to bed while, through the night, we were towed to Swansea. This was to be our routine for the next six months — two shows a night, waking up in a different place every day of the week.

'We used to sleep in the cinema coach and some nights it could be very chilly. We had been issued with those old aluminium hot water bottles that used to be popular then and it was our practice to get them filled with hot water in the station refreshment rooms. One night at Bletchley, I took the bottles in as usual and said "fill them up". When the lady brought them back, she

said "eightpence please"; they were both full of hot tea! That night we kept warm *and* had hot tea in bed. Another time we were alongside an exceptionally noisy shunting yard at Birmingham where the chief shunter had a penetrating horn which he blew all the time. After a while, my colleague Joe Hall (of Brockliss) could stand no more. He opened the window and shouted: "if you can't stop your horn, at least change the damn tune".

'One night in Coventry town hall, we arrived to set up our projectors and found a ladies' whist drive nearing its climax. Joe decided he daren't switch out the lights to wire up the power plug so he stuck his screwdriver into the live socket. There was a tremendous flash, half the screwdriver just disappeared and the hall was plunged into total darkness. The ladies went mad. When the lights came on, all their cards were mixed up on the tables, the near-winners were furious at being cheated out of the top prizes and no one was the slightest bit interested in whether Joe had survived or not.

'The "ironhouse" projection box had steel shutters over the port holes which shut with a bang by pulling a wire release; in this way, the operator and his inflammable nitrate film could quietly burn up without the audience being affected. Even so, most places had two local firemen outside with foam at the ready "just in case". One night during a show in Crewe, the wire broke of its own accord, clang went the shutters and the firemen came roaring at us, axes at the ready and we only just stopped them drowning us and the projectors with foam.

'The film shows were free and a great draw in those days (no telly), especially with the kids. One day, we had a very posh show in that Holy of Holies, the great Shareholders' Room at Euston station. The hall was dark, the film was on and I heard a terrific racket outside. I dashed into the noble hall — to find six kids belting round the polished wood floor on roller skates. It nearly finished our shows at Euston.'
Today A J Potter is manager of British Transport Films.

After 1933, the LMS made a large number of excellent films,

including: *6207: A Study in Steel*, *Passenger Trains of the LMS*, *Building the Corridor Third*, *Engine Sheds*, *Holidays in Scotland*, *Sentinels of Safety* and one classic work *Coronation Scot*. This sound film was made in 1937 and covered the building, trial runs and the famous record-breaking run of *Coronation* when a speed of 114mph was attained near Crewe which Cecil J Allen described so vividly in his book *Two Million Miles of Train Travel*:

'The LMSR plan of campaign was this. Euston to Crewe and back was to be the course of the trial run, and over this stretch of line the only appreciable down gradient on which gravity might have sufficient assistance for a really high speed to be attained was the 6½ miles between milepost 150¼ and milepost 156¾, first for 3¼ miles at 1 in 177 and then for a similar distance at 1 in 269. Driver Clarke was therefore, instructed to run approximately to the new Coronation Scot schedule as far as Stafford, and then to give *Coronation* her head. On the very slight rise from Stafford to Whitmore it should be possible to attain a pretty high speed, and it was then hoped to accelerate to such purpose down Madeley bank that an unbeatable record would be made before it was necessary to brake hard for the two double crossovers leading into Crewe station.

'Out of Euston we started with such vigour that by Watford the speed was up to 86½mph, and the maintenance of just over 80 all the way to the 1 in 330 to Tring, and a passing time of 27 minutes 45 seconds for this initial 31.7 miles, were certainly unprecedented figures. By Tring we were 2½ minutes early, but from here Driver Clarke kept a little more closely to his point-to-point times, though even so by passing Stafford, 133.6 miles, in 109 minutes 56 seconds we gained 5 minutes on booked time. The curve at Trent Valley Junction had not by that date been relaid on its present "two-level" plan, and with scrupulous caution we crawled round it and through Stafford station at no more than 30mph. Not until Norton Bridge, passed at 60mph, did Clarke open his engine out, but from here the proceedings were exciting to a degree.

'Standon Bridge was passed at 75mph and Whitmore at 85; by milepost 150 speed was 93½mph and we had now reached the top of the 1 in 177. The excitement of the three co-timers by now was intense as at the end of successive miles the speed soared upwards to 97, 102½, 106, 108½, 111, and finally, between posts 155 and 156, to an average of 112½mph. Between us we three agreed that a peak of 113mph was admissible — a dead heat with the LNER!

'I have no precise knowledge as to what happened on the footplate during the next mile. Did driver Clarke and Stanier's personal assistant R A Riddles, who also was on the footplate, try to get just a shade more out of the engine at the foot of the 1 in 269, so as to be certain of transferring the record from the LNER into LMSR hands? Personally I think we must have been well into the mile between posts 156 and 157 before steam was actually shut off and a full brake application made, for my times show that the average speed between these posts was 105mph, which would mean that at the 157-mile post, within less than ¾ of the first crossover outside Crewe, speed was still at least 90mph. By now the brakes were on hard, and by the time the highest speed had been halved, we had the feeling that we were travelling quite slowly. But it was a different matter when we hit the point of the first crossover, with its 20mph restriction which we did at fifty-seven miles an hour!

'It says a good deal for the maintenance of the track at this point that we did nothing worse than break the jaws of one or two chairs in the switch and crossing work; the way in which the great engine rode across the succession of double reverse curves without derailing was no small tribute to her design. In the train, to the audible accompaniment of carnage among the crockery in the restaurant car, we passengers preparing to alight were involved in all kinds of involuntary embraces, as the train snaked its way through two crossovers to the left and a final turnout to the right into No 3 platform at Crewe; I have often thought what an astonishing spectacle this sinuous process

must have been to watchers on the platforms at the London end of the station. It will give some realisation of the unique nature of this stop when I say that the 2.1 miles from milepost 156 to the dead stand were run in 1 minute 53 seconds, and the 10.5 miles from Whitmore to the stop in 6 minutes 58 seconds! Also to-day, when every down express starts to brake heavily at Basford Sand Sidings, and then approaches Crewe with the utmost caution, it seems almost incredible that on that July day in 1937 we were doing more than 100mph over more than a mile of that same stretch.

'At the press lunch LMSR vice-president Sir Ernest Lemon, who was in the chair, after various felicitous references to the new train, remarked, "I understand, gentlemen, that you had a slight shaking-up to-day as you were running into Crewe. Of course, we shan't need to do this kind of thing every day." Every day!! Very likely it would have needed no more than a single repetition of what happened for there to have been no more Coronation Scot. At a public gathering in later years, R A Riddles, who as already mentioned was riding on the footplate of *Coronation*, looking back to the experiences of that day remarked "The engine rode like the great lady she is. There wasn't a thing we could do but hold on and let her take it. Take it she did; past a sea of pallid faces on the platform we ground to a dead stand, safe and sound still on the rails." But there was "a thing" that they could have done on the footplate; even at the expense of losing the chance of making a record, they could have applied the brakes early enough to negotiate the crossover curves at a safe speed, and thereby to avoid what was a most reckless proceeding.'

The producer, director and commentator of the film was John Shearman. He conceived the bold idea of inter-cutting newsreel film of the 1937 Coronation with shots of the construction and emergence of William Stanier blue and cream streamlined locomotive at Crewe in which Elgar's 'Pomp and Circumstance March No 4' and William Walton's 'Coronation March' mingle with the cheering of crowds greeting the Coronation coach and Stanier's engine alike. Modesty was not a characteristic of Sir Joshua's LMS company! There are historic shots of Stanier himself, good records of driver Tom Clarke on the *Princess Elizabeth* and *Coronation Scot* runs and impressive aerial shots of the 114mph run. The only regret is that the film is not in colour.

The man in charge was Edgar Anstey, who was later Chief Officer (Films), British Railways Board. He became interested in trains as a schoolboy and used to watch activity at Watford Junction from a park walk nearby. After starting a career in science at Birkbeck College and the Building Research Station, Anstey answered an advertisement in *The Times* and he was selected as a film trainee for John Grierson's famous Empire Marketing Board. 'My training was very simple' Anstey recalls; 'I spent my summer holidays watching the unit at work, was then given a De Vry 35mm camera and sent off to film some London scenes for exactly a day and a half. I had never held a movie camera in my hands before but I was then immediately sent off on my own with some lights, two cameras and a load of film stock on an expedition to Labrador, from which I brought back two films — "Uncharted Waters" and "Eskimo Village". Life was simpler in those days! I then edited "Industrial Britain" for Grierson and Robert Flaherty, worked on "Granton Trawler" and "6.30 Collection" and generally learnt the business with the EMB Unit (later the GPO Film Unit). I had one interesting experience with railway films at the GPO. I did the original research and wrote a complete script for "Night Mail", the story of the Euston-Glasgow Travelling Post Office. Not a single line of my script was used in the finished film!'

After a brief venture with Shell, Anstey joined up with Paul Rotha, Arthur Elton and Donald Taylor to form the Realist Film Unit and later Film Centre. After some notable work, including 'Housing Problems' and 'Enough to Eat', he was asked by Christian Barmen to form the British Transport film unit in 1948; in 1949, the first film 'Wealth of the World: Transport' was made jointly with Peter Baylis and almost simul-

taneously the unit made its own first independent film 'Berth 24'. Since then their work, in staff training, direct sales or general publicity, has been of consistently high quality and many of their main productions like 'Between The Tides', 'Journey Into Spring', 'Wild Wings', 'Terminus', 'Thirty Million Letters', 'Freightliner Story', 'The Midland Pullman', 'The Elizabethan Express', 'Snow' and 'Rail' have not only enjoyed wide distribution but they have also won many awards and diplomas at international film festivals throughout the world.

Edgar Anstey retired in 1974 and died in 1987. In the meantime the work of the film unit, now under the control of the Publicity Department of British Railways continued with John Shepherd (who came from the Admiralty) in charge until it was eventually wound up in 1986. It was perhaps appropriate that the last film dealt with the proposed Channel Tunnel!

Many of the individual films, especially those relating to steam days, will be found under their individual titles; I am indebted to Edgar Anstey and Charles Potter for permission to reproduce entries from their original catalogue.

During the 1960s and 1970s, a very large number of films were produced; the main titles featuring railways include:

London For a Day (1962)
Let's Go To Birmingham (1962)
London's Victoria Line (1969)
Snow (1963)
Forward to First Principles (1966)
Driving Force (1966)
Inter-City (1968)
Class 86 Locomotive (1970)
Wires Over the Border (1974)
Locomotion (1975)
Discovering Railways (1977)
Discover Britain by Train (1978)
Track 125 (1981)
Round Trip to Glasgow (1982)
Stone Carriers (1982)
North Eastern Goes Forward (1963)
Locomotive Jubilee (1962)
Electric Train Driver (1964)
Rail (1967)
Joe Brown at Clapham (1965)
Under The Wires (1965)
Advanced Passenger Train (1969)

Journey Inter-City (1972)
Inter-City 125 (1976)
Rail 150 (1975)
Overture 125 (1978)
New Age for Railways (1979)
Centenary Express (1980)
Train Makers (1981)
Inter-City 1250 (1982)

The British Transport Collection is now looked after by FAME (Barry Coward) from 18-20 St Dunstan's Road, London SE25 6EU.

BROADWAY LIMITED (USA 1941)

A Hal Roach Studios production. Directed by Gordon Douglas. With Victor McLaglen, Dennis O'Keefe, Marjorie Woodworth and Patsy Kelly. A new film star and her temperamental director set out on a long-distance train from Los Angeles to New York. She meets a charming but pennyless doctor and falls in love; the engine driver falls for the director's secretary; a baby, taken on the train for publicity, is pursued by the police looking for a kidnapped baby, all punctuated by good transcontinental railway shots. 35mm, Sound, 75mins, Roach 🚂 🚂

BROADWAY LIMITED AND ROYAL SCOT (Britain 1933)

LMS locomotive *Royal Scot* and the 'Broadway Limited' running towards Chicago during the tour of *Royal Scot* in Canada and America. 16mm, Silent, 4mins, BFI/HA 🚂 🚂 🚂 🚂 🚂

BROKEN CIRCUIT (USA 1924)

Helen Holmes production. An extended version of the serial thrillers which first brought Helen Holmes to fame in 'The Hazards of Helen'. There are the usual collection of villains, young men who make good in the last reel and dangerous stunts by the heroine. The fictional 'C&ERR' is provided by the Los Angeles sheds of the Union Pacific Railroad, with a 4-6-0 express locomotive and great performances by two 0-6-0 freight locomotives Nos 3169 and switcher No 4238 with its strange cutaway tender. 16mm, Silent, 28mins, HA 🚂 🚂 🚂

THE BRUNIG LINE (SWITZERLAND) (Britain 1961)

Made by P B Whitehouse and John Adams. A film made of this Swiss Narrow Gauge electric line between Interlaken and Lucerne shows the working over the cog-driven inclines to the Brunig Pass, and the sole surviving 0-6-0T No 1067.

16/8mm/VID, Silent, Colour, 9mins, CV/NRM/VID

BRUNIG RAILWAY (Britain 1988)

RV Television. A record of the railway from Lucerne, via the Brunig Pass to Interlaken, plus a run up the electric rail coach at 1 in 2 gradient on the Mount Pilatus Railway as well as steam scenes on the Brienz-Rothorn-Bahn.

VID, Sound, Colour, 58mins, RVV

BRUNIG RAILWAY CAB RIDE (Britain 1987)

RV Television. Journey in the cab of a HGe 4/411 locomotive from Lucerne through the heart of central Switzerland to Interlaken in the Bernese Oberland. The trip includes a run through the Brunig Pass.

VID, Sound, Colour, 60mins, RVV

BUILDING A BRITISH RAILWAY: CONSTRUCTING THE LOCOMOTIVE (Britain 1905)

An Urbanora Film. LNWR locomotive being built at Crewe

35mm, Silent, 12mins, NFA

BUILDING OF A LOCOMOTIVE AT CREWE (Britain 1911)

Made by William F Baker. A re-issue of the GWR film on the building of *Prince of Wales* at Swindon in 1911 under a false title.

35mm, Silent, 11mins, NFA

BUILDING OF A TRANSCONTINENTAL RAILWAY IN CANADA (Britain 1910)

A Butcher's Empire picture. The building of the Grand Trunk Pacific Railway.

35mm, Silent, 10mins, NFA

BUILDING THE LOCOMOTIVE PRINCE OF WALES AT SWINDON (Britain 1912)

An Urbanora film. Record of the building of Churchward GWR Star Class No 4041 *Prince of Wales* at Swindon.

35mm/VID, Silent, 12mins, HA/125

BUILDING THE CORRIDOR THIRD (Britain 1937)

An LMS film. A detailed account from drawing board to finished carriage of stock at Derby Works. The finished corridor third is brought out of the works by MR 4-4-0 compound No 1045; the film includes very rare shots of Sir William Stanier, Chief Mechanical Engineer of the LMS.

35/16mm, Silent, 42mins, BTF/HA

BUILDING TOGETHER (France 1963)

Produced by SNCF for the International Union of Railways. The building, installation and inauguration of the headquarters of the International Union of Railways in Paris and the work of the different departments including the General Secretariat, the Board of Management, Committees and Working Parties.

35/16mm, Sound, Colour, 18mins, UIC

BULLDOG JACK (Britain 1935)

A British and Dominions film. Directed by Walter Forde. With Jack Hulbert, Fay Wray, Ralph Richardson, Claude Hulbert, Gibb McLaughlin and Atholl Fleming.

Bulldog Drummond, keyed up to cross swords with the Morelle gang,

has the brakes of his car secretly tampered with, with the result that he crashes into Jack Pennington's car, and breaks his arm. Jack, always thirsting for adventure, volunteers, temporarily to take over Drummond's mission, and, with Algy, Drummond's friend, as his assistant, sets to work to help Ann Manders, an attractive girl, whose grandfather, an expert jeweller, is the unwilling tool of Morelle.

Ann and her grandfather are kidnapped under the very eyes of Jack and Algy, but they trace them to Morelle's hideout in a deserted underground station. Jack forestalls Morelle's plan to force Ann to steal jewels from the Goddess with the Hundred Hands, a figure in the British Museum, but Morelle escapes, and hides in a driverless tube train. When Jack, Ann and Algy come aboard, Morelle sets it going, and it is only the courage of Jack that prevents them all coming to a sticky end. He pulls the train up in the nick of time, and after handing Morelle over to the authorities, offers to become Ann's permanent protector and is accepted.

Although a lot of the Underground scenes were built in the studios, there are some interesting night location scenes filmed at the disused Bloomsbury (British Museum) station on the Central line between Tottenham Court Road and Holborn.

There is an unusual underground tunnel model layout as well as real shots taken from the front of a train with a vast array of lights; the Central line map shows some odd stations, including Camden Hill, Kensington Park, East Perivale and Western Avenue.

35mm, Sound, 72mins, Rank/HA:railway only

BURN 'EM UP BARNES: Episode Seven: Roaring Rails (USA 1934)

Mascot Serials. Directed by Colbert Clark and Armand Schaefer. With Jack Mulhall, Frankie Darro, Lola Lane and Julien Rivero. A racing driver and his son take on a bunch of racketeers. A typical American serial for the cinema in the 1930s; this episode involved a chase between a school bus and an Atchison, Topeka and Sante Fe locomo-

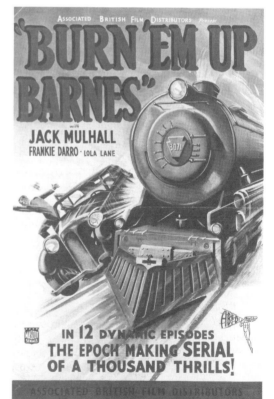

Left:
A scene from 'This Year London' one of the British Transport Films.
British Railways

Below far left:
A young trainspotter gets his ticket clipped during 'This is York' another of the British Transport Films. *British Railways*

Below left:
Advertising promoting a series of 'Burn 'Em Up Barnes' which was released in America in 1934.

Right:
The filming of the LNER film 'Can I Help You' (1946) at King's Cross.

Below:
A scene from the tragi-comedy 'Closely Observed Trains' (1966) which won the 1968 Academy Award for the best foreign film.
National Film Archive

tive No 3071, with a crash involving Burn 'em Barnes riding to the rescue.

35mm, Sound, 20mins, Mascot

BUTCH CASSIDY AND THE SUNDANCE KID (USA 1969)

TCF/Campanile. Produced by John Foreman. Directed by George Roy Hill. With Paul Newman, Robert Redford, Katharine Ross and Strother Martin. The life of two train robbers, partly based on fact. Includes excellent scenes on the Durango and Silverton narrow gauge railroad built by the Denver and Rio Grande Railway Company, mainly featuring D&RGR 2-8-2 No 472 and stock, renamed 'Overland Flyer' and 'Union Pacific' for film purposes. The silent title sequence uses some old Union Pacific stock shots. The blowing up of a coach and its strong box is one of the most notable scenes.

35mm, Sound, Colour, 112mins, TCF

BUTCH AND SUNDANCE: THE EARLY DAYS (USA 1979)

TCF. Directed by Richard Lester. With Tom Berenger and William Katt. Early episodes in the life of the famous outlaws. It ends with a train robbery, using stock shots from the 1969 film and fresh material shot on the Denver and Rio Grande (Silvertown branch).

35mm, Sound, Colour, 112mins, TCF

BUTCHER, BAKER
(Britain 1946)

An LMS film. Specialised railway freight services for the food trade in Britain, illustrated with the LMS area just before nationalisation.

35mm/VID, Sound, Colour, 12mins, BTF/TVP

BUTLER HENDERSON (Britain 1961)

Made by P B Whitehouse and John Adams. The preserved Great Central Railway 'Director' makes a trip out to Romilley for filming after being restored at Gorton Works.

16/8mm, Silent, 5mins, CV/NRM

BY SLIP COACH TO BICESTER (Britain 1960)

Made by P B Whitehouse and John Adams. A record of the last slip coach working on British Railways, the 5.10pm ex Paddington.

16/8mm, Silent, 5mins, CV/NRM/Stirling/RSV

CAB RIDES

There are many. The sophisticated style of **Video 125** includes the following; they are in fact driver's eye views, a slightly different technique:
Settle and Carlisle
1066 D.C. (Hastings to London)
HST West (Exeter to Plymouth)
The Cambrian Coast
Skye Train (Inverness to Kyle of Lochalsh)
Metropolitan and District
Chiltern
Steam to Mallaig (Fort William to Mallaig)
The Far North (Dingwall to Wick and Thurso)
Central Underground
Cornish Branch Lines
Ffestiniog-Conway
HST Far West (Saltash to Penzance)
HST West (Exeter to Plymouth)
The **Railscene** list of cab rides is extensive and includes:
Perth to Inverness
Exeter to Plymouth
Euston to Liverpool
Tunbridge Wells to Eridge
Kings Cross to York
St Pancras to Sheffield
Portsmouth to Cardiff
Dover to Willesden
Bournemouth to Weymouth
Crewe to Holyhead
Salisbury to Exeter
York to Edinburgh
Cardiff to Birmingham
Shrewsbury to Aberystwyth
Machynlleth to Pwllheli
Penrith to Glasgow Central
Aberdeen to Inverness
Uckfield to Victoria
Liverpool Street to Kings Lynn
Sheffield to Cleethorpes
Crewe to Penrith
Carlisle-Newcastle-Carlisle
Carlisle to Newcastle via Gateshead
Hull to Scarborough
Skipton to Carlisle
Brighton to Victoria
Glasgow-Edinburgh-Glasgow
Wolverton to Birmingham
Paddington to Bristol
Redditch to Lichfield
Portsmouth-Eastleigh-Portsmouth
Coalville to Calverton via Nottingham

Waterloo to Salisbury
Merseyrail North
Merseyrail South
Manchester to Barrow
The Cumbrian Coast
Bury-Manchester-Bury
Swansea to Swindon
Stranraer to Glasgow
Dundee to Edinburgh
Cameron Bridge to Mossend
Merehead to Theale

Railfilms have not gone in so much for cab rides but they did carry out a vast cab ride project for British Rail Network SouthEast, recording eight hours of their major routes for internal 'corporate video' use as part of a civil engineering and operations analysis. The material was filmed by Nick Dodson.

CAB RIDE: BLS ALPINE PASS THUN TO BRIG (Britain 1985)

Salford Films. The Lotschberg Pass from Thun to Brig. Colour map supplied with tape.

VID, Sound, Colour, 50mins, SFV

CABARET (USA 1972)

ABC Pictures/Allied Artists. Directed by Bob Fosse. Berlin cabaret in the 1930s, broadly based on the life of Christopher Isherwood. Includes a scene at the Berlin East Station with Pacific Hof locomotives.

35mm, Sound, Colour, 123mins, ABC Pictures

CABLE LAYING JOURNEY (Britain 1958)

Henley Cables. Electrification of the Kent Coast lines and the use of Henley cables.

16mm, Sound, 30mins, RFV

CABLES CARRY THE CURRENT (Britain 1957)

Produced by Stanley Schofield Productions for the Pirelli-General Cable Works. The manufacture and laying of 66kV-oil-filled cables and

their use in a British Railways' electrification scheme in their Southern Region.

16mm, Sound, Colour, 28mins, COI

CADBURY MILK TRAY COMMERCIAL (Britain 1972)

Saatchi Agency. One of the 'mystery man' TV commercials ('All because the lady loves Milk Tray') was filmed on the Nene Valley railway.

16mm, Sound, Colour, 28sec, Saatchi

CAERPHILLY CASTLE (Britain 1961)

Made by P B Whitehouse and John Adams. A journey of this famous engine on a low loader one Sunday morning through London, from Park Royal to South Kensington, destined for the Science Museum.

16mm/VID, Silent, 8mins, CV/NRM/Stirling

CALEY BOGIES FROM PERTH TO AVIEMORE (Britain 1960)

Made by P B Whitehouse and John Adams. This film shows two Pickergill 4-4-0s Nos 54485 and 54486 being prepared at Perth and then working an express from Perth to Aviemore.

16/8mm/VID, Silent, 8mins, CV/NRM/Stirling

CALL OF THE SOUTH (Switzerland 1955)

The story of the St Gothard Tunnel. Its construction and operation (as at 1955).

35mm, Sound, 19mins, NA

CALLANDER-OBAN (Britain 1936)

Scenes at Oban, Loch Etive cantilever bridge, Ballachulish Ferry and Glencoe coach link. Motive power includes LMS 4-6-0 No 5162 (Stanier design, introduced in 1935), and an old Caledonian 'Dunalistair' class engine.

16mm, Silent, 8mins, HA

CALLINGTON BRANCH (Britain 1963)

A brief 8mm record of Callington station and the surrounding area on the old Plymouth, Devonport and South Western Railway, still very much in Southern green. Locomotives include Ivatt LMS 2-6-2T Nos 41291 and 41307 as well as Wainwright SECR 0-4-4T H class No 31278. The line beyond Gunnislake, including Callington, was closed in 1966.

16mm, Silent, Colour, 3mins, HA

THE CAM CAMWELL COLLECTION

One of the great 16mm film collections, W. A. Camwell has given shows of his films for many years to railway clubs and societies; and was always asked back. His work has been available on video through Railscene and the material was grouped together in chronological order:

The Camwell Collection Nos 1 to 6. (1951-54; 1954-56, 1956-58, 1959-60, 1960-62 and 1962-64.)

THE CAMBRIAN COAST (Britain 1988)

Video 125. Written and produced by Peter Middleton. Commentary by Daffyd Hywell. A driver eye view of the 25-mile line from Machynlleth to Barmouth seen from a Class 150 'Sprinter'. This beautiful coast line is well captured and there are fine views of the Barmouth Viaduct. At Tywyn, there is a visit to the Talyllyn narrow gauge railway and a similar look at the Fairbourne railway. A fine example of the Driver's Eye video style.

VID, Sound, Colour, 80mins, VID/125

CAMBRIAN COAST EXPRESS (Britain 1962)

A film by P B Whitehouse and John Adams. The film is described by Pat Whitehouse:

'We open with a record of the then new Western Region Modernisation Plan detailing the changes to the 'lawn' at Paddington Station. For their first stage of the journey to Shrewsbury our locomotive is No 7002 *Devizes Castle*. En route to Banbury we are witness to a 'Castle' making smoke (for the camera?) as it progresses at high speed. After Banbury we go ahead to Shrewsbury to join our next driver finishing his preparation work on No 7803 *Barcote Manor*. Of particular interest are the white buffers and smokebox door hinges, not as we will learn necessarily applied just for our film crew. For practical reasons the journey from Shrewsbury to Aberystwyth was shot over several weekends, and we benefit from views of two other members of the class — Nos 7814 *Fringford Manor* and 7823 *Hook Norton Manor*. For locomotive buffs the appearances of Mogul No 7313 (along with some stray sheep) and the now extinct Swindon inspired BR Standard Class 3 2-6-2T in the shape of No 82033 are a bonus'.

16mm/VID Silent, Colour, 8mins, CV/NRM/VID

CAMP COACH HOLIDAY (GARA BRIDGE) (Britain 1964)

Made by P B Whitehouse and John Adams. Recorded during a visit to the Kingsbridge branch of the GWR.

16/8mm, Silent, 6mins, CV/NRM

CAN I HELP YOU? (Britain 1946)

Verity Films. Produced by Cossar Turfery. Directed by Harold Purcell. With Terry Randall, Hamilton Humphriss, Pat MacGrath and Fred Griffiths, Staff training showing how the driver, the guard, the booking office and the enquiry office all combine to present a public image of a railway; in this case, the LNER at Kings Cross. Made by Merton Park studios.

16mm, Sound, 16mins, Verity/HA

CANADA'S HIGHSPOTS (Canada 1938)

Includes steam-hauled logging train in the area of Vancouver as well as passenger railway traffic in the mountainous regions.

16mm, Sound and silent, 11mins, NA

THE CANADIAN (Canada 1955)

Produced by Canadian Pacific Railways. The age of the diesel comes to a major Canadian system.

16mm, Sound, Colour, 21mins, CPR

CANADIAN MOUNT MAJESTY (Canada 1943)

Associated Screen News for the Canadian Pacific Railway. A train journey from Calgary to Vancouver through the Rockies.

16mm, Silent, 14mins, NA

CANADIAN PACIFIC (USA 1949)

TCF Production. Produced by Nat Holt. Directed by L Mann. Music by Dmitri Tiomkin. Technical Adviser: John Rhodes Study (Canadian Pacific Railway). With Randolph Scott, Jane Wyatt and J Carroll Naish. Opens with a montage of Canadian steam as it was in 1949. Then into reconstruction with a speech by William Van Horne, general manager of the CPR, saying a way will be found through the Rockies by surveyor Tom Andrew. 'Fairly unhistorical but watchable Western' (Leslie Halliwell).

35mm, Sound, Colour (Cinecolour), 95mins, TCF

CANDLESHOE (Britain 1977)

Walt Disney Productions. Directed by Norman Tokar. With David Niven, Helen Hayes and Jodie Foster. An attempt to pass off a fake heiress to an English stately home is frustrated by the resourceful butler. Includes a scene on the Severn Valley Railway, featuring Arley station (re-named 'Hambledon') and a GWR 45XX tank engine.

35mm, Sound, Colour, 101min, Disney

CANNON STREET STATION (Britain 1926)

Empire News. Electrification in progress at Cannon Street station.

35mm, Silent, 50secs, NFA

CANTERBURY-WHITSTABLE RAILWAY (Britain 1951-1953)

Detailed record of the last days of the Canterbury-Whitstable railway including its history (locomotive *Invicta*), the daily running, the last journey, a brief reprieve after the 1953 floods and final lifting of the track and blowing-up of bridges. The main locomotive featured is Wainwright SECR H class 0-4-4T No 31010, with cut-down chimney to negotiate the low bridges on the old 1829 railway. There are also scenes on the main line at Whitstable featuring unrebuilt 'Battle of Britain' class express trains and SECR L1 class 4-4-0 No 31787.

16mm, Silent, 17mins, Endersby/HA

THE CAPE TO CAIRO RAILWAY (Britain 1983)

Nick Lera Collection. A fine study of African steam including South African Class 25s across the Karoo, Zimbabwe's Garratts up to Victoria Falls, and the last steam run to Kilimanjaro in Kenya. There is also archive film made in 1929 of the Cape to Cairo Railway and scenes of the construction of Garratt locomotives at Beyer Peacock Works at Gorton, Manchester.

VID, Sound, Part Colour, 65mins, NLV

CAPE TO CAIRO RAILWAY (Britain 1976)

BBC Television. Produced by Colin Luke. Written and presented by Roy Lewis. From the *World About Us* series.

A wonderful collection of footage of very early days of the building of this famous dream route conceived by Cecil Rhodes. Very detailed account of the use of large steam locomotives. Excellent footage of

Beyer Garratt locos on the East African Railways.

16mm/VID Sound, Colour, 50mins, BBC TV/HA (rail only)

🚂 🚂 🚂

CAPITAL VISIT (Britain 1955)

Produced by British Transport Films. A party of schoolchildren visit London to spend three crowded days in the capital. The adventure starts with the railway journey, and once in London new impressions are collected thick and fast — the streets, the parks, the museums, the shops, the hotel which becomes their temporary home, the Changing of the Guard, St Paul's, the Tower of London — and, at night, the crowded pavements and the bright lights. There is time to visit London Airport and Windsor Castle and to travel by river launch to Greenwich and the Pool.

35/16mm Sound, Colour, 20mins, BTF

🚂

THE CAPTIVE HEART (Britain 1946)

Ealing Studios. Directed by Basil Dearden. With Michael Redgrave and Mervyn Johns. PoW camp drama. Shot of prisoner-of-war train in wartime Germany.

35mm, Sound, 108mins, Weintraub

🚂

CAR GWYLLT (Britain 1934)

An amusing record of the 'wild cars', really just a piece of board, a metal rod and a couple of small wheels made up in the metal shop and used by men to make a fast descent at the end of the day by using the steep inclined planes in the North Wales slate quarry at Dinorwic. Each man owned and maintained his own 'car'; they added another touch of danger to an already dangerous job.

16mm, Silent, 3mins, HA

🚂 🚂 🚂 🚂 🚂

CARDIFF RAILWAY SCENES (Britain 1927-67)

An assembly of scenes including the shipment of GWR No 6000 *King George V* to America in 1927; dock railways in 1927; dock scenes in

1935 with Beyer-Garratt double-engine docks shunter and various privately-owned industrial locomotives; Cardiff General station in 1941; and a visit by LNER No 4472 *Flying Scotsman* in 1967.

16mm, Silent, Part Colour, 11mins, HA

🚂 🚂 🚂 🚂 🚂 🚂

CARDIGAN BRANCH (Britain 1958)

Made by Patrick Whitehouse and John Adams. Journey with GWR Class '45XX' prairie tank No 4558 from Cardigan to Crymmych Arms. A GWR pannier tank is seen working a passenger train.

16mm/VID Silent, 3mins, CV/NRM/Stirling

🚂 🚂 🚂 🚂 🚂

CAREFREE CURVES (Britain 1957)

P&M Ltd. The use of P&M lubricators on the railways.

16mm, Sound, 12mins, P&M

🚂 🚂 🚂 🚂 🚂

CARE OF ST CHRISTOPHER'S (Britain 1959)

Produced by British Transport Films. St Christopher's — for the children of railwaymen. About 100 children are cared for here and this film gives a selection of scenes from a typical day; the breakfast mail, the boy with a problem, the girl with a worry, a visit from two widowers, a birthday teaparty. And most problems are solved by the time the little ones are tucked away in bed.

35/16mm Sound, 13mins, BTF

🚂

CARLSBERG COMMERCIAL (Britain 1991)

Produced by KHBB agency. Made with InterCity On Board Services. 'We sell five million cans of Carlsberg a year on InterCity and so a good relationship was already in existence and giving Carlsberg our full co-operation brought maximum benefits at minimum cost' (Nancy Cullen, Marketing Development Manager, InterCity).

'We try to keep the campaign as fresh as possible and avoid the lads-in-the-pub scenario. A train

compartment for a reunion between our two characters, who had perhaps started a crossword but who needed, after their journey had well advanced, a stimulus to complete. The word was Carlsberg. InterCity reflected the kind of positive environment — stylish and modern — which we were trying to capture, and the ad has produced some very good feedback. It takes the campaign a step further and the train setting undoubtedly helps it stand out' (Colin Clarke, Account Manager, KHBB). The scene was shot in a specially built InterCity carriage in a London studio, with back projected passing scenery. InterCity managed to get their image into the seating, curtains, trolleys and uniforms; Carlsberg got their style — and their name.

16mm, Sound, Colour, 50secs, KHBB

🚂

CARRY ON REGARDLESS (Britain 1960)

Anglo-Amalgamated picture. Includes various BR shots and scenes on the Forth Bridge in the days of steam, with LNER 'A4' Pacifics in evidence.

35/16mm, Sound, 93mins, Anglo-Amalgamated

🚂

CARRYING THE LOAD (Britain 1945)

Central Office of Information. The story of Britain's railways during the war and their contribution to victory, recorded all over the system and the network of the Big Four.

35mm/VID, Sound, 25mins, COI/BTF/TVP

🚂 🚂 🚂 🚂

CASEY JONES (USA 1954-59)

Columbia TV. With Alan Hale as Casey Jones and Bobby Clark as Casey Jones Junior; also Dub Taylor and Mary Lawrence. Despite being essentially a railroad TV series, most of the material was drawn from stock shots, with liberal use of back-projection. A small amount was shot on the Sierra Railroad with Rodgers 4-6-0 No 4493.

35mm, Sound, 25mins per episode Columbia TV

🚂 🚂

CASHEW NUT LINE (East Africa 1959)

East African Railways and Harbours. Building a 24-mile railway to link the main line to the cashew nut plantations of Southern Tanganyika.

16mm, Sound, Colour, 15mins, EAR

THE CASSANDRA CROSSING (Britain/Italy/West Germany 1976)

AGF/CCC/International Cine production. Produced by Lew Grade and Carlo Ponti. Directed by George Pan Cosmatos. With Sophia Loren, Richard Harris, Ava Gardner, Burt Lancaster and Ingrid Thulin.

A terrorist carrying a deadly plague virus boards a transcontinental train. 'A film of no observable film-making technique.' (Leslie Halliwell). This just about sums up the railway interest: 'the studio interiors of the train were almost as ridiculous as most of the plot; the restaurant car appeared to have the dimensions of a baronial drawing room and was just as static, as were the Wagons Lits compartments, which resembled luxury apartments in a block of flats.' Despite liberal use of railway resources, electric and diesel, in Germany and Italy, they too add up to nothing.

There are authentic shots, first at Geneva (our man has stolen the virus from the World Health Organisation!) with trains on their way through Switzerland and then into France for no particular reason.

The grand finale in 'Poland' was shot in Italy. A nice mixed make-up of Wagons Lits, Italian and French stock form a most unlikely train (it turns out the film crew lived in it when not filming). There are good aerial shots from Geneva to Basle with electric-hauled trains which jump to diesel-hauled units in the Jura Mountains area, with single-line operation which switches from overhead electric to diesel almost from shot to shot (supposed to be the same train!) Stock starts to change as we go from SBB to CCF to FFS without a by-your-leave. The climax of this long, tedious film is a crash on a bridge. After some quite

good real train shots, the actual crash is a terrible model bridge, done at a studio in Italy with what looks like a toy set bought in Woolworths.

35mm, Sound, Colour, 129mins, AGF

CASTLE CARY CRASH (Britain 1937)

Results of a spectacular crash which took place on the old North British line from Edinburgh to Glasgow on 10 December, 1937 involving LNER D29 class 4-4-0 No 9896 *Dandie Dinmont* and LNER A3 class 4-6-2 No 2744 *Grand Parade*. The accident happened in snow and killed 13 people.

16mm, Silent, 3mins, HA

CASTLE FROM BRISTOL (Britain 1964)

Made by P B Whitehouse. A journey from Bristol Temple Meads to Birmingham behind various GWR Castle class engines.

16/8mm, Silent, 8mins, CV/NRM

CASTLES AND KINGS (Britain 1959-62)

Produced by Geoff Holyoake. The film includes brief shots of GWR 'King' 4-6-0 Nos 6001, 6006, 6013, 6014, 6015 and 6021: *King Edward VII*, *King George I*, *King Henry VIII*, *King Henry VII*, *King Richard III* and *King Richard II*. For the GWR 'Castle' 4-6-0s, there are Nos 5014, 5016, 5044, 7003, 7004, 7007, 7033 and 7036: *Hartlebury*, *Eastnor*, *Earl of Dunraven*, *Taunton*, *Thornbury*, *Montgomery*, *Goodrich*, *Elmley* and *Great Western*.

8mm, Silent, 4mins, MFS

CASTROL OIL COMMERCIAL (Britain 1966)

On 16-17 April 1966, Gresley Pacific No 4472 *Flying Scotsman*, then owned and run privately by Alan Pegler, was stationed near Cuffley on the Hertford loop for the

making of a Castrol Oil commercial in which oil was poured on to the track and No 4472's wheels spun like mad with no forward movement! 'Even the great Flying Scot can't get a grip against Castrol Oil' said the commentary.

35mm, Sound, 2min, Castrol

CAT BALLOU (USA 1965)

Columbia. Produced by Harold Hecht. Directed by Eliot Silverstein. With Jane Fonda. Lee Marvin, Michael Callan and Nat 'King' Cole. Girl whose father is killed turns outlaw. Major railway scenes were staged on the Durango-Silverton narrow gauge branch line of the Denver & Rio Grande Railroad.

Locomotives include D&RGR 'K' class 2-8-2 Nos 470 and 478; stock includes Combination coach 212, coaches 312, 331 and 335, all painted white. The gauge of the line is 3ft.

35mm, Sound, Colour, 98mins, Columbia

A CAUTIONARY TALE (Britain 1944)

British Transport Commission. Directed by Lister Laurence. A lively and amusing example of a safety film in which a silhouette cartoon character is superimposed on live-action scenes in order to give sharp lessons in safety precautions to railwaymen.

16mm, Sound, 12mins, BTF

CAVALCADE (USA 1932)

Fox. Directed by Frank Lloyd from the play by Noel Coward. With Clive Brook, Diana Wynyard, Ursula Jeans and Herbert Mundin. The story of an upper class English family from the Boer War to World War One. For an American production, there is a pretty good studio reconstruction of a South Eastern and Chatham-type station, including a big domed locomotive in the style of a Drummond 4-4-0. There are no actuality railway scenes.

35mm, Sound, 109mins, TCF

CAVALRYMEN WITHOUT HORSES (Britain 1977)

ARPS. Produced by Barry Wright, Directed by David Bridges. Edited by Brian Trenerry.

'A superb film made for the ARPS but hardly ever shown in public. It is based around a BR steam railtour in 1977, one of those memorable and now unrepeatable trips when four different locomotives worked stages of a run from Newport to Chester. This lovely professional film includes some fine shots of steam on the move, a sequence on the footplate of No 4498 and other gems such as an interview with the late John Bellwood, suggesting that *King George V* would have been a good engine if built at Doncaster!' (Chris Leigh). The locomotives seen are SR 'MN' 4-6-2 No 35028 *Clan Line*, LMS 'Princess' 4-6-2 No 6201 *Princess Elizabeth*, GWR 'King' 4-6-0 No 6000 *King George V* and LNER 'A4' 4-6-2 No 4498 *Sir Nigel Gresley*. There are interviews with George Hinchcliffe, John Bellwood and the Chairman of the 'A4' Society, Julian Riddick. The strange title is a reference to an old loco man who says at the beginning of the film: 'when they took the steam away from us, we were like cavalrymen without horses'.

16mm, Sound, Colour, 28mins, ARPS/HA

CELEBRATION 150 (Britain 1975)

PM Films. A history of the Stockton & Darlington Railway, ending with scenes of the Grand Parade at Shildon in 1975.

8mm/VID, Sound, Colour, 48mins, PMV

THE CENTENNIALS (USA 1984)

Steam Powered Video. Produced by Video Rails. Union Pacific diesel '6900' class 6600hp including an eight-locomotive haul over Sherman Hill.

VID, Sound, Colour, 30mins, SPV

CENTRAL HIGHLANDS AND KYLE LINE (Britain 1988)

RV Television. Commentary by Neil Duncan. Perth to Inverness.

BR Class 37 diesels from Inverness to Kyle of Lochalsh. Also glass blowing, whisky distilling, Highland games, etc. (British Scenic Rail Journeys Series).

VID, Sound, Colour, 30min, RVV

CENTRAL WALES LINE (Britain c1960)

An 8mm amateur record by an unknown railwayman of the line from the old Swansea Victoria station (closed, 1964) through Swansea Bay and Mumbles Road to Gowerton, where it joined the present route on to Llanelli, Llandovery, Llandeilo, Llandrindod, to Knucklas, Knighton, Bucknell and Craven Arms. The ownership of the line was amazingly complex in the old days:

Swansea-Pontardulais: LNWR
Pontardulais-Llandeilo: GWR with LNWR running powers
Llandeilo-Llandovery: LNWR/GWR Joint
Llandovery-Craven Arms: LNWR

So there was always a good mix of motive power, right up to the end of steam.

16mm (from 8mm), Silent, 11mins, HA

A CENTURY OF STEAM (Britain 1963-65)

Made by P B Whitehouse and John Adams. A film record of the world's oldest narrow gauge railway to use steam and still working. The occasion of the film was the centenary celebrations in 1963.

16mm, Sound, Colour, 10mins, BFI/FEST/CV/NRM

CHALLENGE ANNEKA (Britain 1989)

BBC Television. With Anneka Rice. TV item featuring the restoration and reinstatement of the Northiam station on the Kent & East Sussex Preserved Railway.

With 'P' class No 1556 locomotive and the two-coach 'Wealden Pullman'.

TV, Sound, Colour, 28min, BBC TV

CHARING CROSS UNDERGROUND CRASH (Britain 1937)

Newsreel of the scene at Charing Cross after a crash between a District and a Metropolitan train on the line from Charing Cross to Temple. It is made strangely dramatic by the fact that, in those pre-TV days, we see nothing of the crash itself but only the crowds and the activity at the station. Six people were killed and a frightening 60 injured.

16mm, Sound, 4min, VisNews/HA

CHASING CHOO CHOOS (USA 1926)

Monty Banks comedy. A furious chase comedy in the Mack Sennett style, making extensive use of the facilities of the Atchison, Topeka & Santa Fe Railroad, including the yards around Los Angeles and a journey towards the San Fernando Valley and the start of the Sierra Mountains climb.

16mm, Silent (with added music), 20mins, PJ/HA

CHELTENHAM FLYER (Britain 1934)

Gaumont British News Issue No 35/1934. A trick editing device to present news items without a single authentic shot. The signals are LMS, the stock is LNER, the locomotive is an LMS 'Coronation' class; there is one blurred aerial shot which could actually be on the GWR!

35mm, Sound, 2mins, HA

CHESTERFIELD CRASH (Britain 1927)

Silent newsreel of the result of a freight train crash near Chesterfield, due to signalman error.

16mm, Silent, 2mins, HA

CHILDREN'S CORONATION (Britain 1953)

Produced by British Transport Films. The transport services made it possible for millions of people to participate in Queen Elizabeth's

Coronation, and this film reveals a little-known aspect of their work on that day. As a result of collaboration between London Transport, British Railways and the LCC, 30,000 schoolchildren from London and the Home Counties were brought to the Victoria Embankment to witness the passing of the Queen's procession on its way to the Abbey.
35/16mm Sound, 17mins, BTF

CHILTERN (Britain 1990)

Driver's eye View. Video 125. Produced by Peter Middleton. Script by Tony Parkins. Commentary by Philip Hayton. The ex-Great Western/Great Central Joint line from Northolt Junction to the site of the one-time Ashendon Junction in Buckinghamshire. A Class 50 diesel hauling a passenger train from Paddington on the old route to Northolt Junction. Old Great Central line from Marylebone by Class 115 1st generation DMU all the way to Banbury. At this time a major semaphore route out of London with the old station run-through tracks at High Wycombe.
VID, Sound, Colour, 90mins, 125

CINERAMA: No 2 PROGRAMME CINEMA HOLIDAY (USA 1953)

Produced by Louis de Rochment. The programme included a trip through the canyons of the Colorado River as seen from the Vista-Dome of the California Zephyr train on the Southern Pacific railroad. A Vista-Dome railroad car was removed from service and modified to accommodate the huge Cinerama camera. The tinted plexiglass used in the dome was replaced with clear glass to allow standard colour photography. Special platforms were added to enable the camera to work inside and outside the train and the railroad company laid on a special schedule six weeks before the shooting to link with other services. The camera was so precious that it had to be taken off the train at each nightly stop during a four-day shoot. The California Zephyr was hauled by GEC diesel.
Cinerama Three-strip 70mm, Sound, Colour, 123mins

CITIES OF BRITAIN: NEWCASTLE (Britain 1930)

Pathetone Weekly. Newsreel of Newcastle, with commentary by the then Lord Mayor Sir Arthur Lambert. Includes shots of Newcastle LNER station and industrial/docks railways.
35mm, Sound, 4mins, Pathe

CLAPPERBOARD (Britain 1979)

Granada Television. Produced by Graham Murray. Directed by Richard Guinea. Presented by Chris Kelly. John Huntley talks to Chris Kelly about the history of steam railways, including the Liverpool and Manchester (scene from the German 1935 reconstruction and visit to one of the station sites), the speed records of the past (scene from 'Coronation Scot' of 1937), a visit to Carnforth to see *Flying Scotsman* and *Leander* and a look at the Carnforth locations used in making *Brief Encounter*.
16mm, Sound, Colour, 26mins, Granada

CLASS 40 LAMENT (Britain 1985)

First Choice Photographic. 40135 is seen on freight trains; 40079 at Huddersfield, 40012 at Skegness and 40004 on the 'Broadsman' express. At the end, we see five 40s awaiting scrapping.
VID, Sound, Colour, 60mins, First Choice

CLASSIC VIDEO PRODUCTIONS

Largely a miscellany of recent steam railway activity, the collection includes *Eastleigh to Exeter*, *Incident at Afflington* (a mock crash near Corfe Castle in 1992), extensive coverage of the Swanage preserved railway from 1990 to 1992 and a series of studies of preserved steam in action under the title *Steam Unlimited*.

CLEETHORPES TRAIN (Britain 1951)

Arrival of a steel works outing train from Scunthorpe, with LNER Thompson 'B1' locomotive; there

are also scenes of a 10.25in miniature steam railway on the Marine Embankment.
16mm, Silent, 3mins, HA

CLEVEDON (Britain 1910)

Arrival of a GWR train from Yatton at Clevedon station.
16mm, Silent, 2mins, HA

CLOSELY OBSERVED TRAINS (Czechoslovakia 1966)

(American title: Closely Watched Trains)
Ceskoslovensky film (Barrandor Studios). Directed by Jiri Menzel. With Vaclav Neckar and Vladimir Valenta. A boy comes to work on a station at the end of the war, and is involved in the anti-German incidents organized by the senior guard which leads him eventually to be killed. The wartime steam railway backgrounds are superb and very accurate.

The film won an Academy Award as Best Foreign Film. *Closely Observed Trains* made full use of its rural railway setting and of the humour and pathos associated with railways' (Peter Handford).
35mm, Sound, 92mins, BFI

CLOSING OF THE CRYSTAL PALACE HIGH LEVEL LINE (Britain 1954)

A brief newsreel record of the last train from Crystal Palace on 19 September 1954 which made a tour from Crystal Palace round to Richmond, Crystal Palace Low Level and back to the High Level station. The locomotives involved were Wainwright SECR 'C' 0-6-0 Nos 31719 and 31576.
16mm, Silent, 5mins, HA

CLOSING OF THE WYE VALLEY LINES (Britain 1959)

Made by P B Whitehouse and John Adams. A film was made of the last day of operation in January 1959 of the line from Ross-on-Wye to Chepstow, via Monmouth.
16/8mm/VID, Silent, 6mins, CV/NRM/Stirling/RSV

COALPORT RAILTOUR ACTIVITY (Britain 1952)

L&Y 2-4-2T 50703 surging up the bank out of Coalport East Station on a two-coach load, then this loco is joined by an ex-LMS 2-6-2T for SLS Railtour activity with four 'blood and custard' LMS coaches, quite probably on the last day of service on the Coalport East to Wellington line, 2 June, 1952. At Rushton station, on the North Staffordshire lines, L&Y 2-4-2T 50703 on railtour duty, and a passenger in the last coach waves a fond farewell. Made by Patrick Whitehouse.

16mm/VID, Silent, 8min, NRM/Stirling

COAST DAYLIGHT IN THE DAYS OF STEAM (USA 1937)

The first year of the 'Coast Daylight', with 4-8-4 locomotives, filmed at Los Angeles Union Passenger Terminal, through Soledad Canyon, along the Coast, at Santa Barbara, exchange of locomotives at San Luis Obispo, passing the eastbound Daylight around Horseshoe Curve, at Salinas and arrival at San Francisco.

8mm, Silent, 19mins, Blackhawk

THE COAST OF CLYDE (Britain 1959)

Based on the true World War II story. Produced by British Transport Films. In search of the land of his parents, as well as for a holiday, Bernard Braden comes to the Firth of Clyde. Furnished with a Runaround ticket he travels around by train and a steamer. Finally he comes to Arran, and finds the 'Scotland in miniature' whence his grandmother sailed for the New World. It is a holiday of discovery illuminated with typical Braden humour.

35/16mm, Sound, Colour, 20mins, BTF

COASTAL CONNECTIONS (Britain 1936)

LMS Film. The shipping services of the LMS, with special reference to the Holyhead to Ireland route and the theme of 'Holidays in Wales'. (From the 'Just for the Record' series on video).

35mm/VID, Sound, 20mins, RFV/BTF

COCK O' THE NORTH (Britain 1935)

Panther-Mitchell Films. Produced and directed by Oswald Mitchell. With George Carney, Marie Lohr, Ronnie Hepworth, Horace Kenney and Eve Lister. George Barton, an engine driver on the LNER, is selected to drive the new LNER 'P2' 2-8-2 No 2001 *Cock o' the North*. But he is injured in an accident and forced to take early retirement.

His fellow railwaymen stage a charity concert to make his life a little happier. The film only lives in the minds of the small number of people who saw it and can remember it.

35mm, Sound, 84mins, NA (Lost)

COCKLESHELL HEROES (Britain 1955)

Columbia. Directed by Jose Ferrer. With Jose Ferrer, Trevor Howard, Dora Bryan and Victor Maddern. Story of a team who attached limpet mines to enemy shipping. Includes scenes on the Southern Railway as it was including Custom House station and Victoria Dock Road.

35mm, Sound, Colour, 97mins, Columbia

COLLECTORS CORNER, EUSTON (Britain 1984)

Anglia Television. The work of offering railway relics on sale to the public through the Collectors Corner shop at Euston station. With John Huntley (from the *Bygones* series). Produced and directed by David Kenten.

16mm, Sound, Colour, 14mins, Anglia

COLNBROOK (Britain 1963)

A film record by Alan Willmott of GWR '1400' No 1436 and a one-coach auto-train on the line from Uxbridge Vine Street to Staines. Colnbrook closed to passengers in 1965.

16mm, Silent, 2mins, AW

THE COLNE VALLEY RAILWAY (Britain 1962)

Anglia Television. A record of an East Anglian cross-country line that was about to close.

16mm, Sound, Colour, 7mins, Anglia

COMING HOME (Britain 1971)

Flying Scotsman Enterprises (Hon Sir William McAlpine). Directed by Peter Newington. Edited by Peter Wilson. The story of LNER 'A1' 4-6-2 No 4472 *Flying Scotsman* in the United States of America: the near-loss to New York bankers when the tour ran into financial problems; its rescue and journey back to this country via San Francisco and the Panama Canal and Liverpool; an outing on the Torbay railway in Devon.

35mm/16mm, VID, Sound, Colour, 28mins, FSE/HA

COMMERCIALS: CINEMA AND TV

Railways have been used for many years in cinema commercials. The earliest films showing railway scenes were often made without paying fees by giving a big credit to the company concerned. Thus, *A Day in the Life of a Miner* and *London to Glasgow, 1909* and such 'industrials' as *Building a Locomotive at Crewe* all carry a prominent credit: 'By kind permission of the London and North Western Railway'. *The Flying Scotsman* of 1930 credits the 'London and North Eastern Railway' and *The Last Journey* of 1936 gives similar effusive thanks to the 'Great Western Railway'. The Craven A cigarette commercial of 1935, shot in a primitive Dufaycolour system, uses scenes of the Silver Jubilee train ('the world's finest in railway trains; the world's finest in cigarettes') paid for its LNER facilities. Castrol Oil paid for use of LNER 'A1' 4-6-2 No 4472 Flying Scotsman in 1964 for a cinema commercial.

The Severn Valley provided facilities for a Rothmans cigarette commercial in 1960. Today, British Rail want a minimum of £250 an hour for any filming on their territory, although they relented in the case of a Carlsberg commercial in 1991 which gave a big boost to InterCity. Strollers (Confectionery) and Sun Alliance are recent users of BR facilities; not forgetting British Rail's own expensively-made TV commercials ('take off you shoes and R..E..L..A..X').

Nestlé Rowntree's got in on the act with a Kit Kat commercial filmed on the Kent & East Sussex; whilst the DIY enthusiast will recognise the Nene Valley Railway in a B&Q ad filmed in August 1992.

COMMUTERS (Britain 1936)

LMS commuter services around London, featuring both steam and electric. The main scenes are taken at Harrow and Wealdstone station for steam-hauled services and on sections of Euston-Watford to represent the LMS electric suburban operation. There is also an arrival scene at Euston.

16mm, Silent, 6mins, HA

COMPIEGNE (Germany 1940)

Degato film. A German record of the signing of the French surrender to Germany by Pétain, personally accepted by Adolf Hitler on 22 June 1940, which brought about an Armistice and the Occupation of France by the Nazis. It was signed on the same spot in the Forest of Compiègne where Marshal Foch had received the German surrender in 1918 and took place in the same Pullman coach, moved specially for the occasion by the Germany Military Transport Corps.

16mm, Silent, 5mins, HA

CONDEMNED (Britain 1967)

Written and directed by John Inglis. A fascinating record of the early days at Dai Woodham's locomotive scrapyard at Barry, South Wales.

16mm, Sound, 11mins, HA

CONFIRM OR DENY (USA 1942)

20th Century Fox. Directed by Archie Mayo. With Don Ameche and Joan Bennett. A Hollywood story of the London blitz with a pathetic attempt to reconstruct the London Underground.

35mm, Sound, 73mins, TCF

CONQUEST OF RAILWAYS (France 1939)

Pathe. A compilation of various newsreel bits including the replica *Rocket*; the 1927 Iron Horse Centennial on the Baltimore & Ohio; PLM 4-6-2 streamlined locomotive of French Railways; a French Michelin road-railcar; a Michelin railcar; narrow gauge industrial trains in French Morocco; timber trestle viaducts and the French locomotive test bed at Vitry (near Paris) running LNER Gresley 'P2' 2-8-2 No 2001 *Cock o' the North* on trials in 1934.

16mm, Silent, 12mins, HA (from Pathescope RF 9.5mm)

CONTACT WITH THE HEART OF ENGLAND (Britain 1967)

Produced by British Transport Films. 'Introducing the new electric services between the West Midlands, Stoke, London, and the North-West. A service which started 6 March 1967 which is second to none in this country, and indeed, of its type, second to none in the world. Bringing with it a number of new facilities for the passengers together with speed, frequency and electric reliability. Moving travellers across the country at 100 miles an hour much of the time.'

35/16mm, Sound, Colour, 9mins, BTF

THE CONVERSION OF HECTOR THE CHECKER (Britain 1967)

Produced by British Transport Films. The 'Loading by coding' system for goods, sundries on British Rail is well understood by railwaymen, but the bad consequences of wrong coding and wrong loading is not always sufficiently realised. This animated film is shown to railwaymen concerned with Goods Sundries to help shorten transit times and improve deliveries.

35/16mm, Sound, 8mins, BTF

CORNISH FREIGHT LINES (Britain 1989)

Bob Ainsworth Film. This film includes scenes of abandoned freight lines, the current diesel-hauled Cornish clay trains from Lostwithel to Fowey as well as the delivery of Devonport Docks Bagnall 0-4-0ST No 19 to the Bodmin and Wenford railway (including a first steaming in a howling gale) and Hunslet 0-4-0ST *Lillian* built in 1883 for the North Wales slate quarries, now operating on the 1ft 11½in narrow gauge Launceston steam railway.

16mm, Sound, Colour, 10mins, Ainsworth/HA

CORONATION SCOT (Britain 1938)

Made by Captain J Liddell. Colour shots of the Coronation Scot train and locomotives in blue and silver and one shot of No 6225 in maroon and gold.

16mm, Silent, Colour, 2mins, HA

CORONATION SCOT (Britain 1937)

A LMS Railway film. Produced by John Shearman. A record of the construction and trial runs of the Stanier locomotive and train 'Coronation Scot', including a special demonstration run between Llandudno Junction and Rhyl and detailed coverage of the prestige run from Euston to Crewe and back.

35mm/16mm, Sound and silent versions, 11mins, BTF/VID

CORRINGHAM LIGHT RAILWAY (Britain 1949)

SCTS. A journey with an old 1870 coach and a 1917 Avonside industrial locomotive from Corringham to Coryton on the Thames near Tilbury. The line closed in 1952. On the return trip to Corringham, a cow is encountered on the line.

16mm, Silent, 3mins, HA/SCTS

🚂 🚂 🚂 🚂 🚂

CORRIS RAILWAY (Britain 1927)

A simple 9.5mm record of the 2ft 3in narrow gauge railway from Machynlleth to Aberllefenni, closed to passenger traffic in 1931. There are interesting details of the movement and processing of slate for which the railway was originally built. A second film, originally on 35mm, gives excellent details of the locomotives and the journey as it was in 1929.

16mm (from 9.5 and 35mm), Silent, 7mins, HA

🚂 🚂 🚂 🚂 🚂

COUNTY CHAIRMAN (USA 1923)

Keystone. Directed by Edward Cline. With Fatty Arbuckle and Mabel Normand. The first film ever to use the facilities of the Sierra Railroad. Old oil-burners had a pile of wood to cover up the oil tanks on the tenders, big box headlights appeared, cow catchers were extended and great fake balloon smokestacks were added over the years as film makers discovered the joys of this California railway that was originally built for the Mother Lode Gold Mine during the great California Gold Rush and has, since the 1920s, been increasingly used by film and TV companies.

35mm, Silent, 31min, NA (Lost)

🚂 🚂 🚂

COUNTY DONEGAL RAILWAY (Britain 1957 and 1959)

Made by P B Whitehouse. One of the classic films by Pat Whitehouse, this was made first in 1957 as a black-and-white film and then, on a return visit, in colour in 1959. The whole of this 3ft gauge system was dismantled in 1960. The film includes the stations at Strabane, Lough Eske, Donegal and Ballyshannon; locomotives include *Phoenix*, *Drumboe*, *Meenglas* and *Blanche*, plus good shots of the oldest diesel railcars to be introduced in these islands. At one time a total

of 20 railcars were in use, eight of which were articulated.

16mm, Silent, Part colour, 22mins, CV/NRM/VID

🚂 🚂 🚂 🚂 🚂

COURS d'ELECTRICITÉ (France 1948)

SNCF/Service Cinématographie du Métropolitan. The history and workings of the Paris Metro as it was in 1948. It makes effective use of animated diagrams to put across complex technical points.

35/16mm, Sound, 18mins, SNCF

🚂 🚂 🚂 🚂 🚂

COURTESY (Britain 1964)

Produced by British Transport Films. Thousands of passengers pass through London's main stations every day, and during the rush hour the platforms are a sea of faces. How do railwaymen or passengers retain a sense of courtesy in such a situation? How does the station master deal with difficult incidents? These are some of the questions asked in this film, and both staff and travellers put forward opinions. A film more likely to provoke discussion than to provide an answer.

35/16mm, Sound, 18mins, BTF

🚂

COWBOY (USA 1957)

Columbia. Directed by Delmer Davies. With Glenn Ford, Jack Lemmon and Brian Donlevy. A city dweller who becomes a cattle herder. Considerable use was made of the Atchison, Topeka & Santa Fe Railroad, including a spectacular fight in a cattle truck full of frightened animals.

35mm, Sound, Colour, 92min, Columbia

🚂 🚂

CRASH! (Britain 1968)

A film by David Cleveland. Reconstruction, using newspaper cuttings and old engravings, of the head-on collision on the Great Eastern Railway at Brundall (near Norwich) on 10 September 1874 which killed 25 people. The moment of the collision

is recreated by having shots of LNER 'A3' 4-6-2 No 4472 *Flying Scotsman* as the express train and SECR 'P' 0-6-0T No 323 *Bluebell* as the local train.

16mm, Sound, Colour, 11mins, DC/HA

🚂 🚂 🚂 🚂

CRASHES

Railway crashes have featured in literally hundreds of films. Some have been models only as in *A Railway Collision* (Robert Paul, 1898; all in 50sec!), *The Greatest Show on Earth*, *Hatter's Castle* or *Seven Sinners*. Some have been real and staged by smashing up old locomotives and stock, as in *The Wreck*, *The Juggernaut*, *The Wrecker*, *Lawrence of Arabia* and *King Kong*. Others have been a mixture with simulation added to clever editing tricks as in *Train of Events*, *The Young in Heart*, *Mad Love*, *The Wrong Box* and *Crack in the World*. Working out what is real and what is fake can be fun. You will find guidance under individual film titles.

🚂 🚂 🚂 🚂 🚂

CRESSWELL FILM UNIT

This film unit was established in 1956 and went early into video in 1983. In 1986, the name was changed to Transport Video Publishing. The work by S W South was the basis of the first issues by Cresswell Films; he later set up Transport Video as his own company.

🚂 🚂 🚂 🚂 🚂

CROMFORD & HIGH PEAK LINE (Britain 1949-67)

Made by P B Whitehouse and John Adams. A film of this interesting working finishing up with the North London 0-6-0T on Hopton Bank Section. There are freight operations in 1949; a MLS/SLS railtour on 25 April 1953, with Johnson 0-4-4T No 58077 at Wickworth station, leaving for Duffield; and the North London tank engines in action in 1967.

16/8mm/VID, Silent, Colour, 9min, NRM/Stirling

🚂 🚂 🚂 🚂 🚂

CROMFORD AND HIGH PEAK RAILWAY (Britain 1967)

Made by G S Holyoake. Middleton Incline (1 in 8.5) the reservoir and water column at Middleton Top (track lifted). Class 'J94' 0-6-0ST Nos 68006 and 68012 and brake vans on last day of official operations; unsuccessful attempt to climb 1 in 14 Hopton Incline (30 April 1967).

16mm/9.5mm/8mm, Silent, Colour, 11min, MFS/VID

CROOKS IN CLOISTERS (Britain 1963)

Associated British production. Directed by Jeremy Summers. With Barbara Windsor and Dave Kaye. Comedy of a gang of crooks and their hideout. Includes a burlesque on the Great Train Robbery shot at Brent sidings.

35mm, Sound, Colour, 97mins, Weintraub

CROSSING THE RAILWAY SAFELY (Britain 1967)

Compared with the old type of gated, hand-operated railway-road level crossing, the new automatic half-carrier crossing, which is caused to operate by the approach of the train and which displays audible and visual warnings to road users, saves both time and money. This film, for the instruction of schoolchildren, is commentated by Leslie Crowther. It demonstrated the proper and safe ways of using these crossings on foot and on bicycles.

35/16mm, Sound, Colour, 10mins, BTF

CROYDON GAS WORKS RAILWAY (Britain 1927)

A record of an industrial railway system, including delivery of coal from the main line behind SR 'Q' 0-6-0 No 540; industrial saddle tanks within the works and a strange little petrol engined trolley to move individual waggons.

16mm, Silent, 5mins, HA

CYCLISTS ABROAD (Britain 1956)

Produced by British Transport Films. A party of cyclists set out from Victoria station for a tour of Austria. On the boat-train their bicycles are carried in a specially equipped van to Folkestone and transferred to racks for the Channel crossing.

From Calais the party go by train to Buchs, where they start the tour, climbing the magnificent mountains and running down into the lovely valleys of the land of Strauss, Mozart and Schubert. They pause by the wayside to enjoy the sights and sounds of a strange country and eat heartily of Austria's good food.

35/16mm, Sound, Colour, 15mins, BTF

D

DAD'S ARMY (Britain 1986)

BBC Television series. One episode called 'The Royal Visit' had railway scenes made up of some scenes shot on the North Norfolk Railway, stock shots of an LNER 'A4' Pacific and lots of studio mock-ups for the main action. A locomotive No 45 *Colwyn* makes an appearance. A super editing jigsaw.

VID, Sound, Colour, 27mins, BBC Television

DAMNED GOOD TIME (Britain 1990)

Railfilms. Produced by Nick Dodson. Film by Roger Nicholas. Material shot in the 1980s of preserved steam in action, mainly at Carnforth, the Settle & Carlisle line and the Scottish Highlands journey with LMS 5407 and *Maude*.

VID, Sound, Colour, 50mins, RFV

THE DANCING YEARS (Britain 1949)

Associated British production. Directed by Harrold French. With Dennis Price and Giselle Preville. Musical romance set in pre-1914 Vienna. Includes stock shots of old Austrian railway scenes.

35mm, Sound, Colour, 97mins, Weintraub

DARLINGTON CENTENARY, 1925 (Britain 1925)

Kinematographed by Debenham and Company, York.

Part 1: Exhibition opened by HRH Duke and Duchess of York on 1 July, 1925. The Royal party arrive in a 12hp Austin saloon and tour the exhibition at Darlington.

Part 2: 2 July, 1925. Grand parade of locomotives and stock on the Stockton-Darlington track in the presence of HRH Duke and Duchess of York. The parade includes: *Locomotion* (George Stephenson) Stockton & Darlington Railway, 1825; Stephenson Standard long boilered goods engine

Left:
***Lion** (Liverpool & Manchester 1838), **Coronation** (LNWR 1911) and **Coronation** (LMS 1937) in the 1937 LMS film 'Coronation Scot'.*

Below left:
The Grand Parade from 'Darlington Centenary, 1925'.

Bottom left:
In Uhlandstrasse underground station, Berlin, director Compton Bennett shows Walter Gotell (in black coat) how he is to 'murder' Friedrich Joloff for a scene in 'Desperate Moment', by pushing him under the train. *Rank*

Bottom right:
A preserved American locomotive from 'Fair of the Iron Horse' (1927).

No 1275, Stockton & Darlington Railway, 1874; *Derwent* (Timothy Hackworth). Stockton & Darlington Railway, 1847. Replica: *North Star* (R Stephenson). Great Western Railway. (Original built in 1837; replica built at Swindon in 1925); Gresley 'K3' class 2-6-0 No 203 (LNER); Churchward '4700' class 2-8-0 locomotive (GWR); Stirling 4-2-2 8-foot single No 1 (GWR, 1870); Ivatt 'C2' class 4-4-2 No 990 *Henry Oakley* (GNR, 1898); 4-4-2 Raven 'C7' class Atlantic No 2207 (NER, 1911); Fletcher Wordsell 2-2-4 No 66 *Aerolite*. (NER, 1869); 'H1' class 4-4-4T No 2151, (NER); Raven 'B16' class 4-6-0 No 934 (NER); Gresley 'P1' class 2-8-2 No 2393;.Worsdell 'J71' class 0-6-0 No 1163. (LNER); Worsdell 'Q5' class 0-8-0 No 130 (NER); Robinson Valour 'B3' class 4-6-0 No 6169 *Lord Farringdon* (GCR); Gresley 'A3' class Pacific No 2563 *Tagalie* (LNER); LNER 4-6-4 electric locomotive No 13; Holden 0-4-0T 'Y6' class steam tram No 7133 (GER) Experimental Rail-Bus (LNER, 1897); Wordsell 'G5' class 0-4-4T (NER); Gresley Garratt 'U1' class 2-8-8-2 No 2395. (LNER, 1925); Sentinel 100hp railcar; Robinson 'A5' class 4-6-2T No 5088 (GCR); Hughes Baltic 4-6-4T No 11112 (LMS); Churchward 'Hall' class 4-6-0 (GWR); Hughes '8' class 4-6-0 No 10474 (L&YR); Urie/Maunsell 'King Arthur' class 4-6-0 No 449 *Sir Torre*. (SR,1925); Raven Pacific No 2400 *City of Newcastle* (LNER, 1922).

35/16/VID, Silent, 19mins, NFA/HA/125/TVP

🚂 🚂 🚂 🚂 🚂

DART VALLEY RAILWAY (Britain 1969-80)

Extensive film coverage exists on this railway including the opening ceremony attended by Dr Beeching and Ian Allan, with the first train pulled by GWR '45XX' 2-6-2T No 4555; a record of the principal locomotives by Tom Martin and a number of 8mm amateur films. The line was often used by Westward TV and later TSW for both feature and news items.

16mm, Sound, Part colour, 32mins, HA

🚂 🚂 🚂 🚂 🚂

THE DAVID SUTCLIFFE COLLECTION

Originally a private collection on 16mm with films like *Rails to Talsarn* and *Cambrian Steam*, he has recently produced and released a series of video tapes including *Full Steam to Holyhead* (1990), *Ynys Mon Express* (1991), *North Wales Coast Main-Line Steam* (1991) and *Return to Amlwch* (1992).

🚂 🚂 🚂 🚂 🚂 🚂

DAWLISH TO NEWTON ABBOT (Britain 1964)

From the series. A record of the famous Devon Coast route in steam days.

16mm, Silent, Colour, 6mins, HA

🚂 🚂 🚂 🚂 🚂 🚂

A DAY AT SHREWSBURY STATION (Britain 1961)

A film by P B Whitehouse and John Adams. This complex film is described by Pat Whitehouse:

'Shrewsbury provides an ideal setting, with GWR designs supplemented by those of the former LMS together with the (by 1961) inevitable BR Standards and Diesels. We review the necessary locomotive exchange on the Cambrian Coast Express, this time from the other direction as 'Manor' gives way to No 7025 *Sudely Castle*. There are 'Castles' aplenty in '61, but the intrusion of Standard Class 5 4-6-0 No 73049 highlights the more austere lines of the latter. The proximity of the former LMS is typified by the appearance of BR built Class 2 2-6-0 No 46509 hauling an ex-GWR Inspection Saloon. The arrival of a DMU and passing of No 73049 with some coal wagons precedes the departure of Fowler 2-6-4T No 42389 with a passenger serivce destined for Stafford.

'Fowler's successor, ex-Swindon man Sir William Stanier is represented by an ex-LMS '8F' 2-8-0. There is a design link between the '8F' and Hawksworth's 'County' class 4-6-0. We examine and view the departure of No 1017 *County of Hereford*. There was still much to see, another 'Castle' followed by some tank types, firstly the departure of small prairie No 5555, and then pannier No 9657 as it ambles

up the centre road. One particular class always caused a stir . . . the celebrated 'King' 4-6-0s. Our wait is rewarded when No 6018 *King Henry VI* arrives with the 'Cambrian Coast Express' before we take an energetic departure for Aberystwyth. All-too-soon it is time to think of leaving, No 7024 *Powis Castle* provides our last sight of things as they were before we receive a rude awakening.'

16mm, Silent, Colour, 6 mins, CV/NRM/Stirling/RFV

🚂 🚂 🚂 🚂 🚂

A DAY FOR REMEMBERING (Britain 1964)

Produced by British Railway Films. To celebrate the centenary of the world's first underground line — the Metropolitan Railway — London Transport arranged a parade of underground vehicles at Neasden, special stands were erected so that the audience could see rolling stock dating from the inception of underground railways to the modern developments of the present day.

35/16mm, Sound, Colour, 15mins, BTF

🚂 🚂

A DAY IN LIVERPOOL (Britain 1937)

LMS film. Silent film record of various aspects of Liverpool in the 1930s, including Lime Street station and boat trains at the old Riverside station with an LMS Canadian Pacific special arriving with passengers, for the Canadian Pacific transatlantic liner *Duchess of Atholl* at Princess Pier, piloted into the station by two ancient Webb coal tank engines LNWR 0-6-2Ts Nos 27615 and 7738. There are also some shots of the Liverpool Overhead Railway, and very rare scenes of the Railway Air Service at Speke (De Havilland Rapides).

16mm, Silent, 11mins, HA

🚂 🚂

A DAY IN THE LIFE OF A COAL MINER (Britain 1910)

A Kineto film, 'by courtesy of the L&NW Railway.' Includes railway scenes in the yards at Wigan.

35/16mm, Silent, 10mins, NFA/HA

🚂

33

A DAY OUT (Britain 1990)

British Nuclear Fuels. Produced by Uden Associates. A video record of the 'Sellafield Sightseer', a trip organised in association with Flying Scotsman Enterprises and using LNER 'A1' 4-6-2 No 4472 *Flying Scotsman* based on Carnforth. There are aerial views and footplate scenes in what the publicity calls 'steaming into the nuclear age'.

VID, Sound, Colour, 38mins, VID/BNFL

🚂 🚂 🚂 🚂 🚂

DAYLIGHTING THE PADRE TRAIL (USA 1938)

Produced by the Southern Pacific Railroad. One of America's classic railroad routes, still very much in the days of steam.

16mm, Sound, 19mins, RF

🚂 🚂 🚂 🚂 🚂

THE DAYS OF STEAM ON THE L&N (USA 1935-58)

Made by Gene Miller. Locomotives include Pacifics, Consolidations, Mikados and Mountains as well as 0-6-0 and 0-8-0 shunting engines.

16/8mm, Silent, 27mins, Blackhawk/HA

🚂 🚂 🚂 🚂 🚂

DAYS OF STEAM: THE GREAT WESTERN RAILWAY (Britain 1984)

TVS Television. Produced by Peter Williams. Directed by Tony Searle. This programme mixed archive film including Swindon Works in 1935 and the Cornish Riviera in action with material shot at the GWR Society Centre at Didcot, the story of Isembard Kingdom Brunel and the Broad Gauge, Barry Scrap Yards and the Severn Valley Railway. There is a visit to Swindon and Bristol Temple Meads in 1984.

16mm, Sound, Colour, 51mins, TVS TV

🚂 🚂 🚂 🚂 🚂

DAY-TO-DAY TRACK MAINTENANCE (Britain 1951)

Produced by British Transport Films.
Part 1. Plain Line. A film giving instruction in normal maintenance tasks which have to be performed by a permanent-way gang of four men. It shows how all types of fastening on both bullhead and flat-bottomed track are maintained; details the maintenance of rail joints; shows how 'hanging' sleepers should be repacked, and deals with the preservation of correct cant and alignment on curves.
Part 2. Switches and crossings. Continuing the study of the normal tasks performed by a permanent-way gang, this film deals with the maintenance of switches, common crossings and obtuse crossings. These are the fundamental units from which all track layouts however complicated, are built up.

35/16mm, Sound, 52mins, BTF

🚂 🚂 🚂 🚂 🚂

DEATH OF A RAILWAY (Britain 1964)

Anglia Television. Produced and directed by David Kenten. The closing of the railway from March to Cambridge, cutting off passenger services to Histon, St Ives, Somersham and Chatteris.

16mm, Sound, Colour, 11mins, Anglia

🚂 🚂 🚂 🚂 🚂

DEDICATED TO STEAM (1929-59)

Made by R Jeffcoat, D Griffiths and R S Greenwood. A collection of archive film material including L&Y railmotor at Barton; Webb 2-4-2T and LNWR 'George' class at Leamington Spa; steam scenes at King's Cross, Reading and Exeter St Davids; the Lynton and Barnstaple Narrow Gauge Railway, featuring the story of No 759 *Yeo*; a set of films from the Bassett-Lowke collection of 1929 including Euston (LMS No 6111 *Royal Fusilier*), ST Pancras (Midland Compound No 1092), King's Cross (LNER 'A1' No 2546 *Donovan*, Atlantic No 4419 and No 4475 *Flying Fox*); Paddington (GWR 'Castle' No 6004 on the 'Torbay Pullman'), Victoria (SR 'Lord Nelson' class No 859 *Lord Hood* and SR 'King Arthur' class No 796 *Sir Dodinas Le Savage*) and Waterloo (SR 'Lord Nelson' class No 860 *Lord Hood* and SR 'King Arthur' class No 791 *Sir Uwaine*). There is also a set of colour films by Gilbert Kilburn in the 1950s, including a brief series of flashes of 'Britannias', 'Duchesses', 'Black Fives', 'King Arthurs', 'Lord Nelsons', 'Patriots', LMS Compounds as well as sundry 4MTs, 2MTs, '4Fs', 'A4s', 'A3s', 'K1s', 'K2s' and many others.

VID, Silent, Some Colour, 50min, Stirling

🚂 🚂 🚂 🚂 🚂

THE DEFIANT SPIRIT (Britain 1989)

Railfilms. Jointly produced by Railfilms, Stirling Video and Railscene in association with the Birmingham Railway Museum. A history with the Birmingham Railway Museum. A history of GWR 'Castle' 4-6-0 No 5080 *Ogmore Castle* built in 1939 and renamed *Defiant* in 1941 (after the aircraft of that name). It was withdrawn in 1963 and languished at Dai Woodham Scrapyard at Barry until 1974 when it was purchased by the Birmingham Railway Museum as a source of spares for restored 'Castle' No 7029 *Clun Castle*. In 1985 it was decided instead to restore *Defiant* to running order with the aid of the Manpower Services Scheme. The tape includes archive scenes of 'Castles' at work and then follows up the story of the restoration of *Defiant* also telling the history of other locomotives that have been restored at Tyseley.

VID, Sound, Colour, 25mins, RFV

🚂 🚂 🚂 🚂 🚂

THE DEFINITIVE PROGRAMME (USA 1950s)

Steam Powered Video. Produced by Video Rails. Classic Norfolk and Western steam in action, with 'J' class No 611 on run-pasts, Baker valve gear shots and construction scenes.

VID, Sound, Colour, 60mins, SPV

🚂 🚂 🚂 🚂 🚂

DELTICS (Britain 1955-65)

Film material is strangely in rather short supply. There is an excellent record of the building and trial runs of the English Electric prototype but then shots become a bit scattered. There are scenes at Wood Green in

1963; shots in BTF films on diesel power; but the best collection is to be found on the video *Diesel and Electric on 35mm*.

16mm/VID, Silent and sound, Part colour, 34mins, HA/125

🚂 🚂 🚂 🚂 🚂

DELTICS ON VIDEO (Britain 1982)

P Smallwood Video. An assembly of a miscellany of pieces on *Deltic Venturer*, Doncaster works farewell, last Deltic passenger train from King's Cross to York, with 55021, scenes at Peterborough and Finsbury Park, Deltic prototype (English Electric), etc.

VID, Sound, Part colour, 50mins, Ballymoss

🚂 🚂 🚂 🚂 🚂

DEMONSTRATION OF RAILWAY LOCOMOTIVES (Television)

An outside broadcast from Alexandra Palace station of Gresley LNER 'A4' Class 4-6-2 No 2509 *Silver Link* and 'contrasting types of engine'. Programme arranged by the LNER.

BBC Children's Television 3-3.20pm
Saturday, 17 April, 1937

🚂 🚂 🚂 🚂 🚂

DENVER AND RIO GRANDE (USA 1952)

Paramount Picture. Directed by Byron Haskin. With Edmond O'Brien, Sterling Hayden and Dean Jagger. A melodrama of rival railroad companies building lines out West, which includes a battle between the Denver & Rio Grande Railroad and the Canyon City & San Juan Railroad; the D&RG is represented by two fine six-coupled locomotives Nos 268 and 319 which are eventually wrecked in an impressive actual head-on collision. The film also includes a landslide and derailment, caused by explosives and a chase along the line featuring such stations as Canyon Creek, Swallows, Texas Creek and Parkdale. The background music used orchestral variations on the tune *We Were Working on the Railroad*.

35mm, Sound, Colour, 89mins, Paramount

🚂 🚂 🚂 🚂

DEPOT No 1: PLYMOUTH LAIRA (Britain 1989)

Railfilms. Produced and directed by Nick Dodson. Written by Neil Woller. A behind-the-scenes look at a British Rail Depot and its work. Plymouth Laira opened in 1901 and became the centre for Great Western operations in the south-west. In 1961, it was selected as British Rail's first main diesel maintenance depot and this video shows work on its fleet of IC125s, Class 50s and Class 37s.

VID, Sound, Colour, 40mins, RFV

🚂 🚂 🚂 🚂 🚂

DEPOT: SCOTRAIL (Britain 1991)

Railfilms. Produced by Nick Dodson. From 1989 responsibility for the entire freight fleet in Central Scotland was based on Eastfield near Glasgow. It controls depots at Motherwell, Ayr, Millerhill, Grangemouth, Thornton and Perth. A delay on the delivery of the Class 158 Sprinter expresses has meant in recent times that an extra burden has fallen on Eastfield to keep their ageing fleet going. No 3 in the *Depot* series.

VID, Sound, Colour, 50mins, RFV

🚂 🚂 🚂 🚂 🚂

DEPOT: STRATFORD (Britain 1991)

Railfilms. Produced by Nick Dodson. The history of the Great Eastern works which began in 1841 and played a role throughout steam days up to the 'Britannias' in the 1950s and then into the world of electrification (begun in 1945) and the present situation as a Traction Repair Shop, a Maintenance Depot and a 110-strong fleet of locomotives to look after. No 2 in the *Depot* series.

VID, Sound, Colour, 40mins, RFV

🚂 🚂 🚂 🚂 🚂

A DESPERATE CASE (Britain 1958)

Produced by British Transport Films. A cautionary tale of a typical holiday suitcase. Crammed beyond its capacity, imperfectly fastened,

inadequately and confusedly labelled, the railways transport it from station to station, seeking its true abode. Finally, one of the owners comes to the nightmare tribunal where those who maltreat their luggage are dealt with.

35/16mm, Sound, 10mins, BTF

🚂 🚂 🚂 🚂 🚂

DESPERATE MOMENT (Britain)

Fanfare Films. Produced by George G Brown. Directed by Compton Bennett. With Dirk Bogarde, Mai Zetterling and Philip Friend. In Poland, a man imprisoned for a murder he didn't commit escapes and tracks down the real criminal.

Includes a dramatic scene of a man being pushed under a train, shot at the Uhlandstrasse station on the Berlin underground.

35mm, Sound, 88mins, Rank

🚂

DESTRUCTION OF A TRAIN (Britain 1984)

BBC TV News/ITN News. To demonstrate the strength of a nuclear flask on British Rail, a diesel locomotive and three coaches travelling at 100mph were totally wrecked; but the flask survived.

16mm/VID, Sound, Colour, 10mins, BBC TV/ITN/RF

🚂 🚂 🚂 🚂 🚂

DETECTIVES

Detectives in fiction have always been keen on railways. Sir Arthur Conan Doyle himself travelled much by train and so his famous creation Sherlock Holmes was much addicted to the timetables and the country stations as well as the main lines. Thus the first film versions of *The Hound of the Baskervilles* made use of Lustleigh (closed 1959) on the Great Western branch to Moretonhampstead. Since then both film and television versions of Sherlock Holmes stories have made extensive use of preserved railways, notably the Severn Valley and the Bluebell lines. Agatha Christie, whose home overlooked the Torbay line in Devon, was also a stickler for railway timetables. Again the Severn Valley line has been able to provide authentic GWR background for both film and television versions of her books. Overseas locations were provided for *Murder on the Orient Express* mainly by SNCF in France but other adventures of Hercule Poirot for film and television have come from the Nene Valley line (useful for overseas items), the Bluebell, the Torbay and the Severn Valley, with extra backup from the Keighley & Worth Valley preserved railway. American crime stories have followed the same pattern, notably in the many films by Alfred Hitchcock with scenes on transcontinental trains.

THE DEVELOPMENT OF THE ENGLISH RAILWAYS (Britain 1936)

An explanation, using maps and animated diagrams, of the origins and development of the English Railway system from 1800 to 1936. There is one solitary shot of a real train: LMS 'Patriot' 4-6-0 locomotive and LMS stock leaving St Pancras. A GBI instructional film produced by Mary Field.

16mm, Sound, 11mins, GBI/HA

THE DEVELOPMENT OF THE MAJOR RAILWAY TRUNK ROUTES (Britain 1965)

Produced by British Transport Films. A film version of the 1965 Report, with Dr Richard Beeching. How a trunk system can be selected and developed to match the traffic requirements of 1984.

35/16mm, Sound, 17mins, BTF

DEVIL'S DYKE: A VICTORIAN PASTIME (Britain 1987)

John Payne production. Script by Paul Clark. Commentary by John Huntley. A history of Brighton, its architecture, photographs of the 'Daddy-Long-Legs' seashore Railway, the Volks Electric Railway and the early days at Devil's Dyke, including a Cable Car across the Dyke, a Funicular Railway to the village below, a funfair switchback

railway and the line which opened in 1887 from Hove to Rowan Halt, Golf Club Halt and the Dyke. There are photographs of the 'E4s' used on this line including Nos 2492 and 2505 and a rare piece of archive film of the last train with SR 'E4' 0-6-2T No 2494 on an auto train, 31 December 1938.

16mm/VID Sound, Colour, 20mins, Payne/Online/HA (ref)

DEVON BELLE (Britain 1938)

Brief shots of the Devon Belle observation coach as operated in the 1930s.

16mm, Silent, 3mins, HA

DEVONSHIRE RAMBLER RAIL TOUR (Britain 1966)

SCTS. Round tour from Waterloo to Exeter, Taunton, Westbury, Salisbury, Southampton and back to Waterloo. Motive power was provided by SR 'Merchant Navy' 4-6-2 No 35023 *Holland-Afrika Line* and SR 'West Country' 4-6-2 No 34100 *Appledore* (built by BR in 1949).

16mm, Silent, 8mins, HA/SCTS

DIAMONDS ARE FOREVER (Britain 1989)

International Film Associates (Scotland). Glasgow was one of the world's largest locomotive builders. This film is based on the North British Locomotive company with its diamond-shape trademark.

The company was founded in 1852; it built 28,000 steam locomotives, of which 18,000 were exported, going to Russia, China, Egypt, Malaya, Canada, Cuba, South America and, in the Second World War, throughout the whole of Europe. Many hundreds were built for the pre-Grouping companies. A lot of the trains are still running today, many in India and some built in 1911 are still used on everyday scheduled services in Paraguay. Some have been restored and now run on preserved railways. The film includes interviews with many of the men who worked for the company, which came to an end in 1962. The production was master-minded by

Eddie McConnel, who also made *The Emotive Locomotive*.

VID, Sound, Colour, 28mins, IFA

DIDCOT (Britain 1969)

A film by Tom Martin. Scenes of the Great Western Centre, featuring locomotive GWR '14XX' 0-4-2T No 1466 (built 1936) and Auto Trailer No 231 (built 1951). A nice preserved reproduction of a typical GWR branch line.

16mm, Silent, Colour, 6mins, TM/HA

DIDCOT RAILWAY CENTRE (Britain 1969-87)

The Great Western Railway Society centre at Didcot has been filmed for many newsreels, various children's programmes, a study of the 14XX class locomotive by Tom Martin, a visit by *Lion* filmed by Ian Fagg and a trip from Paddington to Didcot with *King George V* in 1979, recorded by Wilf Watters.

16mm, Silent, 29mins, TM/WW/HA/IF/VID

DIESEL AND ELECTRIC ON 35MM (Britain 1990)

Video 125. Produced by Peter Middleton. Written and presented by John Huntley. The early years of Diesel and Electric motive power on British railways, using high-quality 35mm stock shots from Elstree, Pathe and ITC sources. It includes the story of Britain's first mainline diesel electric locomotive No 10000 built by the LMR in 1947 at the English Electric Works and at Derby Works; the 'Deltics' in action, including the prototype; early Great Western classic diesels; a cab view run from Victoria on Southern Electric in the 1940s.

VID, Sound, Part colour, 60mins, 125

DIESEL MANIA (Britain 1983)

B&R Video Productions. An early attempt to see if the video market was ready for diesel; it wasn't. Good scenes of Deltics and diesels in Mid-Wales and on the Cambrian Coast.

VID, Sound, Colour, 59mins, BRV

DIESEL POWER (Britain 1986)

Transport Video Publishing. Mainly Class 40s in action with scenes on the Settle & Carlisle line and the Skegness branch.

VID, Sound, Colour, 40mins, TVP

DIESEL POWER ON BRITISH RAILWAYS (Britain 1965)

Produced by British Transport Films. 'British Railways operate the largest diesel fleet in western Europe. Close co-operation between the locomotive manufacturers and the railways has led to the development of many different types of engine for different purposes, and the wide range in service on British Railways are demonstrated in this film.'

16mm, Sound, Colour, 8mins, BTF

DIESEL TRAIN DRIVER (Britain 1959)

Produced by British Transport Films.
Part 1. An Introduction to the Diesel Train.
Part 2. Driving the Train.
Part 3. Dealing with Faults.
Part 4. Operational requirements.
'Under British Railways modernisation plan diesel traction is taking the place of steam on many lines. The following films are part of a complete visual unit of films, filmstrips and wall-charts which is being used in the mobile instruction coaches and in motive power schools in which men are trained to drive multiple-unit diesel units'.

35/16mm, Sound, 84mins, BTF

DIESEL TRAIN RIDE (Britain 1959)

Produced by British Transport Films. 'The forward-looking front windows of the new diesel multiple-unit trains reveal a new world of signs, signals and railway sights to those who ride behind the driver. Children, particularly, find this a fascinating experience. This film communicates something of their excitement and wonder as well as some of the wry, unconscious humour with which their questions and comments are so often interlarded.' A bit quaint at this distance in time but very much of its era.

35/16mm, Sound, Colour, 11mins, BTF

THE DIESELS ON RAIL (Britain 1956)

Shell film. Diesel training film for railwaymen.

35/16mm Sound, 20mins, PFB

DIFFERENT GAUGES IN EAST GERMANY (Britain 1990)

Videolines. A survey of the various gauges in use in East Germany with a real mix of loco styles, including 0-4-4T, 2-6-2T, 0-8-0T, 0-6-0T and 2-10-2T; and all points in between!

VID, Sound, Colour, 60mins, VLV

THE DIVIDED HEART (Britain 1954)

Ealing Studios. Directed by Charles Crichton. With Yvonne Mitchell and Cornell Borchers. Story of adoption of a child in wartime by a childless German couple. Includes shots of Austrian overhead electric railway and station sequence.

35mm, Sound, 89mins, Weintraub

DMU TEST RUN (Britain 1958)

Made by Tim Hall. An 8mm record of a test run with a brand-new DMU unit from Swindon Works to Kemble, Sapperton Tunnel, Cheltenham (Malvern Road), and back on the old MSWJ line to Cirencester, South Cerney, Cricklade and back to Swindon.

16mm, Silent, Colour, 4mins, Tim Hall/HA

DO YOU REMEMBER? (Britain 1955)

Produced by British Transport Films. Day in, day out, throughout the year, the passengers on London's buses and Underground leave behind them enough property to keep a large staff of sorters and storemen permanently busy. How the lost property is collected sorted, warehoused and, in most cases, restored to its forgetful owners is shown in this film, which reveals an unusual aspect of London Transport's service to the travelling public, gaily described by John Slater.

35/16mm, Sound, 10mins, BTF

DR BEECHING'S VISIT TO THE BLUEBELL (Britain 1962)

A film by Tom Martin. Record of a special from London Bridge to Horsted Keyes and thence to the Bluebell Railway and a trip to Sheffield Park. Among the guests on the train were the then head of the National Railway Museum Dr Scholes and the special guests, Dr and Mrs Beeching who unveiled a plaque.

16mm, Silent, Colour, 14mins, TM/HA

DOCTOR ZHIVAGO (USA 1965)

MGM. Produced by Carlo Ponti. Directed by David Lean. Screenplay by Robert Bolt. With Omar Sharif, Rod Steiger, Geraldine Chaplin, Alec Guinness, Tom Courtnay, Julie Christie and Rita Tushingham. A saga of family life during the years of the Russian Revolution. Like most of David Lean's films, it is punctuated by transport scenes, including electric trams in 'Moscow' (recreated in Spain) and the railways of three countries to provide the 'Russian' scenes, using the State systems of Spain and Finland as well as material shot on the Canadian Pacific.

Almost all the snow was crushed marble dust; not a foot of the film was shot in Russia! Spectacular scenes include the arrival of the Paris express at the Moscow terminus (filmed in Spain), as well as a long train journey with a large 2-6-2

Finnish locomotive and an armoured locomotive and train specially built for the movie.

70/35mm, Sound, Colour, 193mins, MGM

DODGE CITY (USA 1939)

Warner. Directed by Michael Curtiz. With Errol Flynn, Olivia de Havilland and Ann Sheridan. The story of the great Western railroad terminus and how an ex-soldier and a cattle trail boss come to clean it up in the 1880s. Many scenes are filmed on the Sierra Railroad, mainly near Cooperstown, using Baldwin locomotive 2-8-0 No 29790 and a train consisting of coaches Nos 2 and 6, plus Combine No 5 with extra door added.

35mm, Sound, Colour, 104min, Warner

THE DOG IN THE BAGGAGE CAR (USA 1909)

Thanhauser production. A man and his dog try to travel cheap but the dog gets thrown off the train and has to be rescued. Train scenes shot on the Southern Pacific system in the Los Angeles area.

16mm, Silent, 8mins, HA

DONCASTER LOCOMOTIVE WORKS (Britain 1927-46)

W Bassett-Lowke filmed a special visit to Doncaster in 1927, including rare shots of Sir Nigel Gresley and a party of engineers having their photograph taken against a background of LNER 'A1' 4-6-0 No 4470 *Great Northern*. There are also scenes of Doncaster Works from an unknown film made in 1946.

16mm, Silent, 14mins, HA

DONNER PASS: SOUTHERN PACIFIC (USA 1989)

Steam Powered Video. The Sierra Nevada Mountains section of the Southern Pacific, often featured in Hollywood films. This tape covers scenes at Roseville, Auburn, Colfax, Blue Canyon, Norden and Truckee, including the *City of San Francisco* streamliner stranded in snow at Yuba Gap.

VID, Sound, Colour, 60mins, SPV

DOUBLE INDEMNITY (USA 1944)

Paramount. Produced by Joseph Sistrom. Directed by Billy Wilder. Script by Raymond Chandler and James M Cain. With Fred MacMurray, Barbara Stanwyck, Edward G. Robinson, Tom Powers, Porter Hall and Jean Heather. An insurance salesman plots with the beautiful wife of a client to kill her husband. 'Brilliantly filmed and incisively written, the archetypal film noir of the 1940s' (Leslie Halliwell). 'The train is an essential part of the murder story. Indeed, the plot hinges on my favourite part of an American train — the observation platform at the back, as it once was.

Here bandaged Fred MacMurray on crutches keeps his back turned to a passenger taking the night air, wishing —as we wish with him — that the man would go, so that Fred can drop on to the track and pretend he's Barbara Stanwyck's dead husband' (Tony Bilbow).

The railway was provided partly by a Paramount lot privately owned coach and track, supplemented by real scenes on the Atchison, Topeka & Santa Fe in the Los Angeles area.

35mm, Sound, 107mins, Paramount

DOWN AND ALONG (Britain 1965)

Produced by British Transport Films. Londoners are asking what is happening behind the hoardings. This film answers some of their questions. It explains modern techniques of tunnelling, shows miners working a mechanical digging-shield in a running tunnel and the digging by hand of vast underground caverns for junctions and cross-overs. The climax is a 'break-through' to a previously prepared chamber with an accuracy of one inch in more than a mile of tunnelling.

35/16mm, Sound, Colour, 25mins, BTF

DOWN EXETER INCLINE (Britain 1898)

Warwick Trading Company. 'Phantom Ride' on the LSWR. Taken from the buffers of an engine on the L&SWR leaving Queen Street station, travelling down Exeter incline, meeting a train coming up which has an engine at both ends on account of the steep ascent, plunging into Exeter Tunnel, emerging on to the curves beyond, and giving an attractive view of the scenery about.Then, after crossing and re-crossing the points incidental to the junction of this line with the Great Western, the train enters St Davids station and brings the picture to an end. From the Warwick Trading Company catalogue of 1901.

35mm, Silent, 3mins, NFA

DOWN THE LINE (Britain 1990)

Railfilms. Produced and directed by Nick Dodson. A demonstration tape featuring extracts from the Railfilm programmes and marketed at a 'budget' price.

VID, Sound, Colour, 25mins, RFV

DOWN TO THE SEA IN TRUCKS (Britain 1948)

An LMS film. The vast fish train network of the LMS servicing Grimsby, Yarmouth and a number of smaller fishing ports.

35mm/VID, Sound, Colour, 12mins, BTF/TVP

THE DRAGON OF WALES (Britain 1943)

Made by W B Polland. Includes scenes of the Snowdon Mountain Railway.

16mm, Sound, 20mins, NA

DRAGONS OF SUGAR ISLAND (Britain 1983)

BBC Television. Executive producer: Colin Adams. Produced by D Towers. Written and presented by Colin Garratt, from the *Great Little Railways* series.

Colin Garratt looks at the steam hauled sugar cane trains in Negros

DUNKIRK

in the Philippines. Elderly Baldwin narrow gauge locomotives work along impossible looking tracks. The film is beautifully composed with very good railway photography. The working day of the sugar cane workers is graphically portrayed. A train is derailed (with camera crew on board) and is speedily put back by the train crew. Interesting footage of the rare 'Shay' locomotives at work.

16mm, Sound, Colour, 40mins, BBC TV

DRIFTERS (Britain 1929)

Famous John Grierson documentary film made for the Empire Marketing Board. Includes shots of steam-hauled trains on the Forth Bridge.

16mm, Silent, 39mins, HA

DRIVER'S EYE VIEW: HST WEST (Britain 1986)

Video 125. Written and produced by Peter Middleton. Commentary by Anton Rogers. Video of the South Devon railway from Exeter to Plymouth taken from the cab of a High Speed Train. Included is the Royal Albert bridge at Saltash, the Starcross Pumping House of Brunel's Atmospheric railway, helicopter and trackside shots and the whole run from Exeter St Davids alongside the sea to Dawlish, Teignmouth and Newton Abbot, then to Totnes and the Dart Valley, ending at Laira Depot and Plymouth.

VID, Sound, Colour, 85mins, VID 125

THE DRIVING FORCE (Britain 1966)

Produced in association with the Central Office of Information, the British Locomotive & Allied Manufacturers' Association and the British Electrical Manufacturers' Association.

'Britain now operates the most experienced diesel and electric railway in the world and every day Britain's locomotives clock up a mileage equivalent to two round trips to the moon. 150 years ago she invented the steam engine and

introduced a new system of transport and today British Railways and the British locomotive industry have designed, built and proven, in only nine years, enough diesel and electric locos to replace 15,000 steam engines. The transition from steam to the development of new forms of motive power and its effect on railwaymen and passengers is the subject of the film.'

35/16mm, Sound, Colour, 24mins, BTF

DRIVING TECHNIQUE (Britain 1964)

Produced by British Transport Films. Four films for training British Railways electric mainline drivers.
Part 1. The Controls. Explaining the controls of the mainline locomotives of British Railways and their functions.
Part 2. Freight Trains. Special driving techniques applicable to freight trains which are not fully fitted with vacuum brakes.
Part 3. Passenger Trains. The driving techniques applicable to passenger trains.
Part 4. Rheostatic Brake. The principles and correct operation of the rheostatic brake.

35/16mm, Sound, Colour, 53mins, BTF

DRUMS IN THE DEEP SOUTH (USA 1951)

RKO. Directed by William Cameron Menzies. With James Craig and Barbara Payton. An American Civil War story in the style of a Western. Features the Sierra Railroad and Baldwin 2-8-0 locomotive No 29790 of 1906 vintage.

35mm, Sound, Colour, 87min, RKO

DRYSLLWYN CASTLE (Britain 1987)

An account of the life of a BR driver, currently on diesels but previously on steam engines, who comes to Didcot to drive steam locomotives in his spare time.

16mm, Silent, Colour, 12mins, HA

DUEL IN THE SUN (USA 1946)

David Selznick. Directed by King Vidor. With Jennifer Jones and Joseph Cotten. Massive mess of a Western, about a half-breed girl who causes a shoot-out between two brothers. Locomotive Baldwin 2-8-0 of 1906 and a vintage freight train are derailed by outlaw Gregory in the story; the scene of the train going down the hillside loaded with dynamite and finally blowing up was done with a full scale mock-up of the entire train marked 'T&SWRR'.

35mm, Sound, Colour, 138min, Selznick

DUKEDOGS (Britain 1960-71)

The strangley-named GWR locomotives (a mix of the 'Bulldog' class and the 'Duke' class, rebuilt into a new class) have been recorded best by Pat Whitehouse in his film of a trip with two of the class from Shrewsbury to Towyn and Barmouth in 1960 and Tom Martin's film of the restoration of GWR '9000' 4-4-0 No 3217 *Earl of Berkeley.*

16mm/VID Silent, Part colour, 19mins, C/NRM/TM/HA/VID

DUMBO (USA 1941)

Walt Disney. Directed by Ben Sharpsteen. Cartoon. 'In Dumbo the circus train is truly a star vehicle, the scene for the baby's arrival, when the mail stork drops his heavy bundle into the doe-eyed mummy elephant's waggon' (Tony Bilbow). The Walt Disney train is everyone's idea of the perfect model layout, suddenly brought to life.

35mm, Sound, Colour, 64mins, Disney

DUNKIRK (Britain 1940)

A great burden fell on the railways, especially the Southern, with the return of the men from the beaches at Dunkirk. Railway scenes include the handling of Dunkirk specials at Redhill and shots at Dover.

16mm, Silent, 4mins, HA

39

THE DYNAMITE SPECIAL (USA 1917)

A Bison production. Directed by James Davis. Script by George Hively. With Milliard K Wilson and Val Paul.

An engine-driver's daughter is in love with the superintendent's son. Because of the difference in social position the match is discouraged. A dismissed employee who is also in love with the girl, uncouples the dynamite special's engine in an attempt to wreck the superintendent's train. The girl, discovering the plan, climbs on to the footplate and reverses the engine in time to avoid the collision. When her father and the superintendent learn of her bravery they readily consent to her engagement to the boy she loves.

35mm, Silent, 11mins, NFA

DYNAMOMETER CAR (Britain 1927)

A record of the old North British dynamometer car which was later used to record the world record run of *Mallard* at 126mph in 1938 and is now preserved in the National Railway Museum at York.

16mm, Silent, 3mins, HA

E4 AT CAMBRIDGE (Britain 1959)

Made by P B Whitehouse and John Adams. This film shows the last of the 'E4' class 2-4-0s at work at Cambridge.

16mm, Silent, 3mins, HA

THE EAGLE HAS LANDED (Britain 1976)

ITC. Directed by John Sturges. With Michael Caine, Donald Sutherland, Robert Duvall and Jenny Agutter. A plot to kill Churchill with a special German commando group. The early part of the film includes a scene with a German preserved 2-6-0 freight engine No 1070 involved in the transport of Jews to a concentration camp.

35mm, Sound, Colour, 135mins, ITC

EARLY DAYS ON THE GLOUCESTERSHIRE-WARWICKSHIRE RAILWAY (Britain 1983)

An amateur 8mm record of the early days on a preserved line which had a long struggle to get going from 1981 until a move to Toddington in 1983 and the laying of the first main sections of track, leading to the establishment of a steam-hauled train service. The little individual details of getting a railway back into action are well-captured in this film because the photographer was himself directly involved. Fowler diesels 0-6-0DH No 19 and 0-4-0DM No 21 are in action.

16mm, Silent, Colour, 21mins, HA

EARLY RAILWAY SCENES, 1895-1900

British Film Institute. Produced by John Huntley. French 0-6-4 locomotive entering La Ciotat station near Paris (1895); German locomotive entering East station, Berlin (1895); Overhead railway, Alexander-Platz,

Berlin (1895); 4-4-0 Drummond locomotive and State Train, Portsmouth (1897); the 'Black Diamond Express', New York State (1897); Steam elevated railway, New York City (1897); City Imperial Volunteers special train (1900); Lord Kitchener special train, Southampton (1900).

16mm/VID, Silent, 16mins, HA/125

EARLY TRANSPORT SCENES

British Film Institute. Produced by John Huntley. Horse-bus and horse-tram traffic, Paris (1893); Street scene, Berlin (1896); Marseilles Harbour (1896); Paris street scene (1896); St Stephen's Square, Vienna (1896); Hyde Park, Whitehall and the Strand (c1900); Westminster-Tooting tram (1903); Piccadilly Circus (1910); Edgware Road scene (1925); Underground train construction and scene at Golders Green station (1926).

16mm/VID, Silent, 15mins, HA/125

EAST ANGLIAN ROVER (Britain 1984)

An assembly of scenes taken in 1982, including London to Norwich and a general collection taken from 1981 to 1983 across the East Anglian region.

VID, Sound, Colour, 45mins, Cresswell

EAST GRINSTEAD – THREE BRIDGES (Britain 1963)

Made by G S Holyoake. Last push-pull workings with Class H 0-4-4Ts in use. (Nos 31263, 31551 and 31055) and Class M7 0-4-4T No 30379. Two push-pull sets include Nos 601, 602 and 605.

16/9.5/8mm/VID, Silent, Colour, 4mins, MFS/HA/RS

EAST KENT RAILWAY (Britain 1959)

Made by Ivor Gotheridge. A brief 8mm record taken in the area of Tilmanstone Colliery, Eythorne and Sheperdswell, with diesel-hauled freight. The line closed to passengers in 1948.

16mm, Silent, Colour, 4mins, IV/HA

🚂 🚂 🚂 🚂 🚂

ECHO OF AN ERA (USA 1956)

The old New York elevated railway shortly before it was demolished.

16mm, Sound, Colour, 20mins, BFI

🚂 🚂 🚂

THE EDDIE STANBRIDGE COLLECTION

An important assembly of material issued by Railscene under the titles: *Indian Summer A4* and *Steam's Final Frontier*.

🚂 🚂 🚂 🚂

EDGINGTON'S RAILWAYS (Britain 1990)

Produced by John Edgington from the collection of photographs of Dr P Ransome-Wallis deposited in the National Railway Museum in York. Made in association with the Friends of the National Railway Museum. Produced by Gavin Mist and David Sumner.

VID, Sound, Colour, 55mins, P&S

🚂 🚂 🚂 🚂 🚂

EDWARDIAN SCENE, 1902-12 (Britain 1988)

Video 125. Produced by Peter Middleton. Written and presented by John Huntley. (From the *Trains from the Arc* series) *The Great Train Robbery* (1903); *The Jonah Man* (LSWR, Walton on Thames); *An Englishman's Visit to Paris* (SECR); *Lieutenant Daring and the Stolen Plans of the Minefields* (SECR); Port Sunlight (GWR/LNWR Joint); Train crashes (USA); Mount Tamalpais and Muir Woods (USA 1906); Immingham docks (Great Central 1912); Euston to Glasgow (LNWR/Caledonian, 1909); Crewe works (1911); Swindon works (1912); Hereford (GWR 1910).

VID, Sound, 50mins, 125

🚂 🚂 🚂 🚂 🚂

EIGHT-RAIL REPORT (Britain 1968)

Made by British Transport Films. The Freightliner is a familiar sight now in Britain — almost part of the nation's life as the train-loads speed daily up and down the country carrying goods ranging from Royal holiday baggage to fat-stock beef. This is one symbol of continued progress, but there are others including a hot axle box detector; a new platform and barrier indicator at Charing Cross; the speeded up Bournemouth line trains; the luxury lounge car on the Western Region; a huge oil train of 100ton tank wagons; and a 1968 type station for motorists at Pudsey!

35/16mm, Sound, Colour, 13mins, BTF

🚂 🚂 🚂 🚂 🚂

E. K. VIDEOS

A company specialising in overseas railways including *Famous German Locomotives at Work*, *Brig-Visp-Zermatt Railway*, *Steam in Turkey*, *South African Winter Steam*, *Those Giants of Steam* (covers three continents), *Superlatives in Steam* (American railways) and *Big Steam in the West* (USA with Daylight 4449).

🚂 🚂 🚂 🚂 🚂

ELECTRA FILMS

This company specialises in video on Freight Train activity and issues almost unbelievably long tapes of seemingly endless up-and-passed trains all over the country under the title *Freight Train* (Volumes 1 to 7 so far), providing 14hr viewing time. Add to this a further 30hr on such themes as *Salute to the 47s*, *Vulcan's Heritage*, *Railtour Review*, *Railtour Special*, *Power Rail* Vols 1 to 8, *Taking Coals To*, *Loco-Hauled* and it adds up to a glorious 44hr — unless you want to run them through twice. And there are more to come.

🚂 🚂 🚂 🚂 🚂

ELECTRIC TRAIN DRIVER (Britain 1964)

Produced by British Transport Films.
Intended for instructing British Railways electric mainline drivers.
Part 1. Electrical faults-indicated. Ways of detecting and correcting electrical faults in mainline locomotives.

Part 2. Electrical faults-non-indicated. How to detect and correct non-indicated electrical faults in mainline locomotives.
Part 3. Preparation of the BR locomotive. Detailed demonstration of driver's preparation duties.
Part 4. Disposal of BR locomotive. Detailed demonstration of driver's disposal duties.

35/16mm, Sound, 39mins, BTF

🚂 🚂 🚂 🚂 🚂

ELECTRIC TRAINS TO MANCHESTER (Britain 1990)

Railfilms. Produced and directed by Nick Dodson. The story of the Manchester South Junction and Altrincham Railway and the development of electric railways in the Manchester area, including the pioneering 1,500V DC system of 1931. There are interviews with people who remember the old line which lasted until 1971, when the line was re-electrified to fit in with the national network on 25kV and then changed again in the late 1980s to link with the planned Metrolink Light Rapid Transit System. An unusual video on a little known subject.

VID, Sound, Colour, 45mins, RFV

🚂 🚂 🚂 🚂 🚂

ELECTRO-MAGNETIC INDUCTION (Britain 1946)

Gaumont-British Instructional Film. Opens with scenes of old LSWR electric stock in Southern Railway days, probably at Motspur Park. There is also an 00 gauge layout with a model of the Brighton Belle.

16mm, Sound, 12mins, HA (ref)

🚂

ELHAM VALLEY LINE (Britain 1941)

The SER line from Canterbury to Folkestone that was opened in 1889 and finally closed in 1947. It was used during World War 2 for the rail-mounted 18in gun named *Boche Buster* which was assembled at Darlington North Road and travelled to the Elham line via Catterick disguised as a train of three banana waggons. This must have aroused maximum curiosity as bananas were virtually unobtainable in Britain during the war! It never fired in anger but Churchill thought much of it and used to take visitors to Barham to see it in action.

16mm, Silent, 9mins, IWM/HA: ref only

🚂 🚂 🚂 🚂

ELIZABETHAN EXPRESS (Britain 1954)

Produced by British Transport Films for the British Transport Commission. The Elizabethan express covered the 393 miles from London to Edinburgh non-stop at an average speed of over 65mph during the days of steam. The express was a record-holder, and this film captures the speed and excitement of one of those runs. It recalls all the glamour of the great days of steam, as well as the activity of the men who maintained the service. The exciting footplate sequences are probably unique. The locomotive seen throughout is LNER Gresley 4-6-2 No 60017 *Silver Fox*.

35/16mm/VID, Sound, 20mins, BTF/TS/VID BT1

🚂 🚂 🚂 🚂 🚂

ELMER GANTRY (USA 1960)

Bernard Smith Production. Directed by Richard Brooks. With Burt Lancaster, Jean Simmons and Dean Jagger. Story of a discredited revivalist preacher. Includes scenes on an American steam-hauled freight line.

35mm, Sound, Colour, 146mins, TCF

🚂

EMERGENCY (Britain 1962)

Produced by British Transport Films. To test a plan for dealing with major accidents, a mock incident is staged on railway property. After sealing off the area, diverting traffic, hacking through coach roofs, giving blood transfusions on the spot, providing hot cups of tea, and removing the last casualty to hospital, the local authorities and their services – fire, police, first aid, ambulance, hospital, WRVS, telephones – have a clearer idea of how the scheme will work out in practice.

35/16mm, Sound, 15mins, BTF

🚂 🚂 🚂 🚂 🚂

THE EMOTIVE LOCOMOTIVE (Britain 1990)

International Film Associates (Scotland). Produced and directed by Eddie McConnell. A wonderful study of railway enthusiasts of all different kinds, without an ounce of the condescension: collectors, painters, photographers, society members etc. There is an accent on the Scottish scene but the message is universal. The Forth Bridge and LNER 'A4' 4-6-2 No 4488 *Union of South Africa*, temporarily renamed *Osprey*, features prominently. Personalities featured include Lawrie Marshall, Maurice Wilson, David Weston and Ian Allan.

16mm/VID, Sound, Colour, 27mins, IFC (Scotland)

🚂 🚂 🚂 🚂 🚂

EMPEROR OF THE NORTH POLE (USA 1973)

TCF. Produced and directed by Robert Aldrich. With Lee Marvin, Ernest Borgnine, Keith Carradine, Charles Tyner and Malcolm Atterbury. A sadistic train guard attacks hobos hitching a ride. Set in Oregon during the Depression of the 1930s. In the end, it's a duel to the death between Lee Marvin and Ernest Borgnine, with a mass of crazy railroad stunts and an awful lot of talk in between. 'It's hard, contrived, pointless in its thesis, repulsive in its people, joyless in its glorification of the bum and hobo' (Judith Crist). The film makes extensive use of the facilities of the Sierra Railroad, with a lot of locations around the ATSF yards in the Los Angeles area.

35mm, Sound, Colour, 119mins, TCF

🚂 🚂 🚂

EMPIRE STATE EXPRESS (USA 1896)

Biograph. A single railway shot from the early Biograph collection.

16mm, Silent, 40seconds, HA

🚂 🚂 🚂 🚂 🚂

THE ENGINE DRIVER (Britain 1949)

Citizen Film. An educational film featuring the work of an engine driver and fireman. Filmed on what had just become British Railways (Southern Region), it features Nine

Elms sheds and a journey from Waterloo to Bournemouth with SR 'Lord Nelson' class 4-6-0 No 30856 *Lord St Vincent*.

16mm, Silent, 17mins, HA/RF

🚂 🚂 🚂 🚂 🚂

THE ENGINE DRIVER (Britain 1947)

Pathe/British Instructional Film. An educational film on the work of a main-line engine driver on the run from Euston to Manchester. Locomotives include Stanier LMS 'Jubilee' class 4-6-0 No 5614 *Leeward Islands*, Fairburn 2-6-4T No 2681 and Stanier LMS 4-6-0 Black Five No 4815.

16mm, Silent, 9mins, HA

🚂 🚂 🚂 🚂 🚂

ENGINE SHED (Britain 1938)

An account of the work in an engine shed in the days of steam.

35mm, Sound, 20mins, BTF

🚂 🚂 🚂 🚂

ENGINEMEN (Britain 1959)

A British Film Institute production. Directed by Michael Grigsby. Photography by Andrew Hull, Ivan Halleron and Eric Harrison. A study of a group of men in a Lancashire locomotive shed who talk about their approach to the job and the change over from steam to diesel locomotives.

16mm, Sound, 21mins, BFI

🚂 🚂 🚂 🚂 🚂

ENGINES IN STEAM (Britain 1966)

Made by Trevor White. Scenes on the Romney, Hythe & Dymchurch Railway and the Bluebell Line.

16/8mm, Silent, Colour, 5mins, TW

🚂 🚂 🚂 🚂 🚂

ENGLISHMAN'S TRIP TO PARIS (Britain 1904)

Hepworth production. Directed by Lewin Fitzhammon. Early travel film, including scenes of Charing Cross station with SECR 'D' 4-4-0 No 745 (built 1901) and a scene of SECR 'B' 4-4-0 No 1454 fitted with Holden's patent oil-fired equipment. The 'D' class was built by Wainwright; the 'B' class was the last to come from Stirling. There is also a scene of the boat train arriving at Dover Marine.

16mm/VID, Silent, 4mins, HA/125

🚂 🚂

ENTHUSIAST'S SPECIALS NO 1 (Britain 1962)

Made by G S Holyoake. 'Somerset and Dorset Rail Tour' (LCGB) and 'Sussex Special Rail Tour' (RCTS), with shots of such motive power as Terrier No 32636, Class E6 0-6-2, GWR '2251' class and unrebuilt 'Battle of Britain' 4-6-2 No 34064.

16/9.5/8mm, Silent, Colour, 4mins, MFS

🚂 🚂 🚂 🚂 🚂

ENTHUSIASTS' SPECIAL NO 2 (Britain 1962)

'South London Tour' with Class C1-02 0-4-4T No 30199 (REC); 'Home Counties Railway Society Specials' with 4-6-0 Lord Nelson No 30850 and unrebuilt West Country No 34094 *Mortehoe* 'Sussex Coast Special'.

16/9.5/8mm, Silent, Colour, 4mins, MFS

🚂 🚂 🚂 🚂 🚂

ENTHUSIASTS' SPECIAL NO 3 (Britain 1962-63)

Made by G S Holyoake. 'Midland Limited' (LCGB) tour with 'Patriot', 'B16/2' and 'J11' class motive power; shots of 'Schools' class No 30926 *Repton* and restored 'T9' No 120 at Eastleigh; No 45532 *Silver Jubilee* at Bristol; and 'A4' No 60022 *Mallard* at Waterloo, Salisbury, Exeter and Tiverton Junction.

16/9.5/8mm, Silent, Colour, 4mins, MFS

🚂 🚂 🚂 🚂 🚂

ENTHUSIASTS' SPECIAL NO 4 (Britain 1963-64)

Made by G S Holyoake. 'The Cobbler' Rail Tour (SBLC) with Midland class '4F' 0-6-0 No 44414; SCTS Rail Tour with LNER Class A3 4-6-2 No 60112 *St Simon*; LCGB Special with Midland Class 3F 0-6-0T No 47482; LCGB North and West Tour with 'Coronation' class 4-6-2

No 46251 *City of Nottingham*; Ian Allan Tour with No 46245 *City of London*.

16/9.5/8mm, Silent, Colour, 4mins, MFS

🚂 🚂 🚂 🚂 🚂

EQUINOX: RUNNING TO TIME (Britain 1990)

Uden Associates. With the challenge of denationalisation hovering around, many TV programmes and news items turned their attention to the railways in a way that had never happened in quite the same manner before. This programme chose the introduction of the British Rail Class 91 electric locomotives (often known as 'Electras') as its subject, with their introduction on the London to Leeds line in the autumn of 1988. It follows the 'Electras' technical development and shows the testing of the components and the locomotive assembly. Factors affecting body style, economic and marketing requirements are also reviewed until the complete unit finally emerges and goes into service. (A later programme explored the problems of the London-Leeds in the snows of the 1990-91 winter).

VID, Sound, Colour, 28mins, Uden

🚂 🚂 🚂 🚂 🚂

EQUINOX: TROUBLE ON THE LINE (Britain 1990)

Produced by Paul Fabricius. Uden Associates report. A very frank assessment of British Rail's position in 1990, including the threat of privatisation, staffing, freight problems and the government limitations which prevent it from often reaching its full potential. One of the best programmes in recent times on this theme.

VID, Sound, Colour, 28mins, Uden

🚂 🚂 🚂 🚂 🚂

EQUINOX: UNRAVELLING THE UNIVERSE (Britain 1991)

Uden Associates. Produced by David Barlow and Chris Hawes. The 'Superstring theory' of physics, a new interpretation following on from Albert Einstein. One point was made by filming on the Isle of Wight preserved railway at Haven Street,

using an old restored Southern railway carriage and LSWR 'O2' 0-4-4T No W24 *Calbourne*.

VID, Sound, Colour, 28mins, Uden

🚂

EQUIP AND COMPLETE (Britain 1968)

Produced by British Transport Films. A report on the progress of the London Transport Victoria Line.

35/16mm, Sound, Colour, 28mins, BTF

🚂 🚂 🚂 🚂 🚂 🚂

ESCAPE (Britain 1948)

20th Century Fox. Directed by Joseph Mankiewicz. With Rex Harrison and Peggy Cummings. Includes scenes shot on the Dart Valley line.

35mm, Sound, 79mins, TCF

🚂

ESSAIS (France 1946)

SNCF. The workings and the triumphs of steam locomotives on French Railways. Animated drawings explain the technical details; there are big French Pacifics (it's 231 in France; you only count the wheels on one side); a lovely 2-10-0 and a French streamliner with a front exactly like an A4.

35mm, Sound, 18mins, SNCF

🚂 🚂 🚂 🚂 🚂

EUROPE BY TRAIN (Britain 1965)

Produced by British Transport Films. Douglas Brown, journalist and traveller, takes us about Europe retelling his experiences of many different countries; Italy, Switzerland, Germany, Spain. Lingering in stations, or riding on some of the crack Continental expresses, he conveys the excitement of travelling abroad and shows how he makes the journey an interesting part of a holiday or business trip.

35/16mm, Sound, Colour, 25mins, BTF

🚂 🚂 🚂 🚂 🚂

EUROPEAN CINE GAZETTE NO 1 (Germany 1962)

Produced by Deutsche Bundesbahn for the International Union of

Railways. The participation of several European Railway Administrations in a film showing the technical progress and services offered by railways including modern tracks, electrification, modern stations, improved goods, services and the use of snow fences and sheds in Scandinavia.

35/16mm, Sound, Colour, 19mins, UIC

🚂 🚂 🚂 🚂 🚂

EUSTON MAIN LINE (Britain 1929)

Vintage steam action in the Kenton, Wembley and Hatch End areas of the LMS mainline from London, Euston. Looking across the electrified tracks, a parade of ex-L&NWR classes such as 4-6-0 Experiment, 4-6-0 Prince of Wales, 4-6-0 Claughton, 4-4-0 Precursor, and 4-4-2 Precursor Tanks, which passed the camera on services to and from the capital. Also to be seen are an ex-L&Y 4-6-0 *Dreadnought*, Midland 4-4-0 Compounds, LMS Royal Scot 4-6-0 No 6138 *Fury*, which was renamed *London Irish Rifleman* in October 1929, and a 4-6-0 Patriot.

VID, Silent, 10mins, Stirling

🚂 🚂 🚂 🚂 🚂

EUSTON TO BETTWS-Y-COED (Britain 1938)

Originally a 9.5mm amateur record of a journey on the LMS, with lots of old LNWR locomotives still in action on which the unknown photographer concentrates.

16mm, Silent, 7mins, HA

🚂 🚂 🚂 🚂 🚂

EUSTON TO HOLYHEAD (Britain 1936)

A journey behind a 'Royal Scot' via the Menai Bridge through Anglesey to Holyhead, with shots of passengers embarking for Ireland, the hotel, the steam-dominated station and good scenes of some of the LMS shipping fleet, including the *Hibernia*, the *Scotia*, the *Cambria* and the *Slieve More*. One fine shot of the departure of Fowler LMS 'Royal Scot' 4-6-0 No 6155 *The Lancer*.

16mm, Silent, 9mins, HA

🚂 🚂 🚂 🚂 🚂

EVACUEES (Britain 1975)

BBC Television. Produced by Alan Parker. Directed by Mark Shivas. With Maureen Lipman, Ray Mort, Margery Mason and Gary Carp. Dramatic story written by Jack Rosenthal of two Jewish boys from Manchester who are evacuated to Blackpool on the outbreak of war in 1939. Their departure was filmed on the Keighley and Worth Valley preserved railway at Keighley station, using old LMS stock and a GWR locomotive.

16mm, Sound, Colour, 82mins, BBC Television

🚂

EVENING STAR AT SWINDON (Britain 1960)

The building and naming of the last steam locomotive to be built in Britain for BR. It was to become BR 2-10-0 No 92220 *Evening Star* and is now part of the National collection.

16mm, Silent, 6mins, HA

🚂 🚂 🚂 🚂 🚂

EVENING STAR RAIL TOUR (Britain 1964)

SCTS. A tour with BR 2-10-0 No 92220 *Evening Star*, the last steam locomotive built at Swindon in 1960. Other motive power includes two Ivatt LMS '2MT' 2-6-2T Nos 41206 and 41308. The journey starts at Victoria then to Salisbury, Yeovil Junction, Yeovil Town, Seaton Junction and back to Victoria.

16mm, Silent, 6mins, HA/SCTS

🚂 🚂 🚂 🚂 🚂

EVENTS OF 1935 (Britain 1935)

An LMS film. New diesel railcar; launch of LMS Clyde steamers; Heysham to Belfast shipping; Silver Jubilee of trains at Euston; new LMS station at Elm Park; the Turbomotive locomotive (4-6-2 No 6202); opening of railway research laboratory at Derby; naming of new locomotives — *Royal Scots Fusilier* at Ayr and *British Legion* at Euston.

35mm/VID, Sound, 16mins, BTF/TVP

🚂 🚂 🚂 🚂 🚂

EVENTS OF 1936 (Britain 1936)

An LMS film. Naming of *Giggleswick* and *Isle of Man*; launching of LMS ships on the Clyde; first all-steel signalpost; best station awards.

35mm/VID, Sound, 18mins, BTF/TVP

🚂 🚂 🚂 🚂 🚂

EVERY VALLEY (Britain 1957)

Produced by British Transport Films. An impression from daybreak to midnight of the life of the industrial valleys of South Wales and of the growing part played in that life by bus and railway. The free verse spoken by Donald Huston acts as a link on the soundtrack between various arias, choruses and orchestral interludes from Handel's Messiah that utter their own comment, lyrical, ironic or humorous, upon the pictures of Welsh life and landscape that they accompany

35/16mm, Sound, 20mins, BTF

🚂 🚂

EVERYTHING FOR SALE (Poland 1968)

Produced by the Kamera Film Unit. Directed by Andrej Wajda. With Beata Tyszkeiwicz and Elizbieta Czyzewska. A tribute to Zbigriew Cybulski. Includes spectacular steam-hauled railway scenes, with Polish 2-10-0s.

35mm, Sound, Colour, 96mins, Polski

🚂

EXETER FLYER RAIL TOUR (Britain 1965)

SCTS. This tour set out from Waterloo and then on to Basingstoke, Salisbury, Exeter, Barnstaple Junction, Morthoe and Ilfracombe. Main motive power was provided by SR 'Merchant Navy' 4-6-2 No 35022 *Holland-America Line*, plus BR '4MT' 2-6-4T Nos 80039 and 80043.

16mm, Silent, 7mins, HA/SCTS

🚂 🚂 🚂 🚂 🚂

EXILE EXPRESS (USA 1939)

United Players Production. Directed by Otis Gareth. Photography by

John Mescall. With Ann Sten, Alan Marshall and Jerome Cowan. A spy story with railway scenes.

35mm, Sound, 70mins,

EXPERIENCE OF STEAM, THE (Britain 1984)

Cresswell Films. An assembly of steam scenes in South Africa (NCs hard at work), 'Skyliners in Turkey'; Class 44 iron ore bankers in Germany and steam on the Settle & Carlisle line.

VID, Sound, Colour, 30mins, Cresswell

EXPERIMENT UNDER LONDON (Britain 1961)

Produced by British Tansport Films. In preparation of the construction of the new Victoria-Walthamstow line two experimental lengths of tunnels are driven using different lining materials. The film shows in considerable detail the aligning of the cutting equipment, the operation of the shield and cutters and the two techniques of lining.

35/16mm, Sound, Colour, 23mins, BTF

THE EXPERT (Britain 1968-69)

Crime series which had episodes shot at Birmingham New Street, Lapworth, Coventry and Vauxhall. BBC 2 Television (1968-69)

EXPORT BY TRAIN (Britain 1966)

Produced by British Transport Films. 'Transport problems are often a major concern to the businessman who sends goods to the Continent. *Export by Train* illustrates the many facilities offered by BR Train Ferry and Container Services to and from the Continent.'

35/16mm, Sound, Colour, 12mins, BTF

EXPRESS TRAINS (Britain 1898)

A Cecil Hepworth Production. Trains in a cutting in Surrey. 'A photograph taken in a picturesque railway cutting in Surrey. During the

period of the picture no less than three express trains rush through, emitting dense clouds of steam as they pass. The trains come from the extreme distance of the view up into the close foreground, and the effect of their rapid travelling is very fine and quite exciting' (50ft). From the Hepworth catalogue of 1906.

35mm, Silent, 50seconds, NA (Lost)

EXTENSIONS TO LONDON TRANSPORT (Britain 1946)

A record of the first major additions to the London Underground system after World War 2.

35mm, Silent, 11mins, BTF

EYEMOUTH (Britain 1949)

Hurkers Production. The rebuilding of a viaduct on the North British line from Burnmouth to Eyemouth, closed in 1962. A one coach train hauled by NB 'J37' 0-6-0 locomotive marked 'British Railways' reopens the viaduct.

16mm, Silent, Colour, 4mins, HA

F

FAIR OF THE IRON HORSE (USA 1927)

A record of the fair staged by the Baltimore & Ohio to celebrate 100 years of US railroads (also known as the Iron Horse Centennial). A vast parade of historic American steam was on display; Britain was represented by a replica of Stephenson's *Rocket* (with a lady dressed as Britannia on the tender!) and by the first public appearance of GWR 'King' 4-6-0 No 6000 *King George V*.

16mm, Silent, 22mins, HA

FAMOUS TRAINS OF WESTERN RAILROADS (USA 1897-1903)

A Blackhawk Film. Northern Pacific 'Overland Express' (Edison 1900); Northern Pacific 'Fast Mail' (Edison, 1897). Union Pacific 'Overland Limited' (Edison 1902); Union Pacific Sherman Hill tunnel (Biograph 1903); Santa Fe California Limited (Edison, 1898); Southern Pacific 'Overland Mail' (Edison, 1897); Southern Pacific 'Sunset Limited' (Edison, 1898).

16mm, Silent, 11mins, HA

THE FAR NORTH (Britain 1991)

Video 125. Produced by Peter Middleton. Research by David McConnell. Commentary by Paul Coia. A driver's cab ride through 142 miles of spectacular scenery from Dingwall to Wick and Thurso via Georgemass Junction. There are aerial shots and a history of the line that covers some of the remotest territory in Britain.

VID, Sound, Colour, 104mins, VID125

A FAREWELL TO STEAM (Denmark 1968)

Produced by Teknisk Film Company for the Danish State Railways. Directed by Per Larsen. Music by Bert Fabricius-Bjerre. An account of the history of steam locomotives on the Danish State Railways from the original importation of engines from Britain in the 1840s up to the last steam-hauled runs in 1968.

16mm, Sound, Colour, 23mins, DSR/HA

🚂 🚂 🚂 🚂 🚂

FAREWELL TO THE DELTIC (Britain 1983)

P Smallwood Video. The last of the Deltics on display at Doncaster Works in February 1982.

VID, Sound, Colour, 90mins, Ballymoss

🚂 🚂 🚂 🚂 🚂

FARMER MOVING SOUTH (Britain 1952)

Produced by British Transport Films. The true story of a farmer who decided to move his entire stock – cattle, pigs and poultry, machinery, ploughs and tractors south from Stokesley in Yorkshire to Hartfield in Sussex by rail in December, on, as it turned out, the coldest night of the year. In this filmed record, A G Street, writer and broadcaster, discusses some of the unusual problems of the move with Inspector Barr of British Railways.

35/16mm, Sound, 17mins, BTF

🚂 🚂 🚂 🚂 🚂

THE FARMER'S WIFE (Britain 1940)

ABPC. Directed by Leslie Arliss. With Basil Sydney, Wilfrid Lawson and Patricia Roc. A farmer seeks a wife but marries his housekeeper. Includes a scene at Cole Green station on the line from Welwyn Garden City to Hertford, closed in 1951.

35mm, Sound, 82mins, Weintraub

🚂

THE FASCINATION OF STEAM (Britain 1984)

Cresswell Films. Archive scenes of the Euston mainline in the 1930s; steam on the Fort William to Mallaig line in 1984; the British Transport Film *Snowdrift at Bleath Gill* and the Settle & Carlisle line.

VID, Sound, 45mins, Cresswell

🚂 🚂 🚂 🚂 🚂

FENLAND STEAM (Britain 1976)

Anglia Television. Produced and directed by David Kenten. Presented by Dick Joice. A history of the Wisbech to Upwell Tramway and the local museum which contains records of this strange little railway. (From the *Bygones* series).

16mm, Sound, Colour, 11mins, Anglia

🚂 🚂 🚂 🚂 🚂

LA FERROVIA DEL BERNINA (Italy 1913)

Ambrosio film. A railway tour; crossing a viaduct at Brusio; through Poschiavo; over mountains to St Moritz.

35mm, Silent, 6mins, NFA

🚂 🚂 🚂 🚂 🚂

FERRYLOAD (Britain 1960)

Produced by British Transport Films. How can you get a prototype piece of British machinery to an exhibition in Milan in three days? The Transport Ferry Service provides the immediate answer, with regular sailings connecting London with the Low Countries, as well as Lancashire and Northern Ireland. Along with Whitbread tankers, Wall's sausages, and computers, the special load is ferried over, and arrives on time, in one piece, ready for setting up on its stand.

35/16mm, Sound, Colour, 33mins, BTF

🚂 🚂 🚂 🚂 🚂

FESTIVAL OF BRITAIN (Britain 1951)

A Kinocrat Film made for Beyer Peacock. A record of the Festival of Britain with detailed scenes of the railway exhibits including a 660 hp diesel-electric locomotive for the Tasmanian Government by Robert Stephenson and a Beyer Peacock display.

16mm, Sound, Colour, 16mins, Lama

🚂 🚂

FFESTINIOG RAILWAY: 125 YEARS OF STEAM (Britain 1988)

RV Television. Gala Weekend of the Ffestiniog Railway with Fairlie double engine *Merddin Emrys*, the oldest locomotive of the Ffestiniog

— *Prince* — and a visitor from the Welsh Highland Railway *Russell*. Double-headed run with *Blanche* and *Mountaineer*. Outline history of the line.

VID, Sound, Colour, 60mins, RVV

🚂 🚂 🚂 🚂 🚂

FFESTINIOG 150 YEARS (Britain 1986)

SF. Commentary by Stephen Lyons. 19 and 20 April, 1986. *Linda*, *Blanche*, *Earl of Merioneth*, *Prince*, *Mountaineer* (steam) and *Conway Castle* and *Moel Hebog* (diesels) are all featured in runs from Portmadog to Blaenau Ffestiniog.

VID, Sound, Colour, 42mins, SF

🚂 🚂 🚂 🚂 🚂

FFESTINIOG: 150 YEARS (Britain 1985)

Salford Films. A record of 37 Ffestiniog trains at 27 different locations. A mad dash around, but fun.

VID, Sound, Colour, 42mins, SFV

🚂 🚂 🚂 🚂 🚂

FFESTINIOG HOLIDAY (Britain 1985)

Windjammer Production. Written, produced and directed by Alan Willmott. Narrated by Donald Houston. The 13.5-mile long Ffestiniog Railway, linking Portmadog with Blaenau Ffestiniog and one of the major tourist attractions of Wales, was originally built as a gravity line in the 1830s to transport slate from the inland quarries to the coast. The film describes the introduction of passenger services around the turn of the century, as well as the line's history until it finally closed in 1946. Then follows the story of its rebirth by dedicated enthusiasts, who gradually restored the permanent way, the surviving locomotives and the rolling stock to reopen the line. Much information is also included about more recent developments, especially the imagination and hard work required to build a new railway bypass.

16mm/VID, Sound, Colour, 19mins, AW/WJ

🚂 🚂 🚂 🚂 🚂

THE FFESTINIOG RAILWAY (Britain 1976)

HTV Television. Produced and directed by John Mead. A record of the famous 2ft narrow gauge line in North Wales, including some spectacular aerial shots. The 100-year old locomotives *Prince* and *Princess* are featured as well as the double Fairlie *Earl of Merioneth*. (From the *Great Little Trains of Wales* series).

16mm/VID, Sound, Colour, 26mins, HTV/Castle

FIFTEEN-INCH GAUGE RAILWAYS (Britain 1961)

Made by P B Whitehouse and John Adams. Features the Ravenglass and Eskdale Railway and the Romney, Hythe & Dymchurch railway.

16/8mm, Silent, 9mins, CV/NRM

FIFTY CLASS GEA BEYER-GARRATT LOCOMOTIVES FOR THE SOUTH AFRICAN RAILWAYS (Britain 1949)

Produced for Beyer Peacock by the Kinocrat Film Unit. Directed by George Cookson. Photography by Hubert Darey. An account of the construction, delivery and operation of GEA Beyer-Garratt locomotives for South Africa Railways.

16mm, Silent, 42mins, LAMA/BFI/HA

FILM FACILITIES UNIT

Permission to film was originally granted by the General Manager's office of the various pre-grouping companies. It was then left to the Public Relations offices of the 'Big Four' from 1923 to 1948. British Railways applications were dealt with by the British Transport Film Unit at Melbury House, Marylebone, for many years. When the BTF unit came to an end, the job passed to nobody in particular. In September 1990, the BR Film Facilities unit was set up and now controls all film and TV enquiries.

FINIAN'S RAINBOW (USA 1968)

Warner. Directed by Francis Ford Coppola. With Fred Astaire and Petula Clark. A leprechaun tries to get back a crock of gold from an old traveller who has taken it to America. Includes scenes on the Sierra Railroad in California with Rogers 4-6-0 locomotive No 4493 built for the Prescott & Arizona Central Railroad in 1891.

35mm, Sound, 140mins, Warner

THE FIRST GREAT TRAIN ROBBERY (Britain 1978)

United Artists. Produced by John Foreman. Written and directed by Michael Crichton. With Sean Connery, Lesley-Anne Down, Donald Sutherland, Alan Webb, Robert Lang and Wayne Sleep. In 1855, an elegant but ruthless crook picks out a gang to help him rob the Folkestone Express on the South Eastern Railway of a consignment of gold bullion.

'My dream was the historical world was going to be lovingly recreated, and then I was going to shoot *The French Connection* inside it' (Michael Crichton). 'The film gives us trains and railways at their Victorian best. Soot up your nostrils and in your beard, bristly upholstery on first class seats. Feel the wind in your matted hair as you jump from one carriage roof to the next, praying there's enough clearance as the thirteenth tunnel approaches. I still remember the SER train, and the smoke, and the countryside seen through the carriage windows, and the footplate, and Connery hoofing it over the carriage roofs' (Tony Bilbow).

All the railway material was shot in Eire, notably on the CIE area around Bray. Dublin station was used for some of the night locations and all the Irish Republic's collection of old stock and preserved steam locomotives were pressed into service; a tremendous run was set up for the main robbery scenes with helicopters, freight-only Irish lines and, for a few scenes, some of the lines still in use for passengers but happily closed on Sundays! Thanks to the energies of the writer/director, the authentic feel of the old South Eastern Railway is most surprisingly sustained, including cleverly disguised engines.

35mm, Sound, Colour, 108mins, United Artists

THE FISHERMAN'S LINE (Britain 1949)

A brief record of the Kelvedon & Tollesbury Light Railway, closed in 1951.

16mm, Silent, Colour, 4mins, HA

FISHGUARD HARBOUR (Britain 1958)

Made by P B Whitehouse and John Adams. Passenger boat arrived at Fishguard Harbour. Passengers disembark and board the London train, pulled by a 'Hall' class locomotive.

16/8mm, Silent, 4mins, CV/NRM

THE FISHING LINE (WEST HIGHLAND RAILWAY) (Britain 1987)

Series producers: Neil Cameron and Peter Walton. Written and presented by Miles Kington. A journey with a 'Black Five' in the Highlands of Scotland. (From the *Steam Days* series).

16mm, Sound, Colour, 30mins, BBC TV

THE FLOCKTON FLYER (Britain 1972)

Southern Television. A charming railway story with some excellently researched history of the GWR. Extensive use was made of the Dart Valley Railway and the West Somerset Railway, particularly featuring GWR '6400' 0-6-0PT No 6412.

16mm, Sound, Colour, 28mins per episode, Southern Television

FLOODS IN THE NORTH (Britain 1948)

British Transport Films. In August 1948, there were six days of continuous rain and 1,000 sq miles of the Scottish Border Country were flooded; the problems for British Railways are shown clearly in this film.

35mm/VID, Sound, 20mins, 35mm/TVP

FLYING FOX (Britain 1926)

Topical Budget. A newsreel shot entitled 'What a contrast is the Modern Iron Horse! "Grooming" the latest North Eastern monster for the holiday rush'; it shows Gresley LNER Pacific 4-6-2 No 4475 *Flying Fox* being cleaned.

35/16mm, Silent, 35seconds, HA

🚂 🚂 🚂 🚂 🚂

THE FLYING SCOT (Britain 1957)

Anglo Amalgamated Production. Produced and directed by Compton Bennett. Photography by Peter Hennessy. With Lee Paterson, Kay Callard and Alan Gifford. A team of crooks attempt a great train robbery on mail bags containing bank notes scheduled for destruction on their way from the Bank of Scotland via a special compartment on the 'Flying Scot' overnight train from the North to London. The overnight 'Flying Scot' from Edinburgh departs from Paddington; the locomotive and stock are GWR with Birmingham and Shrewsbury destination boards. Shots on route are mainly GWR mainline, with the exception of an LMS stock shot taken at Carnforth for the film *Brief Encounter* and another LMS stock shot from *Night Mail*. The express eventually arrives at its destination – Paddington station!

35mm, Sound, 68mins, Anglo

🚂 🚂 🚂

FLYING SCOTSMAN (Britain 1928-90)

Many films have been made about LNER 'A3' 4-6-2 No 4472 *Flying Scotsman*, some of which are listed individually. The main ones include the 1928 non-stop service, the 1929 feature film *The Flying Scotsman*, the newsreels of the purchase and subsequent running of the engine by Alan Pegler (1963-68), the special non-stop Anniversary run on 1 May 1968, the tour of the United States (various TV programmes), films of the US tour by Terry Robinson, *Coming Home* (return of the locomotive to Britain), various outings under the ownership of Sir William McAlpine and the many private

films that have been made over the past 30 years.

35/16/8mm/VID, Part Sound, Part Colour, Many Hours, TR/WM/Weintraub/HA

🚂 🚂 🚂 🚂 🚂

FLYING SCOTSMAN (Britain 1928)

From the series: *Great Britain's Great Expresses* No 1. A record of a journey from London to Edinburgh on the 10am *Flying Scotsman*; the train at that time carried a ladies hairdressing saloon. Motive power includes Gresley LNER 'A3' Pacific 4-6-2, No 2577 *Night Hawk* fitted with air brake pump, No 4475 *Flying Fox*, a Class D20 4-4-0 and a Raven Class C7 4-4-2 Atlantic.

16mm, Silent, 10mins, HA

🚂 🚂 🚂 🚂 🚂

THE FLYING SCOTSMAN (Britain 1930)

Produced by British International Pictures. Directed by Castleton Knight. Photography by T Sparkuhl. Music by John Reynolds. With Moore Marriott, Pauline Johnson, Raymond Milland and Alec Hurley.

The day before he is due to retire an old engine driver reports his fireman for drunkenness. The man is discharged and threatens to make trouble. As the train is leaving on the driver's last run the injured party boards it, followed by the driver's daughter, who hears of his intentions. During the run the old man discovers what he believes to be an illicit love between his daughter and the new fireman, whom he knocks off the cab with a shovel. He is himself struck down by his former mate, who has clambered along the train, but the girl is there also, and she brings the engine, now parted from the rest of the train, to a standstill, and everything ends as it should.

Castleton Knight managed to obtain the exclusive use for six weeks of Gresley Pacific No 4472 *Flying Scotsman*; then he got running powers on 10 Sunday mornings from Kings Cross to Edinburgh. To this, he added the dedication of a newsreel producer to what was admittedly a melodramatic story and turned the most incredible movie hokum into what is

now a fantastic record of things that could be done to a steam locomotive by determined film men. Cameras are placed on every conceivable foothold offered by the locomotive, tender and stock. Pauline Johnson and Alec Hurley climb out on to the running board at 45mph. Moore Marriott really drives 4472 and a then unknown actor Raymond Milland (known later in Hollywood as Ray Milland) actually tends the fire. There is excellent coverage of many aspects of the Scottish run, notably the King's Cross departure and the Edinburgh approach.

The big action scene was shot on the Hertford Loop on four consecutive Sunday mornings, with a points switch just South of Hertford and the climb out onto the side of the train between Crews Hill, Cuffley and Bayford. The scene of the villain uncoupling the loco from the stock, when the carriages go racing on in pursuit of the engine were a source of great anger to Sir Nigel Gresley!

35mm, Sound, 63mins, Weintraub

🚂 🚂 🚂 🚂

THE FLYING SCOTSMAN (Britain 1970-78)

Video Collection. Produced in association with the then Sir William McAlpine. Three films made by Flying Scotsman Enterprises and its associates including *Raising Steam*, *Once Upon a Train* and *Coming Home*. See individual films for details.

VID, Sound, Colour, 54mins, Video Collection

🚂 🚂 🚂 🚂 🚂

FLYING SCOTSMAN 1964 (Britain 1965)

A Stanley Schofield production. Commentary by Johnny Morris. Directed by Kenneth Rittener. Produced by Alan Pegler owner of the locomotive. The famous locomotive is transformed from its British Railways colours to those of its original LNER days and makes excursions from Doncaster to Cardiff and from Manchester to Marylebone, including a tow through Woodhead Tunnel. There is also a return trip to Scotland after 25 years over some

Above:
Lee Patterson, Kay Callard and Alan Gifford in a scene from 'The Flying Scot' (1957).

Left:
Pauline Johnson in high heels on the running board of the actual *Flying Scotsman* while it travels at 45mph. There were no stuntmen or women to do this for her in the 1930 film 'The Flying Scotsman'.

Overleaf, top:
Another picture of Gresley Pacific No 4472 *Flying Scotsman*, this time showing some of the crew and the camera strapped to the front of the locomotive for the filming of 'The Flying Scotsman' (1930).

Overleaf, bottom:
LNER 4-6-2 No 4472 as 4474 *Victor Wild* as she was disguised for some films. This scene is from 'Flying Scotsman: Tender Memories' (1965-6).

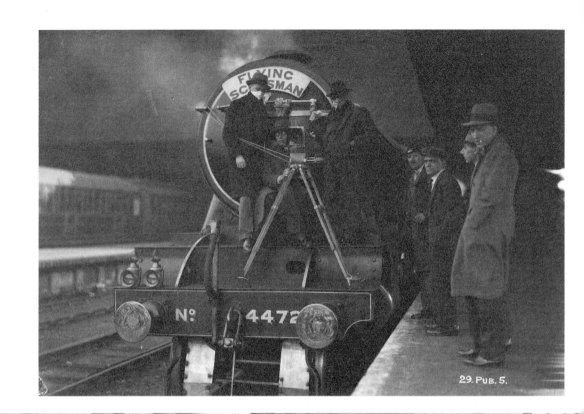

routes never previously travelled, and the train has its portrait painted on the Forth Bridge.

16mm, Sound, Colour, 27mins, HA

🚂 🚂 🚂 🚂 🚂

FLYING SCOTSMAN: A JOURNEY TO THE RED HEART OF AUSTRALIA (Australia 1989)

Flying Scotsman Video. Sunday 6 August 1989. LNER 'A1' 4-6-2 No 4472 *Flying Scotsman* left Melbourne for a 4,000-mile trip through much of Australia, including Australia's barren Red Heart; a parallel run with two massive 'Hudson' class Pacifics Nos 707 and 761; the longest uninterrupted run for a steam locomotive from Parkes to Broken Hill; the Pichi Richi narrow gauge line of the 'Ghan' and much else.

VID, Sound, Colour, 55mins, Flying Scotsman Video

🚂 🚂 🚂 🚂 🚂

FLYING SCOTSMAN AND PENDENNIS CASTLE IN WEST AUSTRALIA (Britain 1989)

Railscene. Film by Kevin J Derrick. Railtours in the Avon Valley, through the Darling Ranges to Toodyay and Northam; to Perth, Merredin, Kalgoorlie, Esperance and Freemantle. As well as other aspects of rail activity in Western Australia, the main feature however is LNER 'A1' 4-6-2 No 4472 *Flying Scotsman* and GWR 'Castle' 4-6-0 No 4079 *Pendennis Castle*.

VID, Sound, Colour, 76mins, RSV

🚂 🚂 🚂 🚂 🚂

FLYING SCOTSMAN AT HIGH WYCOMBE (Britain 1987)

A film by Tom Martin. Scenes of LNER 'A1' 4-6-2 No 4472 *Flying Scotsman* shunting and passing through on various specials.

16mm, Silent, Colour, 7mins, TM/HA

🚂 🚂 🚂 🚂 🚂

FLYING SCOTSMAN DIAMOND JUBILEE CELEBRATIONS (Britain 1983)

Rail Video. RV7 LNER 'A1' 4-6-2 No 4472 *Flying Scotsman* at Don-caster Works on 26 February 1983; trip from Peterborough to York. One of the most staggeringly long videos ever issued on such slim material.

VID, Sound, Colour, 180mins, RVO

🚂 🚂 🚂 🚂 🚂

FLYING SCOTSMAN: TENDER MEMORIES (Britain 1965-6)

A Stanley Schofield Production. Commentary by Johnny Morris. Directed by Kenneth Rittener. Produced by Alan Pegler. The excursions of the *Flying Scotsman* during 1965-6 in which she visited among other places, London, Cardiff and Edinburgh. There are splendid sequences of a sight which is fast becoming a rarity in Britain – a powerful steam locomotive in full cry.

16mm, Sound, Colour, 44mins, HA

🚂 🚂 🚂 🚂 🚂

FLYING SCOTSMAN'S BIRTHDAY (Britain 1983)

BBC Television. Produced by Fiona Johnson. Directed by John Rooney. Presented by Russell Harty. Diamond Jubilee Celebrations of 4472 *Flying Scotsman*, then owned by Sir William McAlpine. There is archive material, a special run to Leeds and an interview with Ray Milland about the making of the 1930 feature film *Flying Scotsman*, followed by scenes from the famous early sound classic.

16mm, Sound, Colour, 33mins, BBC TV

🚂 🚂 🚂 🚂 🚂

FOLKESTONE TRAMWAY (Britain 1938)

Made by C J Barnard. The line between Folkestone Junction and Folkestone Harbour had sections at 1 in 36 and 1 in 30. Originally worked by a variety of locomotives, for a long time it was in the hands of SECR 'F' 4-4-0 and later SECR 'R' 0-6-0T engines which often worked two-in-front and two behind to provide a most spectacular scene as all four locomotives battled to get a heavy boat train up to the Junction.

16mm, Silent, 4mins, HA

🚂 🚂 🚂 🚂 🚂

FOLLOW THE WIRE (Britain 1956)

BICC Cables. Electrification including a run from Sheffield Victoria to Manchester London Road in four minutes. (I wonder where they got the idea from?!)

16mm, Sound, 10mins, RF

🚂 🚂 🚂 🚂 🚂

FOOTPLATE EXPERIENCES (Britain 1934-39)

Made by Mr Garraway. A general title for the fine collection of films made by Mr Garraway, mainly on the LNER for whom he worked. The films have been preserved by his son, Allan Garraway, now with the Boat of Garten preserved railway and one-time manager of the Ffestiniog Railway.

16mm, Silent, 38mins, AG/HA

🚂 🚂 🚂 🚂 🚂

FOOTPLATE EXPRESS (Britain 1955)

PM Films. Scenes from *Rhythm of the Rails* plus 8mm film shot on the footplate. Features the 'Royal Scot'; and a run from Euston to Glasgow.

8mm/VID, Sound, 12mins, PMV

🚂 🚂 🚂 🚂 🚂

FOR THEM THAT TRESPASS (Britain 1948)

Associated British Production. Directed by Cavalcanti. With Stephen Murray and Patricia Plunkett. Drama of a man falsely accused of murder. Includes a LNER scene in a tunnel near Welwyn Garden City.

35mm, Sound, 95mins, Weintraub

🚂

FOR THOSE I LOVED (Britain-USA-Hungary 1990)

TF1 Producers. With Michael York, Brigette Fossey and Jacques Penot. Story of the Warsaw Ghetto. A number of steam scenes were staged in Hungary, using an old 4-6-0 and a big 4-6-2 express engine of the right period. Shown in three parts.

16mm, Sound, Colour, 105mins each part, C4TV

🚂

FOREIGN BODIES

Includes a scene with Marylebone station impersonating Calcutta station in India, complete with hundreds of extras in hot climate marginal clothing freezing to death in the depths of a London winter! (Film not yet released.)

THE FORTH BRIDGE (Britain 1961)

Link Productions. A survey of the famous bridge including steam locomotives of the 'B1', 'V3' and 'J36' classes.

16/9.5/8mm, Silent, Colour, 4mins, MFS

FORTH BRIDGE (Britain 1923-60)

An assembly of material including trains on the bridge in 1923, painting the bridge in 1927, shots of the structure in 1935 and 1948, plus Terence Cuneo painting 4472 *Flying Scotsman* in 1960. There is also a brief shot of a Holmes NBR 4-4-0 of 1912 vintage and a driver's eye view taken in 1932.

16mm, Silent, Part colour, 14mins, HA

FORTIES MEMORY (USA 1940s)

Steam Powered Video. Produced by WB Video Productions. The Denver & Rio Grande and its narrow gauge associated lines like the Silverton. Double and triple headed NMRA specials, two 'Galloping Geese' locomotives and freight working to the top of Marshall Pass. Shot on 16mm colour film with dubbed sound.

VID, Sound, Colour, 60mins, SPV

FORWARD TO FIRST PRINCIPLES (Britain 1966)

Produced by British Transport Films. In the 19th century, railways spread over the country and changed the geography, history and economy, and the life of a nation. But before this, primitive railways were in use (some are shown still working today) which conformed with economic principles rediscovered today as a basis for our newest freight trains.

35/16mm, Sound, Colour, 30mins, BTF

FOUR BACK ROOMS (Britain 1957)

Produced by British Transport Films. Four examples of the work of scientists employed in transport. The research shown covers photoelastic stress analyis used to help in rail design, underwater jets to reduce wave amplitude, the use of a model river bed to test measures against silting and the use of strain gauges in testing of the London Transport Routemaster bus.

35/16mm, Sound, 18mins, BTF

THE FOUR BARRIERS (Britain 1937)

GPO Film Unit. Switzerland, including the place of railways in the nation's development.

35/16mm, Sound, 10mins, COI

FOUR-CAR ELECTRIC MULTIPLE-UNIT TRAIN (Britain 1963)

Produced by British Transport Films. 'Under the British Railways modernisation plan, electric traction is taking the place of steam on many lines. The following films are being used in the mobile instruction coaches and in motive power schools in which men are trained to drive electric multiple-traction motor overload; Part 1 Rectifier fuse faults; Part 2 Fuses (general); Part 3 Airbrake system; Part 4 Main reservoir pipe; Part 5 Train pipe.'

35/16mm, Sound, 60mins, BTF

FOUR'S A CROWD (USA 1938)

Warner. Produced by Hal B Wallis. Directed by Michael Curtiz. With Errol Flynn, Rosalind Russell, Olivia De Havilland and Patrick Knowles. A public relations man has the job of promoting a mean-minded millionaire who has two passions in life — a pack of eight Great Danes and a Lionel Model Railway layout. A large Lionel model American railroad set is featured in the film, including a race scene.

35mm, Sound, 91mins, Warner

FRED THE FUGITIVE STEAM ENGINE (Britain 1988)

Yorkshire Television. Produced and directed by Chris Sutton. With Bill Pertwee and Paul Luty. A children's TV story about Fred, the last steam engine in a goods yard. The time has come for him to go to scrap; it is his destiny to fulfil an order for manhole covers. Fred's driver and fireman are upset to see him go and Fred himself – able to speak in this time of great crisis – expresses his distress. Won over to his side, driver and fireman help in a fight against Messrs Jenkins and Weasel, who have the job of getting Fred to the scrap yard. Will Fred escape his destiny? The forces of good are on his side. Can we doubt the end? Made with the help of the Middleton Railway Trust, Leeds and their North Eastern Tank engine.

VID, Sound, Colour, 22mins, Yorkshire

FREIGHT (Britain 1946)

GWR Sales Film. A detailed record of many aspects of GWR freight services including structural steel, bridge girders, timber, coal, ice cubes, bicycles, cattle, fish, fruit, vegetables and cars from Morris Oxford. There is a shot of a pannier tank and a 0-6-0 freight locomotive at Fishguard Harbour station. There is also a staggering parade of every possible type of GWR road vehicle.

16mm, Silent, 12mins, HA

FREIGHT AND A CITY (Britain 1966)

Produced by British Transport Films. 'The city of Sheffield is renewing itself, but until recently Sheffield's railway network exemplified the confusion and inefficiency created by competitive railway expansion in Victorian times. Now British Railways has swept away the small depots and the conflicting lines, and has centralised its goods operations in a new freight terminal, a diesel maintenance depot, and one of the most modern marshalling yards in Europe, thus providing freight services fit for Sheffield's needs.'

35/16mm, Sound, Colour, 21mins, BTF

FREIGHT TRAIN: VOLUMES ONE AND TWO (Britain 1990-91)

Electra Films. Freight in every possible livery and location. The two volumes add up to over four hours of viewing freight trains.

VID, Sound, Colour, 125mins each, ELV

THE FREIGHTLINER STORY (Britain 1967)

Produced by British Transport Films. *The Freightliner Story* is a film addressed to businessmen not yet committed to the Freightliner as a solution to their transport problems. The film seeks to demonstrate that the product unsuitable for this service has now become the exception. After showing a terminal in action the story moves to the factories of several large companies to examine individual transport problems and the way the Freightliner service has satisfied them. Important customers record their experience of, and, indeed, their enthusiasm for the service.

35/16mm, Sound, Colour, 20mins, BTF

THE FRENCH LIEUTENANT'S WOMAN (Britain 1981)

United Artists. Produced by Leon Clore. Directed by Karel Reisz. With Jeremy Irons, Meryl Streep, Leo McKern and Patience Collier. A comparison between Victorian life and that of our own times. Scenes were shot at the abandoned Lyme Regis station (it closed in 1965) with Windsor Central revamped as Exeter St Davids.

35mm, Sound, Colour, 123mins, United Artists

FRENCH NARROW GAUGE (Britain 1962)

Made by P B Whitehouse and John Adams. Trains on the interesting P O Correze line of SNCF which runs from Tulle to Argentat.

16/8mm, Silent, 9mins, CV/NRM

FRENCH NATIONAL RAILWAYS (Britain 1946-69)

Nick Lera not only recorded films of aspects of the African and South American railways but also nearer home, as well as collecting important historical records. The French railways in the immediate postwar period; the Bastille line in Paris in 1969 with archive items on the 'voitures Imperiales' double-decker suburban coaches and a dynamometer test run with a Pacific steam engine.

16mm, Sound, 9mins, NL

FRENCH STEAM IN THE SIXTIES (Britain 1987)

Rail Video. Last days of French steam.

VID, Sound, 32mins, RVO

FRIEDA (Britain 1947)

Ealing Studios. Produced by Michael Relph. Directed by Basil Dearden. With Mai Zetterling, David Farrar and Glynis Johns. An RAF officer marries and takes back to England a girl who helped him escape from a POW camp. Includes scene at Hartfield Station on the Southern Railway.

35mm/VID, Sound, 97mins, Weintraub/VID125 (rly)

FROM BATH TO EVERCREECH JUNCTION (Britain 1960)

Made by P B Whitehouse and John Adams. The train is hauled by ex-Somerset & Dorset 2-8-0s and shows banking performed by ex-LMS 0-6-0T engines.

16/8mm, Silent, 7mins, CV/NRM

FROM MANCHESTER TO JAVA (Britain 1973)

Made by Nick Lera, with commentary by Nick Lera. A magical film about steam transport in the former Dutch East Indies (now Java), including a steam tram built by Beyer Peacock of Manchester in 1905; another steam tram built by Werktuigen and Spoorwegmaterieel of Amsterdam in 1903, a Swiss Mallet-type locomotive, a German tank engine of 1922 and a magnificent Sharp Stewart 2-4-0, built in Manchester in 1880. The steam tram service is between Udjung and Wonokromo-Kota with trams B1240 and 1242; the Sharp Stewarts work in East Java around the market town of Ponorogo and feature No 5012. The tracking shots are brilliant. (Locomotion Pictures).

16mm, Sound, Colour, 11mins, NL/VID

FROM RUSSIA WITH LOVE (Britain 1963)

United Artists. Produced by Harry Saltzman and Albert Broccoli. Directed by Terence Young. With Sean Connery, Robert Shaw, Pedro Armendariz and Lotte Lenya. A Soviet agent plots to kill James Bond and steal a secret code machine. Mysterious international criminals also figure. 'Arrant nonsense on a big budget' (Leslie Halliwell). A big climax takes place on a train journey from Istanbul into Europe (mainly done with French preserved steam locomotives), but most of the real material is from stock shots. 'The train comes into its own when Connery and Shaw have their pitched battle in a railway compartment. Six-footers and then some, but strictly on 4ft 8.5in, they both have to stoop to get in the door, so it's a bit like two kangaroos having a boxing match in a cupboard under the stairs. It looks as if Bond has, as it were, met his Waterloo... but then there's that special briefcase made in stores just for him.' (Tony Bilbow)

35mm, Sound, Colour, 118mins, United Artists

51

FULL STEAM TO HOLYHEAD (Britain 1990)

Sutcliffe TV Steam Video. Produced by David Sutcliffe. Filmed by Gerallt and Sion Jones, Nigel Roberts, Hywell Williams and David Sutcliffe. Edited by Steve Hewitt. Fifty different locations between Crewe and Holyhead feature in this video which records trips by LNER 'A1' 4-6-2 No 4472 *Flying Scotsman*, LMS 'Princess' 4-6-2 No 6201 *Princess Elizabeth*, SR 'West Country' 4-6-2 No 34027 *Taw Valley*, BR 4-6-2 No 71000 *Duke of Gloucester*, and LNER 'A4' 4-6-2 No 60009 *Osprey*.

VID, Sound, Colour, 55mins, STV

🚂 🚂 🚂 🚂 🚂

FULLY-FITTED FREIGHT (Britain 1967)

Produced by British Transport Films. 'An express steam freight train, now diesel hauled, links manufacturers with their customers at the other end of Britain. This fully fitted freight train from Bristol to Leeds provides an example of merchandise being transported at speed by British Railways. We learn something too, about the men who do the work as well as the goods they handle.'

35/16mm, Sound, 21mins, BTF

🚂 🚂 🚂 🚂 🚂

FUNERAL OF KING EDWARD VII (Britain 1910)

The newsreel records include shots of the GWR Royal train en route from Paddington to Windsor. (125ft)

35mm, Silent, 2mins, NFA

🚂

A FUTURE ON RAIL (Britain 1967)

Produced by British Transport Films. 'British Railways of the future and some of the opportunities they will provide as a result of the modern equipment and methods being introduced in signalling, in marshalling yards and goods depots, in mechanised track-laying and in diesel and electric traction.'

35/16mm, Sound, 10mins, BTF

🚂 🚂 🚂 🚂 🚂

G

GANDHI (Britain 1982)

Columbia/Goldcrest/Indo-British. Produced and directed by Richard Attenborough. With Ben Kingsley, Candice Bergen, Edward Fox, John Mills, John Gielgud, Trevor Howard and Martin Sheen.

The life of the Indian advocate who became a revolutionary, a saint and a martyr. 'It reminds us that we are, after all, human and thus capable of the most extraordinary and wonderful imagination, our will and our sense of right' (Roger Ebert). The film had the official blessing of the Indian Ministry of Information and Broadcasting, so railway facilities were freely used. Nevertheless it was not always easy: 'One of the problems for us was trains. They were the only linking network throughout India during the period of our story, but then of course they were steam trains, not diesels. They also ran sometimes on different gauges from most of those which operate today.

This situation applied to South Africa as well and a certain number therefore had to be re-rigged both inside and out. This was especially important for the major scene in which the young Gandhi was thrown off a train because he was sitting in a first class carriage. Travelling up and down the line, both in Africa and India, with the complication of clearing all other traffic from sections of the track so as not to get sudden modern elements bobbing up. It's very time-consuming; and not much fun for the regular travellers. But nowadays, with so much documentary film available both in the cinema and on television, such sequences only have the ring of truth when they are shot in the actual setting and are historically correct.' (Richard Attenborough).

Among the railways used in the film, the narrow gauge line in the state of Rajasthan was used extensively, including the staging of a derailment of a military train filmed in a yard. The shortage of working locomotives was such that the derailed engine had to be 'rescued' immediately, re-railed and sent back to work! Some all-night locations were done in Bombay on the main line.

35mm, Sound, Colour, 188mins, Columbia

🚂 🚂

GANG MAKING RAILWAY: SOUTH AFRICA (Britain 1898)

Shots of black labourers excavating a clearing, with railway tracks in background.

35mm, Silent, 1min, NFA

🚂 🚂 🚂 🚂 🚂 🚂

GARGOUSSE (France 1955)

French version, using the identical story of rivalry between a bus company and a local railway under threat of closure, to the *Titfield Thunderbolt*, made on a lovely French narrow gauge line and using an old French charabanc.

Only an odd reel seems to survive, featuring a chase between the bus and the train hauled by 'old No 11'.

16mm, Sound, One reel only 10mins, HA

🚂 🚂 🚂

GARRATT LOCOMOTIVES (1925-53)

The Beyer-Garratt locomotives are named after the original inventor Herbert W Garratt, whose patent was acquired by Beyer, Peacock and Co. Each locomotive consists of two distinct engines, practically identical in arrangement and weight, supporting through pivots a heavy girder frame which carries the boiler. The girder frame can be made very large indeed, producing a locomotive of great flexibility coupled with light axle loads and tremendous haulage capacity. Film records include the LNER Gresley-Garratt at the Darlington Centenary Celebrations in 1925; Garratts in Sudan, New South Wales, Queensland, Java, East and South Africa (at one time, Beyer Peacock had their own film unit); and LMS Garratts being built and shipped from the Beyer Peacock works in Manchester. There is one shot of an LMS Garratt working coal trains to Cricklewood.

16mm, Silent and sound, 55mins, HA

🚂 🚂 🚂 🚂 🚂

THE GATE CRASHER (USA 1927)

Silent comedy with railway background and stunts.

35mm, Silent, 22mins, Lost

🚂

GATEWAY TO VICTORY (Britain 1945)

Made by the Southern Railway Film Unit. A history of Southampton docks (owned and managed by the Southern Railway) from 1939 to 1945, including the embarkation of the British Expeditionary Force to France in 1939, the Dunkirk evacuation, the Blitz and D-Day.

There are brief glimpses of SR 'S15' 4-6-0 No 826, SR 'Lord Nelson' 4-6-0 No 853 *Sir Richard Grenville* and USA WD 'S160' No 2822 as well as unique scenes of a wide collection of Southern Railway ships including *Maid of Kent*, *Invicta*, *Isle of Jersey*, *Dinard*, *Isle of Guernsey*, *Maid of Orleans*, *Canterbury* and the paddle steamer *Sandown*.

16mm, Sound, 21mins, HA

🚂 🚂 🚂

THE GENERAL (USA 1927)

A Joseph M Schenck production, distributed by United Artists. With Buster Keaton, Marion Mack, Glen Cavender, Jim Farles and Frederick Vroom. Directed by Buster Keaton and Clyde Buckman. Script by Al Boosberg and Charles Smith. Photography by Dev Jennings and Bert Haines.

The General is a masterpiece of a railway film and is covered here in some detail. Set in 1861, in Marietta, GA, Johnnie Gray, the driver of the Western and Atlantic Express has two loves in his life — his engine and Miss Annabelle Lee. While visiting Miss Lee they hear that Fort Sumter has been fired upon — the Civil war has begun. Annabelle's father and brother go to enlist and Johnnie says that he will too and rushes off to the recruiting centre. The army, however, consider that he will be more useful as an engine driver. Annabelle is encouraged to think that he has been too much of a coward to enlist and she informs him that she won't speak to him again until he is in uniform. A year later Union General

Thatcher and his chief spy, Captain Anderson plot a raid. The plan is to enter the South as civilians then steal a train at Big Shanty, proceed north, burning every bridge, thus cutting off supplies from the Confederate army. Meanwhile Annabelle's father has been wounded and she is travelling to the front to see him.

Her train, driven by Johnnie Gray, stops at Big Shanty. Anderson and his colleagues steal the train — with Annabelle on board. Johnnie gives chase with another engine. The spies pull up some of the track and Johnnie crashes so he borrows a penny farthing. Johnnie warns the Confederate army and he offers to drive a train to pursue the Unionists. Unfortunately, Johnnie forgets to attach the carriages to the engine and the soldiers are left behind. Johnnie is now in sight of the spies. He loads a gun to fire at them but it ends up pointing at himself. By pure chance the Unionists are hit by the shot. They decide to try and block the line in various ways but Johnnie manages to overcome the obstacles. The Southern army, is now retreating and General Parker's victorious army is advancing so that now Johnnie is behind enemy lines. Johnnie abandons the train and finds his way to a house in the forest. The table is laid for dinner and Johnnie, hungry and cold attacks the food hungrily. Then he is surprised by several Unionists chiefs who sit down at the table and start to formulate their plan of campaign. Johnnie is forced to hide under the table where he is in a good position to overhear the enemy's plans.

Annabelle, still a prisoner, is locked in an adjoining room. Late that night, Johnnie creeps from under the table, knocks out two guards and rescues Annabelle.

Johnnie steals an engine, and manages to bring down a telegraph line, so preventing communications between the Unionist soldiers. Johnnie and Annabelle block the bridge at Rock River. They warn the Confederate General of the Unionist plan. Annabelle discovers her wounded father behind the Southern lines. Johnnie joins the Confederates in battle and is the hero of the day.

The Unionists are routed and Johnnie is made a lieutenant as a

reward. Annabelle is now justifiably proud of him.

Buster Keaton's film was based on a spectacular (but not, in real life, very successful) raid which took place during the American Civil War in the year 1862. It was led by a reckless Union raider, civilian volunteer James J Andrews, who, with 21 Union enlisted men disguised in civilian clothes as refugees from the Yankees, set out to destroy the Confederate rail line between Chattanooga and Atlanta with the strategic Chickamauga Bridge a principal target. On 12 April 1862, the group had boarded a northbound train at Marietta, a small Georgia town about 20 miles north of Atlanta.

At Big Shanty, seven miles from Marietta, the train halted and his conductor gave the traditional call, 'Twenty minutes for breakfast.' Between Big Shanty and Chattanooga to the north there were 15 bridges. The daring of Andrew's plan is even more appalling in view of the fact that within a very short distance of the Big Shanty stop was the Confederate troop encampment McDonald where 3,000 fresh recruits were being drilled. The rail platform swarmed with Confederate soldiers. Captain W A Fuller, conductor in charge of the mixed passenger and freight, was understandably startled when he saw the locomotive with three freight cars move out of the station, leaving the detached passenger cars at the platform. He is reported to have remarked to his engineer, Jeff Cain, 'Someone who has no right to do so has gone off with our train', a conservative comment for a man of Fuller's aggressive nature.

Deserters had been reported from Camp McDonald. The CO of the encampment had asked Fuller to be on the lookout for them and to arrest any soldiers attempting to get on the train without passports. Fuller, Engineer Cain and Tony Murphy, who was then foreman of the train's Western and Atlantic railroad shops, assumed reasonably enough that the deserters had stolen the train and would run on up the tracks a short distance to get clear of possible army pursuit and then take to the woods, abandoning the locomotive. Fuller, however, was a proud man. It wounded his pride to have his command stolen

Above:
Harold Lloyd loses his car in the stock yard of the Atchison, Topeka & Sante Fe in 'The Funny Side of Life' (1926).

Left:
All eyes are on Patsy Ruth Miller in 'The Gate Crasher' (1927). Unfortunately the film has not survived into the present day.

Above:
***The General** takes a rest during
the filming of 'The General' (1927).
Six locomotives, two of which
were destroyed, were purchased
for the film.*

Right:
**Buster Keaton in 'The General'
(1927), a film high on most lists of
the best silent comedies.**
National Film Archive

practically from under his flowing black beard so he set out on foot and ran two miles to Moon's station.

The locomotive, *General*, an 1855 product of the Rogers locomotive works of Paterson, New Jersey, was already out of sight. From track hands at Moon's Fuller heard that there were 24 or 25 men aboard the engine and freight cars — a not too grossly exaggerated estimate. The trackmen further reported that while some of the men gathered track tools and loaded them into freight cars, others cut away about a 100 yard section of telegraph lines. The mention of stealing tools immediately brought sabotage to Fuller's mind. For the first time he suspected that the men might be Federals in disguise.

With the assistance of the track hands, Fuller went to work hoisting a hand-car on to the rails by which time Murphy and Cain finally caught up. Fuller was sure that if he and his two cohorts worked hard they could reach Etowah River about the same time the suspect Federal thieves reached Kingston. There he knew that scheduled southbound freight trains would be sure to hold them up. At Etowah River, Fuller knew old *Yonah*, a yard locomotive, was usually steamed up on the sidings at Cooper's iron works. About a mile from Moon's station a short section of track had been torn up. Cross ties were wedged under the rails. The three men lifted their hand car off the rails, pushed it around the obstruction and pumped on toward Acworth. Here they picked up two local citizens and some firearms. Two miles short of Etowah, the five men pumped full speed around a curve and derailed their handcar when it catapulted into an open section of track. The five men were scratched and bruised but within a few minutes they were under way again.

The *Yonah* was where they expected her at Etowah but the tender was turned around backwards with a coal car attached. Six Confederate soldiers standing guard at the iron works volunteered to join in the chase and with Cain at the throttle, old *Yonah*, averaging nearly 60 miles an hour, backed into Kingston.

There Fuller learned that the tall, top-hatted leader of the fugitives had claimed to be a Confederate officer. He had stated that his three freight cars were loaded with ammunition for General Beauregard then at Corinth. So persuasive was Andrews that the agent gave him a switch key and ordered the blockage of freight trains on to sidings. Fuller, finding his own way blocked by the freight engines and their loads which were again on the right of way ran forward and jumped aboard a locomotive standing on the Y heading toward Chattanooga. From information he had gathered from the Kingston station agent he figured that Andrews held about a 15 minute lead.

Within a mile beyond Kingston, Fuller and his volunteer crew, which had grown to nearly a dozen, began to run into ties dropped across the track. Apparently Andrews had gathered a stock of them and was ordering them dumped from time to time as his kidnapped train sped towards Chattanooga.

Four miles from Adairsville, after stopping at least every half mile to remove obstructions, 60 yards of track was found to be torn out.

Making a snap decision, Fuller deserted the stymied locomotive even before Cain could brake it fully and set out at a run calling for the others to follow. At the end of a half mile, the only man still in sight was Western and Atlantic's foreman, Tony Murphy. Fuller apparently was fast on his feet as well as stubborn.

Two miles farther on, Fuller met an oncoming fast freight. He fired his pistol in the air to attract the engineer's attention and fortunately he was recognized by the engineer who stopped the train immediately. Breathlessly Fuller explained the situation. Along with Murphy who by then had puffed up to the scene, Fuller raced to the rear of the train and signalled for the engineer to start backing. 200 yards farther on, Fuller again hit the cinder fill at a dead run, threw a switch shunting the freight cars on to a side track. He, too, uncoupled the train and ordered the locomotive to back down the right of way.

The pursuit crew now consisted of Fuller, Murphy, Pete Bracken, the engineer; Alonzo Martin, a wood-passer; and Fleming Fox, the fireman. From a standstill they covered the distance to Calhoun 10 miles away in 12 minutes. At Calhoun, Fuller spotted the railroad's 12-year-old telegraph operator standing on the platform. As the locomotive slowed on signal, Fuller extended an arm and scooped up the youngster on the run like a mail sack.

While Bracken and his crew forced the locomotive to its utmost, Fuller wrote to General Ledbetter, Commanding Officer at Chattanooga, the following telegram: 'My train captured this am in Shanty. Evidently Federal soldiers disguised. They are heading for Chattanooga, probably with idea to burn the railroad bridges in their rear. If I do not capture them in the meantime, see that they do not pass Chattanooga'.

Two miles beyond Calhoun, Fuller sighted the fleeing locomotive *General* for the first time. The disguised Union soldiers had paused and were frantically tearing up rail. When they spotted their pursuers they unhooked one freight car and hastily clambered aboard their runaway train. Fuller ordered Bracken to keep running and slammed into the freight car at half throttle. Since the car obscured the engineer's vision, Fuller clambered forward on to its top where he could get a view of the track ahead, and from his precarious perch guided Bracken with hand signals. A few miles farther on another of the fugitive's freight cars were detached. Again Fuller ordered Bracken to slam into it without slowing down.

At Resaca the two freight cars were pushed on to a siding. Fuller and his crew continued their chase, still steaming in reverse, since not once during the entire flight had they had an opportunity to head their locomotive.

Two miles north of Resaca, Fuller, who by now had taken up a post on the rear of the tender, saw a short section of T-rail diagonally wedged into the tracks. Too late to signal a full stop, Fuller again took a chance and ordered Bracken to squeeze the throttle. When they slammed into the T-rail at 65 mph, it pinged like a giant tuning fork as it was flung into the brush beside the track.

At the first station beyond Dalton, Fuller dropped off the young telegraph operator with instructions to get a telegram through at any cost. Two miles later he again spotted the fugitives. They had stopped the *General* in plain view of a Confederate regimental encampment and were tearing up the track. The fugitive took off again, fleeing in their 50,300 pound locomotive with its four 5ft iron driving wheels whirling like mad and throwing sparks.

Fuller's locomotive, the *Texas*, had been designed by Danforth and Cooke but was at a handicap running backwards. Despite that the 15 miles of hot pursuit into Ringgold and three miles beyond was made in faster time than Fuller could ever remember in his 22 years experience as a conductor.

Halfway between Ringgold and Graysville near the Georgia-Tennessee border, Fuller's *Texas* closed to within a quarter of a mile of Andrews and the fleeing Union saboteurs. But this time Andrews ordered the long remaining freight car set afire thinking to cut it loose on the next bridge. The smoke from the funnel-stacked *General* was beginning to thin out. She had apparently begun to run out of fuel. As a last frantic gesture Andrews ordered the blazing car cut loose.

The *General*'s crew first flung out the last of its store of ties after debating whether to use them for fuel as a final attempt to derail the oncoming *Texas*. Fuller's men quickly cleared the tracks. They stared aghast as the *General* backed down on them pushing its blazing freight. Fuller was still not beaten. He waved Bracken back, then gently let the burning car touch the tender and signalled Bracken ahead again. Time was running out for Andrews for his last ruse had failed and the *General* was gasping its last breath.

Andrews and his men abandoned their locomotive and headed for the woods to the west of the tracks. Fuller's outfit kicked at the burning rubble and stamped out the blaze in the freight car.

The stubborn conductor had remembered seeing 50 or more military at Ringgold as they had steamed through. He sent Bracken and the *Texas* back to pass the word for the troops to head off the fugitives, while he, Murphy, Fox and Martin set off on foot in the direction Andrews and his men had taken.

Again Fuller was destined to be disappointed for he didn't set eyes on Andrews or any of his men until all 22 saboteurs had been rounded up several days later by cavalrymen. Andrews and seven others were hanged on 7 June 1862.

The recaptured chase-weary *General* was put back into regular service. It was used to haul ammunition to General Johnston in the battle of Kenesaw Mountain and on regular trips carried back wounded soldiers to Marietta. The *General*, too, was also the last Western & Atlantic locomotive to move out of Atlanta with refugees and war materials for Hood's army. The Confederate general moved out of Atlanta retiring before Sherman and destroyed much of the Western & Atlantic railroad as he retreated.

The relevance of the precise facts about the story as recorded in William Pittenger's book *The Great Locomotive Chase* become clear when considering the reviews of *The General*:

'Once when Keaton was asked why he thought *The General* looked so much more authentic than *Gone With the Wind*, he pondered for a moment and then replied with complete modesty: "Well, they went to a novel for their story. We went for history."

The General is unique and perhaps perfect. In form and method it is like no other comedy, not even another Keaton picture. Here, uniquely, the dramatic action and the comic business are one and interdependent. You never feel the story is simply an excuse for the comedy, or that the gags are a decoration planted on the story. Every shot has the authenticity and the unassumingly correct style of a Matthew Brady Civil War photograph.' (David Robinson)

After various attempts to get the real *General* from the old railroad company (they refused to let it go) and trials with some of the regular helpful railroad companies around Hollywood, Buster Keaton decided that he must go farther afield. So he came to Oregon and found that the whole area was covered with hundreds of miles of log-camp railways, many very old and dating back to the Civil War days.

'In *The General*, I took that page of history and I stuck to it in all

detail. I staged it exactly the way it happened. I used the lovely old locomotives that needed only very few modifications to put them back to their 1860s appearance; I put them back to wood burners as they had been — and set fire to the forest on more than one occasion: and it needs a real expert to see that our *General* was not the real original *General*.' (Buster Keaton).

The trains are real, the stock is real, the great crash with a locomotive going to its doom from 50ft above a river on a burning bridge is real. So too is one very simple shot, but one of immense potential danger where Keaton sits down on the connecting rod of a locomotive which then starts up and takes him into the shed, his motionless body describing a series of arcs. Said Keaton: 'Well, the situation in the picture at that point is that my girl says 'never speak to me again until you're in uniform'. So the bottom has dropped out of everything and I've got nothing to do but sit down on my engine and think. I don't know why they rejected me; they didn't tell me it was because they didn't want to take a locomotive engineer off his duty. My fireman wants to put the engine away in the roundhouse and doesn't know that I'm sitting on the cross bar, and starts to take it in. I was running that engine myself all through the picture; I could handle that thing so well I was stopping on a dime. But when it came to this shot I asked the engineer whether we could do it. He said, 'there's only one danger. A fraction too much steam with these old-fashioned engines and the wheel spins. And if it spins, it will kill you right then and there'. So we tried it out four or five times, and in the end the engineer was satisfied that he could handle it. So we went ahead and did it. I wanted a fade-out laugh for that sequence; although it's not a big gag, it's cute and funny enough to get me a nice laugh.'

Such was the extraordinary spirit that dominated the whole of the making of this film. 46 miles of track, six locomotives (two destroyed, one by design and one by accident) and a miscellaneous collection of rolling stock were purchased for the film.

Special roads were laid alongside

the line for over a mile in order to secure detailed 'tracking' shots of the actors and the trains. The old wooden bridge which was set on fire and collapsed with a locomotive into the river below was due for demolition; it is said that the locomotive is still there at the bottom of the river.

In 1991, the special high-quality 35mm nitrate print version, with music composed and conducted by Carl Davis, was made available by David Gill and Kevin Brownlow through the Thames Silents/Thames Video releases. Thus the masterpiece was, after 65 years, again available in its finest form.

35/16/8mm/VID, Silent and sound versions, 77mins, NFA/HA (Ref only)/Thames Video

GENERAL REPAIR (Britain 1938)

General servicing of steam locomotives in the shed at Crewe. There is a very detailed account of all the repair and service operations carried out on LMS 'Jubilee' 4-6-0 No 5605 Cyprus. An LMS film production.

35mm/VID, Sound, 20mins, BTF/TVP

THE GENTLE GUNMAN (Britain 1952)

An Ealing Studios film. Directed by Basil Dearden. With John Mills and Barbara Mullen. Story of two brothers in the IRA. Includes a scene at Holborn Underground station.

35mm, Sound, 86mins, Weintraub

THE GEOFF HOLYOAKE COLLECTION

Geoff Holyoake began filming on 16mm for professional release through his company (Meteor Film Services) in 1959. Originally the films were available for sale on 16mm and 8mm, usually in neat little boxes carrying about 4mins on each subject. After some 30 years of successful distribution in this form, all the railway subjects were sold to Railscene and the other

transport items went to Railfilms for issue on video. This took place in 1991; initial reviews of the material in video were full of praise for Holyoake's work in capturing the last ten years of steam in Britain.

GEORGE BENNIE RAILPLANE (Britain 1929)

A record of the George Bennie Railplane system demonstration built on a steel structure constructed over the LNER line between Milngavie and Hillfoot, near Glasgow. The unit consisted of a rail car suspended from overhead guided rails and was powered by an aircraft engine and propeller. It was never adopted in service.

With the co-operation of the London & North Eastern Railway, the inventor George Bennie erected an experimental track for his 'George Bennie Railplane' at Milngavie, near Glasgow, on a structure built alongside and over an LNER line, and opened it on 3 July, 1930.

The system was a suspended monorail and steelwork for a double-track line line was put up, though only one vehicle is known to have existed. This weighed 7.5 tons, was suspended from two 2-wheel bogies running on a rail beneath the main steelwork and driven by two four-bladed propellors, one at each end. Beneath the car was a guide rail on each side of which horizontal rubber-tyred wheels underneath the car ran, to prevent it swaying on curves or in the wind. The steelwork was supported on trestles about 80ft apart.

Braking was effected by shoes acting on the top and bottom rails. The propellors could be driven by either a diesel engine or an electric motor and were designed to rotate at 800rpm. The car was said to be capable of travelling at 100mph and it was claimed that two or more vehicles could be connected by couplings on the propellor shafts, which rotated with them.

Wooden-platform elevated 'stations' were put up at each end of the demonstration line; access to the platforms was by stairways from ground level. The car had six small windows in each side between two single-width doors. The driver's windscreen was a rather inade-

quate 'porthole' in each sloping end of the vehicle, which was lettered GBR — George Bennie Railplane.

Unfortunately for the inventor, he was unable to sell this revolutionary means of high-speed transport to any backers, though there had been an article on the system in *Tramway & Railway World* of 16 September 1926; a proposal for a railplane route from Lytham St Annes to Southport in 1928 which attracted the attention of *The Manchester Guardian* and the *Lytham St Annes Express*; and a 1935 plan for a railplane route in the north-east suburbs of London, from Waltham Abbey to Dagenham via Tottenham, Walthamstow, Leyton and West Ham.

The test line structure with the single car, slowly rusted above the LNER tracks at Milngavie until World War 2, when most of it was dismantled to provide steel for the war effort.

16mm, Silent, 9mins, HA

GEORGETOWN LOOP (USA 1903)

Biograph. A record of the narrow-gauge railway from Georgetown to Silver Plume, Colorado.

16mm, Silent, 6mins, BFI

GERMAN RAILWAYS (Germany 1896-1969)

There is a brief scene at Berlin East station in 1896, extensive coverage of the railways (including the steam overhead lines) in *Berlin* (1928), the Hamburg Flyer of 1934, an excellent record of the latest in 1935 German steam in *Der Stahltier*, the massive high-speed streamlined express locomotive of 1938 (principal challenger to *Mallard*'s record), various wartime scenes and the fine documentation of the classic HOF Pacifics made by Nick Lera in the last days of steam.

GETAWAYS, THE: THE BLUEBELL RAILWAY (Britain 1979)

BBC Television (South). Produced by John Coleman. The work and operation of the Bluebell Railway and its surrounds as a tourist attraction.

16mm, Sound, Colour, 30mins, BBC TV

🚂 🚂 🚂 🚂

THE GHOST OF THE CANYON (USA 1913)

With Helen Gibson. A tale of bitter rivalry between two railroads for important fast freight contracts and how the rivalry was carried to the extent of fabricating the illusion of *The Ghost of the Canyon*.

Filmed on the San Pedro branch of the Old Los Angeles & Salt Lake — 'The Salt Lake Route' — at or near the stations of Bell and Vernon in suburban Los Angeles as it was then.

16mm, Silent, 27mins, Blackhawk

🚂 🚂 🚂

THE GHOST TRAIN (Britain 1925)

In 1925, Arnold Ridley (best known today for his appearances in *Dad's Army*) was inspired by watching the trains at Mangotsfield in Gloucestershire to write the play whose fascination was described by J C Trewin: 'No one in life enjoys waiting bleakly at midnight, dead of the night's high noon, in a bleaker waiting-room. Never mind, bring the scene to the theatre, and all will respond clamorously. Add a presumed spectral train, a silly-ass comedian, a huddle of assorted passengers, a station master voluble and venerable, and quite absurd explanation about china-clay and gun-running, and everyone will be as happy at the evening's end as any train spotter on the prow of a busy platform.' The station specially created for the play was Fal Vale; the sound of the ghost train was produced with a drum, thunder-sheet, cylinder of compressed air and a garden roller. The play has been frequently revived.

🚂 🚂

THE GHOST TRAIN (Britain 1927)

Gainsborough production. Produced by Michael Balcon. Directed by Geza M Bolvary. From the play by Arnold Ridley. With Guy Newall, Ilse Bois and Louis Ralph. Silent

version, produced partly in Germany. Railway scenes were shot on the Hurtsbourne-Fullerton line of the LSWR; the 'haunted' station was Wherwell. The play was first produced on the stage in 1925 and ran for 215 performances.

35mm, Silent, 82mins, Lost

🚂 🚂

THE GHOST TRAIN (Britain 1931)

Directed by Walter Forde. With Jack Hulbert, Cicely Courtneidge, Ann Todd, Cyril Raymond, Donald Calthrop, Allan Jeayes, Angela Baddeley, Henry Caine, Tracey Holmes, and Carol Coombe.

A ghost story of how a team of smugglers, using a remote branch line in Cornwall attempt to conceal their activities from a group of innocent stranded passengers. An adaptation from the original play includes a scene in which the smugglers go to their doom as their train plunges into a river when a swing bridge is left open (alas, done with a model!).

The GWR provided the facilities for this film. Shots of Paddington and the route to the West Country provide some good shots of 'Kings' and 'Castles' in action. Detailed work was carried out on the Limpley Stoke-Camerton branch (also used for *Kate Plus Ten*, and *The Titfield Thunderbolt*) with one of William Dean's standard 0-6-0 goods engines — No 2381 — much in evidence. The class was launched in 1883 and were officially withdrawn in 1934, although the last did not actually go until 1948; No 2516 is still preserved. Because of extensive night shooting with limited lighting available, the 0-6-0 was painted white for some shots as was the stock used. Substantial 'under cranking' provided spectacular speeded-up effects, as well as allowing a wider margin of exposure. The crash on the swing bridge was done with a model at the studios, intercut with brief shots of GWR '2301' 0-6-0 No 2441. The film is a classic case of a lost film. The negative on nitrate stock deteriorated to the point of total destruction whilst in store. If anyone can find a copy, both the National Film Archive and Huntley Archives will be very happy to hear from you.

Stop press: some parts of this film

have recently been discovered and salvaged by David Meeker of the National Film Archive, including the last reel which features Barmouth Viaduct and the swing-bridge section.

35mm, Sound, 72mins, Part Lost

🚂 🚂

THE GHOST TRAIN (Britain 1937)

BBC Television. Produced by Jan Bussell. With Don Gemmell, Laura Smithson, Hugh Dempster, Daphne Riggs, John Counsell, Joan Lawson, Arther Young, Reni Waller, Clifford Benn, Alex McCringle. First transmission: 20 December 1937. A television presentation of Arnold Ridley's play.

🚂 🚂

THE GHOST TRAIN (Britain 1941)

A Gainsborough picture. Produced by Edward Black. Directed by Walter Forde. Script by J O C Orton, Val Guest and Marriott Edgar. Based on the play by Arnold Ridley. Photography by Jack Cox. Art direction by Vetchinsky. Edited by R E Dearing. Music by Louis Levy. With Arthur Askey, Richard Murdoch, Kathleen Harrison, Peter Murray-Hill, Carole Lynne, Morland Graham, Betty Jardine, Stuart Latham, Herbert Lomas, Raymond Huntley, Linden Travers and D J Williams.

Tommy Gander, a concert comedian; Teddy Deakin, his pal; Jackie Winthrop and her cousin Richard Winthrop; Miss Bourne, a spinster visiting evacuees; Herbert and Edna, an engaged couple; and Dr Sterling, travelling on a train to Cornwall miss their connection owing to a delay and have to spend a night in the waiting room of the eerie Cornish railway junction of Fal Vale. The station master tells them the story of the Ghost Train which is reputed to haunt the station. The story runs that 43 years ago a previous station master fell dead whilst trying to operate a remote control of a swing bridge and a train roared through the gap in the open bridge into the river below. The legend was that some nights a warning bell sounded at the station and the train in phantom form thunders by bringing death to all who gaze upon it.

That night the station master is found murdered. Edna and Herbert leave the station, scared, but return later in a panic pursued by a terror stricken girl, Julie, mental patient, escaped from a nearby home, and eager to gaze upon the fatal Ghost Train. She is in turn followed by Price who claims to be her brother and wishes to take her back. Suddenly the roar of a train is heard in the night and the Ghost Train thunders through the station. Gander and Deakin become suspicious and their investigations reveal that they are the victims of a hoax to cover some criminal activity. A bus has arrived to take the passengers away.

Meantime the Ghost Train has commenced its return journey. Gander reveals that he has opened the control gate, so that if the train goes by the junction it will fall into the river. At this news, Price, Jule and Dr Sterling reveal themselves as members of a gang of fifth columnists gun-running in war-time using the legend of the Ghost Train to enable them to carry their stock to an old jetty on the beach by night. Covering the rest of the passengers with a gun, the criminals rush back in an attempt to signal the driver of the train. But it is too late . . . the train plunges into the river below.

This third screen version of Arnold Ridley's story was enlivened by the personality of Arthur Askey as the concert party comedian but suffered from the fact that it was shot almost entirely in the Lime Grove studios at Shepherd's Bush and is, in consequence, sadly lacking in railway atmosphere. An idea of the respect for truth exhibited by the producers is seen in the first 10 minutes of the film. The train leaves London hauled by a 'King'. It arrives on the sea wall at Teignmouth with a 'Castle' on the front, slows up with bullet-nosed, streamlined *King Henry VII* hauling, whereupon a 'Saint' comes to a halt!

35mm, Sound, 84mins, Rank

🚂

GIANTS OF STEAM (Britain 1963)

British Transport Films. A detailed history of steam railways in Britain, using models, engravings, drawings and museum exhibits. There is a

montage of steam including brief scenes of LMS 'Jubilee' 4-6-0 No 5696 *Arethusa* at St Pancras, LNER 'A4' 4-6-2 No 2512 *Silver Fox*, LNER 'A1' 4-6-2 No 4472 *Flying Scotsman* (as BR No 60103 in this case), MR 'Compound' 4-4-0 No 1000 and Liverpool & Manchester preserved locomotive *Lion*. Elsewhere there are shots of Vale of Rheidol locomotives, GWR Replica Broad Gauge *North Star* (1838), preserved Caledonian 4-2-2 No 123, LMS 'Princess Royal' 4-6-2 No 6201 *Princess Elizabeth*, GWR locomotives on the 'Cornish Riviera' train in the 1930s and a few reasonably detailed shots of LNER 'V2' 2-6-2 with its BR No 60981. A real jigsaw puzzle of a film. Sir Arthur Elton was script consultant. Music was by Ron Grainer; written and directed by John Read.

35/16/8mm/VID, Sound, 40mins, BTF

🚂🚂🚂🚂🚂

THE GIRL IN THE TRAIN (USA 1927)

Directed by Victor Janson. With Mady Christians and Marcella Alboni. A marital melodrama, partly set on a train journey.

35mm, Silent, 103mins

🚂🚂🚂

GIVE YOUR CAR A HOLIDAY (Britain 1967)

Produced by British Transport Films. 'Today trains as well as ships are being designed with the motorist in mind. The film surveys the routes to the Continent and to Ireland and the internal Scottish routes served by British Rail Car Ferries, the facilities at ports and the amenities on board the new ships — with a sight of the research and other work going into the development of the new Harwich/Hook of Holland service.'

35/16mm, Sound, Colour, 18mins, BTF

🚂🚂🚂🚂🚂

GLACIER EXPRESS (Britain 1984)

Highlight International Films. Link House Video. The journey of 170 miles across southern Switzerland

from St Moritz to Zermatt. Three railway companies make up a route network that represents a triumph of engineering. The journey takes 7.5 hours, 291 bridges, 91 tunnels and the crossing of the 6,000ft Oberalp Pass. We leave St Moritz by way of the Rhaetian Railways line through magnificent Swiss scenery then excellent aerial shots. The train weaves through the lush mountains over the famous Landvasser viaduct built in 1902, one of the most impressive rail bridges in Switzerland. At Disentis 90 miles from St Moritz we enter the 'Furka Oberalp' section of the journey. Over the next 60 miles we climb to over 6,000ft with gradients of 1 in 5 on the rack and pinion sections, over the Oberalp Pass then down to Andermatt by way of three long double loops — in and out of tunnels on this rack and pinion section.

At Brig we enter the section run by the 'Brig-Visp-Zermatt Railway' for the last section of the journey. The spectacular engineering and scenery continues throughout the route with splendid aerial photography and good editing keeping a good pace to the film. We emerge from a tunnel (the 91st) into Zermatt station; journey's end.

16mm/VID Sound, Colour, 52mins, Link House

🚂🚂🚂🚂🚂

GLACIER EXPRESS (Britain 1987)

JC/OF. Commentary by Hans Peter Treichler. Produced and directed by John Cocking. Zermatt to St Moritz.

VID, Sound, Colour, 57min, JC/OF

🚂🚂🚂🚂🚂

THE GLORIOUS DAYS OF THE EXPRESS STEAM TRAIN (Britain 1988)

Top Link Video. A potted history of the steam locomotive plus archive material taken mainly from the 1950s and 1960s. To this is added the story of preservation, with a mixed bag of preserved steam runs.

VID, Sound, Colour, 50mins, Top Link

🚂🚂🚂🚂🚂

GLORIOUS DAYS OF THE EXPRESS STEAM TRAIN (Britain 1990)

Railfilms. Produced by Nick Dodson, Steve le Cheminant and Nigel Harris. A major survey of steam railway preservation and running in the past 10 years.

VID, Sound, Colour, 50mins, RFV

GLORY MACHINES (USA 1985-89)

Steam Powered Video. A series of archive films of many aspects of American Railroads issued in the *Golden Archive Series*. Typical items covered include the Chicago & North Western RR, Chicago, Burlington & Quincy RR, the Milwaukee RR ('Hiawathas'), the New York Central RR ('Hudsons' and steeplecab electrics), Pennsylvania RR ('K4' G5 11 pole car), the Santa Fe (Blue Goose) as well as scenes of the Canadian & National and Pacific RR. (Midwestern Railroading 1935-58). The area around St Louis is covered by the Southern Pennsylvania RR ('K4' and streamlined 4-4-4-4s) and the Southern Pacific at Tuscon (4-10-2s), with many scenes made during the war in 1941-45.

VID, Sound, Colour, 34-45 mins each volume, SPV

THE GLORY MACHINES (USA 1928-1950s)

Steam Powered Video. Produced by Herron Rail. 31 American railroads are represented on this tape, including the New York Central, the Lackawanna Delaware & Western, the Norfolk & Western and the Southern Pacific. There are streamlined 'Hudsons', Mallets by the score, and the 'Tweetsie' freight.

VID, Sound, Mainly colour, 64mins, SPV

GN TANK (Britain 1959)

Made by P B Whitehouse and John Adams. A film showing the Great Northern 0-6-0ST No 1247 owned by Capt W Smith of Hatfield. Film made at Hatfield and on a special run to St Alban's Abbey. The locomotive was built in 1897; it has since been transferred to national preserved status.

16/8mm, Silent, 6mins, CV/NRM

GO SLOW ON THE BRIGHTON LINE (also known as) LONDON TO BRIGHTON IN FOUR MINUTES (British 1952)

BBC Television News.
An experiment in slow speed camera work. This journey on the 'Brighton Belle' from Victoria to Brighton is photographed at 2fps; at the normal projection speed of 24fps, a speed of 60mph becomes 720mph on the screen and 70mph is 840mph. An impression of travel at approximately the speed of sound is obtained, with clear record of the topographical features of the country between London and the Sussex coast.
In addition, there are glimpses of the traffic on adjacent lines which includes a flash of steam now and then. To simulate the sound of a high speed run, a recording of a jet aircraft engine was used, mixed with bursts of clapping from a large audience to give the effect of the train passing through platforms and under bridges and tunnels! This simple device sounds unlikely but is in fact extremely effective.

35/16mm, Sound, 4mins, BBC/HA

GO TO IT! (Britain 1990)

Wood Films. Produced by Elizabeth Wood and Paul Chedlow. A film about children with special needs, in which a young boy with disabilities goes train spotting with his elder brother and visits Didcot Railway Centre. The programme highlights the help and support that preserved railways have been keen to offer people with disabilities. In this case, the elder boy explains how his knowledge of the configurations of the locomotives has helped him with his counting; the younger boy himself explains how a steam engine works. Many of Didcot's prize exhibits are on display.

VID, Sound, Colour, 21mins, Wood

GO WEST (USA 1940)

MGM. Produced by Jack Cummings. Directed by Edward Buzzell. With the Marx Brothers, John Carroll, Diana Lewis and Robert Barratt. Groucho, Harpo and Chico meet a Western villain. 'A good start with the ticket office sketch, some pretty soggy stuff in the middle and a rousing finale as they take a moving train to bits' (Leslie Halliwell).
'A brilliantly manic climax as they break up the train they are travelling on to stoke the boiler' (Tony Bilbow). A very elaborate set was built on the MGM lot at Culver City, backed up with some process shots from a lumber camp railway in the nearby San Fernando Valley.

35mm, Sound, 82mins, MGM

GOD'S WONDERFUL RAILWAY (Britain 1980)

BBC Television. Produced by Anna Home and Paul Stone. A series of story programmes in eight parts, based on a script by Avril Rowlands telling the history of the Great Western Railway from the laying of the permanent way through to the days of World War 2. The first group of stories goes from the building of the railway by Brunel and his team up to 1939.
The Permanent Way (The building of the Railway) two parts, 25 minutes each.
Clear Ahead three parts, 25 minutes each. A station boy's story of working at 'Highley Station' during the early 1900s.
Fire on the line three parts, 25 minutes each. 1939. A story of the Railway during the beginning of World War 2.
The films were edited by Christopher Rowlands and photographed by John Williams.
'All filming was imaginatively carried out on the Severn Valley Railway and involved good detail, particularly in the use of the correct rolling stock of the periods portrayed. Very entertaining dramatisation, utilising fully the location resources available' (Robert Ennis).

16mm, Sound, Colour, Episodes as shown, BBC TV

GOING GREAT WESTERN (Britain 1987)

BBC Television. Series producers: Neil Cameron and Peter Walton. Written and presented by Miles Kington. The history of the Cornish Riviera Express; much use was made of the Torbay Railway at Paignton. (From the 'Steam Days' series).

16mm, Sound, Colour, 30mins, BBC TV

THE GOLD RUSH LINE (Britain 1983)

BBC Television. Executive producer: Colin Adams. Produced by Cyril Gates. Written and presented by Simon Hoggart. From the *Great Little Railways* series.

Simon Hoggart travels in the Yukon, from Skagway to Whitehorse recalling the early goldrush days at Skagway for the tourists. The White Pass & Yukon Railway still steam-hauled by No 73 with its rake of timber Parlour cars. The preserved line travels through the spectacular scenery of the Yukon. At Bennett a small town where much of the gold prospecting was carried out, today's passengers alight from the train for a meal at the station, then change trains this time diesel hauled to White Pass. Scenes at Dawson City — then winter track maintenance.

16mm, Sound, Colour, 40mins, BBC TV

GOLDEN ARROW (Britain 1938)

Southern Railway Promotional film for the 'Golden Arrow' including the background to the service, locomotives, stock, etc.

35mm, Silent, 12mins, BTF

THE GOOD AND QUICK (Britain 1983)

BBC Television. Executive producer: Colin Adams. Produced by Bill Lyons. Written and presented by Stanley Reynolds. From the *Great Little Railways* series.

To Ecuador for the journey from Guayaquil to Quito starts before daybreak. Elderly Baldwin locomotives haul old wooden passenger coaches out of Guayaquil, the little Baldwin narrow gauge loco (2-6-0) speeds across the plains. We see the old loco works where veteran locos are cannibalised to keep the railway going. Our train winds through the narrow streets then we change locos for a (2-8-0) to get us to the high mountains — to Devil's Nose. Excellent photography as the little train winds up the mountains. The train zig-zags up the mountain side. The last leg of the journey is by 'auto Fero' (a bus on rails) passing Urbina 12,000ft up in Andes, the highest point on the line. We enter Quito, journey's end, under cover of darkness.

16mm, Sound, Colour, 40mins, BBC TV

THE GOOD COMPANIONS (Britain 1956)

Associated British Picture Corporation. Produced and directed by J. Lee-Thompson. With Eric Portman, Celia Johnson, Janette Scott and Hugh Griffith. The tale of a touring pierrot company, based on a novel by J B Priestley. Includes colour scenes of Welsh valley steam railways.

35mm/VID Sound, Colour, 104mins, Weintraub/VID 125 (Rly)

GOODBYE MR CHIPS (Britain 1969)

MGM. Directed by Herbert Ross. With Peter O'Toole, Petula Clark and Michael Redgrave. Second version of the story of a public schoolmaster. Includes scene shot at Sherbourne station, Dorset, renamed 'Brookfield'.

35mm, Sound, Colour, MGM

GOOLE DOCKS (Britain 1936)

LMS film. A short record of Goole docks, then owned by the LMS. There are no trains; a feature is the steamship SS *Don*.

16mm, Silent, 4mins, HA

GORDON HIGHLANDER ON THE SPEY RIVER LINE (Britain 1961)

Made by P B Whitehouse and John Adams. Great North of Scotland 4-4-0 No 49 working from Craigellachie to Boat of Garten.

16/8mm, Silent, 5mins, CV

DIE GOTTHARDSTRECKE (Britain 1987)

JC/OF. Commentary by Hans Peter Treichler. Produced and directed by John Cocking. Norden to Suden via the Gotthard route.

VID, Sound, Colour, 55min, JC/OF

GPO UNDERGROUND RAILWAY (Britain 1930)

In the early days of sound newsreels, the companies planned a series of tests in the most difficult locations to try out the new sound-on-film recording equipment. The problems of electrical interference, challenging conditions and microphone problems seemed to be at their worst in recording the Post Office underground railway which links various main sorting offices directed with the main-line railway stations. The result was this interesting record of the driverless trains, the narrow tunnels and the method of operating a unique railway system.

16mm, Sound, 6mins, HA

GRAHAM WHISTLER COLLECTION

Based at Bognor Regis, Graham Whistler has specialised in recording preserved railways in their present-day setting. His videos include coverage of the Dart Valley (Paignton and Buckfastleigh lines), Vale of Rheidol, Brecon Mountain. West Somerset and Ravenglass & Eskdale Railways. He has also made 'Driver's Eye View' videos as well as specialised tapes like *How to Drive a Steam Locomotive* and preserved line coverage of the *Ffestiniog* and *Keighley and Worth Valley*.

THE GRAND BRITISH EXPERIMENTAL RAILWAY (Britain 1980)

Granada Television. Produced by Arthur Taylor. Directed by Jonathon

ONLINE VIDEO

Makers of fine transport video tapes

Our staff are professionals working in leading Broadcasting and Television organisations. Archive film is carefully transferred to Betacam SP for editing onto a 1inch VT Reel for quality pictures and sound. We don't use domestic amateur Camcorders, but shoot on High Band Umatic professional tape format, or 16mm Cine film.

Our **Tram** tapes receive many compliments – even from overseas who now want us to edit and produce their tapes for them. Several extracts from our tapes have been shown on Television in Britain. Our **Underground Railway** tapes are written and produced by leading experts in their field. Our recent **Glasgow Underground** has been highly acclaimed, (even in Scotland).

Recently we have branched out into **Buses, Trolleybuses** and even **Shipping**. Most of our videos are made to help raise funds for some preservation societies.

We pay a great deal of importance in accurate commentaries. In most cases we get an expert or two to attend the recording of them to ensure location spotting and correct pronounciations.

You can obtain our tapes from leading shops and outlets of the Ian Allan organisation.

Previous page:
Camerton as 'Fal Vale' station in the 1931 version of 'The Ghost Train'.

Right:
Two members of the 1931 'The Ghost Train' cast, on the footplate during filming.

Centre right:
The Marx Brothers and some of the cast of 'Go West' (1940) on the footplate. *National Film Archive*

Bottom right:
James Garbutt as inventor George Stephenson, with Amanda Boxer as his footplate companion Fanny Kemble, in Granada's one-hour documentary film, 'The Grand British Experimental Railway' (1980).

Lewis. The history of the Liverpool & Manchester Railway. Photographs, graphics, the Rainhill replicas and modern footage were used in this account, plus a fairly elaborate reconstruction of the Trials, with actors in costumes of the period and, again, the replicas.

16mm, Sound, Colour, 52mins, Granada TV

🚂 🚂 🚂 🚂 🚂

GRAND CENTRAL MURDER (also known as GRAND CENTRAL STATION) (USA 1942)

Murder mystery, using mainly Hollywood sets of the station, but a few real shots of the grand staircase and a Pennsylvania Railroad streamlined steam-hauled train departing from Track 12.

35mm, Sound, 72mins, MGM

🚂 🚂

THE GREAT BANK ROBBERY (USA 1969)

Warner. Directed by Hy Averback. With Kim Novak and Zero Mostel. Gag Western about bank robbers who turn up in town disguised as priests. Includes scenes on the Sierra Railroad with Rogers 4-6-0 locomotive No 4493, built in 1891.

35mm, Sound, 98min, Warner

🚂 🚂

THE GREAT BARRIER (Britain 1937)

Gaumont-British film. Directed by Milton Rosmer. Photography by Glen McWilliams. With Richard Arlen, Barrie Mackey and Lilli Palmer. The building of the Canadian Pacific Railway; highlights include the loss of a locomotive in a treacherous bog, a chase after a runaway engine and scenes of the first trains across the Canadian continent. The barrier referred to is a stretch of marshland consisting of bog and quicksand which proved impossible to cross and eventually had to be circumvented by an expensive mountain diversion.

35mm, Sound, 85mins

🚂 🚂 🚂

THE GREAT BRITISH TRAIN ROBBERY (Germany 1967)

Egon Monk Prodis Films. Directed by John Olden and Claus Petter Witt. With Horst Tappert. Hans Cossey, Karl Heinz Hess, Hans Reiser, Rolf Nagel and Harry Engel. Dramatisation of the British *Great Train Robbery*, originally made for television.

The film that was never shown: In 1967, a German company made a feature film based on the Great Train Robbery; it was never shown in Britain or indeed anywhere else. Production facilities were granted by British Railways in the Folkestone area but they were not aware of what was being filmed! The story was not told until a note appeared in *Variety* in July 1968.

'A film about one of the biggest criminal exploits of all time, 80% of which was produced in Britain under conditions of absolute secrecy, can never be shown in England. This cloak and dagger production is now being given its genuine title of *The Great Train Robbery* but when it was in the work in London it was rolling under the phoney title of 'Gentlemen Prefer Cash'.

'The feature, made as a co-production by Steven Pallos, Studio Hamburg, and Nord Deutsche Rundfunk, is based on a series of articles in the German *Stern* magazine by Henry Kolarz, who also did the screenplay. His mag pieces subsequently began serialisation in the London *People*, but after five writs on behalf of men who were serving terms of imprisonment of up to 30 years, who alleged that their characters had been 'blackened' by the articles, publication was suspended.

'It is the threat of similar libel suits brought by the men now in jail which could, presumably, be served against the producers, distributors and all exhibitors showing the film, that have led to the decision not to offer the picture for release in the UK.

'The producers have wound up with a feature running for 110 minutes, plus three 80-minute TV programmes, it is unlikely that *Train Robbery* will be shown theatrically in Germany, though the producers say they have had offers from three major companies in that territory.

'Of the £3 million loot of the August 1963 robbery, some £2 million has yet to be recovered. Of the men who were convicted for the crime the majority received 30-year jail terms, but two have made sensational escapes from jail and the principals are still at large. All the characters are clearly and definitively protrayed in the film, though in all cases their names have been changed.

'As a result of the extensive research done by the author, the film will illustrate how the idea was conceived, the steps that were taken to recruit the gang and how London Airport was held up to get the cash to finance and execute the train robbery. According to the research the gang saw the film *The League of Gentlemen* at least five times to study techniques.

'At no time during production in the various London locations did either producer Pallos or other members of the crew indicate the nature of the yarn which they were filming. However, the underworld picked up the 'info' and during the filming of a location sequence in Folkestone a unit car was broken into and rushes stolen from a camera. Each time the producer was asked what sort of film he was making he tried to bypass the question by indicating that it was just a TV programme.'

In fact, the film did eventually get a limited showing under the title *The Great British Train Robbery* but it has never appeared in Britain. Those who have seen it say it was a shoddy production.

35mm, Sound, 104mins, NA

🚂 🚂 🚂

THE GREAT BRITISH TRAINS (Britain 1987)

MSD Video. An assembly of four major British Transport films including *Coronation Scot* (1937), *Elizabethan Express* (1954), *Blue Pullman* (1960) and *InterCity 125* (1982). See individual items for details.

VID, Sound, Part Colour, 59mins, BTF/MSD VID

🚂 🚂 🚂 🚂 🚂

THE GREAT CENTRAL IN CHESHIRE (Britain c1930)

Remarkable old film on the Cheshire Lines Committee tracks; a tank loco scuttles past a light engine; what appears to be 'G5'

No 67240 arrives, and we seen an N5 0-6-2T.

16mm/VID Silent, 6min, Stirling

🚂 🚂 🚂 🚂 🚂

GREAT CENTRAL JOINT LINES (Britain 1959-63)

Produced by Link productions. Scenes include LNER 'B1' 4-6-0 No 61369 at Seer Green and Marylebone, No 61106 near Wendover, GWR '6100' 2-6-2T No 6138 at Princes Risborough, LMS Fairburn 2-6-4T No 42250 and LMS Stanier 4-6-0 No 45234 at Wendover and GWR 'Hall' 4-6-0 No 5973 *Rollaston Hall* near Princes Risborough. There are also glimpses of a 'Black Five' and a 'King'.

16/8/VID Silent, Colour, 4mins, MFS/VID

🚂 🚂 🚂 🚂 🚂

GREAT CENTRAL RAILWAY

Early material on the Great Central is quite hard to come by. There is a fine scene of a Great Central Royal Train arriving at Immingham docks in 1912, a few brief shots in 1925 of boat trains at Immingham but then not much until Geoffrey Holyoake's *Great Central Joint Lines* in 1959, the films of Richard Greenwood and Richard Willis in the 1960s and the last days with 'Black Fives' at Marylebone, Brackley and Woodford and Hinton (also known as Woodford Halse), including the last train on 3 September 1966. There are extensive film records of the preserved Great Central section and of Marylebone since those days.

🚂 🚂 🚂 🚂 🚂

GREAT EASTERN RAILWAY

Material from the early days is thin on the ground. A feature film of 1935, *The Silent Passenger*, was unusual in having scenes of Liverpool Street and Stratford Works, with 'Claud Hamiltons' and 'N' tanks. There are some 1930s shots of steam at Liverpool Street, the extensive coverage of GER area by G Calloway in the 1960s, Michael Woodward's film of the 'Britannias' and various Anglia Television programmes covering the history of the GER made at the time of electrification.

🚂 🚂 🚂 🚂 🚂

GREAT EASTERN RAILWAY (Britain 1988)

Anglia Television. Produced and directed by David Kenten. Written and presented by John Huntley. The electrification of the line from Liverpool Street to Norwich. The change is centred on the replacement of the old Trowse swing bridge for a complete realignment of the line, removing the old speed restrictions and the swing section now carrying the overhead catenary. The film is also used for a brief history of the Great Eastern Railway including archive film of Liverpool Street in steam days, Britannias en route to Norwich, Brentwood Bank and a large collection of photographs of the GER in its heyday. Details of the electrification process around Diss are also included.

16mm, Sound, Colour, 28mins, Anglia

🚂 🚂 🚂 🚂

THE GREAT HIGHWAY (Britain 1965)

Produced by British Transport Films. 'The main lines between London, Crewe, Manchester and Liverpool have been electrified. Why is this, the first main line system in Britain to be converted to electric traction, drawing its power at high voltage from the National Grid? This film shows, against the vivid and fascinating history of these lines, how they have served the needs of the population and industry since they were first conceived by George Stephenson and the engineers inspired, and compares the new achievements of electrification with the work of the railway pioneers.'

35/16mm, Sound, Colour, 21mins, BTF

🚂 🚂 🚂 🚂 🚂

GREAT: ISAMBARD KINGDOM BRUNEL (Britain 1975)

Bob Godfrey productions. Not a serious historical study this time but rather a highly amusing musical biography of Isambard Kingdom Brunel (1806-59), employing the high quality of animation we normally expect from the director Bob Godfrey. The film covers — in God-

frey's typically anarchic style — all the major inventions and developments of Brunel's career, including the building of the Clifton Suspension Bridge, the development and construction of the Great Western Railway and the building of the steamship *SS Great Eastern*, which was so gigantic that it became stuck in the mud immediately after launching.

35/16mm, Sound, Colour, 38mins, BG

🚂 🚂 🚂

GREAT LITTLE RAILWAYS (Britain 1983)

A BBC Television series which included films on the White Pass & Yukon Railway, Canada ('The Gold Rush Line'); Poland ('The Other Poland'); Greece ('Slow Train to Olympia'); the Philippines ('Dragons of Sugar Island'); India ('Line of Dreams'); Portugal ('Journey to the Land Beyond the Mountains'); and Ecuador ('The Good and the Quick'). From the railway enthusiast's point of view, the series was often criticised for its lack of railway scenes and its preponderance of social and political comment; nevertheless they do amount to a fine collection of railways which most people would never have a chance of seeing for themselves.

🚂 🚂 🚂 🚂 🚂

GREAT LITTLE TRAINS (Britain 1982)

Metro Video. A record of the Ffestiniog, Talyllyn, Vale of Rheidol, Snowdon Mountain and Welshpool and Llanfair preserved railways.

VID, Sound, Colour, 61mins, Metro

🚂 🚂 🚂 🚂 🚂

THE GREAT LITTLE TRAINS OF WALES (Britain 1976)

HTV (Cardiff). Series produced and directed by John Mead. Written and presented by Wynford Vaughan Thomas. Films edited by Terry Elgar and Don Llewellyn. Photographed by Mike Reynolds, Robin Higginson, John Williams, Brian Morgan and Tony Impey. Helicopter pilots and aerial photography by Mike Smith, Lyall Thompson and Mel Davies. A set of six programmes covering the Bala Lake, Ffestiniog, Talyllyn, Welshpool and Llanfair, Vale of Rheidol and Llanberis Lake and Snowdon Mountain railways.

'This superb six-part television series was very much a pioneer series in a number of ways, particularly in the extensive use of aerial shots from helicopters. The programmes were written with a passion for these lovely little railways by veteran broadcaster Wynford Vaughan Thomas and his enthusiasm seemed to have rubbed off on the production team. Until this series, aerial filming was something of a rarity, although today it is almost commonplace. This series is the product of professional film makers who really know their craft. The pace of the editing at most times is gently exciting, intercutting aerial shots to footplate shots beautifully composed, culminating in some very dramatic footage at the summit of Snowdon, a lesson in the art of railway film making which many contemporary video makers would do well to study. The technique of the helicopter running parallel to steam locomotives working through wooded hillsides in medium shot manages to portray the trains in their lovely setting to the best possible advantage. These programmes stand on their own as a forerunner of many television programmes that have since followed in this style of production.' (Robert Ennis).

THE GREAT LOCOMOTIVE CHASE (USA 1956)

Walt Disney. The straight dramatic version of the story used by Buster Keaton for *The General* when Union spies steal a train and go on a rampage of destruction during the American Civil War. 'Good sequences but no overall pace' said Leslie Halliwell. 'Perfectly OK dramatic material,' said Tony Bilbow.

35mm, Sound, Colour, 76mins, Disney

GREAT MALVERN TO WORCESTER (Britain 1962)

See Britain by Rail series. A journey from Great Malvern to Worcester and through the Vale of Evesham. GWR 'Castles' are prominent. (Also called *Between Wye and Severn*)

16mm, Silent, Colour, 5mins, HA/TUA

THE GREAT MISSOURI RAID (USA 1950)

Paramount. Directed by Gordon Douglas. With Macdonald Carey and Wendell Cory. Outlaws Jesse and Frank James in the American Civil War. Railway scenes were done on the Sierra Railroad, using Baldwin 2-8-0 locomotive No 29790 (No 18 on the SR list) built in 1906, renamed *Missouri Railroad*.

35mm, Sound, Colour, 81min, Paramount

THE GREAT NORTHFIELD MINNESOTA RAID (USA 1971)

Universal. Directed by Philip Kaufman. With Cliff Robertson and Robert Duvall. A gang of bandits plan a daring bank robbery in 1876. Includes scenes on the Sierra Railroad with Rogers 4-6-0 locomotive No 4493 of 1891 vintage.

35mm, Sound, 91min, Universal

GREAT ORME RAILWAY (Britain 1936)

LMS film. A record of the cable-operated Great Orme railway at Llandudno, using the San Francisco-style traction cable in a slot in the road driven from a central power station. When this film was made, the system was still worked by stationary steam engines, now replaced by electric motors.

16mm, Silent, 7mins, HA

THE GREAT ORME RAILWAY (Britain 1976)

Anglia Television. From the *Bygones* series. Produced and directed by David Kenten. Written and presented by John Huntley. An account of the cable railway at Llandudno.

16mm, Sound, Colour, 12mins, Anglia

THE GREAT PARADES (Britain 1984)

Online. Anniversary Parade at Shildon for the Stockton & Darlington (1975) and Anniversary Parade at Rainhill for the Liverpool & Manchester (1980).

VID, Sound, Colour, 35min, Online

THE GREAT RACE (USA 1965)

Warner. Directed by Blake Edwards. With Jack Lemmon and Tony Curtis. The first New York to Paris car race in 1908. Includes a scene on the Sierra Railroad with Rogers 4-6-0 locomotive No 4493 of 1891, so vintage about right.

35mm, Sound, 163min, Warner

GREAT RAILWAY JOURNEYS OF THE WORLD (1983)

A massive seven-part series made by a team which included: Series producer: Roger Lawton; Producers Ken Stephenson, Brian James, Tony Morrison, Gerry Troyna, Dennis Marks, and Peter Bartlett. Script and Presentation: Michael Palin, Michael Wood, Miles Kington, Ludovic Kennedy, Michael Frayn, Brian Thompson and Eric Robson. Music by Ian Lynn, Richie Close, 'Achalay', Jade Warrior, Sky, Terry Oldfield and Herbert Chappell. Photography by Nick Lera, David Jackson, David Feig, David South and Ian Punter. Series film adviser, John Huntley.

The journeys selected were: London to Kyle of Lochalsh ('Britain'); from Cape Town to the heart of Africa ('Zambesi Express'); the railways of the Andes in South America ('Three Miles High'); New York to Los Angeles ('Coast to Coast'); across Australia ('The Long Straight'); Bombay to Chochin in India ('Deccan') and London to Budapest ('Changing Trains'). A classic series which has remained a favourite for repeats and for home video.

GREAT RAILWAY JOURNEYS OF THE WORLD: BRITAIN (Confessions of a Train Spotter) (Britain 1980)

BBC Television (Manchester). Produced by Ken Stephenson. Written and presented by Michael Palin. A journey with Michael Palin from London to Kyle of Lochalsh, calling in on the way at the National Railway Museum in York, the North Yorkshire Moors Railway and Steamtown, Carnforth.

16mm/VID, Sound, Colour, 58mins, BBC TV

GREAT RAILWAY JOURNESY OF THE WORLD: CHANGING TRAINS (Journey across Europe). (Britain 1980)

BBC Television (Manchester). Directed by Peter Bartlett. Written and presented by Eric Robson.
Eric Robson sets off from Victoria on a journey by train to Budapest. Early footage of steam days out of Victoria. 'Golden Arrow' with 'Nelsons' working to channel ports. Also steam 'Golden Arrow' in France to Paris. 'Le Cisalpin' Trans Europe Express to Lausanne, excellent on board, trackside and aerial shots. At Montreux we take the steam narrow gauge 'Blonay Chamby Line' now a preserved railway. Following on with early (1931) footage of the only narrow gauge electric Pullman service in Switzerland on the Bernese Oberland the 'Golden Mountain Pullman'. Continuing today on the same line now called the 'Panoramic Express' changing at Zweisimmen for the train for Interlaken on the Bern-Lotschberg-Simplon railway. At Interlaken we change yet again — Swiss Federal Railways this time to the top of the Brunig Pass by rack assistance. Then down to Lucerne. The next lap of the journey is by way of the Vitznau Rigi Bahn electric rack and pinion up the mountainside (Europe's first mountain railway). Steam hauled tourist specials up the Rigi, up to the summit and down the other side. This time a different railway, the Arth Goldau Rigi Bahn, connecting with the federal mainline express to Zurich. Our 'Trans Alpine Express' now leaves Zurich for Vienna over the border and into

Austria — good aerial shots. We break our journey for a side trip to Mayerhofen on the steam narrow gauge Zillertalbahn line (beautifully filmed sequence) from Vienna the last leg of the journey into Hungary by the 'Lehar Express' over the border and under the iron curtain to Budapest. Wartime footage of devastated railways and the rebuilding. Children run the narrow gauge pioneer railway just a few miles out of Budapest training as railway operators of the future. Steam locomotives still shunt and work freight in the twilight of their years. The film closes with SNCF's TGV during development.

16mm/VID, Sound, Colour, 59mins, BBC TV

GREAT RAILWAY JOURNEYS OF THE WORLD: COAST TO COAST (A journey from New York to Los Angeles). (Britain 1980)

BBC Television. Written and presented by Ludovic Kennedy. Directed by Gerry Troyna. A journey across America from East to West.
Starting from Penn station on the 'Broadway Limited', out to Chicago — the start of a 3,000-mile journey. Then from Union station Chicago on the Union Pacific route to the west, stopping at Denver Colorado before continuing via the Denver & Rio Grande Railroad to Salt Lake City. Then over the High Sierras to the Railroad Museum at Sacramento. Onwards to San Francisco and Los Angeles to journey's end. Some of the scenes of the old ladies reminiscing on the train were a bit dull, but the final scenes at Los Angeles were magic.

16mm/VID, Sound, Colour, 60mins, BBC TV

GREAT RAILWAY JOURNEYS OF THE WORLD: DECCAN (Journey through India). (Britain 1980)

BBC Television (Manchester). Directed by Gerry Troyna. Written and presented by Brian Thompson. Brian Thompson travels from Bombay to Cochin, leaving Bombay Victoria by the 'Madras Mail' to Poona with an all-India Rail Pass (£30). The diesel-hauled train climbs

2,000ft to the Deccan Plateau. The second stage of the journey is from Poona to Madras; dinner is served at Daund Junction. At Guntakal the journey continues on the southern system; this time steam takes over for the leg to Bangalore and on to Mysore. The next 96 miles is by road to the narrow gauge rack railway at Ootacamund negotiating a 1 in 12 descent. Next the 'Nilagiri Express', and then the last leg of the journey from Mettupallayam to Cochin by the 'Tea Garden Express'.

16mm/VID, Sound, Colour, 59mins, BBC TV

GREAT RAILWAY JOURNEYS OF THE WORLD: THE LONG STRAIGHT (Journey Across Australia) (Britain 1980)

BBC Television (Manchester). Directed by Dennis Marks. Written and presented by Michael Frayn.
Micahel Frayn travels west from Sydney on the 'Indian Pacific' stopping to see the Great Lythog Zigzag — a preserved steam worked section — across New South Wales to Broken Hill and then Port Pirie in South Australia. Here there is a change of gauge to Adelaide, calling at the preserved Querdi Railway where steam haulage takes Frayn by narrow gauge to Alice Springs. Then across the Nullarbor Plain through Kalgoorlie to Perth, the end of the journey.

16mm/VID, Sound, Colour, 59mins, BBC TV

GREAT RAILWAY JOURNEYS OF THE WORLD: THREE MILES HIGH (Across the High Andes) (Britain 1980)

BBC Television (Manchester). Produced by Tony Morrison. Written and directed by Miles Kington. Photography by Nick Lera who also directed some of the sequences.
Miles Kington travels to the world's highest railway in Peru from Lima station; the train climbs 16,000ft to Huancayo. Then by steam train to Huancavelica. By road to Cuzco; continuing by train to Uno; the crossing of Lake Titicaca (the highest navigable lake in the world) by steamer. Then railcar to La Paz —

in fact Miles Kington didn't make it. He was strike bound and derailment at Viacha saw the end of the rail journey in Bolivia. The scenes where the journey finally ends in a local revolution must be one of the most extraordinary of their kind ever filmed.

16mm/VID, Sound, Colour, 59mins, BBC TV

🚂 🚂 🚂 🚂 🚂

GREAT RAILWAY JOURNEYS OF THE WORLD: ZAMBEZI EXPRESS (From the Cape to the Heart of Africa). (Britain 1980)

BBC Television (Manchester). Produced by Brian James. Written and presented by Michael Wood. Photography by Nick Lera. Michal Wood travels on the 'Blue Train' across South Africa and then northwards by steam to Zimbabwe taking in Mafeking and Transvaal on the way. Journey's end is at the Victoria Falls.

16mm, Sound, Colour, 59mins, BBC TV

🚂 🚂 🚂 🚂 🚂

THE GREAT ST TRINIANS TRAIN ROBBERY (Britain 1966)

British Lion/Braywild production. Produced by Leslie Gilliat. Directed by Frank Launder. With Frankie Howerd, Dora Bryan, Reg Varney, George Cole and Raymond Huntley. The staff of St Trinian's are infiltrated by train robbers but fight back in the end. The film culminates in a major railway chase staged on the Longmoor Military Railway (which closed in 1969). A variety of steam locomotives are seen in action, some disguised. There is also an early Southern DEMU, an SR 0-6-0 diesel shunter (No 3), a Wickham trolley and a pump trolley. Some of the action called for three trains running at speed, all in the same block section; it was a fitting and spectacular memorial to the Longmoor Military Railway shortly before it came to an end.

35mm, Sound, Colour, 94mins, Weintraub

🚂 🚂

GREAT STEAM LOCOMOTIVES

A series of videos issued by Railscene with a volume devoted

to: *Mallard, Clan Line, Somerset and Dorset 7F 2-8-0s, Black Fives, Flying Scotsman, Britannia and the Duke,* and *Princess Margaret Rose.*

🚂 🚂 🚂 🚂 🚂

THE GREAT STEAM LOCOMOTIVES OF FRANCE (France 1960s)

Videolines. This 1960s archive film shows virtually all the classes of steam locomotives then at work in their respective areas on the SNCF. From the 241Ps on the Paris-Clermont Expresses to the 040TX shunters at Vierzon. Rush-hour at Paris Nord with up to four 141TCs in the same shot. The unique Paris Bastille suburban service with 141TBs. Scenes from Lille and the 242TAs. Calais 231E, G and K Pacifics in the days when the 'Flèche d'Or' carried a headboard, the small and large tank locomotives of Boulogne, Rouen, St-German-des-Fosses. Clermont Ferrand, Nevers; Le Mans' oil-burning 141Rs, North British-built locomotives at Argentan. Featuring Nantes, Saintes, Narbonne, Sarreguemines and others. On-train, lineside, shed and station views encapsulating history in scenes now gone forever — semaphore signalling, uniforms, the smoke and grime of the French steam age, including such classes as 230D, 050TD, 050TQ, 040D, 230G, 141TA, 151TC, 140C, 141C, 231D, 141P, 040TA, 050TE, 030TU, 040TG, 231C, 030TA, 151TC, 040TC, 050TD, 141TD and others.

VID, Sound, Colour, 60mins, VLV

🚂 🚂 🚂 🚂 🚂

THE GREAT TRAIN ROBBERY (USA 1903)

Written, photographed, edited and directed by Edwin S Porter for the Edison company. With George Barnes and 'Broncho Billy' Anderson (who plays the parts of bandit, a passenger on the train, a cowboy in the sherriff's posse and the fireman on the engine). Filmed in the New Jersey area and on the Delaware, Lackawanna & Western Railroad, mainly around Paterson, New Jersey.

The scenario is taken from the Edison catalogue of 1904:

Scene 1: Interior of railroad telegraph office. Two masked robbers enter and compel the operator to get the signal block to stop the approaching train, and make him write a fictitious order to the engineer to take water at this station, instead of 'Red lodge', the regular watering stop. The train comes to a standstill (seen through window of office); the conductor comes to the window, and the frightened operator delivers the order while the bandits crouch out of sight, at the same time keeping him covered with their revolvers. As soon as the conductor leaves, they fall upon the operator, bind and gag him, and hastily depart to catch the moving train.

Scene 2: Railroad water tower. The bandits are hiding behind the tank as the train, under the false order, stops to take water. Just before she pulls out they stealthily board the train between the express car and the tender.

Scene 3: Interior of the express car. Messenger is busily engaged. An unusual sound alarms him. He goes to the door, peeps through the keyhole and discovers two men trying to break in. He starts back bewildered, but, quickly recovering, he hastily locks the strongbox containing the valuables and throws the key through the open side door. Drawing his revolver, he crouches behind a desk. In the meantime the two robbers have succeeded in breaking in the door and enter cautiously. The messenger opens fire, and a desperate pistol duel takes place in which the messenger is killed. One of the robbers stands watch while the other tries to open the treasure box. Finding it locked, he vainly searches the messenger for the key, and blows the safe open with dynamite. Securing the valuables and mail bags they leave the car.

Scene 4: This thrilling scene shows the tender and interior of the locomotive cab, while the train is running 40 miles an hour. While two of the bandits have been robbing the mail car, two others climb over the tender. One of them holds up the engineer while the other covers the fireman, who seizes a coal shovel and climbs upon the tender, where a desperate fight takes place. They struggle fiercely all over the tank and narrowly escape being hurled over the side of the tender. Finally they fall, with the robber on top. He seizes a lump of coal, and strikes the fireman on the head until he becomes senseless. He then hurls the body from the swiftly moving train. The bandits then compel the engineer to bring the train to a stop.

Scene 5: The train coming to a stop. The engineer leaves the locomotive, uncouples it from the train, and pulls ahead about 100ft while the robbers hold their pistols to his face.

Scene 6: Exterior scene showing train. The bandits compel the passengers to leave the coaches, 'hands up', and line up along the tracks. One of the robbers covers them with a revolver in each hand, while the other relieves the passengers of their valuables. A passenger attempts to escape, and is instantly shot down. Securing everything of value, the band terrorise passengers by firing their revolvers in the air, while they make their escape to the locomotive.

Scene 7: The desperados board the locomotive with their booty, compel the engineer to start, and disappear into the distance.

Scene 8: The robbers bring the engine to a stop several miles from the scene of the 'hold up', and take to the mountains.

Scene 9: A beautiful scene in a valley. The bandits come down the side of a hill, across a narrow stream, mounting their horses, and make for the wilderness.

Scene 10: Interior of the telegraph office. The operator lies bound and gagged on the floor. After struggling to his feet, he leans on the table, and telegraphs for assistance by manipulating the key with his chin, and then faints from exhaustion. His little daughter enters with his dinner pail. She cuts the rope, throws a glass of water in his face and restores him to consciousness, and, recalling his thrilling experience he rushes out to give the alarm.

Scene 11: Interior of a typical Western dance hall. Shows a number of men and women in a lively quadrille. A 'tenderfoot' is quickly spotted and pushed to the centre of the hall, and compelled to do a jig, while bystanders amuse themselves by shooting dangerously close to his feet. Suddenly the door opens and the half-dead telegraph

operator staggers in. The dance breaks up in confusion. The men secure their rifles and hastily leave the room.

Scene 12: Shows the mounted robbers dashing down a rugged hill at a terrific pace, followed closely by a large posse, both parties firing as they ride. One of the desperados is shot and plunges headlong from his horse. Staggering to his feet, he fires at the nearest pursuer, only to be shot dead a moment later.

Scene 13: The three remaining bandits, thinking they have eluded the pursuers, have dismounted from their horses, and after carefully surveying their surroundings, they start to examine the contents of the mail pouches. They are so grossly engaged in their work that they do not realize the approaching danger until too late. The pursuers, having left their horses, steal noiselessly down upon them until they are completely surrounded. A desperate battle then takes place, and after a brave stand all the robbers and some of the posse bite the dust.

Scene 14: A life-size (close-up) picture of Barnes, leader of the outlaw band, taking aim and firing point-blank at the audience. The resulting excitement is great. This scene can be used to begin or end the picture.

A typical 4-4-0 locomotive of the day and some unique open-vestibule wooden coaches were the main contribution of DL&WR. Main location scenes were shot at Paterson, New Jersey and in the vicinity.

The Great Train Robbery is the most important single film in the first 15 years of the cinema industry. It was shown extensively throughout the world and led many men (including the Warner Brothers, Carl Laemmle and many others) into the motion picture business. It also attracted the attention of a young man by the name of D W Griffith who eventually joined the Edison company and made films with Edwin S Porter before going on to produce *Birth of a Nation*, *Intolerance* and *Way Down East*.

35/16/8/VID, Silent, Part hand-coloured, 14mins, NFA/HA/125

THE GREAT TRAIN ROBBERY (USA 1942)

A Republic Picture. Directed by Joseph Kane. With Bob Steele and

Claire Carleton. Models and actual railway shots (Santa Fe) freely mixed in a film which starts with the title: 'This film has no connection with the picture made by the Edison Company in 1903'.

35mm, Sound, 61mins

GREAT TRAINS: A STEAM TRAIN PASSES (1947-81)

Stylus Video. Three films from Australia and New Zealand in one video. The items are: 'A Steam Train Passes' (1974); 'The Railway' (NSW Railways) and 'Journey of a Nation' (1947). See individual titles for details.

VID, Sound, Colour, 60mins, Stylus

GREAT TRAINS: THE SETTLE AND CARLISLE RAILWAY (Britain 1988)

Stylus Video. Remastered version of a television programme. Commentary by Allan Cartner. A history of the line built by the Midland Railway, followed by scenes at Carlisle, the Eden Valley, and Gill Summit, Arten Gill and Dent Head Viaducts, Blea Moor Tunnel and the Ribblehead Viaduct. The locomotives featured are LNER 'A4' 4-6-2 No 4498 *Sir Nigel Gresley*, LMS 'Coronation' 4-6-2 No 6229 *Duchess of Hamilton*, SR 'LN' 4-6-0 No 850 *Lord Nelson* and SR 'West Country' 4-6-2 No 34092 *City of Wells*.

VID, Sound, Colour, 56mins, Stylus

GREAT WESTERN APPROACHES (Britain 1947)

Made by Gaumont-British Instructional Films for the GWR. A film to promote tourism by using the GWR system. There are occasional glimpses of the 'Cornish Riviera', hauled by a 'King' or a 'Castle' class locomotive, largely unidentified.

Places visited include Weymouth, Torquay, Plymouth, Falmouth, Penzance, Land's End, St Ives, Newquay, Minehead, Weston-super-Mare, Penarth and Tenby.

35/16mm/VID, Sound, 19mins, BTF/TVP

GREAT WESTERN JOURNEY
(Britain 1985)

BBC Television (Manchester). Produced and directed by Barry Bevins. Presented by Anthony Burton. The story of 150 years of the Great Western railway from 1835 to 1985, using mainly modern material with detailed visits to some of the places served by the GWR and much background information; even a jazz concert on the River Thames below Brunel's famous single brick arch bridge.

VID, Sound, Colour, 73mins, BBC TV

THE GREATEST SHOW ON EARTH (USA 1952)

Paramount. Produced and directed by Cecil B DeMille. With Betty Hutton, Cornel Wilde, James Stewart, Charlton Heston and Dorothy Lamour. Love and jealousy under the Big Top. There are various railway shots; the circus train is labelled 'Atlantic Line' of the Atlanta Railroad; a shot of a Pennsylvania General Electric diesel; a big unidentified Pacific steam engine and a spectacular train crash. The crash is nearly all model work, with a diesel on the front and a giant derailment. As it all happens at night, staging a real crash would have been almost impossible to light for the limited exposure range of Technicolor at that time.

35mm, Sound, Colour, 153mins, Paramount

GRESLEY, SIR NIGEL (Britain 1927)

Very little film exists of the great men of the past on the railways. There are a few shots of Gresley taken during a visit to Doncaster by the Institution of Locomotive Engineers on 14 June, 1927. Sir Nigel is reputed to have hated 'film people', after an experience in 1929 when he authorised a film company to use 4472 *Flying Scotsman* and then found they had staged a scene in which the locomotive broke away from the stock and the carriages went racing on, all on their own. As Gresley said,

'it looked as if the LNER had not yet discovered the vacuum brake'. A special title had to be added to the film explaining that 'certain liberties had been taken for dramatic licence with the normal safety equipment of LNER trains'. After that, Sir Nigel never had much interest in the movies.

GRIME AND GLORY DAYS
(Britain 1988)

Stirling. Produced by Dick Griffiths. Archive film by Richard J Willis. A video on Steam in Action in the rundown days of the 1960s, filmed on the old 'Big Four' routes at sites like the Settle and Carlisle, Nottingham, Leicester, Derby, Crewe, Waterloo, Hereford, Wales, Rugby, King's Cross, Essendine, Newcastle, Larbert and Edinburgh.

16mm/VID, Colour, 60mins, VID/Stirling

GRIT OF THE GIRL TELEGRAPHER (USA 1912)

Kalem Production. With Anna Q Nilsson, Hal Clements and Henry Hallem. A girl intercepts a villain and goes in pursuit on a train. Made in Fort Lee, New Jersey. A very odd looking American saddle tank engine and a typical 4-4-0 seem to come from the Delaware & Lackawanna Railroad.

16mm, Silent, 14mins, HA

GROUNDWORK FOR PROGRESS
(Britain 1959)

Produced by British Railways Films. 'With this film, we are taken into the traditionally exciting world of railway civil engineering. Here, we see a length of rail heated until, quite suddenly and dramatically, it buckles. There, a bridge is tested for metal fatigue. The film shows some of the opportunities which British Railways modernisation is providing for the young civil engineer.'

35/16mm Sound, 30mins, BTF

GUNPOWDER MILL AT ROSLIN
(Britain 1948)

An ICI film. A record of a primitive gunpowder plant in Scotland, including a 2ft narrow gauge internal railway which was worked up to closure in 1948 by horses. Roslin, on the North British Railway, lost its passenger service back in 1933.

16mm, Sound, 11mins, HA

H

HALE'S TOURS (USA 1899-1905)

A remarkable development in the story of the cinema which, although, as it turned out, consisted merely of a side issue, nevertheless attracted a great deal of attention at the time and demonstrates only too clearly the relationship seen between the cinema and the railways in those early days. The show was known as 'Hale's Tours' and it was first established in Britain at 165 Oxford Street. Bills announced that one could take a 'trip through the Rocky Mountains' price 6d or go on a 'sight-seeing tour of Wales'. The arrangements were roughly as follows: the audience paid 6d and found themselves seated in a saloon railway carriage of American construction. As soon as enough people had been lured in, a 'conductor' came along, collected the 'fares', then he pulled a cord and a bell clanged. From outside a series of sounds using cylinders of compressed air produced the noise of the hiss of escaping steam; at the same time a series of handles were operated to rotate a collection of wheels and chains, imitating the sounds of a starting locomotive and carriages. A refinement was to have the car mounted on springs and give it a few lurches as it started on its way; men would then continue to rock the car back and forth as the journey proceeded. The lights inside the carriage went out and, as if on the observation platform, scenes of the Rockies or of mountain scenery in Wales would suddenly appear, complete with railway line stretching out before the spectator. When stations were passed the car would slow up, the wheels would reproduce their particular clanking sound, bells would be sounded and the whole thing would be given the sense of life-like imitation. So effective was this particular project that 'Hale's Tours' appeared all over the United States and Europe. In Britain alone there were no less than five of them running at one time in London simultaneously.

The man who started it was George C Hale, ex-chief of the Kansas City Fire Brigade. He had been interested in films as a result of seeing many of the film records showing the turnout of a fire brigade, which were almost as popular as railway scenes during the first years of the cinema. Mr Hale launched the idea of the tours in his native city of Kansas but it was a demonstration at the St Louis Exposition in 1899 that really started him off to world fame; he made £2m in two years!

As far as is known, no material survives from Hale's Tours. The originals were on 35mm film.

HALESOWEN BRANCH (Britain 1962)

Made by P B Whitehouse and John Adams. An SLS special tour from Birmingham New Street via Smethwick to the abandoned Halesowen Branch, which ceased passenger services in 1927. The locomotives are MR Johnson '2' 0-6-0 Nos 58271, 58167 and 58283.

16/8mm, Silent, 8mins, CV/NRM/VID/HA

HALFWAY HOUSE (Britain 1944)

Ealing Film. Directed by Basil Dearden. With Mervyn Johns and Glynis Johns. A fantasy-drama of a strange house to which people with various problems come together. Includes a GWR journey to Wales.

35mm, Sound, 95mins, Weintraub/125

THE HALLADE TRACK RECORDER (Britain 1951)

Produced by British Transport Films. A film to tell gangers and lengthmen how the Hallade track recorder makes a continuous record of the movements of a train during a journey, and so shows up the good and bad places in the track. Hallade records are of value to all permanent-way men because they help in the detection of track faults. This film was made in association with British Transport Films by World Wide Pictures.

35/16mm, Sound, 13mins, BTF

HAMBURG FLYER (Germany 1934)

Dr Kruckenburg's 'Zeppelin on Wheels' was a rail car with a Zeppelin diesel engine and a giant propeller 10ft across in the rear. It was reputed to have achieved 145mph on a trial run from Berlin to Hamburg. The concept was similar to the George Bennie Railplane in Britain. There was only one snag; every time it went through a station without stopping, it swept all the waiting passengers on to the track!

16mm, Silent, 2mins, HA

HAMPSHIRE VENTURER RAIL TOUR (Britain 1963)

SCTS. The tour starts from Victoria then to Wimbledon, Andover Junction, on by the Amesbury and Bulford branch to Bulford Camp station, then to Greatley, Salisbury, Eastleigh, Southampton (the old Canute Road level crossing), Fawley, and again Southampton, Eastleigh and so to Waterloo. Motive power includes SR 'Q' 0-6-0 No 30547, SR 'Q1' Austerity 0-6-0 No 33039, LSWR 'T9' 4-4-0 No 120, SR 'USA' 0-6-0T No 30074 (ex-US Army Transportation, 1942), and SR 'S15' 4-6-0 No 30510.

16mm, Silent, 11mins, HA/SCTS

HANNIBAL BROOKS (Britain 1968)

Produced and directed by Michael Winner. With Oliver Reed, Michael J Pollard and Wolfgang Preiss. A British prisoner of war, along with a saboteur, escape from a Berlin zoo with one of the elephants and plan to cross the Alps to Switzerland. Includes a spectacular railway crash in which a complete train, loaded with (glass-fibre) German tanks is blown up and the whole lot crash down a bank into a river. Staged with an old 4-4-0 locomotive on the only privately owned railway in Austria, the Montafon.

35mm, Sound, Colour, 102mins, United Artists

HAPPY EVER AFTER (Britain 1954)

Associated British Picture Corporation. Produced by Mario Zampi. Directed by Mario Zampi. With David Niven, Yvonne de Carlo, A E Matthews, George Cole, Michael Shepley and Barry Fitzgerald. A new village squire offends the local people who decide to kill him. 'Fairly hilarious black comedy with a good cast entering into the spirit of the thing' (Leslie Halliwell). The railway contribution came from the Buntingford Branch which closed in 1965, and was described by P Paye in his book on the history of the line:-

'The serene atmosphere at Braughing was broken on Sundays 6 and 13 September 1953, when technicians of the Associated Picture Corporation arrived with film stars David Niven, Yvonne de Carlo, Noelle Middleton, Michael Shipley, Robert Urquhart and Barry Fitzgerald to shoot scenes for the film *O'Leary Night*. A comedy, with an Irish setting, the story told of a squire who was loved by all his local villagers. When he dies the new squire, a man of a very different character, played by David Niven, tries to enforce law and order to the extent that the inhabitants unite to rid the village of him.

'To save the film company the expense of going to Ireland, Braughing station was chosen, for suitability and nearness to Elstree, to depict the scenes of the arrival of the new squire at Rathbarney station. The station took on a totally fresh appearance, woodwork on the station buildings and signal box was repainted green and white, flowers were placed in tubs on the station forecourt and planted in the gardens of the platform. New noticeboards, bearing the heading of the Irish railway (CIE) had posters depicting the Dublin Horse Show and Irish whiskey in place of more mundane BR posters. The new nameboards in both Gaelic and English proclaimed "Rathbarney" in place of Braughing.

'A special train composed of ex GER tender locomotive "J15" 0-6-0 No 65464 and a few old coaches spent most of both Sundays steaming back and forth into the up platform, giving way only to the normal service trains, when the Rathbarney notices were temporarily removed, to avoid confusion to passengers.

'Station-master H E Ribbons and his staff did not appear in the film, as actors took their parts, but were fully occupied during the filming in an advisory capacity. Costing £300,000, the title of the film, *O'Leary Night* was changed to *Happy Ever After* before general release.

'For many years until the advent of the "N7" class on freights in the 1940s, trains were handled by the GER "Y14" class and the LNER "J15" designed by T W Worsdell, introduced in 1883. Such was the success of the design that building continued until 1913. All except 19 of the class of 272 0-6-0 tender locomotives were built at Stratford with the others built by Sharp Stewart and Co. No 65464 built in March 1912 as GER No 566 and later renumbered by the LNER in 1924 as 7566 was used for the filming.

'Freshly painted in BR black livery at Stratford Paint Shops 65464 emerged with the BR lion and wheel emblem on the right hand side of the tender and the CIE emblem on the left hand side. The BR number and smokebox numberplate were retained. A Stratford footplate crew worked the locomotive for the filming. During the week of 6-13 September 1953 No 65464 returned to Stratford for normal freight duties but on the way to Buntingford for filming on the second Sunday, worked a Stratford to Hertford East passenger turn. A few days after filming the CIE emblem was replaced by the lion and wheel.

'Before World War 2 through Sunday services from Liverpool Street were often eight-coach close-coupled sets from the Ilford and Romford services. The length of these trains necessitated trains pulling up at the shorter platforms on the branch and so except for use in the film *O'Leary Night* in 1953 they were rarely seen on the branch after the war.

'For the film the four-coach Westinghouse-braked non-articulated close-coupled set was stored at St Margarets for a fortnight before filming when one side was painted green with dirt rubbed in to make it look older. Various compartments were lettered 'first class', 'third class' and 'no smoking' in Irish and English whilst the CIE emblem was painted on the side of each coach. Between filming on 6th and 13th September the coaches were left in the long siding at Braughing.'

35mm, Sound, Colour, 87mins, Weintraub/125

A HARD DAY'S NIGHT (Britain 1964)

United Artists. Produced by Walter Shenson. Directed by Richard Lester. With the Beatles, Wilfrid Brambell and Victor Spinetti. The Beatles come from Liverpool to appear in a TV show in London. Many scenes were shot on British Rail trains on the North West pre-electrification route. Extensive use was made of Marylebone station for the opening sequence, with vast crowds of fans invading the central concourse and the platforms. The journey is in reverse, with Marylebone acting for both Liverpool and London! The train is hauled by unidentified diesels.

35mm, Sound, 85mins, UA/VID

Shooting the scenes at Marylebone station: newsreel.

16mm, Sound, 12mins, HA

HAROLD LLOYD'S FUNNY SIDE OF LIFE (USA 1963)

Harold Lloyd productions. Excerpts from 1920s silent comedies, including some with hilarious train scenes on the old Sante Fe.

35/16mm, Sound, 99mins, Time-Life

HARROW RAIL CRASH (Britain 1952)

Newsreel records of the multiple crash at Harrow and Wealdstone station on 8 October 1952. A local train from Tring to Euston was standing at the fast up line ready for a non-stop run, headed by LMS '4MT' 2-6-4T No 42389, when the overnight sleeper from Perth to London, headed by LMS 'Princess Coronation' 4-6-2 No 46242 *City of Glasgow*, ignoring signals, thundered into the back of the local. One minute later, the Euston to Liv-

Left:
A tense confrontation from 'The Great Barrier' (1937) which was based on the building of the Canadian Pacific Railroad.

Below left:
***The Texas** in Walt Disney's 'The Great Locomotive Chase'.*

Bottom left:
Helen Holmes during the filming of one of 'The Hazards of Helen' episodes.

Right:
Ruth Roland in an early serial based on 'The Hazards of Helen' formula in the 1920s. *National Film Archive*

Far right:
One of 'The Hazards of Helen' series (c. 1914) with Helen Holmes and Henry Vidor.

Below right:
A shot from one of the exterior sequences taken at Filey, Yorkshire for 'Holiday Camp' showing the holidaymakers arriving at the camp station for their well-earned holiday.
Gainsborough Pictures

erpool, double-headed with LMS 'Jubilee' 4-6-0 No 45637 *Windward Isles* and LMS 'Princess Royal' 4-6-2 No 46202 *Princess Anne* ('Turbomotive' engine), making good time, roared into the wreckage with such an impact that both locomotives were totally destroyed. *Princess Anne*, 40ft from front to cab, was reduced to 28ft overall. 112 people were killed and 150 seriously injured.

It so happened that a Pathe newsreel cameraman lived in nearby Hatch End and was soon on the spot. The pictures he captured were so vivid that it led to a public outcry and as a result, a second edition of the newsreel, which appeared three days later, carried what in effect was a public apology.

35/16mm, Sound, 18mins, Pathe/HA (Ref Only)

🚂 🚂 🚂 🚂 🚂

HARTFIELD (Britain 1937)

Made by Peter Tanner. Scenes filmed during the making of shots for a feature film *Bone of Contention* at Hartfield station on the LBSCR line from East Grinstead to Tunbridge Wells. The line was opened in 1866 and closed in 1967. The LBSCR train is hauled by LBSCR 'C2' 0-6-0 No 2533, built in 1893 by R Billinton.

16mm, Silent, 4mins, HA

🚂 🚂 🚂 🚂 🚂

HARVEY GIRLS (USA 1945)

MGM. Produced by Arthur Freed. Directed by George Sidney. With Judy Garland and Ray Bolger. Young ladies going West to work as waitresses and create a new town. There is a massive studio town and railway built for the film; an old 4-4-0 was bought from the Santa Fe for the film. But the star is the Oscar-winning song by Harry Warren and Johnny Mercer: *On the Atchison, Topeka an Santa Fe*. Perhaps not a likely title for a show-stopping number, from the first line 'When I board that train and settle down', it has never looked back.

35mm, Sound, Colour, 101mins, MGM

🚂 🚂

HATTER'S CASTLE (Britain 1941)

A Paramount Picture. Directed by Lance Comfort. With Robert Newton, Deborah Kerr, James Mason, Emlyn Williams, Henry Oscar, Enid Stamp-Taylor and Beatrice Varley. The rise and fall of a Victorian hatter who becomes a tyrant to his wife and family. Includes a reconstruction of the Tay Bridge disaster of December 1879. The model for this scene was built in a tank 60ft by 70ft with nine foot sides at Highbury studios; six wind machines were used to simulate the great gale that destroyed the bridge.

35mm, Sound, 100mins, Paramount

🚂 🚂 🚂

HAYLING ISLAND BRANCH (Britain 1959-62)

The line from Havant to Langston, North Hayling and Hayling Island came to an end in 1963. Towards the finale it was worked by 'Terriers' and undoubtedly helped to preserve quite a number of the class simply because they were so efficient and useful on branch lines that needed a pretty light engine to succeed. P B Whitehouse and John Adams filmed the branch in black and white in 1959 with LBSCR 'A1X' 0-6-0T No 32646. Edward Griffith made a detailed 8mm colourfilm in 1962 of the complete journey with LBSCR 'A1X' 0-6-0T Nos 32646 and 32650. No 32670 was built in 1872, and was at one time No 3 on the Kent & East Sussex Railway and as such appeared in the film *The Loves of Joanna Godden*. It is now back on the preserved KESR, along with two other 'Terriers'.

16mm, Silent, Part colour, 26mins, CV/NRM/HA

🚂 🚂 🚂 🚂 🚂

THE HAZARDS OF HELEN (USA 1914-17)

A famous railroad series of films produced by the Kalem Company, with Helen Holmes. See under individual episodes: *Helen's Sacrifice*, *In Danger's Path* and *The Leap from the Water Tower*.

🚂 🚂 🚂 🚂

HEADLINE VIDEO

This Stirlingshire based video company specialises, unsurprisingly in compilations on Scottish subjects. They work extensively with the Scottish Railway Preservation Society and indeed one of the company's releases, *10 Years Hard*, gives a full account of the creation of that organsiation's Bo'ness and Kinneil Railway. Other subjects covered or under preparation include *Magnificent Maude*, a study of the career of a Springburn-built North British goods locomotive, and *Road of Iron*, a compilation dealing especially with the former iron ore traffic to steel works at Ravennscraig and various steam subjects.

🚂 🚂 🚂 🚂 🚂

HEAT AND DUST (Britain 1982)

Merchant Ivory Productions. Directed by James Ivory. With Julie Christie, Christopher Cazenove and Shashi Kapoor. A look-back at India's history and the days of the British Raj. Includes two scenes with ancient British-built 4-4-0 steam locomoties.

35mm, Sound, Colour, 130mins, Merchant Ivory

🚂

HELEN'S SACRIFICE (USA 1914)

Episode No 1 from the series *The Hazards of Helen*, starring Helen Holmes. Directed by J P McGowan. A Kalem production.

Benton, the day operator at Lone Point signal box, after looking after his sick child the whole night, falls asleep and fails to send a message to stop a train. Helen, the night operator, arrives and seeing the message, rides after the train, jumps on and manages to stop it just before the collision. To protect Benton and his family she takes the blame for not receiving the message and is fired.

35mm, Silent, 15mins, NFA

🚂 🚂 🚂 🚂

HELLINGLY HOSPITAL RAILWAY (Britain 1951)

SCTS. A journey in a brake van on the LBSCR mini-branch from Hellingly on the 'Cuckoo Line' (Groombridge to Polegate), to

Hellingly Hospital station. The line closed in 1965.

16mm, Silent, 3mins, HA/SCTS

HEREFORD STATION (Britain 1910)

A single shot of a GWR 'Aberdare' class locomotive and train entering the station.

16mm, Silent, 45secs, HA

HERITAGE VIDEO

A video company specialising in tapes on preserved narrow gauge lines. Their output includes *Ffestiniog Railway* and *Tallyllyn Railway*.

HERNE BAY (Britain 1958)

Shots taken by SPG Alexander of traffic on the London-Thanet services in steam days, with glimpses of 'Battle of Britain' class locos as well as old SECR types.

16mm, Silent, 4mins, HA

HEROES ARE MADE (USSR 1944)

Produced by the Kievand Ashkhabad studios. Directed by Mark Donskoy. With V Perist-Petrensk. A revolutionary story in which an engine driver introduces a young man to the party and the struggle of the workers leading up to the 1917 revolution. There are extensive scenes in the railway yards at Kiev as they were in 1917.

35mm, Sound, 78mins

HEYSHAM-BELFAST (Britain 1937)

LMS film. The LMS route to Northern Ireland, including LMS ships SS *Duke of Lancaster.* and various dredgers etc. There is a brief steam scene at Heysham docks.

16mm, Silent, 5mins, HA

HIGH NOON (USA 1952)

Kramer. Directed by Fred Zinnemann. With Gary Cooper and Grace Kelly. Classic western about a marshal determined to defend his town against the bad men. The dramatic ending at the railroad depot was shot at Warnerville on the Sierra Railroad during 1951, using the equally classic Rogers 4-6-0 locomotive No 4493 of 1891 and a complete train made up of coaches Nos 2 and 6, plus the Caboose No 9.

35mm/VID, Sound, 85mins, Kramer/VID

HIGHWAY (Britain 1988)

ITV Television. An episode in Harry Secombe's religious programme for Sunday evenings was shot almost entirely on the West Somerset Preserved Railway from Minehead to Bishop's Lydeard.

A second programme was centred on the Romney, Hythe & Dymchurch Railway, featuring Harry Secombe along with Goon Show colleagues Spike Milligan and Michael Bentine.

VT, Sound, Colour, 27mins, ITV

THE HIGHWAY OF STEEL (Britain 1947)

An LMS film. The railway services offered to the steel industry in Britain before both the railways and the steel industry were in line for nationalisation.

35mm/VID, Sound, Colour, 11mins, BTF/TVP

HILLSIDE PUBLISHING

The Hendry's of Rugby originally issued a major series of 8mm silent films covering railways from 1928 to 1939. Lately some have been issued as videos including material on the Isle of Man, Leicester and Rutland and the Southwold Railways.

HISTORIC LOCOS AT CREWE (Britain 1959)

Made by P B Whitehouse and John Adams. The locomotives on display include *Hardwicke*, *Lion* and *Cornwall*.

16/8mm, Silent, 9mins, CV/NRM/VID

HITLER'S SS (USA 1989)

CBS Television production for American CBS network. A scene involving Munich station was done at Kensington Olympia and revamped by designer Richard Hornsby.

16mm, Sound, Colour, 54mins, CBS

HOLBORN STATION (Britain 1928)

In 1928, the Central Line of the London Underground closed British Museum station and rebuilt Holborn. This film shows the opening-up of the tube tunnel to create a new station, with the work carried on with normal traffic. There are good views of the Central Line stock as it was in 1928.

16mm, Silent, 4mins, HA

HOLD-UP OF THE ROCKY MOUNTAIN EXPRESS (USA 1906)

Produced by the American Mutascope and Biograph Company. A fictional one-reel film, similar to *The Great Train Robbery*, photographed on the Ulster & Delaware Railroad at Phoenicia, New York, and on a branch line from Phoenicia to Kaaterskill in the Catskills.

16/8mm, Silent, 12mins, Blackhawk/BFI

HOLIDAY (Britain 1937)

An LMS film. The planning and publication of the LMS Spring and Summer timetables.

35mm/VID, Sound, 22mins, BTF/TVP

HOLIDAY (Britain 1967)

Produced by British Transport Films. In a series of vivid sequences, this film catches all the atmosphere of a traditional holiday by the sea, together with the zest and good humour of ordinary people released from their everyday routine. The action moves at a rhythmic pace to the accompaniment of traditional jazz tunes played by Chris Barber and his band, and the rich variety of candid camera shots captures the behaviour and reactions of people having fun on holiday.

35/16mm, Sound, Colour, 18mins, BTF

HOLIDAY CAMP (Britain 1947)

Gainsborough. Directed by Ken Annakin. With Jack Warner, Kathleen Harrison and Flora Robson. A murderer is on the prowl in a Butlin's holiday camp. The campers arrive at Skegness on what was then still the LNER.

35mm, Sound, 97mins, Rank

HOLIDAY IN NORWAY (Britain 1955)

Produced by British Transport Films. A journey to Norway by train and by ship is itself part of the stimulating holiday in the Hardanger country to which this film takes us. Hardanger has a rich variety of attractions for the holidaymaker, whether he travels by car, coach, rail, bicycle or on foot. It is not possible to see all that Norway has to offer in one visit, but in Bergen, the gateway to the Fjord country, the tourist first experiences the friendliness of the Norwegians and the romantic atmosphere of the country. Produced in association with the Bergen Steamship Company.

16mm, Sound, Colour, 24mins, BTF

A HOLIDAY TRIP TO THE CLYDE COAST OF SCOTLAND VIA L&NWR (1909)

Produced by the Kineto Company. Shots of children playing. The film ends with shots taken from a train — first in the Pass of Leny, then the Pass of Brander with Loch Awe (despite the fact that these locations are not on the Clyde Coast of the title).

35mm, Silent, 11mins, NFA

A HOLIDAY TRIP TO THE CLYDE COAST OF SCOTLAND VIA L&NWR (1909)

Produced by the Kineto Company. The train en route to Scotland with

shots of the dining car, after which the following views are shown: Glasgow Central station, municipal buildings, Sauchiehall Street, the Jamaica Bridge with Caledonian Bridge and Central station, Glasgow; Clyde shipbuilding yards; Dumbarton Rock and Castle; Caledonian steamer leaving Gourock Pier; Hunter Quay and Kirn; Castle Hill, Dunoon, and Highland Mary's Monument; West Bay, Dunoon with crowds on the sands; Wemyss Bay railway station; a destroyer running trials on the measured mile; Wemyss Bay; Rothesay, holiday makers on Rothesay Pier; the pier-rots at Rothesay; the Esplanade at Rothesay; Effrick Bay with children playing on the sands; yachting, Millport; crowds on the beach, Alligator Head, Millport.

35mm, Silent, 23mins, NFA/HA

HOLLYWOOD

In its heyday, three railway systems served Hollywood, either through San Francisco or direct to Los Angeles. The Union Pacific worked from Omaha to Los Angeles and provided services right across the United States from New York to the West Coast, with other lines. The Southern Pacific provided a route to Salt Lake City; to San Francisco; and Los Angeles. The third route was the classic Atchison, Topeka & Santa Fe; all were used by Hollywood film makers but the Sante Fe was a special favourite because it had local lines in the immediate vicinity of the main film studios. (Details under individual films)

HOLLYWOOD CAVALCADE (USA 1939)

TCF. Directed by Irving Cummings. With Don Ameche and Alice Faye. Career of an old-time Hollywood producer. Includes one stock shot of a Southern Pacific steam-hauled train in sand on the Sierra Mountain approaches and a very phoney imitation Mack Sennett comedy train with clumsy modern stock and a most unlikely locomotive.

35mm, Sound, colour, 96mins, TCF

HOLYHEAD TO KINGSTON (Britain 1936)

A record of the LMS ships on the route from Holyhead, with good detail of the boiler rooms, the coaling facilities, the passenger accommodation and the handling of the ships. Featured are RMS *Scotia* and RMS *Cambria*.

16mm, Silent, 5mins, HA

HONITON BANK (Britain 1964)

Made by W Crawforth. An 8mm record of a day watching the trains go by on the Honiton Bank at the exit to the tunnel. There is a profusion of Bulleid Pacifics.

16mm, Silent, Colour, 6mins, HA

THE HOUND OF THE BASKERVILLES (Britain 1930)

Gainsborough Pictures. Directed by V Gareth Gundrey. With Robert Rendell, Frederick Lloyd, John Stuart and Heather Angel. One of the many versions of this classic Sherlock Holmes story, the co-operation of the Great Western Railway was sought for this production, using the GWR hotel at Moretonhamstead as Baskerville Hall and the station at Lustleigh as 'Baskerville' on Dartmoor. An amusing insight into early 'talkie' production is provided in this account by Cecile Leslie from the pages of *Film Weekly* in March, 1930:

Monday

We have been in Moretonhampstead only a week — but how Moretonhampstead has changed! Devonshire cream has slumped badly — farmers' daughters having taken to the 18-day diet.

Fields lie untilled while farmers watch the antics of Mr Gundrey and his merry men. Even local curates gather round us in the hope of film tests.

Today's location centre is the village of Lustleigh, where exteriors of a railway station are to be filmed.

At sunrise, vans carrying our sound, generating and camera equippage start up for the village; for every location centre has to be turned into what is virtually a studio base, and it is a long job. Lights on the set must be linked up with generating engines, camera and mike coupled with the motors by power-conducting cables.

A bewildered stationmaster watches us back lorries into his station-yard, festoon his roof and railings with cables, and turn his waiting-room into the make-up department. Bogus porters in the hired plumes of GWR officials practise wheeling luggage trucks down the platform. The last straw, however, is reached when our carpenters attempt to uproot the signboard proclaiming the name of Lustleigh. 'No! No! No!' says the stationmaster, 'I will not have it'. But we show him a written permit from the railway and offer him a part for his daughter in the film. The stationmaster melts. The signboard is dug up and one bearing the legend 'Baskerville' planted in its place.

Our set ready, we take our first shot. Dr Watson (Frederick Lloyd) is supposed to have arrived by train, and walks through the wicket gate to where the car from Baskerville Hall awaits him. Our second 'take' of this shot is disturbed by the stationmaster, who points excitedly down the line. A puff of smoke heralds the Lustleigh train, and our electricians scatter off the line.

When the train bustles off again the sound department chase it down the platform with the mike. This, I am told, is to record the puff-puff and chook-chook noises to be synchronised later on in the film.

Tuesday

The stationmaster puts up little fight when we descend upon him again this morning and ask whether he would clear the platform for us. We shoot Elizabeth Vaughan (Laura Lyons, the vamp of the film), talking to one of our porters over the station fence. Elizabeth has just extracted the latest village scandal from the porter when the weather plays the best practical joke on us yet.

'Blimey!' the cameraboy has it 'If it ain't a blinkin snowstorm!'

Vamp, lamps, camera and mike are rushed into the waiting-room. Here we wait till late in the afternoon, when we emerge into a changed world. Our sets, the railway platform and station-yard are so completely plastered with snow that they are quite unfilmable.

Wednesday

Seven men with seven mops set out in the early hours to restore what looks like the station of St Moritz to our Lustleigh; but they effect little change. Work, however, will not be greatly handicapped, as the major part of our shooting today is to take place in a railway coach.

And what a coach! The stationmaster assures me it is the one in which Charlie Chaplin travelled up to London. That may be just swank, but at all events the shades of Charlie certainly presided over our activities.

Sherlock Holmes and Dr Watson (Robert Rendel and Frederick Lloyd) sit at one end of a restaurant car. We are to shoot them, the cameras at the far end of the compartment, on the last stages of their journey from London to Dartmoor. Twenty-odd members of the staff seat themselves on the floor. Lights and cameras are held steady by electricians, while the assistant-director plays delightedly with a telephone through which he can talk to the engine driver.

Several difficult conditions have to be fulfiled. Sherlock and Dr Watson must end the last words of a long piece of dialogue, 'Ah, here we are at Baskerville,' as the train steams into the station and stops by the Baskerville signboard. The countryside must fly past the carriage windows at a pace which will photograph clearly. The mike, hidden in Sherlock's tobacco pouch on the table, must pick up the actors' voices distinctly above the din of the train.

'Ten miles an hour is OK for photography,' says the chief cameraman. 'Let's go,' says the assistant-director down the telephone, and the engine driver lets go. Up the line goes the studio on wheels, and Holmes and Watson start up the dialogue.

It seems we have crawled only a yard down the line when the fatal words, 'Ah, here we are at Baskerville,' are spoken. We aren't anywhere near it. Quite a mile away. The actors come to a full stop and stare sheepishly out of the window.

Up the line we go again. This time the engine-driver is to accelerate his pace to 35mph. Down we come. We arrive in 30sec at the Baskerville signboard, but with still a page of the script to go before we

come to 'Ah-here-we-are'.

A third journey at 15mph again leaves us up the line with the unhappy words. But a fourth trek at 25mph synchronises perfectly the signboard and the fatal 'Ah-here-we-are'. Then, without warning, exultantly piercing our sensitive microphone, ring the loudest wedding bells I have ever heard. A maddened recording expert jumps out as the train draws up. The joy-bells have ruined a good take, and we must wait till the happy pair are pealed away.

We repeat the scene till sundown to secure three perfect 'takes' of the arrival at the station.

Thursday

The snow refuses to melt, so the terrace exteriors must wait.

Friday

Snow, rain, mist and blizzard. Shooting out of the question. The production unit retire to the farthest corners of the hotel and devote their day to the new issue of *Film Weekly*

Saturday

We go to a cinema in Exeter to watch production rushes. These are the developed but unedited shots of last week's work on location. If we have slipped into any one of the 101 pitfalls of film making, flat lighting, faulty recording, fogged negative, then shots will have to be taken again.

Fortunately, the rushes are all passed OK, and we return to the hotel enthusiastically awaiting next week's work.

35mm, Sound, 74mins, Rank

THE HOUND OF THE BASKERVILLES (Britain 1968)

Adapted and dramatised from the Sherlock Holmes story by Arthur Conan Doyle. Includes GWR shots taken on the Dart Valley Railway.

BBC Television: Autumn 1968

16mm, Sound, Colour, 83mins

HOW THE OLD WOMAN CAUGHT THE OMNIBUS (Britain 1903)

A Cecil Hepworth Production. Directed by Percy Stow. A knock-about comedy using the Walton-on-Thames station bus (horse-drawn) which used to run between the railway and the old town.

16mm, Silent, 6mins, HA

HOW THE WEST WAS WON (USA 1962)

MGM/Cinerama. Railway sequence directed by George Marshall. With Spencer Tracy, Lee J Cobb, Henry Fonda, Karl Malden, Eli Wallach, Richard Widmark and Andy Devine. Block-busting Cinerama epic about aspects of early American pioneers. The best bit was about the railways, using the Sierra Railroad for some scenes and some giant set pieces built out on location. The best of the preserved 4-4-0s appear, with heavy studio embellishments of balloon spark arresters, massive cow catchers and enormous bells worked on ropes from the cab. MGM already owned their own 4-4-0, left over from countless Westerns and Musicals.

Cineramam Format, Sound, Colour, 162mins, MGM

HUDSONS OF THE NEW YORK CENTRAL (USA 1935-45)

Made by Gene Miller. Action shots of a wide range of Hudsons from 5233 to 5466, both in streamline and wartime economy form.

16/8mm, Silent, 13mins, Blackhawk

HULL NOW (Britain 1967)

Produced by British Transport Films. A concise survey of the seven miles of Hull's dock facilities which include the 'roll-on, roll-off' ferry services for freight, cars and passengers. Extensive new quays with a new arm for larger ships, new suction dredgers, impounding pumps, single-span sheds, mechanical handling of goods such as grain, fish, oil and chemicals are shown all aimed at speed of operation.

35/16mm, Sound, Colour, 15mins, BTF

HUMAN DESIRE (USA 1954)

Columbia Pictures. Directed by Fritz Lang. With Glenn Ford, Gloria Gra-

hame, Broderick Crawford and Edgar Buchanan. A jealous railway engineer, just back from the fighting in Korea, gets sucked into the bleak lives of an unlovely and loveless married couple; the outcome is murder, hatred and fear. 'Fritz Lang at his most detached and unsentimental – in other words, at his best. His examination of the characters is almost clinical, as cold and impersonal as the railway yards against which this chilling story is set' (Tony Bilbow). 'Drab and unattractive remake of La Bête Humaine (Leslie Halliwell). The railway yards and locomotives were provided by Southern Pacific.

35mm, Sound, 90mins, Columbia

HUNDRED YEARS OF RAILWAYS (Britain 1925)

Topical Budget. A newsreel item on the Darlington Centenary celebrations, featuring *Locomotion* and replica train.

35mm, Silent, 1min, NFA/HA

HUNDRED YEARS OF RAILWAYS (Britain 1938)

A television visit to the LMS Centenary Exhibition at Euston Station, including views of rolling stock dating back to 1838 and the latest 'Coronation Scot' class locomotives. 'For the first time television cameras were taken to a big London railway terminus'.

BBC Television 3-3.50pm Sunday 18 September 1938 and 11-11.50am Monday 19 September 1938.

A HUNDRED YEARS UNDERGROUND (Britain 1964)

Produced by British Transport Films. The story of the growth of London's Underground Railways, from the Metropolitan of 1863 to the beginning in 1963 of the Victoria Line. Some of the City's social developments are examined, its population expansion and the corresponding transport problems that led to the 'two-tiered' system. The tale is told by many eminent Londoners including the late Lord Mor-

rison of Lambeth, John Betjeman, Jessie Matthews and sculptor Henry Moore. Made in association with BBC TV.

35/16mm, Sound, 40mins, BTF

HUP AND DAHN THE RAWLWAY LINES (Britian 1939)

Pathetone. A song by Jack Warner. He has described how the song came about:- 'When I started with the BBC, I used to pick up ideas for Cockney songs, mainly in Covent Garden. One day, I heard a chap talking about an old railwayman who had just won the football pools and retired. He was a platelayer and, in the old style, used to walk the tracks every day, checking blocks and ballast and track alignment. In his working days, he used to "walk hup hand dahn the rawlway lines". I used this for a monologue which caught on and was eventually made into a Pathe film item for cinemas. I remember the last bit of the verse now:

So now the station's closed and I just live a life of ease,

But if ever for a change my soul it pines,

I climb hup in a signal box and listen to the whistles

While the trains run hup hand dahn the Rawlway lines'

35mm, Sound, 4mins, Weintraub/Pathe

I AM A LITTER BASKER (Britain 1959)

Produced by British Transport Films. A film designed to encourage the public to adopt tidy habits in the streets and on railway stations.

35/16mm, Sound, 7mins, BTF

I SEE ICE (Britain 1938)

Associated Talking Pictures. Directed by Anthony Kimmins. With George Formby and Kay Walsh. Slapstick comedy about a photographer's assistant. Includes scene on a journey from Manchester to Euston via Birmingham. The stock shown at one point is LNER; the compartments are LMS! When the communication cord is pulled a train hauled by LMS '5XP' 4-6-0 No 5553 *Canada* is shown.

These real scenes are cut in with quite substantial studio reconstructions of an LMS station (With authentic posters, etc) and much back-projection for a studio-built interior of an LMS carriage. Judging by the size of the corridors and gangways, the gauge must have been about 10ft!

35mm, Sound, 81mins, Weintraub/VID RLY ONLY/125

I WAS MONTY'S DOUBLE (BRITAIN 1958)

Film Traders. Directed by John Guillermin. With John Mills, Cecil Parker, Leslie Phillips and Marius Goring. An actor poses as Montgomery to confuse the Nazis during World War 2. Includes scenes at Liverpool Street station and the arrival of LNER 'B17' 4-6-0 No 61606 *Audley End*.

35mm, Sound, 100mins, Film Traders

THE IAN FAGG COLLECTION

Ian and Stella Fagg of Redhill have built up a substantial collection which they have filmed themselves on 16mm. The items include the 'North Wales Coast Express' from Bangor to Holyhead in 1989 with *Taw Valley* and 'Black Five' No 5407; the 'Brighton Belle'; the 'Cumbrian Coast Express'; the Ravenglass & Eskdale Railway and much else. Their films have been shown at Fairfield Hall in Croydon and various other centres in Surrey. A classic film often shown features the now abanded Woodside Line.

IMAGES OF STEAM (Britain 1986)

Transport Video Publishing. The North Yorks Moors Railway, including a footplate ride from Goathland to Grosmont.

VID, Sound, Colour, 30mins, TVP

IN A TRAIN TO EXETER (Britain 1938)

A play by Anthony Shaw adapted from a short story by J Geoffrey Stewart. Produced by Moultric R Kelsall.

BBC Television 14 and 19th July, 14 and 17th October, 1938.

IN DANGER'S PATH (USA 1915)

A Kalem production. An episode from the series *The Hazards of Helen*. Directed by J P McGowan. Script by E W Matlock. With Helen Holmes and Hoot Gibson. A typical example of this famous railroad series in which Helen captures a bunch of crooks.

16/8mm, Silent, 15mins, Blackhawk/BFI

IN OLD CHICAGO (USA 1937)

TCF. Directed by Henry King. With Tyrone Power, Alice Faye and Don Ameche. Events leading up to the great Chicago Fire of the 1880s. A railway scene was shot on the Sierra Railroad, using Baldwin 2-8-0 locomotive No 29790 of 1906 vintage, suitably modified to represent an earlier age.

35mm, Sound, 115mins, TCF

IN THE HEAT OF THE NIGHT (USA 1967)

Directed by Norman Jewison. With Sidney Poitier, Rod Steiger and Warren Oates. Racist tensions in a small Southern town where a murder is being investigated. Southern Pacific provided a train arrival scene at a halt twenty miles north of Los Angeles.

35mm, Sound, Colour, 109mins, United Artists

IN THE VAN (Britain 1932)

Pathetone Weekly. A newsreel item on a two-way radio telephone experiment between Imperial Airways *Heracles* G-AAXC in flight and the 10am *Flying Scotsman* en route to Edinburgh with radio transmitter G5FL in a luggage van, filmed from a De Havilland Puss Moth and on board the 40 passenger aircraft and the train.

35mm, Sound, 3mins, NFA

INCIDENT AT SUMMIT TUNNEL (Britain 1984)

Railfilms. Produced by Nick Dodson for Balvac Whitley Morgan. On Thursday 20 December 1984 a fully loaded petrol tanker train became derailed in the depths of the Summit Tunnel between Littleborough and Todmorden. The fire that followed lasted for two days with spectacular effects when 186,000 gallons of petrol went up, destroying 10 wagons and sending flames 250ft above the ventilation shafts. The video includes material shot by the West Yorkshire Fire Service as well as TV newsreels.

VID, Sound, Colour, 21mins, RFV

INDISCRETION OF AN AMERICAN WIFE (Italy-USA 1954)

David Selznick. Directed by Vittorio de Sica. With Jennifer Jones, Montgomery Clift and Gino Cervi. A sort of Italian remake of *Brief Encounter* staged mainly in the Stazione Termini in Rome, with electric traction much in evidence.

35mm, Sound, 75mins, Selznick International

THE INDUS EXPRESS (Britain 1988)

Railfilms. Produced, directed and photographed by Nick Dodson. The last working steam survivors on Pakistan Railways, including classes SGS, CWD, SGC, HGS, ZB, GS, SP, YD, SPS and YE. Mainly British built railway, with shed scenes, locomotive profiles, dramatic scenery and lineside shots. The SCG class 0-6-0s were based on Great Central Robinson engines. The classics were SPS mainline 4-4-0s. The video goes as far as the Afghan North West to witness the very last steam runs.

VID, Sound, Colour, 60mins, RFV

INDUSTRIAL LOCOMOTIVES (Britain 1927-60)

An assembly of scenes including a Fireless Locomotive in action at Boots (Beeston, Nottingham), engines in Croydon Gasworks, steam shovels and saddle tanks at Corby and a collection of single shots from around the country in the 1930s.

16mm, Silent, 9mins, HA

INDUSTRIAL STEAM (Britain 1991)

Railfilms. Film by Roger Siviter of Mountain Ash, South Wales; Waterside System in Ayrshire; steam in colleries, quarries and factories.

VID, Sound, Colour, 40mins, RFV

INHERITANCE (Britain 1972)

Granada Television. Part of this mammoth serial included a mocked-up train crash in 1846, using a disused stretch of line between Oldham and Ashton, two life-sized coaches of the period built in Granada's workshops in Manchester and full-scale photographic blow-ups of the authentic 1846-vintage Furness locomotive from the National Railway Museum collection.

VID, Sound, Colour, 42mins (one Episode), Granada Television

INLAND VOYAGING (Canada 1938)

Canadian Pacific Railway. Includes railway scenes at Toronto, Port McNicoll and Kenora.

16mm, Silent, 16mins, CPR

INSIDE STORY: RAILWAY (Britain 1991)

Partner TV production. Produced and directed by Charles Stewart and Malcolm Hirst. One of the most penetrating attempts to analyse the recent railway situation by looking closely at the electrified London-Leeds service during the bad weather early in 1991. The withdrawal of the Class 225, the use of HSTs and diesels of Classes 47 and 50 are featured as the railwaymen on the ground struggle to keep the service running. The issue of privatisation is dealt with but the main story is of how 'battered by the great British winter of 1991, both railwaymen and the great British public suffer together from the shortsightedness and poor planning of someone up there'.

VID, Sound, Colour, 28mins, Partner

INSPECTOR MORSE (Britain 1989-93)

Detective thriller series in which Oxford station often appears as Morse intercepts a suspect. With Kevin Whately and John Thaw. One scene included the villain travelling in the last coach from London and emerging in character and costume just as the train pulled into Oxford.

TV, Sound, Colour, 72mins per episode, Thames

INTERIOR NEW YORK SUBWAY (USA 1905)

American Mutascope and Biograph Company. Made for the Hale's Tours system but also part of a Biograph comedy called Reuben in the Subway. Filmed between 14th Street and 42nd Street on the Interborough Subway.

35mm, 5mins, Museum of Modern Art, New York

INLAND VOYAGING (Canada 1938)

THE INTERRUPTED JOURNEY (Britain 1949)

Valiant Film Production. Produced by Anthony Havelock Allan. Directed by Daniel Birt. With Valerie Hobson and Richard Todd. A journalist runs away with another man's wife. On a train he pulls the communication cord and causes a crash. He awakes to find it is all a dream. Mainly railway stock shots.

35mm, Sound, 80mins, Weintraub

INTOLERANCE (USA 1916)

Produced and directed by D W Griffith. Classic silent film which includes a race between a motor car and a train to deliver a letter that will save a man from being unjustly hanged.

35/16mm/VID, Silent, 115mins, NFA/HA (Railway scene only)

THE INTRUDER (Britain 1953)

British Lion. Produced by Ivan Foxwell. Directed by Guy Hamilton. With Jack Hawkins, Michael Medwin and Hugh Williams. Life in post-war Britain as seen through the eyes of an ex-Army officer and an old Army comrade-turned-burglar. Includes railway scenes on GWR Blatchford viaduct near Plymouth with double-headed steam locomotives.

35mm/VID, Sound, 84mins, Weintraub/VID 125 (rly)

INVINCIBLE RETIRES (Britain 1967)

Newsreel record of the end of the steam-operated railway from the Southern Railway station at Farnborough, through the streets of the town, to the Royal Aircraft Establishment. Locomotive Invincible was rescued and brought to the Isle of Wight, where it now runs on the Haven Street preserved railway.

16mm, Sound, 4mins, HA

THE IPCRESS FILE (Britain 1965)

Produced by Harry Saltzman. Directed by Sidney J Furie. With Michael Caine, Nigel Green and

Gordon Jackson. An intelligence man traces a missing scientist. The scientist disappears from a train leaving Marylebone station, steam-hauled by an unidentified locomotive.

35mm, Sound, Colour, 109mins, Rank

🚂

IRISH NARROW GAUGE

The very extensive 3ft gauge system in Ireland went largely ignored by film makers until Pat Whitehouse produced his now classic series of 16mm films of virtually the whole scene, starting with a fine study of the Tralee and Dingle. Apart from John Ford's feature film using the West Clare (The Rising of the Moon 1957), and the early films of the Listowel and Ballybunion, the area was largely ignored for film purposes until it was too late.

🚂 🚂 🚂 🚂 🚂

IRISH NARROW GAUGE (Britain 1958)

Made by P B Whitehouse and John Adams. Film on the County Donegal Railway, of a steam-hauled August Bank Holiday Special, and of steam trains on the Cavan & Leitrim Railway. The Ballycastle Railway, the West Clare and the Londonderry & Lough Swilly Railway.

16mm/VID, Silent, 8mins, CV/NRM/Stirling

🚂 🚂 🚂 🚂 🚂

IRISH RAILWAYS (Britain 1988)

Ulster Television. Produced and directed by Andrew Crockhart. A charming study of preserved Ulster Steam Railways as well as glimpses of the modern scene. It also deals with the fundamental appeal of steam.

16mm, Sound, Colour, 28mins, Ulster TV

🚂 🚂 🚂 🚂 🚂

THE IRON HORSE (USA 1924)

Fox film. Directed by John Ford. Photography by George Schneidermann. Script by Charles Kenyon and John Russell, based on the history of the first American transcontinental railroad. With George

O'Brien, Madge Bellamy, Cyril Chadwick and Fred Kohler.

John Ford, director of The Informer, Stagecoach, How Green Was My Valley and The Grapes of Wrath, was on the threshold of his career in 1924. Although he had been in the industry for 10 years, Ford had so far passed virtually unnoticed. His 48 films up to the end of 1923 were mainly well-made, but conventional Westerns or thrillers, originally made for Universal, the last nine for Fox.

The company was pleased with his work and when he began to make The Iron Horse, it was just another routine assignment which happened to be about the building of a railway. But things began to happen, as John Ford recalls: 'John Russell wrote the original Iron Horse and it was really just a simple little story. We went up to Nevada to do it, and when we got there, it was 20 below zero. All the actors and extras arrived wearing summer clothes; it was great fun – all these boys got up in white knickers – we had a hell of a time. I wish I had time to write the story of the making of The Iron Horse, because more strange things happened. We put the women in circus cars, and the men had to make their own little homes out of the set. (Later, I remember, we were out in the middle of the desert in Mexico and this little guy named Solly came up to George Schneidermann, the photographer, a wonderful guy to work with, and he says "Where's the hotel?" And George says "Hotel? You're standing on it".) But the point is we had to spend more and more money and eventually this simple little story came out as a so-called "epic" the biggest picture Fox had ever made. Of course, if they had known what was going to happen, they never would've let us make it.'

Despite the problems, the film was successful. The distinguished critic and film-maker Paul Rotha wrote: 'The works of John Ford are uneven, but his was the type of film that America can make well if she sets her mind to it. It ranked on the same level with the epic quality of The Covered Wagon and combined the best elements of the Western school with the more sophisticated direction of the Hollywood feature film. The Iron Horse was vast in its

conception, and John Ford, despite the hindrances of a naive love story interest, handled it with a great degree of talent. It was not popular (in England) where audiences have no enthusiasms for railways being thrown across trackless wastes, but as a film, it was fit to rank with any in the class of recorded fact. I remember with feeling ... the far streching landscape across which the track was to run'. (Paul Rotha, The Film Till Now, 1930)

Although the fictional story today looks even sillier than Rotha suggests, the amount of research and trouble to reproduce the true story of the Transcontinental line across America is still impressive. The two-hour film starts with a factual account of the political problems surrounding the passing of the necessary legislation.

On 1 July 1862, the US Congress passed the Pacific Railroad Act, authorising the establishment of the Union Pacific RR Company, granting a right of way 200 feet wide through public land on each side of the roadbed and 100 feet wide on either side of the roadbed through private property. The act also granted 10 alternate sections per mile of public domain on both sides of the railway. Two years later, a second Railway Act doubled the land grants and gave the United States a second rather than a first mortgage on potential loans of £50m. President Lincoln (played in the film by Charles E Bull), on 19 October 1864, established the eastern starting point of Omaha for the central route from Nebraska through to San Francisco.

One interesting feature of the Railroad Act of 1862 was a proviso that President Lincoln established the gauge of the road. Since 5ft gauge tracks already existed in California, Mr Lincoln decided on that gauge. Midwestern rail interests whose lines were largely 4ft 8.5in immediately initiated heated lobbying and Congress finally passed an act declaring that all of the rails through to the Pacific Ocean from the Missouri River over public domain lands should be 4ft 8.5in. This Congressional ruling effectively established what has been today's standard gauge – a gauge all major American railroads were finally forced to adopt a decade or

Left:
**A scene from 'Inheritance' (1972).
A careful study of the photograph
reveals that the locomotive on the
embankment is a two-dimensional
cut-out!** *Granada Television*

Below left:
**All the ingredients of a classic
Western, from John Ford's 'The
Iron Horse'.**

Below:
**An interested crowd watches the
shooting of a scene from 'A
Journey for Jeremy' at Glasgow
Central Station.**

Right::
**Moments before the crash, from
the 'Juggernaut'.**
National Film Theatre

Below right:
**The scene from 'Kate Plus Ten' in
which No 4364 smashes through
the mock-up level crossing gates
at Freshford Station.**

more before the turn of the century.

The Union Pacific, chartered in 1862, began construction in 1864. The Central Pacific, also authorized to build eastward from the coast to meet the UP, had already been incorporated in 1861. Construction on the Central Pacific at Sacramento began in 1863.

Both railroads were granted subsidies of $16,000 a mile in a territory which governmental surveys deemed level, $48,000 a mile for construction through the mountains, and $32,000 for track laid between mountain ranges. The two companies began a dramatic construction race to see which could pile up the greatest amount of subsidies.

Also in 1863, Cyrus K Holliday received a land grant from Congress for three million acres in alternate sections of Kansas and the 35th parallel route. This marked the beginning of the Atchison, Topeka & Santa Fe Railroad. At this time stage coaches still rolled out of Independence, Missouri, to Santa Fe, New Mexico, at a price tag of $250 for a one-way trip. A snag existed for Holliday and his fellow promoters, for not only did the Kansas State Legislature have to pass on the Federal Act in order to accept the land, but it in turn meted out the 20-mile alternate sections only as the line was completed 'in good substantial and workmanlike manner as a first-class railroad'.

Santa Fe's land grant and that of other railroads contained a generous-appearing 'in-lieu clause', which gave the contracting railroad company the right to choose substitute plots of land of equal size to replace those which might already be owned privately in the territory of their alloted 20-mile sections. However, the catch in the 'in-lieu clause' was that the substitution had to be made within 20 miles of the original tract grant, which negated its value for Holliday and his company since nearly all the land in the eastern part of Holliday's grant near Topeka was already held privately.

Holliday's other major stumbling block was a second little Federal Congressional requirement that his railroad must reach the Colorado state line from its starting point at Topeka by 3 March 1873, or both land grant and subsidies would be cancelled.

If any railroad enthusiast feels that the age of railway experimentation was completed by 1860 let him reconsider, for in 1864, after Holliday had been knocking himself out with the idea of a Santa Fe trail railway for a decade, he was replaced as president of the chartered but still-not-under-construction road by S C Pomeroy, a senator from Kansas. This was probably a move of political expediency, for Holliday and Pomeroy remained friendly as Holliday roamed around the country trying to raise funds, though according to records held no official position in the company again until 1868. Official reports and engineers' correspondence seemingly continued to be directed to Holliday and apparently he was still the prospective road's guiding genius. But it was Pomeroy who came up with the cash when the 3 March 1873 deadline moved closer with still no construction work started.

Pomeroy fostered a measure in the Senate in 1866 which seemed to be a grasping-at-straws type of device that would permit the Santa Fe to operate a steam 'railroad' without rails. In order to obtain approval of this, Pomeroy and the Santa Fe agreed to a reduction of the original land grant of ten sections per mile to three sections per mile. At this time Santa Fe promotors were becoming panicky and needed a stalling device. The idea was that the Atchison Topeka & Santa Fe would be a 'railroad' but would omit at least at that time the laying of ties and rails and (shades of the 18th century) would run steam-propelled locomotives with broad, flat-tired wheels capable of pulling 50 tons of freight and cars or a train of 200 passengers at an average of six miles an hour. It was as impractical as suggesting that man could ever fly without wings.

The first shovelful of earth on the Santa Fe wasn't turned until 30 October 1868, nine years after Holliday had made his original application for a charter and five years after the Congressional land grants. The route of the line when it was first started was a curious one. Atchison stockholders were distressed since the line originally had been promised to start at Atchison. They were downright irate when, after it started at Topeka, it headed

almost due south out of Topeka, rather than north towards Atchison. Coal deposits had been located at Carbondale to the south and Holliday figured he could pick up freight by passing through that town and ignored the Atchison objectors. By the end of March 1869, a bridge had been thrown across the Kaw River and an old 4-4-0 yard dog built by the Niles Machine Works, Cincinnati, Ohio for the Ohio & Mississippi Road, was bought and cut down from a 6-foot gauge to 4ft 8.5 in. She was hauled in on Kansas and Pacific track and the first train movement over the Santa Fe was a test run by this former O&M Locomotive over the 300-foot long double Howe truss bridge over the Kaw.

In 1950 the Atchison, Topeka & Santa Fe Railroad Company owned 1,199 steam locomotives, 444 diesels, 1,685 passenger train cars and 80,823 freight train cars as compared to its puny start in the latter part of 1869 when its stock consisted of one second-hand locomotive, a battered day coach bought from the Indianapolis & Cincinnati Railroad, 12 freight cars capable of carrying a total of 120 tons of freight and one handcar. At that time eastern financiers scoffed at the Santa Fe and called it a 'railroad that starts from nowhere and is going nowhere', but 90 years later its rolling stock had covered nearly 55,000,000 train miles, operating over 13,095 miles of track. This was a far cry from 26 April 1869, when the little CK Holliday pulling 13 Santa Fe cars, plus one borrowed from the Kansas & Pacific to offset an opening day jinx, carried its first official train, the Wakarusa Picnic Special, seven miles out of town and back. But by 1870 the Santa Fe dream bubble no longer was in danger of bursting. It had solidified to a reality of a rail line eventually destined to stretch out spider-like to Galveston in the south, Chicago in the northeast, Denver to the north and San Francisco to the west.

In the east, the railroads had moved beyond the building stages. Manipulations for control were beginning. By 1866 the Erie, which seemed destined to be kicked around as a stock football, was under control of manipulator Daniel Drew, who was associated with both Jay Gould and Jubilee Jim Fiske, in operations which were to lead eventually to bankruptcy of the Erie in 1875. Cornelius Vanderbilt now had the New York Central & Hudson River Railroad organisations well in hand. He had already imposed a ruling that once gaily painted locomotives, with ornate, gleaming brasswork, were to be given a dull black monotone finish in the interests of economy, a move that was gradually adopted by other railroads and a depressingly dull colour scheme largely adhered to for 75 years.

Ben Holliday, a swashbuckling westener who had operated one of the greatest pre-railroad transportation companies in the west, the Overland Stage Line, a pony express route, as well as Pacific steamship ventures, at one time had owned 75,000 oxen, 2,700 horses and mules, 100 stage coaches, as well as 500 quarter horses for use on his pony express routes. Holliday saw the trend toward rails. He gave leadership and financing to what was orginally organized in 1863 as the California & Oregon Railroad Company, established to link Sacremento with Portland, a distance which at the time required seven days of stage travel to complete. Almost immediately after organizing, internal friction caused the Oregon supporters of the line to split into two factions, both of which took the name of Oregon Central Railroad Company and started competitive building on the east and west banks of the Willamette River. The two Oregon Central groups were known as the east siders and the west siders. Holliday joined the east side faction but his group's first rail was not laid until 26 October 1869, and to obtain Federal aid authorized by Congress in 1866, 20 miles of the road had to be in operation by Christmas day of 1869.

Holliday dropped all other activies and personally took over direction of construction, including a 380ft bridge across the Clackamas River south of Portland, which he had nearly completed when a flash flood severly damaged it. The race against time was intensified. Holliday sent his construction engine across the river by barge and while the bridge was being rebuilt, he

pushed his line on. One hour short of midnight, 24 December, in another near photo finish, the east side railroad won its purse and on Christmas Day, the OCRR's J B Stephens commenced its regular operation.

Holliday was a driver of men but also less fortunately he proved to be a fast man with a buck. He and his associates squandered money so wantonly that the line, which eventually was to become a part of the Southern Pacific, went through financial uproar half a dozen times before sound reorganisation and direction permitted the line ultimately to reach final completion in 1887.

The era after the turn of the half century railroad-wise was one of over-expansion, poor management and not infrequently out-and-out dishonesty. Typical victims were the stockholders of the LaCrosse & Milwaukee Railroad, milked of assets by New Yorker Russell Sage. Sage somehow managed to get a $2 million third mortgage on the road for less than $300,000 and then, by what the United States Supreme Court termed a 'fraudulent arrangement', managed to have his third mortgage given precedence over first and second mortgages in foreclosing proceedings. The stench that accompanied this trick turned up the fact that Sage, through the LM Railroad's president, had managed to do some first rate buying of political power. In fact, $842,000 worth of LaCrosse & Milwaukee bonds were handed out where bought influence could cover up the machinations to Sage and his stooges' best interests. Governor Bashford got $50,000 worth, and later skipped Wisconsin for residence among the less critical citizenry around Tucson in the Arizona territory. Bashford was a lot smarter than the other bribees. He not only took the 50,000 bonds but since he had to certify that the first 20 miles constructed by the company was in satisfactory, operational condition in order for the company to obtain land grants and Federal subsidy, Bashford refused to do so until the company bought back $15,000 worth of bonds for cash at par value.

When Sage played around with graft, at least he was no fool, for he

saw that $335,000 worth of the bonds were also planted among state assemblymen, $175,000 worth were pushed out surreptitiously to state senators, and $16,000 in bonds went to clerks who were in position to observe any irregularities. Also to protect himself against future repercussions from the press, *Milwaukee Sentinel's* editor, Rufus King, was reportedly slipped $10,000 worth with no cash outlay and Morry Schoeffler, editor of the *Wisconsin Banner* and S Carpenter, editor of the *Wisconsin Patriot*, also got $5,000 apiece. Sage's fraud was to plague the predecessor lines of the Milwaukee Road for many years. Though rate cutting, mergers, double dealings, sloppy management and ruthlessness keynoted much of the rail activity in the east at the time, the western picture was different. Unfriendly Indians still rode the ranges. The mining fever brought with it an era of gang terrorism. Vigilantes were formed and a period of swift border justice existed.

One group of Cheyenne Indians who witnessed their first steam locomotive tried to frighten the steaming beast into submission and retreat. These foolhardy red-skins naively charged the locomotive with their ponies. 20 ponies were killed along with a goodly percentage of their riders. The Cheyenne's animosity towards the Union Pacific was indelibly stamped in the tribesmen's minds as long as the memory of a blood splashed pilot lasted. (This incident is reproduced in the film in modified form).

Section hands and surveyors were killed by bow and arrow snipers. In 1867 the Cheyennes (the Cheyenne chief is played in the film by Chief Big Tree, a descendant of the old tribal chiefs) kidnapped a complete freight train, burned it and in retaliation, perhaps for the earlier head-on collision of ponies versus locomotive, killed the engineer and fireman. The first two graves at Cheyenne, Wyoming were those of Union Pacific section hands killed by Indians.

General Dodge (played in the film by W Rogers) of the Union Pacific, stated 'Every mile of the route had to be laid within the protective range of the musket.' But Indians were not Dodge's only problem.

Whiskey peddlers, gamblers, prostitutes, and thugs caused continuing trouble with Dodge's Irish track layers.

The Union Pacific very shortly established its own police force under the head of General Jack Casement, Dodge's Police Commissioner, who is credited with the origin of the phrase, 'The bad men died with their boots on'. And since the Union Pacific's police force was also law, court and when need be, executioner as well, Casement's statement was probably true. Yet despite these problems, the Union Pacific track layers were trained to drive in 10 spikes per rail, four rails a minute and the line moved steadily forward with 400 rails being laid to the mile. (All accurately reproduced in the film and set to a rythmic song, reflecting the driving of the spikes at the rate of 40 per minute).

The rowdyism, lawlessness and Indian problems were minor by contrast to the graft, bribery and shady financial manoeuvring of the Credit Mobilier which finally came to light as a national scandal in September 1872. Its grandiose graft charges involved US Vice-President Schuyler Colfax, Vice-Presidential nominee Henry Wilson, Speaker of the House Blaine, representatives in Congress by the half dozen, senators and even President-to-be James A Garfield (whose more recent biographers have vindicated him of charges).

The scandal that forced the Union Pacific into receivership and eventual reorganisation quite simply consisted of corrupt practices of the Credit Mobilier, a Union Pacific construction company whose directors were also directors of the Union Pacific. It emerged that for contractual work which cost Credit Mobilier approximately $43m the contractors were paid $94m. Politicians involved, of course, had been given stock bribes in the company in order to approve a highly illegitimate business conducted under government subsidy.

The northern route across the United States from Lake Superior to Portland Oregon, was financed by Jay Cooke and chartered in 1864. That line went into bankruptcy in 1873 and was not to be completed until 1883. Though the Northern

Pacific Railroad's early failure and the collapse of the Jay Cooke and Company banking house precipitated the 1873 financial panic, to the lasting credit of Cooke is the fact that he eventually repaid his creditors. No stigma of purposeful fraud was attached to the line he financed.

In the period through to 1870 no major railroad overcame such tremendous obstacles as those that confronted the Central Pacific Railroad company, which in 1863 started to move its lines east from Sacramento, California. By 10 May 1869, it had extended 690 miles over the Sierra Nevada mountains and across Nevada to Promontory, Utah. Four visionary west coasters had the courage and the determination to make this important section of the trans-continental railway possible. They were Collis P Huntington (played in the film by Charles Newton) and Mark Hopkins (combined and partly translated to the character of Davy Brandon played by George O'Brien), partners in a hardware emporium, Charles Croker, (played in the film by Delbert Mann) a dry goods store proprietor and later state Governor, Leland Stanford, a grocery salesman. The youngest of the group was Stanford, a man of 36. Hopkins, the oldest, was 47. None of the four had ever been connected with any large construction job.

Theodore Judah had, since 1861, been pushing the idea for a transcontinental road and was partially responsible for the final passage of the Pacific Railroad Bill. Yet Judah, Central Pacific's Chief Engineer, on the very threshold of what doubtless would have been an outstandingly brilliant career, contracted malaria and died within a week after the first CP rail was laid in Sacramento on 26 October 1863, and eight days before the *Governor Stanford* went into service over rails that would eventually join with the east.

The first section, 31 miles long from Sacramento to Newcastle, was opened to regular traffic on 10 June 1864. From that point on, building of the Central Pacific was a rugged deal. Dynamite by this time had been produced but was not in general use so the way through and over the granite walls of the Sierra

was made with pick and shovel, one-horse dump carts, hand-driven blasting holes and dangerous-to-handle black powder charges (well reproduced in the film). It was strictly a job of hand carving and the only power tools were locomotives that carted supplies to the rail head. But the locomotives, most of the building materials and the cars that hauled the materials, had been shipped 15,000 miles around Cape Horn from the East, a sea voyage of eight to 10 months.

White labour was scarce in California in those days for there were too many easier ways for white men to make a living. So Chinese labourers were imported. (Los Angeles Chinese extras are prominent in the film; the old chinaman is played by Edward Piel.) In some places such was the difficulty of the terrain that the Chinese workers were swung by ropes suspended in buckets down the sides of sheer cliff faces. Their job was to cut foot paths in the cliff's face so that other workers could have standing room to sledge the holes for the black powder charges to blast away the trail for locomotives.

Financial troubles plagued the Central Pacific just as it had most other railroads. The huge private fortunes of the big four leadership were as nothing compared to the tremendous expense involved in cutting a route through the rugged Sierra Nevada. So severe was the winter weather that tunnelling work on the 16,095ft Summit tunnel and others was saved for this period of the year; grading and track labour was done during the milder seasons.

It didn't take the constructors long to realize that even though the roadbed could be cut through in the milder summer months, something had to be done about the rugged winter snowfalls. Experimental snowsheds were built in the summer of 1867 which that winter proved quite satisfactory. By 1869, 40 miles of snowsheds gave the most rugged sections of the mountain run almost continuous solid covering. One engineer was later to remark, 'I've squeezed throttle on plenty of railroads from coast to coast but this is the first time I've done my railroading in a barn'. The advent of powerful rotary snowploughs gradually did away with the necessity for the snowsheds, so that today less than eight miles of covered track remains.

In 1868, the Sierra Nevada section, including 15 tunnels, had been completed and the road had burst out into the more open plain area of Nevada. (Nevada was the location selected by John Ford for the film; it was 20 degrees below zero for much of the shooting). On 19 June 1868, the railroad's engineers staked out what was to become Reno, Nevada. From there on construction superintendent Strobridge's 14,000 Chinese workers, 2,000 whites, 6,000 horses and half that number of two- and four-wheeled carts really got rolling. In one day, on 28 April 1869, with a $10,000 bet riding on the outcome placed by Tom Durant of the Union Pacific and Charles Crocker of the Central Pacific, Crocker's men laid 10 miles and 56ft of track in less than 12 hours, to shatter the Union Pacific's six miles in 12 hours record and lighten Durant's pocketbook by $10,000. (An incident reproduced in the film).

Since no definite meeting place had been established, in the spring of 1869 the two rival companies roadbed makers passed one another and the grading crews continued on with their work a few yards apart from parallel rail footing. The government finally stepped in and established the official meeting point as Promontory, Utah. On 10 May 1869, the ceremonies for the completion of the colossal construction job were conducted.

Even on the eve of joining of the rails, roughhewn drama was still to play a part. A Union Pacific guest train, which left Omaha, Nebraska, on the Thursday before the final rail linking ceremony was held up on the Wyoming-Utah border by a group of disgruntled Union Pacific workmen who demanded back pay and held the crew and passengers as hostage. (Non-payment of wages is a regular theme in the film.) Finally after two days their demands were met and the train was permitted to continue on its way to the ceremony.

While the ceremony has frequently been referred to as the Last Spike or the Golden Spike ceremony, actually the estimated

12,000-15,000 spectators who gathered at Promontory when the Union Pacific's coal burner No 119 and the Central Pacific's wood burner *Jupiter* (these actual locomotives were used in the film), puffed to a halt where the final rail and tie were to be placed, saw two gold spikes hammered into position. The last tie into which the spikes were driven was made of laurel and bore a silver plaque reading, 'The last tie laid on the completion of the Pacific Railroad, May 1869.' The tie was a gift of Wes Evens, who had sold the Central Pacific ties for its road. The two golden spikes were made of $20 gold pieces, one presented by the State of California and the other a gift of San Franciso financier, David Hewes. Arizona also had given a spike for the occasion made of gold, silver and iron. The Pacific Union Express company supplied the 3.5lb silver maul. Thomas Durant of the Union Pacific and Leland Stanford of the Central Pacific handled the silver sledge. And as if to prove that railroad financing and construction work are totally different trades, both VIP's muffed their first swings and dented the fine silver maul on the rail. At 12.45pm the lines were joined and a telegrapher tapped out the message, 'Done' – four letters in Morse code that signalled to the world that two bands of steel now joined America from coast to coast.

John Ford's film reproduces, in condensed form, some of the financial machinations which coloured the story so sharply as well as bringing in portrayals of a remarkably large group of the people concerned. Naturally, the outdoor locations of the construction of the difficult sections in Nevada, the race to finish and the Indian attacks were the raw material for detailed film sequences; more surprising is the wonderful atmosphere of the temporary railroad towns which sprang up along the line as it advanced into the wilderness, with its mixture of Chinese, German, Irish, Polish, Scandinavian, English and native American workers. John Ford's typical understanding of the Indians is well illustrated, using authentic Cheyenne and Sioux descendants; references to the Pony Express and the problems of handling the locomotives and stock

in such wild conditions are carefully built into the main theme. Looked at in retrospect, *The Iron Horse* is conducted at a level of historical reconstruction not often practical at this distance from events; with the phoney love story removed it would take on the flavour of an old print reproducing stories of bygone days of the American railroads.

This account has been extensive because it relates to a number of films in this book such as *Union Pacific*; it also provides an understanding of the complexity of the railroads that eventually served Los Angeles, Hollywood and, indirectly, the movie industry.

35/16mm, Silent, 119mins, Fox/BFI/VID

IRON HORSE (India 1951)

Indian News and Information Service. Record of first locomotive built entirely in India.

16mm, Sound, 10mins, Indian News and Information Service

THE IRON HORSE (American Television Series)

Produced by Fred Freidberger. With Dale Robertson, Gary Collins and Bob Brandon. A long television series including many railway scenes using preserved American locomotives and stock, mainly from stock shots.

Shown on BBC Television: 1967-69 HA (typical one episode)

THE IRON MULE (USA 1925)

A Tuxedo comedy, distributed by Educational Film Exchange. With Al St John. Directed by Grover Jones.

At one stage in the development of silent one-reel comedy, it was the fashion to produce satires on contemporary feature films. *The Iron Mule* is a parody of John Ford's *The Iron Horse* and included gag attacks by Indians, gamblers on the trail and other pioneer themes. The railway featured is the 1830 'Likskillet & Sassafras' line; the train is the *Twenty Cent Limited*.

The principal prop in this fast-moving silent comedy, directed in the Mack Sennett style and featuring Al St John, one of the first men to work with Charlie Chaplin and himself a Sennett pupil, is a substantially full scale model of the famous De Witt Clinton 0-2-2 locomotive and train. The steeply inclined cylinders high up on the side of the boiler gave the familiar rocking motion; the enormous smoke-stack and a totally exposed footplate present a lively outline in long shot. The large diameter driving wheels are used for a kind of super-roulette, using numbered spokes and short blasts of steam, with the wheels slipping furiously. The smoke-stack is detached on entering a tunnel and carried overground by the driver whilst the fireman takes the train through. Mixed with old jokes – like a cow on the line – is a fantastic scene in which locomotive and train are lashed to large logs and the entire affair, still steaming, sets off down a river, not done with tricks or models but actually staged for the picture. Standard American gauge provides the track, probably on a branch in the immediate vicinity of Los Angeles.

16mm, Silent, 16mins, HA

IRONSTONE LINES OF THE EAST MIDLANDS (Britain 1989)

Railscene. Produced by Jeremy English. Written by David Wilcock and Eric Tonks. Commentary by Peter Woods. Film by Ivo Peters. A very rare example of the work of Ivo Peters on a most unusual theme but beautifully put together.

VID, Sound, Colour, 55mins, RSV

ISLE OF MAN RAILWAY (Britain 1956)

Made by Pat Whitehouse and John Adams. The Isle of Man narrow-gauge railway.

16mm, Silent, Colour, 6mins, WA/BFI

ISLE OF MAN RAILWAYS (Britain 1930-90)

Early film documentation has been secured by the work of Dr R Pre-

ston Hendry and R Powell Hendry, including films of the 1930s. Other material taken from various old publicity films about the Island give a good impression of the railway system. A record by Pat Whitehouse in 1956, various 8mm amateur films and the detailed Alan Willmott production 'Tracks Round the Island' mean that the Isle of Man has been well covered.

ISLE OF WIGHT ENGINES (Britain 1961)

Made by P B Whitehouse and John Adams. This film shows many of the 'O2' 0-4-4Ts at Ryde St John's shed. It also features a trip from Ryde Pier through Smallbrook Junction to Wroxhall, Shanklin and Ventnor.

Locomotives include LSWR 'O2' 0-4-4T No 16 *Ventnor*, No 25 *Godshill*, No 29 *Alverstone*, No 31 *Chale*, No 32 *Bonchurch* and No 36 *Carisbrooke*.

16/8/VID, Silent, Colour, 6mins, CV/NRM/VID

ISLE OF WIGHT RAILWAYS (Britain 1935–)

An excellent film exists of the complex system that operated on the Island back in the 1930s. There are numerous records made during the last years by Pat Whitehouse, Geoff Holyoake and various 8mm amateur films by enthusiasts. The end of steam at Newport, the rescue of some locomotives and stock in the nick of time by the present preservation society, the establishment of the centre at Haven Street and the early days of preserved railway operation also exist. In later days, a series of films have been made by Robert Ennis, including *O2 to Haven Street* and a complete one-hour history of the Isle of Wight Railways. Through the Island Film Archive, he has secured the preservation of much of the Island's history including its railways. He has also made films of the present electric train service from Ryde Pier to Shanklin.

ISLE OF WIGHT STEAM (Britain 1964-65)

Made by G S Holyoake. A survey of the 0-4-4Ts including No 14 *Fishbourne*, No 24 *Calbourne*, No 26 *Whitewell*, No 28 *Ashwell* and No 31 *Chale*.

16/9.5/8mm, Silent, Colour, 4mins, MFS

ISN'T LIFE WONDERFUL (Britain 1952)

Associated British. Directed by Harold French. With Donald Wolfit and Eileen Herlie. Story of the life of a well-to-do English family. Includes scenes on the now abandoned GWR Yelverton to Princetown branch line.

35mm, Sound, 83mins, Weintraub/125

ITALIAN EXPRESS (German 1927)

Volkswochenschau. A German newsreel item on a Pullman express service to Lugan.

35mm, Silent, 7secs, NFA

ITALO-TURKISH WAR (Italy 1911-12)

Pathe. A troop train leaving for Tripoli.

35mm, Silent, 30sec, NFA

IT ALWAYS RAINS ON SUNDAY (Britain 1947)

An Ealing Film. Directed by Robert Hamer. With Googie Withers, John McCallum and Jack Warner. Drama of an escaped convict who is sheltered by a married woman. Ends with a chase filmed at Temple Mills yard, Stratford; LNER 'J69' Nos 8607 and 8591 and an unidentified J39, are seen. 'Some most realistic and dramatic sequences in a shunting yard.' (Peter Hanford)

35mm, Sound, 92mins, Weintraub

ITALIAN RAILWAY SPECTACULAR (Britain 1986)

Salford Films. Rome, Naples, Milan, Turin and Venice, plus Sicily and Sardinia. Mainline, branch lines and preserved sections.

VID, Sound, Colour, 60mins, SFV

🚂 🚂 🚂 🚂 🚂

IT'S A SMALL WORLD (Britain 1974)

BBC Television West. Written and presented by Andy Price. The Pendon Museum with its detailed model of the Vale of White Horse Village, GWR model railway with a Dartmoor background on the Pendon Parva layout and the models of the Madder Valley Railway. A chance to see an unusual private museum/model project in action.

16mm, Sound, Colour, 11mins, BBC TV

🚂 🚂 🚂

THE IVO PETERS COLLECTION

One of the great 16mm film collections. His work was usually associated with the Somerset & Dorset Joint Railway, especially in the Bath-Evercreech Junction area. But his work went much wider than that and covered a vast number of steam scenes in the late 1950s and the whole of the 1960s. Largely unseen for many years, the Ivo Peters collection is now widely known through television and video. The most notable assembly is that put out by Railscene which includes the following Ivo Peters items:

Somerset and Dorset (Volumes 1 and 2)

Westmoreland 1965/67 and Scotland

North Wales Narrow Gauge Steam

Steam in 1960

Ironside Lines

Steam 1961

Steam 1962

Narrow Gauge Scene in the early 1960s

Private Railways 1961 to 1963

🚂 🚂 🚂 🚂 🚂

IVOR THE ENGINE (Britain, various dates)

Smallfilms. Story by Oliver Postgate. Pictures by Peter Firmin. A series of 18 short animated films for children, featuring an engine of the M&LTC Ltd Welsh railway; Welsh backgrounds include the station 'Llanigg' as well as coal mines and Welsh dragons.

VID, Sound, Colour, 4mins per item, Smallfilms

🚂 🚂 🚂 🚂 🚂

JAVA: TROPICAL MOUNTAIN ISLAND (USA 1956)

A travelogue which includes scenes of steam-hauled railways and electric trams.

16mm, Sound, 18mins, HA

🚂

JEEVES AND WOOSTER

A series of television programmes (and sherry commercials) based on the Twenties man-about-town and his butler; stories very much dependent on the recreation of the atmosphere of the Jazz Age. Preserved railway lines have been used on four occasions in the course of the ITV programmes, first with the Severn Valley and then with the Bluebell; one programme used the Keighley & Worth Valley. For their visits to America, stock shots of American trains of the Twenties were cut in, sometimes with dubious accuracy.

🚂 🚂 🚂 🚂 🚂

JERSEY RAILWAYS (Britain 1935)

A single shot of the 3ft 6in narrow gauge line which closed in 1936, probably taken from an amateur holiday film at St Helier.

16mm, Silent, 1min, HA

🚂 🚂 🚂 🚂 🚂

JESSE JAMES (USA 1938)

TCF. Produced by Nunnally Johnson. Directed by Henry King. With Tyrone Power, Henry Fonda, Nancy Kelly, Jane Darwell and Randolph Scott. Two brothers take up train robbing when unscrupulous railroad men harass and cheat their family. A superb collection of old 4-4-0s, some actually owned by 20th Century Fox, are used in various settings representing the 'St Louis Midland Railroad', plus old 'No 8' on loan from Universal. It is nice to see a real in-out US-type regulator, a very real-looking Wells Fargo office and waggon and some great scenes on a branch of the Southern Pacific. A theme of the film is anti-lawyers, with the classic line: 'If we are ever to have law and order in the West, first we have to shoot all the lawyers!'.

35mm, Sound, Colour, 106mins, TCF

🚂 🚂

JOE BROWN AT CLAPHAM (Britain 1965)

British Transport Films. Produced by Edgar Anstey, Direct by Norman Prouting. 'The Railway Song' by Harry Dawson. With Joe Brown and the Bruvvers. A lighthearted history of railways which uses old prints, rare pieces of film as well as 1965 material to tell the story from Stephenson's *Rocket* to the new diesel and electric expresses. Pop singer Joe Brown, an ex-railwayman himself, comperes the film from the Railway Museum at Clapham as it then was. The story takes in the Stockton & Darlington Railway of 1825, the Liverpool & Manchester of 1829-30, Brunel and the GWR, the London to Birmingham in 1838, the 1851 Crystal Palace Exhibition and the GWR conversion from broad to standard gauge in 1892. Locomotives on display in the Museum include LNER Gresley 'A4' 4-6-2 No 4468 *Mallard* (just moved to the museum), LBSCR Stroudley 0-4-2 No 214 *Gladstone*, and LBSCR 'A1X' 0-6-0T No 380S *Boxhill*. There is archive film of Hyde Park Corner in 1896, crossing the Tay Bridge (1897), Henley-on-Thames station (1898), Liverpool Overhead Unit No 19, 'Castle'-hauled 'Cheltenham Flyer' (1932), GWR diesel railcar (1933; streamlined version), LNER 'N2' 0-6-2T No 4743, LNER 'A4' 4-6-2 No 2509 *Silver Link* (with 'Silver Jubilee' train, 1935), LMS 'Princess Coronation' 4-6-2 No 6220 *Coronation*, LNER 'V2' 2-6-2 No 60961 as well as English Electric diesel D208, a 'Deltic', the 'Midland Pullman' and electric locomotive E3079. There are also shots of St Pancras and Paddington, bombed in World War 2 and a scene of NER 'B16' 4-6-0 No 61415 being broken up, probably at Doncaster. It all adds up to a kind of high-speed, lighthearted version of what later became *Giants of Steam*.

36/16mm, VID, Sound, 18mins, BTF/VID

🚂 🚂 🚂 🚂

JOE HILL (Sweden, 1971)

SVI. Directed by Bo Widerberg. With Tommy Berggren and Anja Schmidt. The Ballad of Joe Hill. Immigrants from Sweden arrive in the United States in 1902. Freight cars, including Caboose No 5 and Combine No 5 were used for scenes of hobos riding the railroad. These scenes were made on the Sierra Railroad with Rogers locomotive 4-6-0 No 4493, built in 1891, very suitable for the story line.

35mm, Sound, Colour, 115min, SVI

🚂 🚂 🚂

JOHN BETJEMAN GOES BY TRAIN (Britain 1962)

Produced by British Transport Films. From King's Lynn through the wide, flat fields of Norfolk to the unique, half-timbered, unposted station of Wolferton, the station for Sandringham. Then through a land of 'red farms and flint churches' standing amongst the silver birches of Snettisham, with its name cut in a box hedge. And so to Hunstanton and the sea: an unusual and enchanting journey, illumunated by John Betjeman's engaging personality. Made in association with BBC TV.

35/16mm, Sound, 10mins, BTF

🚂 🚂 🚂 🚂 🚂

JOHN COCKING COLLECTION

A major set of videos, mainly of European railways but also featuring the Bluebell (*Bluebell Railway Souvenir*), *Duchess of Hamilton*, *Mallard '88*, the Talyllyn, Mid-Hants and Ffestiniog.

🚂 🚂 🚂 🚂

THE JONES GOODS (Britain 1962)

Made by P B Whitehouse and John Adams. The film shows preserved HR Jones 4-6-0 No 103 making an historic journey from Kyle of Lochalsh to Dingwall on the old Highland Railway. The Jones Goods is famous as the first 4-6-0 tender locomotive in the British Isles. At the time, it was painted in Stroudley's 'improved engine green' — actually bright yellow!

16/8mm, Silent, 12mins, CV/NRM/VID

🚂 🚂 🚂 🚂

JOURNEY ACROSS THE ALPS (Britain 1990)

Videolines. The Albula and Bernina Passes. Rhätische Bahn 2-6-0T and 2-8-0s with Ge 3/4, Ge 4/6, Ge 6/6 Krokodil, and various classes at the RB Centenary Celebrations. The Arlberg Pass with the powerful 1020 class on banking duties. French motive power at the Gare de Nord and Gare de Lyon (Paris), including the TGVs.

VID, Sound, Colour, 60mins, VLV

🚂 🚂 🚂 🚂 🚂

A JOURNEY FOR JEREMY (Britain 1949)

New Realm. Directed by James Hill. Photography by William McLeod. With Robin Netscher, Audrey Manning, Katherine Page and Harry Douglas.

Jeremy is a normal little boy with a passionate interest in trains. He and his friends take down engine numbers. In fact so great is his interest in trains that he is caught not paying attention in class and severely reprimanded by his master.

On the way home, after watching the Scots express go by, he has an encounter with a large dog whilst carrying a dozen eggs; his friend Caroline tells him she is going for a long journey; a little boy called Pinkie, persists in following him around — and with all this and his homework — on his mind he goes to bed in a somewhat confused state.

And whilst asleep he dreams that his model railawy has started to work by itself and on going to find out what is wrong he suddenly finds himself in the Glasgow engine sheds — and that he has turned into an engine driver.

From that moment he is accepted as an engine driver and takes the 'Scots Express' to Euston, having several adventures on the way. Eventually he finds himself in a railwayman's tavern where things are too much for him and he wakes up — only to find that things are not quite the same as the night before.

All the railway material was shot on the LMS between Glasgow and London. After shots on an O gauge LMS *Royal Scot* model, the scene moves to Polmadie Motive Depot,

Glasgow. Jeremy first takes the stock of the 'Midday Scot' into Glasgow Central station with the aid of LMS tank locomotive No 15224. He then transfers to the cab of Stanier LMS 'Coronation' class 4-6-2 No 6253 *City of St Albans* and drives her all the way from Glasgow, through Carlisle and Crewe, to Euston. The same locomotive is used with admirable consistency.

'This is a very pleasant film suitable for old and young. Anyone who likes engines and trains will appreciate the excitement and accuracy of the trip depicted. Jeremy is a natural boy, acting with obvious enjoyment and seriousness, and except for some repetition of scenes, this film will be enjoyed by everyone.' *Monthly Film Bulletin*

16mm, Sound, 34mins, Rank

🚂 🚂 🚂 🚂

A JOURNEY FROM HELSINKI TO THE ARCTIC CIRCLE (Britain 1961)

Made by P B Whitehouse and John Adams.

16/8mm, Silent, 12mins, CV/NRR

🚂 🚂 🚂 🚂 🚂

A JOURNEY FROM RYDE TO VENTNOR (Britain 1962)

Made by P B Whitehouse and John Adams. A film which shows well the operation of the Isle of Wight Railways by the LSWR 'O2' 0-4-4T locomotives, one of which is still preserved in running order on the Isle of Wight Steam Railway at Haven Street.

16/8mm, Silent, 6mins, CV/NRM/VID

🚂 🚂 🚂 🚂 🚂

JOURNEY OF A NATION (Australia 1947)

Australian Film Board. Produced and presented by John Heyer. A film that highlights the absurd situation which used to exist in Australia where the various states had adopted different gauges, making a trans-Australia journey impossible without constant changes. This has since been corrected.

35/16mm/VID, 20mins, AFB/VID

🚂 🚂 🚂 🚂

JOURNEY TO THE LAND BEYOND THE MOUNTAINS (Britain 1983)

BBC Television. Executive producer: Colin Adams. Produced by Brian James. Written and presented by Ray Gosling. From the *Great Little Railways* series.

Ray Gosling takes us on a train from Oporto in Portugal to the Tras-Os-Montes region in the north. Within two hours the splendid scenery of the Douro Valley opens out — the area of the port wine vineyards. Our journey continues up the mountains diesel hauled with two small passenger coaches from Germany. Journey's end is near the Spanish border — very much a rural railway to this primitive corner of Portugal.

16mm, Sound, Colour, 40mins, BBC TV

🚂 🚂 🚂 🚂 🚂

THE JUGGERNAUT (USA 1915)

Vitagraph production. A spectacular real crash film, which culminates in an old 4-4-0 charging off a collapsing wooden trestle viaduct into the river below, taking a train of four coaches with it. The only bits of the story that survive lead up to the magic moment (which, in his excitement, the cameraman almost misses completely!); there is a follow-up as the two coaches that have remained on the track are pushed over into the river in a somewhat unconvincing manner.

16mm, Silent, 7mins, HA

🚂 🚂 🚂 🚂 🚂

JULIA (USA 1977)

TCF. Produced by Julien Derode. Directed by Fred Zinnemann. With Jane Fonda, Vanessa Redgrave, Jason Robards Jnr and Maximilian Schell.

Lillian Hellman reflects on the fortunes of her friend Julia, filled with 1930s dedication to European causes but who is eventually killed by the Nazis.

Includes many highly-atmospheric steam train scenes to depict the 1930s, using preserved SNCF 230G353, which Peter Handford described as 'probably the most frequently filmed locomotive in Europe'.

35/16mm, Sound, Colour, 117mins, TCF

Film on how the railway scenes were shot exists separately:

16mm, Sound, Colour, 9mins, HA

🚂 🚂

JUST FOR THE RECORD (Britain 1985)

Railfilms. Produced by Nick Dodson. Written by Nigel Harris. Volume One. An assembly of archive film from various sources including the BBC Outside Broadcast of the attempt to wreck a 'King' class 4-6-0 locomotive on the Longmoor Military Railway (it didn't work!), the 100mph crash with BR Class 46 No 46009 hauling a nuclear flask (it did work!), BBC Television film *London to Brighton in Four Minutes* (1953), LMS training film for firemen (1938), the Southern 'Golden Arrow' film, *Trains De Luxe* (Golden Arrow train in the 1930s), the Bulleid double decker EMU and the 1948 British Rail locomotive exchanges, with a Bulleid Pacific at Euston and a Stanier 'Princess Coronation' at King's Cross.

VID, Sound, 45mins, RFV

🚂 🚂 🚂 🚂 🚂

JUST STEAM ALIVE (Britain 1982)

Metro Video. A record of six preserved railways featuring Midland Railway locomotives and sections of Midland lines that have been kept running.

VID, Sound, Colour, 60mins, Metro

🚂 🚂 🚂 🚂 🚂

JUST THE TICKET (Britain 1967)

Produced by British Transport Films. Travel by train is for holidays, travel by train is for work, and travel by train can be a pleasure in itself. Howard Marion Crawford advises us in verse to take advantage of all three possibilities and shows us impressions of a wide variety of journeys, destinations and amenities. A selection of railborne experiences include the luxury of Pullman travel, the thrill of arriving at the seaside, and a journey through the highlands.

35/16mm, Sound, Colour, 8mins, BTF

🚂 🚂 🚂 🚂 🚂

K

KAMERADSCHAFT (Germany 1931)

Nerofilm. Directed by G W Pabst. With Ernst Busch and Fritz Kampers. A mine disaster on the Franco-German border. Includes a scene at a provincial railway station with a fine old DBB 4-4-0 and train of old stock leaving just as the mine disaster strikes.

35/16mm, Sound, 92mins, BFI

KANSAS PACIFIC (USA 1953)

Allied Artists. Directed by Ray Nazarro. With Sterling Hayden and Eve Miller. An American Civil War story about the sabotage of a new railroad system. Once again, this film made great demands on the Sierra Railroad, using their two locomotives, Rogers 4-6-0 No 4493 (1891) and Baldwin 2-8-0 No 29790 as well as all the coaching stock, all renamed 'Kansas Pacific RR'.

An old Virginia and Truckee Railroad 4-4-0 was borrowed from Paramount Pictures to add to the stock.

35mm, Sound, Colour, 73min, Allied Artists

KATE PLUS TEN (Britain 1937)

Produced by Richard Wainwright. Directed by Reginald Denham. With Jack Hulbert, Genevieve Tobin, Noel Madison, Francis L Sullivan, Arthur Wontner and Frank Cellier. Adaptation and scenario by Jeffrey Dell. Dialogue by Jack Hulbert and Jeffrey Dell. From an original story by Edgar Wallace. Photography by Roy Kellino. Art direction by D W Daniels. Sound recording by M R Cruickshank. Edited by E M Hunter. Music by Allan Gray. A Wainwright production.

Kate Westhanger is a beautiful but notorious crook whose criminal associates number 10. Inspector Mike Pemberton, CID, meets her at the house of Lord Flamborough where she is posing as the great man's secretary and, wondering

what fresh scoop she is planning, follows her. He is just in time to save her from being knifed by Tolmini, an escaped convict who owes his term of imprisonment to having disobeyed Kate's orders. Kate gathers her gang together and explains the details of their next 'job' — the robbery of a £600,000 gold bullion train during its trip from Seahampton to London. Mike is further mystified when he discovers Kate in close conversation with Sir Ralph Sapson.

The first inkling of what is afoot comes to him following a successful raid by the gang on Lord Flamborough's bank, as a result of which Kate obtains all the information necessary to her plans, Lord Flamborough being in control of the gold supply.

Mike, extremely mystified by the gang's departure for Seahampton, becomes perturbed when he finds that Lord Flamborough has left for the same destination and when it comes to his knowledge that Sir Ralph Sapson is also making the journey his alarm knows no bounds. Sapson, he discovers, owns the railway running between Seahampton and London.

He tries to communicate with the magnates by 'phone but they are busy watching the disembarkation of the gold and refuse to speak to him.

The crooks get away with the train and bring it, by means of disused tracks, to an old mine, where under Kate's instructions, they start to blast the steel safes containing the gold.

Mike traces the gang to their hideout, arriving just in time to witness a mutiny against Kate. Furious at this behaviour she gives instructions that the waiting lorries loaded with the gold are to be delivered to Lord Flamborough's London house. When the crooks discover the lorries are going in the wrong direction they set out in cars to head them off leaving Mike and Kate stranded, but together they start up an old engine with which they are able to block the way of the gang at a level crossing. With the arrival of the police the crooks are taken into custody while Kate is sentenced to marry Mike.

The years 1929 to 1938 saw a flood of films using various forms of

transport locations. For this film, the company used the services of the Port of London Authority, the New Zealand Shipping Company, the London, Midland & Scottish Railway and the Great Western Railway. The main railway scenes were shot in and around Bath as well as on the much used Limpley Stoke-Camerton line. Night locations during the early months of 1937 took place on the single track line between 9pm and 6am each night during a particularly cold spell. Frost, mist and fog interrupted shooting several times; once the camera froze. The oil in the spindles and chain drive became so thick that the motor drive failed; filming was only got going when the camera was warmed up under the arc lights.

The principal locomotive used in this film was the GWR mixed traffic Churchward 2-6-0 No 4364. Amongst other adventures, 4364 had to smash through her shed doors and shatter a pair of wooden mock-up level crossing gates at 45mph.

The chase scene starts in Brentford docks (freight only) with what is reputed to be Churchward's own saloon vehicle and a pannier tank on the front. The scene moves to the Westbury-Bathampton main line; the level crossing scene was done at Freshford station. The action finally jumps to the old Somersetshire coal field and an abandoned colliery before ending up on a level crossing just outside Camerton station. The colliery was a real one — Dunkerton, which, until 1925, was served by its special halt.

35/16mm, Sound, 81mins, NA/rail scene only: HA

KELLY'S HEROES (USA/Yugoslavia 1970)

MGM. Directed by Brian G. Hutton. With Clint Eastwood, Telly Savalas and Donald Sutherland. World War Two melodrama about an American platoon that abducts a German general and discovers a hoard of gold. Includes scenes filmed on Yugoslavian Railways, with stock relabelled as if German plus a number of Yugoslavian locomotives, some of German origin, including a

Krupp 4-4-0.
35mm, Sound, Colour,
143min, MGM

KENT AND EAST SUSSEX RAILWAY (Britain 1950-75)

Film records made by Wilf Watters, Peter Goddard and Peter Wood. An 8mm film shows the line at Rolvenden, Frittenden Road and Headcorn Junction in its working days, with LBSCR 'Terriers' and SECR 'V' 4-4-0 No 31065. The line closed in 1954. Further film shows the first arrival of the preservation society, with the delivery of Manning Wardle 0-6-0ST No 14 *Charwelton* (built in 1955) and the first steaming of LBSCR 'A1X' 0-6-0T No 32670, still with its BR number. There is further material made by J Liddell.

16mm, Silent, Colour, 16mins, WW/HA/VID

KENT & EAST SUSSEX RAILWAY (Britain 1948)

One of Colonel Stephen's empire of minor railways, the K&ESR provides an active scene for the camera just five months after Nationalisation. An 'A1X' backs on to a one-coach train: vintage stock abounds; 'A1X' No 3 visibly displays the K&ESR initials on its tankside, an 'A1X' plus coach arrives in the platform.

16mm/VID, Silent, 9min, NRM/VID

KENT TOUR (Britain 1957)

SCTS. A visit to the Bowater Paper Mills Light Railway (now part preserved) and a trip on the 2ft 6in narrow gauge train from Sittingbourne to Kemsley Mills and Ridham dock (River Sway) with Bagnall (2472) 0-6-2T *Alpha* built in 1932 (now on static display). The line dates back to 1906; the locomotives were fitted with American-type spark arresters. The tour continued with a visit to the Romney, Hythe & Dymchurch Miniature Railway.

16mm, Silent, 9mins, HA/SCTS

KENYA: EAST AFRICAN RAILWAYS (Britain 1963)

Made by Tim Hall. Journey from Mombassa to Nairobi by train with old steam locomotives *Galla* and *Kenani*, plus various Garratts, views of the bush, a baby Garratt and double-headed freight trains.

16mm, Silent, Colour, 9mins, TH/HA

THE KEY TO SCOTLAND (Britain 1938)

Strand Films. History of Edinburgh, with some LNER railway scenes.

16mm, Sound, 10mins, R F

KEY TO THE TOR (Britain 1964)

Harold Baim production. Travelogue of Torquay and Devon, including one shot of diesel-hauled 'Torbay Express'.

35mm, Sound, Colour, 20mins, HB/HA

KHARTOUM (Britain 1966)

United Artists. Directed by Basil Dearden. With Charlton Heston, Laurence Olivier, Ralph Richardson and Richard Johnson. The story of General Gordon and the British Empire in the Sudan. Includes a scene when General Gordon meets Mr Gladstone on a railway station, filmed at night on Horstead Keynes station on the Bluebell Railway, using a SECR 'P' 0-6-0T bearing a false LNWR-style number plate '2650', with the old Bluebell 'Chesham' stock.

35mm, Sound, Colour, 134mins, United Artists

KILSBY (Britain 1988)

A film by John Payne. Commentary by John Huntley. A history of Kilsby Tunnel on the London to Birmingham Railway; the work of Robert Stephenson; problems and flooding; final opening; the tunnel today.

16mm/VID, Sound, Colour, 21mins, JP/HA/Online

KING AND QUEEN AT A RAILWAY STATION (Britain 1914-18)

The King and Queen at an unknown railway station

35mm, Silent, 7sec, NFA

KING GEORGE V (Britain 1970)

National Coal Board. Directed by Paul Barnes. A study of GWR 'King' 4-6-0 No 6000 *King George V* at that time trapped in a short length of track at Bulmers Cider at Hereford. A historical review includes scenes of the "King" at the Fair of the Iron Horse in America in 1927, details of Swindon works, and a plea for the return of the "King" to main-line running at a time when steam was totally banned on British Rail. The film was shown at the Royal Film Performance in 1970 and is said to have influenced BR to think again about steam specials; especially as HM the Queen is supposed to have liked the film and said to the Chairman of BR: 'Why can't we have those lovely old steam engines back in action again?'

16mm, Sound, Colour, 11mins, NCB/ARPS/HA

THE KING GOES TO PADDINGTON (Britain 1979)

Produced by Wilf Watters and Nick Lera. A record of a journey from Paddington to Didcot, headed by GWR 'King' 4-6-0 No 6000 *King George V*. This was the first time that steam had been seen at Paddington in nearly 15 years. The King left in the midst of normal HST traffic and discreetly made the journey on the slow line! The plan was to make a return trip from Didcot in the afternoon but a bearing ran hot and the turn-round had to be abandoned.

16mm, Sound, Colour, 11mins, WW/NL

KING KONG (USA 1933)

RKO Radio picture. Produced by Merian C Cooper. Directed by Merian C Cooper and Ernest Schoedsack. A film producer on safari brings back a giant ape which terrorises New York. Includes a scene, done entirely with models and studio sets, when King Kong attacks the Third Avenue El by smashing a whole section out of the track and creating a gap into which the approaching train falls, with mass destruction. There is a great shot when King Kong rises up in the centre of the shattered track as seen from the motorman's position.

35/16mm/VID,   Sound,   100mins, RKO

KING OF THE LUMBERJACKS (USA 1941)

Warner Bros. Directed by William Clemens. With John Payne and Stanley Fields. Lumber-camp melodrama including spectacular runaway steam trains scenes originally used in *The Valley of the Giants*.

35mm,   Sound,   59mins

KING SOLOMON'S MINES (USA 1985)

Cannon films. Directed by J Lee Thompson. With Richard Chamberlain, Sharon Stone and Herbert Lom. A fast and furious remake of the old familiar story, rather like an over-heated *Indiana Jones*; the *Sunday Mail* said 'the cinema's equivalent to junk food'. There is a major railway scene using old EAR locomotives and ancient 'colonial' stock on an extensive single-line section in Zimbawbe, with very strange ballast that looks like elephant droppings!

35mm,   Sound,   Colour, 100mins,   Cannon

KINGSBRIDGE BRANCH (Britain 1960)

Two classes of engine are shown principally. The '4500' class, introduced by G J Churchward in 1906 as part of his standardisation plan, and the '4575' class of 1927. The bulk of the latter were numbered in the 55XX series and thus became referred to as 'fifty-fives'. Both types are seen as are some superb former LMS and LNER carriages. We view the journey to Kingsbridge and back again to Brent in time to see a

'Manor' class 4-6-0 arrive with a main line connection.

16mm,   Colour,   5mins, CV/NRM/HA

KING'S CROSS STATION (Britain 1935)

Pre-World War 2 activity at London King's Cross. 'A3' 2578 *Bayardo* backs onto a train in Platform 10, and departs vigorously; an 'N1' 0-6-2T is seen in Platform 8; 'N2s' are in Platforms 12 and 13; mid-1930s enthusiasts crowd the end of Platform 10 as 'A3' 2508 *Brown Jack* departs with a set of LNER teak coaches. 'A3' 2743 *Felstead* is seen, too, together with 'A3' 2746 *Fairway*, and an 'N2' 0-6-2T arrives on the empty Pullman coaches for the 'Queen of Scots'.

VID,   Silent,   7min,   Stirling

KIRTLEY, JOHNSON & COMPANY (Britain 1962)

Maded by P B Whitehouse and John Adams. The preserved engines from Derby Works have a journey to Worksworth for Railway Roundabout. Kirtley 2-4-0 No 158A, Johnson 4-2-2 No 118 and 4-4-2T *Thundersley* hauled by Midland Compound No 1000.

16/8mm,   Silent,   6mins, CV/NRM

KISS IN THE TUNNEL (Britain 1900)

Produced by George Albert Smith of Hove. Three shots linked together to tell a simple film story (for the first time ever?). A train on the LSWR enters a tunnel. (Shot 1). Mock-up of the interior of a first class carriage where an elderly well-dressed gentleman with a top hat proceeds to kiss a distinguished looking lady, apparently to the mutual satisfaction of both parties. (Shot 2). A real shot of the view from the train as it emerges from the end of the tunnel. (Shot 3). The real shots are taken from 'View from an Engine Front: Shilla Mill Tunnel' (qv), simply by cutting the original 'Phantom Ride' scene in half. The carriage interior was built

in the grounds of Smith's house in Wilbury Avenue, Hove.

35/16/VID,   Silent,   1min, NFA/HA/125

KISS IN THE TUNNEL (Britain 1900)

A Bamforth film. A railway cutting is seen with a train entering a tunnel. In a compartment a young couple are seated opposite each other. The young man throws away his cigarette and kisses the girl as the train enters a tunnel. The train emerges from the tunnel and finally draws up at a station.

This is an exact copy of the George Albert Smith film of the same title, also of 1900. Who made the film first? No one knows. In the Bamforth film, Shot 1 of the train entering a tunnel, is a high shot of the south portal of the Queensberry Tunnel on the old Great Northern Railway between Bradford and Halifax. Shot 2 is in the little 'post card' studio of the Bamforth Company in Holmfirth. Shot 3 is of a Johnson Derby-built 4-4-0 of the Midland Railway, with Midland stock all clearly marked 'MR' entering Monsal Dale station on the Peak Forest line between Matlock and New Mills.

35/16/VID,   Silent,   1min, NFA/HA/125

KNIGHT WITHOUT ARMOUR (Britain 1937)

London Films. Produced by Alexander Korda. Directed by Jacques Feyder. With Robert Donat, Marlene Dietrich and Irene Vanbrugh. Russian aristocrat escapes from Russia in 1917. Includes 'European' train scenes, using stock shots, elaborate studio sets and a 'Russian' locomotive mocked up on the Longmoor Military Railway, as well as a complete railway section (full size) built in the grounds of Denham studios using two LNER 'J15' class locomotives Nos 7835 and 7541, bought by London Films from the LNER and mocked up as Russian locomotives.

35mm,   Sound,   107mins, London Films

L

THE LADY KILLERS (Britain 1955)

An Ealing Studios film. Directed by Alexander Mackendrick. With Alec Guinness and Cecil Parker. Comedy of a gang of robbers who come to a bad end. Sequences at and near King's Cross, including a scene at the south face of Copenhagen Tunnel just outside King's Cross. A great deal of superb steam scenes of trains setting out from King's Cross on the long climb up to Finsbury Park and beyond were shot and never used in the finished film. These 'out takes' have since been salvaged by Video 125 and incorporated into their production *Steam on 35mm*.

35mm/VID, Sound, Colour, 90mins, Weintraub/125

LADY ON A TRAIN (USA 1945)

A Universal picture. Directed by Charles David. With Deanna Durbin and Ralph Bellamy. The film begins with location scenes of a train approaching New York.

35mm, Sound, 94 mins, Universal

THE LADY VANISHES (Britain 1938)

Gaumont-British/Gainsborough production. Directed by Alfred Hitchcock. With Margaret Lockwood, Michael Redgrave and Dame May Whitty. An old lady (actually a spy) disappears on a train across Europe. Like most of Hitchcock's films with a railway background, it is a weird mixture of studio scenes, models and bits of the real thing. His directorial skill keeps it all moving where others might fail. In this case, there are two complete 'studio' stations and one full-size studio steam locomotive. Then there are a series of large model layouts, including the train trapped in the snow, the border check point, a train crossing a viaduct and a station departure, complete with wheel slip; all strictly O gauge by Bond and Bassett-Lowke. Into this come

real shots of PLM trains at speed, French Pacifics in action, a British Southern Railway Boat train and some fragments supposed to have been filmed on the Longmoor Military Railway. Sometimes, the mix is masterly; a real train swings round a bend towards a tunnel, cut to a model train entering the tunnel. All the carriage interiors are studio-built, with rather clumsy back-projection for the passing scenery, most of which looks reasonably Continental. The famous 'Harriman's Herbal Tea' label stuck on the carriage window is entirely studio-concocted, as is Redgrave's climb out of the carriage window. So a hotch-potch of the Gaumont-British Shepherds Bush studios and a miscellany of French railway stock shots from many different angles is made, in the hands of the master, to add up to what Leslie Halliwell called: 'Superb, suspenseful, brilliantly funny, meticulously detailed entertainment'.

35/16mm, Sound, 97mins, Rank

THE LADY VANISHES (Britain 1978)

A Rank/Hammer production. Directed by Anthony Page. With Cybill Shepherd, Elliott Gould, Angela Lansbury and Herbert Lom. Remake of the 1938 film, 'in which everything goes wrong: wrong shape, wrong actors; wrong style' (Leslie Halliwell). Peter Handford saw some of it happen:

'For the 1978 version of *The Lady Vanishes* exterior scenes were filmed in Austria with OBB 2-10-0 No 50.1171 and a train of six coaches. All the railwaymen involved were exceptionally helpful and the driver and firemen, who came with the locomotive from the Graz Köflacher Bahn, calmly accepted even the most extraordinary demands and performed the most complicated and occasionally dangerous manoeuvres to perfection. One particularly hazardous operation, most unlikely to have been given high level management approval, took place at Feistritz im Rosental, a station on the single line between Klagenfurt and Rosenbach. It was necessary for the camera to be on a moving train and for another

train to be seen passing in the opposite direction. The camera was set up inside a coach, hauled by a diesel locomotive which moved away on the single line to a position some distance from the station. The 2-10-0 moved the train of six coaches back to the points at the far end of the station loop line, then, with all the brakes hard on, the driver put the engine in full forward gear, opened the regulator wide, whistled and hoped for the best. The diesel and single coach accelerated down the single line towards the station and as the diesel approached the points at the rear end of the loop, the driver of the 2-10-0 at the far end released the brakes and with an almighty roar the engine took off, taking the train through the station on the loop line, at the end of which the points had been hurriedly changed as soon as the diesel had passed over them. This extraordinary operation was repeated three times, mercifully without any disaster!

35mm, Sound, Colour, 97mins, Rank

THE LADY WITH A LAMP (Britain 1951)

British Lion. Produced by Herbert Wilcox. Directed by Herbert Wilcox. With Anna Neagle, Michael Wilding and Felix Aylmer. The life of Florence Nightingale. Includes a scene with a train hauled by the little Liverpool & Manchester locomotive of 1838 *Lion*, filmed at Cole Green station, which closed in the year the film was made.

Hatfield Shed provided a footplate crew in period costume; *Lion* had to have wheel flanges specially profiled for the occasion.

35mm, Sound, 110mins, Weintraub

LANCASHIRE AND YORKSHIRE RAILWAY (Britain 1919)

Scenes of a cotton train, headed by a Hughes 0-8-0 freight engine, with a similar banker in the rear. There are also scenes of L&Y road transport, including horse-drawn vehicles and some old World War 1 Leyland trucks.

16mm, Silent, 4mins, HA

LANCASHIRE STEAM (Britain 1967-68)

Made by Nick Lera. A fine study of the last days of steam notably on the L&Y at Copy Pit with freight workings with 'Black Fives' and '8Fs'. including many heavy trains being banked up a 1 in 66 climb across the viaduct. There are also steam scenes at Horton-in-Ribblesdale, Scout Green, Lostock Hall, Rose Grove, Leeds, Hoghton, Hellifield, Clapham and Manchester Victoria. LMS '5' 4-6-0 Nos 44819, 45310, 45200, 44781, 44819, 44899, 45231, 44871, 44814, 45190, 45110 and 45156 are all seen, as are LMS '8F' 2-8-0 Nos 48519, 48247, 48297 and 48151.

The very last days of steam in the north-west (and also on British Rail) include a series of specials with LNER 'A1' 4-6-2 No 4472 *Flying Scotsman* (at Copy Pit); LNER 'A4' 4-6-2 No 4464 *Bittern* (at Leeds); and BR 'Britannia' 4-6-2 No 70013 *Oliver Cromwell* (at Hellifield and Copy Pit). There is also a special, double-headed out of Manchester Victoria by two 'Black Fives', and seen on the outskirts of Manchester and again at Copy Pit, the main subject of this film. An Inspector's Saloon, also hauled by a 'Black Five' No 45231 is likewise crossing the viaduct at Copy Pit signalbox. The very occasional diesel makes a brief appearance in the background, seemingly much to the annoyance of the film maker!

16mm, Silent, Colour, 17mins, NL

THE LAND OF INVENTION (Britain 1941)

British Films Ltd. Directed by Andrew Buchanan. Achievements of Scottish inventors and engineers. Includes a brief account of the work of James Watt (1736-1819) and fragmentary scenes of LNER 'C15' 4-4-2T No 9003, LMS 'Royal Scot' No 6119 *Lancashire Fusilier* and North British Glasgow-built locomotives being shipped overseas.

16mm, Sound, 11mins, HA/SFC

LAST DAYS OF STEAM ON THE SOUTHERN (Britain 1967)

A film by Peter Goddard. A journey from Waterloo to Bournemouth behind various Bulleid Pacifics including SR 'Battle of Britain' 4-6-2 No 34052 *Lord Dowding*. There are scenes from the lineside and shots of the sheds at Bournemouth. Original material on 8mm.

16mm, Silent, Colour, 11mins, Goddard/HA

LAST DECADE OF STEAM (Britain 1989)

Rail Video Production. Film by Gavin Morrison. This first tape covers part of the South of England and also further North around Lancashire and Yorkshire. The locations used include Basingstoke, Branksome, Bournemouth Central, Bradford, Leeds, Cleckheaton Branch, Goole, York, The Waverley Route, Bacup, Bury, Hellifield, Shap, Scout Green, Hooton, Gargrave and Kingmoor. Loco classes featured include Bulleid Pacifics, Standard Class '4s', '5s', 'Britannias', '9Fs', 'B1' 4-6-0s, 'Black Fives', Jubilees, 'A4s', Ivatt '2MT' 2-6-0s, Crab 2-6-0s, Stanier '8Fs', WD 2-8-0s, Fairburn 2-6-4s and a few diesels in BR green livery.

VID, Sound, Colour, 30Mins, RVO

THE LAST DELTICS (Britain 1983)

Rail Video. RV2. Deltics in green livery; various run-pasts; and the 'Deltic Scotsman Farewell' trip. An interesting early experiment in recording the more recent scene on video.

VID, Sound, Colour, 60mins, RVO

THE LAST JOURNEY (Britain 1936)

Twickenham Studios production. Directed by Bernard Vorhaus, photography by William Luft and Percy Strong. Art direction by James Carter. Music by W L Trytel. Edited by Jack Harris, with Hugh Williams, Godfrey Tearle, Julian Mitchell, Judy Gunn, Michael Hogan, Nelson Keys, Eliott Makeham, Viola Compton and Frank Pettingall.

The story of an engine driver's last journey. As a result of brooding over his impending retirement and doubting his wife's faithfulness, he goes mad and drives his train at terrific speed, disregarding all signals, and disaster is only averted at the last moment. The various people who are brought together by fear include a young criminal who has just made a bigamous marriage to a rich girl, two small-time crooks making a get-away, a disguised detective and a brain specialist called to perform an operation in the country and who eventually saves the train by bringing the engine driver back to his senses.

This picture was the subject of a detailed report in the December 1935 issue of the *Great Western Railway Magazine*.

'Twickenham Film Studios desire to express their grateful thanks to the Great Western Railway Company for the facilities which they have courteously extended to them in connection with the filming of *The Last Journey*.

'Apart from the interest which the portrayal of a great railway system on the screen must arouse, it is, perhaps, amusing to reflect that, actually, the Great Western would be the very last railway on which the events pictured in the film could actually happen, as it has become a recognised truism with the travelling public that the Great Western Railway is not only the fastest and most comfortable, but also the safest railway system in the British Empire.

'Film-goers will read this tribute as the foreword to a thrilling railway film which is being released shortly, and they can sit back in their seats with an assurance of 60 minutes' entertainment packed full of excitement.

'The story on which the film is based is by J Jefferson Farjeon, and is a mixture of drama and comedy. Practically all the action takes place on board an express train, which is in the charge of driver Bob Holt, who is making his last journey after 40 years on the footplate. This fact, coupled with an unfounded suspicion of an intrigue between his young wife and his fireman, Charles Disher, causes Holt's mind to become temporarily unbalanced. He decides to take revenge by dashing the train to destruction at "Mulchester", the terminus station and end of his last run. He ignores all signals, passes all "stop" stations and, taunting Disher with his intrigue, forces him, at the point of a revolver, to keep firing.

'There are plenty of thrills in the footplate fight while the train is roaring along the iron road, and it is only when disaster seems inevitable that Disher escapes from the footplate by scrambling back over the tender and carriage tops, to swing himself, with his last ounce of strength, down and along the side of the swaying train and into one of the coaches. Here he tells his breathless story to some of the now terrified passengers.

'On the train, the passengers were at first ignorant of the fact that the express was in charge of a man temporarily insane, and various little comedies and dramas, centred around a variety of passengers, have been taking place. These are skilfully used to relieve the central melodrama – but soon fear is aroused when it becomes realised that something is wrong as the train hurtles through stations at which it is scheduled to stop.

'Among the passengers is a famous brain specialist making a dash against time to perform an urgent operation. He answers the call made through the train for a doctor and, when he hears Disher's story, risks his life to save the train load of terrified passengers. By picking a perilous path to the footplate, and by means of a rapid psycho-analysis, he brings Holt to reason and the train to a stop only a few inches from the buffers of "Mulchester".

'The part of Bob Holt is played by Julien Mitchell; that of Charles Disher by Michael Hogan (of the "Buggins Family" fame), and the role of specialist by Godfrey Tearle.

'The making of this remarkable film called for extensive co-operation between the film company and the railway management, especially as certain liberties with recognised railway practices had to be taken in order to meet the film company's need to produce a "thriller". The facilities which the Great Western Railway Company provided included the running of special trains and coaches, occupation of sections of track and signal boxes, the use of locomotive depots, the loan of a considerable variety of material, technical advice, and general assistance.

'The actual filming extended from May to July, and during that period special runs were made from Paddington to Plymouth and Bristol. On these trains coaches were adapted for the film company's requirements, and some of the windows in a saloon were removed so as to permit the filming of passing trains and the making of certain other "shots".

'On two Sundays in June a special train of main line coaches, drawn by a "Castle" locomotive, was run, leaving Paddington with the film unit of some 60 passengers aboard at 8.30am for the Basingstoke branch, where occupation was given between trains on both lines between 9.30am and about 8.00pm. A dining car was included in the make-up of these trains, and this was the canteen of the unit for the day. A goods engine was also sent from Reading locomotive shed to form a goods train with the wagons which had been concentrated in the neighbourhood for this purpose.

'It was here that some of the most thrilling parts of the film were made, including one where the express, minutes ahead of time, is overhauling a lumbering goods train. This is, indeed the high spot of the film, and most spectators will find themselves expecting, and knowing, that the express is going to crash into the back of the goods train. That it does not do so is due to some smart work on the part of the actor-signalman who switches the goods train into a siding only a fraction of a second before the wheels of the express would have reached it.

'Train "noises" were made at many places on the company's system. Paddington, being the departure station of the film express, came in for a full share, and the film actor-enginemen were "shot" on the footplates of outgoing expresses just prior to their departure. Elsewhere "shots" were made of train movements and passengers on the platforms and boarding the trains, also waiting the arrival of the express at intermediate stations and losing their hats – and wigs- as it rushed through instead of stopping.

'The camera operators were called upon to photograph from all manner of places, and in peculiar positions; they took full advantage of the opportunities offered by overbridges, water towers, signals, etc. They also used an aeroplane to get pictures of a motor car racing the train, their cameras being strapped to the wings of the plane for this purpose.

'Swindon has played a part in the making of a dozen or more films during the last year or so. In most cases this has not been very apparent, but in The Last Journey evidences of Swindon are very much in the limelight. As some of the "shots" in the film could not be done on actual trains, all the fittings and fixtures required for first and third class compartments, corridors, and dining car were sent from the Great Western Railway Swindon works for erection in the studios at Twickenham. Sheaves of blue prints and various photographs were also despatched, and finally a man from the carriage and wagon shops, to superintend the fitting together of the many parts.

'For some of the footplate scenes the tender, cab, and part of the boiler of a "Castle" locomotive were built to scale, in three-ply wood, from Swindon drawings and photographs, and a fitter from locomotive works was sent to the studios to reassemble the cab fittings, including gauges, pipes, regulators, injector gear, automatic train control apparatus, reverse gear, look-out windows, water pick-up gear, coal watering pipe, sand gear, fire hole door, and fireman's tools. The "engine" was built up on a low framework, instead of on wheels, and had curves under supports, like a rocking-chair. This enabled the swaying motion of an engine at speed to be reproduced by the simple method of levering the structure from behind. At the same time, from behind the screen at the back of the "engine", a film of the countryside, taken from the carriage window of a Paddington-to-Bristol express, was projected, giving the appearance, from the front, of a moving engine.

'The illusion of speed was carried

still further. The waving of planks in front of lights at irregular intervals created shadows supposedly made and cast over the engine by lineside trees and buildings, while a "wind" machine and a tattered silk rag on a long stick, waved in the air current, gave the light streaky effect of rushing air. All kinds of means and processes were employed to obtain realistic effects. The fire, fiercely burning, was an electric one protected by mattresses from the very genuine coal which Michael Hogan shovelled many times through the fire hold door. Among the most ingenious "fakes" were wooden button moulds, as used in ladies' dressmaking, to represent the rivet-heads on the engine tender and cab.

'Swindon supplied also the uniforms for the screen station masters, inspectors, guards, porters, signalmen, and engine drivers; also the cotton waste, dating press, platform ticket machine, and the tickets.

'To help the actor-engineman to become word and action perfect, arrangements were made for a retired main-line driver to attend the studios in an advisory capacity during the filming of the footplate scenes.

'Suffice it to say that *The Last Journey* abounds in "Stars", "Halls", "Castles" and "Kings", embellished by 0-6-0 and 0-4-2T engines as well as liberal glimpses of stations, signalboxes and stock on the way from Paddington to the West Country. And the scene of a slow-moving goods train being pursued up the track by a "Castle" hauled express has to be seen to be believed.'

The wonderful collection of locomotives seen include GWR 'Star' 4-6-0 No 4020 *Knight Commander*, GWR 'Hall' 4-6-0 No 4953 *Pitchford Hall*; GWR 'Castle' 4-6-0s No 5004 *Llanstephan Castle*, No 5012 *Berry Pomeroy Castle* and No 5013 *Abergavenny Castle*; and GWR 'King' 4-6-0s No 60045 *King George II* and No 6022 *King Edward III*. The goods train appears with four different locomotives on the front (all supposed to be the same train!); it starts with a pannier tank, goes to a '2800' class, then to a '4300' class and finally to *King Edward III*. And the strange thing is that it doesn't seem to matter when you are watching the film; just adds to the fun.

The film contains a bonus for transport enthusiasts: an old Mercedes sports car; and an Avro 594 Avian G-AAAT at Heston.

35/16mm, Sound, 66mins, NFA/HA/TUA

LAST STEAM THROUGH THE CHILTERNS (Britain 1966)

Made by G S Holyoake. 'Black Fives' in action on the Great Central Line; 'Merchant Navy' class No 35030 on Great Central Rail Tour (LCGB) for the last day of passenger service (3 September 1966).

16/9.5/8mm, Silent, Colour, 4mins, MFS

LAST STEAM TRAIN FROM NORWICH (Britain 1962)

Anglia Television. Special train hauled by GER 'J17' 0-6-0 No 65567.

16mm, Silent, Colour, 4mins, Anglia

LAST STEAM TRAIN: LYMINGTON TO BROCKENHURST (Britain 1967)

A film by Peter Goddard. Shot on 8mm, this is a detailed record of the final steam-hauled trains on 2 April 1967, from Lymington Pier, now served by diesel units. There are glimpses of main-line steam between Bournemouth and Weymouth; the principal action is reserved for LMS '2MT' No 41295 and No 41320, and BR '4MT' 2-6-4T No 80146. There are scenes of the shipping at Lymington Pier.

16mm, Silent, Colour, 8mins, Goddard/HA

LAST TRAIN (Australia 1963)

A TVT6 (Tasmania) television film. A record of a preservation society outing in Tasmania, Australia.

16mm, Sound, 10mins, HA

LAST TRAIN FROM ABERGAVENNY TO MERTHYR (Britain 1958)

Made by P B Whitehouse and John Adams. A record of an SLS Special to celebrate the end of the line, taking in scenes at Ebbw Vale High Level station (LNWR), Govilon and Merthyr. The train was double-headed by LNWR Bowen-Cooke 0-8-0 No 49121 and LNWR Webb 0-6-2T coal tank No 58926 of 1882 vintage, now preserved.

16mm, Silent, 4mins, CV/NRM/VID

LAST TRAIN FROM ALDEBURGH (Britain 1966)

British Film Institute. Made by Bruce Beresford. The end of passenger service on the Saxmundham-Aldeburgh line on 10 September 1966.

16mm, Silent, 12mins, HA

LAST TRAIN FROM BALA TO BLAENAU FFESTINIOG (Britain 1961)

Made by P B Whitehouse and John Adams. Record of the last passenger train from Bala to Blaenau Ffestiniog on the line which is now closed because of the building of a new reservoir.

16/8mm, Silent, 7mins, CV/NRM/HA

LAST TRAIN FROM BALA TO BLAENAU FFESTINIOG (Britain 1961)

Newsreel record with train hauled by GWR pannier tank, the issue of the final tickets, the crowds on the route, the band and all the trappings of a farewell to a local line in the Beeching era.

16mm, Silent, 9mins, HA

THE LAST TRAIN FROM GUN HILL (USA 1959)

Paramount. Produced by Hal B Wallis. Directed by John Sturges. With Kirk Douglas, Anthony Quinn, Earl Holliman and Carolyn Jones. A marshal tracks down a man who raped and murdered his wife. The end is like a *High Noon* situation; notably a lovely 4-4-0 No 22 and carriages Nos 15 and 4 marked 'South Western RR' and also used the Sierra Railroad.

35mm, Sound, Colour, 98mins, Paramount

THE LAST TRAIN FROM MADRID (USA 1937)

Paramount. Directed by James Hogan. With Dorothy Lamour, Lew Ayres and Lionel Atwill. A very phony account of an episode in the Spanish Civil War. Despite the title, the railway content is small — a very unlikely train on the Paramount lot in Hollywood.

35mm, Sound, 85mins, Paramount

🚂

LAST TRAIN ON THE BRILL BRANCH (Britain 1935)

A maddeningly brief record of the last days on the line from Quainton Road to Brill, taking the London Underground (Metropolitan) system to within 11 miles of Oxford! There are views of Westcott station, the opening of a level crossing gate by the train crew and a glimpse of London Transport tank engine L41. The line opened to Brill in 1872 and closed completely in 1935.

35/16mm, Silent, 3mins, HA

🚂 🚂 🚂 🚂 🚂 🚂

LAST TRAIN ON THE SHROPSHIRE & MONTGOMERYSHIRE (Britain)

Made by P B Whitehouse and John Adams. Last run on the line from Shrewsbury to Llanymynech, which finally closed in the 1960s.

16/8mm, Silent, CV/NRM

🚂 🚂 🚂 🚂 🚂

THE LAST TRAIN TO MEDICINE HAT (Canada 1990)

Produced by Arnie Gelbart and Charles Ohayan. Directed by Josh Freed and Tom Puchnaik. Presented by Murray Sayle. The end of the 7,000-mile railway from the Atlantic to the Pacific, with its spectacular passage through the Rocky Mountains and the link created with Montreal, Toronto and Vancover, as well as obscure one-house towns like Coral Rapide. The most famous section from Sudbury to Thunder Bay, Kenora, Winnipeg, Regina, Swift, Maple Creek, Calgary, Banff and Medicine Hat, from which the programme takes its title, all came to an end in January 1990. Thus, the film not only takes in the great trunk route but many of the fasci-

nating local lines that were equally doomed; although certain sections where roads were non-existent, have been retained, as with the part on the Hudson's Bay Polar Route running to the very edge of the Arctic Circle. Another of the Great Railway Journeys of the World had gone.

16mm/VID, Sound, Colour, 58mins, Cleo 24

🚂 🚂 🚂

LAST WEEKS OF STEAM ON THE SOUTHERN (Britain 1967)

A film by Tom Martin. Filmed at Surbiton, Berrylands and Woking, with a vast parade of 'Merchant Navy', 'Black Five' and 'West Country' locomotives. The last great display of steam on the Southern Region.

16mm, Silent, Colour, 10mins, TM/HA

🚂 🚂 🚂 🚂 🚂

LAWRENCE OF ARABIA (Britain 1962)

Columbia. Directed by David Lean. With Peter O'Toole and Alec Guinness. Includes a sensational railway crash and various railway scenes done on location in the Middle East with authentic locomotives and stock.

70/35mm, Sound, Colour, 222mins, Columbia

🚂

LBSCR OVERHEAD ELECTRICS (Britain 1909)

A brief record of the original LBSCR electric train service from Victoria to Crystal Palace. It was known as the 'Elevated Electric Railway', working at 6,700V with equipment from AEG, Germany. There is a short scene of Gypsy Hill station.

16mm, Silent, 4mins, HA

🚂 🚂 🚂 🚂 🚂

LEADER CLASS LOCOMOTIVE: BULLEID

Material on this famous experimental locomotive has always been sought after. In recent times quite a lot has come to light. Issued for example by Transport Video Publishing in their *Reflections on Southern Steam*.

🚂 🚂 🚂 🚂 🚂 🚂

THE LEAP FROM THE WATER TOWER (USA 1915)

An episode from the series *The Hazards of Helen* starrring Helen Holmes. A Kalem production.

Helen saves the train at the last moment and captures a bunch of bullion robbers.

The locomotive most prominently in evidence is interesting. No 3001 of the Santa Fe, star of *The Leap from the Water Tower* (along with Helen Holmes), was one of a series of 10 that were, in 1914, the largest engines that had ever been built.

No 3001 started out in 1904 as Santa Fe's 2-10-2 No 957. But the need for more power was so great that, in 1911, the Santa Fe had the Baldwin Locomotive Works construct 10 2-10-2s, part in the 900 series, built in 1904, and part in the 1500 series, built in 1905. The resulting monsters were 2-10-10-2s, the first (new) section being the low pressure unit, the original section a high pressure unit. They were only a limited success and beginning in 1916 they were separated into 20 2-10-2 locomotives, the front portion of No 3001 becoming No 3022, the back portion 3013.

The action sequences in this film were photographed in the vicinity of Cajon Pass in California, while the major yard scenes were taken at San Bernardino.

16mm, Silent, 18mins, Blackhawk

🚂 🚂 🚂

LEAPFROG (Britain 1965)

Produced by British Transport Films. Leapfrog was a name given to a new method of handling bulk liquid containers. The film shows how special tanks holding 4,000gal of liquid were transferred easily from road to rail and vice-versa, thus ensuring an efficient door-to-door service.

16mm, Sound, Colour, 8mins, BTF

🚂 🚂 🚂 🚂 🚂

LEAVING JERUSALEM BY TRAIN (France 1896)

Lumière film. Departure of a train from Jerusalem station.

35mm, Silent, 48seconds, NFA

🚂 🚂 🚂 🚂 🚂

LEEK & MANIFOLD LIGHT RAILWAY (Britain 1927-32)

This film record was made between Waterhouse and Hulme End on the Staffordshire and Derbyshire boundaries. It shows the countryside in which the railway was set as well as locomotives and rolling stock. This 2ft 6inch narrow gauge line was opened in 1904 and closed in 1935. The railway was built by two military gentlemen who had built the Indian Barsi Light Railway for the Army. The line had a strictly 'Empire' look with tramcar-like bogie saloons, 'caboose' style 1st/3rd/brake van, military precision-working (despite total absence of passengers) and the only two locomotives were named after the officers who built the line: Kitson 2-6-4T No 1 *E R Calthrop* and No 2 *J B Earle*.

Mr Calthrop's patent narrow gauge transporter was famous; it allowed a standard gauge waggon (milk or coal) to transfer straight across from the exchange station at Waterhouses (North Staffordshire Railway, later from 1923 LMS) piggyback style, to a narrow gauge truck fitted out to carry a short piece of 4ft 8.5 track mounted on a 2ft 6in platform. What a gem this line would be in today's preservation scene; handy for the M1, lovely countryside along the valleys of the Rivers Hemp and Manifold, and a trip to Sparrowlee, Beeston Tor Halt, Grindon Halt, Thor's Cave, Redhurst Crossing, Wetton, Butterton Halt, Ecton and Hulme End! In fact, thanks to Sir Josiah Stamp of the LMS, much of the trackbed has been retained as a nature walk; there is a bit of it you can drive along, including passing through Swainsley Tunnel (154yd). Much of the original is well captured in what is two films combined into one.

35/16mm, Silent, 10mins, HA

THE LEIGHTON BUZZARD NARROW GAUGE RAILWAY (Britain 1988)

Red Triangle Video. A detailed account of the railway, featuring the locomotive *Chaloner*. History of the line.

VID, Sound, Colour, 40mins, Red Triangle Video

LET'S GO TO BIRMINGHAM (Britain 1962)

Produced by British Transport Films. Five and a half minutes from Paddington to Birmingham, Snow Hill, in the driver's cab of the Blue Pullman; to the accompaniment of Johann Strauss's *Perpetuum Mobile*, the camera makes the journey at a speed of about 960mph! Inside the train, passengers eat and drink, sleep or read, oblivious of the speed at which they travel.

35/16mm, Sound, Colour, 6mins, BTF

LET'S IMAGINE A BRANCH LINE (Britain 1963)

BBC Television West. Produced by Brian Johnson. Made with the simpliest of resources, this regional programme featured John Betjeman on the Somerset & Dorset Joint, notably at Evercreech Junction and on the branch to Highbridge. It has some classic Betjeman throwaway lines, like 'By the way, you will notice, because it's been paid for by the BBC, that I am actually travelling first class'.

16mm, Sound, 14mins, BBC TV

LETTER FOR WALES (Britain 1960)

Produced by British Transport Films. Watching the Night Mail Train leave Paddington Station, a Welshman Donald Houston, remembers the engine he wanted to drive as a child: the one that climbs Snowdon! This recalls other memories; of bridges, boats and dolphins, of first love, and slate quarries. Then with the launching of the lifeboat at Tenby, the spray dissolves to steam and our Welshman is back at Paddington.

35/16mm, Sound, Colour, 25mins, BTF

A LEVEL CROSSING AT JOINVILLE-LE-PONT (France 1896)

Pathe. A train at a level crossing in France.

35mm, Silent, 43seconds, NFA

LEVEL CROSSING GATES (Britain 1956)

Produced by British Transport Films.

Part 1: General Salient points in the mechanism of various types of level crossing gates are shown and explained.

Part 2: Mechanism One representative type of level crossing gate is selected and its mechanism and working principles shown in detail.

Part 3: Maintenance The linesman and his assistant are shown inspecting, cleaning and adjusting the parts of a typical mechanically-operated level crossing gate.

35/16mm, Sound, 45mins, BTF

LEWISHAM CRASH (Britain 1955)

Newsreel record of the crash on 2 December 1955, when a Cannon Street-Ramsgate train, hauled by SR 'Battle of Britain' 4-6-2 No 34066 *Spitfire*, crashed into the back of a Charing Cross-Hayes that was standing at signals. The accident took place in fog and by an unhappy chance, the locomotive's tender was flung against the stanchions of the overbridge that carried the Nunhead line over the main tracks, bringing down two massive girders which crushed and killed many passengers in the second and third coach of the Ramsgate train. In all, 90 people were killed and 109 injured. The newsreel brings out the full horror of the collapsed bridge as well as shots of a train on the Nunhead-Lewisham route above, which, despite the fog, was brought to a stop literally above the wreckage below onto which it seemed destined to fall had it not been for the alertness of the driver who spotted the girders distorting, even though he only had restricted visibility.

16mm, Sound, 8mins, HA (ref)

LICHFIELD RAILWAY CRASH (Britain 1946)

Newsreel of the result of a crash near Lichfield station on 1 January 1946 when a fish train, hauled by LMS '5' 4-6-0 No 5495, ran into the

Left:
A stuntman in German uniform falls victim to 'Kelly's Heroes'. As is common in such scenes he is falling into a specially prepared pit filled with cushioning material lightly covered with earth.

Below:
From 'Khartoum', General Gordon (Charlton Heston) awaits his meeting with Prime Minister Gladstone.

Overleaf, top:
A carefully posed still of a dramatic moment from Hitchcock's classic 'The Lady Vanishes'. The photo also gives a good impression of the studio-built carriage interior.

Overleaf, bottom:
From Hitchcock's 'The Lady Vanishes' – who is lying disguised by the bandages?

back of a local train standing at the station, with LNWR 'Prince of Wales' 4-6-0 No 25802 on the front. The cause was a mis-interpretation of signals by the fish train driver. 20 people were killed and 21 injured. A contributing factor was frozen ballast on a set of points.

16mm, Sound, 4mins, Visnews/HA (ref)

🚂 🚂 🚂 🚂 🚂

THE LICKEY INCLINE (Britain 1950)

Much effort from two 'Jinties' as they latch on to an uphill train in Bromsgrove Station; the Midland Railway *Big Bertha* 0-10-0 No 58100 is at rest; and the huge LNER Beyer-Garratt 2-8-8-2, introduced in 1925, trundles through the yards at Bromsgrove in 1950.

16mm/VID, Silent, 8mins, CV/NRM/Stirling

🚂 🚂 🚂 🚂 🚂

LIEUTENANT DARING AND THE PLANS OF THE MINEFIELD (Britain 1911)

From the *Lieutenant Daring* series. Produced by British and Colonial. Directed by Dave Aylott. A long chase forms the main part of the action, showing scenes by road, rail and in the air between Charing Cross Station, Folkestone Harbour and France.

The film provoked a letter by Mr Haines to the editor of the *Kinematograph and Lantern Weekly* (6 March 1913) which is not without interest:

'I was greatly interested and not a little amused to observe the effect upon a Guernsey audience of a set of moving pictures, more or less of a modern trend. A moment's reflection makes it obvious that the people of a small island are going to receive totally different impressions from a set of pictures than an ordinary English audience viewing the same films would experience. For instance, you would see nothing of extraordinary interest in watching a train passing across the picture. In Guernsey, however, a large percentage of the population has never seen a train of any description and their first introduction to such a thing usually takes place at the photoshow. In Jersey, it

is true, there is a small railway — the pride of the islanders and envy and despair of their keen rivals the Guernseyites. One often hears it boasted by a Guernsey man that he has been to Jersey, and seen or even used the railway of his more fortunate brother, the Jerseyite. Taking into consideration this one fact, the following incident will sufficiently explain itself.

'One evening I strolled into a picture show in St Julian's, the People's Picture House, a theatre accommodating about a thousand, at a rough guess, thriving well under the management of Mr Bartlett. A "Daring" film was showing — I believe it was the *Plans of the Mines* — packed with exciting incidents from start to finish. An anarchist had got away with some plans, and eluded Daring by boarding the boat train, which the enterprising Lieutenant endeavoured to overtake on a motor-cycle. The road ran parallel with the railway, and as the cyclist shot round the bend, the express steamed into view from under a bridge.

' "Look, oh look," I heard from various parts of the hall.

'I glanced up at the picture quickly — thinking I had missed some important piece of work. All seemed in order — Daring was safe on his motorcycle, and the train was not derailed or anything.

' "A train," I heard whispered around me. Then I understood. Many of those in the theatre had never seen a train in the pictures before — let alone a real one — hence the excitement. Those who had either been to Jersey and seen the trains there, or who had crossed to England, were subjected to much examination as the reality of the train on the screen — for many were sceptical and insinuated that the picture was a "fake".

' "Are they really like that — and do they go as fast?" asked a little Guernsey servant maid of her youthful cavalier from the Fort.

' "Yus, mi dear, course they do — an' a lot faster".

' "I wonder however people manage to hold on — I know I would fall off," she murmured.

' "Oh no you wouldn't, leastways, not if I was there to hold you _."

' "Look!" she broke in, interrupting his amorous speech — she'd heard

these Irish Tommies before.

' "What's the marrer?", he asked rather grumpily.

' "Can't you see, they've made a horrible mistake, the train must have got off the line; it's running right into that big house with a glass roof. Oh! There'll be an accident now," and she broke off, covering her face up with a muffler until the awful catastrophe was over. Tommy laughed, and when he had finished, the train was standing quietly alongside the platform.

'The maid looked up and saw it.

' "Didn't it run into the house after all?", she asked.

' "Course not, you silly, that's not a house, it's a station."

' "Please?", queried the girl.

' "A station, that's a place where the trains go to get passengers. That glass roof is to keep the rain out when you're waiting for a train".

' "Well, how did it get in there without knocking down the house-part?" demanded she.

' "Cause there's lines laid through the station and a space let for trains so they shan't knock walls and things down".

' "Please, what else is there in a station?" she pursued.

' "Well," meditatively sucking his pipe, "There's a buffet, that's a place where you can stick your luggage if you like, a cloakroom, and where you can send telegrams and telephone messages. Oh, all sorts of things; you jes' wait until you see 'em.

' "What wonderful places they must be. Oh, I should love to see one. Do you ever think I shall?" she concluded moving closer to him. But Tommy, wise to his generation, drew attention to the crowd of passengers leaving the train at Folkestone. Amongst them was the anarchist and his accomplice in whom interest had waned owing to the extraordinary phenomenon of a train in a station.

'During the chase I believe an aeroplane from the B&Cs sheds figures conspicuously, but this did not excite much interest for most Guernsey people have seen the real thing. Grahame White, it will be remembered, paid the Island a visit.

'The education value of the moving picture is far wider in Guernsey than in this country, for, although in England the film may bring near to us delightful Swiss scenery, or mountains and lakes, yet we have most of us seen the charms of nature in our own country, in minature, whilst the Islanders have no mountains, no rivers, no wide plains, large forest lands, and lastly railway or river bridges, which seem to possess a remarkable fascination for these Island people.'

The last part of the film is a kaleidoscope of 1911 transport as Daring goes in pursuit of the Folkestone boat train. First, he borrows an old Rudge motorbike, then a horse, then a lovely old Darracq (X716) and finally some extremely rare shots of a British and Colonial (later Bristol) Boxkite at Brooklands, before moving to Filton.

A location shot at Charing Cross has a SECR 'F1' 4-4-0 in the background and a good action shot of a Wainwright SECR 'D' 4-4-0 No 729; there are also shots of Folkestone Harbour station and an SECR ship setting out for France. The film was made at the Walthamstow studios of British and Colonial.

35/16mm/VID, Silent, 12mins, NFA/HA/125

THE LIFE AND TIMES OF JUDGE ROY BEAN (USA 1972)

National General. Directed by John Huston. With Paul Newman, Ava Gardner and Jacqueline Bisset. An account of the famous outlaw judge and the old Wild West of America. Includes railway scenes shot on the Sierra Railroad, with very proper 4-4-0 Baldwin locomotives.

35mm, Sound, Colour, 124mins, National General

LIFE OF CHARLES PEACE (Britain 1905)

Produced by William Haggar. The activities of a famous Victorian villain. Includes a scene on the GWR (location unknown), recognised only by the scrolly brass door handles unique to the GWR at that time.

16mm, Silent, 14mins, NFA/HA

LIGHTWEIGHT ALUMINIUM TRAINS FOR TORONTO (Canada 1957)

The Aluminium Development Association. The construction and operating of lightweight suburban trains in Toronto.

16mm, Sound, Colour, 21mins, HA

LILLE-BASLE (Britain 1963)

Made by P B Whitehouse and John Adams. One of a number of excursions made by the *Railway Roundabout* team to record aspects of European travel.

16/8mm, Silent, 12mins, CV/NRM/VID

LIMESTONE SPECIAL (Australia 1963)

A TVT6 (Tasmania) television film. A television film of a diesel-hauled, narrow gauge quarry railway.

16mm, Sound, 6mins, HA

LIMPLEY STOKE — CAMERTON BRANCH

One of the classic lines for film makers, it ranks alongside the Basingstoke-Alton as a much loved route for the production of railway-oriented films. It was first used for the making of the original version of *The Ghost Train* in 1931, when Camarton became 'Fal Vale'. It was used again in 1938 for *Kate Plus Ten*, including Camerton and Dunkerton Colliery Halt. The master film was, of course, *Titfield Thunderbolt* when Monkton Coombe and a section of the line back to Bathampton and on to Bristol Temple Meads was featured.

Camerton closed to passengers back in 1925 as did the rest of the line; freight traffic kept it alive for a while but it was always a 'ghost' line from about 1930 onwards. At Midford, the line was crossed at Midford by the Somerset & Dorset Joint, providing the opening shot for *Titfield Thunderbolt* with a Southern Bulleid Pacific on the viaduct and a GWR '1400' tank below on the Camarton line. The S&DJ came to an end in 1966.

LINE OF DREAMS (Britain 1982)

BBC Television. Executive producer: Colin Adams. Written and prdouced by Gerry Troyna. Presented by John Shrapnel. From the *Great Little Railways* series.

John Shrapnel takes us on a journey through Rajastan from Jodhpur to Jaipur in India. The steam railway is a way of life to many — the only way to the Royal Palace — a six hour journey from Jaipur. This film tells the story of a 12-year-old boy who rides the train earning his keep singing to the passengers, constantly escaping the eyes of the train's company detective. The huge marshalling yards at Phalera are shown — the largest metre gauge system in India.

O P Dixit the railway detective tells of his exploits and demonstrates some of his many disguises. The Maruda Express eventually pulls into its journey's end, Jaipur, the Pink City.

16mm, Sound, Colour, 40mins, BBC TV

THE LINE THAT REFUSED TO DIE (Britain 1979)

BBC Television. Produced by Robin Bootle. Written and presented by Robert Symes. The story of the Ffestiniog Railway with good modern coverage by aerial shots as well as plenty of old photographs and archive film.

16mm, Sound, Colour, 50mins, BBC TV

LINK SPAN (Britain 1956)

British Transport Films. 24 hours in the life of British Railways Channel Ferryboats including the 'Night Ferry' for passenger services to Europe and the 'Lord Warden: for freight traffic. (From the *Just for the Record* series on video.)

VID, Sound, 20mins, BTF/RFV

LINK SPAN (Britain 1956)

A second version, produced by British Transport Films for the

British Transport Commission. 24 hours in the story of the British Railways Channel ferryboats, the link 'spans' directly joining the roads and railways of Britain with those of France and all the Continent. The *Lord Warden*, laden with an assortment of road vehicles, and the Night Ferry, carrying passengers from Dover, bound for Paris, Vienna or Rome, are two of the ferries illustrated in this film.

35/16mm, Sound, 25mins, BTF

🚂 🚂 🚂 🚂 🚂

LION

Locomotive *Lion*, built in 1838 for the Liverpool & Manchester Railway as their No 57, went to the Grand Junction Railway in 1845 and in 1859, it became a stationary pumping engine in Mersey docks. It was re-discovered in 1929 and was put back into full working order at Crewe for the 1930 Centenary Celebrations of the L&M. Here, it was filmed by W Bassett-Lowke, running round a circular track at Aintree. It was used for 'Victoria The Great' at Bricket Wood in 1937, for the London-Birmingham Centenary Celebrations in 1938 with newsreels and an early TV outside broadcast, for *The Lady with a Lamp* at Cole Green in 1951 and then to the final triumph as *The Titfield Thunderbolt* in 1952. During the production work on the Limpley Stoke to Camerton branch, it got a rather nasty clout. It was decided that it was too valuable as a relic to loan out to film makers and *Lion*'s career as a film star came to an end!

🚂 🚂 🚂 🚂 🚂

LION (Britain 1962)

Made by P B Whitehouse and John Adams. A film made at Dunchurch on one of the rare occasions when this famous old engine ran under its own steam. It was about to be passed back to the care of the Liverpool Industrial Museum.

16/8mm, Silent, 4mins, CV/NRM/HA

🚂 🚂 🚂 🚂 🚂

LION AT DIDCOT (Britain 1988)

A film by Ian and Stella Fagg. A record of the Liverpool & Manchester 1838 locomotive running and providing short trips at the Great Western Centre at Didcot in the summer of 1988.

16mm, Sound, Colour, 8mins, Fagg/HA

🚂 🚂 🚂 🚂 🚂

A LION IN SUMMER (Britain 1988)

A film by Don Sykes. A detailed record of the delivery, preparation and running of the Liverpool & Manchester Railway 0-4-2 *Lion*, built in 1838 at Steamport, Southport in June 1988.

16mm, Silent, Colour, 18mins, Sykes/HA

🚂 🚂 🚂 🚂 🚂

LISTEN TO BRITAIN (Britain 1941)

A Crown Film Unit production. Directed by Humphrey Jennings. Made for the Ministry of Information.

The sounds of wartime Britain, including a troop train at night, scenes at Waterloo station and a steam locomotive hauling a train-load of tanks from a factory. There are some highly atmospheric railway sounds including the clank of shunted goods wagons and a Gresley Pacific stopping and starting up from signals at night.

35/16mm, Sound, 20mins, COI/BFI

🚂

THE LISTOWEL & BALLYBUNION RAILWAY (Britain 1920)

Producer: unknown. A brief but effective record of the extraordinary twin engines of the Lartigue Railway Construction Company who built the Listowel & Ballybunion Railway. There are shots showing the 0-3-0 steam locomotive with its twin boilers, running on trestle rails. The problem of turning the locomotives, which involved a series of trestles radiating from a turntable, is clearly shown, despite the fact that surviving copies of the film are of poor quality. The line began in 1887 and was dismantled in 1924.

16mm/VID, Silent, 6mins, HA/125

🚂 🚂 🚂 🚂 🚂

LITTLE AND OFTEN (Britain 1947)

LMS Railway. A film to demonstrate the most economical way of firing a locomotive. LMS mixed traffic 4-6-0 No 4777 is shown; with a flat truck used as a camera platform inserted between the locomotive and tender in order to accommodate the camera and lights for the firing scenes. The main material was shot on the Hemel Hempstead branch line.

16mm, Sound, 20mins, NA

🚂 🚂 🚂 🚂 🚂

LITTLE TRAIN'S STORY (Yugoslavia 1967)

Produced by Yugoslavian State Railways. A record of the Ohrid narrow gauge line. The line dated back to the days of the Austro-Hungarian Empire, with locomotives coming from Berlin in 1917. This delightful film gives an excellent impression of a little country line and the charmingly informal nature of its operations. But a new road was built into the hills and the railway came to an end in 1967.

35/16mm, Sound, 19mins, HA

🚂 🚂 🚂 🚂 🚂

THE LITTLE TRAIN TO LYNTON (Britain 1987)

BBC Television (West). The story of the 2ft gauge Lynton & Barnstaple Light Railway which operated from 1898 to 1935. Archive film, photographs, scenes from 'then and now' and personal recollections of people who worked and travelled on the line were linked with a reconstruction of the past, using the Launceston preserved steam railway.

16mm, Sound, Colour, 60mins, BBC TV

🚂 🚂 🚂 🚂

LITTLEWORTH (Britain 1926)

A brief record of a feeder railway from nearby fields to the yard at Littleworth on the old Great Northern Railway in Lincolnshire between Spalding and Peterborough; the station closed in 1961. The agricultural railway uses an old World War 1 petrol-driven engine; its load is delivered to the care of a train headed by LNER 'J3' 0-6-0

No 4109, a Gresley rebuild of an 1892 Stirling/Ivatt design.

16mm, Silent, 2mins, HA

🚂 🚂 🚂 🚂 🚂

LIVERPOOL OVERHEAD RAILWAY (Britain 1935-56)

Various records exist of this railway. Material was shot by Patrick Whitehouse; it was featured in the film *Waterfront* (1950); in an LMS film in 1935; and in *Northern Journey* (qv). Some is now on video; other items are on film only. There is an excellent full-scale video available.

16mm/VID, Silent, 12mins, HA/Online

🚂 🚂 🚂 🚂 🚂

LIVING WITH LIZZIE (Britain 1987)

Railfilms. Produced by John Wildy. A detailed study of one locomotive: LMS 'Princess Royal' 4-6-2 No 6201 *Princess Elizabeth*. John Wildy has described the making of the video and the principles behind the production itself:

'When I first toyed with the idea of making a one hour video about a single locomotive, I had some doubt as to whether it would sustain interest for that long. I even wondered whether I could get enough material together.

'In the end, I had much more film than I needed! This has been put together in a way that is just a little bit different, hopefully to keep you glued to the screen for the full 60 minutes.

'By its very nature the video concentrates on the locomotive itself, and those who are solely concerned with its maintenance, testing and operation. What should not be forgotten is that this is only part of the whole. Without money raised from rail tours, sales and donations, distributed by the treasurer; without the membership secretary bashing out newsletters; the safety officer's checks; the secretary administering; the chairman keeping everyone in order and, finally, the ordinary working members, *Princess Elizabeth* would probably be razor blades by now. I, and many others, owe these un-paid professionals a deep debt of gratitude.

'On 7 February 1987 *Princess Elizabeth* hauled a 575ton train of mostly Pullmans, plus *Ethel*, between Leeds and Appleby. The weather was fine and dry and, despite indifferent coal quality (compared to her normal diet) the locomotive put in a magnificent performance, with spectacular columns of steam and smoke exhausting from her chimney; managing to keep more or less to time. This is thought to be the heaviest loaded passenger train ever successfully hauled by a preserved steam locomotive over the "Long Drag".

'Five weeks later 14 March) a reverse working was scheduled with one coach less. This is the story.

'The fire was lit at Carlisle Upperby at 11.30pm, the previous night. It began to rain, with a bitterly cold gusting wind; not a crashing downpour, just insidious and spitting with drizzle constantly mixed in, driving across the dimly lit yard, and moving south towards the mountains. The fireman was alternately frozen or smoked on the footplate.

'By 8am the following day 6201, gurgling nicely, was lubricated, had its daily exam', and nameplates fitted. Final cleaning took place, *Ethel* arrived and was attached. The rain had stopped and the rails were dry by departure time.

'An uneventful trip to Appleby followed. *Ethel's* brakes had given problems at Carlisle, and again at Appleby, but had seemed OK thereafter.

'6201 took water, backed down onto her train and pulled it into the station off the link line to Warcop, ready for the off, the fireman building up a big fire for the climb ahead.

'We left on time. By Helm tunnel speed was 30mph, full regulator, 30 per cent cut-off boiler pressure 230psi, when there was a bang. I think I was the only one to hear it – and only because this was the third time it had happened with me being on the footplate. The fireman's front lookout had broken, hit by a lump of tunnel roof lining. It looked quite dramatic, stuck half in and half out of the window, but there was no time to contemplate it, as coming out of the tunnel we had our first slip, not serious, well controlled, and away again. Sanders were used as needed for the rest of the trip.

'By Crosby Garrett conditions were about the same; From here there is a pw slack of 30mph to Kirby Stephen. Occasional slipping, low speed, but no real problems.

'It must have been around this time that I noticed that the rails had become greasy from the southwards moving rain. The weather had been closing in since we had begun the climb; now a thick drifting mist, with a cold side breeze predominated. Icicles, formed from melting snow, had frozen solid on the trackside rocks.

'We went through Kirby Stephen with partly opened regulator, 40 per cent cut-off, 230psi boiler pressure, between 20 and 25mph, and the slipping got worse and worse. The driver did an excellent job of controlling it, and the fireman the fire; but the train was steadily loosing momentum.

'A 20mph pw slack around Mallerstang did not help. Despite the fireman and inspector trying to assist by throwing grit from the lineside under the wheels, and the driver using the steam-operated sanders, speed dropped to walking pace, with slipping, then to a crawl, with more slipping, and we finally came to a stand on the last bend, between Hangmans Bridge and Ais Gill viaduct, about a mile from the summit.

'Fortunately, we have always carried spare dry sand in our support coach and this was applied in liberal quantities for some 100yd, or so on both rails in front of the loco. With 540 tons hanging onto the tender, on a curve, at 1 in a 100, the driver got us moving again and over the summit with only a couple more slips; the last of which you see on the video. The whistle, I might add, was blown with considerable relief!' (John Wildy)

(From the *Lineside View* series)

VID, Sound, Colour, 60mins, RFV

🚂 🚂 🚂 🚂 🚂

LLANBERIS LAKE AND SNOWDON MOUNTAIN RAILWAYS (Britain 1976)

HTV Television. Produced and directed by John Mead. Presented by Wynford Vaughn-Thomas. A narrow gauge passenger carrying railway starting at the historic Dinorwic Quarry workshops (now part of the National Museum of Wales) and

running along the shores of the Llanberis lake, using the trackbed of the former slate railway line to Port Dinorwic, with excellent views of Snowdonia. Which leads easily to the only rack and pinion railway in the British Isles which climbs up the slopes of Snowdon to the hotel at the top, often rising up through the clouds. The Llanberis Line is two miles; the Snowdon is four and three-quarter miles long. (From the *Great Little Trains of Wales* series).
16mm/VID, Sound, Colour, 26mins, HTV/Castle

🚂 🚂 🚂 🚂 🚂

LMA FILM EXTRACTS (Britain 1949)

Production shots made during the shooting of The Locomotive.
16mm, Silent, Colour, 7mins, Lama/HA

🚂 🚂 🚂 🚂 🚂

LMS AND LNER STEAM IN THE SIXTIES (Britain 1988)

Rail Video. Filmed in the 1960s this tape shows locos from these two rival companies hard at work on BR locations such as North Wales, Euston, Camden, King's Cross and York are the settings for many loco classes including 'Duchesses', 'Royal Scots', 'Jubilees', 'Black Fives', '8Fs', 'A1s', 'A2s', 'A3s', 'A4s', 'B1s', 'K1s' and a few BR Standards.
VID, Sound, Colour, 30mins, RVO

🚂 🚂 🚂 🚂 🚂

LNER/GREAT EASTERN MEMORIES (Britain, 1950)

Very soon after Nationalisation, 2-4-2T 'F5' No 67193 displays its new tankside lettering, a 'J15' 0-6-0 passes an elegant signalbox, and a 'J69' 0-6-0T is in action on the Kelvedon & Tollesbury Light Railway. A 'B1' passes on an embankment heading a mix of tank wagons and parcel cars, and 'J15' 65477 is seen at work. Another 'J15' 5420, complete with a tender-cab is on passenger service.
16mm/VID, Silent, 9mins, NRM/VID

🚂 🚂 🚂 🚂 🚂

LNWR HISTORY AT CHESTER (Britain 1948)

Allocated the BR number 58010, the very last 4-4-0 'Precursor' No 25297 *Sirocco* is seen in bright sunshine active at Chester, shortly before her withdrawal and the total demise of this famous LNWR 1904-built class.
16mm/VID, Silent, 7mins, NRM/Stirling

🚂 🚂 🚂 🚂 🚂

LNWR 1950 (Britain 1950)

Made by P B Whitehouse. A record of the few classes of the former LNWR locomotives which still survived including shots of *Hardwicke* (N790) and *Cornwall* (No 3020) at Crewe Works.
16mm, Silent, Colour, 8mins, CV/NRM/VID

🚂 🚂 🚂 🚂 🚂

LOCO NUMBER ONE (Britain 1948)

Empire Film. Directed by Francis Miller. Photography by Paddy Kingham. With Frank Hawkins and Gladys Tudor. 'Old Loco', once an engine driver, is now a model train enthusiast. In the film he relives one of his runs and describes the route from Mallaig to Glasgow. His friends discuss the run from Fraserburgh to Edinburgh.
35mm, Sound, 45mins Empire

🚂 🚂 🚂 🚂 🚂

LOCO SPOTTERS (Britain 1957-58)

A record of the activities of loco spotters at King's Cross and Euston stations. At King's Cross, they record in their Ian Allan books LNER 'A4' 4-6-2 No 60030 *Golden Fleece*, 'A1' 4-6-2 No 60113 *Great Northern*, 'V2' 2-6-2 No 60832 and 'L1' 2-6-4T No 67774. At Euston, they list LMS '4F' 0-6-0 No 44352, 'Jubilee' 4-6-0 No 45669 *Fisher*, 'Royal Scot' 4-6-0 No 46115 *Scots Guardsman*, and 'Princess' 4-6-2 No 46210 *Lady Patricia*. There is a useful record of the old Euston and a rare look at the youngsters of 35 to 40 years ago, still with a wide variety of steam to tick off in the little booklets that began life in 1942.
16mm, Silent, 14mins, HA

🚂 🚂 🚂 🚂 🚂

THE LOCOMOTIVE (Britain 1949)

Produced for the Locomotive Manufacturers Association of Great Britain by Furneaux-Weber Ltd, Produced by Rupert Furneaux. Technical advice by A J Lane. Written and directed by Cecil Musk. A short history of the steam locomotive and an extensive study of locomotive construction in Britain. There are shots of British Railways 'K1' class 2-6-0 Nos 62012 and 62015 coming off the production lines, a Bulleid British Railways West Country Pacific locomotive leaving Waterloo, a Beyer-Garratt leaving Gorton works and various steam locomotives on overseas railways, including a 2ft 6in gauge wood burner and steam locomotive on Indian Railways.
16mm, Sound, Colour, 29mins, Lama/HA

🚂 🚂 🚂 🚂 🚂

LOCOMOTIVE JUBILEE (Britain 1962)

Produced by British Transport Films. A visit by HRH Prince Philip adds further interest to an exhibition of locomotives in honour of the jubilee of the Institution of Locomotive Engineers. Among the engines on display was the record breaking *Mallard*, as well as the latest diesels now coming into service.
16mm, Sound, Colour, 10mins, BTF

🚂 🚂 🚂 🚂 🚂

LOCOMOTIVE LORD NELSON (Britain 1947)

SR 'Lord Nelson' 4-6-0 No 850 *Lord Nelson* is well featured in this film which is actually about road safety, a fact that is only revealed in the final moments. A schoolboy talks to the driver of *Lord Nelson* and imagines he is driving the train.
16mm, Silent, Colour, 9mins, HA

🚂 🚂 🚂 🚂 🚂

LOCOMOTIVE MAINTENANCE CONTROL (Britain 1966)

Produced by British Transport Films. This film explains a new concept in the control of diesel and electric locomotives, both in traffic and maintenance, which had then recently been put into practice on the London Midland Region. 'Centralised control and records, and a drastic reduction in the number of locomotive depots combine with the use of new equipment and methods to bring locomotive deployment and maintenance into line with the requirements of a modern locomotive fleet.'

25/16mm, Sound, 20mins, BTF

🚂 🚂 🚂 🚂 🚂

LOCOMOTIVE PRESERVED: ADAMS RADIAL (Britain 1964)

A film by Tom Martin. A record of preserved Adams LSWR '0415' 4-4-2T No 488 (30583), originally introduced in 1882. This locomotive was sold by the LSWR after reboilering to the East Kent Railway but was bought back by SR for use on the difficult Lyme Regis branch where these engines proved to be the best at coping with tricky curves and steep gradients. It is now preserved on the Bluebell Railway where this film was made.

16mm, Silent, Colour, 9mins, TM/HA

🚂 🚂 🚂 🚂 🚂

LOCOMOTIVE PRESERVED: AVELING & PORTER LOCOMOTIVE (Britain 1967)

A film by Tom Martin. A detailed record of the preserved single-cylinder geared locomotive built in 1926 for the Portland Cement Works at Snodland, Kent. It is now preserved on the Bluebell Railway. Named *Blue Circle* (works No 9449) it is rated as 2-2-0TG.

16mm, Silent, Colour, 8mins, TM/HA

🚂 🚂 🚂 🚂 🚂

LOCOMOTIVE PRESERVED: PIXIE (Britain 1967)

A film by Tom Martin. An RCTS special was the occasion for the making of this film record of Kerr/Stuart 0-4-0ST No 4260 Pixie on the Leighton Buzzard narrow gauge railway at Pages Park; it was built in 1922.

16mm, Silent, Colour, 7mins, TM/HA

🚂 🚂 🚂 🚂 🚂

LOCOMOTIVES (Britain 1934)

Produced by the GPO Film Unit. The début of Humphrey Jennings who later became celebrated for his films reflecting life in wartime London. Made with the cooperation of the Science Museum, this film shows model trains doing imitation duty for their real-life counterparts and ends with some actuality footage shot at King's Cross. An experimental film by a great director of the future, here learning his craft. Railway sights and sounds often featured in his later films, like *Listen to Britain* and *Spare Time*.

35/16mm, Sound, 1min, GPO

🚂 🚂 🚂 🚂 🚂

LOCOMOTIVES FOR ABROAD (Britain 1922-45)

Hundreds of British locomotives were built for overseas use. This reel contains a brief selection including Armstrong-Whitworth locos for Australia, North British for India, Beyer Peacock for Africa and Australia and wartime 'Austerity' locomotives built by North British in Glasgow and bound for Europe after the D-Day invasion.

16mm, Sound and Silent, 12mins, HA

🚂 🚂 🚂 🚂 🚂

LOCOMOTIVES FOR D-DAY (Britain 1943-44)

Some 1,800 USA S.160 locomotives were shipped to Britain in the build-up to the D-Day landings in June 1944. This American 'Austerity' design was a committee job between US builders, including Alco, Baldwin and many others. Rather than have them standing around in store, a large number were put into use on British railways, with allocations to all four companies: GWR, SR, LNER and LMS. They steamed freely and were much liked by British loco men except for one snag. It was very difficult to read correctly the water level in the boiler, especially in the blackout. As a result, there were two or three disastrous accidents, notably when one blew up in the Watford tunnel, killing the crew. They all went to Europe after June 1944, but three have since been

brought back to Britain and can be seen in action. The film shows the arrival of the locomotives, their assembly at Eastleigh, a brief scene of one working a freight train in the south and their shipment through Southampton Docks to France.

16mm, Silent, 6mins, HA

🚂 🚂 🚂 🚂 🚂

LOCOMOTIVES OF LONDON TRANSPORT (Britain 1961)

Made by P B Whitehouse and John Adams. Scenes at Neasden shed of steam locomotives followed by shots at Rickmansworth of the change over of steam to electric traction, featuring ex-Metropolitan Locomotive *Sherlock Holmes*.

16/8mm, Silent, 7mins, CV/NRM

🚂 🚂 🚂 🚂 🚂

LOCOMOTIVES OF THE SNOWDON MOUNTAIN RAILWAY (Britain 1966)

Made by Trevor White. The principal items of motive power.

16/8mm, Silent, Colour, 7mins, TW

🚂 🚂 🚂 🚂 🚂

LONDON-BRIGHTON IN FOUR MINUTES (Britain 1952)

BBC Television. An experiment in slow-speed camera work. The journey on the 'Brighton Belle' from Victoria station to Brighton was photographed at 2fps; at the normal projection speed of 24fps a speed of 60mph becomes 720mph on the screen and 70mph is 840mph. An impression of travel at approximately the speed of sound is obtained, with a clear record of the topographical features of the country between London and the Sussex coast.

35/16mm, Sound, 4mins, HA

🚂 🚂 🚂 🚂 🚂

LONDON EXPRESS (Britain 1898)

A Robert Paul production. GNR express at Wood Green.

35mm, Silent, 40secs, HA/125

🚂 🚂 🚂 🚂 🚂

LONDON TERMINUS (Britain 1943)

Raylton Productions. Activities of railway workers at a London Terminus.

35/16mm, Sound, 16mins

LONDON UNDERGROUND REVIEW (Britain 1989)

Online Video. Volume 1. Film from 1974 to 1989 by John Baker. An extensive look at the London Underground over the past 20 years; there is a major sequence on a railtour with Metropolitan electric locomotive *Sarah Siddons*. Produced by Wilf Watters.

VID, Sound, Colour, 55mins, Online

LONDON UNDERGROUND REVIEW (Britain 1989)

Online. Produced by Wilf Watters. Commentary by David Coleman. Photographed by John Laker. Material recorded since 1974, featuring many aspects of the London Underground system, including the Jubilee, Victoria and Bakerloo lines; 'D' stock on the District line; battery locomotives; Metropolitan locomotive *Sarah Siddons*; Acton Works; 1956 stock on the Northern Line; 1960 prototype stock on the Central Line; 1938 stock on the Bakerloo Line; withdrawal of 'R' stock in 1983; problems of the severe winter of 1982.

VID, Sound, Colour, 60min, Online

LONDON'S TRANSPORT (Britain 1959)

Produced by Kinocrat and the Central Office of Information for the Foreign Office. From the series *People and Places*: Arabic Teleview. With the daily life of London as his backgrond, Ali Nour, well-known Arab painter, reports on the intricate organisation behind London Transport. A daily average of nearly 10 million people use the city's many forms of transport, and Mr Nour sees something of the everyday routine in cleaning and checking the vehicles, and of the training given to conductors and drivers. He learns about the research which is carried out in order that London Transport operators and vehicles maintain their world-renowned reputation for efficiency and public service.
In Arabic only.

16mm, Sound, 12mins, COI

THE LONEDALE OPERATOR (USA 1911)

American Biograph production. Directed by D W Griffith. Photographed by G W (Billy) Bitzer with Blanche Sweet.

This is a dramatic account of a railway crash averted at the last moment and a significant advance in the development of film montage. Griffith here made strides in the cinematic or conjunctive method of narration: the tempo of continuity-movement was heightened; action-speed within the shot was increased; and very close shots were used both for detail and suspense. The technique of cross-cutting was also further developed.

This was one of the pioneer films made by the Biograph company in California; Hollywood as such was only a few months old. The line selected for the location work was the Santa Fe and the film contains excellent shots of Santa Fe American-type locomotive No 9, a design of the 1870's which was scrapped by the Santa Fe in Topeka in 1914.

35mm, Silent, 14mins, NFA

THE LONG ARM (Britain 1956)

Ealing Studios. Directed by Charles Friend. With Jack Hawkins, Dorothy Alison and Geoffrey Keen. A Scotland Yard detective solves a series of robberies. Includes scenes of Midland Region steam hauled trains.

35mm/VID, Sound, Weintraub/VID 125 (Rly)

THE LONG DRAG (Britain 1963)

Photographed and edited by Peter Boocock. Script and narration by Tom Blackburn. Directed by Donald Horsfall. A superbly detailed account by three railway enthusiasts of the Settle to Carlisle line which is now so famous but was, perhaps, almost unknown to those outside the area until this film won a 'Ten Best Award' organised by the magazine *Amateur Cine World* in 1964. When the Awards show was presented at the National Film Theatre, it was decided that it was too long to show in full, so an 18 minute extract was prepared and screened to great acclaim. Although the full version was shown later at the NFT, there is now some doubt as to whether the full version still survives.

Shot on 16mm Bolex camera, the full film covered the whole line from Settle, to Horton-in-Ribblesdale, Ribblehead, Dent, Garsdale, Kirkby Stephen West, Appleby, Appleby West, Culgaith, Armathwaite, Cotehill and Carlisle, in some cases with an examination of the station buildings and town itself. Motive power is at a magic moment when diesel traction was just beginning to appear, represented by what are now historical exhibits in the form of D153, D158 and D165. Steam abounds, with LNER 'A4' 4-6-2 No 60023 *Golden Eagle*, BR 'Britannia' 4-6-2 Nos 70023 *Venus* and 70048 *The Territorial Regiment 1908-1958*, LMS '3' 2-6-2T No 40075, LMS '4F' 0-6-0 Nos 44149 and 44554 and LMS '5' 4-6-0 No 45232 as well as an old Midland steam crane. The study of the camp that once served the building of Ribblehead Viaduct and scenes in the snow in the winter of 1962-63 are masterly.

16mm, Sound, Colour, 58mins/18mins ext, Boocock/ACW/IAC/BFI/HA (ref)

LONGMOOR AND AFTER (Britain 1983)

Rail video. The Longmoor Military Railway on an Open Day in 1968 with BR '9F' 2-10-0 No 92203; SR 'West Country' 4-6-0 No 34023 *Blackmore Vale*; the last day at Longmoor in 1969 with *Errol Lonsdale* and *Gordon*; and the dispersal of the locomotives from Longmoor to other preservation sites (RV4).

VID, Sound, Colour, 60mins, RVO

LONGMOOR MILITARY RAILWAY

The Longmoor Military Railway was established around the turn of the century. It was used by film makers from the 1930s including *The Lady Vanishes* (1938) the documentary *The Army Lays The Rails* (1942), *Bhowani Junction* (1956), *The Inn of the Sixth Happiness* (1958), *Runaway Railway* (1965), *The Great St Trinians Train Robbery* (1966); for a famous outside broadcast on TV of a locomotive and train being derailed; and the very last film, after the railway had technically closed, *Young Winston* (1972).

LONGMOOR MILITARY RAILWAY VISIT (Britain 1959)

SCTS. On this trip, the locomotives seen were Alfred Dodman (Kings Lynn) 0-4-2WT *Gazelle*, built in 1893 and at one time on the Shropshire & Montgomery Railway; and Avonside WD 0-6-0ST No 74 *Woolmer*. The day included a derailment demonstration, a World War 2 track wrecker in action and a forklift truck providing rides for children. A train is seen departing from Liss.

16mm, Silent, 5mins, HA/SCTS

A LONG TIME DYING (Britain 1967)

An uncompleted film, of which only the 'rushes' survive, about the sad scene, notably at Liverpool Street station, during the last days of steam on British Rail. The material is full of run-down steam atmosphere and it is sad that the film was never completed. There is no record with the raw material as to who made the film.

16mm, Silent, 22mins (rushes only), HA

LOOK AT LIFE: DRAW THE FIRES (Britain 1963)

Look at Life series No 17. Report on the modernization of the railways. The accent is on the end for the steam locomotive.

35/16mm, Sound, 9mins, Rank/HA

LOOKING AT TRANSPORT (Britain 1956)

Produced by British Transport Films. The design of London Transport's trains and vehicles, buildings, equipment and furniture reveals a style which is characteristic of the whole undertaking, a style which this film shows dates from 1916 when Frank Pick commissioned a new type-face for use in all London's public transport notices. Since then, and not least in its printing and posters, London Transport has sought to maintain a high standard of good looks throughout the wide field in which it operates.

35/16mm, Sound, 13mins, BTF

THE LOST FREIGHT CAR (USA 1911)

A Kalen Production. The yardmaster objects to Jim, a freight conductor, as a suitor for his daughter. Out on his run, Jim loses a freight car and is dismissed. Determined to clear his name Jim sets out to search for it. He sees a train in which the President is travelling, approach a burning bridge, Jim manages to stop the President's train in time, and at the same time discovers the missing freight car by the bridge. To mark his return to favour, the yardmaster gives his blessing to Jim and his daughter.

35mm, Silent, 8mins, NFA

LOVE ON THE DOLE (Britain 1940)

Produced and directed by John Baxter. With Clifford Evans and Deborah Kerr. Social drama of Lancashire life in the depression. Includes scenes at Blackpool station and on Lancashire sections of the LMS.

35mm, Sound, 90mins, NFA

THE LOVE MATCH (Britain 1955)

Group Three Production. Produced by John Baxter. Directed by David Paltengi. With Arthur Askey, Thora Hird and Robb Wilton. Football fans come from Lancashire to London. Includes steam railway scenes on the London Midland Region of British Railways, mainly stock shots but one action scene with a railway setting.

35mm, Sound, 85mins, Weintraub

LOVE ME TONIGHT (USA 1932)

Paramount picture. Produced and directed by Rouben Mamoulian. With Maurice Chevalier and Jeanette MacDonald. A Parisian tailor accidentally moves into the aristocracy. The film ends in a chase between a man on horseback and a train. The 'French' train looks very much indeed like one of those 4-4-0s left over from a Western as indeed does the stock, despite an optimistic 'Nogent-Vin' written on the cabside!

35mm, Sound, 104mins, Paramount

THE LOVES OF JOANNA GODDEN (Britain 1947)

Ealing Studios. Produced by Michael Balcon. Directed by Charles Frend. With Googie Withers, John McCallum, Jean Kent and Derek Bond. Romney Marsh at the turn of the century. Includes Kent and East Sussex locomotive No 3 and old SECR stock filmed near Lydd.

35mm, Sound, 89mins, Weintraub

LOW COMMOTION (Britain 1937)

A Kinograph production. Produced by William Duncalf. Commentary by Geoffrey Sumner. The film visits two large-scale O gauge layouts: 'Wingate' and 'Leaford', representing LNER and LMS; miniature railways at Amberley and Farnborough; the Bassett-Lowke factory at Northampton and well as scenes of toy and tinplate models. Odd US railroad stocks are scattered about; there are nine GWR run-passes (including streamlined, bullet-nosed No 6014 *King Henry VII*) and the film ends with a mock melodrama played by children on a garden miniature railway. (Unidentified).

16mm, Sound, 18mins, RF/HA

Left:
The train rolls into town in 'Last Train From Gun Hill'.

Below left:
A train may feature in the title and in the poster but is not such a major player in the film itself.

Overleaf, top left:
A train comes under attack from 'Lawrence of Arabia' and his Arab comrades. Violent and spectacular attacks on Turkish trains figure importantly in the plot and the development of Lawrence's character.

Overleaf, top top right:
From the British Transport Film 'Link Span', freight wagons being drawn off the *Norfolk* ferry.
British Railways

Overleaf, bottom:
The Majorca Electric Railway, as filmed by the author in 1955.

ACR
SOLLER
Ferrocarril Eléctrico

LSD (Britain 1964)

Produced by British Transport Films. Lost, Stolen, Damaged – the £2 million a year problem of claims against the British Railways is debated in this film, in which railwaymen, transport police and businessmen put their different points of view vividly and sometimes provocatively.

35/16mm, Sound, 30mins, BTF

LUCERNE: STEAMSHIPS, RAILWAYS, SCENERY (Britain 1988)

RV Television. A tourist's video which includes scenes on the Rigi Bahn Railway from a steam special to the summit.

Vid, Sound, Colour, 60min, RVV

🚂 🚂 🚂 🚂 🚂

LUMBER CAMPS RAILWAYS

The lumber camp railways of the United States were famous for their Shay-type locomotives, with a great mass of gearing on the side and the odd appearance of the cylinders. The film item gives excellent details of the Shay in action and the lumber operations it is designed to serve. There is a fascinating scene of a Shay hauling Palace stock car No 15610; the locomotive belonged to the Denver & Rio Grande Railroad and was filmed in 1911. The collection is completed with Chadwell O'Connors film of the Louisiana Cyprus Tree Lumber Camp railway, with LLC 4-6-2 No 1, oil-fired and in action. But perhaps the finest record of a lumber camp railway must still go to Buster Keaton and *The General*!

16mm, Silent, Part colour, 18mins, HA

🚂 🚂 🚂 🚂 🚂

LUMIERE FILMS: LIVERPOOL SCENES (Britain 1896)

When the Lumière Brothers presented their original film programmes in Britain from February 1896 onwards, they supplemented the shows with material filmed in this country, probably by their operator and technician Etienne Trewey. One item was a brief record of Lime Street station, Liverpool, and a short trip on the Liverpool Overhead Railway.

35/16mm, Silent, 4mins, LUM

🚂 🚂 🚂 🚂

LUMIERE PROGRAMME (France 1895)

The programme of the first public film shown in Britain, given at the Regent Street Polytechnic on 20 February, 1896; the subjects shown included *Arrival of a Train at La Ciotat Station* (filmed in July 1895) also called *The arrival of the Paris Express*. La Ciotat is a small seaside town on a branch line of the PLM from Marseilles; the locomotive is a PLM Bourbonaisse class 2-4-2 and is recorded in an almost classic three-quarter view. Not bad for 1895!

35/16mm/VID, Silent, 52secs, NFA/HA/125

🚂 🚂 🚂 🚂

LUZERN-STANS-ENGELBERG RAILWAY (Britain 1987)

RV Television. Cab ride from Luzern to Engelberg via the Obermatt rack and pinion section at 1 in 4, plus details of workshops, control system, postal sorting service and the modern trains themselves.

VID, Sound, Colour, 45min, RVV

🚂 🚂 🚂 🚂 🚂

L&Y SPECIAL (Britain 1961)

Made by P B Whitehouse and John Adams. An enthusiast's special hauled by Aspinall L&Y 2-4-2T No 50850 and Aspinall L&Y 0-6-0 No 52271 around little-used lines in the Manchester area.

16/8mm/VID, Silent, 7mins, CV/NRM/VID

🚂 🚂 🚂 🚂 🚂

LYNTON AND BARNSTAPLE RAILWAY (Britain 1933-35)

This record of the 1ft 11.5in narrow gauge line, which opened in 1898 and closed in 1935 is made up of various films taken by professional newsreels and amateur holidaymakers movies. There are good scenes of many of the locomotives including the Manning Wardle 2-6-2Ts *Yeo*, *Exe* and *Taw* as well as the distinctive US Baldwin 2-4-2T *Lyn*. There are scenes at Barnstaple Town, Chelfham, Bratton Fleming, Woody Bay and Lynton and Lynmouth. Lynton station was 250ft above sea level and the seaside town of Lynmouth, where most people were going. It became a casualty of a bus service when the road improved. At a protest meeting to save the railway in 1935, 80 people attended. They had all come to the hall by car, except the man from Waterloo who had come to close it down!

16mm, Silent, 12mins, HA

🚂 🚂 🚂 🚂 🚂

M

THE MAD TRAIN (USA 1925)

(See The Overland Limited)

THE MAGIC OF THE SEVERN VALLEY RAILWAY (Britain 1989)

Steam Reflections. A record made over two years of 21 locomotives (including seven visitors) on the famous line. Was ever a preserved railway recorded quite so massively?

VID, Sound, Colour, 120mins, SRV

THE MAGNET (Britain 1950)

Ealing Studios. Directed by Charles Frend. With Stephen Murray and Kay Walsh. Adventures of a small boy and his magnet. Includes a sequence on the now dismantled Liverpool Overhead Railway.

35mm, Sound, 79mins, Weintraub

MAGNUM (USA 1978)

NBC Television. American TV series which included episodes at Marylebone with John Roker.

TV, Sound, Colour, 28mins, NBC TV

MAIN LINE 1988 (Britain 1989)

Preserved steam on video. A comprehensive album of events in 1988 and includes the Settle-Carlisle line, *Mallard* 88, Salisbury, Welsh Marches, Marylebone-Sheffield, West Highland line, Shakespeare Ltd etc etc. All of the material was taken from the lineside and the film also features a brief commentary.

Locos included are: 92220 *Evening Star*, 5305 *Alderman A E Draper*, '8F' 48151, 7029 *Clun Castle*, 5080 *Defiant*, 4498 *Sir Nigel Gresley*, 34092 *City of Wells*, 5593 *Kolhapur*, 4468 *Mallard*, 'K1' 2005, 80080, 6201 *Princess Elizabeth*,

4472 *Flying Scotsman*, 5407, 44932 and 35028 *Clan Line*.

VID, Sound, Colour, 120mins, PSO

MAIN LINE KING (Britain 1987)

Railfilms. Produced by John Wildy. From the *Lineside View* series). A study of one preserved locomotive; a similar record was later made of *Princess Elizabeth*. GWR 'King' 4-6-0 No 6000 *King George V* was built in 1927 at Swindon, sent to America for the Fair of the Iron Horse, was in service until 1962, preserved at Bulmer's Siding at Hereford from 1968 and returned to the main line to haul Specials from 1972. This video picks up the story from 1983 to 1987 with a wide number of runs being documented, shed scenes, lineviews and a chance to watch one locomotive in action for three-quarters of an hour!

VID, Sound, Colour, 45mins, RFV

MAIN LINE STEAM ROUTES (Britain 1960-68)

Stirling Video. Produced by Dick Griffiths. From the 16mm Collection of Richard J Willis. Virtually the whole country is covered in the two volumes of this video; perhaps the largest 1960s steam assembly of them all.

(Volumes 1 and 2; each 50mins).

VID, Sound, Colour, 50mins each Volume, Stirling

MAINLINE STEAM ALBUM, 1985-88 (Britain 1989)

Steam Reflections. A survey of preserved steam outings of many different types recorded over a period of four years.

VID, Sound, Colour, 120mins, SRV

MAINTENANCE OF ELECTRICAL SIGNALLING EQUIPMENT (Britain 1958)

Produced by British Transport Films. *Part 1 – Outside Equipment*: the linesman and his assistant

inspecting and adjusting electrical equipment. *Part 2 – Outside equipment*: continuation of work shown in part 1. *Part 3 – Equipment at the Box*: The adjustment and maintenance of electrical equipment inside the signalbox.

35/16mm, Sound, 63mins, BTF

MAJORCA ELECTRIC RAILWAY (Britain 1955, 1990)

A film by John Huntley. The Siemens Schuckert Electric Railway on the island of Majorca between Palma and Söller. The film features the terrain, the journey and shed scenes at Söller, with locomotives Nos 3 and 4. The railway opened to steam in 1912 and was electrified with Carde and Escoriaza Bo-Bo saloon motor coaches with Siemens electrical equipment. It is still a considerable tourist attraction, especially for the plush padded first class coaches.

16mm, Silent, 6mins, HA

The railway was filmed in 1990 by Robert Ennis and was found to be much as it was in 1955.

16mm, Silent, 20mins, Ennis

MAJORCA STEAM RAILWAYS (Britain 1955)

A film by John Huntley. At one time, there was quite a network of steam railways from Palma to various parts of the island. This film records the shed at Palma with No 22 *Salinas*, No 32 *Lloseta* and a Nasmyth Wilson 2-4-2 No 14 *Arta* built in Manchester in 1887; as well as the departure of trains from the terminus.

16mm, Silent, 6mins, HA

MAKING A RAILWAY ENGINE (Britain 1909)

A Charles Urban film. Construction of a 1909 locomotive, at Crewe works of the LNWR.

35mm, Silent, 11mins, NFA

MAKING TRACKS (Britain 1956)

Produced by British Transport Films. 'Of the thousands of miles of railway lines in Britain hundreds are renewed every year. No longer is each rail manhandled by the men of the permanent way. Mobile cranes remove the old track, complete with sleepers, and replace it with prefabricated lengths. This has made the work less arduous, and the period during which the line is closed to traffic is considerably shortened.' This account of the workman seen from the point of view of the crane inspector is a version for public audiences of the staff instructional film *Mechanised renewal of plain line.*

35/16mm, Sound, 17mins, BTF

🚂 🚂 🚂 🚂 🚂

MALLARD: THE DRAKE'S PROGRESS (Britain 1990)

Anglia Television. Produced and directed by David Kenten. Written and presented by John Huntley. A celebration of the day in July 1938 when *Mallard* broke the world's speed record for a steam locomotive for all times at 126mph. The line between Little Bytham (closed 1959) and Essendine (also closed 1959) as it is today. The picture of *Mallard* on the village inn sign. Posters of the 1930s for *Mallard.* The history of LNER locomotives in the early days, including a stunt newsreel with a race between 'The Flying Scotsman' train, a De Havilland Puss Moth aircraft and a speed boat on the River Ouse at Oxford, near Huntingdon; Doncaster works in the 1930s; rare shots of Sir Nigel Gresley as host to a visit by the Institute of Locomotive Engineers in 1927 (with group photograph around *Great Northern*); the debut of No 10000 'Hush-Hush', Gresley's experimental Yarrow-boilered 450 psi engine of 1929 and scenes of LNER 'P2' 2-8-2 No 2001 *Cock o' The North* on test at Vitry in France and No 2002 *Earl Marischal* running near Welwyn Garden City.

There are scenes of the 'Silver Jubilee' train of 1935, including very rare shots in colour of LNER 'A4' 4-6-2 No 2509 *Silver Link* and No 2510 *Quicksilver* followed by a general selection of scenes of 'A4s' in action. Four of the men involved in the 1938 record breaking run recall the event, which was a joint effort between the LNER and the Westinghouse Brake Company, at

that time carrying out tests. The moment of triumph is recalled by Driver Duddington. The film continues with a brief history of *Mallard* since then, to the point when it was transferred to the National Railway Museum. The story ends with the restoration of *Mallard* to full working order, the museum setting, a Post Office Special and a journey from York to Scarborough, including aerial shots and footplate scenes.

16mm/VID, Sound, Colour, 28mins, Anglia/Stylus/HA (ref)

🚂 🚂 🚂 🚂 🚂

MAN HUNT (USA 1941)

20th Century Fox. Directed by Fritz Lang. With Walter Pidgeon, Joan Bennett and George Sanders. Nazi thriller including London Underground scene as reconstructed in Hollywood. American-style stock, small windows, wrong sound and other defects made it very 'studio' despite accurate Underground signs ('Piccadilly Line. Cockfosters via Hammersmith') but the villain was electrocuted on the centre (earth return) rail of the Piccadilly line system instead of the outer positive rail! There was no pit between the rails; and the insulators were of US design.

35mm, Sound, 102mins, TCF

🚂

THE MAN IN THE WHITE SUIT (Britain 1951)

An Ealing Studios film. Directed by Alexander Mackendrick. With Alec Guinness and Joan Greenwood. Comedy of a chemist who discovers an indestructible material. Includes a sequence at Stonebridge Park Underground station.

35mm, Sound, 85mins, Weintraub

🚂

MAN OF THE WEST (USA 1958)

United Artists. Directed by Anthony Mann with Gary Cooper and Lee J Cobb. Arizona 1874. A retired gunman is persuaded to help some of his old mates rob a bank. Includes scenes on the Sierra Railroad with Rogers 4-6-0 Locomotive No 4493, built in 1891, so quite accurate.

35mm, Sound, Colour, 100mins, United Artists

🚂

MAN WHO LOVES GIANTS (Britain 1990)

Start/Pickwick Video. A record of David Shepherd and his work for the World Wildlife Fund, as an artist and a fund raiser. His paintings of elephants in the wild first brought him to fame. His other 'giant' interest is steam engines. He owns two ex-BR steam locomotives in working order and is Chairman and Founder of the East Somerset Railway at Cranmore in Somerset. This video shows many aspects of David Shepherd's life and includes scenes of his railway paintings being made in 1967 at Nine Elms on the Southern taken from the film *The Painter and the Engines* by Paul Barnes.

VID, Sound, Colour, 75mins, Start

🚂 🚂 🚂

THE MAN WHO WATCHED THE TRAINS GO BY (Britain 1952)

Raymond Stross production. Directed by Harold French. With Claude Rains and Marta Toren. A meek Dutchman goes to Paris on stolen money to enjoy the good life but ends up attempting suicide. Extensive use is made of various Continental railway locations, including Dutch electrics on a full barrier crossing ('Post 37'). 'Quevy' station on the route from Amsterdam to Paris and a major location in an SNCF yard on the outskirts of Paris (Paris Cabine No 3, with Sacré Coeur in the far distance) involving steam locomotives and a night scene.

35mm, Sound, Colour, 80mins, Stross

🚂 🚂

THE MAN WITH A MOVIE CAMERA (USSR 1928)

Directed by Dziga Vertov. Photography by M Kaufman. A 'Kino-Eye' documentary of Moscow which includes a number of railway scenes.

16mm, Silent, 90mins, BFI

🚂 🚂

THE MAN WHO WOULD BE KING (USA 1975)

Columbia. Directed by John Huston. With Sean Connery, Michael Caine and Christopher Plummer.

India in the days of Rudyard Kipling. Includes a scene of the arrival of a steam-hauled train in a remote area, filmed with the help of Indian Railways.

35mm, Sound, Colour, 129mins, Columbia

MANCHESTER-SHEFFIELD-WATH RAILWAY ELECTRIFICATION (Britain 1956)

British Insulated Callender's Constructions. The first mainline electrification scheme in Britain using the overhead system.

16mm, Sound, 15mins, BICC

MANCHURIA EXPRESS (Britain 1989)

Central Television. Produced and directed by John Bird. Presented by Julian Pettifer and Maggie Whitehouse. Interpreter and representative of China National Railways is Ning Fang. Maggie Whitehouse, an expert on Chinese railways, was on her fifth visit when joined by the film unit. The 27 hour train journey took the Chinese and English pair from Beijing to the far North-East forestry area just 200 miles from the Soviet border (an area where few Westerners have ever been) and to a small logging town called Langxiang. There are excellent scenes of the engine workshops at Changchun where the giant steam engines are stripped down to their frames and rebuilt in a Dickensian world of dirt and darkness; the shunting yards to see the engines watered and coaled up; and the Manchurian countryside where the trains still travel on rails laid by the then-occupying Japanese. Here, steam is not a tourist attraction but part of the complex logistics of running a railway in China, where it is necessary to limit the number of passengers on the station concourse and where the railway, still mainly steam-powered, acts as a primary form of national transport.

VID, Sound, Colour, 46mins, Central

THE MANCHURIAN CANDIDATE (USA 1962)

United Artists. Produced by Howard W Koch. Directed by John Frankenheimer. With Frank Sinatra, Laurence Harvey and Angela Lansbury. A Korean war hero comes back a brainwashed zombie, programmed to kill a liberal politician. His first steps to sanity come during a train journey from New York to Washington (diesel-hauled, on the New York Central) and filmed on a real train, not a studio mockup. 'Although it's a thriller, it may be the most sophisticated political satire ever to come out of Hollywood.' (Pauline Kael).

35mm, Sound, 126mins, United Artists

MANHANDLING (Britain 1962)

Produced by British Transport Films. 'It ain't what you do, it's the way that you do it' – the popular song is particularly apposite when you lift heavy weights, as many railwaymen know to their cost. The wrong way can produce aches, pains, strains, sprains, and even slipped discs. With the help of a young weight-lifting lady this film shows how to avoid all the strains and make the job easier into the bargain.

35/16mm, Sound, 10mins, BTF

MANX ELECTRIC RAILWAY (Britain 1967)

Made by Trevor White. Impressions of a ride on the railway.

16/8mm, Silent, Colour, 4mins, TW

MARCH TO HINTON (USA 1957)

Steam Powered Video. Produced by Video Rails. 5,000ton coal trains steam hauled in West Virginia in winter, with scenes in snow and frost. C&O Locomotive No 614. *Railway World* said it was 'simply one of the most exciting tapes on the market'.

VID, Sound, Colour, 30mins, SPV

MARGATE MINIATURE RAILWAY

Only a couple of shots from an 8mm holiday film, it features DMR 0-4-4 No 359 Ford 10hp petrol engine locomotive with BR double-bogie diesel engine outline.

16mm, Silent, Colour, 2mins, HA

MARVELLOUS TRIP (France 1975)

French Railways. A history of rail-cars in France, including the Lyon-Bordeaux route.

16mm, Sound, 14mins, SNCF

THE MARX BROTHERS GO WEST (USA 1940)

MGM. Directed by Edward Buzzell. With the Marx Brothers, John Carroll and Diana Lewis. Comedy Western. The elaborate scene of taking a moving train to bits was made using almost the whole length of the Sierra Railroad from Oakdale to Tuolumne and featuring Baldwin locomotive 2-8-0 No 29790 of 1906 vintage as well as an elaborate studio mock-up of a 4-4-0.

35mm, Sound, 82min, MGM

MARYLEBONE EXHIBITION (Britain 1964)

Made by P B Whitehouse and John Adams. A display of steam and diesels using two plaforms of the old Marylebone layout.

16/8mm, Silent, 8mins, CV/NRM/VID

MATLOCK RAILWAY CLUB

Run by L W Henshaw, this society has for many years specialised in the presentation of an amazing series of film shows of transport material, unearthing rare films from specialised sources to supplement the more familiar railway classics. Les Henshaw and his colleague, Mr K Plowman, have also presented film shows in the Derbyshire area; they have also preserved some of the New Zealand railway films which are no longer available through the normal channels.

A MATTER OF LIFE AND DEATH (Britain 1946)

Archers film. Written and directed by Michael Powell and Emeric Pressburger. With David Niven and Kim Hunter. Fantasy. London Passenger Transport Board, in conjunction with Rownson, Drew and Clydesdale, were called in to build a giant escalator, fitted with a two-gear 12hp engine, giving speeds of 30-60ft/min, carrying camera crew and lights as well as the actors. The escalator moved between the earth and heaven!

35mm, Sound, Colour, 104mins, Rank

MAUNSELL HAULED (Britain 1961-66)

Made by G S Holyoake. Classes 'U', 'N', 'Q' and 'S15' at Reigate, Partridge Green, Comshall, Basingstoke, Wimbledon and Virginia Water. LCGB 'S15' Commemorative Railtour and a special on Meadstead Bank are featured.

16/8mm/VID, Silent, Colour, 4mins, FMS/VID

MAURITIUS RAILWAYS (Britain 1965)

Made by P B Whitehouse and John Adams. World traveller Pat Whitehouse visited this unusual location for a wide range of steam locomotives, many of them very ancient.

16/8mm, Silent, 11mins, CV/NRM/VID

THE MAVERICK QUEEN (USA 1955)

Republic. Directed by Joe Kane. With Barbara Stanwyck, Barry Sullivan and Scott Brady. A lady rustler and a detective sent to unmask her fall in love. 'Tedious Western in bilious colour' (Leslie Halliwell). The attack on a train was staged on the Durango-Silverton preserved railway.

35mm, Sound, Colour, 90mins, Republic

MAVERICK'S SERIES: STOCKBEDS AND STEAM (Britain 1983)

BBC Television. Written and presented by Geoff Hamilton. A detailed look at the narrow gauge line with ex-Welsh Quarries locomotives Hunslet 0-4-0ST Gwynedd and George Sholto, as well as views of the traction engine collection and preserved BR 'Britannia' 4-6-2 No 70013 Oliver Cromwell.

16mm, Sound, Colour, 26mins, BBC TV

MARYLEBONE STATION

Ever since it was used for the first-ever appearance on the screen of the Beatles in 1964, the star of London termini in the cinema was undoubtedly Marylebone, tucked away behind the Marylebone Road and quiet enough to give film crews the chance to work in peace and away from the public view. Before the 1989 announcement of the ambitious £74 million route modernisation, the future of the Chiltern line looked uncertain, and it was widely rumoured that Marylebone was to be closed. The departure of a major section of the administration of British Rail from the old Marylebone hotel fuelled the flames of doubt about its future. But it has now been completely renewed. What was good for commuters from Great Missenden and Seer Green spelled the end of Marylebone as a mini-Hollywood. Incidentally, it also wrecked the schedules of the steam specials from Marylebone for 'Sunday Shakespeare' trips and Santa outings, much to the annoyance of Flying Scotsman Enterprises and other operators.

The former traffic manager at Marylebone in film making days was John Roker, who often was pushed into appearing in various roles himself. 'The closure of the line seemed imminent,' Roker remembers, and it was as much to raise morale among the staff as anything else that two colleagues and myself decided to put the word about that Marylebone, with its 1899 features almost intact, would make an ideal film venue.' It worked. A Hard Day's Night, The

Ipcress File two Miss Marple films At Bertrams Hotel and 4.50 From Paddington, In Sickness and in Health, Foreign Bodies and many others were made there. Roker found himself hosting scenes from American television series such as Magnum and Remington Steele, looking after Joan Hickson in the Miss Marple films and playing a porter driving a parcel trolley for Warren Mitchell's classic In Sickness and in Health, with script by Johnny Speight.

MEASURED FOR TRANSPORT (Britain 1962)

Produced by British Transport Films. A transformer, weighing 123 tons, is required for a remote site at Blaenau Ffestiniog in North Wales. First the rail and road journey must be planned, then the transformer fitted to cope with the complexities of the route; and finally the special transportation equipment and crews must carry the job through.

35/16mm, Sound, Colour, 13mins, BTF

MEASURED PACKING (Britain 1953)

Produced by British Transport Films. Part 1. Straight Track: Loose, uneven packing of ballast causes uncomfortable riding, and shortens track life. Measured packing is the scientific way of making track firm and level by placing accurately calculated quantities of stone chippings under individual sleepers. The film shows the special equipment used and demonstrates in detail the various steps necessary to deal with a section of straight track. Part 2. Curved Track: The additional factor of cant must be taken into account when applying measured packing to curved track. The film gives a quick recapitulation of measured packing on straight track, and then shows how cant is allowed for on curved track.

35/16mm, Sound, 67mins, BTF

MEASURED SHOVEL PACKING (Britain 1938)

An LMS film. An instructional film explaining in detail the method of laying and packing sleepers on both straight and curved track.

35mm/VID, Sound, 10mins, BTF/TVP

MECHANICAL HANDLING OF TRAFFIC (Britain 1948)

Produced by British Transport Films for the British Transport Commission. This film shows some of the many mechanical devices used by British Railways for the handling of freight.

35/16mm, Sound, 21mins, BTF

MECHANICAL POINT OPERATION (Britain 1954)

Produced by British Transport Films. *Part 1. Layout of Rodding and connections*: A simple explanation mainly for the recruit, of the rods, cranks, and other fittings, and their function in the system of transmitting movement from the levers in the signalbox. *Part 2. Maintenance of rodding and connections*: The lineman and his assistant are shown doing their regular inspection, cleaning and adjusting the parts of a typical mechanically operated points system, from the lever trail under the box through the leadaway and the rodding run to the points. *Part 3. Maintenance of points and fittings*: Some examples of various point layouts are followed by a more detailed explanation of the operation and maintenance of a set of facing points. The use of the lineman's gauge is demonstrated in checking the clearances at the facing-point lock of double-ended points. Double-ended points are shown out of adjustment. The lineman and his assistant carry out the necessary work to bring them back to normal operation.

35/16mm, Sound, 68mins, BTF

A MECHANICAL RAIL CREEP ADJUSTER (Britain 1951)

Produced by British Transport Films. This film shows in some detail the adjustment of rail-creep on a section of line where some expansion gaps have closed too much while others have opened too wide. A mechanical device, the creep adjuster, is used to correct rail-creep. This is a horizontal screw jack which can be attached to the rail at a joint, and which can push or pull several hundred yards of rail at a time. This film was made in association with British Transport Films by World Wide Pictures.

35/16mm, Sound, 18mins, BTF

MECHANICAL SIGNAL OPERATION (Britain 1955)

Produced by British Transport Films. *Part 1 Layout of signal connections*: An explanation of the main types of mechanical signal and of the mechanism which transmits movement from levers to signal. *Part 2 Maintenance of signals and connections*: The lineman and his assistant are shown carrying out regular inspection, cleaning and adjusting the parts of a typical mechanically operated signal system from the lever tail through the leadaway and wire run to the signals.

35/16mm, Sound, 64mins, BTF

MECHANISED RENEWAL OF PLAIN LINE (Britain 1956)

Produced by British Transport Films. The weekly cycle of operations covers pre-assembling, building of new sections at the depot, the removal of old track from the site and its replacement by new. Timing is arranged to cause least interference to the running of trains. The film also shows measuring up on the site and how the data is employed as the basis for pre-assembly. There is a version of this film for public audiences under the title *Making Tracks*.

35/16mm, Sound, 33mins, BTF

MEET NEW ZEALAND (INDUSTRY AND TRANSPORT) (New Zealand 1948)

Produced by New Zealand National Film Unit. 'Although New Zealand is an agricultural country, only one worker in five is employed directly on the land. This film shows the growth of industry and industrial research; and dwells particularly on the expansion of the transport system, by rail, road and air, showing its importance for business purposes, as well as for the holiday maker.'

16mm, Sound, 10mins, NZF

MEMORIES OF STEAM AT HORSESHOE CURVE (USA 1930-50)

Locomotives include 'K4' Pacifics, and the 2-10-0 and 4-8-2 engines that frequented this section of the line.

8mm, Silent, Colour, 4mins, Blackhawk

MEN OF THE FOOTPLATE (Britain 1938)

An LMS film. An account of the progress of a trainee from engine cleaner to fireman and eventually to engine driver. There are many depot and shed scenes as well as views of LMS passenger and freight trains in action. The truth behind the basic 1930s belief that 'every schoolboy wanted to become an engine driver'.

35mm/VID, Sound, 21mins, BTF/TVP

MEN ON THE MEND (Britain 1956)

Produced by British Transport Films. Joe Miller, injured in the Western Region railway workshops, goes to the Rehabilitation Workshop at Swindon. There, together with other men, he exercised his injured limb on machines specially built or adapted for the purpose, and turns out articles necessary to British Railways. After a reduced period of convalescence he returns, fully recovered, to duty.

35/16mm, Sound, 13mins, BTF

THE MERCENARIES (Britain 1968)

MGM. Directed by Jack Cardiff. With Rod Taylor, Yvette Mimieaux and Kenneth More. A fortune in diamonds is brought out in an armoured train by a group of mercenaries in the Belgian Congo in 1960. Some of the action was shot in Spain, and it was Spanish Railways that provided a mock-up armoured train and suitably disguised old 4-4-0 locomotive. The main scenes were staged in the area around Seville on freight-only lines.

35mm, Sound, Colour, 100mins, MGM

🚂 🚂 🚂

METROLAND (Britain 1973)

BBC Television. Produced by Edward Mirzoeff. Written and presented by John Betjeman. An old film *A Trip on the Metro* made in 1910 and preserved by the National Film Archive, became the inspiration for this superb study of the line from Baker Street to Aylesbury. The early material is cut with modern scenes, showing the countryside that has changed so much over the years, the plans of the Metropolitan Railway to develop in a very positive way the places covered by the line and how the residential areas reflect a way of life over a period of some 70 years. All this could have been pretty dull; it is transformed into sheer magic by the poems and commentary by John Betjeman.

16mm, Sound, Colour, 49mins, BBC TV

🚂 🚂 🚂 🚂 🚂

METROLAND (Britain 1981)

BBC Television and Video. Written and presented by John Betjeman. The story of the Metropolitan Rilway from Baker Street to Verney Junction and its links with the Midland Railway. The programme takes in Chiltern Court at Baker Street, the British Empire Exhibition at Wembley in 1924, the houses designed by Norman Shaw and Voysey. Chorley Wood and the owner of a cinema organ in his house. Interspersed with an old archive film of a journey from Baker Street to Aylesbury made in 1910. A slightly altered version of the classic 1973 BBC programme. Superbly presented.

VID, Sound, Part Colour, 47mins, BBC Video

🚂 🚂 🚂 🚂 🚂

METROPOLITAN AND DISTRICT: A DRIVER'S EYE VIEW (Britain 1990)

Video 125. Produced by Peter Middleton. Commentary by Rob Curling. The Hammersmith and City line from Hammersmith to Whitechapel includes the very first section of public underground railway in the world. The 'C' stock train is changed for a District line 'D' stock at Whitechapel as the journey continues along the Circle line from Tower Hill to Gloucester Road and thence out in the open from Earls Court to Ealing Broadway. The film was made with no artificial lighting, a technique made possible by a special Sony ultra-fast video camera.

VID, Sound, Colour, 85mins, 125

🚂 🚂 🚂 🚂 🚂

METROPOLITAN RAIL TOUR (Britain 1961)

SCTS. A tour with a five-coach train to Wembley Park, Stanmore, Baker Street, Farringdon Street, New Cross Gate and Surrey Docks. Motive power includes Metropolitan 'E' 0-4-4T No 1, built at Neasden in 1896, worked as L44 from 1938 and now preserved as No 1 at the Buckinghamshire Railway Centre at Quainton Road; and Metropolitan Railway Electric Locomotive No 16 *Oliver Goldsmith*, one of the rebuilt batch from Metropolitan Vickers in 1922.

16mm, Silent, 9mins, HA/SCTS

🚂 🚂 🚂 🚂

THE MFD RERAILING EQUIPMENT (Britain 1956)

Produced by British Transport Films. An introduction to equipment designed to raise and rerail rolling stock without the use of cranes. Hydraulic jacks of various patterns, having a lifting capacity ranging from 10 to 150 tons, together with ancillary components, are shown under demonstration and in use following an actual derailment.

35/16mm, Sound, 30mins, BTF

🚂 🚂 🚂 🚂 🚂

MIDHURST BELLE RAIL TOUR (Britain 1964)

Made by G S Holyoake. Rail tour organised jointly by RCTS and LCGB with five changes of motive power.

16/8mm/VID, Silent, Colour, 4mins, MFS/VID

🚂 🚂 🚂 🚂 🚂

MIDLAND COMPOUND 1000 (Britain 1959)

Made by P B Whitehouse and John Adams. Film showing the rebuilding of this famous engine, its trials and first official run. A beautiful and detailed record of a superb-looking preserved locomotive.

16/8mm, Silent, 9mins, CV/NRM/HA

🚂 🚂 🚂 🚂 🚂

THE MIDLAND PULLMAN (Britain 1960)

Made by P B Whitehouse and John Adams. Early record of a famous diesel-hauled British Rail unit which makes a useful supplement to the official BTF film.

16/8mm, Silent, Colour, CV/NRM

🚂 🚂 🚂 🚂 🚂

MIDLAND RAILWAY (LONDON EXTENSION) CENTENARY 1869-1968 (Britain 1968)

A film by Jack Middleton. An assembly of archive film including scenes at Elstree Tunnel, St Albans station and St Pancras. There is an interesting collection of LMS '3P' 2-6-2T locomotives, both as station pilots and on local services, including Nos 23, 27 and 33; LMS 'Royal Scot' 4-6-0 No 6156 *The South Wales Border*; sundry LMS 0-6-0s; LMS English Electric diesel No 10000; BR/Sulzer Co-Co diesel No D98 *Royal Engineer*, a glimpse of the Blue Pullman and very new-looking DMUs.

16mm, Silent with tape commentary, 19mins, JM/HA

🚂 🚂 🚂 🚂 🚂

MIDNIGHT ALARM (USA 1923)

Silent melodrama with railway background.

36mm, Silent, 50mins, Lost

🚂

Left:
Postal sorters hard at work, from 'Mallard: The Drake's Progress'.

Below far left:
A dangerous moment from 'The Man who Watched Trains Go By'.

Below left:
Present day London Underground passengers may find it hard to believe, but the giant escalator built for 'A Matter of Life and Death' efficiently carried the characters in the film up to heaven.

Right:
A scene from the superb 'Metroland' showing a train to Harrow around the turn of the century.

Below:
Train and level crossing incidents have long been a favourite of film makers from the earliest days to the most modern car chases. This is from the Vitograph melodrama 'Midnight Alarm' (1923).

MIDNIGHT LIMITED (USA 1940)

A Pathe film. Directed by Howard Bretherton. With John King and Marjorie Reynolds. A railroad murder mystery in which a detective rounds up a train robber and killer. Some good railway material on the Santa Fe at Los Angeles and on the Chicago route.

35mmm, Sound, 62mins, Pathe

MILLIONS LIKE US (Britain 1943)

Gainsborough Films. Produced by Edward Black. Directed by Frank Launder and Sidney Gilliat. With Patricia Roc, Gordon Jackson and Eric Portman. The Home Front during World War 2. Contains one or two LMS stock shots, and an LMS departure with two of the cast from an unidentified station.

35mm, Sound, 103mins, Rank

MINIATURE RAILWAY (1930s-1990s)

There have been many films over the years of film coverage of miniature railways; detail will be found under many individual systems.
Some of the railways and their sources are:
Kenton Miniature Railway (1930s), RF
Radwell Miniature Railway (1930s), RF
Great Orme Railway (1951), RF
Ravenglass & Eskdale Railway (1915, 1950s, 1980s), RF
(1928, 1956, 1987), HA
Blackpool Miniature Railway (1934, 1950s, 1984), RF
Southend Pier Railway (1948), RF
(1935, 1938, 1949), HA
Hunstanton Pier (1955), RF
Paignton Zoo Miniature Railway (1955), RF
Surrey Border and Camberley (1938), RF/HA
Wickstead Park Miniature Railway (1950), RF
Stapleford Park (1960s), RF
(1970s), HA
Great Cockrow Miniature Railway (1970s), DH/HA
Southern Railway Orphanage, Woking (1928), HA

Romney, Hythe & Dymchurch (many films: see under main title).
Fairbourne Miniature Railway (1950s), HA
and lots more, both on film and video.

MINIATURE RAILWAY AT RAYNES PARK (Britain 1926)

Gaumont British News. A newsreel item titled *The Southern Railway Runs a Special!* shows the layout of a miniature railway with 'Pacific Type Loco' at the Southern Railway annual flower show at Raynes Park.

35mm, Silent, 1min, NFA

MINISTRY OF FEAR (USA 1944)

Paramount. Produced by Seton I Miller, Directed by Fritz Lang. With Ray Milland, Marjorie Reynolds, Carl Esmond, Hillary Brooke, Dan Duryea, Percy Waram and Alan Napier. World War 2 tale of how a former mental patient becomes involved in confusing intrigues. A totally phoney London, with weird Hollywood tourist buses mocked up to be supposedly London Transport and some extremely unlikely trains (cow catchers on the Barnet line?). But it does have tension: 'Atmospheric and surefooted, the images linger on — the open carriage door of a train, and a cloud of hissing steam from which the blind man emerges, still tapping his stick. Vintage Fritz Lang.' (Tony Bilbow).

35mm, Sound, 85mins, Paramount

MISHAP (Britain 1957)

Produced by Wallace Productions for the British Transport Commission. A film of interest to the railway operating staffs. The operating procedures necessary for protection on a double track in the event of a mishap to a train which fouls the opposite line. The film also illustrates steps to be taken by station staff in such an emergency, and shows how normal working is resumed.

35/16mm, Sound, 20mins, COI/BTF

MISS MARPLE: 4.50 FROM PADDINGTON (Britain 1987)

BBC Television. Directed by T R Bowen. With Joan Hickson, David Horovitch and Maurice Denham. Miss Marple solves the mystery of a murder witnessed as the fast train overtakes the slow train, somewhere on the Great Western Railway. There are real scenes at Paddington station, without revealing the motive power, but the Severn Valley Railway and the Dart Valley provide lots of genuine GWR scenes. The dramatic scene of the trains passing each other used the full resources of the double track sections of the SVR in the area of Bewdley. Fine scenes of Great Western stock in chocolate and cream were rather spoilt by locomotive BR Class 4MT No 80079 on the front.

35mm, Sound, Colour, 112min, BBC TV

MR SATOW'S IMPROVED TRAVELLING MACHINE LOCOMOTION (Britain 1975)

Anglia Television. Produced and directed by David Kenten. Presented by Dick Joice. The story of the building of the replica of the 1825 engine *Locomotion* by Mike Satow and his team.

16mm, Sound, 25mins, Anglia

LE MISTRAL (Britain 1960)

Made by P B Whitehouse and John Adams. Films of a journey from Nice to Paris, firstly behind a 141R to Marseilles and 241P to Valence with BB and CC electrics for the remainder of the journey.

16/8mm, Silent, 8mins, CV/NRM

MISTRAL (France 1957)

French Railways. Journey from Paris to Nice on the 'Mistral' express.

16mm, Sound, Part colour, 38mins, SNCF

MRS MINIVER (USA 1942)

MGM. Directed by William Wyler. With Greer Garson and Walter Pidgeon. American impression of wartime Britain; there is a most unlikely train to 'Belham' but a SR-style railway station set is a little more successful.

35mm, Sound, 133mins, MGM

🚂

MODEL TRAINS (Britain 1939)

A demonstration of model locomotives by Colonel R Henney CMG, DSO, Vice Chairman of the Model Railway Club.

BBC Television: 3.15pm. Saturday 4 August 1939.

🚂 🚂 🚂

MODELLING FOR THE FUTURE (Britain 1961)

Produced by British Transport Films. A model of a proposed Terminal to serve the Channel Tunnel demonstrates the facilities it will offer and shows the possibilities of an age-old dream, a dry land crossing between England and France!

35/16mm, Sound, Colour, 8mins, BTF

🚂 🚂 🚂

THE MODERN COAL BURNING STEAM LOCOMOTIVE (USA 1948)

Produced by the Norfolk & Western Railroad Co. Photography by Bryon Beard and Frank Rader. The construction and operation of giant steam locomotives in the final period of steam progress in America. There are very fine scenes of steam locomotives in action as well as a detailed sequence on how the locomotives are maintained.

16mm, Sound, Colour, 23mins, HA

🚂 🚂 🚂 🚂 🚂

MONTREAUX-OBERLAND BERNOIS AND CONNECTING RAILWAYS (Britain 1984)

RV Television. Metre gauge line up through Zweisimmen, Lenk and the Bernese Oberland with the 'Panoramic Express' and the 'Golden Mountain Pullman'. Mixture of electric and diesel traction, passenger and freight. Includes scenes of the Rochers-de-Naye rack railway, the Blonay Chamby museum

tourist line and steam in action, plus rotary snow plough avalanche clearance.

VID, Sound, Colour, 60min, RVV

🚂 🚂 🚂 🚂 🚂

THE MOONLIGHTER (USA 1953)

Warner. Directed by Roy Rowland. With Fred MacMurray and Barbara Stanwyck. A cattle rustler decides to reform; originally in 3-D. The Sierra Railroad locomotive Baldwin 2-8-0 No 29790, built in 1906, features in a number of scenes.

35mm, Sound, 3-D, 77min, Warner

🚂

MORE POWER TO YOUR ELBOW (Britain 1953)

Produced by British Transport Films. 'The handling of goods which have to be transhipped several times during their road or rail journey has always presented a problem. The first stage in a programme of modernisation has been the introduction of 'Palletisation' — the stacking together on simple platforms or pallets of all packages for the same destination, thus enabling small consignments to be combined into larger 'unit loads'. The film shows examples of mechanised handling which have saved warehouse space, speeded up the transit of goods and resulted in the more efficient use of manpower.'

35/166m, Sound, 15mins, BTF

🚂

MORE THAN JUST A LINE (Britain 1972)

Saga production. A detailed film record of the Fairbourne 15in miniature railway in its original form. A journey from Fairbourne to Barmouth Ferry involves two of the steam locomotives and the diesel that was used on the line after WW2. Arrival at Fairbourne is behind 'GWR' '4300' 2-6-0 No 7314.

16mm, Sound, Colour, 17mins, HA

🚂 🚂 🚂 🚂

THE MOSCOW UNDERGROUND (USSR 1942)

Central Newsreel Studios, Moscow. Detailed record of the remarkable architectural achievements of the Moscow Underground as well as scenes of the stock, operating methods and impressions of a journey.

35mm, Sound, 20mins, ETF

🚂 🚂 🚂 🚂 🚂

MOST EXCLUSIVE CLUB (Britain 1964)

Made by P B Whitehouse. A record of some of the rarest items in the world of preservation, including items at the National Railway Museum.

16/8mm, Silent, CV/NRM

🚂 🚂 🚂 🚂 🚂

THE MOUNT PILATUS RAILWAY (Britain 1900)

Warwick Trading Company. A journey up and down the line.

35mm, Silent, 43seconds, NFA

🚂 🚂 🚂 🚂 🚂

MOUNT TAMALPAIS AND MUIR WOODS RAILWAY (USA 1906)

A detailed visit to what was called 'the crookiest railway in the world'. This lovely steam-hauled scenic railway in San Francisco Bay no longer exists.

16mm, Silent, 12mins, HA

🚂 🚂 🚂 🚂

MOUNT WASHINGTON COG RAILWAY (USA 1923)

A brief film of vertical boilered *Old Peppersass* on the New Hampshire cog railway which dates from 1869.

16mm, Silent, 3mins, HA

🚂 🚂 🚂 🚂

MOUNTAINS AND FJORDS (Britain 1955)

Produced by British Transport Films. 'The traveller by train and sea to Norway's east coast should not miss an opportunity to see the magnificent Sogne-Fjord or the grandeur of the Nordifjord and the Geirangerfjord. Follow this film through Bergen and to Balestrand by the exciting Flam railway, to Oldem and Loen and finally to Geiranger, which many regard as the loveliest Fjord in Norway. A single holiday providing a variety of scenery which no other country can better.' Produced in association with the Bergen Steamship Company.

16mm, Sound, Colour, 22mins, BTF

MOVIN' (Canada 1967)

Canadian Pacific Railways. Directed by David Main. Modernization of the Canadian railway system.

16mm, Sound, Colour, 20mins, CPR

MOVING MILLIONS (Britain 1948)

Produced by the Crown Film Unit and the Central Office of Information for the London Passenger Transport Board. A comprehensive survey of the vast organisation needed to run the various forms of transport serving London's huge population during the late 1940s. The routine of cleaning and checking buses and underground railways, training schools for conductors and drivers, and the constant research into new safety devices are described.

35/16mm, Sound, 16mins, BTF/COI

THE MOVING SPIRIT (Britain 1953)

Produced by Halas and Batchelor for the British Petroleum Company. A film illustrating, in cartoon form, the development of the horseless carriage of the 1880s to the streamlined automobile of today. It also shows the railways' challenge to the stagecoach and the evolution of petrol-driven motors through the various stages that led to modern mass-production methods.

35/16mm, Sound, Colour, 18mins, Petroleum Film Bureau

A MUGS GAME OR HOW TO SQUASH A LEMON HEAD (Britain 1967)

Produced by British Transport Films. Pogo and Yo-Yo are two kids with good ideas – but in the same crowd there's a boy they call 'Splat'. He's a bit of a problem, because he's such a show-off. He's liable to lead others into trouble which may involve serious risk on the railway unless they think for themselves. This film, made in a new puppet technique – Macro Figure Animation – was a contribution to the campaign against unthinking vandalism which endangers passengers and railwaymen.

35/16mm, Sound, Colour, 4mins, BTF

MUDDLE AND GO NOWHERE RAILWAY (Britain 1978)

Anglia Television. Produced and directed by David Kenten. A detailed history of the Midland & Great Northern Joint Railway (M&GN), including scenes at Sutton Bridge, Melton Constable and a vast collection of photographs of the entire system before closure. There are interviews with men who worked on the railway and the son of its General Manager. Unfortunately very little material was ever filmed when the railway was flourishing; the main movie items relate to the last days and the lifting of the track.

16mm, Sound, Colour, 27mins, Anglia/HA

MURDER ON THE ORIENT EXPRESS (Britain 1974)

EMI. Produced by John Brabourne and Richard Goodwin. Directed by Sidney Lumet. From the novel by Agatha Christie. With Albert Finney, Ingrid Bergman, Lauren Bacall, Wendy Hiller, Sean Connery, Vanessa Redgrave, Michael York, Martin Balsam, Richard Widmark, Jacqueline Bisset, Jean-Pierre Cassel, Rachel Roberts, George Coulouris, John Gielgud, Anthony Perkins and Colin Blakely.

In the 1930s, Hercule Poirot solves a murder on a train. 'Reasonably elegant but disappointingly slackly-handled version of classic mystery novel. Albert Finney overacts and his all-star support is distracting, while as soon as the train chugs to a halt in the snowdrift, the film stops moving too, without even a dramatic "curtain".' (Leslie Halliwell). 'Audiences appear to be so hungry for this type of entertainment that maybe it hardly matters that it isn't very good.' (Judith Crist)

'The outdoor shots were filmed by courtesy of SNCF on a freight-only line in the Jura Mountains. Istanbul proved hopeless – far too many modern intrusions. The rest of the real route was equally unhelpful. So Landy depot, stabling point for the 'Night Ferry' and the 'Nord Express' and servicing Paris (Nord) station was used for the departure from Istanbul as well as intermediate stations. It all looked good but if the Fourgon Luggage van No 1283, built in Britain in 1928 and prominently featured in the film had perhaps run on occasions on the 'Simplon-Orient Express', no Pullman car, not even first class, was ever included in that famous train in the whole of the 1930s.' (Jean Des Cars and Jean-Paul Caracalla)

The film makers took their cue, not from the real 'Orient Express' but from the romantic memories of a young and impressionable Agatha Christie; the only real link with the novel was the fact that the train was snowbound – an incident which actually happened to the author. But the film makers decided to go for the best. They tracked down the fact that some old Wagons-Lits stock had been abandoned in Belgium and managed to buy up various pieces of carriages, equipment, cutlery and, most especially, marquetry panels from the restaurant. So although the interior of the train was entirely built up in the studios at Elstree, much original material was used in the sets. In addition, the marquetries of two sleeping cars originally built in Leeds by the Leeds Forge Company in 1922 were also used in the Elstree set building. A fine set of original glassware was also purchased and used by the cast.

All the studio shots made extensive use of back projection, not always entirely satisfactory and often leading to colour fringing. The exterior scenes were most effective. At first, it did not snow as planned and the film company spent a lot of money having convoys of lorries bring down snow and ice from the mountains. As soon as it was all in place, it actually started to snow; so much so that the film unit itself got cut off for a couple of days!

Once you know that the Istanbul-Calais on the side of the four beautiful Wagons-Lits Pullmans with their superb blue livery and gold emblems is actually at an SNCF depot, it all becomes obvious, with the depot concrete floor, no platforms and rather clumsily placed 'Turkish' extras. But the departure of the four-car train, headed by SNCF 2-3-0 (British 4-6-0) No 230-G-353, with the music of Richard Rodney Bennett, is one of the great moments in the film. Eventually 230-G-353 runs into the snowdrift in the Jura Mountains; and, as many critics have noted, the film seems to die from that moment onwards. Alfred Hitchcock would never have stopped the train!

35mm, Sound, Colour, 131mins, Weintraub

MUSIC

Many films have included song and dance numbers based on railways. Some of the best known are the Academy Award-winning number 'The Atchinson, Topeka and Santa Fe; (from *The Harvey Girls*), 'Chattanooga Choo Choo' (Glenn Miller in *Sun Valley Serenade*), 'Lydia the Tattooed Lady' (*At the Circus*), 'Casey Junior' (*Dumbo*), 'Toot Toot Tootsie, Goodbye' (*The Jazz Singer*), 'When the Midnight Choo Choo Leaves for Alabam' (*Easter Parade*), 'Shuffle Off to Buffalo' (*Forty-Second Street*) and the 'Miss Turnstiles' number from *On the Town*. Music ranges from the Arthur Honegger 'Pacific 231' to the most often used piece of music in all the railway documentaries of the 1940s and 1950s — 'Coronation Scot'.

MY LITTLE CHICKADEE (USA 1939)

Universal. Directed by Edward Cline. With W C Fields and Mae West. A shady lady and an inefficient cardsharper unmask a villain in a comedy Western. A long sequence was filmed on the Sierra Railroad, using Baldwin locomotive 2-8-0 No 29790 and Combine Car No 5 (renumbered No 12) and coaches Nos 2 and 6, involving an attack by Indians, filmed on the flat section from Warnerville to Cooperstown.

35mm, Sound, 83min, Universal

MYSTERY JUNCTION (Britain 1951)

Directed by Michael McCarthy. With Sydney Taffler, Barbara Murray, Martin Benson, Pat Owens, Christine Silver and David Davies. Thriller fantasy of a writer's tale about his fellow passengers on a train.

35mm, Sound, 67mins, Lost

NARROW GAUGE CATSKILL MOUNTAIN RAILWAY (USA 1906)

A record of the Catskill Mountain Railway, a 3ft gauge line running from Catskill Landing on the west bank of the Hudson River.

16/8mm, Silent, 12mins, Blackhawk/BFI

NARROW GAUGE FROM VOLOS (Britain 1963)

Made by P B Whitehouse. Part of a major European tour to document railways made by Pat Whitehouse from 1962 to 1963.

16/8mm, Silent, 12mins, CV/NRM

NARROW GAUGE IN BRITTANY: COTES DU NORD (Britain 1956)

Made by P B Whitehouse. A further item in an earlier tour of Europe made by Pat Whitehouse, exploring various aspects of the narrow gauge for a book and taking the opportunity to film lines that were about to disappear.

16/8mm, Silent, Colour, 14mins, CV/NRM

NARROW GAUGE IN THE LEVANT (Britain 1968)

A film by Nick Lera. Record of narrow gauge railways in Yugoslavia, Greece (60cm on the Volos-Milaei line), a rack railway in Lebanon and narrow gauge in Jordan.

16mm, Silent, Colour, 10mins, NL

NARROW GAUGE TO SILVERTON (USA 1953)

A film by Mac Owen. A detailed record of the narow gauge Durango-Silverton branch of the Denver & Rio Grande Railroad with D&RGRR 2-8-2 (Mikado) No 476 and a full train of tourists making the journey out into the 'Wild West'.

Above left:
Supposedly Istanbul but in fact Landy depot on the SNCF, from 'Murder on the Orient Express'.

Left:
From 'Night Mail Two', Post Office staff load the train at Euston station.

Above:
One of the Norfolk & Western's big Mallet locos, from the 1948 documentary film on the line.

Right:
A sinister figure on the hillside in the foreground watches as the train crew repair sabotage to the line in 'North West Frontier', but is there a traitor aboard the train carrying the young prince to safety?

This line has been used in many feature films.

16mm, Silent, 18mins, HA

THE NARROW MARGIN (USA 1950)

RKO Radio. Produced by Stanley Rubin. Directed by Richard Fleischer. With Charles McGraw, Marie Windsor, Jacqueline White and Queenie Leonard.

Police try to guard a prosecution witness on a train from Chicago to Los Angeles. 'A taut, breathlessly fast and highly suspenseful 'sleeper' par excellence.' (Time Out) 'Claustrophobic train background. Menace everywhere, no glance is what it seems, every image we see contains the seeds of doubt.' (Tony Bilbow). The Atchison, Topeka & Santa Fe provided the steam railway facilities for this one, although, in the tradition of the cheaper RKO 'B' movies of the day, all the real action is in the studio. Claustrophobic indeed.

35mm, Sound, 70mins, RKO Radio

A NATION TURNS TO OIL (USA 1920)

Sinclair Consolidated Oil Corporation. A documentary on oil which includes shots of oil burning locomotives in Cuba.

35mm, Silent, 51mins, NFA

NATIONAL FILM THEATRE

There have been three eras of Railway Film Shows at the National Film Theatre on the South Bank in London, some of which were later reflected in the Regional Film Theatres developed by the British Film Institute. The original shows organised by John Huntley arose in a somewhat unusual way. The catalogue department of the National Film Archive (then run by Roger Holman) was having problems with the large number of 'Trains Entering Stations' items which they could not identify. It was then suggested that a rather fun way of solving this problem would be to make prints from the precious nitrate masters and then show them at the NFT.

The railway buffs would do the rest and provide the information. The first shows were attended by such people as O S Nock, L C T Rolt, Cecil J Allan and Alan Pegler.

The information positively flowed in: 'That's LNWR at Llandudno' . . . that's LSWR at Southampton . . . it's Midland at Monsal Dale'. The shows continued all through the 1960s, bringing in the new material, arranging for the screening of new British Transport films, often with Edgar Anstey in attendance. A great moment was when *Terminus* was selected as the short film to open the 1961 London Film Festival. It was a British Transport production and had been directed by an unknown man by the name of John Schlesinger. The feature film that night came from Columbia and some of their executives were present in the audience. They saw *Terminus*; before the evening was over, John Schlesinger had been signed up to direct a feature film for Columbia. He later made *Sunday, Bloody Sunday*, *A Kind of Loving*, *Billy Liar* and *Midnight Cowboy*.

By the end of the 1960s, the shows had become so popular that some were transferred first to the nearby Queen Elizabeth Hall and then to the Royal Festival Hall.

The second era of NFT shows was devoted to the work of Nick Lera. During the 1970s, he personally presented assemblies of his own films, many shot in various parts of the world including Africa, Vietnam and Germany, supported by items from the National Film Archive. The superb photographic quality of Nick Lera's films was much appreciated by NFT audiences.

The 1980s saw yet another chapter in the story. Two stalwart enthusiasts, Andrew Youdell (of the British Film Institute) and Alan Willmott (formerly of British Transport Films), now 'Windjammer Films' arranged between them a series of special film programmes at the National Film Theatre, London, devoted to some of the best films available – both feature and documentary – which involved railways or other forms of surface transport, both in Britain and aboard. All these proved very popular, and gave many people an opportunity to see some very rare gems, especially the documen-

taries, some of which had not been seen on a cinema screen for over 40 years.

Many of the film programmes consisted of some of the best productions of the famous British Transport Film Unit, set up in 1949 and led for 25 years by Edgar Anstey, one of the pioneers of the British documentary. Mr Anstey, and other former members of the unit now working in the feature film world, attended most of these events, and introduced many of the films, which added interest.

Other programmes were devoted to films made by the former mainline railway companies in Britain, for prestige and travel promotion purposes. These included some of the output of the former London Midland & Scottish, and Southern Railways, which had their own film sections between the years 1935 and 1949.

Two very rare films were screened concerning railways during the last war *Carrying the Load* (1946) – the vital role of railways in Britain during 1939-45 – and *Women at War* (1945) which explained the duties performed by the 'fairer sex' on vital railway jobs during those war years. Each film programme, which was carefully selected to give as much variety as possible, and to appeal to as many transport tastes, included complete old favourites such as *Oh, Mr Porter* (1937), *The Titfield Thunderbolt* (1952) and other feature films such as *The Last Journey*, made on the GWR in 1935.

Documentary classics such as *The Flying Scotsman* (1929), *Night Mail* (1936) and *Pacific 231* (1949) were also screened.

More recent films, on the subject of preserved steam railways in Britain, were also included in the programmes, such as *Tracks around the Island* (1986) (the Isle of Man Railways), *Ffestiniog Holiday* (1983) and *Return to Bewdley* (1987), all of them produced by Alan Willmott's 'Windjammer Films'.

No doubt in the future further similar programmes will appear from time to time at the 'NFT' – for as long as the interest in railway films remains!

NE REGION (Britain 1963)

Link Productions. A survey of the North Eastern Region on 9th-10th September 1963, including scenes south of Durham, Piercebridge and Darlington. Motive power includes Class '8F', 'V2' and 'A3'.

16/8mm/VID, Silent, Colour, 4mins, MFS/VID

NEASDEN PARADE 1963 (Britain 1963)

A film by Tom Martin. A record of the London Transport Parade at Neasden in 1963 including three steam locomotives:- Metropolitan 'F' class of 1901; London Transport No 23 (now in the London Transport Museum) and London Transport No LT44 (Now LT1 on the Buckinghamshire Railway). There was also Underground stock new in 1963, Electric locomotive *Sarah Siddons* and old 'Dreadnought' stock, some of which eventually went to the Bluebell Railway.

16mm, Silent, Colour, 9mins, TM/HA

NED KELLY (Britain 1970)

Woodfall Film. Produced by Neil Hartley. Directed by Tony Richardson. With Mick Jagger and Allen Bickford. The career of a 19th century outlaw in Australia, famous for his iron armour. Includes 19th Century train scene, using old 1887 locomotive and restored stock from the Melbourne Preservation group.

35mm, Sound, Colour, 103mins, United Artists

NEW BLACK DIAMOND EXPRESS (USA 1900)

An Edison Film. A second version of Edison's shot of the 'Black Diamond' express in New York state.

35mm/VID, Silent, 2mins, NFA/HA/125

NEW RAILWAY FOR BULGARIA (USSR 1953)

USSR Today Newsreel No 3. The introduction into Bulgaria of electric locomotives built in the USSR.

16mm, Sound, 4mins, ETV

NEW ROUTE TO THE NORTH (Germany 1963)

Produced by German State Railways. A record of the principal engineering work carried out by the German State Railways since the war, including the building of the 'Bee-Line', the shortest route between Germany and Scandinavia.

35/16mm, Sound, Colour, 52mins, DSB

THE NEW WAIRARAPA RAILWAY (New Zealand, 1958)

Produced by the New Zealand National Film Unit. The building of the world's longest main-line tunnel, running 13.5 miles under the mountains between Wellington, NZ, and the farmlands of Wairarapa. Various ingenious devices for track-laying, levelling, and ballast-tamping are seen at work. The film recalls the rigours of the former long rail-climb over the Fells and shows the inaugural celebrations for the new service.

16mm, Sound, 11mins, COI/NZF

NEWCASTLE CENTRAL (DMU) (Britain 1958)

Made by P B Whitehouse and John Adams. The early days of DMUs in the Tyneside area where they appeared at the start of the DMU project.

16/8mm, Silent, 6mins, CV/NRM

NEWCASTLE TO CARLISLE (Britain 1989)

Written and produced by Ian Heys and Garry Price. A journey from Newcastle Central Station (explored in some detail), via Hexham and the Tyne Valley, to Carlisle. (Cross Country Series No 2)

VID, Sound, Colour, 60mins, Branch Line Video

NEWMARKET RAILWAY STATION (Britain 1980)

Anglia Television. Produced and directed by David Kenten. Presented by Dick Joice. From the Bygones series. The remains of the old Newmarket station.

16mm, Sound, Colour, 3mins, Anglia

NEWSPAPER TRAIN (Britain 1941)

A Realist production for the Ministry of Information. The work of circulating the newspapers, despite blitz conditions, via road and rail. There are good railway scenes at Paddington and Euston.

35/16mm, Sound, 16mins, COI

NEWTON HEATH SHED (Britain 1962)

Made by P B Whitehouse and John Adams. A good selection of LM locomotives including some rare L&Y Classes.

16/8mm, Silent, 6mins, CV/NRM

NEXT OF KIN (Britain 1942)

An Ealing Studios production. Directed by Thorold Dickinson. With Mervyn Johns and Nova Pilbeam. Includes a sequence in which a spy is arrested on a night train. (Studio reconstruction only).

35mm, Sound, 101mins, Weintraub

NEXT STOP SCOTLAND (Britain 1968)

Produced by British Transport Films. Swimming, skating, sailing, mountaineering, water skiing, pony trekking, or leisurely motoring and cruising in the beautiful landscape of the Highlands and Western Islands; visits to see the manufacturers of traditional tartans, and to the distillers of single malt whiskies; steamer trips on the Firth of Clyde and Loch Lomond – these are some of the pleasures which Raymond and Lesley Suffield and Alan and Sibella Fowler enjoy when they take their cars from London to Scotland by Motorail for the summer holidays.

35/16mm, Sound, Colour, 30mins, BTF

NIGHT BOAT TO DUBLIN (Britain 1946)

Associated British Film. Directed by Lawrence Huntingdon. With Robert Newton, Raymond Lovell and Guy Middleton. Spy melodrama of an atomic scientist working in Devon. Includes a Southern Railway departure sequence at Waterloo station.

35mm, Sound, 100mins, Weintraub

NIGHT MAIL (Britain 1936)

A GPO Film Unit production. Directed by Harry Watt and Basil Wright. Produced by John Grierson. Music by Benjamin Britten. Verse by W H Auden. Sound by Cavalcanti.

A documentary of the Night Postal Special from Euston to Scotland. The train leaves Euston and a message is passed from Euston to Crewe control. The train is seen from various viewpoints; aerial shots, passing a signal box, a platelayer's glimpse, from a shunted local, from a farmer in a field near the line. Crewe is reached after some mail bags have been picked up. English crew are exchanged for Scots, engines are changed and there is a short delay to a late connection. The journey continues up north and the mail is sorted. As dawn comes up, Beattock is climbed and the train races across the border. These scenes are accompanied by verses written by W H Auden:

This is the night mail crossing the border,
Bringing the cheque and the postal order,
Letters for the rich, letters for the poor,
The shop at the corner and the girl next door,
Pulling up Beattock, a steady climb,
The gradient's against her but she's on time.
Past cotton grass and moorland boulder,
Shovelling white steam over her shoulder,
Snorting noisily as she passes
Silent miles of wind-bent grasses;
Birds turn their heads as she approaches,
Stare from the bushes at her blank-faced coaches;
Sheepdogs cannot turn her course
They slumber on with paws across,
In the farm she passes no one wakes,
But a jug in a bedroom gently shakes.

The voice of John Grierson is heard in a section of blank verse as the train goes towards Glasgow:

Dawn freshens, the climb is done.
Down towards Glasgow she descends
Towards the fields of apparatus, the furnaces
Set on the dark plain like gigantic chessmen.
All Scotland waits for her;
In the dark glens, beside the pale-green sea lochs
Men long for news.

There now follows a final section of rhythmic verse, set to shots of wheels and pistons, rabbits scattering in a field, a sheepdog running, all punctuated by flashes of steam:

Letters of thanks, letters from banks,
Letters of joy from the girl and boy,
Receipted bills and invitations
To inspect new stock or visit relations,
And applications for situations,
And timid lovers' declarations,
And gossip, gossip from all the nations,
News circumstantial, news financial,
Letters with holiday snaps to enlarge in,
Letters with faces scrawled on the margin,
Letters from uncles, cousins and aunts,
Letters to Scotland from the South of France,
Letters of condolence to Highlands and Lowlands,
Notes from overseas to the Hebrides;
Written on paper of every hue,
The pink, the violet, the white and the blue,
The chatty, the catty, the boring, adoring,
The cold and official and the heart's outpouring,
Clever, stupid, short and long
The typed and the printed and the spelt all wrong.

Against shots of Scottish cities and scenery, ending with cleaners at work outside the Glasgow locomotive sheds, is heard a final section of blank verse:

Thousands are still asleep
Dreaming of terrifying monsters
Or a friendly tea beside the band at Cranston's or Crawford's;
Asleep in working Glasgow, asleep in well-set Edinburgh,
Asleep in granite Aberdeen.
They continue their dreams
But shall wake soon and long for letters.
And none will hear the postman's knock
Without a quickening of the heart,
For who can bear to feel himself forgotten?

The film provides an excellent opportunity to study the working of the LMS in the steam-dominated days of the mid-1930s. Naturally, the 4-6-0 Fowler 'Royal Scot' locomotives are very much in evidence, notably No 6115 *Scots Guardsman* and No 6108 *Seaforth Highlander*. At Crewe, there are connecting trains, one hauled by a 2-6-0 'Crab', another by a 4-4-0 Midland Compound. The main locations at Euston, Bletchley, and across the border are all genuine, except that Broad Street station 'doubled' for Crewe in one or two night shots and the interior of the Travelling Post Office sorting van was built in the GPO Film Unit studios at Blackheath.

The editing of the film contains some interesting presentations of railway activity, as Mr H A V Bulleid noted in an excellent analysis published in *Amateur Cine World* in 1940.

'The Signalbox

Long shot of a signalbox. Cut to signalbox interior, where the signalman telegraphs: "Can you take Postal Special?" Mix to telegraph wires. Mix to next box, receipt of message, line clear indicators: then:

(a) CMS The signalman moves away from the indicator.

(b) CMS (low angle, from behind signal levers) he pulls one, then ...(first clang)

(c) CS (high angle, levers and name plates behind) . . . he pulls another (second clang)

(d) CMS (as b) . . . he pulls the third.

(e) CS A signal: it goes down . . . (third clang)

(f) CS The indicator needle moves over to train on line. (Sound of train in distance)

(g) LS (from inside box, levers in

foreground). The train approaches, passes. (Sound swells up).
(h) FLS The train on and away: the solitary signal against the twilight sky drops back to danger. (Sound fades into the distance).

This is a lovely sequence: note in particular a brillant cut at (d) to (e), the three clangs coming incisively from the excellent sound track (though we wish it had been a silent-background recording) and the anticipated sound of train, before we actually see it, at the moment of swingover of the indicator. The last shot is memorable, so lovely is the sky.

Crewe
Fade-in. LS a smoky greyness, two tall chimneys, two lights . . . "Crewe: main junction for the Midlands". Cut to dim LS, awaiting empty platform trucks. Then the connecting trains arrive: one hauled by a 2-6-0 'Crab', one by a Midland Compound. The bustle and activity of handling the mail bags is excellently portrayed, the night-time photography having a grand air of reality. Suddenly a tracking-forward CS shows a note on the arrival board: the Holyhead connection is running nine minutes late; the station staff decide they'll have to hold the Postal four minutes. Good establishing LS introduced the Control, and one of the controllers confirms that the Postal may be delayed. Dark, dramatic LS shows the Postal speeding on, the low angle again well used with the towering high smoke-box of the 'Royal Scot' locomotive CS, signals drop to safety. TS, the rails fly back beneath us. Pan MS a taper-boiler Class 5XP locomotive slowing down. LS a parallel-boiler "Baby Scot" Class 5XP draws the Postal into the platform. This triple error not only shatters the continuity, but forces doubt on to the film's overall accuracy, which in a documentary should be impeccable.

'The 13 minutes booked stop at Crewe is well handled: the crews change over, some coming out of the refreshment room: mailbags are thudded on to trucks: engines are changed, the coupling of the new engine being excellently shown in two angles well out on action. Then an official shouts up "Where's that Holyhead stuff?". CS the late notice. Wheel tapper proceeds imperturbably. LS, a group of men

waiting (an excellently timed effect, it exactly conveys the impatience of delay).

Then in LS the Holyhead arrives. Wrongly, the producers have used for this another shot of the same train with 2-6-0 locomotive as previously shown. An excellent high angle shot shows the platform trucks, laden, snaking along to the Postal . . . "about time, too . . ." The natural sounds are ideal. Then comes the slamming of doors, and right away, the whistle, and . . .
(a) CMS Driver turns away from window.
(b) MS Wheels and motion start moving: TILT UP to engine moving . . .
(c) MS In cab, driver looks out.
(d) MS Post offical swings himself . . .
(e) MS (taken from train) . . . on to the train.
(f) LMS Two railway officials talking, train moving behind them.
(g) MS (as c) but now steam throws the dark of the cab into relief.
(h) The engine proceeds, pale steam around it.
This is nicely done, particularly a brilliant cut at (d) to (e). A documentary film should avoid showing process errors, hence the leaving open of the firehole door in (c) when the fireman is not firing should not have been shown. Conversely, the cloak of steam in (h) is dramatically effective and permissible, even though it may upset the running shed foreman.'
Apart from noting such strange faults as the unexplained steam of a banking engine on Beattock and other points noted above, Mr Bulleid made an extremely interesting point on the use of the verse in the final sequences:
'Admirable and memorable though we find the words and rhythms of W H Auden, we recall that this is a film we are watching, the one medium wherein rhythm can be controlled with extreme finesse: and the cutter should at least have used three-shots-and-a-long in his montage down the bank, giving the triple rhythm:
Words, 'Letters of thanks',
Wheels, Ta-ta-ta Tum,
Shots, Short, short, short, long.
This might well have become a classic example of the use of metric montage. It would have had the

advantage of preventing two errors: the first, that this is a carriage-wheels rhythm (adjacent pairs of bogie wheels clicking over the rail-joints) whereas only engine-wheel shots are used: the second, that there is a pause between every set of four beats, whereas the poet wrongly cut the pause. Compare (wicked anomaly, that a silent film could create a more memorable sound rhythm!) the railway carriage scenes in *The Spy* (1928, by Fritz Lang) where a six-wheel bogie followed a four-wheeler, and hammered into Gerda Maurus's brain the serial number of the carriage . . . 33133 . . . three three One three three . . . Had Wright and Watt recalled the carriage wheels, then we would have been happy indeed to see the later labour of the sorters, not to mention their unsteady attempts at tea, against the rollicking roll of the train.'
Railway enthusiasts are traditionally critical of the vast number of errors and stupidities perpetrated by film companies over the years. *Night Mail* too, has its errors, as we have seen. Yet, as H A V Bulleid also agrees, the general quality of the shooting and the overall atmosphere is, in this case, sufficient to ride out the technical faults. When a modern audience has gasped a little at the jumps in motive power, they usually end up by giving this 35 year old film a spontaneous round of applause. After all, perhaps at this distance in time, there is something to be said for seeing a taper-boiler 5XP followed immediately by a parallel-boiler '5XP Baby Scot' rather than not see them at all'.

35/16mm, Sound, 21mins, NFA/Post Office/HA/VID

SON OF NIGHT MAIL (Britain 1989)

There have been various attempts, direct or indirect, to imitate the great classic of 1936. The Post Office themselves made one in 1964.

The best version is perhaps the one that gives the fullest credit to the original – by showing it in full right from the beginning – *Night Mail Two*.

NIGHT MAIL TWO (Britain 1989)

TVS Television. Music by James Harpham. Poems by Blake Morrison. In the 1980s update, 11 tons of first class letters travel on the night plane to Edinburgh; some go further, to Port Athair on the Island of Barra where the Royal Mail collection van serves as the local bus. The widespread use of mail order has resulted in a significant growth of mail to the island. Trains, however, still play an important role in the transportation of post.

The nightmail service moves 42 million letters every 24 hours. Sorting is carried out on the trains, just as in the past. And we must not forget the Post Office has its own railway still very much in action, 80ft underground in Central London, as it links the main line stations and the principal sorting offices of the metropolis. It has all grown out of a service that first carried letters from Liverpool to Manchester over 150 years ago.

VID, Sound, Colour, 42mins, TVS

THE NIGHT OF THE DEMON (Britain 1957)

Columbia pictures. Produced by Frank Bevis. Directed by Jacques Tourneur. With Dana Andrews and Peggy Cummins, Naill MacGinnis, Athene Seyler and Maurice Denham. An occultist despatches his enemies by raising a giant medieval devil. The final spectacular scene, when the villain is run down by a steam train which assumes the image of the devil, was shot at Bricket Wood on the St Albans Abbey to Watford line of the one-time LMS. The scenes were all shot at night and the station was very atmospheric with gaslights and lots of steam.

35mm, Sound, 87mins, Columbia

NIGHT OF THE RIO GRANDE (USA 1937)

Republic. With William Boyd. Western melodrama about a lone ranger in trouble. Includes scenes shot on the Sierra Railroad with locomotive

No 30 from the White Mountain Scenic Railroad in Arizona.

35mm, Sound, 87mins, Republic

NIGHT TRAIN (Pociag) (Poland 1959)

Directed by Jerry Kawalerowicz. Photography by Jan Laskowski. Music by Andzej Trzaskowski, based on *Moon Rays* by Artie Shaw. With Lucyna Winnicka, Leon Niemezyk and Zbigniew Gybulski. A study of humour, drama and human psychology as revealed by a group of people on a night train.

16mm, Sound, 90mins, BFI

NIGHT TRAIN TO MEMPHIS (USA 1946)

A Republic film. Directed by Lesley Selander. With Roy Acuff, Allan Lane and Adele Mara. Railway melodrama about a railroad president who tries to run the town by force. 'Some very nice shots of trains and a most entrancing "hand-car" which rushes up and down the line among very pleasant scenery.' (MFB)

35mm, Sound, 64mins, Republic

NIGHT TRAIN TO MUNICH (Britain 1940)

Produced by Edward Black. Directed by Carol Reed. Photography by Otto Kanturek. With Rex Harrison, Margaret Lockwood, Paul von Henreid, Basil Radford and Naunton Wayne. Story of an escape from Nazi Germany. There are some authentic shots of German steam locomotives and spectacular scenes on an aerial railway on the Swiss-German border.

35mm, Sound, 95mins, TCF

NINE ELMS LOCOMOTIVE SHED (Britain 1960)

Link Productions. A tour of Nine Elms Motive Power Depot of the Southern Region dominated by many steam locomotives as it was in 1960.

16/9.5/8mm/VID, Silent, Colour, 4mins, MFS/VID

NORFOLK & WESTERN RAILROAD

The classic American steam-operated railroad. It clung to steam right up to the end and many of the films from Steam Powered Video and others have extensive coverage of the system. The line was basically from Norfolk in Virginia, westward to Roanoke (the 'Swindon' of Norfolk & Western) and on to Williamson, Portsmouth and to Cincinnati in Ohio. There were a few branches, notably to Columbus, Ohio. Its enthusiasts were as keen and as faithful as those for the Great Western in Britain, well, almost!

NORFOLK & WESTERN RAILROAD: THE MODERN COAL BURNING STEAM LOCOMOTIVE (USA 1948)

A detailed study of the N&WRR system, its great locomotives of the last days of steam, its freight and passenger services and its maintenance procedures. A unique final epitaph to the steam locomotive.

16mm, Sound, Colour, 21mins, HA

NORTH BY NORTH WEST (USA 1959)

MGM. Directed by Alfred Hitchcock. With Cary Grant, Eva Marie Saint, James Mason and Leo G Carroll. A businessman is mistaken for a spy. Includes scenes of the 'Twentieth Century', diesel-hauled from New York, with various scenes on the New York Central system between New York and Chicago. The interiors of the trains were entirely built in the studio.

35mm, Sound, Colour, 136mins, MGM

THE NORTH EASTERN GOES FORWARD (Britain 1962)

Produced by British Transport Films. Keeping pace with rapidly developing social and industrial needs is the aim of modernisation on the North Eastern Region. The building of new marshalling yards, the improvement of passenger and freight facilities and the design of modern aids for speed and safety on the track are among the features shown.

35/16mm, Sound, Colour, 20mins, BTF

🚂 🚂 🚂 🚂 🚂

NORTH EASTERN STEAM IN THE SIXTIES (Britain 1988)

Rail video. Filmed by Barry Eagles, this tape gives rare coverage of some of the last steam at work in the North East. Most of these workings were freight and many examples of 'J27' 0-6-0s, 'Q6' 0-8-0s, 'WD' 2-8-0s and 'K1' 2-6-0s are shown in action. In addition some LNER 'A2', 'A3' and 'A4' Pacifics are seen on railtour duties away from their native areas.

VID, Sound, Colour, 30mins, RVO

🚂 🚂 🚂 🚂 🚂

NORTH FROM YORK (Britain 1960-61)

Link Productions. Steam locomotives at York, at South Otterington station, near Danby Wiske and near Croft; motive power includes locomotives of Classes 'A', 'A1', 'A2', 'A4', 'K3', 'V2' and J72'.

16/9.5/8mm, Silent, Colour, 4mins, MFS/VID

🚂 🚂 🚂 🚂 🚂

NORTH WALES, ENGLAND: THE LAND OF CASTLES AND WATERFALLS (Britain 1907)

From the *Picturesque Wales* series. An Urban Company film, by courtesy of the London & North Western Railway company. Chester, Llandudno Junction, Llandudno, Conway, Menai Straits, Llanberis Pass, Snowdon, Caernarvon, Bettws-y-Coed and Swallow Falls. Early scenes are linked by shots taken from a moving train.

35mm, Silent, 13mins, NFA

🚂 🚂

NORTH WEST FRONTIER (Britain 1959)

Rank production. Directed by J Lee Thompson. With Kenneth More, Lauren Bacall, Herbert Lom and Ursula Jeans. In 1905 during a rebellion an English officer escorts a young Hindu prince on a dangerous railway escape. Great period

atmosphere is obtained by the extensive use of real Indian railway stock and locomotives, the main star *Victoria* being an old Beyer Peacock tank engine originally called *Empress of India*. There are scenes of a train leaving an Army camp, shots in the roundhouse, a race through a tunnel to beat the rebels and the last-minute crossing of a bridge about to be blown up. With the help of the Indian State Railways, all the scenes are real, with never a model in sight, although some of the footplate scenes were made in the studios.

'Thoroughly enjoyable *Boys' Own Paper* adventure story with excellent set pieces and a spot-the-villain mystery.' (Leslie Halliwell) 'Northwest Frontier seems to have borrowed its eccentric engine from *The General*, its hazardous expedition from *Stagecoach* and its background of tribal violence from *The Drum*.' (Tony Bilbow)

35mm, Sound, Colour, 129mins, Rank

🚂 🚂 🚂

NOWHERE TO GO (Britain 1958)

Ealing Studios. Directed by Seth Holt. With George Nader and Maggie Smith. Convict on the run after a jail breakout. Opening sequence on derelict station platform at Kew Bridge.

35mm, Sound, 87mins, Weintraub

🚂

NUMBER SEVENTEEN (Britain 1932)

British International Pictures. Produced by John Maxwell. Directed by Alfred Hitchcock. With Leon M Lion, Anne Grey, John Stuart, Donald Calthrop, Barry Jones and Garry Marsh. A girl jewel thief reforms and helps the police track down her former gang. 'Minor Hitchcock thriller largely confined to a single interior until the final train chase, which, despite obvious models, remains exhilarating.' (Leslie Halliwell) 'I couldn't do much with the boring play scenes which the producer insisted on retaining just as they did on the stage, but I did start to get going a bit with the final railway chase.' (Alfred Hitchcock) The final chase is indeed quite

complex. It starts as the villains make their escape on the night ferry train, filmed in the yard and around the south face of Copenhagen Tunnel.

Now onto the scene comes the locomotive we are to stay with for the whole of the chase: LNER 'A1' 4-6-2 No 2547 *Doncaster*; in the first shot, there is a quaint little 'J55' LNER saddle tank engine. The goods train of European International goods waggons sets off but the hero is left behind. He has seen a page from the *Illustrated London News* of 1932 describing 'The Ferry That Carries Trains to the Continent from Harwich' (Hitchcock had also seen it and it was his inspiration for the whole sequence).

As the train races away to the 'Ferry' (actually filmed on the Hertford Loop of the LNER at night), the hero hijacks a Greenline coach (then only just introduced in 1932) and goes in pursuit (Registration: GF 48).

All the action now on the train, including an attack on the guard and the villain's hunt for the jewels, is a mixture of real night shots of 2547, studio-built bits of the goods train and lots of real shots of the journey. It culminates in a scene where the villains are on the footplate, having shot the fireman and the engine driver having passed out, racing away to the terminus; which in this case is the ferry. Real shots of 2547 cross-cut with the Greenline coach mix furiously with studio effects (including a Gresley footplate which seems to have everything except a regulator handle, making it difficult for the villains to control its onward rush!) until the approach to the 'Ferry'. Now a massive O gauge model, built on a stage at the old Shepherds Bush studios by Bond and Bassett-Lowke takes over; it includes a model of the Greenline coach, 2547, the 'Night Ferry' and the pierhead. In the ensuing crash, the villains perish and the hero saves the heroine.

35/16mm, Sound, 63mins, Weintraub

🚂 🚂 🚂

NÜRNBERG JUBILEE PARADE OF TRAINS (Britain 1985)

John Cocking. A collection of 70 trains from *Adler* (Eagle) replica of

1835 to Class 120 locomotives, including old and new Rheingold, Trans-Europe Express, Lufthansa Airport Express, Gläserner Zug, Deutsche Weinstrasse Zug, TUI Ferienexpress, etc.

VID, Sound, Colour, 60min, JC/SF

NÜRNBERG 1985 PARADE OF TRAINS (Britain 1985)

Salford Films. 70 trains on parade for the German 150th Anniversary Celebrations.

VID, Sound, Colour, 45mins, SFV

O2 TO HAVEN STREET (Britain 1988)

Produced and directed by Robert Ennis. Commentary by John Huntley. The story of the Haven Street preserved railway on the Isle of Wight and the line from Haven Street to Wooton. One of the principal class of locomotives that worked the island service in Southern Railway is featured LSWR 'O2' 0-4-4T No W24 *Calbourne*.

16/8mm/VID, Sound, Colour, 28mins, Ennis/West/HA ref

O. WINSTON LINK (USA 1990)

Produced by Berwick Universal Pictures. A film by Paul Yule. A portrait of perhaps the greatest photographer of the age of steam, who, from 1955 to 1960, made a series of night pictures by flash on the old Norfolk & Western Railroad. He kept these extraordinary pictures hidden away until 1984, when he was finally persuaded to show them to fellow railway enthusiasts and have some of them published. We meet some of the people who helped him with these romantic night images and men of the railroad itself, who were there at the time. In 1960, Link bought a Norfolk & Western steam locomotive which he has been patiently re-building for the past 30 years. He sets up, just for old times sake, a photograph using 30,000 flash bulbs; alas, it doesn't work!

16mm, Sound, Colour, 48mins, Berwick Universal

OCTOPUSSY (Britain 1983)

Eon Films. Produced by Albert R Broccoli. Directed by John Glen. With Roger Moore, Maud Adams and Louis Jordan. James Bond takes on an evil Afghan prince in a hunt for Tsarist treasures. Includes powerful sequence filmed on the Nene Valley Railway.

35mm, Sound, Colour, 131mins, Eon

OCTOPUSSY BEING MADE AT PETERBOROUGH (Britain 1982)

Anglia Television. A record of the elaborate stunts in which a car has to be fired into the air across the bows of a speeding train and a fight staged on the roof of the carriages. With Greg Barnes. Produced and directed by David Kenten.

16mm, Sound, Colour, 9mins, Anglia

ODETTE (Britain 1950)

Produced and directed by Herbert Wilcox. The story of a woman in the French Resistance in World War 2 Includes steam scenes on SNCF at Annecy, Cannes, Cassis and Marseilles. Sound recorded by Peter Handford.

35mm, Sound, 123mins, Weintraub

OFF THE BEATEN TRACK (Britain 1960)

Produced by British Transport Films. 'Would you like to sleep in a castle, pony-trek in Wales or relax on the beaches of Northern Ireland? Would you like to climb mountains or paddle your own canoe on Loch Lomond? By train, bus, ship, cycle or 'Shanks's pony' the countryside is yours and with the facilities provided by the Youth Hostels Association your holiday can be expansive rather than expensive.' Produced in association with the Youth Hostels Association.

35/16mm, Sound, Colour, 17mins, BTF

OH! MR PORTER (Britain 1937)

A Gainsborough picture. Directed by Marcel Varnel. Script by J O C Orton, Val Guest and Marriott Edgar. Photography by Arthur Crabtree. Art direction by Vetchinsky. Edited by R E Dearing and Alfred Roome. Music by Louis Levy. With Will Hay, Moore Marriott, Graham Moffat, Sebastian Shaw, Agnes Lauchlan, Percy Walsh, Dennis Wyndham and Dave O'Toole.
The Story
William Porter, an incompetent wheel tapper, has one ambition in life — to become a station master.

After accidentally wrecking the naming ceremony of *Silver Link*, he is sent to Buggleskelly on the Southern Railway of Northern Ireland as a station master through the influence of his brother-in-law. Here he finds a derelict station, completely off the map, and staffed by Jeremiah Harbottle and Albert. These good-for-nothings make a comfortable living out of goods they steal, and pay for what they have to buy with railway tickets. Will decides to run a day excursion to liven things up. All the tickets are bought by a one-eyed man for his 'football team'. Will despatches the train and it disappears. Frantic enquiries up and down the line bring no news of it. Will, Jeremiah and Albert then get out *Gladstone*, an ancient engine 'with beautiful lines', and start in search. They find the train in a tunnel on a disused loop. And Will makes the further discovery that his excursionists are gun-runners. Will, Jeremiah, and Albert are chased into a windmill. They escape down the sails, uncouple the excursion engine, attach *Gladstone* to the other end, and off they go, with the gun-runners on board. A hectic and hilarious journey ends at the terminus with the capture of the gang. The beaming Will is anxious to share the congratulations with *Gladstone*. But alas, the excitement has been too much for him — or her. With one final gasp *Gladstone* blows up!

Reviews

'And every night when the moon gives light,
The Miller's Ghost is seen
As he walks the track
With a sack on his back
Down to the black borheen.'

'*Oh! Mr Porter* is Hay's most well-loved comedy. It was made in the same year as *Good Morning, Boys* and is the second film he completed with Marcel Varnel. This is that rare phenomenon; a film comedy without a dud scene. Everything "comes off". Direction, acting and writing are beautifully integrated. *Oh! Mr Porter* is probably Hay's funniest film. It hasn't the scathing satire of *Convict 99* and *Old Bones of the River* or the subtle implications of *Good Morning, Boys*, but for sheer belly-laughs, *Oh! Mr Porter* is in a class of its own. Marcel Varnel had the idea that if the technicians on the floor laughed during the shooting of a comedy, then there was something wrong. The joke which appeared so funny to the technicians would not raise even a smile from an audience in the cinema. All one can say about *Oh! Mr Porter* is that the men and women working on it must have resembled corpses.

'In *Oh! Mr Porter* the team work of Moore Marriott, Graham Moffatt and Hay is seen at its best. The beautiful sense of timing, the comic invention and the subtlety of their playing are superb. Nothing is laboured, nothing is lost.

'There is a golden timeless quality about this film. The backgrounds and characters are real enough, but the whole thing is set in a poetic limbo, where nothing will ever change; where the signal box will still be used as a greenhouse; where Harbottle will continue to have his liquid supper every night; and the four marble clocks, three white and one black, will still tick away gloomily on the mantlepiece, until the end of time.' (Peter Barnes)

'He haunts the hill
He haunts the mill
And the land that lies between.'

'So chants the sinister village postman in an attempt to make the new station master's flesh creep. "Is he a house agent?" asks Will Hay, and returns to his stationmastering. What sublime practicality, and yet what ridiculous nonchlance, is summed up in that simple sentence. Behind it lie the gutsy uplands of the British music-hall tradition, whose rich soil the British film industry is at last beginning to exploit. Better late than never; for here is something entirely British, which can be set in independent glory over against the vaudeville and slapstick tradition of America whose first stimulus, it is true, came from our original seeds, but which has grown up differently in the atmosphere of a new world. Film comedy in Britain has so far — with a few exceptions — been an undistinguished failure, chiefly because neither producers nor directors have understood the value of teamwork, and the necessity of achieving a special genre not merely in subject-matter but also in the character of each separate comedian. For that is the secret of American comedy, from the days of Keystone to the days of the Marx Brothers; and our own neglect of it has too often wasted the talents of a Claude Dampier or a Gracie Fields. But tradition will out. Gainsborough Pictures have found the formula for transmuting the magic of the Will Hay music-hall turn into an equal magic of the screen. The original schoolmaster act, after a long innings, has now been jettisoned. The divine Harbottle remains, and the team is strengthened by the authentic Fat Boy of Graham Moffat. And Will Hay himself, precariously avoiding the beckoning finger of fantasy, wins richer laurels than ever before.

'*Oh! Mr Porter* tells of his adventures as the stationmaster at a dilapidated and reputedly haunted railway station on the borders of the Irish Free State and Northern Ireland. The possibilities are endless, and are well-exploited. To see Will Hay despatching what he thinks is an excursion train to Connemara but which departs — in the wrong direction — on a gun-running expedition, is an object lesson in comedy. Marcel Varnel, who directed, is responsible not merely for the rapid rhythm of the film, but also for a Gallic exuberance which is beautifully welded to the more phlegmatic atmosphere of the Hay team. His treatment of the final chase in the train (piloted by an adorable mid-Victorian engine named *Gladstone*) is particularly brilliant.' (Basil Wright: *The Spectator*, 5 November 1937.)

The Railway

The material for this film was shot mainly on the abandoned Basingstoke-Alton branch line of the Southern Railway; various additional shots were taken of different sections of the same system. The titles are set against a background of scenes taken from various points on the Waterloo-Southampton line; sections of a third rail electrified track appear on some of the shots, with the train going in the wrong direction ie on the right-hand track! The editor just reversed his negative at one stage in preparing the title backgrounds, causing them to come out reversed on the final print. Buggleskelly was in real life the station of Cliddesden and was in a semi-derelict condition before the Gainsborough film company added

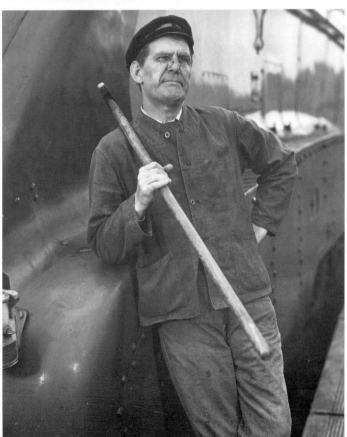

Will Hay and his gang in action
during the classic 'Oh Mr Porter'.

their own embellishments. Indeed, the line was being dismantled while the film was being made and the crew working on the lifting of the track occasionally helped the film people with a difficult bit of railway manipulation.

Not surprisingly motive power, carriages and wagons came from various items of ex-London & South Western Railway stock. The express engine was William Adams X2 class 4-4-0 No 657 of 1895 vintage; the excursion train was drawn by Adams class 0-6-0 No 3509 of 1885, a Neilson-built goods engine. These two engines were ex-LSWR; to change their appearance for the film they had shorter LBSCR chimneys fitted.

Gladstone was borrowed from the Kent & East Sussex Railway. It was one of two 2-4-0 tanks built by Hawthorn Leslie in 1899 for the opening of that line under its original name of the Rother Valley Railway on which they were No 1 *Tenderden* and No 2 *Northiam*. Alas, both engines were sold for scrap in 1941. It was No 2 that ran light to and from Basingstoke for the filming. The nameplate *Gladstone* replaced its own nameplate for the occasion and, whereas the two LSWR engines had lower chimneys fitted for the occasion, *Gladstone* was made higher with a spiked top. The LSWR engines retained their cab side number plates but the wording of 'OF NORTHERN IRELAND' was painted in below the name 'SOUTHERN RAILWAY'.

For certain action scenes, the camera crew worked from a wooden platform built on the side of No 657; for location scenes of the fight on the roof Graham Moffatt was tied by one leg (out of view of the camera) to the roof of the train. The final chase and crash was done in Basingstoke yard.

As the Basingstoke and Alton was used so extensively in both *The Wrecker* and *Oh! Mr Porter*, it might be useful to end with a note on the history of the line taken from an article by Charles Klapper published in *Railway World*:

'The Basingstoke and Alton, first light railway to be sanctioned by the 1896 procedure, had a melancholy story and can serve to epitomise the fate of light railways in general. In the first instance the London &

South Western Railway, its sponsor, was not really interested in the welfare of the area it traversed. However silly its prospectus may read to us of the 1960s, in 1895 the intentions of the promoters of the Portsmouth, Guildford & Basingstoke Railway Company seemed serious and menacing to the directors of the London & South Western Railway. That company's blocking line to fill up the territory between Fareham and Alton, the Meon Valley line, was authorised in 1897 and opened on June 1, 1903.

'From Alton to Basingstoke the new light railway drill was put into operation and the Light Railway Commissioners issued in 1897 their first order to permit its construction. Once the power to build was secured three years were allowed to pass after the ceremony of cutting the first sod before its completion on June 1, 1901. There were no great communities to serve en route and the route seemed deliberately to avoid the villages after which stations were named. Although cheapness was obviously sought in the very adoption of a light railway and the route was meandering there were nevertheless some heavy earthworks. The LSWR board soon felt they had paid dear for foiling the PG&B plans.

'It was offered as a sacrifice in the 1914-1918 war and the track was lifted and sent overseas. No attempt was made to restore but abandonment powers were strongly opposed when the Southern sought them in 1923 and the newly grouped company made the best of it and agreed to reinstatement subject to review after 10 years. Reopening came on 18 August 1924, but abandonment was again sought in 1933, with greater success. The northern part of the line remained open for freight but passenger services were withdrawn as from 12 September 1932, and freight facilities followed on 1 June 1936.'

Oh! Mr Porter was filmed between May and July 1937 as the track was being lifted. There was no tunnel on the branch so the one seen in the film was built by Gainsborough in a cutting. K&ESR locomotive No 2 was noted at Basingstoke on 13 June 1937 but was

back in Kent by the beginning of August. Interior scenes were shot at the Gainsborough studios at Shepherd's Bush during August and the film was released at the end of the year.

35/16/8mm, Sound, 85mins, Rank/rail, only: HA/production shot: AW

OH! WHAT A LOVELY WAR (Britain 1969)

Paramount. An Accord production. Directed by Richard Attenborough. With Laurence Olivier, John Gielgud, Michael Redgrave, Ralph Richardson, John Rae and Mary Wimbush. World War 1 fantasydrama. Scenes were shot on 16 June at Brighton station using restored LSWR 'M7' Class 0-4-4T No 245 together with two former ambulance coaches and a Longmoor Military Railway coach.

35mm, Sound, Colour, 144mins, Paramount

OHRID EXPRESS (France 1963)

Directed by Legrand-Dasque. A look at the narrow gauge railway in the south of Yugoslavia near Skopje which runs to Lake Ohrid.

16mm, Sound, Colour, 10mins, UniFrance

OKLAHOMA CRUDE (USA 1973)

Columbia Pictures. Directed by Stanley Kramer. With Faye Dunaway and John Mills. An itinerant oil worker assists a lady oil-well operator. Includes scenes on the Sierra Railroad with Rogers 4-6-0 locomotive No 4493 built in 1891, repainted as 'Oklahoma Central RR' for the film.

35mm, Sound, Colour, 111mins, Columbia

ON GREAT COCKROW TRACKS (Britain 1967)

A film by Derek Henderson. The fascinating minature railway with its large collection of beautiful miniature locomotives, of which LMS 'Princess Coronation' 4-6-2 No 6230 *Duchess of Buccleuch* is prominent. The quaintly named stations seen include 'Hardwick Central', 'Allan Water' and 'Jungle Halt'.

16mm, Sound, Colour, 11mins, DH/HA

🚂 🚂 🚂 🚂 🚂

ON THE CENTRAL WALES LINE WITH A G2 (Britain 1961)

Made by P B Whitehouse and John Adams. A trip on the line Swansea Victoria to Craven Arms.

16/8mm, Silent, 9mins, CV/NRM

🚂 🚂 🚂 🚂 🚂

ON THE END OF A PLATFORM: BRISTOL (Britain 1985)

A film by Rob Foxon. A day spent watching the motive power in action at Bristol Temple Meads station.

16mm, Silent, Colour, 20mins, TUA

🚂 🚂 🚂 🚂 🚂

ON THE END OF A PLATFORM: CARLISLE (Britain 1985)

A film by Rob Foxon. Another survey of the various aspects of motive power to be seen at Carlisle in the mid-1980s.

16mm, Silent, Colour, 20mins, TUA

🚂 🚂 🚂 🚂 🚂

ON THE END OF A PLATFORM: LEICESTER (Britain 1977-1978)

A film by Rob Foxon. An earlier study of a typical day on a platform; it includes rare shots of the Advanced Passenger Train (APT).

16mm, Silent, Colour, 14mins, TUA

🚂 🚂 🚂 🚂 🚂

ON THE ISLE OF MAN (Britain 1964)

Link Productions. The horse trams, the Manx Electric Railway and the narrow gauge railway; the locomotives include No 10 *G H Wood* and No 11 *Maitland*.

16/9.5/8mm, Silent, Colour, 4mins, MFS

🚂 🚂 🚂 🚂 🚂

ON THE NORFOLK & WESTERN (USA 1950)

Made by Fred McLeod. 2-8-8-2, 4-8-4 and 4-8-2 locomotives photographed in Virginia in the later days of steam.

16/8mm, Silent/sound, 8mins, Blackhawk

🚂 🚂 🚂 🚂 🚂

ON THE PENNSYLVANIA (USA c1950)

Made by Fred McLeod. 2-10-4, 2-10-2, 2-8-2 and K4 Pacifics filmed mainly in the area of the Horseshoe Curve, near Altoona, Philadelphia.

16/8mm, Silent/Sound, 8mins, Blackhawk

🚂 🚂 🚂 🚂 🚂

ON THE TRACK (USA c1940)

Produced by the Association of American railroads. A hard sell for going by rail in the USA, suggesting, amongst other things, that US railroads were subsidising the building of new roads and thus paving the way for their demise. Good coverage of many US systems, with lots of steam.

16mm, Sound, Colour, 20mins, TUA

🚂 🚂 🚂 🚂 🚂

ON THE TRACK (USA 1946)

Association of US Railroads. A documentary on the future of American railways and the chances of survival under self-financing conditions. It didn't work, except for freight.

16mm, Sound, Colour, 19mins, RF

🚂 🚂 🚂 🚂 🚂

ONCE UPON A LINE (Britain 1946)

Video Workshop. Video issue of an old film about model railway societies, intermixed with archive railway shots.

VID, Sound, 30mins, Video Workshop

🚂 🚂 🚂 🚂

ONCE UPON A LINE (Britain 1947)

Normans Film Productions. The activities of model railway clubs

around London, inter-related to actuality shots of railways past and present.

35/16mm, Sound, 21mins, HA

🚂 🚂 🚂 🚂

ONCE UPON A TIME (Yugoslavia 1989)

Belgrade Film School Production. Directed by Ales Verbic. With Bernarda Gaspercic, Emil Filipcic, Toni Ziherl, Nadja Vidmar, Anica Sadar and Marinko Banjac. A film showing life as a railway journey: some passengers get off, some continue on their way and some miss the train altogether. There is no commentary and the film is shot in a sepia tone. The movie is dedicated to the Italian 'Spaghetti Western' director Sergio Leone, who once travelled on the route shown.

35mm, Sound, Sepia Tone, 19mins, Yugofilm

🚂 🚂 🚂 🚂 🚂

ONCE UPON A TRAIN (Britain 1987)

Flying Scotsman Enterprises. (Hon Sir William McAlpine). A film by Jeremy Monson. Photography by Frank Gell and Tony Goggans. A mixed bag of railway history including the replica of *Locomotion*; *King George V* in action from Hereford to Newport; GWR '45XX' 2-6-2T No 4555 on the Dart Valley Railway at Staverton; a study of the Royal coaches at the National Railway Museum in York and three American preserved railroads: the Strasburg in Pennsylvania with a four-mile run behind a Baldwin 2-10-0; the Reader Railroad in Arkansas with a 23-mile line built in 1925 with a hundred timber trestles; and an old Norfolk and Western 2-10-0 still working to feed scrap metal to the North Western Steel and Wire Company of Illinois.

16mm/VID, Sound, Colour, 21mins, HA/Video Collection

🚂 🚂 🚂 🚂 🚂

ONE DAY IN SEVERN (Britain 1990)

Video 125. Produced by Peter Middleton. Commentary by Anton Rogers. A very detailed record of a working day in the country's largest surviving mechanical signalbox –

the Severn Bridge Junction box at Shrewsbury. Multiple cameras were installed inside the signalbox, still operating a vast array of semaphore, and the work of this 180-lever box was recorded through the daylight hours on 30 June, 1990, in company with Bernard Hitch, the Area Movements Inspector who discusses operations with Arfon Haines Davies. A unique video record.

VID, Sound, Colour, 105mins, VID/125

ONE DAY IN SOVIET RUSSIA (USSR 1943)

Central Newsreel Studios, Moscow. Film by 97 cameramen of one day in Russia. Includes scenes on the Moscow Underground and the trans-Siberian railway.

35mm, Sound, 48mins, ETV

ONE WAY OF SEEING THE ISLAND OF FUNEN (Denmark 1963)

Produced by Danish State Railways. A journey on the mainline of the island of Funen from Nyborg station up to the Little Belt bridge, as seen from the interior of the driver's cab.

35/16mm, Sound, Colour, 10mins, DSB

ONE WAY TICKET (Britain 1983)

P Smallwood video. The last 'Deltic' run from Kings Cross to York in December 1981. Locomotive No 55021.

VID, Sound, Colour, 80mins, Ballymoss

ONLINE VIDEO

Run by Wilf Watters and using much of his own private collection, this company covers many aspects of transport. Their railway output includes *Glasgow Underground, Irish Railways, Liverpool Overhead Railway, Trains Remembered* (three volumes), records of many preserved railways like the Kent and East Sussex, the Mid-Hants and the Swanage line and very

extensive coverage of London's Underground system, plus one on the Paris Metro.

ONGAR TO EPPING UNDERGROUND RAILWAY (Britian 1977)

Anglia Television. From the series *Probe*. Problems of survival for a special bit of the London Underground system.

16mm, Sound, Colour, 8mins, Anglia

THE OPEN TRACK (USA 1915)

An episode from the series *The Hazards of Helen* starring Helen Holmes. A Kalem Production. Helen, as a telegraph operator at the station, outwits a gang of counterfeiters. There is a spectacular chase in an Atlantic-type locomotive in the Los Angeles area.

16/8mm, Silent, 15mins, Blackhawk/BFI

OPENING OF IMMINGHAM DOCKS (Britain 1912)

Gaumont newsreel. The opening of the Great Central Docks at Immingham, including the arrival of King George V and Queen Mary in a Royal train hauled by a Robinson GCR 'Atlantic' of 1905 vintage. The opening ceremony was conducted by means of a tour of the docks on a GCR 'Humber' paddle steamer *Killingholme*. The plan was to rename this paddle steamer *Queen Mary* but Buckingham Palace took the greatest possible exception to an old paddler being given the Royal title! At the end of the day, Sam Fay, General Manager of the Great Central, was knighted on the spot.

16mm, Silent, 14mins, HA

OPERATION BLUEBELL (Britain 1960)

Made by Trevor White. A record of the work of the Bluebell Railway Preservation Society.

16/9.5/8mm, Sound, 7mins, TW/BFI/MFS

OPERATION BULLSHINE (Britain 1959)

Associated British Picture Corporation. Directed by Gilbert Gunn. With Donald Sinden, Barbara Murray, Carole Lesley, Ronald Shiner, Naughton Wayne and Dora Bryan. In 1942, complications ensue when an ATS private suspects her officer husband of infidelity. 'Despite the cast, a flabby comedy with few laughs.' (Leslie Halliwell) Includes a scene of an LNER 'N7' tank arriving at Braughing station with a set of old Great Eastern corridor coaches repainted in LNER livery. All the coaches were scrapped within a week of the filming. Alas, the LNER exterior shots are followed by an LMS compartment interior! Some material shot in the making of this film was used in the video *Steam on 35mm*.

35mm, Sound, Colour, 84mins, Weintraub

OPERATION SNOWBOUND (Britain 1947)

GWR Unit, Paddington. An interesting experiment by the GWR at snow clearance, using two Whittle jet engines mounted on a flat waggon and pushed slowly forward to clear the snow. It was tried out at Dowlis Top in February 1947. The jet engines certainly shifted the snow. Alas, they also shifted most of the blocks, half the ballast and cut a neat slot in the sleepers! A nice try in the last days of GWR enterprise.

16mm, Silent, 6mins, HA

ORIENT EXPRESS (Britain 1971)

BBC TV. From the *Nairn's Journey* series. 14 August 1971. A rail journey from Paris to Bucharest on the reconstructed Orient Express. A mixture of electric and diesel across Europe, with a glimpse of steam in the last lap from Bucharest to Istanbul (not part of the official trip). Produced and devised by Barry Bevins. Photographed by Bob Sleigh. Edited by Peter Marsh.

16mm, Sound, Colour, 29mins, BBC TV

THE OTHER POLAND (Britain 1983)

BBC Television. Executive producer Colin Adams. Produced by Lyn Webster. Written and presented by Brian Blessed. From the *Great Little Railways* series. Brian Blessed travels to the rural areas of Poland by way of the narrow gauge line from Warsaw to Krakow. The narrow gauge line from Komancza to Cisna in the south and the Pultusk to Nasieisk in the north – interesting narrow gauge railways film showing something of everyday life in rural Poland.

16mm, Sound, Colour, 40mins, BBC TV

THE OTHER WAY WEST (Britain 1980)

Westward Television. Produced and directed by Tony Smith. Written and presented by Robert Adley, MP. The rise and fall of the 'Withered Arm', the old LSWR route from Waterloo to Padstow. The film deals with the competition between the GWR and LSWR, its adoption by the Southern Railway in 1923, the continued competition with the Great Western for the routes to the West Country, the days of the 'Atlantic Coast Express' and the collapse of much of the route after 1948. There are archive steam scenes in the 1950s, the Lyme Regis branch, the Lynton & Barnstaple Railway and a reconstruction, using LSWR '0415' Radial Tank 4-4-2T No 488, of the special locomotives dating back to 1882 which were kept specially to work the difficult severe curves and gradients of the Lyme Regis branch. These scenes were filmed on the Bluebell Railway where the Adams Radial is preserved.

16mm, Sound, Colour, 26mins, Westward

OUR CANTEENS (Britain 1951)

Produced by British Transport Films. This film was shown to all new recruits to London Transport's canteen service. It opens by revealing the complexity of the canteen organisation. After this, conditions of work in various canteens are contrasted and explained, the aims of training are dealt with, and the new employees are shown how they should fit in with their fellow canteen-workers. Advice is given about coping with some of the difficulties which arise on the job and the film ends by emphasising the importance to transport workers of efficient and friendly canteens. This film was made in association with British Transport Films by Trident Films.

35/16mm, Sound, 13mins, BTF

OUR CLUB MAGAZINE No 18 (Britain 1946)

A Wallace Production. Scenes of the Romney, Hythe & Dymchurch Railway.

35mm, Sound, 3mins, CFF

OUR HOSPITALITY (USA 1923)

Metro. Directed by Buster Keaton and Jack Blystone. With Buster Keaton, Natalie Talmadge and Joe Keaton. A Southerner in the United States returns to his home property to find himself in the middle of a blood feud. Notable for a quite extraordinary reproduction of the famous American De Witt Clinton train, built on a vast scale and followed by one of Keaton's equally famous logging railroad trains.

35mm, Silent, 70mins, NFA

OVER AND UNDER (Britain 1964)

Produced by British Transport Films. London Transport's new underground line from Victoria to Walthamstow was the largest work of its kind since the early years of this century. The film, introduced by C E Dunton, then Chief Civil Engineer describes the work at Oxford Circus, probably the most complicated engineering problem of the whole project, from early 1963 until the summer of 1964.

35/16mm, Sound, Colour, 28mins, BTF

OVER SHAP 1963 (Britain 1963)

Produced by Link. Photographed in Ektachrome March/April 1963. A journey by Euston-Glasgow express from Lowgill past Langdale Fell by the river Lune through Tebay past Scout Green to Shap Summit SE. At Tebay a goods train headed by Stanier 4-6-0 waits for banking engine Fairburn 2-6-4T No 42278 before proceeding up Shap. A similar train headed by 4-6-0 No 45083 with 2-6-4T No 42110 nearing the summit. Other locomotives seen between Lowgill and Shap Summit include 'Patriot' 4-6-0 No 45526 *Morecambe & Heysham*, Class 9F No 92018, Class 5 Stanier 4-6-0 No 45083, 'Royal Scot' 4-6-0 No 46162 *Queen's Westminster Rifleman*, Class 4MT 2-6-0 No 43029, Jubilee 4-6-0 No 45627 *Sierra Leone*, 'Britannia' 4-6-2 No 70002 *Geoffrey Chaucer*, Class 5 4-6-0 No 45284, and English Electric Type 4 diesels No D304, D321 and D325.

16/9.5/8mm, Silent, Colour, 8mins, MFS/VID

OVER THE ALPS: THE BUILDING OF A RAILWAY (Britain 1985)

TVS Production. Music by Doc Cox. Written and presented by Murray Walker. 'Over the Alps' was the affectionate name given to the steeply graded section of the British Railways (Southern Region) secondary route between Alton and Winchester in Hampshire. Although closed as uneconomic in 1973, much of its route through unspoilt countryside now forms part of the 10-mile Mid-Hants preserved steam railway between Alton and Alresford. Most of this route's track between Ropley and Alton had to be completely relaid and the stations, signalling, steam locomotives and rolling stock, acquired from British Rail, had to be restored – most of the work being done by volunteers. This film tells the impressive story of the rebuilding of the railway, its gradual reopening to passenger traffic, and its ultimate goal of reaching the British Rail station at Alton, where the first Mid Hants train steamed up on 25th May 1985.

16mm, Sound, Colour, 27mins, TVS

OVER THE MOON (Britain 1939)

London Film Production. Produced by Alexander Korda. Directed by Thornton Freeland. Photography by Harry Stradling. With Merle Oberon, Rex Harrison and Ursula Jeans. Romantic comedy; includes LNER express scenes and the 'Blue' train.

35mm, Sound, Colour, 78mins, London Films

THE OVERLAND LIMITED (USA 1925)

In 1925 Gotham Productions made *The Overland Limited* (English title: *The Mad Train*) which received a favourable review in *The Bioscope* magazine (Review 8 October 1925).

'Hair-raising sequence showing an express train driven by an imbecile towards a dangerous bridge is the great big thrill of this luridly sensational railway story. The episode compares with such classic thrills as the climax of *Way Down East*, and will undoubtedly ensure the success of a production which, in other respects, is just sound, straightforward melodrama. The action passes almost entirely in the impressive mountain gorge where the bridge is constructed, and on the railway line leading thereto. Though doubtless a model scene, the destruction of the bridge is convincingly realistic.'

It was a model; but it was not very convincing!

35mm, Silent, 71mins, Blackhawk/HA

OVERTURE (Britain 1978)

British Transport Films. In the mid-1970s, the now familiar Inter City 125 high-speed trains were introduced on many major routes radiating from London. This seven-minute impressionistic film was made to show the advantages of travelling on board. Exciting visuals and specially composed music by David Gow are brought together to enhance the mood and rhythm of the journey.

35/16mm, Sound, Colour, 7mins, BTF

PACIFIC 231 (France 1929)

Made by Professor Alexander Lazlo. A silent film interpretation, designed to be shown with a 'live' performance of the music by Arthur Honegger. The film has not survived.

35mm, Silent, 14mins, Lost

PACIFIC 231 (France, 1949)

Written and directed by Jean Mitry. Photography by Andre Tadie, Andre Perie and Jean Jarret. Music by Arthur Honegger. A visual interpretation of Honegger's locomotive tone-poem of a fast run on a train hauled by one of the powerful Pacific 231 Class locomotives of French railways. An opening sequence uses only natural sound, which serves to accentuate the dramatic moment when the music starts in time with the first massive movement of the wheels and connecting rods as the locomotive begins its run. There are some remarkable shots during the journey, notably of the valve gear in action at speed and a very low angle view of the track ahead as the train races through the open countryside. The locomotive used throughout the film is 231.

The film was awarded a special prize for Editing at the Cannes Film Festival in September 1949.

35/16mm, Sound, 11mins, HA

PACIFIC EXPRESS (USA 1947)

A film to exploit the introduction of the North Western diesel-hauled trains, with scenes of old preserved 4-4-0s for contrast.

16mm, Sound, 20mins, North Western

PADDY'S ENGINE: LMS 5407 (Britain 1989)

Railfilms. The story of Paddy Smith, owner of preserved LMS '5MT' 4-6-0 No 5407, based on Carnforth but often seen on the West High-land line from Fort William to Mallaig. There is extensive coverage of this run, including lineside and aerial shots. Produced and directed by Nick Dodson.

VID, Sound, Colour, 45mins, RFV

THE PAINTER AND THE ENGINES (Britain 1967)

A film by Paul Barnes. 'David Shepherd made the paintings. Paul Barnes made the film,' says the final title on this excellent record of the last days of steam on the Southern, notably at Nine Elms, made in company with the painter who has since been involved extensively not only in railway art but also, through the East Somerset Railway, the world of perservation. Locomotives seen in various states of decay and collapse include, most interestingly in view of their subsequent preservation, SR 4-6-2 'Merchant Navy' No 35028 *Clan Line* and 'West Country' No 34023 *Blackmoor Vale*, as well as 'Merchant Navy' No 35013 *Blue Funnel*, 35027 *Port Line*, 'Battle of Britain' No 34060 *25 Squadron*, BR '5' 4-6-0 No 73029 and BR '4' 2-6-4T No 80085.

16mm, Sound, Colour, 20mins, Barnes

PALACE ON WHEELS (Britain 1984)

Central Television. Produced by Zia Mohyeddin. Directed by Sid Kilbey. Presented by Hilary Minster. An item in the *Here and Now on 4* series. With 7,000 steam trains in daily active service in India on 60,000km of railway track, this journey through Rajastan with the film's writer, researcher and presenter Hilary Minster presents plenty to satisfy the steam enthusiast and tourist alike. We join the train at the beginning of its journey at Delhi, and spend a week travelling through Jaipur, Uidaipur, Baratpur and Agra, past such sites as the Taj Mahal, a deserted Mogul city and the Baratpur bird sanctuary.

Our journey is aboard the 'Palace on Wheels', a tourist train hauled by a combination of diesel and steam locomotives, with carriages dating from 1898. At the peak of Indian steam locomotion in 1963, there were some 6700 standard 5ft6in gauge locos, 3700 metre-gauge and 410 narrow gauge (2ft and 2ft6in) – this from the birth of Indian locomotion in April 1853, when British 240 tender engines hauled some 14 carriages a distance of 34km. The 'Palace on Wheels' runs on the metre gauge.

Hilary Minster explores a lifestyle created by the Maharajas as he tours the luxurious carriages (which, without corridors, rely on regular stops for movement around the train), with spacious bedrooms, bathrooms, lounges and bars. For many, however, the attraction lies simply in the job of being hauled by steam locos during the week long journey.

16mm, Sound, Colour, 38mins, Central

PANORAMA PRIS D'UNE TRAIN EN MARCH sic (France 1899)

Taken from the top of a centre carriage of a moving train, the film shows the tops of the preceding carriages and engine as it winds its way past stations, under bridges and viaducts. On one of the stations the words 'Bel-Air-Ceinture' are distinguishable. George Melies star film in the style of a 'Phantom Ride'.

35mm, Silent, 1min, NFA

PARCELS SERVICE (Britain 1959)

Produced by British Transport Films. A sequence on the art of Judo, another on making fruit bowls, set this film's theme: 'Start Right-Keep Right-and Finish Right'. The advice can be applied to each stage of a parcel's journey: delivery and collection, acceptance by the parcels office clerk, loading and unloading barrows, guard's and parcels vans and delivery vehicles. Right handling at each stage can save time, trouble, loss and damage and help to bring in extra traffic as well. This film was made in association with British Transport Films by Pilot Films.

35/16mm, Sound, 35mins, BTF

PARIS-LILLE (France 1962)

French Railways. Electrification of the line from Paris to Lille at industrial voltage.

16mm, Sound, 18mins, SNCF

PARIS TERMINI (Britain 1963)

Made by P B Whitehouse and John Adams. Part of a major European tour, this film concentrates on the remaining steam operations in the Paris area.

16/8mm, Silent, 9mins, CV/NRM

PASSENGER TRAINS OF THE LMS (Britain 1935)

LMS Film Unit. A detailed survey of the main service of the LMS in the 1930s from Euston and St Pancras to Manchester, Scotland, the Midlands and right through to Kyle of Lochalsh. (From the 'Just for the Record' series on video).

35mm/VID, Sound, 28mins, BTF/RFV

PASSPORT TO PIMLICO (Britain 1948)

Ealing Studios. Directed by Henry Cornelius. With Stanley Holloway and Margaret Rutherford. London comedy. Sequence on the District line of the London Underground near South Kensington station.

35mm, Sound, 84mins, Weintraub

THE PAST AT WORK: RAILWAY MANIA (Britain 1980)

BBC Television. Series producer: Michael Garrod. Produced by Suzanne Davies. Written and presented by Anthony Burton. A tour of the many preserved steam railways that have sprung up in recent years; a sort of second 'Railway Mania'. There is a vist to the National Railway Museum in York and a trip on a steam special from York to Harrogate.

16mm, Sound, Colour, 25mins, BBC TV

THE PAST AT WORK: STEAM ON THE MOVE (Britain 1980)

BBC Television. Series producer: Michael Garrod. Produced by Suzanne Davies. Written and presented by Anthony Burton. The various uses of steam power including industrial and freight trains; beam pumping engines; the preserved Middleton Railway, one of the oldest railways in the world, authorised by Parliament in 1758 (in those days, for horse power only); and, in action, the replica of the 1825 0-4-0 Stephenson locomotive No 1 of the Stockton & Darlington Railway's *Locomotion*.

16mm, Sound, Colour, 25mins, BBC TV

PENNINE STEAM: VOLUME ONE (Britain 1990)

Jumpcut Video. Film by Geoffrey Whitwam. Recorded on the line from Huddersfield to the Standedge tunnel and the village of Golcar. Scenes in the 1960s with LMS '8Fs', 'Black Fives' and 'Jubilees' as well as BR standard classes and a '9F', one of which is an ex-Crosti-boilered example. These are contrasted with Pacers, Super Sprinters and locomotive hauled stock in trans-Pennine livery.

VID, Sound, Colour, 30mins, JMC

THE PENNSY ELECTRICS (USA c 1960)

Scenes on the 'Pennsy Speedway' between Philadelphia and Washington showing GG1, B2, FF1, 8-5 and 4-6-4 electric locomotives, some shots are taken on the Shuylkill River Bridge, Philadelphia.

8mm, Silent, Colour, 4mins, Blackhawk

THE PENNSY'S ELECTRIFIED SPEEDWAY (USA c 1960)

Scenes around Harrisburg, Pennsylvania and Princeton, New Jersey, of a variety of forms of electric traction.

8mm, Silent, Colour, 4mins, Blackhawk

PENNSYLVANIA STEAM LOCOMOTIVES (USA 1939-50)

Scenes of 'K4' Pacifics, 10-wheelers, Consolidations and duplexes of the Pennsylvania line.

8mm, Silent, Colour, 8mins, Blackhawk

PEOPLE LIKE US (Britain 1962)

Produced by British Transport Films. 'With your head bursting with trains and people asking you a question every minute, it isn't always easy to remember that passengers are people. But if, through the eye of an often candid camera, you see yourself dealing with them, it is only too obvious that they are "people like us".'

35/16mm, Sound, 9mins, BTF

THE PERILS OF PAULINE (USA 1947)

A Paramount picture. Directed by George Marshall. With Betty Hutton and John Lard. Biography of Pearl White, the serial queen. Includes some lively railway rescue stunts, staged in the studio.

35mm, Sound, Colour, 94mins, Paramount

PERMANENT WAY RENEWAL (Britain 1949)

Produced by British Transport Films for the British Transport Commission. A staff instructional film which shows modern methods of re-laying railway tracks.

35/16mm, Sound, 16mins, BTF

PERTH SHED (Britain 1960)

Made by P B Whitehouse and John Adams. A film of locomotives seen on a normal shed visit, in old Caledonian and North British territory.

16/8mm, Silent, 6mins, CV/NRM

THE PETER GODDARD COLLECTION

A wide-ranging collection going back some 30 years, partly on 8mm

and some of 16mm. It covers many aspects of the Southern region such as the Redhill-Guildford-Reading line in steam days (steam ended in 1965), vintage electrics including the Ouse Valley Viaduct and Copyhold Junction; the Ardingly branch; the Bluebell Railway and many other scenes.

PETER HANDFORD AND HIS RECORDINGS (Britain 1980)

Anglia Television. Conversation between Paul Barnes and Peter Handford, specialist in making highly-prized recordings of steam locomotives with shots of preserved No 6100 *Royal Scot*.

16mm, Sound, Colour, 8mins, Anglia

THE PETER WOOD COLLECTION

This is a very wide-ranging 8mm collection, covering many aspects of preservation – the Kent & East Sussex, the Ffestiniog, the Talyllyn, many trips with *Clan Line*, aspects of Southern Electric, overseas trips in America and Holland as well as early items like a 1964 record of an 'M7' on the Caterham branch and a 1963 film of the Three Bridges to East Grinstead line. Peter Wood has been much involved himself in the preservation of the Great Little Trains of Wales and is closely associated with the *Clan Line* support group. He is a Council Member of the Lloyds Railway Society.

PHANTOM EXPRESS (USA 1925)

A Banner production. Directed by John Adolfi. With David Butler and Ethel Shannon. A railroad story of rivalry and deliberate wrecks. Reputed to have been made with the help of Southern Pacific.

35mm, Silent, 77mins, Lost

PHANTOM EXPRESS (USA 1932)

Directed by Emory Johnson. With J Farrell MacDonald, William Collier Jnr, Sally Blane, Hobart Bosworth and Eddie Phillips.

The Phantom Express concerns a railroad which has been troubled

with repeated wrecks. In each case the engineer's story has been identical. On a dark, moonless night a shrieking express has come roaring into the road, speeding straight at his engine. He has braked his train violently to avoid a collision and a wreck has resulted. But in each instance investigation shows no trace of another train. MacDonald finally wrecks his train in the same manner and is discharged. The President's son (Collier) a reformed ne'er-do-well who loves MacDonald's daughter (Sally Blane) proves his mettle by tracking down the mystery of the 'phantom' train that has been causing all the trouble. The main action was filmed on the Atchison, Topeka & Santa Fe Railroad.

35mm, Sound, 66mins, NA

THE PHANTOM LIGHT (Britain 1934)

Gainsborough. Directed by Michael Powell. With Gordon Harker and Binnie Hale. Wreckers try to scare off a new lighthouse keeper and cause a shipwreck. Includes scenes of the Ffestiniog railway in its original form.

35mm, Sound, 75mins, Rank

PHANTOM RIDE: CHAMONIX (Britain 1900)

A Robert Paul Film. Views from an engine.

35mm, Silent, 3mins, NFA

PICCADILLY INCIDENT (Britain 1946)

Associated British Picture Corporation. Produced and directed by Herbert Wilcox. With Anna Neagle, Michael Wilding, Coral Browne and A E Matthews. During World War 2, a girl believed drowned comes back to find her husband remarried. Includes railway scenes on the Southern Railway and wartime Waterloo.

35mm/VID, Sound, Colour, 102mins, Weintraub/VID 125 (Rly)

PICCADILLY LINE EXTENSIONS (Britain 1964)

New additions to the Piccadilly line and work in progress on new lines.

35mm, Sound, 12mins, BTF

PICTURE AND SOUNDS

A video company which broke new ground by making tapes exclusively with still photographs. The pictures come mainly from the collection of John Spencer Gilks which goes back to 1952. The main items include: *Cumbria* (Vol 1); *North Riding of Yorkshire* (Vol 2); *Scottish Highlands* (Vol 3); *Mid and North Wales* (Vol 4); *Bristol-Bournemouth-Weymouth* (Vol 5); *East Anglia* (Vol 6) and *The West Country* (Vol 7). There are a further two tapes assembled by John Edgington of the National Railway Museum, York, they cover the work of P. Ransome-Wallis and R. D. Stephen.

PICTURESQUE NIAGARA, ONTARIO, CANADA: GRAND TRUNK RAILWAY SYSTEM (Britain 1910)

Butcher's Film Service. Railway scenes around Niagara Falls, including the Grand Trunk Steel Arch Bridge.

35mm, Silent, 5mins, NFA

PIER RAILWAYS

Films of pier railways are rare, with the exception of Southend. There are good records of the original Crompton/Falcon Works electric cars which were in use from 1890 to 1949 and were filmed in 1928, 1938 and 1946. New gleaming stock was supplied by AC Cars of Thames Ditton in 1949 and some of the old originals were transferred to the Volks Railway in Brighton. The new cars were filmed in their first ` weeks of operation by John Meredith. There are little bits of Herne Bay (c 1956), Hythe (1948), Ryde (1910, 1964 and 1967) and Margate (1948).

PIERRE OF THE PLAINS (USA 1942)

MGM. Directed by Geoge B Seitz. With John Carroll and Ruth Hussey. Tale of a cheerful trapper in Canada's North West Territory. Use was made of Baldwin locomotive 2-8-0 No 29790, built in 1906 and often modified with such additions as a massive fake balloon smokestack, box headlight and other brass trimmings to suit each occasion; the scenes were shot on the Sierra Railroad in California.

35mm, Sound, 66mins, MGM

PILOTES DU RAIL (France 1947)

SNCF. An excellent, if somewhat poetic, impression of the work of the footplate crew on French main-line rosters, with many nice domestic details not usually included in this type of film.

35/16mm, Sound, 20mins, SNCF/RF

THE PLYMOUTH EXPRESS (Britain 1990)

LWT. An Agatha Christie Poirot story with a railway background. It used Hull Paragon station to represent Paddington, Bristol and Plymouth! The designer on the film explains: 'with a wide shot from the booking office, we had a train steaming out from underneath the arch, which gave a good impression of a London terminus. For Bristol, we hung up a sign – just that! For Plymouth, just another sign of the right period and a sailor whistling in the shot. We always have to hide the arrivals and departures television screens, usually cloaked with baskets of flowers or hanging signs.' (Ron Harris)

TV, Sound, Colour, 52mins, LWT

POISON PEN (Britain 1939)

Associated British Production. Directed by Paul L Stein. Photography by Philip Tonnura. With Flora Robson, Ann Toddy, Edward Rigby and Edward Chapman. Location shots of a typical LMS small country station; LMS tank loco pulling a

rather modern set of LMS coaches.

35mm, Sound, 78mins, Weintraub

PORT OF MANCHESTER (Britain 1942)

Educational Film Bureau, Tring. Includes shots of steam locomotives and trains in the area of the Bridgewater Canal and Transporter Bridge.

16mm, Silent, 20mins, Lost

LES PORTES DE LA NUIT (France 1946)

Pathé Cinema. Directed by Marcel Carné. With Pierre Brasseur, Yves Montand, Nathalie Nattier, Serge Reggiani and Jean Vilar. Various people in postwar Paris are drawn into a pattern woven by Destiny, who is represented by a melancholy tramp. Includes scenes shot on the Paris Metro.

35mm, Sound, 106mins, Pathe

POSTCARD TO DEVON (Britain 1946)

Pathe/British Instructional Films. The journey of a postcard from London to Ivybridge in Devon. Includes a series of the overnight Travelling Post Office train from Paddington to Plymouth.

16mm, Sound, 10mins, Pathe

POSTMAN'S KNOCK (Britain 1961)

MGM British. Produced by Robert Kinnoch. Directed by Robert Lynn. With Spike Milligan, Barbara Shelley and Wilfrid Lawson. A postman from a quiet country area moves to work amid London's confusing bustle. He finds fame by foiling a criminal gang. 'Mildly amusing star vehicle rising to good comic climaxes.' (Leslie Halliwell) Scenes are filmed on the Buntingford branch of the old Great Eastern, which finally closed in 1965. The filming was described by P Paye in his history of the line:-
'Fame came to the Buntingford line when Metro-Goldwyn Mayer took over West Mill station, one

Sunday early in 1961 for outside location work for the film *Postman's Knock*. Spike Milligan played the title role of the village postman, who went to the big city in search of ambition. West Mill station, renamed Upper Fringly for the occasion, was the departure point for the postman, who was cheered on his way by the local villagers, played in the film by extras. For the journey 'J15' class 0-6-0 locomotive No 65460 and two Gresley bogie suburban coaches were provided and spent most of the day steaming into and out of the station.'

35mm, Sound, 88mins, MGM

🚂

POWER RAIL: VOLUMES 1 AND 2 (Britain 1990-91)

Electra Films. Guaranteed 391 locomotives in Volume 1; Volume 2 has only a modest 354 engines on view.

VID, Sound, Colour, 120mins each, ELV

🚂 🚂 🚂 🚂 🚂

POWER-SIGNAL LINEMAN (Britain 1954)

Produced by British Transport Films. 'Strategically sited throughout London Transport's railway system, at immediate call, are Power-Signal Linemen, ready to put right any faults that may occur. The film, which is part of London Transport's training course for power-signal linemen, shows a possible fault and how the lineman makes repairs. It emphasises the conditions of urgency and stress under which a lineman must work, and the patient, methodical skill he must nevertheless bring to any problem if it is to be solved successfully as well as speedily'. This film was made in association with British Transport Films by Basic Films.

35/16mm, Sound, 16mins, BTF

🚂 🚂 🚂 🚂 🚂

POWER TO THE PANTOGRAPH (Britain 1960)

Produced by Cas Productions for British Insulated Callender's Cables Ltd. The installation of AC overhead equipment for British Railways, as part of their modernisation and electrification scheme. The film gives a detailed account of the surveying, planning, design and manufacture of the equipment and records the work involved during its installation at the multiple-tracked Crewe Junction.

35/16mm, Sound, Colour, 35mins, BICC

🚂 🚂 🚂 🚂 🚂

POWERFUL GIANTS (USA 1951)

Westinghouse. Building diesel and electric locomotives for the Argentine and Netherlands.

16mm, Sound, Colour, 20mins, RF

🚂 🚂 🚂 🚂 🚂

PRAIRIE EXPRESS (USA 1947)

Monogram Film. Directed by Lambert Hatton. The rounding up of a gang who organize attacks on a freight line out West. AT&SF stock shots.

35mm, Sound, 55mins, Monogram

🚂 🚂 🚂

PRAISE BE! (Britain 1989)

BBC Television. Today, countless TV programmes use railways as a background; it would take a book four times this size to take them all in! An edition of Thora Hird's religious programme *Praise Be!* on 6th August 1989, featured a scene at York station, where an HST power unit was named 'Songs of Praise' in company of Ernie Marshall, a retired railwayman and a confirmed Baptist.

BBC Television, Produced by Noel Vincent

🚂 🚂

THE PRE-GROUPING YEARS, 1913-23 (Britain 1989)

Video 125. Produced by Peter Middleton. Written and presented by John Huntley. Port Sunlight (1919); 'A Trip on the Metro'; LSWR Electrics (1916); Listowel and Ballybunion (1921); LMS Scenes (1923); Crash at Abermule (1923); GWR Buses; Crash from *The Wrecker*; Darlington Centenary Celebrations (1925).

VID, Sound, 50mins, 125

🚂 🚂 🚂 🚂 🚂

PRESERVED RAILWAY VIDEOS

A number of preserved railways issued their own videos, including the Romney Hythe & Dymchurch (six volumes by Festival Videos); North Yorkshire Moors (*Moors Steam Celebration*) and the Leighton Buzzard Narrow Gauge Railway (Red Triangle Video).

🚂 🚂 🚂 🚂 🚂

PRESTRESSED CONCRETE (Britain 1948)

R Costain Ltd. Production of concrete sleepers. Relaying track in the Tring area on the London Midland Region.

16mm, Silent, 15mins, Costain

🚂 🚂 🚂

PREVIEW (1986)

Salford Films. One of the many 'preview' tapes issued by the pioneer companies. This one cost £10 outright, with a £5 voucher against first purchase. Many sections from the European railway videos in which Salford specialised, plus Ffestiniog 150.

VID, Sound, Colour, 15mins, SFV

🚂 🚂 🚂 🚂 🚂

PRE-WAR LONDON UNDERGROUND (Britain 1938)

A sub-surface cab ride in 'Standard' 31/34 Stock, and vintage station adverts provide a fascinating insight into London's transport scene 50 years ago. Vintage Bakerloo Line stock at Wembley Park and also the old wooden compartment stock on the Metropolitan line. At Baker Street two electric locos, Nos 7 *Edmund Burke* and 14 *Benjamin Disraeli*, are seen in service.

VID, Silent, 6mins, Stirling

🚂 🚂 🚂 🚂 🚂

PRE-WAR PADDINGTON (Britain 1935-39)

A view of the concourse in the 1930s; a 4-6-0 Castle arrives on an express, and 2-6-2T 6121 pulls out on clerestory suburban coaches, Castle pulls out on an express, Ealing Broadway to watch a 4-6-0 King in full flight. A 4-6-0 'Star' passes, a look at the signalbox, and a 4-6-0

'Hall' runs through bound for Paddington. At Ruislip and Icken-ham, in GW/GC Joint territory a 4-4-2 'County' is seen, then LNER 'A5' 4-6-2T No 5045 departs and another A5 is seen on GC metals between Finchley Road and Wembley Park.

VID, Sound, 4mins, 125 (from Steam on 35mm Vol 1)

THE PRIVATE LIFE OF SHERLOCK HOLMES (Britain 1970)

United Artists. Directed by Billy Wilder. With Robert Stephens, Colin Blakely, Genevieve Page and Christopher Lee. A secret manuscript by his aide Watson outlines cases in which Sherlock Holmes became involved with the women in the plot. Includes scenes with L&Y '2F' 0-6-0 No 52044 repainted green and labelled 'LNWR', filmed on the Keighley and Worth Valley railway.

35mm, Sound, Colour, 125mins, United Artists

PROBLEMS AND PROGRESS (Britain 1967)

Produced by British Transport Films. At King's Cross the complex remodelling of a ticket hall and interchange passageways; at Oxford Circus a department store is supported on a concrete raft over the southbound station tunnel; at Tottenham ground-freezing techniques are employed for the construction of an escalator shaft; and at Finsbury Park running lines are diverted through new tunnels. Finally, surveying and laying the permanent way.

35/16mm, Sound, Colour, 27mins, BTF

THE PROUD VALLEY (Britain 1939)

Ealing Studios. Produced by Sergei Nolbandov. Directed by Pen Tennyson. With Paul Robeson, Edward Chapman, Edward Rigby and Rachel Thomas.
A black stoker off a ship helps Welsh miners to reopen their pits. Includes GWR railway scenes in

the Welsh Valleys with autotrains and goods traffic.

35mm/VID, Sound, 76mins, Weintraub/VID 125 (Rly)

PUFF BUFFS IN BAVARIA (Britain 1985)

Anglia Television. Dick Joice visits the 150th Anniversary Celebrations of German Railways in Bavaria; British exhibits; replica of *Rocket* and *Der Adler*, steam trips. Produced and directed by David Kenten. Guest: Adrian Vaughan.

16mm, Sound, Colour, 30mins, Anglia

PUFFING BILLY PUFFS AGAIN (USA 1930)

A short newsreel of 'Puffing Billy' at the South Carolina Rail Road in 1830 Centenary celebrations; the line was originally opened on 25th December 1830 with a locomotive called *Best Friend of Charleston*, which blew up in 1831 and was rebuilt in 1832 as *Phoenix*. Other early locomotives included *West Point* and *South Carolina*.

35mm, Silent, 2mins, NFA

PULLMAN BRIDE (USA 1916)

A Mack Sennett Keystone comedy. Directed by Mack Sennett and Clarence Badger. With Mack Swain and Gloria Swanson.
The pretty young girl has to marry the big fat business man. They go on the honeymoon via the Pullman; on board too are the rejected suitor, Oklahoma Pete, a gunman, a drunk and other odd characters. Windows are lowered, causing soup to fly, newspapers to wrap round people's faces, soot to cover everything and buckets of water to wash away passengers! A furious chase through the cars introduces the Sennett Bathing Belles and includes one very lively railway joke. The hero is being pursued by the villain and climbs out of the carriage window. He is about to be shot when he leaps on to a mail gantry alongside the track; seconds later he is scooped up by a hook on the mail-van at the rear of the train and is back into the fray.

Once again the AT&SFRR provides locomotives, stock and track. Pullman car No 103 is the main location carriage used, along with a profusion of motive power, all supposed to be the same train. The departure is double-headed, then cuts twice to different single hauled shots outside Los Angeles, followed by two double-headed scenes and a final tunnel entrance with a 4-4-0 locomotive emerging from the tunnel as 2-6-2.

16mm, Silent, 26mins, HA

QUAI DES ORFEVRES (France 1947)

Majestic Films. Directed by Henri-Georges Clouzot. With Louis Jouvet, Bernard Blier, Suzy Delair, Pierre Larquey and Simone Rennant. A music hall artiste is accused of murdering the man he took to be seducing his mistress. Includes scenes on the Paris Metro.

35mm, Sound, 105mins, Majestic

QUAINTON ROAD (Britain 1969)

A film by Tom Martin. Scenes at the Buckinghamshire Railway Centre, featuring Hunslett 0-6-0ST *Juno*, built in 1958, one of the last of the 'Austerity' Hunslett's built for the Ministry of Supply.

16mm, Silent, Colour, 7mins, TM/HA

QUEENSBURY TUNNEL (Britain 1898)

A Bamforth film, made in Holmfirth. Scenes of GNR trains entering and leaving Queensbury Tunnel on the old line from Bradford to Halifax.

35/16mm, Silent, 1.5mins, NFA/HA

Left:
An old impression of the filming of one of the many 'Phantom Rides'.

Below left:
As well as L&Y No 52044, Class J72 No 69023 also featured in the filming of 'The Private Life of Sherlock Holmes' on the Keighley & Worth Valley Railway.
Ian G.Holt

Bottom left:
The cast of 'The Railway Children' take a break during filming. Bernard Cribbins, Dinah Sheridan and Jenny Agutter are among those sharing a joke. *R. Higgins*

Right:
The innocent victim is thrown from the train in a suitably melodramatic advertising illustration for 'A Railway Tragedy'.

Below right:
Sheep replace the more usual cattle blocking the line in this scene from 'The Red Sun'.

Below far right:
The Keighley and Worth Valley's 47279 in its usual role but still showing some of the markings applied for the making of 'Resurrection' a short time previously. *Ian G. Holt*

QUEST FOR SPEED (Britain 1987)

BBC Television. Series producers: Neil Cameron and Peter Walton. Written and presented by Miles Kington. A series of steam specials on British Rail, using some of the classic locomotives involved in various speed records, including *City of Truro*, the Stirling Single from the Races to the North and a Gresley A4 Pacific. (From the 'Steam Day' series).

16mm, Sound, Colour, 30mins, BBC TV

THE QUIET MAN (USA 1952)

Republic Production. Produced and directed by John Ford. With John Wayne, Maureen O'Hara, Barry Fitzgerald, Victor McLaglen and Ward Bond. The plot of Shakespeare's *The Taming of the Shrew* translated to an Irish Village, with an ex-boxer who has retired to the land of his fathers and needs a wife, however tempestuous. There is a lovely railway scene on the line from Sligo to Limerick at Ballyglunin.

35/16mm, Sound, Colour, 129mins, Republic/HA: Rly scene only/ref

QUIET WEDDING (Britain 1940)

A Paramount picture. Directed by Anthony Asquith. With Margaret Lockwood and Derek Farr. A family story which includes 'Throppleton' station, established by a GWR single line shot showing the token being passed from a pannier tank engine and local station shots, 'somewhere on the Great Western'.

35mm, Sound, 80mins, Paramount

RACE AGAINST TIME (Contre la Montre) (France 1956)

French Railways. Directed by Andrew Perie. The creation of the world rail speed record of 205.6mph on consecutive days in March 1955 by the two French Railways electric locomotives CC7107 and BB 9004.

35/16mm, Sound, 23mins, SNCF

RACE TO THE NORTH (Britain 1985)

BBC Television (Scotland). Produced by Michael Marshall. Directed by John MacPherson. Presented by James Cameron. The story of the competition between the North West and North East routes to Scotland which came to a climax in 1895, using archive film and modern reconstruction of the days of the Railway Mania and the major events of the 19th century. There are scenes of *Flying Scotsman*, *Coronation Scot*, *Silver Link* as well as old locomotives like LNWR 2-4-0 No 790 *Hardwicke*, which took part in the original races.

16mm, Sound, Colour, 47mins, BBC TV

A RACE WITH TIME (USA 1913)

A Kalem production. Two railroad companies compete for a contract to carry mail. When one company sabotages the other's train, the station agent's daughter saves the situation by transferring the mail to another locomotive, which arrives just in time to win the contract.

35mm, Silent, 8mins, NFA

RAGE AT DAWN (USA 1955)

RKO. Directed by Tim Whelan. With Randolph Scott and Forrest Tucker. A fake train robbery is staged to attract real robbers into a trap. Filmed on the Sierra Railroad in California with Rogers 4-6-0 locomotive No 4493 and a train made up of their Coaches No 2 and No 6

as well as Combine No 5 and Caboose No 9, renamed 'Ohio & Mississippi Railroad'.

35mm, Sound, 86min, RKO

RAIL (Britain 1967)

Made by British Transport Films in association with Geoffrey Jones (Films) Ltd. Produced by Edgar Anstey. Directed by Geoffrey Jones.

Rhythmically edited scenes imaginatively allied with music by Wilfred Josephs to celebrate the age of steam and then the railway age of electricity that has succeeded it.

'Cathedral-like stations, engines looming through the steam, a white plume passing along a distant viaduct, these are the images which have given place to the power-bearing cable the illuminated control panel and the steel, glass and gay colours of tomorrow's railway.'

35/16mm, Sound, Colour, 14mins, BTF

RAIL FREIGHT TODAY (Britain 1989-91)

TeleRail Productions. A set of rail freight tapes in four volumes: Vol 1 *North West*; Vol 2 *Midlands*; Vol 3 *Scotland*; Vol 4 *North East*. Some of the areas covered include: Northumberland Coalfields, Boulby potash, Eastgate cement, Newcastle, Redmire Branch, ICI Wilton Billingham, oil traffic to Jarrow, Lackenby Steel, Middlesbrough, industrial cab rides, Durham Coal fields, Seal sands, ECML, Northallerton, Class 60 cab ride, Tees yard, aluminium traffic, Speedlink traffic, snow scenes, Trip workings, industrial locomotives. Produced by Steve le Cheminant

VID, Sound, Colour, 58mins per volume, Telerail

RAIL STRESS (Britain 1959)

Produced by British Transport Films for the British Transport Commission.

New forms of diesel and electric traction introduced as a result of modernisation gave rise to special problems of rail stress. This film gives a brief account of the research then being carried out in this field by the British Railways Board Research Service.

35/16mm, Sound, 10mins, BTF

🚂 🚂 🚂 🚂 🚂

RAIL VIDEO

Based on Bournemouth, this was one of the pioneer video companies, specialising in offering amateur collections, mastered from 8mm and 16mm by filmmakers like Gavin Morrison, Barry Eagles, Max Lock, Jim Oatway, John Shaw and C R L Coles and made mainly in steam days in the 1950s and 1960s. They were founder members of the Railway Video and Film Guild.

🚂 🚂 🚂 🚂 🚂

RAILFILMS

One of the major video producers, this company is run by Nick Dodson. In contrast to the many 'Driver's Eye View' videos, Railfilms have made a speciality in recent times of 'Lineside Views', notably with the work of John Wildy. Starting up in 1984 alongside Railscene, their catalogue was originally a wide ranging one, with a *Portfolio of Railway Film and Video* as the mainstay, they also introduced a *Depot* series and have ventured overseas with the work of Colin Garratt and videos on the railways of Germany, Pakistan and China. Other productions include *The Woodhead Route*, *Tropicana Steam*, *Steam in Retrospect* (four volumes), *Pride of the Park* and *Planet Project*. Details of two further productions follow below.

🚂 🚂 🚂 🚂 🚂

THE RAILFILMS COLLECTION (Britain 1989)

Railfilms. Produced by Nick Dodson. Aerial shots of LMS '5MT' 4-6-0 No 5407 during the making of the film *Paddy's Engine* in 1985. Then: 'A Brew of Steam': Wilson's Brewery celebrating 150 years of traditional beer with LNWR Webb 0-6-2T No 1054 and an observation coach on a trip from Manchester Victoria to the brewery. Also scenes of LNER 'A1' 4-6-2 No 4472 *Flying Scotsman*. 'The EM2 Special': 200 rail enthusiasts on a trip to Holland

for a week of vintage electric traction and preserved steam. Cab ride aboard *Electra*. EM1 scenes of the Woodhead route. 'Tyseley: Alight for Railway Museum': a visit in 1985 by HRH the Duke of Gloucester. GWR '49XX' 4-6-0 No 4930 *Hagley Hall* on a Post Office Special from Birmingham Moor Street to Tyseley. 'Les Tindall's Sawmill': a model sawmill owned by a North American railroad enthusiast. 'The Mull & West Highland Narrow Gauge Railway': 10.25in miniature railway on the Isle of Mull, run by Graham Ellis. Roger Nicholas at the controls of *Lady of the Isles*. 'Paddy's Engine', Black Five' No 5407, owned by Paddy Smith, heading south from Carnforth in 1989 and passing through Mobberley (Paddy's home station) on its way to Chester.

VID, Sound, Colour, 80mins, RVF

🚂 🚂 🚂 🚂 🚂

RAILFILMS COLLECTION (Britain 1989)

Railfilms. Produced by Nick Dodson. Volume Two. Night shots of LMS Stanier '5MT' 4-6-0 No 44871 *Sovereign* at Eastfield Depot, Glasgow. 'Damned Good Time': a Roger Nicholas film on the Settle and Carlisle line and NBR 0-6-0 No 673 *Maude* on the route from Fort William to Mallaig (a Lineside film of 1984): 'Incident at Summit Tunnel': also available as a separate video. 'Up and Down the Drag': Settle and Carlisle fight for survival, 1989. 'The Poppy Line Celebrates': North Norfolk Railway with GER 'J15' 0-6-0 No 564 and Hunslet 0-6-0ST *Ring Haw* plus Chairman David Morgan. 'Sterndale': Donald Avery's 'N' gauge railway layout with a Peak District theme. The video ends with the first train to Holt on the North Norfolk railway.

VID, Sound, Colour, 80mins, RFV

🚂 🚂 🚂 🚂 🚂

RAILROAD BUILDERS OF THE NORTH (Canada 1963)

Produced by Canadian National Railways. A record of recent years during which Canada has been building miles of new railway lines to open up the expanding North, to

provide transportation facilities for the tremendous industrial development in mines, forests and waterpower.

16mm, Sound, Colour, 28mins, CNR

🚂 🚂 🚂 🚂 🚂

THE RAILROAD INSPECTOR'S PERIL (USA 1913)

A Kalem production. A railroad inspector held prisoner on a train by a gang of thieves is rescued by his sweetheart in a motor car.

35mm, Silent, 8mins, NFA

🚂 🚂 🚂

RAILROAD RAIDERS OF '62 (USA 1911)

A Kalem production. An early film version of the story of the Andrews Raid in the American Civil War.

16/8mm, Silent, 12mins, Blackhawk

🚂 🚂 🚂

THE RAILROAD SIGNAL (USA c1938)

Produced by the Motion Picture Bureau of the New York Central System. From the *Running the Railroad* series. A prewar survey of the signalling systems in use on the New York Central lines.

16mm, Sound, 6mins, HA

🚂 🚂 🚂 🚂 🚂

THE RAILROADER (Canada 1965)

National Film Board of Canada. With Buster Keaton. Buster Keaton stars as himself in this short film in which he sees a travel advertisement in *The London Times* about Canada, swims the Atlantic to get there and once on the spot finds a motorised railway trolley (belonging to Canadian Pacific Railway) and takes us on a tour, at the same time recreating some of his celebrated railway gags.

35/16mm, Sound, Colour, 21mins, NFBC/HA

🚂 🚂 🚂 🚂 🚂

RAILROADERS (Canada 1958)

MGM. Maintenance of the Canadian Pacific line.

35/16mm, Sound, 20mins, MGM

🚂 🚂 🚂 🚂 🚂

RAIL-ROADING IN THE EAST (USA 1896-1906)

Philadelphia Express Jersey Central (Edison, 1897); Black Diamond Express (Edison, 1902) 'West Shore' Local (Biograph, 1906); Ulster and Delaware Switcher (Biograph, 1906); Horseshoe Curve Pennsylvania (Edison, 1900); Sarnia Tunnel, Grand Trunk (Biograph, 1903); Working Rotary Snow Plows (Edison, 1902); Black Diamond Express, Lehigh Valley (Edison, 1903); Empire State Express New York Central and Hudson River (Biograph, 1902); The Ghost Train (Biograph, 1903); Empire State Express (Edison, 1905).

16mm/8mm, Silent, 15mins, Blackhawk/BFI

RAILS IN WALES (Britain 1967)

Made by Trevor White. Scenes of the Welshpool and Llanfair, Talyllyn and Vale of Rheidol railways.

16/8mm, Silent, Colour, 5mins, TW

RAILS THROUGH LEICESTER AND RUTLAND (Britain 1929-70)

Hillside Video. A history of railways in one area including pre-World War 2 scenes of the LMS and LNER, Market Harborough in steam days, the long-abandoned Uppingham branch and aspects of the Great Central. The story ends on the early diesels.

VID, Sound, 30mins, Hillside

RAILS TO TALSARN (Britain 1958)

Produced by David Sutcliffe. A record of a horse-drawn narrow gauge slate quarry railway in its original form.

16mm, Silent, 4mins, Sutcliffe

RAILSCENE

A major video producer specialising in the video 'magazine' market. Jeremy English has provided one of the best summaries of the 'First Era' of video production in this country:

'Once upon a time, there was a world without videos. It seems to us a long time ago with a catalogue of over 100 titles but it was only 10 years or so that Dick Griffiths and one or two others "dipped their toes in" and produced the first tailor-made railway videos. *Railscene* started in October 1984. The guiding lines behind our magazine have been worked out with major feedback from our subscribers. Since we're enthusiasts ourselves we make our programmes as much for our own pleasure as for sale. We try not to take ourselves too seriously. Although railways are a serious subject, I feel a slight sense of humour is always welcome. Alongside *Railscene* has been the growth in the number of archive productions, the logical successors to Dick Griffiths' pioneering work and this has played an increasingly important part in our work, using the title *Steamscene*. Both Dick and I have always been convinced that archive material should be pure, so we have tried to make the *Steamscene* programme without being "padded out" with modern footage, non-railway sequences, repeats or presenters — they are pure, unadulterated railway films which is how it used to be. Thus we have presented the major archive collections over the years — W A "Cam" Camwell, Patrick Whitehouse and John Adams, Ivo Peters, Geoff Holyoake, and Eddie Stanbridge.'

But the mainstream *Railscene* magazine has produced the most consistently good reviews; here are two widely separated examples:

'*Railscene No 1 — The Railway Video Magazine*
45min Video (VHS, Beta or V2000). Railscene Ltd.

With the abundance of railway videos now available, new ones must have a new angle — this one has; also, the film quality must be of the highest standard — this one is; and it must be reasonably priced — this one is unbeatable! Thus far, rail videos have been the film equivalents of books; this is that of a rail magazine and, as such, it has a wide variety of subjects and lengths. Opening with a very up-to-date news section, it then moves to a lengthy 'article' on the Hastings-Tonbridge line, viewed from the cab of a "201" demu. This is followed by archive film of the building of the first main-line diesel, LMS 10000; then a competition, a feature on the North Yorkshire Moors Railway and it closes with more news. Throughout, the filming is flawless, the commentary is informative and the right amount; it is educational and well-linked piece-to-piece; and for most of the modern shots, the camera gets away from the well-worn angles, even on the Settle & Carlisle — no small feat! And the highlights come thick and fast. Bringing the magazine format alive, with sight, sound and movement, this has been put together with imagination — especially the use of computer titling throughout, keeping you informed as you go — and, although you cannot hope to please all the people all the time, I found the whole thing fascinating. At the price, it is a must and I eagerly await No 2; and on this example, Railscene's film of Hastings to Charing Cross — available by order — should be well worth the owning.'
(MJS *Railway Magazine*)

'*Railscene 24*
Approximately 2hr video, (VHS), Railscene Ltd

If for nothing else, Railscene is invaluable if you want to be a railway couch potato; you can sink into your sofa and watch the railway world of the UK glide into your living room. But this apart, it consistently comes up with high standard viewing that keeps you abreast of recent events. No one person can be everywhere, but with a small handful of cameramen, *Railscene* can and does provide a highly aesthetic and entertaining review of virtually everything worth watching, and with such as the 1990 steam at Amersham, views of varying angles cleverly segued. The return of steam on the Met this summer makes for a very pleasing feature, including delightful behind-the-scenes views at South Ruislip Depot and a lot of organisation obviously went into this. Gloucester 150 is interestingly seen through the eyes of visiting railtours; Class 60s are seen in action — itself a rarity so far! — at varying locations; a feature on Railfreight around Grimsby/Immingham Docks is very interesting; and preserved steam is well captured, with 14 different engines seen including a superbly atmospheric shot of *Flying Scotsman* crossing the Menai Bridge. But my favourites this time are the views of the Middleton Railway, with vintage footage of newly-restored pioneer LMS diesel shunter 7401 and a fascinating view of a sextuple-header! With plenty of news, a celebration of the Talyllyn's 40th year in preservation and the usual high standard of filming, this is a another goody.' (MJS *Railway Magazine*)

A typical two hour *Railscene Video Magazine* usually consisted of current items (Newslines); a Cab Ride a visit to a Preserved Railway; a main line outing; and an Archive selection.

🚂 🚂 🚂 🚂 🚂

RAILSCENE PROGRAMMES

It would take another book this size to list every single item that has been included in the *Railscene* magazines! So it is necessary to restrict to a listing of some of the major items over the past 10 years. As Jeremy English has said: 'We've covered many items from the demise of the 1940s, the rise of the 1960s, and the rise and fall of the 1990s and the rise of the Settle and Carlisle and steam in Scotland, North, South, East and West Wales and all over England and . . . just all over!' Here is a representative list of items covered:

Cab ride: Hastings-Tonbridge Line (201 DEMU)
First LMS Main Line Diesel No 10000 (1947)
North Yorkshire Moors Railway report
Settle and Carlisle Line
Hastings to Charing Cross
Cab Ride: King's Cross to York (1985)
Dart Valley Preserved Railway
GWR 150 Celebrations
LMS 'Black Five' 4-6-0 No 5407: (Swindon 1985) West Highland Line
Mid-Hants Preserved Railway; line to Alton
Tunbridge-Eridge before closure
Euston to Liverpool: Cab Ride, via old Crewe layout
Great Central Preserved Railway: Loughborough to Rothley
Enginemen's films of Nine Elms and Waterloo
Run by GWR Dean 4-4-0 No 3440 *City of Truro*
Didcot and Tyseley Open Days
Iron Duke replica in Hyde Park and on show

Steam on the West Highland ('K4' and two 'Black Fives')
Newcastle to Carlisle Cab Ride
Forest of Dean Preserved Railway at Parkend
Sittingbourne and Kemsley Light Railways
Electra in the Netherlands
North Wales Coast Steam
Cab Rides: Brighton to Victoria: Hull to Scarborough
Preserved Deltics on the Severn Valley, North Yorks Moors, Butterley and Keighley and Worth Valley.
West Anglia News: LNER 'N7' to Cambridge, '73' to Fen Drayton, '91s' and ICI 125s to Cambridge, freight to King's Lynn and first train to Stansted Airport
Industrial Displays: Middleton, Rutland, Tanfield and Padiham.
A signalbox interior in South Wales.
LNER 'A4' 4-6-2 No 60009 *Union of South Africa* (now *Osprey*) on the Forth Bridge
Holborn Viaduct station and layout
BR '8P' 4-6-2 No 71000 *Duke of Gloucester* in action
Excerpts from the Ivo Peters, Pat Whitehouse and 'Cam' Camwell archive collections
Steam at Amersham (1990); Steam on the Met
RailFreight at Grimsby and Immingham Docks
Flying Scotsman crossing the Menai Bridge
The Middleton Railway (LMS 0-6-0DM No 7401 — 1032 pioneer diesel shunter)
Talyllyn 40th Anniversary Celebrations
Cab Ride on the Cumbrian Coast line
Behind the Scenes at Eastleigh Works
Preserved GWR locomotives
Bluebell Railway developments
GWR '78XX' 4-6-0 No 7819 *Hinton Manor* and GWR 'Hall' 4-6-0 No 4930 *Hagley Hall* double-headed along the seafront at Teignmouth
Cab Ride from Exeter to Plymouth
BTF film *Single Line Working* (BTF film on the SDJR at Shepton Mallet, 1958)
The Mid-Hants Railway
Steam Comes Back to Marylebone
Crossing the Tay Bridge
Cab Ride: Perth to Inverness
Engine on Shed: LMS 'Royal Scot' 4-6-0 No 6170 *British Legion*
The Severn Valley Railway

SR 'Merchant Navy' 4-6-2 No 21C10 *Blue Star* at Barry Scarp Yards.
Strathspey Railway at Aviemore
Dart Valley Railway
Bescot Open Day
Cab Ride: Dover to Willesden
BR site visits: Toton
Southern Main Line Steam: Salisbury to Yeovil with *Clan Line, Sir Lamiel, Burton Agnes Hall, Sir Nigel Gresley.*
W A Camwell film on the last days of the Welshpool & Llanfair before closure
Severn Valley Railway revisited
The Didcot, Newbury and Southampton Railway
Local trains on the Settle & Carlisle
Eastleigh Open Day 1986
Network South East and Chris Green
Cab Ride: St Pancras to Sheffield
Isle of Wight: archive film of 'O2s' in 1963 (Edward Trotman) and B&W film in 1953 (W A Camwell) plus Open Day at BR and Haven Street in 1986
Further visit to the Ffestiniog Railway
W A Camwell archive scenes of the Mersey railway.
Southern steam in 1965, the Cromford and High Peak railway, Dinorwic
Quarries and Great Western steam scenes
Inverness Open Day
Didcot 25th Anniversary
GWR 150th Anniversary Celebrations: *Iron Duke* replica; 'Castles' at Dawlish; Bristol to Plymouth Steam run; Tyseley Events; Didcot-Swindon-Gloucester freight special with GWR '2800' 2-8-0 No 2857
Stone Traffic with Class 59s
Cab Ride: Portsmouth to Cardiff
The Severn Tunnel
Dutch Weekend 1986
The Keighley and Worth Valley revisited
South African steam (Ray Freeman items)
W A Camwell archive film: steam on BR in the 1950s.
Depot visit: Inverness TMD of ScotRail
The Kent & East Sussex Railway Santa Specials in action
Ivo Peters classic films of the Somerset & Dorset Joint Railway
Cab Ride: King's Cross to York
GWR '2800' 2-8-0 No 2857 at Newport

SR 'West Country' 4-6-2 No 34092 *City of Wells* on the Cumbrian Coast Express.
ARPS Celebrations on the Talyllyn (1990)
Nuclear Trains
Gravity powered train on the Ffestiniog
Kent & East Sussex to Northam
Llangollen on Deeside
'S160' locomotive on the Mid-Hants
Bahamas at Keighley
Freight workings on the Middleton
Last Days at Dinting

RAILTOUR SPECIAL (Britain 1990)

Electra Films. Works visits, shed tours and depot open days.

VID, Sound, Colour, 120mins, EFV

THE RAILWAY (Australia 1979)

New South Wales, Australia, Rail Authority. Current rail activity as it was in 1979. Introduced by David Hill. Like British Transport Films *Report on Modernisation*.

35/16mm/VID, 20mins, NSW Rail/VID; Stylus

RAILWAY BYEWAYS: CUMBRIA (Britain 1990)

Pictures and Sounds production. Written and presented by John Spencer Gilks. An assembly of photographs by John Gilks taken on the Settle and Carlisle, Ravenglass & Eskdale, Penrith & Windermere lines. Produced in association with the Friends of the National Railway Museum. An interesting and successful experiment in using 'stills' as against moving images. Produced by Gavin Mist and David Sumner.

VID, Sound, Colour, 21mins, P&S

RAILWAY BYEWAYS: NORTH RIDING OF YORKSHIRE (Britain 1991)

Pictures and Sounds production. Written and presented by John Spencer Gilks. An assembly of photographs by John Gilks covering the whole of the old North Riding of Yorkshire area, dominated by the LNER. Made in association with the Friends of the National Railway Museum in York. Produced by Gavin Mist and David Sumner.

VID, Sound, Colour, 25mins, P&S

RAILWAY CARRIAGE HOMES (Britain 1981)

Anglia Television. Produced and directed by David Kenten. Presented by Eddie Anderson. The use of old railway carriages as homes, chicken sheds and bungalows. From the *Bygones* series.

16mm, Sound, Colour, 8mins, Anglia

THE RAILWAY CHILDREN (Britain 1957)

BBC Television. Early TV version of the Victorian novel by E Nesbit. Railway scenes were filmed on the Guildford-Christ's Hospital LBSCR line, notably at Barnyards station, featuring LSWR Class T9 No 30310 and two LSWR coaches; LSWR class No 30026 was also used in action shots.

16mm, Sound, BBC TV

THE RAILWAY CHILDREN (Britain 1970)

EMI. Produced by Robert Lynn. Directed by Lionel Jefferies. From the novel by E Nesbit. With Dinah Sheridan, William Mervyn, Jenny Agutter, Bernard Cribbins, Sally Thomsett and Gary Warren. 'Lionel Jeffries performs a small miracle with his treatment of the E Nesbit classic. We are in Edwardian England, where a middle-class family (mother and three children) are forced, because father has been wrongfully imprisoned, to rough it — relatively speaking — in a cottage in Yorkshire, with a railway line running at the bottom of the garden. All comes right in the end, of course, but while the children plot to help their father, they also inhabit the private world of childhood that Nesbit was able to recall so well and which, with the greatest possible sensitivity, his enormous paw feather-light in its touch, Lionel Jeffries enables us to share. We watch these mini-adults — from a respectful distance, of course — as they go about their daily tasks of looking after Momma when she is poorly, helping passing revolutionaries and bolshie station masters, and saving lives. It's an Edwardian idyll, dappled in sunlight. Jeffries never strikes a false note.' (Tony Bilbow)

'Fresh and agreeable family film with many pleasing touches to compensate for its meandering plot.' (Leslie Halliwell)

This film did for preserved railways what *Genevieve* did for old cars. The massive assistance of the Keighley & Worth Valley was a key element. The line from Keighley to Oxenhope was practically taken over by EMI for five weeks during the filming. The main station was Oakworth, where Bernard Cribbins is Station Master and the entire staff.

The main motive power used in the film included an 1887 L&Y 'F16' 0-6-0 No 52044 (this number was shed for the movie people) introduced by Barton Wright in 1876. In the film, it looks resplendent in new colours, with the number '957' and 'GN&SR' on the tender. The big scene when the children stop the 11.29am from running into a landslip introduces a rather strange engine for a Yorkshire local train. The un-numbered GN&SR loco (still to this day kept in *Railway Children* livery) is played by ex-GWR '5700' 0-6-0PT No 5775, which later became L89 on London Underground before being rescued by the Keighley & Worth Valley.

Nearly all the railway scenes carry great conviction; the only jarring note is the appearance of some modern concrete sleepers and a strange lack of ballast on some of the scenes. The lovely old pre-grouping NER carriage is still known as 'the old gentleman's coach'. It was built originally in 1871 by the Stockton & Darlington Railway as a third class saloon. In 1884 it was converted into an inspection saloon for the use of the Locomotive Superintendent at Gateshead. In 1904, the vehicle was extended by a further 10ft, when a small kitchen, toilet and attendant's compartment were added. It was in the restored NER condition that the carriage was used in the film.

35mm/VID, Sound, Colour, 108mins, Weintraub/EMI

🚂 🚂 🚂 🚂

RAILWAY CITY: CARLISLE (Britain 1980)

Border Television. Directed by William Cartner. Written and presented by Chris Rogers. The story of railways in and around Carlisle, including many photographs, archive footage, steam scenes in the 1950s and the modern scene.

16mm, Sound, Colour, 20mins, Border

🚂 🚂 🚂 🚂

THE RAILWAY DAY BY DAY AND ON HOLIDAY (Belgium 1961)

Produced by SNCB. After a short history, the film shows the routine daily activity of the railway as well as visits to various holiday resorts.

35/16mm, Sound, Colour, 21mins, SNCB

🚂 🚂 🚂

RAILWAY DEMONSTRATION (Television)

An outside broadcast from Alexandra Palace station of Gresley LNER 'A4' No 4482 *Golden Eagle* and a demonstration train. Presented by Leslie Mitchell.

BBC Children's Television 3-3.20pm, Saturday, 6 March 1937 BBC

🚂 🚂 🚂 🚂 🚂

RAILWAY ELECTRIFICATION AT INDUSTRIAL FREQUENCY (Britain 1960)

Produced by British Transport Films for the British Transport Commission.

A technical explanation of the system used in transferring power from the grid to the new 25kV locomotives of British Railways. This specialised film illustrates one of the outstanding achievements of modern electrical engineering involved in the electrification programme for British Railways.

35/16mm, Sound, Colour, 28mins, BTF

🚂 🚂 🚂 🚂

RAILWAY ELECTRIFICATION IN BRAZIL (Britain 1956)

British Insulated Callender's Cables. Electrification in Brazil.

16mm, Sound, 12mins, BICC

🚂 🚂 🚂 🚂 🚂

RAILWAY HORSES (Britain 1911-84)

Vast numbers of horses were once used by the railways. The earliest shot occurs in the 1911 record of Crewe Works. There are a number of scenes in *Women at War* (1945) and a detailed record of the last railway on shunting work at Diss in 1984.

16mm, Silent, 12mins, HA

🚂 🚂 🚂 🚂

RAILWAY JUNCTION (Poland 1962)

Polish State Railways. Directed by Kazimierz Karabasz. A record of a busy junction on the Polish State system.

35mm, Sound, 9mins

🚂 🚂 🚂 🚂

RAILWAY MARSHALLING: THE MODERN WAY (Britain 1955)

Produced by R A Lister and Company.

'Replacement of worn out and uneconomic steam shunters by diesel electric shunters is the modern answer to efficiency in shunting yards, be they modern automatic 'hump' yards or older flat yards with manually operated points. This film shows the construction and operation of a modern diesel electric shunting locomotive as used by British Railways. The diesel unit is a 350hp *Lister Blackstone* six-cylinder vertical engine. Many shots are taken in the Locomotive Works of British Railways at Darlington from whence came many famous steam locomotives in the past. Shunting is shown taking place over the 'hump' and on the flat and is carried on without fuss, cleanly and efficiently in this *The Modern Way*. The film is of interest to both technical and non-technical audiences.'

16mm, Sound, Colour, 25mins, SFV

🚂 🚂 🚂 🚂 🚂

RAILWAY PRESERVATION SOCIETY OF IRELAND (Britain 1968)

A detailed film record of the Society formed in Belfast in 1964. At that time, it had care for an industrial saddle tank previously used by Guinness, GSWR No 186 and GNR 'S' 4-4-0 No 171 *Slieve Gullion*. A tour took place from Belfast to Athlone and back, as recorded in this film. Earlier steam scenes were filmed on 8mm in the Roberts collection, covering 1953, 1957 and 1959.

16mm, Silent, Colour, 32mins, HA

🚂 🚂 🚂 🚂

RAILWAY RESEARCH (Britain 1937)

A film dealing with many aspects of railway research for the LMS. Subjects include the testing of fabrics, paint, water supplies, tail lamps, track chairs, flywheels for motor vehicles, hot boxes and locomotive tyres.

There is material shot by a 16mm camera during tests on movement of wheel flanges on the track during running, a model of a coaling plant and a demonstration of the use of a wind tunnel during the design stages of LMS locomotives, including the 'Coronation Scot'.

16mm, Silent, 27mins, HA

🚂 🚂 🚂 🚂 🚂

RAILWAY RIDE OVER THE TAY BRIDGE (Britain 1897)

Four-stage journey across the Tay Bridge taken from the front of a slow-moving locomotive; uneven cylinder thrust is reflected in the gently 'riding' motion on the front beam.

Section I: Starting out from the Fife bank with the signalbox controlling the westward and eastward junction south of the bridge on the left, across the Wormit arches of the bridge. A train hauled by a Wheatley NBR 'P' Class 2-4-0 locomotive passes on the up track. Bridge and track maintenance crews are seen at various points.

Section II: The High Girders. The passage through the enclosed high girders of the main bridge span are illuminated by shafts of light at regular intervals. Track and bridge maintenance staff are glimpsed in the shadows.

Section III: Journey across the northern approach arches. A second train hauled by a Wheatley NBR 'P' Class 2-4-0 locomotive is again seen approaching and passing on the up line. A track maintenance crew is seen at one point.

Section IV: Passing through Tay Bridge station on the Dundee side of the river and running alongside the Tay Bridge sheds and yard, in which are seen some goods wagons, carriages, another Wheatley NBR 2-4-0 locomotive and an NBR (later LNER) 'J36' Class 0-6-0 locomotive.

35/16mm, Silent, 4mins, HA/125

RAILWAY ROUNDABOUT: VOLUME 1 (Britain 1958-62)

Stirling Video. Film by Patrick Whitehouse and John Adams. Compiled and produced by Dick Griffiths. Research by Colin Jacks. Commentary by Robin Whitting. Sound effects by Dennis Feltham. This was one of the master videos made from the BBC *Railway Roundabout* material including 'Recording the Last Years of Steam'; 'Branch Line Closures' (Westerham, Bewdley, Tenbury Wells, Wollferton Junction, Monmouth, Ross-on-Wye and Chepstow); 'From the Museum to the Main Line' (Midland Compound No 1000, the Jones Goods and the Caledonian Single); 'Castle Swan Song' GWR 'Castle' 4-6-0 Nos 5054 *Earl of Ducie* and No 7029 *Clun Castle* (a remastering of an earlier video issue). Volume 1 (re-master). Also known as *Railway Roundabout Revisited*.

VID, Sound, Part Colour, 55mins, Stirling

RAILWAY ROUNDABOUT: VOLUME 2 (Britain 1958-62)

Stirling Video. Film by Patrick Whitehouse and John Adams. Compiled and produced by Dick Griffiths. Research by Colin Jacks. Commentary by Robin Whitting. A video made up of lines that were closing and steam locomotives that were to be withdrawn.

They include 'Last Train from Abergavenny to Merthyr'. 'Craven Arms to Llandovery' (this line was rescued); and 'Last Train from Brecon to Merthyr'. Plus a mixed collection of 1960s in many different locations. (Volume 2). Also known as *Roundabout Sixty*.

VID, Sound, 55mins, Stirling

RAILWAY ROUNDABOUT: VOLUME 3 (Britain 1958-62)

Stirling Video. Filmed by Patrick Whitehouse and John Adams. Compiled and produced by Dick Griffiths. Written and narrated by David Jenkinson. A set of seven items from the BBC *Railway Roundabout* series including: 'Swindon Engines'; 'Two Dukedogs to Barmouth'; 'The Cardigan Branch'; 'The Wye Valley Lines'; 'The Bristolian in the days of Steam', 'Caerphilly Castle in London' and 'The Cambrian Coast Express'. (Volume 3). Also known as *Western Steam: The Final Years*.

VID, Sound, Part Colour, 60mins, Stirling/NRM

RAILWAY ROUNDABOUT: VOLUME 4 (Britain 1958-1962)

Stirling Video. Filmed by Patrick Whitehouse and John Adams. Video production by Dick Griffiths. Research and script by Colin Jacks and John Harris. A vast assembly of steam railways taken from the Pat Whitehouse collection, plus three of his major works: 'Two Glens to Fort William'; 'Southern Branch Lines' (Exmouth, Okehampton, Hayling Island, etc.); and 'The Lickey Incline'. (Volume 4 re-mastered).

Also known as *Steam Around Nationalisation* and *The Lickey Incline*.

VID, Sound, 60mins, Stirling/NRM

RAILWAY ROUNDABOUT: VOLUME 5 (Britain 1929-62)

Stirling Video. Filmed by Patrick Whitehouse. Produced by Dick Griffiths. Compiled and researched by Colin Jacks. Commentary by Robin Whitting. Additional film by C R L Coles.

This video is made up of various archive pieces collected by Pat Whitehouse including: 'The *Royal Scot* in the USA' (1933); 'The Silver Jubilee' (1935); and sections from the films made before World War 2 by the Southern, the LNER and the GWR, as well as glimpses of the Liverpool Overhead Railway and the London Underground. Three major Whitehouse films are included: 'Irish Narrow Gauge'; 'Post War Years'; and 'The Cromford and High Peak railway'. (Volume 5. Also known as *Steam Archive Favourites*).

VID, Sound, Part Colour, 60mins, Stirling

RAILWAY SCENES, 1930-39

Made by C J Barnard. Brief records of steam in the 1930's in Britain, including scenes at Folkestone, Waterloo, London Bridge, King's Cross, Portsmouth and shots of the 'Cheltenham Flyer'.

9.5mm, Silent, 15mins, CJB

RAILWAY SCENES, 1938-53

Made by C J Barnard. 'Brighton Belle' 1939; LNER run, 1938-9; Isle of Wight scenes, 1953; Folkestone scenes, 1953.

16mm, Silent, Part colour, 15mins, CJB

RAILWAY SCENES, 1938-53

Made by C J Barnard. LNER scenes, 1938-39; Ireland — Strabane, Londonderry, Ballymoney and Ballycastle, 1953; GNR scenes, Dundalk Works, Cork and Cobh, 1947.

16mm, Silent, Part colour, 15mins, CJB

RAILWAY SCENES 1947-53

Made by C J Barnard. Irish scenes, 1947-50; Cromer, 1952; Sussex lines, 1952; Ash and Longmoor, 1953; Portsmouth and Bishops Waltham, 1953.

16mm, Silent, Part colour, 15mins, CJB

RAILWAY SCENES AROUND NIEDEROSTERREICH (Britain 1988)

RV Television. Austrian Railways steam locomotive 310.23, a four cylinder with 6ft 11in driving wheels, on a run from Vienna to Wiener Neustadt during which it achieved a speed of 110kph. Also scenes of the Engerth type 0-8-4 steam locomotive on the 760mm gauge from Gmund to Gra Gerungs and a cab ride from St Valentin to Kleinreifling via Ennstal in a class 1141 electric locomotive.

VID, Sound, Colour, 50min, RVV

RAILWAY STATION SCENE (USA 1897)

International Film Company. Typical 'Train entering a station' film, taken at Elizabeth, New Jersey on the Pennsylvania Railroad.

35mm, Silent, 28secs, AFI

RAILWAY TRAFFIC (Britain 1898)

Prestwick Manufacturing Company. Scenes in the Barnet area.

35mm, Silent, 1min, NFA

A RAILWAY TRAGEDY (Britain 1904)

A Gaumont production. A woman joins a train of non-corridor coaches and is attacked and thrown from the train. She finds she has been robbed by a fellow passenger. She is rescued from the side of the track and the villain is apprehended at the next station. The station entrance and train scenes were filmed at North Dulwich station on the LBSCR. The interior of the coach was built out of doors at the Gaumont studios on Fellows Cricket Ground at Dulwich; hence the convenient use of a nearby station. When the door of the compartment is flung open and the woman thrown from the 'moving' train, there is a clear view of the cricket ground!

16mm/VID Silent, 8mins, HA/125

RAILWAY WONDERS OF THE WORLD (Britain 1983)

Nick Lera Collection. Part One. An assembly of individual films including *Hot Pacifics*, *Austrian Iron Mountains*, *From Manchester to Java* as well as material from France and India.

VID, Sound, Colour, 60mins, NLV

RAILWAY WONDERS OF THE WORLD (Britain 1983)

Nick Lera Collection. Part Two. An assembly of individual films including *Steam in the Andes*, *Portuguese Steam Museum*, *Dolomite Steam Spectacular* and *Jungle Rack Lines of Indonesia*.

VID, Sound, Colour, 60mins, NLV

THE RAILWAYMAN (Britain 1947)

Crown Film Unit for Ministry of Transport and the Central Office of Information. Produced by Alexander Shaw. Directed by Richard McNaughton. Photography by Edwin Catford. Music by Temple Abady. A 'vocational guidance' film on the numerous jobs on the railways.

35/16mm, Sound, 23mins, COI

RAILWAYS (Britain 1966)

Produced by Tim Hewardt for Granada Television. Nearly all the railway systems in the world lose money and this film looks at what were then the latest trains, electrification schemes, timetabling and area coverage in Britain, Japan, America, Russia and France to find out why.

16mm, Sound, 25mins

RAILWAYS AROUND EUROPE (Britain 1988)

RV Television. Removing Garsdale Turntable on the Settle & Carlisle line; Keighley & Worth Valley Railway; Railways on the Jungfrau region in Switzerland; British BR Class 25 diesels in profile; Cab ride on the Centovalli Railway from

Locarno to Camedo in Southern Switzerland; Railways of Basle (SBB, DB plus trams). (*Video Railway Magazine*, Volume No 1)

VID, Sound, Colour, 60min, RVV

RAILWAYS IN HOLLAND (Britain 1983)

PM Films. Assembly of material shot in the 1970s with Dutch 0-4-0T locomotives around Apeldoorn.

8mm/VID, Silent, 14mins, PMV

RAILWAYS OF INDIA (Britain 1986)

Chess Valley Films. Commentary by Hugh Ballantyne. A mad dash around India with all sorts of images, not with much continuity. Some good examples of British built locomotives still running.

VID, Sound, Colour, 28mins, Chess Valley

THE RAILWAYS OF THE ISLE OF WIGHT (Britain 1986)

Transport Video Publishing. Filmed by Geoffrey Utton. A history of the Island railways in colour film shot by Geoffrey Utton at Ryde, Ventnor, Cowes, Newport, Shanklin, Sandown, Wroxall and Haven Street. Covers rolling stock, preservation developments, the post-1967 electric services with commentary by David Rees.

VID, Sound, Colour, 45mins, TVP

RAILWAYS OF THE JUNGFRAU REGION (Britain 1984)

Salford Films. Steam Rack Railway, plus Swiss Country Festival.

VID, Sound, Colour, 60mins, SFV

RAILWAYS OF THE JUNGFRAU REGION (Britain 1988)

SF. Commentary by Paul Brown. Wengernalbahn; Bernese Oberland Bahn; Interlaken to Lauterbrunnen and Grindelwald; metre gauge LMB from the Lauterbrunnental to Mür-ren; Bern-Lötschberg-Simplon Rail-way; Schynige Platte Bahn; steam and electric locomotives.

VID, Sound, Colour, 60min, SF

🚂 🚂 🚂 🚂 🚂

RAILWAYS ON THE RIGI (Britain 1989)

RV Television. The mountain rail-ways developed by Niklaus Riggen-bach at the end of the 19th century, including the Arth-Rigi-Bahn and the Vitznau-Rigi-Bahn in Central Switzerland.

VID, Sound, Colour, 60min, RVV

🚂 🚂 🚂 🚂 🚂

RAILWAYS TODAY (1947)

March of Time series. 13th Year, No 1. The problems facing the rail-ways of Britain and America in 1947.

35/16mm, Sound, 16mins, NFA

🚂 🚂 🚂 🚂 🚂

RAILWAYS WITH A HEART OF GOLD (USA 1952)

Made by Carson Davidson. A light-hearted account of the Talyllyn Rail-way as seen through the eyes of a visiting American. 'Shot on the Talyllyn by an American visitor in the early 1950s, it is a truly wonder-ful film, capturing all the joy and fun of the early days of preservation — as well as the pitfalls and the some-times painful learning processes. Watch for the hand shunter! I won-der if he is still involved?

'What is so amazing is the quality, when British enthusiasts were mak-ing the best of handheld clockwork, 8mm monochrome technology of the sort that gave home movies a bad name, this transatlantic visitor is a miniature William Wyler. He deserves our gratitude, for he has produced a fine record of the start of preservation, absolutely unique, the reality behind the *Tittfield Thun-derbolt*, which itself was inspired by the early days of the Talyllyn.' (Chris Leigh).

35/16mm/VID, Sound, Colour, 21mins, Tally/CV/HA

🚂 🚂 🚂 🚂 🚂

THE RAINBOW JACKET (Britain 1954)

Ealing Studios. Directed by Basil Dearden. With Kay Walsh, Bill Owen, Edward Underdown and Robert Morley. A boy jockey is blackmailed into losing a big race by crooks. Includes a scene of BR 'Britannia' 4-6-2 No 70011 *Hotspur* leaving platform 10 at Liverpool Street station and an LNER 'B1' 4-6-0 arriving with a train at New-market station. (Complete scenes are included in the Video 125 pro-duction *Steam on 35mm*.)

35mm, Sound, Colour, 99mins

🚂

THE RAINHILL STORY (Britain 1980)

BBC Television. Produced by Mar-tin L Bell. Presented by Anthony Burton. The story of the Liverpool & Manchester Railway and the Rain-hill Trials, with particular reference to the building and running of the replica locomotives, including *Rocket*, *Locomotion* and *Sans Pareil*. The work of Michael Satow was covered and the background to the 150th Celebrations was intro-duced. The event itself was later covered by newsreel units and a BBC Outside Broadcast.

VID, Sound, Colour, 48mins, BBC TV

🚂 🚂 🚂 🚂 🚂

RAISING STEAM (Britain 1965)

Flying Scotsman Enterprises (Hon Sir William McAlpine). Produced by John Huntley. Directed by David Kenten. Commentary by George Hinchcliffe. The process of raising steam on a locomotive, using LNER 'A1' 4-6-2 No 4472 *Flying Scots-man* as a demonstration of what is involved. A training film for railway preservationists.

16mm, VID, Sound, Colour, 10mins, FSE/HA

🚂 🚂 🚂 🚂 🚂

RAMBLES ON THE READING (c1960)

The journey of the 'Reading Ram-bler', a railfan special, from Williamsfront, Pennsylvania, beside the Susquehanna River, through Lewisburg, Sunbury, Shamokin, Reading to Tamaqua, hauled by Reading 4-8-4 No 2124, which then backs from Tamaqua to Reading. The remainder of the tour was hauled by two diesel-electric hood units.

8mm, Silent, Colour, 8mins, Blackhawk

🚂 🚂 🚂 🚂 🚂

RAMSGATE STATION (Britain 1926)

Gaumont British News. The open-ing of a new station at Ramsgate, including shots of some traffic.

35mm, Silent, 2mins, NFA

🚂 🚂 🚂 🚂 🚂

RAMSGATE TUNNEL RAILWAY (Britain 1949)

8mm record of the 2ft gauge 460V DC railway which made use of the old LCDR tracks through a tunnel down to the beach at Ramsgate. It opened in 1936, closed in 1939, was used as a vast air raid shelter during World War 2 (valuable as being dangerously near the Battle of Britain airfield at Manston), reopened at Whitsun 1946 but did not survive. The equipment was built by English Electric.

16mm, Silent, Colour, 5mins, HA

🚂 🚂 🚂 🚂 🚂

THE RARE BREED (USA 1966)

Universal. Directed by Andrew V McLaglen. With James Stewart and Maureen O'Hara. A cattle story about an English bull that goes to America to breed with longhorns. The American cattle train is drawn by Sierra Railroad Rogers 4-6-0 locomotive No 4493 of 1891, with old box cars and Caboose No 9.

35mm, Sound, 97min, Universal

🚂

RAVENGLASS AND ESKDALE (Britain 1967)

Made by Trevor White. A ride on the 15in gauge line.

16/8mm Silent, Colour, 4mins, TW

🚂 🚂 🚂 🚂 🚂

THE RAVENGLASS & ESKDALE RAILWAY (Britain 1961)

Made by P B Whitehouse and John Adams. Story of a journey from Ravenglass to Dalegarth showing the two steam engines *River Esk* and *River Irt*.

16/8mm, Silent, 7mins, CV/NRM

🚂 🚂 🚂 🚂 🚂

RAY FREEMAN VIDEOS

A video firm specialising in overseas tapes, including Brazil (EFTC Railway); China (The West and the East); and three volumes on South African Steam.

🚂 🚂 🚂 🚂 🚂

THE REBEL (Britain 1960)

Associated British Production. Directed by Robert Day. With Tony Hancock and George Sanders. Story of an office worker who becomes an avant-garde artist. Includes BR Southern Region electric suburban line from 'Fortune Green South' to Waterloo 'Fortune Green' was in reality Bingham Road station on the now abandoned Woodside line from Beckenham to Selsdon.

The gag of crossing from one train to another when both are standing at the platforms would no longer be permitted by British Rail; indeed, they recently turned down just such an incident for a TV Commercial.

35mm, Sound, Colour, 105mins, Weintraub

🚂

THE RECORD BREAKERS (Britain 1988)

Yorkshire Television. Produced by Mike Best. Directed by David Wilson. Presented by Richard Whiteley. This programme heralded the advent of electrification of the East Coast main line and at the same time takes a nostalgic trip back to the pioneering days of Britain's railways and the race for speed between the London, Midland & Scottish's West Coast main line and the London & North Eastern's East Coast main line (and before that, the pre-Grouping companies).

The programme relives some golden moments of railway history through archive film and talking to people who saw it happen. It goes right back to the start of the railways as we know them when, in 1825, the steam engine *Locomotion* travelled from Darlington to Stockton at 15mph. Since then, many remarkable achievements have been recorded and great legends created. One locomotive stands supreme as a world beater: LNER 'A4' 4-6-2 No 4468 *Mallard*, which broke the world speed record for a steam engine for all times in 1938 at 126mph. This film includes material shot in July 1988 when *Mallard* came back for a 50th Anniversary run between Doncaster and Scarborough. A result was that Scarborough Council decided to make a major contribution to the full restoration of *Mallard* in association with the Friends of the National Railway Museum. Two railwaymen who were there when the LMS made their crack run with LMS 'Princess Coronation' 4-6-2 No 6220 *Coronation* (Harold Forster and Bill Dale) in 1937 are interviewed.

16mm, Sound, Colour, 28mins, Yorkshire

🚂 🚂 🚂 🚂 🚂

THE RED SHOES (Britain 1948)

Archers production. Directed by Michael Powell and Emeric Pressburger. With Anton Walbrook, Moira Shearer, Leonide Massine and Robert Helpmann. Ballet world drama; ends with a suicide scene filmed on the French Riviera line of SNCF.

35mm, Sound, Colour, 136mins

🚂

THE RED SUN (France, Italy, Spain 1971)

Corona. Directed by Terence Young. With Charles Bronson, Toshiro Mifune, Alain Delon and Ursula Andress. A 'European' Western about a Japanese Samurai and a Wild West outlaw in 1870, both in pursuit of a stolen sword. Includes scenes shot on Spanish Railways near Barcelona using an old Spanish 4-4-0 mocked up with balloon stack and cow-catcher to look like a Wild West train in Arizona in the last century.

35mm, Sound, Colour, 108mins, Corona

🚂

REDBRICK (Britain 1951)

Made by Brian Coe. A record of life at Hull University, including steam scenes at Hull Paragon station and various level-crossings.

16mm, Silent, 16mins, HA

🚂

THE REDEMPTION OF RAILROAD JACK (USA 1913)

A Selig production. With Adele Lane and Tom Santschi. Railroad Jack stops a train robbery and wins a pardon from the Governor.

35mm, Silent, 11mins, NFA

🚂 🚂 🚂

REFLECTIONS ON SCOTTISH STEAM (Britain 1989)

Transport Video Publishing. West Highland Steam in the 1950s and 1990s. Steam on the Aberdeen to Glasgow and Edinburgh in the 1960s. The Strathspey Railway at Aviemore. LNER 'A4' 4-6-2 No 60009 *Union of South Africa* (now *Osprey*).

VID, Sound, Colour, 50mins, TVP

🚂 🚂 🚂 🚂 🚂

REFLECTIONS ON SOUTHERN STEAM (Britain 1990)

Transport Video Publishing.
Archive Film from the prewar years of steam at work on the Isle of Wight, and on the former London and South Western System.
Freight Traffic on the Southern in the 1930s.
Freight Traffic in and around Feltham Yard in the 1960s showing a wide range of classes at work.
Rare colour film showing steam at work in and around Waterloo in the years before Nationalisation.
The Merchant Navy Class, looking at their development in the 1940s, plus a look at *Swanage* on the Mid-Hants Railway.
A study of Bulleid's 'Leader' design, using rare black and white film of the engine on test at Brighton.
Bulleid passenger coaches.
The Hayling Island Branch, and Guildford to Horsham Line.
Railways of the Isle of Wight.
30 Years of the Bluebell Railway.
Railtours on the Southern.

VID, Sound, Part Colour, 55mins, TVP

🚂 🚂 🚂 🚂 🚂

REGIONAL FILM ARCHIVES

A number of newly-established regional film libraries have issued their own videos which include transport scenes in their areas. The best known are the East Anglian Film Archive (Norwich) with many scenes of steam railways in East Anglia; and the North West Film Archive with items on Altrincham to Mobberley (1909); Stalybridge Station (1927) Holinwood to Oldham Werneth (1919) and holiday trains at Blackpool (1957).

REINFORCED CONCRETE TRANSVERSE SLEEPERS IN MAIN LINES (Britain 1942)

GWR Unit, Paddington. The laying of an experimental section of main line track at Slough, using concrete sleepers manufactured by Stanton Ironworks and Stent Pre-Cast Concrete Ltd. There is a detailed record of the laying of the sleepers, using a 'John Machine'; most of the work is still done by hand, including the handling of the rail lengths.

16mm, Silent, 11mins, HA

REMINGTON STEELE (USA 1981)

CBS Television. American TV show which included episodes taken at Marylebone station, with John Roker.

TV, Sound, Colour, 27mins, CBS TV

REPORT ON MODERNISATION 1 (Britain 1959)

Produced by British Transport Films. 'As the modernisation scheme for British Railways enters its sixth year, its effects become increasingly apparent in every aspect of railway work throughout the Regions: in track improvements, in electrification and signalling in new depots, marshalling yards and stations; in the latest coaches and traction units, and in the railway training schools. It is these visible signs of progress that the camera examines as the commentary interprets their even greater significance for the future.'

35/16mm, Sound, Colour, 20mins, BTF

REPORT ON MODERNISATION 2 (Britain 1961)

Produced by British Transport Films. 'As the thousands of passengers move about Britain every day, the railway system they use is being transformed: soaring concrete sustains new stations, a hillside is moved to make a new marshalling yard, express freight trains carry complete loads of oil, limestone, cars, frozen foods; griddle cars and Blue Pullmans, road-railers and driverless trucks — these are only a few of the changes and innovations brought about by the Modernisation Plan.'

35/16mm, Sound, Colour, 20mins, BTF

REPORT ON MODERNISATION 4 (Britain 1963)

Produced by British Transport Films. 'The fourth film in the series draws attention to the new pattern that is emerging as the modernisation scheme progresses. It refers now and again to work shown in previous editions, and compares it with today's scene. This includes freight, transport, marshalling yards, shipping and passenger services.'

35/16mm, Sound, Colour, 20mins, BTF

REPORT ON MODERNISATION 5 (Britain 1965)

Produced by British Transport Films. 'Behind Britain's railway modernisation lies research, design and development. Research ensures that in various ways passengers travel fast, safely and in comfort. Design and development yield new vehicles, equipment and methods; from motor-car conveyors to micro-wave communications. The electrification of the busiest main line in the world also depends on research, design and development.'

35.16mm, Sound, Colour, 80mins, BTF

RESEAU BRETON & RESEAU VIVARAIS (Britain 1963)

Made by P B Whitehouse.

16/8mm, Silent, 8mins, CV/NRM

RESEAU DE VIVARAIS (Britain 1961)

Made by P B Whitehouse and John Adams. A film taken on metre gauge branch line not far from St Etienne, showing workings of 0-6-0 + 0-6-0 Mallet tanks.

16/8mm, Silent, 7mins, CV/NRM

RESHAPING BRITISH RAILWAYS

A video of the major Beeching plan as published in 1963, plus two reports on BR modernisation plans in 1959 and 1961.

VID, Sound, Part colour, 63mins, VID/BTF/TV10

RESHAPING BRITISH RAILWAYS (Britain 1963)

Produced by British Transport Films. The film version of Dr Richard Beeching's plan for the reshaping of British Railways, showing some of the problems involved, the research necessary, and the answers that were produced.

35/16mm/VID, Sound, 23mins, BTF

RESURRECTION (Britain 1968)

BBC Television. Russian historical reconstruction. Includes scenes of LMS '3F' 0-6-0T No 47279 disguised as Russian loco No 31 and filmed on the Keighley and Worth Valley line.

16mm, Sound, Colour, 28mins (part serial), BBC 2 Television

RETARD AND ADVANCE (Britain 1966)

Produced by British Transport Films. The development and application of the Dowty system and automatic wagon speed control in railway hump marshalling yards, such as Tinsley near Sheffield. With this equipment the speed of each wagon is controlled throughout the movement by retarders and boosters which sense the speed of the vehicle and retard or accelerate it to the ideal speed for the vehicle and for the section of the yard which it has to transverse. This system has virtually eliminated damage to goods and waggons during marshalling yard operations.

35/16mm, Sound, Colour, 15mins, BTF

RETURN OF FRANK JAMES (USA 1940)

TCF. Directed by Fritz Lang. With Henry Fonda and Gene Tierney. Jesse's brother avenges a murder in this typical Western. Scenes were shot on the Sierra Railroad, using Baldwin 2-8-0 No 29790 of 1906 vintage.

35mm, Sound, Colour, 92min, TCF

RETURN OF JESSE JAMES (USA 1950)

Lippert. Directed by Arthur David Hilton. With John Ireland and Ann Dvorak. Villain impersonates Jesse James in a series of bank robberies and is tracked down by the real man. A train robbery was staged on the Sierra Railroad, using Combine No 5 and Caboose No 9, plus Baldwin 2-8-0 locomotive No 29790 of 1906.

35mm, Sound, 75min, Lippert

RETURN OF KING AND QUEEN FROM CANADIAN TOUR OF 1939 (Britain 1939)

Shown on Baird big screen television at various London cinemas including the Tatler. Good shots of train entering the station at Waterloo.

BBC Television: 22 June 1939

RETURN OF THE KING AND QUEEN FROM INDIA (Britain 1912)

The newsreel includes shots of the Royal train at Portsmouth and Waterloo.

35mm, Silent, 1min, NFA

RETURN TO BEWDLEY (Britain 1987)

Windjammer production. Produced, written and directed by Alan Willmott. Commentary by Anton Rogers. The Severn Valley Railway, which links Kidderminster in Worcestershire with Bridgnorth in Shropshire, is one of the most popular steam-operated private lines in Britain. On a typical autumn day, Bewdley, the main intermediate station on this 16-mile line, is the centre of much activity, and this film records the arrivals and departures of trains and their passengers from mid-morning to early evening. It also shows the scenic attractions of the route, and describes interesting features of its history, stations, locomotives and rolling stock, as well as the dedication of the many people — both permanent staff and volunteers — who operate the services.

16mm/VID, Sound, Colour, 19mins, AW

RETURN TO EVERCREECH (Britain 1984)

BBC Television (West). Produced by Dennis Dick. Directed by Andrew Johnston. The original unveiling of the superb Ivo Peters collection on the Somerset & Dorset Joint Railway. Using the 'then and now' technique, it includes interviews with Ivo Peters and intercuts his master material with the scene as it was in 1984, nearly 20 years after closure.

16mm, Sound, Colour, 30mins, BBC TV

RETURN TO LANCASHIRE: THE OPENING OF THE EAST LANCASHIRE RAILWAY FROM BURY TO RAMSBOTTOM (Britain 1987)

Produced by the Bury Cine Society. A good example of two enthusiasts'

groups coming together in common cause. The East Lancs Railway joins up with the local Cine and TV Society to make a useful historical record of the opening of the line on 25 July, 1987.

VID, Sound, Colour, 30mins, Bury Cine Vid

RETURN TO YESTERDAY (Britain 1940)

Capad Productions. Directed by Robert Stevenson. With Clive Brook & Anna Lee. A stage star tries to recapture his youth. Includes GWR main line scenes from Paddington to Teignmouth.

35mm, Sound, 68mins, Weintraub

THE REVEREND TEDDY BOSTON COLLECTION

A substantial record of railways of all kinds, including the Leicester & Swannington Railway (1962) and LMS Centenary Grand Parade of Transport at Wavertree (1930).

8mm/items above on 16mm, Silent, 14mins, TUA

THE REVIVAL OF STEAM (Britain 1986)

Transport Video Publishing. *Clan Line*, *Duchess of Hamilton* and *Sir Nigel Gresley* in action on the Marylebone workings in 1985. Locations include Saunderton Bank, Thame, Bicester, Aynho Junction, King's Sutton, High Wycombe, Gerrards Cross, Stratford-upon-Avon, Bearly Junction, Hatton Bank and Leamington Spa. There is a review of the railway itself and its history. Filmed from January to July 1985. (Originally issued under the Cresswell Video label.)

VID, Sound, Colour, 40mins, TVP

RHÄTISCHE BAHN: GLACIER EXPRESS (Britain 1985)

SF. Volume One. Commentary by Martin Oldfield. Rhaetian Railway including St Moritz to Disentis; the Engadine, the valley of Poschiavo, the Prattigau, the Davos area, the Grisons Oberalp, the Albula Tunnel, the Landwasser Viaduct, Albula and Bunder Oberland, etc. 243 route miles of narrow gauge network.

VID, Sound, Colour, 60min, JCV/SFV

RHÄTISCHE BAHN: VOLUME TWO (Britain 1985)

SF. Commentary by Paul Brown. The Prattigau valley, Klosters, Davos, Castione to Grono, Schanfigg Valley, Langwies Viaduct, Bernina line, Brusio Viaduct, the Engadine, St Moritz, etc.

VID, Sound, Colour, 60min, JCV/SFV

RHODESIAN RAILWAYS: ROYAL TRAINS (Britain 1947)

A Kinocrat production. A short colour record of the Royal tour of Rhodesia in a train hauled by a GEA Beyer-Garratt locomotive.

16mm, Silent, Colour, 4mins, Lama

RHYTHM OF THE RAILS (Britain 1955)

Directed by Frank Green. Commentary by John Snagge. Produced by Ace Films for the British Iron and Steel Federation. A behind-the-scenes film on British Railways, containing spectacular shots of the 'Royal Scot', which has maintained a daily service from London to Scotland for over a century. Various little-known aspects of railway technique, such as the speed testing of locomotives on a stationary fast bed, and the utilisation of an engine's own power to swing it on a turntable, are illustrated. Locomotives seen include LMS 'Princess' 4-6-2 Nos 46247 *City of Liverpool*, 46220 *Coronation* and 46239 *City of Chester*, LMS '3P' 2-6-2T Nos 40051 and 40054; LMS 'O1' 2-8-0 No 63760 and, on the test bed at Rugby, BR '9F' 2-10-0 No 92013. There are good scenes at Crewe Works the old Euston and Shap Summit.

16mm, Sound, 21mins, HA

THE RICHARD J WILLIS COLLECTION

Richard Willis was one of the great documentary 16mm film makers of the 1960s. His speciality was the Great Central which he recorded in great detail during the last days of steam, notably around Nottingham and Leicester but also taking in Marylebone and less well covered areas like Charwelton and Aylestone. But his interests were very wide and took him to the Midland Main Line, the East Coast Main Line as well as parts of the Great Western, the North Western and as far as Holyhead and the last days of steam on the Southern. The quality of his 16mm masters were ideal for good quality video and his original collection was issued through Dick Griffiths and the Stirling label. One of the best of the 1960s film makers, his tapes were accompanied by excellent and detailed notes. More recently, the collection has been re-issued by Railscene in four volumes: *Main Line Steam Routes* (Vols 1 and 2), *Grime and Glory Years* and *Oases of Steam*.

RICHARD S GREENWOOD COLLECTION

Richard Greenwood documented mainly the final days of steam in the 1960s, both on film and in photographs. His work has been used for various archive videos and he has documented important scenes from the early preservation days, notably on the Keighley & Worth Valley line.

RICHARD TAKES A TRAIN RIDE (Australia 1952)

Produced by the Australian National Film Unit for the Australia Department of the Interior.

Richard a small Australian boy, is taken by train from Murray Bridge to Adelaide. On the journey he sees various things which excite him; a goods train loaded with cargo, different kinds of engines, level crossings, tunnels, and the men who run the railways. Particularly suitable for young children.

16mm, Sound, 11mins, COI/Australia

RICHARD WAGNER (Britain 1989)

United Artists. Directed by Ken Russell. With Richard Burton and Vanessa Redgrave. Life of the composer. Scenes depicting Munich and Venice were made by mocking-up sections of the Peter Allen Building at the National Railway Museum in York, with static locomotives well covered by smoke machines to disguise their origin.

35mm, Sound, Colour, 119mins, United Artists

A RIDE BEHIND STEAM ON TWO TOURIST PIKES (c1960)

Made by Craig Faulkner. East Tennessee & Western North Carolina 4-6-0 No 12 on the North Carolina 'Tweetsie' 3ft gauge railroad and White Pass & Yukon 2-8-0 No 192 (renamed *Klondike Kate*) on the Tennessee 'Rebel' 3ft gauge railroad.

8mm, Silent, Colour, 11mins, Blackhawk

A RIDE ON AN EXPRESS ENGINE (Britain 1899)

Unidentified 'Phantom Ride' film

35mm, Silent, 1min, NFA

RIO GRANDE WORK TRAIN (USA 1981)

Steam Powered Video. Produced by Video Rails. Mountain railroads on the Denver & Rio Grande system with a 'Jordan Ditcher'.

VID, Sound, Colour, 60mins, SPV

THE RISE AND FALL OF THE STEAM LOCOMOTIVE (Britain 1982)

Spa Films. Commentary by Laurie Brooks. An early video featuring the *Rocket*, *Lion*, the Stirling Single, the GWR De Glehn, *Dryslwyn Castle*, *Lord Nelson*, *Stowe*, *Great Marquess*, *Sir Nigel Gresley*, *Mallard*, *Blackmoor Vale*, *Evening Star* 'and many others', all in 30 minutes! Happy days.

VID, Sound, Colour, 30mins, Spa Films

ROAD OF IRON (Canada 1953)

National Film Board of Canada. The building of the 360 mile iron ore Ungavaline.

35/16mm, Sound, 42mins, NFBC

THE ROB FOXON COLLECTION

All shot on 16mm colour film, the collection covers the period from 1983 in a variety of locations:

Mallard at the National Railway Museum undergoing restoration (1985) and at York station for 50th Anniversary (1988)

4472 *Flying Scotsman* at Peascliffe tunnel, Newark (1983) and Nottingham Midland (1984)

4498 *Sir Nigel Gresley* at Derby (1987)

Nuclear Flask demonstration crash at 100mph with a Class 46 diesel (1984)

Exeter St Davids station (1987)

Crewe Royal Train: Crewe Heritage Centre (1987)

Opening of new Leicester North station (1991)

Castle Donnington power station open day (1988)

Hulme End 10.25in gauge miniature railway of the Leek and Manifold (1988)

Coalville Open Day (1988)

Detailed account of Leicester resignalling operation (1987)

Last 'Peak' class diesels at Leicester (1988)

Carlisle station with the APT (1986)

Loughborough station: 59 and 60 class diesels (1990)

Bristol Temple Meads: Class 50 diesels (1981)

16mm, Silent, Colour, TUA

Famous for his 'live' film presentations throughout the country, Rob Foxon has also been involved in the production of many videos, often with a transport background. He has a very large archive of railway films of all kinds.

In the last days of steam, he began filming himself on 8mm in 1968 and later went over to 16mm. Despite his video work, he has remained a 'film' man; he has written many articles on aspects of railway films, including a detailed account of the process of mounting railway film shows.

ROBBERY (Britain 1967)

A Paramount Picture release. Produced by Michael Deeley and Stanley Baker. Directed by Peter Yates. Script by Edward Boyd, Peter Yates and George Markstein. Photography by Douglas Slocombe. Music by Johnny Keating. With Stanley Baker, Joanna Pettet, James Booth, Frank Finlay, Barry Foster and William Marlowe.

The original Great Train Robbery took place in 1963. 20 lawyers worked on the script of this film version to ensure that there would be no libel or other actions following release. The result was a film that gives an accurate description (taken direct from the court proceedings) of the actual robbery but surrounded by entirely fictitious characters and subsequent incidents. The original robbery took place near Cheddington, Buckinghamshire; it lasted 22 minutes and involved a well-organised assault on the overnight Glasgow-London Mail Train. The film version was staged at Husbands Bosworth near Market Harborough, Leicestershire, took 29 hours to film, and used an identical diesel-hauled train including a 54ft long maroon Royal Mail coach at Cheddington. The real robbers stole about £3m; the film cost about £2,600,000!

The real robbers had a fine night; the film unit worked over a fortnight of wet, cold nights. British Railways provided a complete crew for the train; the film company duplicated each man with an actor for the cameras. A frequent cry on location was 'Are you the real driver?' A strong 'Yes' in a thick Midlands accent usually settled the matter.

Shortly after the film was finished Michael Deeley, co-producer with Stanley Baker, was falsely arrested in a Mayfair gunsmiths for being in possession of firearms without a license — two guns used as props on the film. He was awarded £100 damages for wrongful imprisonment.

35mm, Sound, 114mins, Paramount

ROBERT CARTWRIGHT PRODUCTIONS

Enthusiast Robert Cartwright has produced two volumes on the history of the Leek and Manifold Light Railway, mainly using documents and photographs. A small amount of moving picture film does exist of this narrow gauge line which closed in 1934.

THE ROBERT ENNIS COLLECTION

Robert Ennis lives on the Isle of Wight and, although his film collection ranges widely over 8mm and 16mm, his speciality has been to build up the Island Film Archive, along with the local cine society and John Bartlett. This includes the greatest collection anywhere of films on the railways of the Isle of Wight going back in steam days to the 1930s and taking the story right up to the end of steam and the closure of most of the island's system. Since then, he has made his own films on 16mm of all the later developments; the preserved railway at Haven Street, the London Transport tube stock on the line from Ryde to Shanklin and the extension of the Haven Street project to Smallbrook Junction.

Bob has recently completed a one-hour major history of the Isle of Wight railways, established a film viewing centre at the Mountbatten Theatre at Newport IoW and has his own cinema museum and projection theatre at his base at Field Lane Holiday Park at St Helens. A great TV and video addict, he assisted in the listings for this book.

THE ROCK ISLAND RAILROAD (USA 1950s-1970s)

Steam Powered Video. Produced by Green Frog Productions. The Rock Island line closed down, bankrupt, in 1980, abandoning 7,500 miles of track across 14 states. This tape recalls many of the locomotives that worked the line including classes 'E', 'GP', 'U', 'RS', 'F2', 'E3A', 'DL109' and 'AB6'. Some of the named trains that once worked the line are shown, including the 'Imperial', 'Rocky Mountain Rocket', 'Peoria Rocket', 'Golden State Limited' and the quaintly named 'Quad Cities Rocket'.

VID, Sound, Colour, 60mins, SPV

Left:
Munich station recreated inside the National Railway Museum at York for the filming of 'Richard Wagner'.

Below left:
The train crew fall victim to the villains in 'Robbery'.

Below:
Two MGM film stars, the English actress Diane Wynyard and child star Jackie Cooper, are overshadowed by the gleaming frontage of the *Royal Scot* during the filming of the 1933 US visit.

Right:
Typical action from 'Santa Fe'. One of the train crew is already dead as the gang closes in.

Below right:
Actors and crew stand ready at Horsted Keynes during the filming of 'Savage Messiah'. *K.D. Chown*

THE ROCKET

One of the world's most famous engines, it has been the subject of many replicas which have appeared in films. A replica was sent to America for the Fair of the Iron Horse in 1927 and was photographed (complete with Britannia in attendance in the form of the Railway Queen!). It was also shown in 1930 at Liverpool, and on various occasion, as at Rainhill in 1980, with Mike Satow's working replica of *Locomotion* and at the Darlington Centenary Celebrations in 1925. In Germany, a quite passable replica of *Rocket* was built for the film *Der Stahltier* in 1935.

🚂 🚂 🚂 🚂 🚂

ROCKET 150 (Britain 1980)

BBC Television. Produced by Martin Bell, Presented by Brian Redhead. The grand parade at Rainhill which took place over three days before vast audiences and involved everything from replicas of *Rocket* and *San Pareil* to the doomed Advanced Passenger Train (APT).

16mm, Sound, Colour, 60mins, BBC TV

🚂 🚂 🚂 🚂 🚂

ROMANCE OF A RAILWAY (Britain 1935)

Directed by Walter Creighton. With Carl Harbard as Brunel and Donald Wolfit as Daniel Gooch.

The film records the main events connected with the history of the Great Western Railway from 1835 to 1935, including the 1833 Bristol meeting at which Robert Bright's speech aroused great enthusiasm for the idea of the railway, the meeting at Bristol on 30 July 1835, when it was decided to form the company, the commissioning of Brunel as chief engineer, the opening of the Paddington to Maidenhead line in 1838, the building of the Severn Tunnel, the hectic days when Sir Daniel Gooch salvaged the company from financial crisis in the 1860s and the changing of the gauge from broad to standard in 1892. This is followed by a survey of the GWR as it was in 1935; the towns and cities served, the freight traffic, operating procedures and a detailed survey of Swindon locomotive works, including the building of

a 'King'. A final sequence gives a glimpse of streamlined, bullet-nosed No 6014 *King Henry VII*.

In addition to the professional actors, members of the Great Western Railway Amateur Dramatic and Operatic Society took part in the crowd scenes; in the gauge-conversion scenes, permanent way men dressed up in the clothes of their fathers to re-enact the 1892 events. A full scale replica of R Stephenson's *North Star* built at Swindon works for the Darlington Centenary in 1925 was used for a number of scenes, along with a full-scale reproduction from original drawings of the 1838 Maidenhead (Riverside) station. Locomotives seen include GWR 'Castle' 4-6-0 No 5011 *Tintagel Castle*, GWR 'King' 4-6-0 No 6013 *King Henry VIII*, various pannier tanks in the docks and a privately-owned small Beyer-Garratt double engine: East Moors Iron and Steel GKB No 12 *Vivian* (Cardiff works).

35/16mm/VID, Sound, 58mins, BTF/TVP

🚂 🚂 🚂 🚂 🚂

ROMANCE OF THE RAILS (USA 1902)

An Edison production. Directed by Edwin S. Porter. A short advertising film for the Delaware & Lackawanna Railroad company.

16/8mm, Silent, 5mins, Blackhawk/BFI

🚂 🚂 🚂 🚂

ROMANCE OF THE RAILS (USA 1912)

An Edison production. With Harry Eytinge.

35mm, Silent, 14mins, NFA

🚂 🚂 🚂

THE ROMANCE OF TRANSPORTATION IN CANADA (Canada 1952)

Produced by the National Film Board of Canada. An animated cartoon film in light vein, tracing the successive stages in the development of land, sea and air transportation across the vast distances of Canada; beginning with the first painful progress on foot by early explorers and proceeding through canoe, barge and steamboat, ox-

cart, railway and automobile to the aircraft of tomorrow.

35/16mm, Sound, Colour, 11mins, NFBC

ROMANCE ON THE ORIENT EXPRESS (Britain/USA 1986)

Directed by Lawrence Gordon Clark. With Cheryll Ladd, Stuart Wilson and John Gielgud. Very dull made-for-TV cheap movie, exploiting the then-new Simplon Orient Express. The real train is used extensively, first at Venice station and then on through Paris to London. Italian FFS electric locomotives haul the train for most of the scenes.

35mm, Sound, Colour, 84min, ITV

🚂 🚂

ROME EXPRESS (Britain 1932)

Gaumont-British. Produced by Michael Balcon. Directed by Walter Forde. With Conrad Veidt, Esther Ralston, Harold Huth, Cedric Hardwicke and Gordon Harker.

The prototype train thriller with a mixed group of people thrown together on a continental journey. It was a great success as this review from the seriously minded *Cinema Quarterly* (Winter 1932 issue) reveals:

'If this is the sort of production the new Gaumont-British studios are going to turn out, we can look happily forward to an era of technical brilliance, clever observation, and good entertainment. Whether we can look forward to some sensible subject-matter remains an open question.

'Here, at any rate, is a first-class craftman's job. The restrictions of the set (except for the opening scene, the whole story takes place on the train) might well have overpowered the interest of the story had not Forde concentrated every effort in building up the authentic atmosphere of a long-distance continental express. In every shot the impression of movement is retained, either by sound and vibration or by faint shadows passing across the set, but mainly by clever running of passing scenery outside the windows. I think there is no doubt that this concentration on detail and atmosphere saves the film.

'The acting — with a *Grand Hotel* cast — is very encouraging. The stagey atmosphere is disappearing, and it is noteworthy that the two best pieces of pure movie-acting came from two of our best stage-actors, Hardwicke and Vosper. Veidt is, of course, as grand as ever, and Gordon Harker's suburbanite is gorgeous.

'But the real heroes of *Rome Express* are the studio technicians and the supers — especially the supers — from station passers-by to Cook's men and Wagon-Lits attendants. They never strike a false note.'

As may be gathered, this was largely a studio reconstruction of a railway but there are some interesting shots of the real activities of the PLM and the Gare de Lyon as well as good details of the track and locomotives of a famous prewar Continental run. The story was remade in 1948 under the title *Sleeping Car to Trieste*.

35/8mm, Sound, 94mins, Rank

ROMNEY, HYTHE & DYMCHURCH RAILWAY

There are good amateur records of the RHDR in the 1930s; the famous armoured train of 1940 (with a visit from Winston Churchill); the formal reopening by Laurel and Hardy in 1947; fine colour records of the Jubilee Celebrations in 1977 and a trip on the railway in 1979.

ROMNEY, HYTHE & DYMCHURCH RAILWAY (Britain 1961)

Made by G S Holyoake. A survey of the main motive power of the line in action.

16/9.5/8mm, Silent, Colour, 4mins, MFS

THE ROMNEY, HYTHE & DYMCHURCH RAILWAY (Britain 1977)

Movietones production. Directed by Peter Hampton. Commentary by Norman Dahl. Celebration of the 50th Anniversary of the RHDR, featuring Davey Paxman locomotives 4-6-2 No 1 *Green Goddess*, No 2

Northern Chief, No 3 *Southern Maid*, No 7 *Typhoon* and No 8 *Hurricane*, 4-8-2 No 6 *Samson*; YEC (2294) 4-6-2 No 9 *Winston Churchill* and Krauss (8378) 0-4-0TT No 4 *The Bug*. Scenes of the armoured train on the RHDR in 1940 and the visit by Laurel and Hardy in 1947 for the formal reopening are included as well as brief glimpses of other locomotives in the sheds, under repair, etc.

16mm, Sound, Colour, 21mins, HA

ROMNEY, HYTHE & DYMCHURCH RAILWAY INTO THE 1990s (Britain 1991)

Festival Video. All 13 of the railway's main line locomotives are seen on the 13½-mile journey from Hythe to Dungeness. Behind the scene views of the sheds and workshops. The story brings the RH&DR into the 1990s.

VID, Sound, Colour, 48mins, Festival Video

ROOM FOR TWO (Britain 1940)

Directed by Maurice Elvey. With Frances Day and Vic Oliver. A comedy with typical railway shots of the period. A Southern Railway 'King Arthur' Class leaves Victoria station; in the next shot it is a GWR 'Castle' bound for Reading.

35mm, Sound, 77mins

ROTHER VALLEY SPECIAL (Britain 1958)

Made by P B Whitehouse and John Adams. A film was made on the occasion of an enthusiasts' special run, over the old Kent & East Sussex Railway from Robertsbridge to Tenterden. This special train was operated with a Brighton Terrier at each end, one of them being the special engine *Brighton Works*.

16/8mm, Silent, 7mins, CV/NRM

ROTTEN TO THE CORE (Britain 1965)

Tudor production. Produced by Roy Boulting. Directed by John Boulting. With Eric Sykes, Charlotte Ram-

pling, Avis Bunnage and Kenneth Griffith. A plot to steal the Army payroll. Railway scenes were shot at Christ's Hospital station with 'N' class locomotive No 31405; the station was renamed 'Longhampton' for the filming.

35mm, Sound, 88mins

ROTTERDAM STEAM TRAM (Britain)

Made by P B Whitehouse and John Adams.

16/8mm, Silent, CV

LA ROUE (The Wheel) (France 1919-23)

Produced by Charles Pathe. Directed by Abel Gance. Photography by Burel, Bujord and Duverger. With Severin-Mars, Ivy Close, Gabriel de Gravone, Pierre Magnier, Teroff, Maxudian and Gil Clary.

The main railway locations were in the Alps and at the Nice railway yards. Abel Gance provides his own detailed account of how the film was made:

'I had to arrange for railway facilities from PLM in the south, find a locomotive we could use all the time and get 30km of track for the exclusive use of the film unit. I also had to find a suitable location between the railway lines so that I could put the set right in the middle of the railway.

'I found a crossroads in the rails where I put Sisifs' house, so that the rails parted at this point and went to left and right. So this house was right in the middle of the trains; out of the door one came upon either a train taking water or another one passing by.

'It was quite dangerous and I had to have a lookout to make sure we had plenty of warning of approaching trains. We shot a lot of the film in conditions surrounded continuously by trains; in the sheds, in a locomotive "cemetery" where we shot the scenes of the crash of Sisifs' engine. Much was in and around Nice. Incidentally, Sisif crashes because he doesn't want to fall into anyone else's hands. He'd rather make the engine commit suicide.

'After this, I had to do the "white symphony". I went to St Gervais which is next to Chamonix and there went to work on a funicular railway in the Grand Moulais area. I wanted to build a set but there was a station platform which was in my way. So one night I came up on the last train and got my workmen to take down the platform. By morning it had gone and I was able to start shooting, but when the first train of the day came up, they found they had lost their platform!

'Back in Nice, we nearly had a disaster when a platform indicator disc struck the camera platform we were using to film the motion and the wheels. Just before, I had asked if the platform camera was really safe and the railway people said yes for an extra £5 it could be even better. We paid up; and it was the best £5 I ever spent!'

There was, as Bardeche and Brasillich suggested, a very deep feeling behind the making of La Roue, even if it did look a little quaint in execution. 'The Film,' Gance wrote, 'is the poetry of light. Yet I am able less and less to feel that the cinema can create real works of art. Everyday I draw back from big projects because the mechanics of film making are at present too imperfect to make the 'Cathedrals of Light' of which I dream. At present (1919) I am searching for a dramatic and eternal subject which can use the best in the world of cinema. I came on the world of trains, rails and smoke; and, for contrast, a world of snow peaks and solitude. A white symphony succeeding a black symphony. I felt the need to make feelings of catastrophe in humans and machines go together, each as big and significant as the other; to show the ubiquity of everything that fights, be it a human heart or a steam valve. I must show the pathos in 'things' and put them on the same level as for humans. I am haunted by the laments of machines. I must make a tragedy about machines and human hearts together, at the same time; my trains must go on two rails, one physical, the other spiritual.'

Gance began to work on La Roue in 1919 first in Nice, then in the Col de Voza and the Bossons glacier, finishing it by 1921. It was so long

that it cost 2.5 million francs and could only be shown in a curtailed version. Like Griffith's *Intolerance* and von Stroheim's *Greed* it is one of the monstrosities of the cinema, but an extraordinarily important monstrosity.

'The story is unbelievably complicated. An engine driver finds a little girl in the wreckage of a train smash that has killed her parents. He adopts her and falls in love with her, as does his son, but he marries her off to an engineer. There are accidents and catastrophes galore, the engine driver goes blind, his son and the engineer are killed, leaving the modern Oedipus and his Antigone together. This gloomy tale, redolent of Zola and his *La Bête Humaine*, of Hugo and a dozen other romantic writers, would have been laughed off the screen had not everything else been effected by its technical mastery and a very genuine and even nobly poetic quality which this technique served to express.

'The early part of the film vividly re-creates the mechanical world of steel and smoke and steam and tracks. No one had realised before how amazingly the film can express the modern world or to what extent a new type of panthesism can endow inanimate things with soul, with a life of their own. It was because he did this and not because of the plot he developed that Gance's work had real worth. Signals and wheels, pistons and manometers seemed to live. The camera with a hitherto unknown flexibility, with almost startling ubiquity hovers over all of them, revealing them in unfamiliar guises and aspects, lending them an epic quality. Inevitably at times Gance goes wrong: the engine expiring amid a bank of flowers is almost comic. Yet virtually throughout the film the moment he turns from human beings to the mechanical world he sweeps us irresistibly along with him.

'What is more, La Roue was the first work of any real scope to be composed according to an exact rhythmical pattern. "The film", Gance has said, "is the poetry of light." He regarded the rhythm of a film as being akin to that of Latin verse, with its long and short feet; and La Roue was actually based on

a careful metrical pattern, with blank film punctuating the end of scenes and sequences. In imitation of "Donogoo", Gance made use of rapid cutting to give an impression of simultaneous happenings and discovered how to achieve an accelerated tempo by means of shorter and shorter shots to give the feeling of flight, of giddy descent and of inevitable catastrophe. The most stirring moments of La Roue are those which this brilliant and unhesitating technical ability emphasises . . .'
(*History of the Film* by M Bardeche and R Brasillach)

35mm, Silent, 122mins, NFA

🚂 🚂 🚂 🚂

LA ROUE (France 1956)

Produced by André Haguet. Directed by Maurice Delbez. With Jean Servais, Pieree Mordy, Francois Guerin and Chamarat.

A railway engineer, Pelletier, takes in a little orphan named Norma in 1940. Norma is brought up in Lyon with Roland, an adopted son aged five. However, Pelletier, badly wounded during the battle for the Liberation, is transferred from the workshops. The years pass; soured by his new employment, Pelletier cannot but own a certain jealousy he feels towards his son, now an engineer. At the same time he is troubled by the presence of Norma, now grown up to be a lovely woman. She, worried, flees to Paris. The day arrives when Roland, at the controls of an electric locomotive breaks the world's speed record. Norma re-appears on this occasion, but Pelletier does not try this time to make her stay. While the future appears good for the young couple, it seems now to be the time for him to retire.

This film is interesting because it contrasts the old and new. There is some excellent steam material in the early part of the film (the story begins in 1930), including well-documented scenes at Lyon. The son, however, becomes driver of electric locomotive BB9004, the fastest in the world when the film was made. SNCF gave facilities to the producers to shoot extensively on the Paris-Lyon network and the electric locomotive high-speed scenes are authentic. Unhappily the film is badly made as a whole and is rarely shown anymore.

35mm, Sound, 92mins, Films de France

🚂 🚂 🚂

ROUGH CUTS (Britain 1986)

Railscene. An extension of the 'magazine' formula. Volume 1 was typical with material shot on other video projects but not previously released including scenes shot in 1984-86: Settle to Carlisle, 'Cumbrian Coast Express', Scarborough, 'Spa Express', Fort William to Mallaig and Newcastle to Carlisle.

VID, Sound, Colour, 55mins, RSV

🚂 🚂 🚂 🚂 🚂

ROYAL SCOT IN THE USA (Britain 1933)

In 1933 the LMS was invited to take part in the Century of Progress Exhibition in Chicago, USA. We see No 6100 *Royal Scot* (felt by many to have actually been No 6152) and her smart train taking part in some spectacular America showmanship as a 'race' is staged with Pennsylvania Railroad 4-6-2 No 5436 (note the views of the other cameraman to be seen). Finally the LMS 4-6-0, in truly pristine condition, is seen en route for the Chicago Fair in June 1933.

16mm/VID, Silent, 12min, HA/Stirling

🚂 🚂 🚂 🚂 🚂

ROYAL TRAIN IN SOUTH AFRICA (Britain 1947)

Produced for Metro-Cammell by Kinocrat Films. Directed by Gerald Cookson. Photography by Lewis Lewis. The stock and locomotive SAR *City of Cape Town* used on the Royal Tour of South Africa; there are many action shots of the train en route from Cape Town to Johannesberg and on tour.

16mm, Sound, Colour, 18mins, Lama/HA

🚂 🚂 🚂 🚂 🚂

ROYAL TRAIN WITH THE DUKE AND DUCHESS OF YORK (USA 1901)

Edison Film. A royal train with two locomotives on the front and a banker in the rear climbing Mount

Hector with two Pullmans. Three locomotives to two coaches; seems they were not taking chances!

16mm, Silent, 4mins, HA

🚂 🚂 🚂 🚂 🚂

ROYAL TRAINS (Britain 1959)

BBC Television production. Directed by D A Smith. Commentary by Bruce Wyndham. Some of the rolling stock, compartments and furnishings used by British royalty during more than a hundred years of travelling by rail.

16mm, Sound, 19mins, BFI

🚂 🚂 🚂 🚂 🚂

RUNAWAY RAILWAY (Britain 1965)

A Fanfare Films production. Produced by George H Brown. Directed by Jan Darnley-Smith. Script by Henry Geddes and Michael Barnes. Photography by John Coquillon. Music by Ron Goodwin. With John Moulder-Brown, Kevin Bennett, Leonard Brockwell, Roberta Tovey, Syndey Taffler, Ronnie Barker, Graham Stark and Hugh Lloyd.

It is a sad day for a group of children who are waiting at Barming station for the Barming Loop to be closed and their favourite engine, *Matilda*, is to be broken up.

Inspired by an unwitting suggestion the children decide to borrow time by a minor act of sabotage. Unhappily they succeed beyond their expectations and *Matilda* runs amock with fatal results to her well-being. Ironically, a telegram arrives from the eccentric Lord Chalk announcing his intention to take over *Matilda* and the Barming Loop providing all is in working order.

The children set about the apparently impossible task of repairing *Matilda* and receive unexpected help from Mr Jones and Mr Galore, who pose as railway enthusiasts but are in fact planning to use *Matilda* in a mail-robbery.

A trial run is planned at dawn with the unsuspecting children driving. Too late they realise what Jones and Galore are really up to. In the ensuing scuffle *Matilda*'s controls become jammed and she careers madly on to the main line, narrowly missing collision with other trains. All lines are cleared and, gushing

steam and smoke, she finally comes to a thunderous halt at the main terminus buffers. *Matilda* is wrecked once more but the mail train robbers are outwitted.

Lord Chalk, however, has duly been impressed by *Matilda*'s astonishing performance and offers to buy her and the Barming Loop, if the children will join him as partners, which they do!

The film was made with facilities provided by the army at Longmoor, Hampshire. One of their preserved locomotives was brought out, put in working order and run for two months between Bordon and Longmoor to provide scenes for the film company. Bordon station became Barming and the locomotive was renamed *Matilda*. Children from Bordon County Junior School joined in for some of the 'crowd' scenes.

35mm, Sound, 55mins, CFF

🚂 🚂 🚂

RUSH HOUR (Britain 1970)

British Transport Films. This unique film was originally intended to show station planners the movement of passenger flow during the morning rush-hour peak (8.20-9.20am) at London's Waterloo station. When the results had been analysed, it was decided that this material should be compiled into an entertaining short to show how many people do use the station every morning. Now we can watch the thousands of Waterloo commuters arrive and depart — all in the space of under three minutes!

35/16mm, Sound, Colour, 3mins, BTF

🚂 🚂 🚂 🚂 🚂

RUSSIAN ENGINEERS (Britain 1962)

Made by P B Whitehouse and John Adams. The adventurous spirit of these pioneer film makers had already led to them being arrested in Yugoslavia. Now, posing as tourists, they sneaked some fascinating bits of Russian steam in the days when it was a novelty and the USSR very much a closed society.

16mm, Silent, 6mins, CV/NRM

🚂 🚂 🚂 🚂 🚂

S

SAFE TRANSIT (Britain 1956)

Produced by Pilot Films for the British Transport Commission. The correct methods for handling freight if damage and loss during rail transit is to be prevented. A film to encourage the freight-handling staff of British Railways to adopt the safest and most up-to-date techniques and so reduce not only the cost of damage to freight in transit but also the apprehensions of the trader.

35/16mm, Sound, 41mins, BTF

🚂 🚂 🚂 🚂 🚂

SAFETY ON ELECTRIFIED LINES (Britain 1961)

Two of a series of safety films made for showing to railway staff in areas of Britain where the 25kV AC single-phase overhead electric system had been introduced. Both these films were made in association with British Transport Films by Tara Films.
Part 1: Traffic Staff. 'To ensure their own safety under the conditions brought about by electrification, traffic staff have to learn to change certain of their working habits so as to conform with the new rules and regulations.'
Part 2. Rescue and First-aid. 'Observance of basic rules and regulations ensures safety but, should an accident occur, a knowledge of rescue procedure and the prompt and efficient rendering of artificial respiration – particularly the latest 'mouth-to-mouth' technique can often save life.'

35/16mm, Sound, 24mins, BTF

🚂 🚂 🚂 🚂 🚂

SAFETY ON THE TRACK (Britain 1951)

Produced by British Transport Films. This film was shown to all recruits in London Transport's railway departments, and teaches commonsense practices to be followed when working on electrified track, or in depots. London Trans-port's 'four-rail ' permanent way is explained in detail, and it is shown that both negative and positive current rails are dangerous. Correct behaviour when working or walking on or near the track is shown, and the examples are given of methods of handling and disposing of tools. This film was made in association with British Transport Films by Rayant Pictures.

35/16mm, Sound, 13mins, BTF

🚂 🚂 🚂 🚂 🚂

SAFETY PRECAUTIONS ON ELECTRIFIED LINES (Britain 1964)

Produced by British Transport Films. A series of safety films made for showing to railway staff in areas where the 25kV AC single-phase overhead electric system was in operation. Part 1: General Maintenance. Painters, plumbers, and permanent-way men can all put themselves in danger from the overhead wire if they don't follow the rules. This film shows the precautions they must take, and explains why new regulations are necessary. Part 2: Construction. Contractors' staff engaged on the construction of the overhead wire system are reminded of the dangers of working on the railway, and advised how to avoid them. Part 3: Overhead line maintenance. Tells the story of an emergency repair to the overhead line, showing in detail the working of the routine precautions to ensure the safety of the maintenance gang. Part 4: Electric Depots. Shows how the live wire is made safe in a district electric depot for work to be done on rolling stock and how the staff should co-operate for their own safety. Part 5: Switching stations. The safety routing enabling maintenance work to be done on the oil circuit-breakers in a switching station is described in detail.

35/16mm, Sound, 71mins, BTF

🚂 🚂 🚂 🚂 🚂

SAFETY: THE TRUMP CARD (France 1966)

Produced by SNCF for the International Union of Railways. A montage film produced under the aegis of the Sixth Committee of the Inter-national Union of Railways on the occasion of the 1966 International Safety Fortnight. Eight European railways participated in the production.

35/16mm, Sound, Part colour, 32mins, UIC

🚂 🚂 🚂 🚂 🚂

SALUTE TO THE CLASS 47 (Britain 1991)

Electra Films. 'The ultimate class 47 sightings video'. Non stop uninterrupted no-nonsense train spotting.

VID, Sound, Colour, 125mins, EFV

🚂 🚂 🚂 🚂 🚂

SANDLING JUNCTION TO HYTHE (Britain 1937)

A 9.5mm amateur film showing Southern Railway traffic at Sandling Junction (including boat trains bound for Folkestone) and featuring a high-speed run on the branch line to Hythe by trick photography. A sort of early London to Brighton in Four Minutes.

16mm, Silent, 9mins, HA

🚂 🚂 🚂 🚂 🚂

SANTA COMES TO ROMNEY (Britain 1991)

Festival Video. A record of the Santa Specials on the miniature Romney, Hythe & Dymchurch Railway, showing how the trains are got ready and then a run with Santa on board.

VID, Sound, Colour, 20mins, Festival Vid

🚂 🚂 🚂 🚂 🚂

SANTA FE (USA 1951)

Columbia Pictures. Produced by Harry Joe Brown. Directed by Irving Pichel. After the Civil War, the eldest of four westbound brothers tries to prevent the others becoming permanent outlaws, despite some attacks on the railroads. There is a major railroad robbery scene staged on the Sierra Railroad, with additional scenes staged on the Atchison, Topeka & Santa Fe Railroad in the hills above Hollywood.

35mm, Sound, Colour, 89mins, Columbia

🚂 🚂 🚂

SANTA FE TRAIL (USA 1940)

Warner. Directed by Michael Curtiz. With Errol Flynn and Olivia de Havilland. A cavalry officer captures the famous John Brown. Includes scenes on the Sierra Railroad with Baldwin 2-8-0 locomotive No 29790, built in 1906.

35mm Sound, 110mins, Warner

🚂 🚂

THE SAVAGE MESSIAH (Britain 1972)

MGM. Produced and directed by Ken Russell. With Dorothy Tutin, Scott Anthony and Helen Mirren. The life of the painter Gaudier and Sophie Brzeska. Includes scenes filmed at Horsted Keynes on the Bluebell railway with glimpses of LBSCR 'A1X' 0-6-0T No 55 *Stepney*.

35mm, Sound, Colour, 103mins, MGM

🚂

SCENES ON THE LNER (Britain 1936-39)

Made by Major W B Greenfield. Blow-up from 9.5mm, of a series of fragmentary shots of LNER steam in the late 1930s, including 'Silver Jubilee' and 'Coronation' expresses.

16mm (from 9.5mm), Silent, 5mins, HA

🚂 🚂 🚂 🚂 🚂

SCHOOL FOR SCOUNDRELS (Britain 1960)

Associated British Picture Corporation. Produced by Hal E Chester. Directed by Robert Hamer. With Ian Carmichael, Alastair Sim, Terry-Thomas and Dennis Price. Includes railway scenes in the Salisbury area with ex-Southern Railway trains.

35mm/VID, Sound, 94mins, Weintraub/VID 125 (rly)

🚂

THE SCHOOL TRAIN: ZILLERTAL BAHN (Britain 1961)

Made by P B Whitehouse and John Adams. Part of the hunt by these two filmmakers for the unusual in the European scene in the 1960s, often discovering railways that were later to be preserved or become better known.

16/8mm, Silent, Colour, 8mins, CV/NRM

🚂 🚂 🚂 🚂 🚂

SCIENTIFIC RESEARCH (Britain 1938)

An LMS film. The founding in 1935 of the Railway Research Establishment in Derby and the nature of the work done there on all aspects of railway safety.

35mm/VID, Sound, 22mins, BTF/TVP

🚂 🚂 🚂 🚂 🚂

THE SCOTTISH BELLE (Britain 1963)

Made by G S Holyoake. Caledonian Railway 4-2-2 No 123 and the LSWR 'T9' 4-4-0 No 120 on a visit to the Bluebell Railway; other motive power on the Bluebell Line is included.

16/9.5/8mm, Silent, Colour, 4mins, MFS

🚂 🚂 🚂 🚂 🚂

SCOTTISH EXPRESS (Britain 1946)

Paul Barrelet production. Directed by Paul Barrelet. A survey of preparations and subsequent journey by rail from King's Cross to Edinburgh.

35/16mm, Sound, 35mins, HA

🚂 🚂 🚂 🚂 🚂

SCOTTISH HIGHLANDS (Britain 1953)

Produced by British Transport Films. From Glasgow or Edinburgh, Scotland may be explored by train or long-distance coach, and this film includes a coach tour from Edinburgh to the Isle of Skye. The route taken meets the Highlands at Killin, and then goes over Rannoch Moor and through Glencoe to Ben Nevis, the entrance to the Great Glen. Here we meet the West Highland Railway line, and follow it on its journey through the Bonnie Prince Charlie country to Mallaig. Returning to the Great Glen we rejoin the coach route out through Glen Foyne and Glen Shiel to Kyle of Lochalsh, and take the ferry over to Skye.

16mm, Sound, Colour, 20mins, BTF

🚂

SCOTTISH HISTORICAL LOCOS AT DUNSHOLME (Britain 1923)

Made by P B Whitehouse and John Adams. Part of a tour made for

BBC *Railway Roundabout*, with views of some of the locomotives that later became part of the Scottish Industrial Museum; others were later used on preserved lines in Scotland.

16/8mm, Silent, CV/NRM

🚂 🚂 🚂 🚂 🚂

SCOTTISH STEAM IN THE THIRTIES (Britain 1938)

Edited by John Huntley. Journey from Euston to Glasgow. Annan. Dumfries, Ballachulish Ferry station, Loch Etive, Callander to Oban by observation coach.

16mm, Silent, 20mins, HA

🚂 🚂 🚂 🚂 🚂

THE SEA SHALL NOT HAVE THEM (Britain 1954)

Eros Production. Directed by Lewis Gilbert. With Dirk Bogarde, Michael Redgrave, Bonar Colleano and Nigel Patrick. Survivors of an air crash adrift in a dinghy await rescue. Incudes scenes of the old Felixstowe Pier station and an 'F6' arriving at Felixstowe Town station.

35mm, Sound, 93mins, Eros

🚂

THE SEASIDE TRAINS (Britain 1989)

BBC Television. A series produced by BBC Bristol on various branch lines, using film from the Ivo Peters collection and also amateur film. A most unusual item dealing with the Weston, Clevedon & Portishead Railway, which came to an end in 1940. It used the small amount of material that has survived, as well as stories by people who knew the line and an O-gauge model.

VID, Sound, Colour, 28mins per episode, BBC TV

🚂 🚂 🚂 🚂 🚂

SEATON JUNCTION (Britain 1961)

Made by P B Whitehouse and John Adams. A good selection of Southern Region engines are seen in this film made in Summer of 1961 when there was still plenty of steam about and not all the branch lines had been shut down.

16/8mm, Silent, 6mins, CV/NRM/VID

🚂 🚂 🚂 🚂 🚂

SECOND GLANCE: STEAM (Britain 1982)

International Film Associates (Scotland). A film by Eddie McConnell. A brief nostalgic look at steam trains and those who tend them. There are locomotives both large and small, as tourist amusements and working engines. The material is set to a brisk musical accompaniment.

16mm, Sound, Colour, 9mins, IFA (Scotland)

SECOND NATURE (Britain 1967)

Produced by British Transport Films. Railwaymen moving into the age of electricity. In *Second Nature* they interpret in their own words the great technological changes and the human problems of adaptation each has to face. As with seamen and farmers, railwaymen even today remain curiously close to nature; and gain flexibility of mind from the relationship. An incident at Rugby provides the starting point for thoughts going beyond the new machines and the new methods.

35/16mm, Sound, Colour, 23mins, BTF

SECOND REPORT ON MODERNISATION (Britain 1960)

Produced by British Transport Films for the British Transport Commission. 'Recent progress in the modernisation and electrification scheme for British Railways. The film illustrates some of the new architectural and engineering techniques employed in building railway stations, flyovers, marshalling yards, freight trains and de luxe Pullman carriages. Electronics and automation are prominent features of the new face worn by British Railways' tracks, stations and offices, and a glimpse of modern training and living facilities for staff is included.'

35/16mm, Sound, Colour, 21mins, BTF

THE SECRET AGENT (Britain 1936)

Gaumont British. Directed by Alfred Hitchcock. With John Gielgud, Robert Young, Peter Lorre and Madeleine Carroll. An amateur spy is ordered to kill a man who is endangering the organisation. One railway sequence was filmed on the Longmoor Military Railway.

35mm, Sound, 83 mins, Rank

SELLING TRANSPORT (Britain 1935)

An LMS film. A training film for railway employees on selling themselves and the service offered by the railways. In those days, they were still known as 'Railway Servants'!

35mm/VID, Sound, 25mins, BTF/TVP

THE SEMMERING LINE (Britain 1961)

Made by P B Whitehouse and John Adams. A film showing the electrification of this line in Austria with both steam and electric locomotives.

16/8mm, Silent, 5mins, CV/NRM

SENTINELS OF SAFETY (Britain 1936)

An LMS film. The West Coast main line, following the passage of a train between three signal boxes and tracing the course of the 'Lakes Express' from Euston to Windermere.

35mm/VID, Sound, 23mins, BTF/SPV

THE SERVANT (Britain 1963)

Springbok Films. Directed by Joseph Losey. With Dirk Bogarde and Sarah Miles. Domination of a rich young man by his manservant. Includes diesel-hauled arrival at St Pancras.

35mm, Sound, 115mins, Rank

SERVICE FOR SOUTHEND (Britain 1957)

Produced by Data Films for the British Transport Commission. The extension of the electrification of the Southend railway line from Shenfield to Southend in the English county of Essex. The last steam train leaves Liverpool Street station in London for Southend and makes way for a new stage in a big modernization plan for British Railways. The film tells the story of how it was done and the men behind the service.

35/16mm, Sound, 10mins, BTF

SERVICE FOR THE SERVICES (Britain 1945)

Southern Railway film. The contribution of the Southern Railway during the war years from the Expeditionary Force, Dunkirk and the build-up to the D-Day invasion.

35mm/VID, Sound, 30mins, BTF/TVP

THE SETTABELLO (Britain 1961)

Made by P B Whitehouse and John Adams. Yet another episode in the 'Grand Tour' made by the *Railway Roundabout* experts.

16mm, Silent, 12mins, CV/NRM

THE SETTLE AND CARLISLE RAILWAY (Britain 1984)

Cresswell Films. A survey of the history, operations, architecture and locomotives of the line, including steam and diesel hauled trains. It was not to be the only time this line was the subject of a video camera.

VID, Sound, Colour, 60mins, Cresswell

THE SETTLE & CARLISLE RAILWAY (Britain 1984)

Video 125. Produced by Peter Middleton. Made in association with the Railway Development Society. A driver's eye view of the famous line, made when the future of the line was still in jeopardy. The first work of Video 125.

VID, Sound, Colour, 60mins, 125

SETTLE TO CARLISLE LINE (Britain 1987)

Railway Consultants. Commentary by Sidney Weighell. A driver's eye view of the line from start to finish, with additional scenes in signal-boxes, at the main points along the route and scenes of some of the surrounding countryside, including Settle Junction, Ribblehead Viaduct, Garsdale and Blea Moor.

VID, Sound, Colour, 150mins, Railway Consultants

SEVEN BAD MEN (USA 1954)

Universal. With Randolph Scott. A typical Western-type story with some scenes shot on the Sierra Railroad, using locomotive Baldwin 2-8-0 No 29790 (1906)

35mm, Sound, Colour, 86mins, Universal

SEVEN MORE STATIONS (Britain 1948)

British Transport Films. Produced by Edgar Anstey. The opening of the Eastern Extension of the London Transport Central Line from Wanstead to Newbury Park.

35mm, Sound, 11mins, BTF

SEVEN PER CENT SOLUTION (USA 1976)

Universal. Produced and directed by Herbert Ross. With Nicol Williamson, Joel Gray, Robert Duvall, Alan Arkin, Vanessa Redgrave, Laurence Olivier and Jeremy Kemp. Dr Watson lures Sherlock Holmes to Vienna so that Professor Freud can cure him of his persecution complex and cocaine addiction (the 'seven per cent solution'). 'Sherlock Holmes is placed under hypnosis by Sigmund Freud and the audience is then placed under hypnosis by director Herbert Ross.' (Michael Billington)

A major 'continental' railway scene was staged on the Severn Valley Railway with heavy (but not always impenetrable) disguises, like BR '2MT' 2-6-0 No 46443 (the Sherlock Holmes Red Loco); LMS '5' 4-6-0 No 45110 *RAF Biggin Hill* (the Baron's Loco) and glimpses of LMS '8F' 2-8-0 No 8233 and GWR

'45XX' No 4566. A short piece of the Wyre Forest line was reopened by the film company for aerial shots, where two of the trains converge in a chase scene.

35/16mm, Sound, Colour, 114mins, Universal/TUA:HA:ref rail only

SEVEN SINNERS (Britain 1936)

A Gaumont-British production. Directed by Albert de Courville. With Constance Cummings, Edmund Lowe, Thomy Bourdelle, Henry Oscar, Felix Aylmer, Joyce Kennedy, O B Clarence, Mark Lester and Allan Genine.

The flim opens at a carnival ball in Nice where Harwood, an American detective, is awaiting the arrival of a London insurance agent, Mr Fenton, who is to work on a case with him. 'Mr Fenton' proves to be Caryl Fenton, an attractive young woman. Meanwhile Harwood has found a murdered man in the hotel. The body subsequently disappears and Harwood and Caryl leave for England. The train is wrecked and Harwood finds the body of the murdered man in the wreckage. This gives him the idea that the accident to the train was planned to cover up the murder. The Prefect of Police and Caryl are equally sceptical about this theory. The solution of the mystery takes Harwood and Caryl to a mysterious house in Paris, to the Guildhall, and to a village in Hampshire, where they witness another railway crash. Eventually the villain stages a third crash to dispose of Harwood, Caryl and members of his gang. Harwood and Caryl escape and the wrecker dies in a gun battle with the police in front of a newsreel of the smashes he has caused.

Many of the old Southern Railway shots (the film uses material taken during the making of *The Wrecker* in 1929) including the Foden lorry/South Eastern and Chatham locomotive collision were used. A train crash on the Continent is mostly done with models and old newsreel shots. As in *The Spy* it involves a single carriage uncoupled and left standing in a tunnel (the ease with which stock travelling at speed is uncoupled remains one of the more charming myths of rail-

way fiction films). An express thunders into the tunnel and the hero just has time to look out of the rear and see it coming. The villains are not so fortunate and there is one tremendous shot in *Seven Sinners* achieved by back projection. The interior of the carriage is built up on the studio floor with pull-away fittings and sides. A back projection screen fills one end, on which a locomotive is seen rushing right into camera (probably a reverse shot). As the engine appears to crash into the coach, the whole sides collapse around the screaming occupants. It is among the most imaginative of all railway crash shots, even though it was carried out in the studio.

The use of the shots from *The Wrecker* comes in the second smash in Hampshire. They are assembled as follows:

1. LS	Car on road with Harwood and Caryl.
2 LS	Lorry (not original steam lorry from *The Wrecker*).
3. LS	Train approaching.
4. MS	Man in carriage.
5. LS	View through spectacle showing view of countryside and boiler dome ahead.
6. MS	Harwood and Caryl run in horror towards camera, staring at crash (not seen).
7. LS	View through spectacle (as shot 5).
8. MS	Driver shutting off regulator.
9. MS	Harwood and Caryl; Caryl covers face.
10. Insert.	Locomotive 1060 racing towards camera (reverse printed shot).
11. LS	Actual crash (from high angle).
12. CS	Detail of crash; locomotive overturns.
13. MS	Crash from rear; carriages moving forward.
14. LS	Locomotive tearing up ground, carriages overturning (high angle).
15. MS	Harwood and Caryl; Caryl covering up her face. (Shots 3, 5, 7, 8, 10 (reversed), 11, 12, 13, 14 are from *The Wrecker*.)

The final crash is complex in its editing pattern:

Above left:

A desperate need for fuel is met in a way familiar from a number of films _ this time from the 'Seven Percent Solution'.

Above:

The film crew and railmen at work during the making of the training film 'Single Line Working'.
British Railways

Left:

The actor David Niven meets the real engine driver during the making of 'The Silken Affair'.

Above right:

A characteristic freight scene from 'Sullivan's Travels', shot on the Southern Pacific.

Above far right:

The studio reconstruction of Paris Gare de Lyon used during the making of 'Sleeping Car to Trieste'. *Rank*

Right:

A young star of John Schlesinger's 'Terminus' seems none too happy with his role, Waterloo Station, 1961.

Model Shot: Tunnel Mouth.
PAN to show express approaching in the distance.

MS   Harwood, Caryl and group in carriage; Harwood runs to rear door (camera PANS to follow).

MS   Harwood tries to open door; it is jammed. Rest of group join him.

MS   Wrecker's henchmen run to door at other end.

Model Shot: Express enters tunnel at speed.

MS   Harwood and Crayl open carriage end doors: see train approaching in tunnel (back projection).

MS   Reverse angle: Harwood and Caryl stare out from carriage end door.

MS   Train approaching in tunnel (real)

MS   Harwood and Caryl dash to side door.

MS   Harwood and Caryl leap towards side door (another angle).

LS   Locomotive and train approaching at speed in tunnel (real; unmistakably British locomotive).

MS   Interior of cariage with tables, wall and the train wreckers. Locomotive leaps forward and blurred outline of locomotive wheels swamps all. (Back projection, with foreground action.)

Insert.   Blurred effect of collapsing steel and timber; train wheels and frames; steam. FADE OUT.

35mm, Sound, 70mins, Rank/16mm, rail only HA (ref)

SEVENTH RAIL REPORT — Speed the Payload (Britain 1967)

Produced by British Transport Films. 'The speed-up on British Rail is not confined to faster schedules. In many aspects of railway working modern methods and structures are making for quicker results. This report shows how sending coal by the continuous merry-go-round trains is regularising the supply from pit to power station, how the Motorail terminal at Olympia speeds the holidaymaker and his car comfortably on their way. It also suggests that British Rail's adoption of the hovercraft shows it will try new ways of speeding the payload.'

35/16mm, Sound, Colour, 15mins, BTF

SEVERN & WYE (Britain 1962)

Made by P B Whitehouse and John Adams. In 1961 a SLS Special was run over the lines of the old Severn & Wye Railway in the Forest of Dean. Two GWR Pannier tanks and three autocoaches made up the train.

16/8mm, Silent, Colour, 6mins, CV/NRM/VID

SEVERN VALLEY 1988 (Britain 1989)

Preserved Steam on Video. Featured are the following locos: 5080 *Defiant*, 5593 *Kolhapur*, 6960 *Raveningham Hall*, 4566, 2857, 7819 *Hinton Manor*, 5960 *Leander*, 8233, 80079, 46443, 5000, 47393, 686 *The Lady Armaghale* and 34027 *Taw Valley*.

VID, Sound, Colour, 120mins, PSO

SEVERN VALLEY STEAM (Britain 1982-85)

Video Line. An updated version of an earlier video, featuring 17 locomotives in steam, with a visit by GWR No 3440 *City of Truro*.

VID, Sound, Colour, 75mins, Video Line

SHADOW OF A DOUBT (USA 1943)

Universal. Directed by Alfred Hitchcock. With Joseph Cotten, Teresa Wright and Hume Cronyn. A murderer on the run ends up in a small Californian town as a welcome uncle to the family he originally came from. Includes scenes on the California section of the Southern Pacific Railroad, still in steam days.

35mm, Sound, 108 mins, Universal

SHANGHAI EXPRESS (USA 1932)

Paramount. Directed by Josef von Sternberg. With Marlene Dietrich, Clive Brook and Anna May Wong. A British officer and an old girl friend meet up on a train pursued by bandits. The 'Chinese' railway has a strong American flavour! Perhaps two location shots of an actual Chinese train, then those wheels going round (Baldwin Works much in evidence), lots of chimney smoke in the night and wailing whistles and train bells straight out of any Western. The carriage interiors (studio built) seem to be only suitable for at least a 10ft gauge system!

35mm, Sound, 84mins, Paramount

THE SHINING RAILS (USA 1950)

Produced by General Electric USA Inc. A short history of railway development in the USA, leading to the first diesels and electrics in the 1930s and on to the super-diesels of the 1950s.

16mm, Sound, 20mins, TUA

SHINING THROUGH (USA 1991)

TCF. This is the film that turned St Pancras into Zurich in the 1940s; and caused a great stir amongst railway fans as to what was going on! Barrie Keeling, Film Facilities Manager of British Rail, explained at the time: 'It was a month from the first request to the first day of shooting. They wanted two steam trains to be painted in the colours of Swiss Railways but it had to be easily washed off. 20th Century Fox spent all Saturday transforming the station and it looked fantastic. At six o'clock the following morning the filming started, with stars Michael Douglas and Melanie Griffith, and they had wrapped by eleven at night.'

35mm, Sound, Colour, 124mins, TCF

SHOAH (France 1990)

Produced and directed by Claude Lanzmann. Nine-hour documentary on the World War Two holocaust in Poland involving the slaughter of the Jews. Includes very sustained shots of railway operations all over Poland, notably with electric train to Auschwitz, steam-hauled goods trains throughout the entire system, a long slow approach to Treblinka station (with views of an old and somewhat eccentric engine driver leaning out from the footplate), diesel shunters at work in Auschwitz yard and goods yards in the surrounding area. There are details of big Polish 2-8-0 goods locomotives and an interview with the then Chief Programme Planning Officer, Head Office of Eastern Traffic, Reichsbahn HQ, Warsaw, whose job was to schedule the 'Resettlement Specials' which transported the Jews to the extermination camps at Auschwitz and Treblinka. A surviving Working Order from 1942 traced a double-headed 'merry-go-round' train which hauled 50 Continental-size closed goods waggons on a 24hr schedule from various parts of Poland to Treblinka, each carrying 4,000 Jews. These death trains worked to tight timetables: 'arrival at Treblinka 11.24; unloading and cleaning; depart Treblinka 4.29'. The SS Ministry had to pay the Ministry of Transport for each person carried at the 'Party Outings' rate; the only difference was that the passenger journey was strictly one way.

35mm, Sound, Colour, 540mins, Lanzmann/French Ministry of Culture

SHUNTER BLACK'S NIGHT OUT (Britain 1941)

Ministry of Information. A Verity film. Directed by Maxwell Munden. An off-duty railway shunter helps to control a fire in the marshalling yards at Feltham following an incendiary raid. Based on an actual event.

35mm, Sound, 7mins, NFA/IWM

SIERRA (USA 1950)

Universal. Directed by Alfred E Green. With Audie Murphy and Wanda Hendrix. Old outlaw is wrongly accused of murder. Both principal locomotives of the Sierra Railroad were used for some

scenes: Rogers 4-6-0 No 4493 (1891) and Baldwin 2-8-0 No 29790 (1906).

35mm, Sound, Colour, 82mins, Universal

THE SIGNAL ENGINEER (Britain 1962)

Produced by British Transport Films. Practical work in shop and signalbox, on gantry and by track side, coupled with instruction in mechanics, electricity, electronics and draughtsmanship, these lead the apprentice into the intricacies of design, the excitement of research and experiment, and the intense satisfaction of being in on a big 'changeover' from old semaphore to a new colour-light scheme.

35/16mm, Sound, Colour, 26mins, BTF

THE SIGNALMAN (Britain 1976)

BBC Television. Produced by Rosemary Hill. Directed by Lawrence Gordon Clark. With Denholm Elliott, Bernard Lloyd and Carina Wyeth. A ghost story by Charles Dickens, dramatised by Andrew Davies. A lonely signalman is haunted by a hooded figure which seems to warn of danger. But what exactly is the danger? This superb piece of railway atmosphere was filmed on the Severn Valley preserved railway, using Kidderminster Tunnel and its approach signal box; a specially strong (and rather bogus) red signal light was mounted on the face of the tunnel for film purposes. The train used was hauled by GWR '5700' 0-6-0PT No 5764, with two-toned ex-GWR stock (three coaches); a simulated crash was quite convincing. The sound of the bells and the clicks of the old block instruments were used to great effect.

16mm, Sound, Colour, 48mins, BBC Television

SIGNAL SUCCESS (Britain 1930)

British Screen Tatler. A magazine item on the work of the Portobello Junction signalbox on the Great Western Railway outside Paddington; there are some good glimpses

of locomotives and stock of the day passing the box.

35/16mm, Silent, 3mins, HA

SIGNPOST (Britain 1955)

Produced by British Transport Films. A short film illustrating the reconstruction and electrification of the main railway line between Manchester and Sheffield and presenting this as an example of what the British public may expect from the plan of modernisation and re-equipment of British Railways. Produced for television by the BBC during the evening that the plan was debated in Parliament.

16mm, Sound, 5mins, BTF

SILENCE ON ROULE (France 1959)

French Railways. Experiments with rubber tyres on French Railways.

16mm, Sound, 10mins, SNCF

THE SILENT PASSENGER (Britain 1935)

A Phoenix film. Produced by Hugh Perceval. Directed by Reginald Denham. Script by Basil Mason. Based on a story by Dorothy Sayers. Photographed by Jan Stallick. Art direction by R Holmes Paul. Edited by Thorold Dickinson. With John Loder, Peter Haddon, Mary Newland, Donald Wolfit, Austin Trevor, Leslie Perrins and Aubrey Mather.

An unpleasant blackmailer is murdered and his body hidden in a trunk. John Ryder eventually finds himself in possession of both the dead man's railway tickets and his luggage, and at Calais, the Customs officials make what the headlines describe as 'a gruesome discovery'. The outlook for John Ryder seems black, especially as his wife, who had been behaving indiscreetly with the blackmailer obviously does not believe a word he says but, fortunately for him, Lord Peter Wimsey happens to be on the train and he is a master amateur detective. After many adventures the true murderer is tracked down in an exciting climax in a locomotive repair shed.

All the railway scenes involved

night locations. The hero sets out from Liverpool Street on a train hauled by former Great Eastern Railway 4-4-0 No 8788. Arrival at Stratford is accomplished by a train drawing into a different platform at Liverpool Street. The star of the shed drama is played by 0-6-2T 'N7' Class locomotive No 2616, which runs down the hero and villain in the pits and eventually crashes its way through the shed doors until brought under control by a swift-footed driver.

35mm, Sound, 88mins, Weintraub

THE SILKEN AFFAIR (Britain 1956)

Dragon Films. Directed by Roy Kellino. With David Niven, Genevieve Page and Wilfrid Hyde White. An accountant enjoys a powerful life style by cooking the books. Includes a railway scene at an unknown station (named Wormley in the film) and BR 4MT 2-6-4T No 80064.

35mm, Sound, 96mins, Dragon

THE SILVER JUBILEE (Britain 1936)

A4 2509 *Silver Link* departs from Newcastle Central, and 2510 *Quicksilver* arrives in King's Cross, emerging gracefully from Gasworks Tunnel and rolling into Platform 7. Buffer stop scenes show a multitude of passengers disembarking as well as plenty of station interior detail in the summer of 1936.

VID, Silent, 7mins, Stirling

THE SILVER STREAK (USA 1934)

RKO Radio. Directed by Tommy Atkins. With Sally Blane, Charles Starrett, Hardie Albright, William Farnum, Arthur Lake and Edgar Kennedy. A streamlined train makes its first run from Chicago to Boulder Dam where a victim of infantile paralysis must be got into an iron lung. 'Pretty absurd, yet exciting and fast. There's scarcely a stunt known to the railroad picture formula that hasn't been employed.' (*Variety*) The real 'Silver Streak' line

– the Southern Pacific – gave full facilities for this production, with the latest in 4-6-2 Pacific streamliners out of Chicago and heading west. Some of the railway detail was done a little nearer home for Hollywood – the yards at Los Angeles. Mixed in are shots of the 'Burlington Zephyr' of 1934.

35mm, Sound, 85mins, RKO Radio

THE SILVER STREAK (USA 1976)

TCF. Produced by Martin Ransohoff and Frank Yablans. Directed by Arthur Hiller. With Gene Wilder, Jill Clayburgh, Ned Beatty and Patrick McGoohan. On a trans-continental train, a young publisher discovers a murder and is at the mercy of the culprits. '1970s performers trapped in this fake 1930s mystery comedy, which is so inept you can't even get angry.' (*New Yorker*) 'The 'Silver Streak' is a transcontinental train running from Los Angeles to Chicago; Gene Wilder spends all his time dodging some murderers. The end is great.' (Tony Bilbow)

Southern Pacific Railroad this time refused all co-operation; the ATSF had no more crack trains left. So it all had to be done in Canada, using the CPR railway and its facilities. It too, was heading for the end of its trans-continental services. The big crash was staged in a Boeing aircraft factory hangar and is all done with specially constructed mockups.

35mm, Sound, Colour, 113mins, TCF/HA:rail only

SIMPLON TUNNEL (German 1958)

A DEFA film. Directed by Dr Gottfried Kolditz. With Hans Finchr, Brigitte Krause, H Weinheimer and Gerry Wolff. The story of the building of the Simplon Tunnel from 1898 to 1905. 12.25 miles long, up to a depth of 7,000ft, the temperature was so high at times that the men could only work by being constantly sprayed with cold water. Hot and cold springs were encountered but the completed tunnel cut 70 miles off the existing route into Italy.

35mm, Sound, 91mins, DEFA

SING AS WE GO (Britain 1934)

Associated Talking Pictures. Directed by Basil Dean. With Gracie Fields and John Loder. Adventures of a mill girl in Blackpool. LMS excursion trains arriving and leaving Blackpool.

35mm, Sound, 80mins, Weintraub

SINGLE LINE WORKING (Britain 1958)

British Transport Film. Staff Training Film. The unit hunted around for a suitable line which could be used on Sundays for filming and came upon the S&DJ. They selected Shepton Mallet as the centre of activity and they had just started shooting when they heard that the line in question was in the pipeline for closure. So phoney station names were invented, along with relabelled block signal instruments to conceal a long term training film being made on a dying line. The secret seemed secure with BR '4' 4-6-0 No 75071; and then up bobbed Fowler S&DJ 2-8-0 freight locomotive exclusively associated with the S&DJ! All was revealed, despite the subterfuge.

35/16mm, Sound, Colour, 38mins, BTF

SIXTH RAIL REPORT — The good way to travel (Britain 1965)

Produced by British Transport Films. 'The best in ideas, the newest of materials, the most modern methods are being employed to make sure that British Rail becomes indisputably the good way to travel. Amongst the many subjects included are: Neptune, an automatic and electronically equipped track fault recorder; an underfloor lathe for re-profiling worn wheels tyres and flanges; a cab simulator at Willesden for training drivers; the new electric multiple-unit stock for service for Euston; the launching of the SS *Dover*; and the ticket hall at Liverpool Street station.'

35/16mm, Sound, Colour, 19mins, BTF

SIXTIES SOUTHERN (Britain 1960-68)

Films by Geoff Holyoake. A video assembly of the principal works of Mr Holyoake, using all the material he made on the Southern Region, including items like Enthusiasts' specials, 'South Western Limited', 'Maunsell-hauled' and many others.

VID, Sound, Colour, 55mins, RS

SIXTIES STEAM IN ACTION (Britain 1987)

Rail Video. Volume One. Filmed by John Shaw this tape uses locations such as the Hawkhurst Branch, Bluebell, Saunderton, Westbourne Park, Morthoe, Upwey, Bushey, Troughs and Lickey Incline (13mins). Locos include 'O1s', 'Cs', Bluebell locos, 'J52s', 'Kings', 'Castles', 'Halls', Panniers, '63XXs'. Bulleid 'Merchant Navies' and West Countries', 'Ns', 'Us', 'Black 5s', 'Royal Scots', 'Duchesses', 'Britannias', Standard '4s', '5s', '9Fs' and LMS 'Jubilees'.

VID, Sound, Colour, 30mins, RVO

SIXTY GLORIOUS YEARS (Britain 1938)

Imperator Film. Directed by Herbert Wilcox. With Anna Neagle and Anton Wallbrook. Second film on the life of Queen Victoria, 1840-1901, with period railway scenes, facilities provided by the LMS.

35mm, Sound, Colour, 95mins

THE SKYE LINE (Britain 1959)

Made by P B Whitehouse and John Adams. One of the loveliest journeys in the British Isles is that from Fort William to Mallaig in Western Scotland. This film was made when steam was still supreme and shows the journey behind a 'K2' Class 2-6-0. Shots include the departure of a MacBraynes's boat for the Western Islands.

16/8mm, Silent, Colour, 7mins, CV

SKYE TRAIN (Britain 1987)

Video 125. A Class 37 diesel takes a train over the ex-Dingwall & Skye Railway from Inverness to Kyle of Lochalsh. The 64 mile journey was filmed from the driver's eye view, from a helicopter and from various key points on the route. Signalling was semaphore to Dingwall and RETB to Kyle. Produced by Peter Middleton. Commentary by Paul Coia.

VID, Sound, Colour, 90mins, 125

SLEEPERS AWAKE: HARBORNE BRANCH, BIRMINGHAM (Britain 1950)

Made by P B Whitehouse.

16/8mm, Silent, CV

SLEEPING CAR (Britain 1933)

Directed by Anatole Litvak. With Ivor Novello, Madeleine Carroll, Kay Hammond and Stanley Holloway. Romance on a transcontinental train across Europe. Mainly studio reconstruction of stations, locomotives and stock with a few genuine PLM shots, mainly in and around Paris.

35mm, Sound, 72mins

SLEEPING CAR TO TRIESTE (Britain 1948)

Two Cities Film. Produced by George Brown. Directed by John Paddy Carstairs. With Jean Kent, Albert Lieven, Derrick de Marney, Paul Depuis, Rona Anderson, David Tomlinson and Bonor Colleano. Re-make of *Rome Express* using much of the same technique as the original, with big studio set piece built at Denham and a collection of stock shots of European steam-hauled trains scattered along the way. 'This is solid entertainment and includes a cast most of whose members grew old and distinguished in the business.' (Tony Bilbow). Finlay Currie appeared in *Rome Express* and, 16 years later, in this one.

35mm, Sound, 95mins, Rank

SLITHER (USA 1972)

MGM. Directed by Howard Zieff. With James Caan and Peter Boyle. A comedy-thriller in which gangsters and others hunt across California for hidden loot. Includes scenes with Sierra Railroad Baldwin Model S12 diesels.

35mm, Sound, 96mins, MGM

SLOW TRAIN TO OLYMPIA (Britain 1983)

BBC Television. Executive producer: Colin Adams. Produced by Derek Towers. Written and presented by Michael Wood. From the *Great Little Railways* series. Michael Wood takes us on a journey from Athens to Olympia. The film starts with the nightlife of Athens for the tourists. Various scenes around Athens by day. The main station of the Peleponnesian Railway is crowded with young tourists seeing the real Greece. The diesel local train will take us through rural countryside — first stop Elefsis. Then on to cross the Corinth Canal and into the Peleponnese mountains stopping at Argos. The line now heads to the southern mountains calling at villages on the way. At Zevgolatio we change trains for the Western coast and the journey's end at Olympia.

16mm, Sound, Colour, 40mins, BBC TV

SLS SPECIAL: 'HARBORNE AND HALESOWEN BRANCHES' (Britain 1959)

Made by P B Whitehouse and John Adams. Story of a special train organised by the Stephenson Locomotive Society over closed or little used lines in the Midlands.

61/8mm, Silent, 6mins, CV/NRM

SMALL FOR ITS AGE (Britain 1978)

Produced by the Romney, Hythe & Dymchurch Railway. A detailed survey of the miniature and its history.

16mm, Sound, Colour, 20mins, RHD/VID

SMALL STEAM (Britain 1979)

Produced by Smiths Industries. A journey on the RHDR; there are views of Davey Paxman 4-6-2 locomotives No 1 *Green Goddess* and No 6 *Samson*, and 4-8-2 No 5 *Hercules*, and Krauss 0-4-0T No 4 *The Bug*. There is a short episode devoted to a fine 0 gauge layout.

16mm, Sound, Colour, 12mins, HA

🚂 🚂 🚂 🚂 🚂

SMALL WORLD (Britain 1979)

BBC Television (West). Produced by Paul Smith. Written and presented by Eric Thomson. A study of two model railway layouts: Mike Sharman's period and historical model railways and the Rev Peter Denny's Great Central Railway model layout at his home at Buckingham.

16mm, Sound, Colour, 10mins, BBC TV

SNAEFELL MOUNTAIN AND MANX ELECTRIC RAILWAYS (Britain 1967)

Made by Trevor White. A camera record.

16/8mm, Silent, Colour, 5mins, TW

🚂 🚂 🚂 🚂 🚂

SNOW (Britain 1963)

Made by British Transport Films. Produced by Edgar Anstey. Directed by Geoffrey Jones. A great 'classic' prizewinning documentary. Railwaymen, trains and travellers in a battle against the winter of 1962-63. Individual shots are rhythmically composed to form a unity with a score which has been electronically edited and arranged. It won 13 international accolades. One recalls how train spotters hated it because the locomotives were gone in a flash!

35/16mm, Sound, Colour, 8mins, BTF

🚂 🚂 🚂 🚂 🚂

SNOW JET (Britain 1947)

See: Operation Snowbound.

🚂 🚂 🚂 🚂 🚂

THE SNOW TRAIN (Britain 1963)

Made by P B Whitehouse and John Adams. The re-opening operations and snow clearance with steam locomotives of the Swiss Narrow Gauge Furka Oberalp Bahn with Brig to Disentis.

16/8mm, Silent, 15mins, CV/NRM

🚂 🚂 🚂 🚂 🚂

THE SNOWDON MOUNTAIN RAILWAY (Britain 1960)

Made by P B Whitehouse and John Adams. Story of a journey from Llanberis to the Summit.

16/8mm, Silent, Colour, 8mins, CV/NRM

🚂 🚂 🚂 🚂 🚂

SNOWDRIFT AT BLEATH GILL (Britain 1955)

Produced by British Transport Films. A freight train travelling between Kirkby Stephen and Barnard Castle becomes snowbound in the Westmorland Hills. The Motive Power, Operating and Engineering Departments go to work with snowploughs to reach the trapped train. The team dig clear and thaw out moving parts, and finally two rescue engines help to clear the line.

35/16mm/VID, Sound, 10mins, BTF/VID BT1

🚂 🚂 🚂 🚂 🚂

SO THIS IS LONDON (Britain 1948)

National Talkies Production. Photography by Eric Cross. Good shots of the underground and an effective shot of a Southern steam-hauled train taken from a lattice bridge outside Waterloo.

16mm, Sound, 16mins, NA

🚂

SOME LIKE IT HOT (USA 1959)

United Artists. Produced and directed by Billy Wilder. With Jack Lemmon, Tony Curtis, Marilyn Munroe, Joe E Brown, George Raft and Joan Shawlee. Two unemployed musicians are innocent bystanders to the St Valentine's Day Massacre and have to flee in disguise with an all-female band. 'A

milestone of film comedy. Constantly flogs its central idea to death and then recovers with a smart line or situation.' (Leslie Halliwell) 'As Lemmon, Curtis and the band travel to Florida on the train, Lemmon has delicate problems when he bunks up to Marilyn Munroe.'

There is a lovely train scene when the band rehearse and Munroe sings. The rhythm of the song (*Running Wild*) is very cleverly cut to the rhythm of the wheels and motion of an old 4-4-0 in action, taken from stock shots but given a new life by the editing. The train interiors are strictly studio: but good.

35mm, Sound, 122mins, United Artists

🚂

SOMERSET AND DORSET RAILWAY (Britain 1958-66)

Not much attention was paid to this fascinating line until after World War 2. From then until its closure, coverage was extensive. It featured in the BTF film *Single Line Working* in 1958, in John Betjeman's superb *Let's Imagine a Branch Line* (1963). Pat Whitehouse's study of the Fowler 2-8-0s in action, an amazing 8mm film which recorded every single station from Bournemouth to Bath; but dominating all, the magnificent work of the late Ivo Peters, happily available on video and something of a monument to the dedicated work of a railway enthusiast.

🚂 🚂 🚂 🚂 🚂

SOMETHING ABOUT FREIGHT TRAINS (USA 1950)

Hump marshalling and general freight operations on American railroads.

16mm, Sound, 10mins, TUA

🚂 🚂 🚂 🚂 🚂

SONS OF THE SEA (Britain 1939)

British Consolidated Pictures. Directed by Maurice Elvey. With Leslie Banks, Cecil Parker and Kay Walsh. Naval spy drama, which includes a GWR train at Dartmouth.

35mm, Sound, Colour, 82mins

🚂

SORRY! WRONG NUMBER (USA)

A Paramount Picture. Directed by Anatole Litvak. With Barbara Stanwyck and Burt Lancaster. Includes scenes on the New York Subway system.

35mm, Sound, 92mins

SOUND RECORDING

An integral part of modern film and TV production is the sound track. Until about 1954, despite some amazing pioneer work with an early primitive domestic tape recorder and a mass of car batteries used by Jack Law and Victor Jones to record the sounds of the last London trams (now a classic LP) in 1952, all sound tracks were either on primitive 78 rpm discs (acetate on aluminium or shellac pressed 78 rpm discs in rare cases); or on the elaborate optical sound-on-film equipment used in feature films. In 1954, Peter Handford, working on the David Lean feature film *Summer Interlude*, shot entirely on location in Venice, used 'wild' 0.25in tape on a portable machine, also powered by car batteries, and a rotary converter which could 'play up' pretty badly. In 1955, Handford took an early Ferrograph, again with car batteries and a rotary converter on a four-wheel luggage trolley for a full day's recording at Euston station. The main recording of LMS 'Princess Coronation' 4-6-2 No 6247 *City of Liverpool* is now a classic; it was originally issued on a 78 rpm record. By the end of 1955, Handford had recorded 'Big Bertha' on the Lickey Incline and issued his first LP under the Transacord label.

Meanwhile, Argo Records had started up in Bournemouth in 1951 with primitive 78 rpm records for the enthusiast but, in 1957, had become part of Decca Records. All three elements came together in 1961 when Peter Handford also joined Argo/Decca. Under the Argo label, Handford's work has become internationally famous and we owe it to him that the last days of steam on British Rail were so well captured, just in the nick of time. Today's simple equipment has made sound recording commonplace; it is, of course, usually on a video complete with the pictures.

Despite this fact, feature films and TV producers still get it wrong! As Peter Handford put it so well in his book *Sounds of Railways*:

'Any railway enthusiast cinema-goer must have seen examples of almost total ignorance and a general disregard for authenticity in railway matters. For instance, in a sequence involving a railway journey, it was not uncommon for a character to be seen joining a train of GWR coaches which, when it pulled out of the station had mysteriously become a train of LMS coaches, hauled by a Stanier Pacific, accompanied on the sound track by a three-cylinder exhaust beat and the sound of a Southern Railway whistle; during the supposedly continuous journey the train might become the Silver Jubilee, hauled by an 'A4' Pacific and it could well arrive at its Scottish destination behind a GWR 'King', accompanied on the sound track by an LMS whistle. When sound libraries are asked to provide sound tracks of trains it is rare for any details to be given, since it is a widely held opinion that, apart from the obvious differences between steam, diesel and electric all engines and trains sound the same, even in different countries.'

In recent years, these things have become a bit less common; mainly because railway enthusiasts in their droves usually write in to complain.

THE SOUTH AFRICAN RAILWAYS (South Africa 1925)

Produced by South African Railways and Harbours. A survey of the principal routes, stations, engineering works, motive powers and main line stations of South African Railways.

35mm, Silent, 15mins, NFA

SOUTH EASTERN RAMBLER RAIL TOUR (Britain 1967)

SCTS. Times were now changing for the Society. Gone were all the steam-hauled tours; this one featured Sulzer Type 3 diesel-electric No D6529. The tour was from London Bridge to Lewisham, Catford, Selsdon, Oxted, Uckfield, Lewes, Brighton, Polegate, Hailsham, East-bourne, St Leonards, Rye, Appledore and back to London.

16mm, Silent, 4mins, HA/SCTS

SOUTH LONDONER RAIL TOUR (Britain 1958)

SCTS. A tour with a two coach train hauled by an SECR 'H' 0-4-4-T locomotive to Admiralty Spur, Birkbeck, Norwood Junction, Wimbledon, Merton Park, Merton Abbey (closed to passengers in 1929), Waddon Marsh and on to West Croydon.

16mm, Silent, 6mins, HA/SCTS

SOUTH WESTERN LIMITED (Britain 1962)

Made by G S Holyoake. Southern Counties Touring Society 'South Western Limited' tour on 2 September 1962 and scenes at Salisbury, Honiton Bank, Exeter and Exmouth. Motive power includes Classes '6F', '4', '2', 'Lord Nelson' and 'King Arthur' at Surbiton on SLS/RCTS tour; 'A4' 4-6-2 *Mallard* on Ian Allan Rail Tour at King's Cross.

16/9.5/8mm, Silent, Colour, 4mins, MFS

SOUTH WESTERN RAMBLER RAIL TOUR (Britain 1964)

SCTS. A journey from Waterloo via Barnes, Andover, Luggershall, Salisbury, Templecombe and on the SDJR to Blandford Forum, Broadstone, then Hamworthy junction, Bournemouth and back to Waterloo. Motive power includes BR 'Britannia 4-6-2 No 70020 *Mercury*, BR '9F' 2-10-0 No 92209 and a GWR pannier tank for the ride on the SDJR.

16mm, Silent, 8mins, HA/SCTS

SOUTH WESTERN RAMBLER RAIL TOUR (Britain 1961)

SCTS. The journey goes from Waterloo to Hampton Court Junction, Salisbury, Sidmouth, Ottery St Mary, Budleigh Salterton, Exeter, Eastleigh, Andover Junction,

Southampton Central and back to Waterloo via Woking. Motive power includes SR 'Lord Nelson' 4-6-0 No 30861 *Lord Anson*, SR 'N15' 4-6-0 No 30770 *Sir Prianius* as well as an 'M7' tank, a BR Standard tank and an old Drummond '700' 0-6-0 goods engine built for the LSWR in 1897.

16mm, Silent, 9mins, HA/SCTS

🚂 🚂 🚂 🚂 🚂

SOUTHAMPTON DOCKS: SOUTHERN ENGINES (Britain 1959-60)

Made by P B Whitehouse.
16/8mm, Silent, CV/NRM

🚂 🚂 🚂 🚂 🚂

SOUTHAMPTON HARBOUR (Britain 1958)

Made by P B Whitehouse and John Adams.
This film shows American shunters, 'B2s', 'Battle of Britain' and 'Lord Nelson' classes. It also shows the radio control of shunters.

16/8mm, Silent, 5mins, CV/NRM

🚂 🚂 🚂 🚂 🚂

SOUTHAMPTON RAIL TOUR (Britain 1966)

SCTS. A circular tour from Waterloo via Tooting, Wimbledon, Salisbury, Southampton, Andover (with trip to Luggershall) and back to Waterloo. Motive power includes one of the surviving US Army Transportation Corps 0-6-0T locos purchased after World War 2 by SR for use in Southampton docks (BR No 30072), 'Battle of Britain' 4-6-2 No 34052 *Lord Dowding* and (old regular on SCTS tours) 'Merchant Navy' 4-6-2 No 35023 *Holland Afrika Line*.

16mm, Silent, 8mins, HA/SCTS

🚂 🚂 🚂 🚂 🚂

SOUTHDOWN VENTURER (Britain 1966)

SCTS. A trip from Victoria to East Croydon, Crowborough, London Road (Brighton), Hove, Havant, Fareham, Gosport, Portsmouth and Portsmouth Harbour. Motive power includes SR 'WC' 4-6-2 No 34013

Okehampton, SR 'N' 2-6-0 No 31411 and BR Sulzer 'Bo-Bo D' No D6543.
16mm, Silent, 7mins, HA/SCTS

🚂 🚂 🚂 🚂 🚂

SOUTHERN COUNTIES ENTERPRISE RAIL TOUR (Britain 1963)

SCTS. A tour from Waterloo to Hamworthy Junction, then to the Isle of Portland, Easton, Weymouth, Bridport, West Bay and Yeovil. Motive power includes LNER 'A1' 4-6-2 No 60112 *St Simon*; an 'M7' 0-4-4Tank and two GWR '5700' 0-6-0PTs Nos 4689 and 7782.

16mm, Silent, 8mins, HA/SCTS

🚂 🚂 🚂 🚂 🚂

SOUTHERN COUNTIES TOURING COLLECTION

Films of tours taken from 1948 to 1967 by Geoffrey Ashwell, Jack Law, John Meredith, Victor Jones and John Bearman. This society, most energetically directed by Bill Crawforth, organised an amazing number of transport excursions by bus, tram, trolleybus and train. The outings were documented by a team of cameramen who worked first on 9.5mm and later on 16mm. The films were originally shown to the AGM of the Society and were then often put aside. In 1987, the entire collection was resuscitated and many of the 9.5mm films copied onto 16mm film. They have since been widely shown and some of the material has been used in various transport videos. The film collection was looked after for many years by Mr Crawforth's son, Ted Crawforth, himself an 8mm enthusiast.

🚂 🚂 🚂 🚂 🚂

THE SOUTHERN KNIGHTS (Britain 1983)

Rail Video. RV3 records of SR 'LN' 4-6-0 No 850 *Lord Nelson*; SR 'N15' 4-6-0 No 777 *Sir Lamiel*, both on various tours including Hereford, Carnforth-Keighley and Leeds-Carlisle. Plus scenes of 'Merchant Navy' 4-6-2 No 34092 *City of Wells* and LMS '2MT' 2-6-2T No 41241.
VID, Sound, Colour, 120mins, RVO

🚂 🚂 🚂 🚂 🚂

SOUTHERN RAILWAY WORKS, ASHFORD (Britain 1926)

Empire News Bulletin. An item called 'Royalty and Railwaymen', the newsreel shows the Duke and Duchess of York visiting the Southern Railway Works at Ashford, Kent. There are shots of SR 4-6-0 No 850 *Lord Nelson* with the Duke and Duchess on the footplate.

35mm, Silent, 2mins, NFA

🚂 🚂 🚂 🚂 🚂

SOUTHERN RAMBLER RAIL TOUR (Britain 1967)

SCTS. This tour went from Victoria to East Croydon, Selsdon, Parks Bridge Junction, Brighton, Eastbourne and Polegate. Most of the trip was with a BR '4' Standard tank but part featured SR 'West Country' 4-6-2 No 34108 *Wincanton* and, at Selsdon, a brand new diesel No E6016.

16mm, Silent, 5mins, HA/SCTS

🚂 🚂 🚂 🚂 🚂

SOUTHERN STEAM IN THE SIXTIES (Britain 1989)

Rail Video. This tape is a compilation of the *Southern Steam in the Sixties* series of tapes volumes 1-4 edited together to produce the first two-hour archive video tape. This is the entire archive footage shot by Jim Oatway of SR steam in action. The tape features various classes including Bulleid Pacific, 'King Arthur', 'Lord Nelson', 'S15', 'H16', 'N', 'U', 'Q', 'Schools', 'M7', 'O2', 'G16', 'W', 'Q1', 'A1X', Standard '2', '3', '4', '5' and a 'Britannia'. Locations include Waterloo, Clapham Junction, West Byfleet, Horsham, Feltham, Hayling Island, Isle of Wight, Nine Elms and the Bluebell Railway.

VID, Sound, Colour, 120mins, RVO

🚂 🚂 🚂 🚂 🚂

SOUTHERN WANDERER RAIL TOUR (Britain 1965)

SCTS. A tour from Victoria via Crystal Palace, Sutton, Horsham, Poole and to Southampton Central; then on to Broadstone, Highbridge, Templecombe, Salisbury and back to Victoria. Motive power includes BR

'5' 4-6-0 No 73022 (Derby 1951), Fowler LMS '4F' 0-6-0 No 44560 and SR 'Merchant Navy' 4-6-2 No 35023 *Holland Afrika Line*.

16mm, Silent, 6mins, HA/SCTS

🚂 🚂 🚂 🚂 🚂

SOUTHWELL BRANCH (Britain 1958)

Made by P B Whitehouse. A trip on the branch from Rolleston Junction to Southwell with MR 0-4-4T No 58085 of 1881 vintage.

16mm, Silent, 6mins, CV/NRM/VID

🚂 🚂 🚂 🚂 🚂

THE SOUTHWOLD RAILWAY (Britain 1928-29)

Hillside Video. Archive film of the old Southwold 3ft narrow gauge railway from Halesworth on the Great Eastern to Southwold on the East Coast which started in 1879 and came to an end in 1929. A victim to an early and energetic bus service. The attractive locomotives (*Southwold*, *Halesworth*, *Blyth* and *Wenhaston*) and the tramway-type stock are all well captured in this video, based on the Stretton-Ward collection.

VID, Sound, 30mins, Hillside

🚂 🚂 🚂 🚂 🚂

THE SOUTHWOLD RAILWAY (Britain 1929)

Produced by A Barrett Jenkins and the Gaumont Mirror. A record of the narrow gauge line from Halesworth on the ex-GER line from Saxmundham to Bungay to the east coast resort of Southwold, opened in 1897 and closed in 1929. There is good coverage of the little 2-4-0T locomotives; the six-wheeled carriages, some of which had end doors and outside platforms in the American manner; the fine scenery of some parts of the line; and the delightful little station bus which served the town and the various hotels.

This rare film material has been preserved through the personal enthusiasm of A Barrett Jenkins, historian to the line and responsible for the preservation of its relics in the Southwold museum.

The railway was a 3ft line; the four locomotives were named after the stations on the line: No 1 *Southwold*; No 2 *Halesworth*; No 3 *Blyth*; No 4 *Wenhaston*. The line opened in 1879 and closed in 1929. It remained in situ until 1942 and only finally went for scrap as part of the war effort. There was a time when you could have bought one of the 2-4-0T engines for £18! The six six-wheel Clemison flexible wheelbase tramway-type saloons were reputed to have been built for the Woosung tramway in China. They went bust so the Southwold then took them instead. The *Gaumont Mirror* newsreel was originally on 35mm; the 16mm material was made by Mr Barrett Jenkins. The railway was once the subject of a series of comic postcards with all the traditional jokes about sleepy branch lines, including a cow on the line (there once was one on the line but it turned out to be a bull). Reprints of the cards are still available.

35/16mm/VID, Silent, 18mins, BJ/VID/HA

🚂 🚂 🚂 🚂 🚂

SOUTHWOLD RAILWAY (Britain 1965)

Anglia Television. Produced and directed by David Kenten. History of the Southwold Railway which closed in 1929, using archive film and an interview with A Barrett-Jenkins, the acknowledged expert on the narrow gauge line from Halesworth to Southwold.

16mm, Sound, 7mins, Anglia

🚂 🚂 🚂 🚂 🚂

SOVIET SCRAPBOOK (USSR 1942)

Central Newsreel Studio, Moscow. A new method of laying railway tracks over long distances.

35mm, Sound, 3mins, ETV

🚂 🚂 🚂 🚂 🚂

SPEAKING OF FREIGHT (Britain 1960)

Produced by British Transport Films. When a business tycoon allows himself to be 'snared' into seeing some films in a railway traffic manager's office, there must be a reason for it. In this case, it's a particularly giant-sized transport problem. But before he's convinced that the railways can help him solve it, there is an atmosphere of battle in the room, and some interesting and unexpected facts are hurled about in the course of the argument.

35/16mm, Sound, Colour, 28mins, BTF

🚂 🚂 🚂 🚂 🚂

SPECIAL OPERATIONS ON THE LICKEY (Britain)

Made by P B Whitehouse and John Adams.

16/8mm, Silent, 7 mins, CV/NRM

🚂 🚂 🚂 🚂 🚂

SPEED IN THREE ELEMENTS (Britain 1930)

Pathestone Weekly. A race between the 'Flying Scotsman' train, a De Havilland Puss Moth (piloted by Geoffrey De Havilland) and an outboard motorboat with Miss Elto Mycroft at the wheel. The scene is set in a field near the line near Huntingdon where details are agreed. Unfortunately, the cameras could only record one or two basic shots of the race with Gresley LNER Class A3 4-6-2 No 4475 *Flying Fox* so others were added for effect which are all supposed to be the same train. First, a GNR 'C1' 4-4-2 is seen and then Gresley Class 'A3' 4-6-2 No 2549 *Persimmon* bobs up to complete one of those carefree newsreels of the early days.

35/16mm, Sound, 4mins, Pathe/HA (ref)

🚂 🚂 🚂 🚂 🚂

SPEED THE SCRAP (Britain 1955)

British Iron and Steel Federation. Recycling of scrap metal; includes some railway scenes.

16mm, Sound, 18mins, RF

🚂 🚂

SPEEDRAIL TO THE SOUTH (Britain 1967)

Produced by British Transport Films. 'Between London, Southampton and Bournemouth, electricity replaces steam with travel fit for the seventies — clean, quiet, fast and frequent. Extra, faster trains now make commuting much quicker. After a glimpse of the old days of steam the film follows various travellers – commuters and holiday makers – as they experience the pleasures of travel on this route. Businessmen discuss their work in comfort or relax at the buffet bar, and at the end of a day a group of young folk come up to London for a gay evening.'

35/16mm, Sound, Colour, 11mins, BTF

🚂 🚂 🚂 🚂 🚂

SPENDER (Britain 1990-)

BBC Television. Thriller series in which Newcastle Central station features regularly. Scenes to be shot between Durham and Newcastle had not reckoned with the speed of the train and the scene was not complete, so they had to go to Darlington to give more time to get the shot in the can.

TV, Sound, Colour, 54mins per episode, BBC TV

🚂

SPICK AND SPAN (Britain 1962)

Produced by British Transport Films. Two and a half million passengers every day all over the country; thousands of trains, each to be cleaned at the end of its journey. This film shows in detail the various types of cleaning undertaken at stations, between journeys and at the cleaning depots.

35/16mm, Sound, 18mins, BTF

🚂

SPIONE (Germany 1927)

Produced and directed by Fritz Lang. Script by Fritz Lang and Thea van Harbou. With Gerda Maurus, Willy Fritsch, Rudolph Klein-Rogge, Fritz Rasp, Lupu Pick, Lien Deyers, Hertha von Walther, Craighall Sherry, Paul Hoerbiger and Grete Berger.

The tale of a master mind who directs a vast network of criminals and killers from his wheelchair in a secret hideout until he is eventually tracked down and disposed of by a government agent and his girlfriend. The film includes a spectacular railway crash when the 'Nord Express' collides head-on in the curved Altmuhl Tunnel with a coach detached

from a preceding train by some of the spy's henchmen. The hero is saved at the last minute when he goes to the end coach and looks out to see the front of the approaching express.

Since *The Cabinet of Dr Caligari* (1919) almost everything in German films was staged in the studios. In this case, much of the train sequence, including countryside, track tunnel, locomotives and stock were built in the Neubabelsburg Studios in Berlin. The method of shooting was largely imitated in *Rome Express* produced in Britain a few years later. The studio shots were then intercut with skilfully recorded actuality material taken from a camera platform lashed to the side of the locomotive and at the entrance to a tunnel. The sequence starts with the departure of the train carrying the hero. The girl, who is travelling on another train, notes the number of his carriage through an open window- 33133. There are studio shots of the train interior and the rhythm of the wheels, picked out in good actuality shots taken under a moving train, repeat the number 33133. (Although the action is all supposed to be at night, one shot from below the train reveals a daylight background.) A fine night location shot, marvellously lit by arcs at the tunnel mouth and on the front of the locomotive, dramatises the entrance into the scene of the crash. The carriage with the hero on board is detached by the crooks and he is awakened just in time to dash to the rear and see another train approaching. The front of the approaching train is a night location shot with full lighting but the crash itself and the wreckage is cleverly done in the studio. There follow shots of rescue teams being called from stations nearby (a mixture of studio and actuality); the girl, having heard of the crash, is seen on the footplate of a locomotive, arriving at the tunnel mouth (real). She enters the tunnel (real) and finds the wrecked coach (33133) in which the hero is trapped (studio). He is rescued and the pair make their way out into the daylight (real).

35/16mm, Silent, 120mins, BFI

🚂 🚂

THE SPOILERS (USA 1942)

Universal. Directed by Ray Enright. With Marlene Dietrich, Randolph Scott, John Wayne and Harry Carey. Fights in the old West over land rights and a saloon entertainer. Includes a big train crash effectively staged on the Universal back lot, using old preserved engines.

35mm, Sound, 87mins, Universal

🚂

SPOTLIGHT ON THE NIGHT MAIL (1948)

Rayant Films. Directed by Anthony Gilkinson. The work of GPO sorters on the night mail train between London and Aberdeen.

35/16mm, Sound, 19mins, TCF

🚂 🚂 🚂 🚂 🚂

SPOTTERS (Britain 1989)

Royal College of Art. Produced by Carl Prochezer and Peter Salmi. Directed by Peter Cattaneo. A short drama which looks at the lives of a family of train spotters who are enthusiastic about diesel locomotives (what a nice change!). There are love intrigues and touches of teenage rebellion to update the story.

16mm, Sound, Colour, 14mins, RCA

🚂 🚂 🚂 🚂 🚂

SPY TRAIN (USA 1943)

A Monogram Picture. Directed by Harold Young. With Richard Travis and Catherine Craig. A timebomb thriller set on a long-distance train.

35mm, Sound, 61mins, Monogram

🚂 🚂

SQUADRON LEADER X (Britain 1943)

RKO Radio. Directed by Lance Comford. With Eric Portman and Ann Dvorak. Wartime drama; includes scenes of Waterloo station.

35mm, Sound, 99mins, RKO Radio

🚂

DER STAHLTIER (Germany 1935)

Reichebahndirektion Film. Directed by Willy Otto Zielke. English Title: *The Iron Horse*.

'More, perhaps, than that of any other art, the history of the cinema is littered with unfinished projects, half-completed films. Willy Otto Zielke's *Der Stahltier* is an even stranger case. Here is a film that was certainly finished; it has just not been seen. Indeed, had it not been for the accident of fate and the fact that the Cinémathèque Française practises a policy of taking what it can get without being too choosey, it probably would never have been seen by anybody. Except Goebbels.

'The story begins in 1934. Zielke, who had previously made what seems to have been a highly interesting film called *The Unemployed*, was commissioned by the German State Railways to make a film celebrating the hundredth anniversary of the German railway. This was to be a big propaganda production, and during the year it took to make, tremendous publicity was put out concerning the film. Zielke and his crew had their own train which circulated all over Germany, advertising on the outside the forthcoming great production. When it was completed, propaganda minister Goebbels was the first to see it. It has not come down to us what he actually said on that occasion, but Mr Zielke soon found himself behind the walls of an insane asylum, and this extremely expensive and highly publicised film was never released.

'What upset Goebbels so much? Partly the fact that this film to the glory of the German railways paid glowing tributes to French and English rail pioneers, Stephenson and his *Rocket* and all the others. 'As if this wasn't enough, the film, far from being a paean to the German genius, was instead a symphonic poem, an abstract hymn to the beauty of rail and engine. Zielke attached his camera to the driving shafts of the locomotives, under the bogies, to the cow-catcher; he created fantastically beautiful montages of points, signals: a triumph of Neue Sachlichkeit; the 'New Objectivity' movement which raised objects to the status of pure works of art.

'Zielke was sprung from his insane asylum through the personal intervention of Leni Riefenstahl who wanted him to work on her Olympic Games film. He is, in fact responsible for the camerawork on the prologue of the film.

'Sad to say, it appears that once he had done this, he was sent straight back to his insane asylum where he remained until the end of the war. Zielke is still alive, living in west Berlin, and most of this information about his life was gathered this winter by the American filmmaker Kenneth Anger *Scorpio Rising*. An admirer of the film ever since days when he worked at the Cinémathèque Française, Anger took advantage of a recent visit to Berlin to try to see if Zielke had survived. Much to his surprise, he found that he had, and that far from being broken he was still working in the cinema, making short films.

'There was even some talk of finally releasing *Der Stahltier*. Apart from the print in Paris (which got there after the war as captured alien property by the French Army), there does exist a negative in the archives of the Federal Railways.

'Apart from the purely formal beauty of photography and montage, *Der Stahltier*, if it ever does come out again, will astonish many in the highly accomplished way in which, 15 years before *Miss Julie*, it intermingles past and present into a kind of free-flowing continuum. In so far as the film has a plot, it concerns the training of a locomotive engineer who is sent out on various trail runs. During his training period, he tries to communicate to his colleages his own enthusiasm, and his passion for railways. And it is during the course of these conversations that the historical incidents are effortlessly interspersed.

'But ultimately, whatever its technical interest or its beauty of photography, *Der Stahltier* would not be worth reviving were it not for the degree of emotion, of frenzy, even, with which it is informed. Unlike Gance, in whose film *La Roue* railways play chiefly a dramatic role, for Zielke they are the subject, the only subject. And he makes us care'. (Richard Round, *The Guardian*)

The film was based on the complete new building of the locomotive *Alder* (*Eagle*) from original drawings carried out on the occasion of the 1935 centenary celebrations of the German state railways. *Adler* was built by Robert Stephenson in 1835 for the first German public steam railway from Nuremberg to Fürth.

35/16mm, Sound, 72mins, HA

STAPLEFORD MINATURE RAILWAY (Britain)

Made by P B Whitehouse and John Adams.

16/8mm, Silent, 11mins, CV/NRM

THE STARS LOOK DOWN (Britain 1939)

Grand National. Directed by Carol Reed. With Michael Redgrave, Emlyn Williams and Margaret Lookwood. Brief shots of GWR pannier tank hauled local trains in the Welsh valleys are included in this story by A J Cronin of a Welsh mining disaster.

35/16mm, Sound, 103mins, BFI

STEAM (Britain 1979)

Produced by the British Tourist Board. A fast and furious look at the many steam-operated preserved private railways in Britain, both standard and narrow gauge. Briefly seen are the Keighley & Worth, the Bluebell and the Ffestiniog railways.

11mm, Sound, Colour, 14mins, BTA

STEAM ALIVE (Britain 1983)

B & R Video Productions. A brisk run round some preserved steam railways, grabbing quickly what came in view. From the early carefree days of video when all that mattered was to use the word 'Steam'.

VID, Sound, Colour, 60mins, BRV

STEAM AT WORK (Britain 1987)

Online. Produced by Wilf Watters. Commentary by David Coleman. Industrial steam locomotives

recorded in 1970-71; fireless locomotive at Gravesend, Kent; six
locomotives at work in a cement
works in Swanscombe; coal mines
near Dover; CEGB station at Bedford; power station at Acton; London Transport steam engines:
Neasden depot to the City with an
LT steam crane; South Wales colliery locomotives at Mountain Ash,
Blaenavon, Maesteg, Pontypool,
Pontardulais, Aberfan. spoil trains
at Belfast.

VID, Sound, Colour, 55mins,
Online

STEAM DAYS (Britain 1990)

A BBC Television series presented
by railway enthusiast Miles Kington.
The six-part collection included the
Settle and Carlisle line ('Travels
with a Duchess'); the West Highland Line ('The Fishing Line');
Steam Specials on BR ('Quest for
Speed'); freight trains
('Workhorses'); GWR main line
steam ('Going Great Western'); and
LNER 'A1' and 'A4' Pacifics ('A Tale
of Two Scotsmen'). Produced by
two Open University producers, this
was a much appreciated series for
its concentration on the railways
themselves.

VID, Sound, Colour,
27mins each, BBC TV

STEAM DEPARTURES (Britain 1986)

Transport Video Publishing. A
series of departures from Marylebone in 1985 and 1986, with City of
Wells, Flying Scotsman and Sir
Nigel Gresley.

VID, Sound, Colour, 35mins,
TVP

STEAM ENGINE (Britain 1947)

Produced by G B Instructional for
the British Council. The story of the
development of the steam engine,
shown principally by animated diagrams, from the early inventions of
Newcomen and then James Watt
and George Stephenson to the
streamlined locomotive of the present day.

16mm, Sound, 20mins, HA

STEAM FANTASY (Britain 1983)

B & R Video Productions. Impressions of steam locomotives at work,
much of it recorded on the Dart Valley Railway.

VID, Sound, Colour, 61mins,
BRV

STEAM FAR WEST (Britain 1985)

Bob Ainsworth Film. A lively record
of a steam special on 8 April 1985
(as part of the GWR 150 celebrations), featuring a journey from Plymouth via Exeter St Davids to Bristol with GWR '78XX' 4-6-0 No 7819
Hinton Manor and GWR 'Hall' 4-6-0
No 4930 Hagley Hall.

16mm, Sound, Colour, 9mins,
Ainsworth/HA

STEAM FAR WEST (Britain 1988)

Movieland. Films produced and
directed by Bob Ainsworth. A video
assembly of six films including
Branch Line Supreme (Dart Valley),
Plymouth to Bristol (steam trip in
1985), Nostalgia in Miniature
(model and minature railways in
Devon and Cornwall), Cornish
Freight Lines and Shadows on the
Moor (then and now record of the
old Yelverton to Princetown branch
line of the GWR across Dartmoor.
Archive film by John Huntley).

VID, Sound, Colour, 53mins,
VID/Movieland

STEAM FINALE: LICKEY INCLINE (Britain 1960-62)

Made by P B Whitehouse.

16/8mm, Silent, Colour,
CV/NRM

STEAM IN FINLAND (Britain 1968)

Made by P B Whitehouse.

16/8mm, Silent, Colour,
CV/NRM

STEAM IN IRAN (Britain 1964)

An amateur record of a car expedition into Iran in the days before the
revolution and the wars. Detailed

scenes of double-headed steam
workings.

16mm, Silent, Colour, 12mins,
HA

STEAM IN RETROSPECT: EAST AND WEST COAST MAIN LINE (Britain 1991)

Railfilms. Volume 3. Film and sound
by Roger Nicholas. 'A4' Pacifics
and 'Princess Coronations' still running in the last years of steam in
the 1960s. Also many other survivors of the LNER and the LMS
from the days of the 'Big Four'.

VID, Sound, Colour, 50mins,
RFV

STEAM IN RETROSPECT: NORTH WEST AND MAINLINE STEAM (Britain 1988)

Railfilms. Film and sound by Roger
Nicholas. Volume Two. Crewe
works in 1963. Bulleid Pacifics from
Waterloo, with lineside shots at Surbiton, Weybridge, Woking and Salisbury. Sustained scene of Semley
Summit and Greene King. Lineside
sequence at Saltney Junction
(Chester); 'Crabs' at Edgeley Shed;
'8F' in action in Derbyshire; Manchester to Buxton line in 1965, with
LMS survivors and LMS '5XP' 4-6-0
No 5705 Seahorse.

VID, Sound, Colour, 50mins,
RFV

STEAM IN RETROSPECT: STANIER STEAM IN RETROSPECT (Britain 1988)

Railfilms. Film and sound by Roger
Nicholas. Volume One. Standard
and Super 8mm film of Crewe to
Carlisle in 1963. The accent is on
the locomotives of Sir William
Stanier – rebuilt 'Royal Scots',
'Jubilees', 'Duchesses' as well as
class '5s' and '8Fs'. The use of
actual sound recorded simultaneously is a bonus.

VID, Sound, Colour, 40mins,
RFV

STEAM IN SPAIN AND PORTUGAL (Britain 1983)

PM Films. Major steam lines,
including Salamanca and Pam-

plona; industrial systems; express services in Portugal; narrow gauge lines around Oporto and the Douro Valley.

VID, Sound, 58mins, PMV

🚂 🚂 🚂 🚂 🚂

STEAM IN THE WEST (Britain 1985)

Nick Lera collection. Part of the GWR 150th Celebrations. Footplate ride on GWR 'Castle' 4-6-0 No 7029 *Clun Castle* in Cornwall; GWR Dean 4-4-0 No 3440 *City of Truro*; two 'Castles' battling up the South Devon banks, plus various freight locomotives and branch line engines.

VID, Sound, Colour, 40mins, NLV

🚂 🚂 🚂 🚂 🚂

STEAM INTO SUMMER (Britain 1979)

BBC Television (South West). Produced by David Spires. Presented by Tom Salmon. An affectionate look at the Dart Valley Railway and the present-day working of the line from Buckfastleigh to Totnes. Locomotives featured include GWR '1400' 0-4-2T No 1420 *Bulliver* and GWR '1600' 0-6-0PT No 1638 *Dartington*.

16mm, Sound, Colour, 30mins, BBC TV

🚂 🚂 🚂 🚂 🚂

STEAM LOCOMOTIVES IN VIDEO (Britain 1983)

C & C Video. A tour in primitive video of six preserved steam railways in 1983.

VID, Sound, Colour, 55mins, CCV

🚂 🚂 🚂 🚂 🚂

STEAM NORTHBOUND (Britain 1985)

B & R Video Productions. A wide ranging collection of scenes notably with Caledonian Railway 4-2-2 No 123; Great North of Scotland Railway 4-4-0 No 49 *Gordon Highlander* as well as sundry 'A4s', 'Black Fives' and *George Stephenson* on the run from Fort William to Mallaig.

VID, Sound, Colour, 60mins, BRV

🚂 🚂 🚂 🚂 🚂

STEAM ON 35mm (Britain 1989)

Video 125. Produced by Peter Middleton. Written and presented by John Huntley. An assembly of professionally made stock shots from feature films to illustrate the story of steam railways on the 'Big Four' in the 1930s, 1940s and 1950s. It includes scenes from *Train of Events* (1949), *I See Ice* (1938), *The Long Arm* (1956) for the LMS; *Temptation Harbour* (1947), *Piccadilly Incident* (1946), *Frieda* (1947) and *School for Scoundrels* (1947) for the Southern; *Return to Yesterday* (1939), *The Proud Valley* (1939), *The Long Arm* (1956), and *The Good Companions* (1956) for the Great Western; and newsreels plus *The Lady Killers* (1955). There are 'Jubilees', 'A4' Pacifics, 'M7' tanks, 'Castles', 'R' tanks, GWR autotrains and many others.

VID, Sound, Part colour, 60mins, 125

🚂 🚂 🚂 🚂 🚂

STEAM AND THE DRAGON: THE LOCOMOTIVES OF NORTH EAST CHINA (Britain 1989)

Railfilms. Produced and directed by Nick Dodson. Music by Graham D'Ancey. Steam scenes, with many lineside shots of Beijing (The Forbidden City), Harbin Yard, Harbin, Wong Gang Bank, Harbin Shed, Nancha Shed, branch line to Wuyiling, main line to Jaimusi, Langxiang Narrow Gauge Timber railway, Harbin Forest Locomotive Works, Tieli timber trains, main line at Suiha, Tieli, Langxiang, Changchun, Dalien, Anshan, Fushun and Nenxi. Locomotives include Classes 'RM', 'SL', 'OJ', 'SY', 'YJ', 'S1', 'S160' and 'USATC'.

VID, Sound, Colour, 50mins, RFV

🚂 🚂 🚂 🚂 🚂

STEAM ON THE MID-HANTS (Britain 1989)

Online. Commentary by Jim Palm. Start of the preservation effort in 1973; arrival of *Errol Lonsdale* from the Longmoor Military Railway via the KESR; SR 'N' class No 31874 used to reopen the line in 1977 from Alresford and Ropley; locomotives of the Mid-Hants, including *Bodmin*, *Swanage*, ex-WD 2-10-0

Sturdee, LSWR Drummond 'T9' No 120, SR 'S15' class and BR Standard 4 No 76017; Santa Specials in 1988.

VID, Sound, Colour, 58mins, Online

🚂 🚂 🚂 🚂 🚂

STEAM ON THE NORFOLK AND WESTERN (USA c 1940-50)

Nine different Norfolk and Western locomotives of the 100, 600, 1200, 1300, 1400 and 2000 series, filmed at Roanoke, Virginia and Portsmouth, Ohio.

8mm, Silent, Colour, 4mins, Blackhawk

🚂 🚂 🚂 🚂 🚂

STEAM ON THE READING (USA 1930)

Scenes taken at Reading Terminal, the 10th and Green Street Enginehouse of the Reading in Philadelphia, along the main line to Valley Forge, on the Bethlehem Branch, at Stowe Yard in Pottstown, along the mainline south of Pottstown and on the Reading Seashore line.

8mm, Silent, 28mins, Blackhawk

🚂 🚂 🚂 🚂 🚂

STEAM ON THE SETTLE AND CARLISLE (Britain 1990)

The scenic 72-mile Settle and Carlisle line has taken on a new lease of life since its formal reprieve by British Rail in 1990. Many hundreds of miles of video tape and countless quantities of film must have been used to document this line since the days when, 20 years ago, it was first scheduled for closure. This, too, is one of many TV programmes; but it is a good representative example, being made by Border in Carlisle.

The history of the line; interviews with Julian Riddick (Chairman of the 'A4' Locomotive Society), George Gordon (retired Inspector), Alan Dugdale (signalman at Culgaith); views of the Dales National Park and the beautiful Eden Valley and a journey from Carlisle Citadel station to Ribblehead Viaduct are all featured. The motive power is provided mainly by LNER 'A4' 4-6-2 No 4498 *Sir Nigel Gresley*, with support from SR 'Lord Nelson' 4-6-0 No 850 *Lord*

Nelson, SR 'Merchant Navy' 4-6-2 No 35028 *Clan Line* and LMS 'Princess Coronation' 4-6-2 No 6229 *Duchess of Hamilton*.
VID, Sound, Colour, 42mins, Border

🚂 🚂 🚂 🚂 🚂

STEAM OVER SHERMAN (USA 1950s)

Steam Powered Video. Produced by WB Video Prods. From the Golden Archive series. A wide variety of 1950s studies including Big Boy 4-8-8-4s, Challenger 4-6-6-4s, 2-8-8-0s, 4-12-2s and 4-8-4s (what a lot of wheels!). Also Cheyenne Yard and Engine Shed. From 16mm silent film with dubbed sound.
VID, Sound, Colour, 52mins, SPV

🚂 🚂 🚂 🚂 🚂

STEAM POWER (Britain 1983)

B & R Video Productions. Mainline preserved steam, with *King George V* much in evidence.
VID, Sound, Colour, 59mins, BRV

🚂 🚂 🚂 🚂 🚂

STEAM POWERED VIDEO

This video company has specialised in the release of many American railway videos that have proliferated in the past 10 years. A vast amount of archive film has emerged in the United States over this period, backed by freshly produced videos on aspects of the current preservation scene. A valuable service has been created which avoids the complex process of trying to locate the many American independent video makers like Herron, Mark 1, Green Frog, Video Rails and countless others. Their list is extensive. In addition to titles mentioned in the general alphabetical sequence it includes:

Alcos, Iron Ore and More (USA 1988)

The Alco pioneer diesels in the Upper Peninsula of the Michigan zone.
Sound, Colour, 60mins

Allegheny Rails (USA 1959) Volume 1.

The Baltimore & Ohio in steam days. Shot on 8mm.
Sound, Colour, 60mins

Allegheny Rails (USA 1958) Volume 2

Steam action on Western Maryland. Shot on 8mm.
Sound, Colour, 60mins

America on Rails (USA 1934-60)

A kaleidoscope (known as the 'Complete Collection') of inter-urban services and all forms of steam, diesel and electric, including pre-war items like the Burlington Zephyr.
Sound, Mainly colour, 85mins

Articulated 3985 V 1218 (USA 1989)

Two preserved articulated Mallet-type locomotives.
Sound, Colour, 60mins

Assault on Snow (USA 1985)

Union Pacific rotary snowplough in action and F7s battling through snow.
Sound, Colour, 62mins

The Battle up Sherman Hill (USA 1955-90)

Union Pacific operations with Big Boys, Gas Turbines, Centennials and Super Cab SD60s.
Sound, Colour, 60mins

The Birth of a Locomotive (USA 1989)

Drawing board to finished locomotive at General Motor's Canadian Centre at London, Ontario.
Sound, Colour, 38mins

Cab Ride: Harrisburg to Huntingdon (USA 1988)

A trip on the Pennsylvania Railroad to Rockville Bridge, Lewistown and to Mount Union.
Sound, Colour, 100mins

Cab Ride: Huntingdon to Johnstown (USA 1988)

A trip on the Pennsylvania Railroad to Tyrone, Altoona and the Horseshoe Curve.
Sound, Colour, 100mins

California Limiteds (USA 1920-30)

The Atchison, Topeka & Santa Fe and the Southern Pacific; the scenes in the 1920s, when these were the two main routes to Hollywood.
Sound, 33mins

California Zephyr (USA 1965)

A special diesel express in the twilight of American crack railroads. Very soon, it would be all over.
Sound, Colour, 70mins

Chama Turn: Cumbres Pass Route (USA 1958)

3ft narrow gauge freight line from Chama to Alamosa.
Sound, Colour, 60mins

Classic Collectors Volume 1 (USA 1941)

Southern Pacific 'Daylight' Expresses and Cab forward freights.
Sound, Colour, 30mins

Classic Collectors Volume 2 (USA 1947)

Union Pacific 'Big Boys' in action.
Sound, Colour, 30mins

Classic Collectors Volume 3 (USA 1945-85)

Southern Pacific steam in the 'Golden Age'.
Sound, Colour, 30mins

Diesels 86 (USA 1986)

Diesel action, with yard shunting and run-pasts.
Sound, Colour, 45mins

Diesels on the Union Pacific (USA 1983-84)

Diesel action at Sherman Hill including Centennials.
Sound, Colour, 120mins

Donner Pass (USA 1989)

The Sierra Mountains section of the Southern Pacific with diesels of up to 40,000 hp trains climbing the gradients. A section often used in Hollywood movies.
Sound, Colour, 60mins

The East Broad Top (USA 1950-1970)

3ft narrow gauge coal traffic line in Pennsylvania.
Sound, Colour, 120mins

First Generation Diesels (USA 1988)

A late hunt for old diesels built by EMD, ALCO and LIMA, intercut with earlier archive film. 'A Search for Survivors' (sub-title).
Sound, Colour, 52mins

A Forties Memory (USA 1940s)

The Denver & Rio Grande Railroad in the 1940s including narrow gauge.

Sound,   Colour,   23mins

Forty-Four Years of the 8444 (USA 1946-90)

A history of preserved Union Pacific 4-8-4 No 8444.

Sound,   Colour,   60mins

Frisco 1522 (USA 1989)

Preserved steam locomotive from the Southern Pacific.

Sound,   Colour,   70mins

The Glory Machines (USA 1928-52) Volume One.

A kaliedoscope of American steam.

Sound,   Mainly Colour,   64mins

The Glory Machines (USA 1944-62) Volume 2

Mallets on the Norfolk & Western; articulated locomotives on the Baltimore & Ohio; Shays on lumber camp railways.

Sound,   72mins

The Glory Machines (USA 1935-58) Volume 3

Mid   Western   scenes,   with Hiawathas to Blue Goose, the Pennsylvania to Rock Island etc

Sound,   Mainly colour,   47mins

The Glory Machines (USA 1940s) Volume 4

Southern Pacific at Tucson, Arizona;   the   Pennsylvania,   the Wabash, and the Frisco.

Sound,   Colour,   37mins

Lackawanna Legacy (USA 1990).

The Wickerliner EMU story. A history and recent scenes.

Sound,   Colour,   60mins

Last Breath of the Fire (USA 1959)

A day with a Mikado on freight on the GTW.

Sound,   Colour,   30mins

Last Days of the Newfoundland Railway (USA 1975)

The end of a narrow gauge diesel operated system in Canada.

Sound,   Colour,   35mins

CP Rails Rogers (USA 1989)

18,000 hp, six-engine bankers ('pushers' in Canada) up Rogers Pass on the Canadian Pacific.

Sound,   Colour,   55mins

Last Steamers of the Colorado and Southern (USA 1950s)

Heavy steam locomotives at work.

Sound,   Colour,   52mins

Life Begins at Forty (USA 1986)

A study of NKP Berk No 765 in action. Known as the 'Greyhound with the shotgun exhaust'.

Sound,   Colour,   60mins

The Magnificent GG1 (USA 1990)

A celebration of the preservation of the Pennsylvania GG1 8000 hp electric locomotive.

Sound,   Colour,   60mins

Manitoba Steam (1950s)

Archive steam in Canada in the 1950s.

Sound,   Colour,   30mins

Milwaukee's Mighty Electrics (USA 1989)

The Little Joes and Boxcabs in their last years.

Sound,   Colour,   36mins

Montage Series No 1 (USA 1988)

Video magazine featuring L&N 152, NKP 765 and CP 2317.

Sound,   Colour,   58mins

Montage Series No 2 (USA 1989)

Video Magazine featuring Blue Mountain and Reading, C & NW 1385, N & W J 611, and NKP 765.

Sound,   Colour,   60mins

Montage Series No 3 (USA 1989)

Video magazine featuring N & WA 1218, Pennsylvania K4 1361, the Gettysburg Railroad and the American Steamtown.

Sound,   Colour,   60mins

Norfolk and Western Class A 1218 (USA 1987)

One of the last great classic American locomotives from the last great stronghold of steam.

Sound,   Colour,   60mins

Pennsylvania Glory Volume 1 (USA 1950-58)

A basic 1950s collection including GG1s,   Camelbacks,   K4s, Decapods, Mountains and the Atmospheric.

Sound,   Colour,   46mins

Pennsylvania Glory Volume 2 (USA 1950s)

Known to some as the 'Standard Railroad of the World' (what price the Premier Line'!), this video looks at some of the classic sites including Altoona, Rockville, Sandusky and the famous Horseshoe Curve where the *Royal Scot* was proudly seen in 1933.

Sound,   Colour,   43mins,

Pocahontas Glory Volume 1 (USA 1946-67)

Scenes   at   Columbus,   Ohio; Portsmouth   and   Kenova   with 2-6-6-4 Malletts of the A, J and Y class.

Sound,   Colour,   42mins

Pocahontas Glory Volume 2 (USA 1950-58)

Norfolk and Western steam in the 1950s.

Sound,   Colour,   48mins

Pocahontas Glory Volume 3 (USA1950-58)

Steam scenes along the Shenandoah.

Sound,   Colour,   48mins

Pocahontas Glory Volume 4 (USA 1950-57)

Heavy coal movements on the Tipple to Tidewater route.

Sound,   Colour,   42mins

Railfanning the Silverton (USA 1985)

A detailed study of the Silverton Line, so frequently used in feature films. A narrow gauge branch of the Denver & Rio Grande Western Railroad, it's a sort of American Wild West version of the Ffestiniog.

Sound,   Colour,   110mins

Rails to Steel City (1990)

The surviving railways of the Pittsburg area.

Sound,   Colour,   60mins

Reflections of American Railroads (USA 1935-66)

Golden Age of steam with Inter-urbans and express services.

Sound, Part Colour, 78mins

FT 103, The Diesel that Revolutionized American Railroading (USA 1990)

Very detailed record of First Generation diesels in America plus the restoration of FT 103.

Sound, Colour, 115mins

Ride the Sandy River Railroad (USA 1935)

Maine 2ft narrow gauge line.

Silent, 30mins

Rio Grande of the Rockies (USA 1950s)

The Tennessee Pass with 2-8-8-2 bankers to the Monarch branch on the narrow gauge system.

Sound, Colour, 60mins

The Rio Grande Today (USA 1982-85)

Diesel-operated railways in the Great Rocky Mountains, the Tennessee Pass and at Moffat.

The Rock Island Railroad (USA 1950-70)

Classic diesel operations of the early days plus Southern Pacific 4501 at Chicago.

Sound, Colour, 60mins

Rotary on the Rio Grande Narrow Gauge (USA 1975-76)

Snow scenes at Cumbres and Toltec near Chama.

Sound, Colour, 70mins

Saluda Mountain (USA 1950s-70s)

America's steepest climb for three miles; a sort of USA version of the Long Drag. Its history and scenes over the years with steam but mainly diesel power.

Sound, Colour, 75mins

A Salute to Soldier Summit (USA 1950s)

Diesel on the Denver & Rio Grande Railroad at Utah.

Sound, Colour, 60mins

Santa Fe Odyssey (USA 1950s-80s) Volume 1.

Very detailed record of diesel operations over 30 years from 1950 to 1980 on the ATSF.

Sound, Colour, 126mins

Santa Fe Odyssey (USA 1970s)

Illinois to California over a period of 23 days in the late 1970s. Volume 2.

Sound, Colour, 108mins

Santa Fe's Seligman Sub and New Mexico Main (USA 1980s)

Red, silver and yellow Warbonnets and action in a diesel-orientated system.

Sound, Colour, 120mins

Slim Rails Through the San Juans (USA 1990)

Cumbres & Toltec narrow gauge scenic railroad. The American Vale of Rheidol?

Sound, Colour, 51mins

Snowplows (USA 1984)

Action on Canadian National with class F7s.

Sound, Colour, 55mins

St Louis 1990 Steam Spectacular (USA 1990)

Cotton Belt 819, UP 844, Frisco 1522, N&W 1218 and loco mounted mini cam.

Sound, Colour, 120 mins

Steam in the 1950s (USA 1950s)

From Chicago to the Blue Ridge Mountains of Virginia (sounds like Laurel and Hardy).

Sound, Colour, 41mins

Steam Memories of Ontario, Canada (Canada 1950s)

Four loco men recount their experiences, backed by archive film.

Sound, Colour, 60mins

Steam Over Sherman (USA 1950s)

Union Pacific steam in the 1950s with Big Boys, Challengers, 4-12-2s and early diesels.

Sound, Colour, 52mins

Steamfest 1990 (USA 1990).

SP & S 700, SP4449 and GW 51.

Sound, Colour, 120mins

Steaming to LA (USA 1989)

SP4449 and UP 8444 in the Los Angeles area and climbing Cajon Pass.

Sound, Colour, 105mins

Super Cabs and Steam (USA 1991)

Union Pacific diesel and steam.

Sound, Colour, 88mins

Susquehanna Spectacular (USA 1990)

Documentary on the classic 'Susie Q'.

Sound, Colour, 107mins

Tehachapi (USA 1983-84)

Atchison, Topeka & Santa Fe and Southern Pacific diesel-hauled trains.

Sound, Colour, 120mins

Twilight of the Rio Grande Trilogy (USA 1950s)

Material on the Denver & Rio Grande Railroad and its narrow gauge branches.

Sound, Colour, 85mins

Union Pacific Last Steam Giants: Heavy Freight (USA 1958-90)

Big Boys, Challengers, 800s plus preserved 3985 on freight train.

Sound, Colour, 80mins

Cajon Pass/Tehachapi Loop (USA 1986)

Diesel-hauled trains in the Cajon Pass and the Tehachapi Loop.

Sound, Colour, 120mins

Western Maryland (USA 1950s)

Last days of First and Second generation diesels.

Sound, Colour, 70mins

Wheels of Steel (USA 1967)

Norfolk and Western 1218. Powerful steam action.

Sound, 60mins

Steam Powered Video has also issued tapes on British railways:

The Bluebell Railway (Britain 1989)

A study of the preserved railway.

Sound, Colour, 28mins

The Last Deglehn (Britain 1987)

75th Anniversary study of a famous locomotive.

Sound, Colour, 20mins

Romney Hythe & Dymchurch Railway (Britain 1984)

Sub-title: 'The Biggest Little Railway in the World'.

Sound, Colour, 23mins

Upminster Open Day (Britain 1990)

Special Metropolitan and Underground show, with Metropolitan 'E' 0-4-4T No 1 (until lately L44).

Sound, Colour, 31mins

Winchfield 150 (Britain 1988)

Anniversary rail show of the London to Basingstoke line.

Sound, Colour, 25mins

SPV also issue films on railway modelling covering a series of American layouts and technical instruction on Weathering, Airbrushing and building Scenery for railway models.

THE STEAM RAILWAY (Britain 1983)

Video Workshop. A jigsaw of sections from many films. Professional films with commentary by Alvar Liddel and a few pieces of W A Camwell's films.

VID, Sound, 50mins, Video Workshop

STEAM SAFARI (Britain 1986)

Transport Video Publishing. South African steam, including the De Aar-Kimberley line, the Knysa branch and various narrow gauge steam operations.

VID, Sound, Colour, 45mins, TVP

STEAM SPECIAL: THE KEIGHLEY & WORTH VALLEY RAILWAY (Britain 1988)

RV Television. Narrated by Paul Brown. Features 'Jinty' No 47279, USA Class S160 2-8-0 No 5820, Haydock Foundry 0-6-0WT

Bellerophon, GWR Pannier Tank No 7752, Manchester Ship Canal 0-6-0 Side Tank No-31 *Hamburg*, SR USA 0-6-0T No 72, diesel-electric 0-6-0 No D0226, and Class 25 No 25059. There are also scenes of Oakworth and Damens stations.

VID, Sound, Colour, 60mins, RVV

STEAM SPECIAL: GMUND TO GROS GERUNGS (Britain 1986)

RV Television. Energth type 0-8-4 articulated locomotives haul special trains on the border of Czechoslovakia and Austria to Gmund. 43km long line on 760mm gauge track from Gros Gerungs.

VID, Sound, Colour, 60mins, RVV

STEAM SPECIAL: THE BRIENZ ROTHORN BAHN (Britian 1988)

RV Television. A famous mountain railway, steam operated on this occasion, up gradients of 1 in 4 to 7,700ft above sea level with views of the Bernese Oberland.

VID, Sound, Colour, 60mins, RVV

STEAM SUNDAY (Britain 1990)

Falkman Television for Channel Four. An outside broadcast, with film inserts, from the Bluebell Railway, to open the Channel Four *Going Loco* series. Presented by Mike Read, with Joe Brown, Samantha Brown, Miles Kington and Pete Waterman; historical material from Huntley Archives. Music by Instant Sunshine. An insert paid a visit to the Keighley & Worth Valley Railway. In the middle of the Bluebell OB, with views of various preserved locomotives, the skies opened up and the entire production was nearly washed away! There was much debate afterwards as to how successful this programme had been in introducing the world of preservation to a wider audience.

VID, Sound, Colour, 46mins, Falkman

STEAM SURVIVORS (Britain 1985)

Transport Video Publishing. Steam in action in Turkey, including the Izmir Suburbans, the Skyliners and the Burdur system. Filmed in 1981-86.

VID, Sound, Colour, 50mins, TVP

STEAM THROUGH THE GOLDEN VALLEY (Britain 1985)

Railfilms. Produced by John Wildy. From the *Lineside View* series. Part of the GWR 150 Celebrations, this tape was unusual in having no commentary or sub-titles but inviting the viewer to read off a set of numbered notes, giving the chronological progress of filming days in one single month. John Wildy explained the idea:

'1985 was the year in which railway enthusiasts celebrated the 150th Anniversary of the incorporation of the Great Western Railway. Of all the events organised for the celebrations the most successful must surely have been the running of 26 steam-hauled trains from Swindon to Gloucester and back using 'Chocolate and Cream' MK 1 coaches. Strong winds and heavy rain were a feature of one of the wettest Augusts on record and the fear of getting the recording equipment wet severely restricted the choice of locations used.

'Both the use of commentary and sub-titles were tried and discarded in favour of the use of a printed sheet with corresponding numbers appearing on the screen at each change of location.'

It started like this:

1, 6 August *Hagley Hall* approaching Standish Junction with the 18.50 departure from Gloucester to Swindon.

2, 7 August *Hagley Hall* at Ryeford with the morning departure, from Swindon.

In all, 47 Numbers were used and the sights included: *Hinton Manor*, *Drysllwyn Castle*, *Hagley Hall*, *Clun Castle*, *King George V* and *City of Truro*. From the *Lineside View* series.

VID, Sound, Colour, 47mins, RFV

STEAM TO MALLAIG (Britain 1985)

Video 125. Driver's Eye View. Produced by Peter Middleton. Commentary by Anton Rogers. The 42-mile 'Road to the Isles' runs through some of the most magnificent scenery in Britain. This *Driver's Eye View* follows Class 5 locomotive *George Stephenson* from Fort William along the shores of Loch Eil over the famous Glenfinnan Viaduct to Lochailort; then across Keppoch Moss to the shores of the Atlantic at Mallaig.

'Filmed on video to full broadcast standard, the quality of picture is virtually faultless; this whole tape is good enough to be a television programme. The commentary by Anton Rogers is some of the best yet heard. It is extremely informative, knowledgable and historically packed with facts. This again has taken much research and perfectly matches the excellence of the filming.' (MJS)

VID, Sound, Colour, 56mins, 125

STEAM TO REMEMBER (Britain 1983)

B & R Video Productions. A mixed assembly, mainly of amateur 8mm material, of pre-1968 steam; but not much before 1960.

VID, Sound, Colour, 60mins, BRV

STEAM TO THE BORDERS (Britain 1989)

Railfilms. Produced by Nick Dodson. Steam parade at Reisa. Narrow gauge industrial lines. Lineside shots including Saxon Meyer 0-4-4T at Mugeln and street running at Bad Doberan. A visit to East Germany before the Wall came down.

VID, Sound, Colour, 45mins, RFV

STEAM TOURS OF THE EARLY SEVENTIES (Britain 1983)

Rail Video. GWR No 6000 *King George V* from Newport to Shrewsbury (1972); LNER 'V2' 2-6-2 No 4771 *Green Arrow* and LNER

'A4' 4-6-2 No 4498 *Sir Nigel Gresley* from Tyseley to Didcot and back (1973) and SR 'Merchant Navy' 4-6-2 No 35028 *Clan Line* from Hereford to Chester, with *King George V* (1975).

VID, Sound, Colour, 60mins, RVO

A STEAM TRAIN PASSES (Australia 1974)

Australian Film Board. Produced by Anthony Buckley. Directed by David Haythomwaite. Music by George Dreyfuss. Archive film from a newsreel of 1943 introduces a new steam train service called the 'A38' on its first run out of Sydney. This film continues with a reconstruction of this journey, from its preparation in the engine sheds to life on the footplate, track and local stations. Now recognised as one of the truly great evocations of the steam era. Presented by Jack Sparkes, ex-fireman/driver of locomotive No 3801.

35/16/VID, Sound, Colour, 20mins, AFB/HA/VID

STEAM VIEW

A Steam video magazine. 'Steam View offers comprehensive coverage of the steam scene in the UK, with features looking at topical aspects of steam operations, both on British Railways and on the preserved lines. In addition, archive film is regularly included of steam at work prior to August 1968.' (*Transport Video Publishing*). During the years that it has been issued, it has covered many subjects including:

Regal Steam: A 'Princess', a 'Duke' and a 'Duchess'
Osprey in Scotland: Perth-Dundee-Forth Bridge
East Somerset Railway: LNER 'J72' 0-6-0 No 69023; plus *King Edward I*.
Settle and Carlisle Railway
Bluebell Extension
Bescot Open Day
Dart Valley Anniversary
'A4s' in the 1930s and 1960s
Winter Steam in the South East: Mid Hants, KESR and Bluebell
Steam at Marylebone
Nene Valley Railway

Keighley & Worth Valley Railway
Great Central Railway
Industrial Railways of the North East
Steam Spectacle of 1989
Santa Specials on the Mid-Hants Railway
North Yorkshire Moors Gala
Edinburgh Suburban Steam Specials
North Wales Coast Steam
The Great Marquess Story
Chesham Branch Centenary
The Swanage Railway
Hartlepool Open Day
Gwili Railway
West Somerset Railway
Flying Scotsman in Australia
Llangollen Railway
Didcot Diary
Profile of Scottish Steam
Winter Steam 1988: Keighley & Worth Valley, Severn Valley and Bluebell Railway
1988 Settle & Carlisle Report
Great Western Branch Freight
Steam in the West Highlands
Lizzy on the Main Line (LMS 'Princess' 4-6-2 No 6201 *Princess Elizabeth*)
Mallard on the Settle & Carlisle Railway
City of Wells on the Scarborough line
Port Line on the Bluebell Railway

STEAMING BACK TO MARYLEBONE (Britain 1985-88)

Online. Produced by Wilf Watters. Commentary by David Coleman. Steam in the 1960s from Marylebone to Harrow, Brackley, Nottingham etc., mainly 'Black Fives'; *Sir Nigel Gresley* at Marylebone in 1985 with a Post Office promotion; *Sir Nigel Gresley*, *Clan Line*, *Duchess of Hamilton*, *Flying Scotsman*, *Sir Lamiel*, *Green Arrow*, *Black Five* and *Mallard*, all at Marylebone; journeys to Stratford. Originally issued in 1985; revised version issued in 1988.

VID, Sound, Part colour, 60mins, Online

STEAMING ON (Britain 1987)

British Railways Board. An assembly of three British Transport Films including, *The Driving Force* (1966), *Rail 150* (1975) and *This is York*

(1953). See individual items for details of films.

VID, Sound, Part-Colour, 57mins, BTF/MSD

STEAMPIPES

Railway preservation has stimulated interest in shows of films specifically about aspects of railway working, made by the Railways themselves, by independent bodies or often by amateurs who simply wished to place on record the railway activities that interested them. Typical of this type of film show is *Steampipes*, an annual event held in London each December.

Steampipes arose from quite humble origins unconnected with the cinema. In 1966 the first of a series of annual joint meetings took place between the members of the London groups of the three premier Welsh narrow gauge railway societies – the Ffestiniog, the Talyllyn and the Welshpool & Llanfair. In the years 1972 and 1973, through the agency of FRS member Ross Gregory, full length feature films with a railway theme, such as *Train of Events* and *Titfield Thunderbolt*, were shown at these meetings, which were held at the Botany Theatre of University College. The success of these two meetings prompted John Smallwood, a committee member of the Cinema Organ Society as well as the TRPS, to suggest the exploitation of the combined interest of many people in both steam engines and the pipe organ. And so for the 1974 show a move was made to the New Gallery in Regent Street, a West End cinema still with its original 1925 Wurlitzer organ, but no longer in regular public use. Here the first *Steampipes* took shape, although the title 'Steampipes' was not adopted until the third show.

The format decided upon comprised of a selection of short films and clips: a mixture of sound and silent, colour and black-and-white, archival and more up-to-date, with the silents accompanied by the Wurlitzer organ in traditional style. The main theme of the show would of course be the traditional steam railway, but at this larger theatre a wider public appeal would be needed. Supporting comedies and cartoons were therefore included in the programme – the silents providing more scope for the organist, who also gave a couple of short solo selections. The date was fixed for Thursday 12 December, with the late David Hamilton as organist and Ross Gregory as compere. The Christmas lights in Regent Street added to the sense of occasion, and an audience of around 900 gave the show an enthusiastic reception to the delight and relief of the organisers.

This was the prelude to an event held each December ever since, except for one year when the New Gallery ceiling fell in, enabling it to be said that the previous year's show brought the house down! Running *Steampipes* is almost a continuous process: early spring each year sees the start of the preparations for the following December. The formula remains essentially the same. Films shown have ranged from some of the earliest known sequences of trains to the latest BR releases, from the main line to branch line backwaters, and from many countries. Of course the narrow gauge has not been forgotten, and not just in preservation: rare clips of prewar narrow gauge have been shown. Supporting items have ranged from Buster Keaton and the Marx Brothers to Tom and Jerry: even those dreaded St Trinian's girls once got in on the act!

After the first show Welshpool & Llanfair member and radio broadcaster Paul Barnes took over as compere until he moved to Anglia Television; he was succeeded by Jim Palm, the compiler and presenter of the *Rail* programme heard on local radio. Organists appearing at *Steampipes* have included Douglas Reeve, Ena Baga, William Davies, Nigel Ogden and many other famous names. Indeed, it was at the New Gallery organ at a *Steampipes* event that Miss Baga recorded the sound track for a new film of the narrow gauge *The Fathew Flyer*. And there is one name that must not be forgotten: *Steampipes* film adviser and projectionist Alan Willmott, formerly of British Transport Films, now Windjammer Films.

STEEL RIDE (Britain 1954)

United Steel Company. The manufacture of locomotive wheels, tyres and springs.

16mm, Sound, 32mins, USC

THE STING (USA 1973)

Universal. Produced by Richard Zanuck and David Brown. Directed by George Roy Hill. With Paul Newman, Robert Redford, Robert Shaw, Charles Durning, Ray Walston and Eileen Brennan. In the 1920s Chicago, two con men stage an elaborate revenge on a big time gangster who caused the death of a friend. 'A visually claustrophobic, mechanically plotted movie that's meant to be a roguishly charming entertainment.' (*New Yorker*) 'The menacing Shaw regularly plays a select game of poker – which he always wins – on board a train. All this to the music of Scott Joplin.' (Tony Bilbow) The railway is an old bit of the Long Island Railroad; old enough to give the true feel of the 1920s. But most of the action is in the studio.

35mm, Sound, Colour, 129mins, Universal

STIRLING NO 1 (Britain 1938)

A film by Kenneth Leech. A record in both black-and-white and rare early colour of outings made by Patrick Stirling's Great Northern 4-2-2- No 1 of 1870. This was probably the first time that a preserved steam locomotive ever ran in service on mainline tracks.

Kenneth Leech has provided one of the earliest of all photographer's notes on chasing locomotives and finding suitable sites for both still and cine-photography.

16mm, Silent, Part-colour, 12mins, Leech/Garraway/HA

STOCKER'S COPPER (Britain 1991)

Channel 4 TV. Directed by Jack Gold. With Bryan Marshall and Jane Lapotaire. Reconstruction of 1913 Cornish Tin Mine strike. Includes a GWR train on a branch line, using GWR '45XX' 2-6-2T No 4555 and GWR autotrain stock on the Dart Valley Railway.

TV, Sound, Colour, 96mins, C4TV

STOP PRESS GIRL (Britain 1949)

Aquila production. Directed by Michael Barry. With Sally Ann Howes and Gordon Jackson. Comedy about a young girl possessing the power of stopping all types of machinery; includes various railway scenes.

35mm, Sound, 77mins, Aquila

THE STORY OF DR WASSELL (USA 1943)

A Paramount Picture. Directed by Cecil B De Mille. With Gary Cooper. Includes scenes of steam-hauled hospital train in Java, using revamped American locomotive and stock superimposed on a jungle background.

35mm, Sound, 114mins, Paramount

STORY OF THE MALLARD (Britain 1988)

(Correct title: MALLARD: The DRAKE'S PROGRESS)

In this programme from Anglia Television, John Huntley recounts the story of Sir Nigel Gresley's famous locomotive which broke the speed record in 1938, reaching 126mph in a test run over a section of the former LNER East Coast main line near Little Bytham. The history of the *Mallard* is told from its launch in 1938 to its subsequent preservation after its withdrawal in 1963 and its eventual return to steam. The *Story of The Mallard* combines original stills of the locomotive's record-breaking run with vibrant footage shot at the time of her 50th anniversary rerun in 1988, and includes a visit to her home at York Railway Museum.

16mm/VID, Sound, Colour, 22mins, Anglia/HA/VID

STORY OF THE WHEEL (Britain 1934)

GPO Film Unit. The film ends with views of a steam train.

35/16mm, Sound and Silent, 12mins, Post Office

STRANGERS ON A TRAIN (USA 1951)

Warners. Produced and directed by Alfred Hitchcock. With Farley Granger, Robert Walker, Ruth Roman, Leo G Carroll, Patricia Hitchcock and Marion Lorne. The strangers meet on a train and discuss solving each other's problems by swapping murders. The one with the motive will then be able to have a perfect alibi. One then carries out the crime. Typical dialogue: 'Some people are better off dead – like your wife and my father, for instance.' 'You may not take it seriously but you certainly don't have time to think about much else.' (Richard Mallett) The train is provided by shots of the New York Central but only a few scenes are real. All the interiors of the club car and various parts of the train interior are in the Hollywood studio.

35mm, Sound, 101mins, Warner

STRANRAER-LARNE (Britain 1937)

LMS film. Brief scenes of the Stranraer terminus and the LMS ship TS *Princess Mary*.

16mm, Silent, 3mins, HA

STRATFORD-UPON-AVON AND MIDLAND JUNCTION RAILWAY (Britain 1952)

Ettington station and an LMS '3F' 0-6-0 arriving on a two-coach train. Made by Patrick Whitehouse.

16mm/VID, Silent, 8mins, NRM/VID

STREAMLINE EXPRESS (USA 1936)

A Mascot Picture. Produced by Republic Pictures. Directed by Leonard Fields. With Victor Jory, Evelyn Venables, Esther Ralston, Ralph Forbes, Sidney Blackmer,

Eric O'Brien Moore, Vince Barret and Clay Clement.

Patricia Wallis, Broadway stage star, runs out on her show in a temperamental fling, deciding to marry Freddy Arnold, scion of a wealthy family. Jimmy Hart, producer of the show and Patricia's manager, runs after the girl, telling the stage manager he will only be a minute. He does not catch Patricia, however, until she has boarded a train leaving on its inaugural run to the coast. Jimmy, not possessing a ticket, is not allowed aboard. By bribing a steward, however, he persuades the man to change places with him, hoping that once aboard he will be able to make Patricia return to the show.

His expectations are not realised, however, and he becomes involved in a theft. There are many people aboard the express, and, by the scheming of one of them, he is accused of stealing a valuable diamond pendant. Patricia denies knowing him at first, but later relents and tells the investigators that he is a well-known Broadway producer.

The mystery is finally cleared up, Patricia discovering that she loves Jimmy and therefore, deciding to return to the show in New York.

'Six experts, working day and night, studied plans to create a train of the future, and found it was necessary to build a model which would anticipate the rail transportation of the future,' said the publicity leaflet when this film first appeared.

'They worked upon the idea that eventually railroad tracks would have to be widened so that travelling cars would give greater freedom of movement to the public.

'Their next innovation was to arrange a double-decker train, with stairs leading up to a top deck which was in the middle of an observation platform. The interior, more than double the width of the average train of today, contained within it a barbers shop, beauty parlour, pool hall, small dance floor and other forms of recreation for the passengers. A special telegraph station could actually be installed in such a train so that passengers might send wires whilst the train was in motion.

'Some railroad engineers visited the studios, saw the shining copper model on the process stage – found it entirely practical and estimated that it could attain a speed of 150mph.'

Be that as it may, the film has a certain minor fascination in that it did relate to developments then taking place in America and the model is interesting to compare with trains that eventually did achieve a speed of 150mph.

35/16mm, Sound, 71mins, Republic/HA

🚂 🚂 🚂

STREAMLINED ENGINE KING HENRY VII (Britain 1936)

British Paramount News. Record of GWR 4-6-0 No 6014 *King Henry VII* at Swindon works.

16mm, Sound, 3mins, BFI

🚂 🚂 🚂 🚂 🚂

STRUGGLE WILL END TOMORROW (Czechoslovakia 1953)

Czechoslovak Films. The building of the Slovakian railway in the 1930s.

35/16mm, Sound, 80mins, Plato

🚂 🚂 🚂 🚂 🚂

STUDY IN STEEL (Britain 1937)

LMS Film. Made by Commerical and Educational Films Department, Topical Press Agency. The design and construction of the LMS 'Princess Royal' 4-6-2 No 6207 *Princess Arthur of Connaught* at Crewe works. This is a shortened but sound version of the silent film *6207: A study in Steel*.

35mm/VID, Sound, 42mins, BTF/TVP

🚂 🚂 🚂 🚂 🚂

THE SUBURBANITE (USA 1904)

American Mutascope and Biograph Company. A story of early commuting into New York. Includes scenes on the New Jersey Central Railroad.

35mm, Silent, 8mins, Lost

🚂 🚂 🚂 🚂 🚂

SUBWAY (France 1985)

Gaumont. Directed by Luc Bresson. With Isabelle Adjani and Richard Bohringer. The hero and the villains fight it out, mainly on extensive night location shooting on the Paris Metro.

35mm, Sound, Colour, 104 mins, Gaumont

🚂 🚂 🚂

SUBWAY (Britain 1992)

BBC Television: First Tuesday series. Documentary about a New York Cop John Frawley who hunts down crooks, drug dealers and gun men on the New York Subway. The area covered is from Wall Street to the Bronx, the world's busiest underground railway. The cars shown are gleaming glass and aluminium, without graffiti, some in dark brown livery; express and local services are featured. The New York Subway is a third-rail system, still with long elevated sections, especially in the suburbs. Four people a week commit suicide and there are 20 murders a year on 'Subway City'.

VID, Sound, Colour, 25mins, BBC Television (First transmitted on 4 February 1992)

🚂 🚂 🚂 🚂 🚂

SULLIVAN'S TRAVELS (USA 1942)

A Paramount picture. Directed by Preston Sturges. With Joel McCrea and Veronica Lake. Comedy melodrama with social comment. Much of the action takes place on freight trains and includes some good action shots of steam locomotives on American railroads.

35mm, Sound, 91mins, Paramount

🚂 🚂 🚂

SUNDAY WITH A TRAIN SET (Britain 1975)

Anglia Television. A visit to the Leighton Buzzard Narrow Gauge Railway featuring the locomotive of 1921 from India, Baguley 0-4-0T *Rishra*. Produced and directed by David Kenten. Presented by Dick Joice.

16mm, Sound, Colour, 27mins, Anglia

🚂 🚂 🚂 🚂 🚂

THE SUNDOWNERS (Britain/Australia 1960)

Warner Bros. Produced by Gerry Blatner. Directed by Fred Zinneman. With Robert Mitchum, Deborah Kerr, Glynis Johns and Peter Ustinov.
Includes 1920s steam-hauled train marked 'Flinders' shot on preserved railway in Queensland

35mm, Sound, Colour, 133mins, Warner

🚂

SUNDRY QUESTIONS (Britain 1967)

Produced by British Transport Films. 'Every year an enormous amount of sundries traffic is handled in our depots. But there is a great deal of capacity for even more. A new specialist organisation has been set up – the British Rail Sundries Division – a lot of people, staff as well as customers, want to know how it's going to work. Huw Thomas asks questions and its first General Manager, R L E Lawrence, gives the answers.'

35/16mm, Sound, 11mins, BTF

🚂 🚂 🚂 🚂 🚂

SURREY RAMBLER RAIL TOUR (Britain 1966)

SCTS. A trip from Victoria, over Grosvenor Bridge, to Balham Junction, Redhill, Guildford, Woking, Latchmere Junction, Kensington Olympia, Lillie Bridge Depot, West Brompton, Epsom Downs, West Croydon, Sutton, Wimbledon and Victoria. Motive power includes SR 'Merchant Navy' 4-6-2 No 35027 *Port Line*, BR '4' 2-6-4T No 80154 (last locomotive to be built at Brighton, 1957) and SR 'Battle of Britain' 4-6-2 No 34089 *602 Squadron*.

16mm, Silent, 6mins, HA/SCTS

🚂 🚂 🚂 🚂 🚂

SUTCLIFFE VIDEO see DAVID SUTCLIFFE COLLECTION

SWINDON: ALL CHANGE (Britain 1985)

HTV West. Produced and directed by Terry Miller. A tribute to the skills of the craftsmen who built the locomotives and stock for the Great Western Railway at Swindon Works. The plant closed in March 1986 and this film explores the history of the works through archive film and interviews with people like Stan Tinklin from Bristol who has driven both steam and high-speed diesels and lectured on railway safety. In 1985 he took the controls of a steam train for the first time again after many years when he drove *King George V* at the start of the GWR 150th Anniversary celebrations. Joyce Murgatroyd, daughter of a Swindon engineer, recalls the times when the entire Swindon workforce and their families piled into special trains for trips to the seaside at Weston-super-Mare – as many as 26,000 people in 32 Specials!

The Great Western adopted a highly paternalistic tradition at Swindon, building, in effect, a complete town, with their own schools, hospitals, and workers' houses. The only thing was that they didn't like Unions much and kept them out until the 1920s. It was at Swindon that the last steam locomotive to be built in this country was constructed: BR '9F' 2-10-0 No 92220 *Evening Star*, which went into service in 1960 and is now preserved in the National Collection.

VID, Sound, Colour, 29mins, HTV

SWINDON ENGINES (Britain 1960)

City of Truro is seen midway during her first return to service outside the works in the summer of 1960. There follow profiles of Dean Goods No 2516 and 'Star' class 4-6-0 No 4003 *Lode Star*. Collett's development of the latter class is represented by No 7023 *Penrice Castle* and No 7037 *Swindon*. Steam construction continued at Swindon after the demise of the Great Western Railway in 1948 – with both GWR designs (initially) and the new BR Standards. While not Swindon-built 'Britannia' Pacific No 70025 carried a GWR name – *Western Star*. Final manifestation of Western independence, a 'Warship' diesel-hydraulic No D823. Made by Patrick Whitehouse.

16mm/VID, Silent, Colour, 7mins, NRM/Stirling

SWISS RAILWAY JOURNEYS No 1: THE BRUNIG RAILWAY (Britain 1987)

RV Television. Another version of this journey, taking in the aerial cableway to Titlis, the Mount Pilatus Railway at 1 in 2 and steam on the Brienz-Rothorn-Bahn. The basic trip is from Lucerne to Interlaken.

VID, Sound, Colour, 55mins, RVV/SFV

SWISS RAILWAY JOURNEYS No 2 (Britain, 1987)

RV Television. Jungfrau Railway through the Eiger Mountain to Europe's highest railway station at Jungfraujoch. Bern-Lötschberg-Simplon-Bahn via the Kander Valley. Brig-Visp-Zermatt-Bahn to Zermatt at the foot of the Matterhorn. Also cable cars, paddle steamers, chairlifts etc.
(Swiss Railway Journeys: Interlaken-Brig).

VID, Sound, Colour, 60mins, RVV/SFV

SWISS RAILWAY VIDEO SPECTACULAR (Britain 1988)

RV Television. Basle, Gottard Pass, Chiasso, Waldenberg, Mount Pilatus, Rigi, Jungfrau, Luzern-Stans-Engelberg, Landwasser Viaduct, 'Glacier Express' from Chur to Zermatt, Gornergrat-Bahn, Montreux-Oberland-Bernois, Rochers-de-Naye, Blonay-Chamby etc.

VID, Sound, Colour, 60mins, RVV/SFV

SWISS TRAIN FORMATION (Britain 1986)

Salford Films. 138 Swiss freight and passenger trains. A test of video stamina!

VID, Sound, Colour, 55mins, SFV

SWISS TRAIN FORMATION (Britain 1988)

RV Television. Swiss Federal Railways standard gauge including international trains from Germany to Yugoslavia, the 'Swiss Express', modern Mark 4 coaches of the Fed-

eral Railway, Wagons-Lits, ex-Rheingold observation cars, freight trains with bankers on the Gottard route and a study of Swiss main line stations.

VID, Sound, Colour, 55mins, RVV/SFV

THE SWITCH TOWER (USA 1913)

An American Biograph production. Directed by D W Griffith. With Henry B Walthall, Lionel Barrymore, Jack Dillon, Charles West and Claire McDowell. A signalman who has been showing his small son how to manipulate the levers, sees his wife fall into the hands of a gang of counterfeiters. Leaving his son to signal the express, he goes to her rescue but is overpowered. After fulfilling his duty, the boy succeeds in saving his father with the aid of a toy pistol.

35/16mm, Silent, 11mins, BFI/HA

T9 TO TAVISTOCK (Britain 1960)

Made by P B Whitehouse and John Adams. This shows the 'Atlantic Coast Express' leaving two coaches at Oakhampton which are put on the local train to Tavistock and hauled by a 'T9'.

16/8mm, Silent, Colour, 8mins, CV/NRM

TAKING COALS TO . . . (Britain 1991)

Electra Films. 'Two hours of just coal traffic'. Part of the Loco Spotters *Track Experience* series.

VID, Sound, Colour, 120mins, EFV

THE TAKING OF PELHAM 123 (USA 1974)

United Artists. Produced by Gabriel Katzka. Directed by Joseph Sargent. With Walter Matthau, Robert Shaw, Martin Balsam, Hector Elizonda and Earl Hindman. A New York subway train is held for ransom by a criminal gang. How can they collect the money and escape? 'Full of noise and squalling and dirty words used for giggly shock effects.' (*New Yorker*)
    'Four killers kidnap a subway train in New York. A pacy thriller with no messages. It's given weight by the always welcome presence of Walter Matthau.' (Tony Bilbow) A massive studio reconstruction of part of the New York subway is backed by some real shots of the system, especially in the finale. The switch from studio to real is very well done and the use of locations for the climax gives a strange sense of release.

35mm, Sound, Colour, 104mins, United Artists

A TALE OF TWO SCOTSMEN (Britain 1987)

BBC Television. Series producers: Neil Cameron and Peter Walton. Written and presented by Miles

Kington. The story of the 'Flying Scotsman' train and the 'Elizabethan Express', including scenes from the old 1930 feature film *The Flying Scotsman* and scenes from the British Transport Film on the 'Elizabethan'. (From the *Steam Days* series.)

16mm, Sound, Colour, 30mins, BBC TV

THE TALL TARGET (USA 1951)

MGM. Produced by Richard Goldstone. Directed by Anthony Mann. With Dick Powell, Adolphe Menjou, Paula Raymond and Marshall Thompson. An attempt to prevent the assassination of Abraham Lincoln. 'This is another of those rare "small is beautiful" movies. Most of the action takes place on a train and the claustrophobic atmosphere is played for all its worth.' (Tony Bilbow). MGM already owned its stable of early 4-4-0s and sundry stock and track, so they were able to do most of this film on the studio lot, punctuated with a few stock shots of old 'Wild West' style engines and stock.

35mm, Sound, 78mins, MGM

THE TALYLLYN RAILWAY (Britain c1948)

A record made when the railway was still in private hands. The locomotive *Dolgoch* is prominent. (1866 vintage.)

16mm, Silent, 10mins, TAL/HA

TALYLLYN RAILWAY (Britain 1950)

A record of the Talyllyn Railway during the last days of its old ownership. The death of its owner, Sir Henry Haydon Jones, and its rebirth under the auspices of the Talyllyn Railway Preservation Society is recorded, along with details of one of the preserved locomotives at Tywyn Pendre workshops — the 1866 0-4-0WT No 2 *Dolgoch*.

16mm, Silent, Colour, 22mins, TAL/CV/NRM

THE TALYLLYN RAILWAY (Britain 1976)

HTV Television. Produced and directed by John Mead. Presented by Wynford Vaughan-Thomas. The narrow gauge line from Towyn to Abergynolwyn which originally served the slate industry, fell into near dereliction and became the first-ever major preservation project in this country in 1950 when a group, led by Rolt, Nock and Whitehouse, decided to try and rescue it, using volunteer labour. It became the inspiration for the feature film *The Titfield Thunderbolt*. This film features Hunslet 0-4-0ST *Rough Pup* making the climb to 380ft above sea level. (From the *Great Little Trains of Wales* series.)

16mm/VID Sound, Colour, 26mins, HTV/Castle

THE TANAT VALLEY LINE (Britain 1948)

Filmed in May, 1948, this Great Western branch line headed west, branching away from the Southbound line from Oswestry at Llynclys Junction. We see a '58XX' 0-4-2T at Blodwell Junction, action at Nantmawr, and No 5803 trundles across the A495 road. A month later, in June 1948, south to Carmarthen in a search for a Dean Goods 0-6-0; activity on the ex-LMS branch line to Llandeilo.
Made by Patrick Whitehouse

16mm/VID Silent, 7min, NRM/Stirling

THE TED CRAWFORTH COLLECTION

Mr R E Crawforth filmed extensively on 8mm in the later days of steam, (1950s and 1960s). His films covered all the main action on the old 'Big Four' territories, some Continental railways, the M&GN, the Isle of Man, the Isle of Sheppey and many other sites. One of his classic films is a day spent watching the trains go by on Honiton bank, dominated by Bullied Pacifics. He has contributed to film programmes at Fairfield Hall, Croydon, and was for many years custodian of the Southern Counties Touring Society films, which he has now made available for screening.

TEDDY BOSTON TRIBUTE (Britain 1987)

Anglia Television. Dick Joice visits the Rev Teddy Boston at Cadeby; his museum and miniature railway. Books and models.

16mm, Sound, Colour, 7mins, Anglia

TELERAIL PRODUCTIONS

Yet another video company that specialises in railfreight coverage. Eleven volumes of *Rail Freight Today* have been issued, each approximately one hour in length and covering the various regions of BR. They have also produced a history of the Bicester Military Railway.

TEMPTATION HARBOUR (Britain 1947)

An Associated British Picture Corporation production. Directed by Lance Comfort. Photography by Otto Heller. With Robert Newton, Simone Simon and William Hartnell. Thriller in which an innocent observer becomes involved in a murder mystery. Includes scenes of the signal box at Newhaven and Newhaven-Dieppe channel crossings on the Southern Railway. 'The railway scenes, the arrival of the ship, the cranes, the signalbox, the trains are all there beautifully and technically perfect'. (*Monthly Film Bulletin*).

35mm/VID Sound, 102mins, Weintraub/VID 125 (Rly)

TERMINUS (Britain 1961)

Produced by British Transport Films. 'On the concourse and platforms of a large railway station you can hear the rhythm of the city and watch the most poignant moments of private lives become public property: grief, joy, meeting and parting, high comedy and near tragedy. Here, for a brief moment, the traveller may confront the station staff with a personal crisis while his neighbour looks on, or passes by to catch a train.' To the accompaniment of Ron Grainer's music, and Julian Cooper's songs, this film captures the atmosphere of London's Waterloo station. The film

was directed by John Schlesinger.

35/16mm/VID, Sound, 33mins, BTF/VID BT1

TERMINUS STATION

(see *Indiscretion of an American Wife* .)

TERROR BY NIGHT (USA 1946)

Universal. Produced by Howard Benedict. Directed by Roy William Neill. With Basil Rathbone and Nigel Bruce. Sherlock Holmes recovers a stolen jewel and solves a murder aboard the LNER train from London to Edinburgh. Some stock shots of the LNER 'Pacifics', mixed with ridiculous carriage interios and passing scenery taken in the San Fernando Valley!

35mm, Sound, 60mins, Universal

TEXAS RANGERS (USA 1951)

Columbia. Directed by Phil Karlson. With George Montgomery and Gale Storm. A Western, in which Civil War veterans become Rangers. Scenes filmed on the Sierra Railroad, using Baldwin 2-8-0 locomotive No 29790 (1906) and coaches Nos 2 and 6.

35mm, Sound, 73min, Columbia

THAMESIDER RAIL TOUR (Britain 1959)

SCTS. A trip around London with LSWR 'M7' 0-4-4T and ex-LBSCR stock to Kensington Olympia, Richmond, Malden, Raynes Park, East Putney, Lewisham Junction, Angerstein Wharf and Bricklayers Arms. Deptford Wharf is briefly glimpsed as is a hand-operated lift bridge over the Surrey canal.

16mm, Silent, 7mins, HA/SCTS

THANET BELLE (Britain 1948)

The introduction of the steamhauled 'Thanet Belle' service from Victoria to Margate, Ramsgate and Broadstairs, with SR/BR 'Battle of Britain' 4-6-2 No 21C120 *Manston*.

16mm, Sound, 5mins, HA

THEY HAD AN IDEA (Britain 1953)

Produced by British Transport Films. In every industry men need skill and knowledge, but the addition of a dash of imagination will often mean more pleasure from the job as well as greater efficiency. The film presents two examples; the invention of a ratchet device for turning rails; reshaping worn spanners at a locomotive works; speeding up the replacement of old escalator slats by means of an attachment to a drill; and, finally, the thoughtful porter working at a country station who goes out of his way to warn a regular passenger of a change in the timetable.

35/16mm, Sound, 14mins, BTF

THEY STEAMED TO GLORY (USA 1962)

International Film Bureau. Directed by Bill Warwick. Documentary of the steam engine and the part it played in the westward expansion of the United States, from its earliest beginnings in 1831 when the *John Bull* was brought from England, to the last run of a main line steam locomotive in 1960. Sequences include the historic race in 1831 between the *Tom Thumb* and a horse pulling a wagon; the Pioneer, first locomotive to run out of Chicago which was destined to become the nation's rail centre; the *William Mason*, the engine that pulled Lincoln's inaugural train; the *General* and its role in the Andrew's raid during the Civil War; the Union Pacific's 119 and the *Jupiter* at the wedding of the rails at Promonotory Point, Utah in 1869; the New York Central's 999, claimed as the first locomotive designed to exceed a speed of 100mph (did it ever do so? No one knows).

In Part Two, there is a summary of the steam locomotive in the 20th century, ending with the zenith of steam in 1958. It includes the early American 'Pacifics' like No 614 and the Pennsylvania 'K4' class 4-6-2s (just like our 'A' Pacifics and just as long lived); the 4-6-4 'Hudson' class on the New York Central; the 4-4-2s of the Milwaukee Railroad; the Norfolk & Western 'Super Mountain'

4-8-2s and the 'J' class as well as, at the end of steam, the N&W vast Mallet-type engines of the 'Y6' and 'A' classes. The Southern Pacific Cab Front Mallets of the Southern Pacific; the 2-10-2s of the Santa Fe (later going to 2-10-4s) and finally the Union Pacific Mallet-type 'Big Boys' the ultimate in steam locomotive power. And in 1934, a look to the future: the 'Burlington Zephyr', bound for the Chicago World's Fair.

VID, Sound, Part colour, 18mins, BFI/HA Part Two.

THIRD AVENUE EL (USA 1956)

Written, directed and photographed by Carson Davidson. A photographic impression of the now-demolished Third Avenue overhead electric railway in New York, which includes glimpses of the many types of passengers who used to travel on the system with nostalgic scenes of the old-fashioned stations and trains. The musical accompaniment is provided by a recording of Haydn's Concerto in D for harpsichord, played by Wanda Landowska.

16mm, Sound, Colour, 11mins, BFI

THE THIRD MAN (Britain 1949)

British Lion. Produced by Alexander Korda. Directed by Carol Reed. With Joseph Cotten, Trevor Howard, Alida Valli and Orson Welles. The famous hunt for Harry Lime through the very real streets of postwar Vienna. It includes one scene at Vienna main station with glimpses of steam locomotives and old prewar Austrian stock.

35mm, Sound, 100mins, Weintraub

THE THIRD SAM (Britain 1962)

Produced by British Transport Films. Sam Smith is taught to drive an electric locomotive. He learns the new job without difficulty but one day his train breaks down and Sam summons up three sides of his character to deal with the emergency. First Sam couldn't care less; Second Sam flies into a terrible panic; but Third Sam solves the problem! With narration, in typical rhyming monologue, by Stanley Holloway, this is an amusing and original approach to instructional film making.

35/16mm, Sound, 10mins, BTF

THIRTY MILLION ACRES (Britain 1948)

An LMS film. A survey of the very large-scale special goods stations and yards servicing agriculture with a vast number of special trains in the years before the big trucks and the motorways.

35mm/VID, Sound, Colour, 14mins, BFT/TVP

THIRTY MILLION LETTERS (Britain 1963)

Produced by British Transport Films. 'Every day the minds and emotions of Britain's citizens are changed by the coming and going of thirty million letters. This film shows how it is done, who does it, and what they think about it, whether it be a postman in the Outer Hebrides, a sorter on the postal special out of Euston or an engineer supervising the working of a new automatic letter-facing machine.' Produced in association with the General Post Office.

35/16mm, Sound, Colour, 30mins, BTF

THE THIRTY-NINE STEPS (Britain 1935)

Gaumont British Picture. Produced by Ivor Montagu. Directed by Alfred Hitchcock. From the novel by John Buchan. With Robert Donat, Madeleine Carroll, Godfrey Tearle, Lucie Mannheim, Peggy Ashcroft, John Laurie, Wylie Watson, Helen Haye and Frank Cellier. A spy is murdered and her benefactor is the suspect. He decides to make a dash for it, based on a slim clue in the form of a map of Scotland. He manages to elude the police until a chase across Scotland, where he becomes involved with a girl, but eventually gets to London and the final unmasking of the real villains in the music hall where the story began.

'A miracle of speed and light.' (Otis Ferguson) 'Marvellous comedy thriller with most of the tricks found not only in Hitchcock's other work but in anyone else's who has tried the same vein. It has little to do with the original novel and barely sets foot outside the studio but it makes every second count and is unparalleled in its use of timing, atmosphere and comedy relief.' (Leslie Halliwell) The point about the studio is interesting for very few scenes are filmed on the real locations, even when it would seem to be essential by modern film-making standards. Take the case of the Forth Bridge scene which is made up of the following shots:
1 MS. Hannay opens carriage door. Studio, with back projection of bridge girders.
2 MS. Looking forward along the carriage and engine moving across the bridge. Hannay steps out from one carriage door, moves forward and goes into a door further forward. A real shot taken from a real train, with the last half section of carriage built on the studio to match exactly the real train moving forward. An extraordinarily complex and clever split screen shot.
3 Studio. LS. The empty corridor of the train.
4 Studio. MS. The detectives pull the emergency cord.
5 Studio. LS. The train corridor as train stops.
6 Studio. MS. Hannay passes through to next carriage.
7 Studio. MS. Hannay in corridor.
8 Studio. MS. Hannay continues to race down corridor.
9 Studio. MS. Detectives racing down corridor.
10 Studio. MS. Hannay opens restaurant car door, looks.
11 Studio. LS. Restaurant. Waiter offers a seat.
12 Studio. MS. Hannay mouths a 'No'.
13 Studio. LS. Hannay runs through restaurant car; nearly knocks over waiter with tea tray. Detectives race after him; waiter nearly demolished.
14. Studio. MS. Hannay opens door to next carriage: runs through.
15. Studio. GV. It's the guards van with three Alsatian dogs looking very nasty.
16. Studio. MS. Hannay looks; backs away; shuts door.

17. Studio. MCS Hannay; looks behind; detectives are closing fast.
18. Studio. Alsatians barking.
19. Studio. MS. Detectives advance nervously; the boss man lets his subordinates go first.
20. Studio. MCU.Dogs bark around detectives' legs.
21. Studio (or was it?) LS. Exterior shot of half a carriage on right, framed by girders of bridge as detectives jump down, hunting their man. Very slight 'camera pan' to left reveals Hannay clinging to bridge main girder, out of view.
22. Studio. CS. Hannay clinging to bridge superstructure; he looks down.
23. Real. GV. Looking down from bridge to Firth of Forth below; small boat goes past.
24. Studio. MCU. Hannay looks around, still clinging precariously to bridge superstructure.
25. Studio. MS. Detectives climb aboard train through guards van door; half carriage only seen; moves off slowly to right, disappearing off-screen. Repeat of slight 'camera pan' to left. The bridge girder. Hannay has gone.
26. Real. GV. Forth Bridge from a distance; sounds of morse and broadcasts of wanted man.

In the whole of this sequence, there are just 2.5 real shots. The last scene on the bridge looks very real but we know there were pieces of carriage in use from Shot 2. Nevertheless the men's breath suggests cold air. The answer: it is believed that the scenes involving shots 21, 22, 24 and 25 were done on the roof of the old Islington studios, with the piece of coach being wheeled out at the right moment. At least it was done in the open air!

The film is famous with railway enthusiasts for a classic error. Hannay makes his escape by catching the train to Scotland from King's Cross. There are location scenes at the LNER terminus, again with many studio inserts. The 'LNER' feel of the studio-built stock is quite good, as is the restaurant car. So the train heads north from King's Cross. Meanwhile, the landlady has arrived at his apartment and discovers the body. She turns towards camera and opens her mouth to scream. Now Hitchcock breaches the 'One-should-see-what-one-hears' rule as the lady opens her mouth to

the scream of a powerful train whistle. But Hannay is heading north on the LNER to Edinburgh; the shot is of a Great Western 'King' on an express train bursting out of the west portal of Box Tunnel near Bath! One can only quote Alfred Hitchcock: 'There is something more important than logic; it is imagination.'

35mm/16mm/VID, Sound, 81mins, Rank/VID

THE THIRTY-NINE STEPS (Britain 1959)

Rank. Produced by Betty Box. Directed by Ralph Thomas. With Kenneth More, Taina Elg, Barry Jones, Faith Brook, James Hayter and Brenda de Banzie. Remake of the 1935 Hitchcock film, with the same basic script and plot line. 'Just to show that stars and story aren't everything, this scene-by-scene remake muffs every opportunity for suspense or general effectiveness, and is practically a manual on how not to make a thriller.' (Leslie Halliwell)

This failure is interesting because it is far more accurate in railway detail than either of the other two versions of the story. For example, in this case, the company was able to use the actual Forth Bridge quite extensively, including real parts of the girdering and a little trap door between the tracks for maintenance purposes through which Kenneth More makes his escape, although a shot of him clambering over the girders is very much a studio back-projection job. The old maroon stock is actually on an Edinburgh-Aberdeen train and there is an 'A4' Pacific on the front. In one shot, the negative has been turned round to get a different eyeline for the detectives; but you can clearly see 'OCS' as part of a reversed "Scotland" on one of the carriages.

For an approaching train, there is a real shot of LNER 'A4' 4-6-2 No 60147 *North Eastern*. There is a perfect example of how the original Hitchcock humour was ruined in the remake. In the 1935 film, Hannay races through the restaurant and 'nearly' overturns a waiter with a tea tray; in the remake, the waiter is struck and empties a tureen of soup over an elderly passenger — from

subtle comedy to slapstick in one easy stage.

35mm/VID, Sound, Colour, 93mins, Rank

THE THIRTY NINE STEPS (Britain 1978)

Rank. Produced by James Kenelm. Directed by Don Sharp. With Robert Powell, Karen Dotrice, John Mills, Eric Porter, David Warner, George Baker, Ronald Pickup and Timothy West. Third version of this story, the film returns to the original period of the John Buchan novel — just before World War 1. 'Not bad but rather spoils itself with a ridiculous cliffhanger climax on the face of Big Ben.' (Leslie Halliwell)

This time, the Forth Bridge was not available so Hannay goes to Scotland by a rather unusual route — from Marylebone via the Severn Valley Railway and Victoria Bridge. The journey starts at Marylebone with many steam effects rather than actual motive power. It transfers (after the rescue of a clergyman whose clothes have been stolen in the 'real' Marylebone Gentleman's toilet) to the Severn Valley with a train of dubious pre-1914 stock, with maroon Mk 1 carriages optimistically labelled 'Midland'. The locomotive on the front is BR '2MT' 2-6-0 No 46443, built in 1950! To make it look more 'Midland', the first and last number had been painted out on the smokebox and cabside displays, to become '644'. Despite all this, the scene in which Hannay escapes from the train while it is halted on the Victoria Bridge across the Severn (again after the communication cord has been pulled) is very effective, especially a real Robert Powell, with some help from a double for the more acrobatic bits, hanging on by the skin of his teeth to the girders of the bridge.

35mm/VID, Sound, Colour, 102mins, Rank

THIS IS ME (Britain 1982)

Central Television. Produced by Lewis Rudd. Directed by Michael Connor. Associate producer: Ron Olsen. The story of Joe Bowmer, a 16 year old from Nottingham who spends his spare time as a trainee fireman on the Great Central Railway preserved section based on Loughborough. His work takes him to LNER 'B1' 4-6-0 No 1306 *Mayflower* (with excellent aerial shots), LNER 'N2' 0-6-2T No 69532 and trips on a visiting locomotive — Patrick Stirling GNR 'Single' 4-2-2 No 1, on loan from the National Railway Museum. There is also a visit to the Barry Scrap Yards run by Dai Woodham.

16mm, Sound, Colour, 26mins, Central

THIS IS MY RAILROAD (USA 1951)

Made by Gene K Walker for the Pacific Railroad. An account of the great railway network covering the West of the United States, and how it has developed into the vast Pacific Railroad.

16mm, Sound, Colour, 30mins

THIS IS YORK (Britain 1953)

Produced by British Transport Films for the British Transport Commission.
Historical York, industrial York and the surrounding countryside form the background to this film; but the main setting is York station. We spend there the hours from dawn to dark on an autumn day. Our guide is the Station Master, who shows us something of the planning, hard work, and human interest behind the scenes at a key point in the British Railways system.

35/16mm, Sound, 20mins, BTF

THIS YEAR — LONDON (Britain 1951)

Produced by British Transport Films. Candid cameras follow the adventures of the staff of a Midland boot factory on their day off. They participate in the fun and pleasure of the train journey to Town, and in a sight-seeing trip round the Capital. Lunch is followed by an afternoon cruise on the Thames from Richmond to Hampton Court, with tea in the Tilt Yard. Afterwards, amid the noise, the bustle and the lights of a West End Saturday night,

our party enjoys what few hours remain of their day.

35/16mm, Sound, 25mins, BTF

THOMAS THE TANK ENGINE (Britain various dates)

Britt Allcroft Productions. Based on the Railway Scenes by the Rev W. Awdry. Produced by Britt Allcroft. Directed by David Mitton. Stories told by Michael Angelis. Music by Mike O'Donnell and Junior Campbell. Elaborately produced interpretations of the original stories, using large scale models of the engines and the backgrounds (plus occasional cell animation). All the model engines have the familiar faces on the front, with giant eyes that move. The excellent studio work was done at Shepperton. The Thomas the Tank Engine theme has been picked up and successfully exploited by many railway preservation societies, despite copyright clashes with Britt Allcroft who own all the rights in the theme.

VID, Sound, Colour, 5 mins per episode, Britt Allcroft

THORNABY SHED (Britain 1962)

Made by P B Whitehouse and John Adams. Last days of steam in the North East.

16/8mm, Silent, 8mins, CV/NRM

THOSE MAGNIFICENT MEN IN THEIR FLYING MACHINES (Britain 1965)

TCF. Directed by Ken Annakin. With Sarah Miles, Robert Morley, Eric Sykes, Terry-Thomas and James Fox. The London to Paris Air Race of 1910 and some of the aircraft and men who took part. Includes a railway scene shot on the Bedford-Hitchin branch line (including Old Warden tunnel), using preserved HR 4-6-0 No 103, with tender re-labelled 'N.O.R.D.' and a set of ex-Midland Railway suburban coaches. Other scenes were shot in the area around Shefford.

70mm Todd-Ao, Sound, Colour, 133mins, TCF

THREE BRANCH LINES (Britain 1958)

Made by P B Whitehouse and John Adams. A Terrier locomotive works the Hayling Island train, 0-6-0 No 16518 on the Halesowen branch and 0-4-4T No 58085 on the Southwell branch.

16/8mm, Silent, 7mins, CV/NRM

THREE RAILWAYS TOUR (Britain 1961)

SCTS. Visits to the Eastbourne Miniature Tramway, Princess Park, Eastbourne (afterwards transferred to Seaton, Devon); Volks Electric Railway at Brighton, with original four-wheel cars at Black Rock; and the Bluebell railway, with SECR 'P' 0-6-0T No 27 *Primrose* and GWR 'Dukedog' 4-4-0 No 3217 *Earl of Berkeley*.

16mm, Silent, 8mins, HA/SCTS

THRILLING EMOTION (Britain 1948)

Union Films. Documentary, including sequence on the model railway at Chessington Zoo.

35mm, Sound, 34mins

THROUGH THE TRIENT VALLEY (Switzerland 1941)

Made by Swiss Federal Railways. A railway journey from Martigny.

16mm, Silent, 16mins, SFR

THUNDER (USA 1929)

MGM Directed by William Nigh. With Lon Chaney, James Murray, George Duryea and Phyllis Haver. A train driver has trouble with his sons. 'An almost forgotten star melodrama with a great railway background.' (Leslie Halliwell) The film about an ailing locomotive engineer was made more poignant by the fact that Lon Chaney was a very sick man when he made it; he died a few months later in 1930. He will always be most remembered for the original silent version of *The Phantom of the Opera* but in this film he drives No 2329, a big American

Left:
A superb Baltimore & Ohio scene from the documentary 'They Steamed to Glory'.

Below:
HR 4-6-0 No 103 and its train of Midland coaches during the final day's filming for 'Those Magnificent Men and Their Flying Machines'. *Peter T. Waylett*

Alco Pacific on the Chicago North Western run. There are great scenes in the snows of the High Sierras.

35mm, Silent, 90mins, MGM

🚂 🚂 🚂

THE THUNDER OF STEAM IN THE BLUE RIDGE (USA 1958)

Norfolk & Western Railroad between Roanoke and Bedford, Virginia with big Mallet-type 2-6-6-4s on freight trains and 4-8-4s on passenger trains. There are also scenes of a Mallet 2-8-8-2 in action.

16mm, Sound, 18mins, HA

🚂 🚂 🚂 🚂 🚂

THUNDER ROCK (Britain 1942)

Charter Films. Directed by Roy Boulting. With Michael Redgrave, Lilli Palmer, James Mason and Barbara Mullen. A writer-turned-lighthouse keeper conjures up the people who went down in a wreck in 1849 and debates whether a world at war is worth living in. Includes a double-headed Italian steam train stock shot, plus a rather poor reconstruction of Italian carriage interiors.

35mm, Sound, 112min, Charter

🚂

A TICKET TO TOMAHAWK (USA 1950)

TCF. Produced by Robert Bassler. Directed by Richard Sale. With Anne Baxter, Dan Duryea, Rory Calhoun and Walter Brennan.
A stagecoach line tries to delay the coming of the Western railroad. Made extensive use of the classic Durango & Silverton narrow gauge railroad, built by the Denver & Rio Grande Railroad in 1882, including combination coach No 212 and coaches 306, 320 and 280, all painted yellow-orange for the fictitious 'Rio Grande Gold' train hauled by 470 series ('K28' class) Denver & Rio Grande 2-8-2 locomotives No 470 and 478 as well as RGS engine No 20 (renumbered No 1 and named 'The Emma Sweeney'), now in the Colorado Railroad Museum. The Silverton branch was used throughout; Silverton station was renamed 'Epitaph'.

35mm, Sound, Colour, 90mins, TCF

🚂 🚂

TIME FREIGHT TO TIDEWATER (USA c1950)

Norfolk & Western Freight No 86 from Columbia, Ohio to Norfolk, Virginia, hauled by a variety of later-day steam locomotives.

8mm, Silent, 22mins, Blackhawk

🚂 🚂 🚂 🚂 🚂

TITFIELD THUNDERBOLT (Britain 1952)

An Ealing Studios film. Produced by Michael Balcon. Directed by Charles Crichton. Script by T E B Clarke. Photography by Douglas Slocombe. Music by Georges Auric. With Stanley Holloway, George Relph, Naunton Wayne, John Gregson, Godfrey Tearle, Hugh Griffith, Gabrielle Brune and Sidney James.
Opens with the closing of the Titfield-Mallingford branch line. When the notices go up, all inhabitants of Titfield protest loudly except Messrs Crump and Pearce who own the Titfield Road Transport Co Ltd. They have just bought a smart new, single-decker bus. Led by the Reverend Weech, an ardent railway enthusiast, some of the villagers get together and decide to buy the railway and run it themselves. Their first problem, which is to find finance for the venture, is solved by Mr Valentine, a local old-world drunk who is happy to give the railway his fiscal support on the assurance that a bar will be installed in the coach, thus enabling him to take his first gin at 8.47am.
Titfield is granted a Light Railway Order for a probationary period of one month. During this time the enthusiastic amateurs must prove their professional ability to the satisfaction of the Ministry of Transport. The engine is driven by the Vicar, guarded by the Squire and fired by Dan, a former railway worker who has long since retired and taken up the more casual occupation of poaching from the disused railway coach in which he lives. Business flourishes on the railway while the Crump and Pearce bus rattles emptily on its lonely way. Sabotaging the railway is the only way to save the bus, and, when the day for the Inspector's final test is about to dawn, the villains attack. They hire the steam-roller driver to tow the train away in the middle of the night and send it to destruction over an embankment.

It seems the end of the Titfield railway, until the vicar has the idea of getting the old original locomotive out of the museum. By the morning the *Thunderbolt* is ready and Dan's former home has replaced the wrecked coach. To the Vicar's consternation the arrival of a bishop is announced — indicating some form of censure to engine-driving clergymen — but all is well. The Bishop of Selchester is none other than old Olly Matthews, a fellow enthusiast who is allowed to fire the engine all by himself.

The inspector arrives and so, driven by the Reverend Weech and fired by the Bishop of Selchester, the gallant old *Thunderbolt* sets off for Mallingford to defend the title of the Titfield line which, after many adventures, it does with great success.

T E B Clarke, author of *The Titfield Thunderbolt*, described at the time how the story came to be written:

'Never again will I smile unkindly at the plight of the man who catches mumps in his mid-40s. Though personally I said goodbye to this complaint at the respectable age of seven, I had to wait until the 1950s to contract an even commoner childhood fever.

'I had no ambition in early life to drive an engine — it never even occured to me to spot one. My father was allowed to play with my most expensive Christmas present unhampered by me. I regarded trains as smelly things liable to make one sick, their only virtue being the power they had to squash a half penny placed on the line into the size of a penny.

'Came the dangerous 40s and a visit to North Wales, where in the summer of 1951 I found myself standing on a station of the narrow-gauge Talyllyn Railway, blinking incredulously at a notice which said "Volunteer Platelayers Required". Curiosity had to be satisfied, and my inquiries brought the information that this was a private line run through the summer months by railway enthusiasts from all parts of the country, who spent their holidays as engine-drivers, firemen, guards or booking clerks.

'Thus was born the idea of *The Titfield Thunderbolt*: the idea of a village with sufficient love of its little branch-line railway to buy it up and run it with an amateur staff when it came to suffer the fate of so many pleasant but uneconomic little branch lines in these materialistic times.

'Two days of fact-finding with the enthusiasts of the Talyllyn line, and I succcumbed to the mania as completely as any clergyman in the land. Or perhaps you are not yet aware of the affinity that exists between the Cloth and the Boiler Suit? Almost my first discovery was the extraordinarily large number of clerics who are held in thrall by fascination of railways; it presented me at once with my leading character, the Reverend Samuel Weech.

'The appearance of a few paragraphs in the newspapers about plans for this film brought a flood of helpful correspondence. "It occurs to me that you might care to make use of a delightful incident which took place some years ago on a small branch line . . ." Never was a writer so inundated with gloriously usable material.

'Such enthusiasm is very infectious. By now I had developed and satisfied the long-delayed ambition to drive an engine, and it was becoming a question of whether my preoccupation with railway lore would make serious inroads on my work as a screenwriter. By this I do not mean to suggest that the railway enthusiast has no time for films. I asked one to make sure of that. 'Oh, I go quite a lot to the pictures,' he said. "I saw *Train of Events, Night Train to Munich, The Ghost Train, Oh! Mr Porter* . . ."

'Well, I finished my work on *The Titfield Thunderbolt* last summer, and now that I have added to my record the supreme satisfaction of driving Thunderbolt herself, I think I can safely say that the crisis is past and. . .

"Hello! That you, Clarke? Not too busy, I hope?"

"Well, I'm just writing something I've got to finish in time for . . ."

"Because I'm at Paddington — and what do you think I've just seen here? The new Gas Turbine — 18100".

"Not really? Oh, I say! Wait for me — I'll be with you in 20 minutes." '

The script of the film called for a good single line standard gauge railway in beautiful countryside (suitable for Technicolor) with an attractive station, bridges, viaducts and a junction with a main line as well as a reasonably old tank engine and a very old veteran locomotive. A good steam-roller and some old-world stock were needed to complete the inventory.

The seven-mile line between Limpley Stoke and Camerton provided the answer, as it had done for *The Ghost Train* and *Kate Plus Ten* many years before; Bristol provided the junction point. The branch line had been open for freight traffic until 1950 (to serve some small collieries) and in 1951 the track was still there. Limpley Stoke became the headquarters for the film unit; an old disused mill was used as a projection theatre for the daily 'rushes'. Monkton Coombe, a derelict but redeemable village station, was used for many of the scenes; boys from Monkton Coombe Preparatory School appeared in various scenes and provided a cricket match for a particular lineside shot. The principal passenger coach was an old saloon with end balconies which had come from the Kelvedon & Tollesbury Light Railway, originally it had been built for the Wisbech & Upwell tramway and was later restored for preservation but was broken up instead; the steam-roller was *Invicta*, loaned by Messrs Barnes Bros of Southwick, Wilts.

The particular problem was to obtain a really effective genuine early locomotive for the last part of the story. *The Lion* was the final choice. Built by Todd, Kitson and Laird of Leeds in 1838, *The Lion* became engine No 57 on the Liverpool & Manchester Railway, the first exclusive passenger steam railway in the world. In 1845, she was transferred to the Grand Junction Railway and later became No 116 on the books of the London & North Western. In 1859 she was sold to the Mersey Docks and Harbour Board for £100, and was used as a pumping engine at the Princess graving dock until 1928 when she was rescued by the Liverpool Engineering Society for their museum.

Visually *The Lion* was a perfect film star, in locomotive terms. Her construction is poetically simple. The boiler and tank is contained in a fine wooden casing, pleasingly offset by a brass hood over the fire-box, and a tall elegant funnel collared and crowned with brass sunbursts, while the coal-bearing half of the ensemble is strengthened by a dado of wrought-iron. The one handbrake controls the rear-wheel brakeblocks which are made of wood and plugged with resin and one control lever deals with start, stop and reverse. The buffers are horsehair stuffed leather 'cushions'.

When approached by Ealing Studios for a loan of *The Lion*, the Society thought hard but were finally persuaded when they saw Clarke's lively script. They agreed that she could be transported to Limpley Stoke and they also allowed her to have her dignified colouring of ark green and mauve changed to a more conventional nursery red and green for the benefit of the Technicolor camera, on the reasonable understanding that her normal appearance was resumed after filming. *The Lion* travelled to the location in two stages. She made the major part of the journey from Crewe to Westbury, Wilts, on a low-loader. In the yards at Westbury she was overhauled and put under steam. Found to be in perfect working condition, she was able to make the final 20 miles from Westbury to Limpley Stoke under her own power. Apart from one hectic day's work in a fish bay at Temple Meads station in Bristol, the film life of *The Lion* was spent entirely on the Limpley Stoke-Camerton line. During the eight weeks of location shooting *The Lion* manifested only one serious weakness; she had to be driven a matter of four miles to the nearest turntable every time the director wanted to turn her round!

'Undervalued on its release in the wake of other Ealing comedies, this now seems among the best of them as well as an immaculate colour production showing the England that is no more; the script has pace, the whole thing is brightly polished and the action works up to a fine climactic frenzy.' (Leslie Halliwell)

'I was never really sure if we had got this one right; somehow it never seemed to me that we were matching up to the script.' (Sir Michael Balcon)

'A train enthusiast's delight. Shades of *Passport to Pimlico*, of course, and it came at the fag end of the Ealing comedies, but it now seems one of the best of the bunch.' (Tony Bilbow)

But at last word must go to T E B ('Tibby') Clarke, who recalled some aspects of the film's production in an interview with Jim Palm, published in *Railway World* in October 1990:

'Jim Palm: "Why was the film called *Titfield Thunderbolt*?"

Tibby Clarke: "Well, I lived at the time in Limpsfield and the next village was Titsey; so I just combined the two and made it 'Titfield'."

Jim Palm: "The scene with the locomotive running along the road must have been a problem?"

Tibby Clarke: "Yes, it was. It was a locomotive outline built on a lorry chassis and the driver was, I think, lying down inside with a little peep-hole in front of him. That sequence was shot at Woodstock in Oxfordshire and I know that the driver said afterwards that it was done very early in the morning. Even so, he'd never seen so many people fall off their bicycles at the sight of the engine coming along the main road!"

Jim Palm: "You seem to have gone to great lengths to get the detail right?"

Tibby Clarke: "In none of my films — except this one — did I base a character on a real person. In the film, they couldn't think how to raise the money they needed to reopen the line and someone suddenly thought of Mr Valentine, the rich old alcoholic played by Stanley Holloway. He had the money if only they could persuade him to invest and they did that by putting on a buffet car so that he could have a drink at any time. Naturally, he put up the capital at once! Now, Mr Valentine was based on a character that I came across while I was on holiday; I was in the hotel bar one day when this old gentleman came in and said, 'Landlord: wine for the company!' Apparently he did this every so often and bought everyone a drink. His 'wine' was always gin and he would propose a toast: 'To our magnificent generals: General Gordon and General Booth!' This was a great character, I thought, so when I came to do *The Titfield*

Thunderbolt, I remembered this and based Stanely's part entirely on that old gentleman — even to the toast 'To General Gordon and General Booth.' Stanley never met him, of course, but he did it so perfectly that when the film came out, the man's friends said, 'Why, that's old so-and-so!' and they persuaded him to go to the pictures to see it. He was very much against the idea, though — he hadn't been inside a cinema for 30 years! Then, when the titles came up, he said, 'But the damned thing's in colour. I can't watch anything in colour!' So he got up and stamped out, and never did see himself on the screen!" '

The film has been on television a number of times and was shown during the Channel Four 'Going Loco' season. It has been issued on video, originally by EMI Video. In 1991, it was decided by Video 125 to go back and see if any of the material shot during the making of the film had survived. At the vaults at Pinewood were discovered a number of 'takes', including variations on the opening shot with the SDJR meeting the GWR at Midford. But they were on old-fashioned 'three strips Technicolor', a process which is now almost obsolete and immensely costly to copy. However, it was decided to go ahead and the best shots are now in *Steam on 35mm*, issued by Video 125.

35/16/VID, Sound, Colour, 84mins, Weintraub/125

🚂 🚂 🚂

TO BUILD AN ISLAND'S FUTURE (Britain 1961)

Brush Electrical Engineering Company. The building and operation of diesel-electric locomotives for the Ceylon Government.

16mm, Sound, Colour, 7mins, Brush

🚂 🚂 🚂 🚂 🚂

TO THE SUMMIT IN STEAM (Britain 1966)

Made by Trevor White. A trip to the top of the Snowdon Mountain Railway.

16/8mm, Silent, Colour, 7mins, TW

🚂 🚂 🚂 🚂 🚂

TOCCATA FOR TOY TRAINS (USA 1957)

Made by Charles and Roy Eames. A delightful study of Victorian children's toy trains.

16mm, Sound, Colour, 15mins, BFI

THE TOM MARTIN COLLECTION

Tom Martin began filming in the early days of the Bluebell Railway and many of his films feature the history of the preserved line as well as individual studies of particular locomotives such as the Adams Radial and the Terriers. His film shows were once a regular feature of Bluebell meetings and many Bluebell members came to more recent presentations of items from his archive shown at the Fairfield Hall at Croydon and elsewhere in the South. He has also filmed extensively on 16mm all over the preservation scene; a notable part of his work has been on the Great Central line, including the last days of steam working and extensive coverage of steam specials out of Marylebone on more recent times. In addition, he has covered events like the Brighton 150 celebrations, the return of steam to Folkestone, the story of the preserved Black Fives and many other activities which are listed under individual film titles such as his film on the historic (and still surviving) Wimbledon to West Croydon line.

🚂 🚂 🚂 🚂 🚂

TOMMY'S LOCOMOTIVE (Britain 1907)

Clarendon Films. A comedy about a boy who has a large toy engine which tows away his little sister in her baby frame.

16mm, Silent, 11mins, HA

🚂

TORBAY EXPRESS (Britain 1983)

Stirling Video. Film made by J F Traxler of Grantham showing a journey in 1938 from Torquay to Paddington, with 'Kings' and 'Castles'. There are also some early Dufaycolour scenes at Paddington, including the departure of the 10.30

'Cornish Riviera'. (Material also incorporated into *Pre 1968 British Steam*.)

16mm/VID, Silent, 12mins, Stirling/RF/HA

TRACK BUCKLING AND ITS PREVENTION (Britain 1951)

Produced by British Transport Films. The expansion of rails in hot weather might cause dangerous buckling of the track unless proper maintenance is carried out. Buckling may result from (1) rail-creep, which causes expansion gaps to close up: (2) seized fishplates, which may prevent the free movement of the rail-ends during expansion; (3) lack of proper ballast or bad sleeper-packing, either of which may allow sleepers to shift out of place. This film shows what precautions were taken and what maintenance practices were followed in the fifties.

35/16mm, Sound, 16mins, BTF

A TRACTIVE EFFORT (Britain 1962)

Brush Electrical Engineering Company. The building and running of British diesel-electric locomotives.
16mm, Sound, Colour, 30mins, Brush

TRAGIC RAILWAY

(See *The Block Signal*.)

TRAILER TAPE (Britain 1982)

Stirling Video. When video was very new, people needed to know what they could expect. Dick Griffiths issued this tape, using sections from his Great Western, Pat Whitehouse and 1964-65 Steam Memories to attract business. The tape was 'available for hire at £3 per week, with a deposit of £10.'

VID, Sound, Part colour, 30mins, Stirling

THE TRAIN (USA 1964)

Produced by Jules Bricken. Directed by John Frankenheimer. Script by Franklin Coen and Frank Davis. Based on *Le Front de l'Art* by Rose Vailand. Photography by Jean Tournier and Walte Wottitz. Music by Maurice Jarre. With Burt Lancaster, Paul Scofield, Jeanne Moreau, Michel Simon, Suzanne Flon, Charles Millot and Albert Remy.

It is 1944 and the Allies are almost at the gates of Paris. A German officer's car passes through the empty streets of occupied Paris. Colonel Franz Von Waldheim is on his way to his offices at the Jeu de Paume Museum.

In the museum he admires the paintings — from homes and collections all over France. Surprised by the curator, Mlle Villard, he drops the information that the paintings — modern paintings considered degenerate by Hitler but still priceless — are to be taken out of Paris by train.

Furious when the train that was to have carried the looted paintings is cancelled, Von Waldheim is brought face to face with Labiche, a French SNCF Area Inspector. Labiche tells Von Waldheim that the train cannot move without permission from General Von Lubitz, because of the evacuation of Paris. Bearding the harassed and unsympathetic general in his office, Von Waldheim is forced to tell him the value of the paintings — translated into cash on the open market. He then receives authorisation to assemble his train.

Meanwhile, Labiche climbs aboard a shunting engine where he is warmly greeted by Papa Boule who has known Labiche since he was a child. Labiche has been protecting Papa Boule, but by going over Labiche's head, he has obtained the job of taking the art train to Germany. When Papa Boule sees Labiche's reaction to this news, he grows angry realising that Labiche has, all along, kept him in safety from the hated Germans. Dropping from the cab of Papa Boule's engine, Labiche makes his way through the bustling marshalling yards where the Germans are loading an armament train for the front. Alongside the yard, in a barge where members of the Resistance meet, Labiche is introduced by Mlle Villard. With her are her collaborators. Mlle Villard explains that the art, France's heritage, is being looted. The problem is to prevent the train from reaching Germany. Labiche opposes the idea because of its danger to human lives — something more important to him than paintings. After her departure, the quartet discuss their real mission — how to stop the armament train from reaching the front. If they can halt the train for a few minutes at a certain spot at a predetermined time, high-altitude bombers can destroy it. In the meantime, Papa Boule, convinced of the importance of the art aboard his train, sabotages the engine.

At the marshalling yards of Vaires, Labiche, in a control tower with Major Dietrich, the German officer in charge of the yards, waits nervously for 10am, the time the yards will be bombed, but the armament train is ready to pull out. Somehow, the resistance men manage to hold the train up until the sound of an air raid alarm is heard. At the same moment, Papa Boule's train comes chugging through the yards. Labiche narrowly saves it from being derailed, and dives for safety himself as the bombs rain down.

When the sabotaged engine is returned from Rive-Reine to the smouldering yards at Vaires for repair, Papa Boule's trick is discovered by Major Herren, the German officer responsible for keeping the art train running. The old man is later executed despite Labiche's pleas. Labiche escapes from Von Waldheim's vigilance and sets up a a desperate stratagem to stall the train. It is shuttled around Paris without the guards on board knowing that they are not on their way back to Germany. When morning comes, they are back where they started. By crashing two locomotives together and slamming another into the rear of the art train, it is blocked in front and behind. As Von Waldheim forces his men to clear the wreckage, he is unable to keep Labiche from mounting a daring night-time raid to mark the train with white paint so that it will not be bombed by the allies. Labiche is hidden after the raid by Christine, and after she has dressed his wounded leg and fed him, they fall into each other's arms. Von Waldheim drives workers throughout the night to clear the rails. When all is ready he climbs aboard himself to take command, determined that this time nothing shall go wrong. With hostages mounted on the locomotive, the train pulls out. Labiche, who must work alone, wounded and tired, with supreme effort is able to derail the engine for good. The German soldiers realise the end has come. They abandon their leaders and join the retreating troops. In their final confrontation, the now obsessed enemies Labiche and Von Waldheim meet. The German dies. And Labiche walks away, abandoning the train filled with priceless paintings.

Shooting on *The Train* began in France in early August 1963. The first day with the cameras came in the marshalling yard at St Ouen, in Paris, where the French army had agreed to work with the production. On hand were 25 tanks, 500 extras and soldiers dressed in German uniforms, a 35-car train and dozens of cannons, half-tracks and guard dogs. All milled around the steaming locomotives that would play such an important role in *The Train*.

From the very beginning, Frankenheimer kept his cameras in motion in order to capture in black and white the full cinematic flavour of his recreated war-time operations. He perched it on top of cranes, smuggled the camera into tanks and hung it outside the cabs of racing locomotives. One of his favourite tools was the newly developed Mitchell Mark II camera with its powerful zoom lens. Frequent use of the wide-angle lens, almost a Frankenheimer trademark, brought in the surrounding atmosphere but meant that every background detail had to be precisely arranged. For two weeks *The Train* unit filmed with the army at St Ouen, and aboard a barge moored at the quay there. Because of the vastness of the area, and the overpowering sounds of the tanks, locomotives and other equipment, a new technique had to be developed for getting the troops into action and then letting them know when to 'cut'. The signal for 'get ready' was three short blasts on a locomotive in steam. One long blast meant 'action', and another meant 'cut'.

From there the unit moved on, along with its armament train, to Vaires, some 40 miles out of Paris, where for three weeks scenes were shot leading up to the bombard-

ment of the arms train and the narrow escape of the art-laden train. Here, crew members and cast got their first real taste of railway operations. The Vaires marshalling yards are one of the most important in the Paris area. Here a special signalbox was constructed and then blown up with dynamite, 'in order to save the construction boys having to tear it down', as the Hollywood special effects man Lee Zavitz put it. At Vaires, Burt Lancaster and Michel Simon practised driving locomotives on long empty stretches of track until they had mastered the art; it is traditional that all actors in railway films drive the trains! During these sequences, experts from SNCF helped the film makers by recalling tricks they had pulled to delay German trains during the war. Many of the identical 'accidents' — blocked points, jammed stop lights, sabotaged oil lines, and fake arguments — were recreated. Unfortunately, though an extensive search had been made, none of the original members of the crew of the art train were still alive.

On 19 September, the company, some 175 strong, moved to Acquigny, a village in Normandy, where for eight weeks they shot some of the film's major sequences. While the majority of the crew moved into a selection of hotels in Rouen, a 45 minute drive from the shooting site at the unused Acquigny station, Burt Lancaster, Paul Scofield and John Frankenheimer, stayed at a nearby country inn. It was in Acquigny that Jeanne Moreau joined the cast and crew for 10 day's filming in the tiny station hotel taken over by the company, not for sleeping, but for use as a natural location. Rain and unseasonable day-long fogs cut into the production schedule as the build-up of men and equipment went on in the station. First the art train was pulled in, carrying aboard it much of the unit's equipment — a technique that was to continue throughout the filming of the picture.

It was in Acquigny that one of the principal crashes was staged. To begin with, a locomotive was derailed. By accident its speed got out of hand, and it smashed three of the five cameras filming the action. Fortunately, no one was hurt, and the scenes were dramati-

cally captured by one small camera, remotely run and embedded at railheight where the locomotive went off the tracks. Only one day's shooting was missed because of the accident.

On 17 October, the big crash took place. With nearly 100 journalists on hand a second locomotive travelling at nearly 60mph, was crashed into the already derailed engine. Extensive safety precautions were taken for this scene. It could be done only once. Families were evacuated from their homes in the area; a cafe across the street from the station and in the possible path of the crash, was heavily insured; a representative from Lloyds of London was on hand to see the crash for himself, and had already agreed a price for it from the owners!

All electricity and gas in the area was shut off during the hours spent preparing and shooting the scene. Railway experts feared the locomotive boiler might explode. Special pits were dug along the rails to catch the runaway engine. The scene was shot with seven different cameras. By the time Frankenheimer had finished at Acquigny and moved into the surrounding countryside for the final sequence of the film, the station held three crashed locomotives, half a dozen demolished box cars, and the local residents had become used to the sight of their daughters talking freely with 'Nazi' soldiers and officers.

Moving into the countryside after his stay in Acquigny, Burt Lancaster's next stunt was to blow a section of track with dynamite, in an attempt to halt the train. Real dynamite was used, and when the track blew, the driver expertly stopped his locomotive with just the front wheels hanging over into the hole caused by the dynamite. Location filming ended in mid-December 1963.

Shooting was resumed on 31 March, 1964 when Lee Zavitz, the special effects man, blew up an entire marshalling yard at Gargenville, outside Paris. For more than six weeks Zavitz supervised a crew of more than 50 technicians and members of the French Army Ordnance Engineers in preparing the mile-square area for this key scene, which simulated the destruction of the Vaires marshalling yards in France by high-flying Allied bombers towards the end of World War II. For planting charges of TNT, 150 holes were dug with a powered welldigger. Wires were run through almost two miles of trenches to a control bunker from which demolition men, linked by telephone with Zavitz, but unable to see the marshalling yards, made the electrical contacts which set off the detonations. Through six switches and more than 20,000m of cable, 140 individual explosions were set off in just over 50sec. In order to duplicate, as nearly as possible, the concentrated Allied bombing raids of 1945, charges of dynamite and large plastic containers of high-octane petrol were placed in the trucks, buildings, sheds, control towers, and a 22-car train which were to be blown up. In all, the destruction required nearly two tons of TNT and dynamite and some 2,000gal of petrol. Nine cameras recorded the scene, all of them in bunkers or metal pillboxes, but only two of them manned; the other seven were remote-controlled.

The company then went out in to the French countryside again, shooting a few nights each at railway stations in such rural towns as Longueville, Provins, Troyes, Louviers, Acquigny, and others to film what was called the 'rondelay' sequence, in which *The Train* headed east out of Paris, then took a great oval route which brought it back to the station from which it had left, while the German guards on board, fooled by signs changed along the way by resistance workers, believed they were heading for Berlin. During the last week of shooting, at the end of May, Frankenheimer had a Spitfire brought over from England, with 'Taff' Rich, a Welsh RAF veteran of wartime Spitfires, as pilot. Shooting near Elbeuf, just outside Rouen, in a tree-covered ravine leading to a railway tunnel, Frankenheimer filmed the sequence in which the locomotive of the train just manages to reach safety in the tunnel ahead of the Spitfire's four guns. One more short night scene, filmed at the now familiar station at Acquigny, completed *The Train* at the end of May after 186 days of shooting.

'What I tried to do,' Frankenheimer said, 'was first of all tell a dramatic adventure story. But more than that, I wanted all the realism possible. There are no tricks in this picture. When trains crash together, they are real trains. There is no substitute for that kind of reality.' John Frankenheimer had re-discovered what the Vitograph Company first found out in 1914.

'Coming hot on the heels of the *Manchurian Candidate* and *Seven Days in May*, *The Train* (Odeon, Leicester Square) is yet another superbly bizarre thriller which demonstrates John Frankenheimer's uncanny ability to make the ordinary seem extraordinary. Elaborated from a brief anecdote in *Le Front de l'Art*, Rose Vailand's history of the Nazi looting of art treasures during the war, the script tells of the heroic efforts of a group of French railway Resistance workers to prevent a German general escaping from Paris just before the Liberation with a train-load of priceless Impressionist paintings.

'Frankenheimer, however, is more interested in the efforts than the heroism, and a brilliant pre-credits sequence establishes his thriller priorities. A German officer prowls through the deserted Musée du Jeu de Paume, pausing here and there to stare fascinatedly at a Gaugin or a Renoir; a lady curator, jealous of her treasures, emerges to offer fervent thanks for his help in preserving them from destruction; and he immediately disillusions her by ordering their despatch to Germany. Here the accent is firmly placed on strangeness and mystery; the footsteps echoing through the corridors, the forlorn stacks of paintings lying around, the wall-light snapped on to pick out a painting from the surrounding darkness, the angular lady emerging from nowhere.

'From there on it is trains and excitement all the way as two obsessions clash mightly. The German is fanatically determined to get the paintings he adores safely to Germany; and the Resistance leader, supremely disinterested in art, finds that once he has unwillingly been started out in opposition, he cannot stop, and must go on finding new ways and means of delaying the train for an hour here,

a day there. So the screen becomes a giant chess board on which huge, lumbering trains are manoeuvred skilfully about as pawns in a desperate battle to find the fatal weakness.

'The whole paraphernalia of trains, tracks and shunting yards — once a favourite symbol of romantic despair and longing for the cinema — acquires an almost hypnotic fascination, as if one were watching some terrible, primaeval struggle taking place. Engines charge blindly down the tracks and crash into each other, toppling slowly over like wounded monsters. An armoured engine crawls threateningly out of its shed, only to roll helplessly back again as a saboteur switches the points. A train, with its brakes full on, slides painfully towards a damaged sector of the track; another scurries like a beetle away from a preying aircraft, or comes screeching to a halt inches away from the mouth of a sheltering tunnel while the frustrated aircraft hovers, overhead; yet another snakes its way with maddening deliberation through a series of shattering explosions as raiding bombers rake the marshalling yards.

'If one chooses to be churlish, it is easy to pick several holes in the film's superstructure. There is, for instance some self-conscious talk about the Resistance workers who died, and about art as a national pride and heritage (the latter cunningly put into the mouth of a spinster, and therefore discountable); there is an interlude with Jeanne Moreau to provide the love interest (mercifully tactful and devoid of clinches); the accents are very polyglot, with rather crude dubbing of some of the French members of the cast; and although Burt Lancaster gives his usual sound performance as the Resistance leader, Paul Scofield is inclined to be stagey as the German.

'But none of this really affects the film. What matters is Frankenheimer's iron control of his narrative, his obvious delight in the mechanical devices at his disposal, and of course his strong dash of wit. There is a brilliant sequence, for instance, in which the French, by changing station signs in an operation of split-second timing, deceive the Germans into thinking that their train is entering Germany; as the German officer in charge of the train sighs with relief and indicates the safe crossing of the frontier on his map. Frankenheimer laconically pulls back his camera to focus on the real location, right back where they started from in France. Hitchcock, it would seem, now has a strong rival in the thriller stakes.' (Tom Milne, *Financial Times*, 30 October 1964)

'The Train, produced in France, with some early scenes directed by Arthur Penn, who was later replaced by John Frankenheimer, included some of the most realistic train crashes ever seen on the screen; they were achieved by crashing redundant locomotives and stock supplied by the SNCF and filming the destruction with a number of cameras.' (Peter Handford)

35mm, Sound, 140mins, United Artists

THE TRAIN (Sweden 1948)

A Kinocentralen production. Directed by Gosta Werner. Photography by Sten Dahlgren. Music by Sven Erik Back. An impression of the magic of a journey from the south to the north of Sweden.

35/16mm, Sound, 20mins, BFI/HA

TRAIN 523 (France 1947)

Midi Films. A kind of poor-relation version of *La Bête Humaine*, shot between Paris (St Lazare) and Gisors, with locations mainly in the Réseau de L'État.

35mm, Sound, 97mins, Midi

TRAIN AT MADELEINE STATION (France 1929)

SNCF. First scene made by the Service Cinématographique of the Chemin de Fer Métropolitan in 1929. They have made many films since, including a series on railway safety, tourism in Paris, Sprague-Thomson equipment as well as offering facilities for film companies wishing to film on the Paris Metro, including *Rendez-vous Champs-Elysées*, *Métropolitan*, *Dernier*

Metro, *Les Portes de la Nuit*, *Antoine and Antoniette* and *Quai des Orfèvres*.

35/16mm, Silent, 8mins, SNCF

TRAIN ENTERING AND DEPARTING FROM HOVE STATION (Britain 1896)

Made by Hove portrait photographer George Albert Smith in May 1896 as a result of seeing the Lumière programme at the Empire, Leicester Square, in February 1896, with its scene of a train entering La Ciotat station. The LBSCR train is hauled by a Stroudley LBSCR 'Gladstone' 0-4-2, originally recorded as Class B and later as 'B1'. *Gladstone* was withdrawn in 1927, bought for £140 by the Stephenson Locomotive Society and is now in the National Collection.

35/16/VID, Silent, 52secs, HA/125

TRAIN ENTERING A COUNTRY STATION (France 1896)

A train enters a country station.

35mm, Silent, 44secs, NFA

TRAIN ENTERS A STATION (France c1899)

Unidentified railway shot.

35mm, Silent, 24secs, NFA

TRAIN JOURNEY THROUGH THE ALPS (Britain 1947)

Boulton-Hawker Films. Journey from Milan via the Simplon tunnel.

16mm, Silent, 9mins

TRAIN OF EVENTS (Britain 1949)

An Ealing Studios film. Produced by Michael Balcon. Directed by Sidney Cole, Charles Crichton and Basil Dearden. Script by Basil Dearden, T E B Clarke, Ronald Millar and Angus Macphail. Photography by Lionel Banes and Gordon Dines. Art Direction by Malcolm Baker-Smith and Jum Morahan. Music by Leslie Bridgwater. With Valerie

Hobson, Jack Warner, John Clements, Irina Baronova, Susan Shaw and Joan Dowling.

An express train speeds northwards across the flat countryside of the Midlands. Its driver peers ahead, watching the line and the signals. Suddenly a horrified look comes into his face. His hands go to the emergency brake, driving it hard home. Grinding and screeching, the great train begins to pull up. The brakes scream to a crescendo. And then blackness... sudden absolute silence.

Behind the crash lie some hundreds of human stories, the stories of the passengers, the stories in particular of four different sets of people.

The story, for instance, of the engine driver, Jim Hardcastle (Jack Warner). He's a genial, middle-aged man with a sympathetic wife (Gladys Henson) and a modern daughter, Doris (Susan Shaw). He is on the point of getting promotion, but his hopes are jeopardized because his prospective son-in-law, Ron Stacey (Patrick Doonan) fails to turn up to work on the railway after a quarrel with Doris. Jim drives Ron's engine for him.

There is the story of a London waif (Joan Dowling) and an escaped German prisoner-of-war (Laurence Payne), very much in love, very broke and terrified of the consequences when the girl steals money from their landlady in order to help the German.

The third story is gay – the story of a romantic composer-conductor Raymond Hillary (John Clements) who is having an affair with a solo pianist, Irina Norozova (Irina Boronova) until his wife Stella (Valerie Hobson) steps in to handle it in a cool and humorous manner, gained from long experience of her husband's interest in the opposite sex. The unfortunate husband, assuring the wife that she is really the one he loves, finds himself in the difficult situation of having to explain to Irina that their romantic interlude is over.

The fourth story is melodramatic — a highly-strung actor (Peter Finch) who murders his faithless wife (Mary Morris) and puts her strangled body into his theatrical basket. The basket accompanies him on his journey to Liverpool...

All four episodes merge on the train. The crash solves problems for all of them – happily for the engine-driver and for the composer; ironically for the German, tragically for his girl-friend; and inevitably for the actor.

'Ever since those far-off days in 1905 when a wondering public in a 5-cents Pittsburg theatre saw *The Great Train Robbery*, the first film with a story, trains have been cinema's most constantly popular actors. Quite rightly, because they are big and handsome and fulfil a basic screen requirement. They move.

'Even all those swaying corridors in *Night Trains* to every imaginable European capital cannot spoil their charm for me, and I am glad of another excellent one, in the Gaumont timetable from today, called *Train of Events*.

'This train is the 3.45pm from Euston to Liverpool. It starts from Platform 13, and the film isn't five minutes old before we see it come to a gruesome end. Then in the *Bridge of San Luis Rey* manner we go back a few days to see the lives of four different sets of its passengers. Suspense is maintained because we do not learn until the very end who is killed and who injured, and how the various tangled problems are resolved.

'Three directors have handled the different stories leading up to the crash and have achieved harmony if insufficient pace at times, and special credit must go to Basil Dearden who sets a near-French quality of squalor about his gin-soaked murder in a room over a pub while a gramaphone grinds out *These Foolish Things*.

'In a long list of excellent performances Joan Dowling has real pathos as the girl who loves the German, Jack Warner is exactly the man I always want to have driving my trains, Valerie Hobson with a quiet, wry smile damps the temperamental fireworks of Irina Baronova, Gladys Henson has one superb moment and Miles Malleson makes a delightful job of an enthusiastic chicken keeper.' (Felix Barker, *Evening News*, 18 August 1959)

The London, Midland & Scottish Railway (absorbed into British Railways while the film was being made) provided the facilities for the main locations. The star started the film as LMS 4-6-0 'Royal Scot' Class No 6126 *Royal Army Service Corps* and ended it as BR No 46126.

The crash was staged at Wolverton Carriage Works and a vast amount of excellent film was recorded between Euston and Bletchley, hardly a foot of which was used in the finished film (and then only behind the opening titles). The negatives on high-quality 35mm film were rescued from the vaults at Elstree Studios and used in the video *Steam on 35mm*

Jack Warner himself set down his own account of the making of the film: 'I was told I was the envy of every boy in Britain (and a good many chaps well out of their boyhood) when I made the film *Train of Events*, because I really did drive an express train.

'When Sir Michael Balcon asked me if I would like to play the part of an engine driver in this film I replied that I would on condition that I was coached well enough to drive the express train properly. 'If I'm going to play this part I want it to be authentic,' I added.

'Micky agreed and that was how I actually drove the Euston-Liverpool express out of Euston station. Not very far and not very fast, I must admit, but nevertheless I did drive – and without slipping the wheels which, according to my tutor, was as common a fault with engine drivers under tuition as slipping the clutch is with the learner drivers of cars. Mind you, I was an amateur and remained an amateur. My teacher was a great big fellow named Ned Sparks who always wore a bowler hat. His name has always stuck in my memory because the only other Ned Sparks I ever heard of was the American movie comedian who always uttered his dry jokes in an unvarying monotone and usually chewed on a fat cigar.

'As I stood in the cab with 85 tons of machinery pulsating in front of me and we took bends at speed, the monster looked more than a little awesome to me, but it was all a schoolboy's dream come true. Manipulating the mechanical mass, which professional drivers seemed to think possessed a soul, was absolutely fantastic.

'On the initial journey to Liverpool, the train was driven by a little chap no more than 5ft tall who sat on a stool. I need hardly say that the view from the footplate is vastly different from that one gets on a journey looking out of a compartment window, or even standing on a station or from a road or field as the train goes by. As we approached Tring Tunnel at about 70mph, the mouth seemed so small that I said in alarm, "It won't go through there." The under-sized driver, who was looking out of the side of the cab, didn't bother to turn around. He just shouted over his shoulder, "The old cow went through yesterday, guv'nor."

'In the meantime, Ned Sparks had handed me a duster which he told me to put over my face as we reached the tunnel. When we emerged, I asked him why the face protection had been necessary. "Well," he said, "sometimes the windows in the side of the cab get a bit loose and with the vacuum created by the wind as we pass through the tunnel they may shatter so that the glass is thrown into your face..."

'The accident looked so realistic in the completed film that it was difficult to believe it hadn't really happened. It was a clever combination of model craftsmanship and actual wreckage. Once again, we were in the hands of technicians with expertise.

'A studio team went from Ealing to Wolverton Carriage Works in Buckinghamshire and constructed a 'wreck' from old derelict railway stock provided by British Railways. They were assisted by railway officials well versed in the technicalities of crashed debris. The shooting of this sequence took three nights, with our technicians working from eight in the evening until seven o'clock the next morning. 100 Wolverton people were engaged to play the roles of passengers involved in the crash and we used regular ambulancemen and rescue squads. A model train in Ealing Studios was brought into operation for the actual impact. It was quite small and was fixed to a table only a few feet wide, but by the time the genuine and the fake had been fused on film it was impossible for the eye to separate them. I tried to buy the model but the studio wouldn't sell and it's been used since in other films. Model boats are similarly employed for filming in the same way, but unless great care is taken, they are easily detected, especially if they are filmed in fresh water.

It was in this film that I nearly broke my back. The camera was in the driver's cab of the real train and I, as the driver, was wrenching on the brakes at the moment I sighted an obstruction on the track. Too realistically, I fell backwards and collided with solid iron. The hefty clout I took in the spine affected a leg and hip and this is the reason why, today I sometimes suffer pain from arthritis when I'm walking.

'The stupid and ironic thing about this regrettable incident was that it was deleted in the cutting room!!!' (Jack Warner died in 1988.)

35mm/VID, Sound, 89mins, Weintraub/125

TRAIN OF EVENTS (Britain 1966)

British Insulated Callender's Construction Co film. The story of the overhead electrification on the London (Euston) to Crewe, Liverpool and Manchester line. It covers the demolition of the old Euston Terminus (see *Arch at Euston*) up to the opening of the new line.

16mm, Sound, Colour, 13mins, BICC

TRAIN RIDE TO DEVIL'S BRIDGE (Britain 1962)

Written and directed by Alan Willmott. A detailed record of the journey from Aberystwyth to Devil's Bridge on the BR-operated Vale of Rheidol Light Railway; there is good coverage of the various locomotives used on the line.

16mm, Sound, Colour, 11mins, BTF/AW

TRAIN TIME (Britain 1950)

Produced by British Transport Films for the British Transport Commission. 'A film which takes for its theme the operation of British Railways, the busiest and most complex railway system in the world. The integration of Britain's goods and passenger services calls for a constant review of timetables to meet varying local needs. For example a sudden demand for extra locomotives in West Cornwall may affect the tin-plate traffic from South Wales, or the fast traffic to clear fish from Scottish ports may affect rail demands in the Midlands. All these alterations to carefully prepared schedules mean new train times.'

35/16mm, Sound, 30mins, BTF

TRAIN TO LYMINGTON (1989)

Picture Palace Productions. Produced by Malcolm Craddock. Directed by Richard Simpson. With Chris Good and Claire Parker. A four-minute drama of two people alone in a railway carriage.

VID, Sound, Colour, 4mins, PPP

TRAINS (Germany c1924)

Unidentified general railway scenes; probably Germany.

35mm, Silent, 1min, NFA

TRAINS AT NEWCASTLE-UPON-TYNE (Britain 1961)

Made by P B Whitehouse and John Adams. In addition to many Pacifics we see the station pilot in North Eastern livery and 'J21' class No 65033.

16/8mm, Silent, 5mins, CV/NRM

TRAINS AT SEA (Sweden 1959)

The building and operation of a new train ferry.

16mm, Sound, 16mins, BTF

TRAINS AT WORK (Britain 1958)

Made by P B Whitehouse and John Adams. A film made at York Station before the days of the main line diesel.

16/8mm, Silent, 4mins, CV/NRM

TRAINS IN THE ISLE OF WIGHT (Britain 1959)

Made by P B Whitehouse.

16/8mm, Silent, Colour, CV/NRM

TRAINS: MIDLAND & N E REGIONS (Britain 1959)

Link Productions. Scenes between Shep and Tebay, through Troutbeck station, at Kirkby Stephen and Darlington. Locomotives include 'Coronation', 'Royal Scot', 'Jubilee', 'A3' and 'J72' Classes.

16/9.5/8mm, Silent, Colour, 4mins, MFS

TRAINS – NOT WAGONS (Britain 1964)

Produced by British Transport Films. 'The coal industry is rapidly modernising; the market for coal is continally changing. *Trains — Not Wagons* examines the way in which British Railways is meeting the problems created by the changing pattern of coal distribution, the peak winter demand, and the waste that arises from single wagon-load delivery.'

35/16mm, Sound, Colour, 16mins, BTF

TRAINS OF THE MOUNTAINS (Australia 1953)

Produced by Charles Wolnizer. Directed by Bill Veitch. Commentary by Bert Wicks. The Mount Lyell mountain railway, using the ABT Rack system, at Queenstown, Tasmania. It is a good example of the adhesion and rack procedure and dates from 1896.

16mm, Sound, 21mins, HA

TRAINS ON THE LICKEY (Britain 1958)

Made by P B Whitehouse and John Adams.

This film depicts a typical summer Saturday in 1958 on the Lickey Incline, with scenes at Bromsgrove and en route to Blackwell.

16/8mm, Silent, 7mins, CV/NRM

TRAINS REMEMBERED (Britain 1985)

Edited by Wilf Watters. Commentary by David Coleman. Volume One. 1930s colour film of 'Coronation Scots'; scene at Silloth; London Commuter Services; 1940s 'A4s' in black livery; Underground trains, Swindon works; Belfast to Larne, etc; 1950s and 1960s motive power sheds; 'A4s' retire; last steam to Euston and Paddington; Clapham Museum, Victoria line opens, end of the 'Brighton Belle'; 1980s — diesels scrapped; preservation work, etc.

VID, Sound, Part Colour, 55mins, Online

TRAINS REMEMBERED (Britain 1986)

Edited by Wilf Watters. Commentary by David Coleman. Volume Two. Steam scenes at Little Kimble, Marlow, Colnbrook, Epping, Chesham, Weymouth Quay, Corfe Castle, Newport Pagnell (Alan Willmott collection). ECML in 1959, with 'A4s', 'A2s', 'N2s', 'B1s' and 'B17s' (Ralph Cooper). Deltics, Class 76 electrics on the Woodhead Tunnel line. Isle of Man steam railways (1964 and 1971). Steam at Kingmoor depot, Carlisle in 1964 (Ken Attwood), preserved railways (1969-74) including the KESR. Snow Hill press visit (1986), Marylebone Specials (1986).

VID, Sound, Part colour, 60mins, Online

TRAINS REMEMBERED (Britain 1987)

Online. Produced by Wilf Watters. Commentary by David Coleman. Volume Three. 1940s — 'Terriers' at Eastleigh Works, Waterloo in snow, with steam-hauled 'electrics' 1947. 1960s — last steam trains on the Paddock Wood line to Hawkhurst 1961; Carlisle station, with steam specials hauled by *Clun Castle*, *Kolhapur*, *Blue Peter* and *Oliver Cromwell*, filmed by Ken Attwood; 1968-69. Longmoor Military Railway (Wilf Watters); Leeds area double-headed steam, 1967 (Alan Willmott); 1970s — Derwent Valley Preservation Railway; Swindon Works; diesel Classes 42 and

52; *Iron Duke* replica in Hyde Park. 1980s — end of Swindon Works; Ffestiniog Anniversary, 1986; London and Greenwich Railway Anniversary; steam trips from Marylebone.

VID, Sound, Part colour, 60mins, Online

TRAINS: SOUTHERN REGION (Britain 1961)

Made by G S Holyoake. Scenes at Waterloo include 'Merchant Navy' and 'King Arthur' class locomotives. Scenes at Victoria include the last steam-hauled 'Golden Arrow' train on 11 June 1961.

16/9.5/8mm, Silent, Colour, 4mins, MFS

TRAINS TO TENTERDEN (Britain 1987)

Online Video. Produced by Wilf Watters. Commentary by David Coleman. Archive film of the line as it was includes a scene in the 1930s at Bodiam station and trains going from Rolvenden to Headcorn Junction in the 1950s. There is also film shot in 1961 when the goods service to Robertsbridge was hauled by 'Terriers'. Closure came in 1967 and the preserved railway opened its first section to Wittersham Road in 1974. Many aspects are covered in this study of a preserved line.

16mm, Sound, Part colour, 60mins, Online

TRAINS: WESTERN REGION (Britain 1959)

Link Productions. Scenes at Reading station, Paddington, West Drayton, Slough and near Sonning. Locomotives include Castles and Halls.

16/9.5/8mm, Silent, Colour, 4mins, MFS

TRALEE AND DINGLE (Britain 1950)

Made by P B Whitehouse.

16/8mm, Silent, Colour, CV/NRM

TRANSCONTINENTAL LIMITED (USA 1926)

Metro. Directed by Art Croft. With Lionel Barrymore and Madge Bellamy. An engine driver is believed to have caused an accident but the real culprit is eventually revealed with the help of his daughter. All filmed on the Atchison Topeka and Sante Fe Railroad.

35/16mm, Silent, 82 mins, HA

TRANSPORT (Britain 1948)

Produced by the Pathe Documentary Unit for the British Transport Commission. (Taken over by British Transport Films in 1950.) Produced by Peter Baylis. Directed by Peter Bradford. One of the *Wealth of the World* series. The story of the rapid development of canals, railways and road transport services in this country up to the reorganisation and nationalisation of 1948. There are many stock shots from films like *Painted Boats* and *Passenger Trains of the LMS*; even a shot of KESR locomotive No 3 at Lydd from *The Loves of Joanna Godden*. There are good steam scenes at Liverpool Street, an unidentified 'Castle' and a shot of LMS 'Princess Royal' 4-6-2 No 6205 *Princess Victoria*.

35/16mm, Sound, 21mins, BTF

TRANSPORT IN MERSEYSIDE AND LANCASHIRE (Britain 1954)

Made by Geoffrey Ashwell, Victor Jones and Jack Law. The Mersey Railway and Wirral Electric lines, the Liverpool Overhead Railway and aspects of the work of municipal and company operators in Lancashire.

16mm, Silent, 12mins, HA

TRANSPORT IN NORTH WALES (Britain 1954)

Made by Geoffrey Ashwell, Victor Jones and Jack Law. A record of the Llandudno and Colwyn Bay Electric Railway and the Great Orme Railway in 1954.

16mm, Silent, 10mins, HA

TRANSPORT IN VISION: DIESEL POWER

Five British Transport Films including *Diesel Train Ride* (1959), Blue Pullman, *Let's Go to Birmingham* (1961), *Overture 125* and *InterCity 125* (1985).

VID, Sound, Colour, 55mins, VID/BTF

🚂 🚂 🚂 🚂 🚂

TRANSPORT IN VISION: DIESEL TRAIN DRIVER

Four British Transport Films for staff training on one tape, including 'Introduction to the Diesel Train', 'Driving the Train', 'Dealing with Faults' and 'Operating Requirements'.

VID, Sound, 75mins, VID/BTF

🚂 🚂 🚂 🚂 🚂

TRANSPORT IN VISION: WEST COAST ELECTRIFICATION

Three British Transport Films including *Under the Wires* (Euston to Crewe and Manchester, 1965), *Wires Over the Border* (North to Glasgow, 1974) and *Driving Techniques: Freight Trains* (1964).

VID, Sound, Colour, 50mins, VID/BTF

🚂 🚂 🚂 🚂 🚂

TRANSPORT SPECIAL (Britain 1982)

Anglia Television. An item from *Anglia Reports*. The fight to sustain local money in maintaining railway services. With Ray Buckton, James Urquhart, Sidney Weighell and Jim Foxon.

16mm, Sound, Colour, Anglia

🚂 🚂 🚂 🚂 🚂

TRANSPORT STORY (Britain 1959)

Produced by Kinocrat and the Central Office of Information for the Foreign Office. From the series *Report From London: Persian Teleview*. A film similar in subject and content to the above, but introduced on the screen by a prominent author, broadcaster and journalist from Iran — Hussein Massudi. In Persian only.

16mm, Sound, 11mins, COI

🚂 🚂

TRANSPORT VIDEO PUBLISHING

(formerly Cresswell Video until 1986)

'The Video Magazine for the Steam Enthusiast,' this was one of the video magazines that began in the height of the 'Video Mania' in the mid-1980s. Called *Steam View* its purpose was to stick to the theme of steam only and its formula included such items as Locomotive Profile, Preservation Feature and News and Events. The news magazine was supplemented by individual tapes, mainly of an archive flavour, like *Reflections on Southern Steam*, *The West Coast Main Line*, *Reflections of Scottish Steam*, *Branch Lines in the South East* and *East Coast Main Line*.

Typical items in the magazine include:

Flying Scotsman in Australia including film of the locomotive's tours in 1968 and good coverage of the Australian tour.
Locomotive Profile: *The Great Marquess* (Archive).
The HOF Pacifics of Germany (1981)
Summer Days on the Settle & Carlisle railway
BR '9F' 2-10-0 No 92220 *Evening Star* on the North Yorks Moors Railway (1985)
Steam to Stratford-upon-Avon, with *Kolhapur* and *Clun Castle*
City of Truro on the Severn Valley Railway
Profile of *King George V*; British Rail Journeys
Last days of steam on the Hope Valley Line
British Rail tours with GWR 4-4-0 No 3440 *City of Truro*, plus visits to Severn Valley.
Andover Steam Weekend (1985)
LMS 'Princess' 4-6-2 No 6229 *Duchess of Hamilton* on the Settle & Carlisle line
LNER 'A4' 4-6-2 No 60009 *Union of South Africa* on the Settle & Carlisle line
Marylebone workings with *Flying Scotsman*, *Sir Lamiel*, *Kolhapur* and *Clun Castle*
Preserved Steam: the Ffestiniog Railway
Steam specials to Hereford
Steam railways of Portugal and Turkey

Scarborough to Hull with LNER 'A4' 4-6-2 No 4468 *Mallard* (1986)
Footplate ride: GWR 'Castle' 4-6-0 No 7029 *Clun Castle* to Marylebone (1986) and recent coverage
Preservation Feature: steam on the West Somerset Railway, with SDJR '7F' 2-8-0 No 53808 and a visit from BR '9F' 2-10-0 No 92220 *Evening Star*.
Steam on the Nottingham-Lincoln line
LNER 'A4' 4-6-2 No 4498 *Sir Nigel Gresley* on the line from Marylebone with specials.
LNER Gresley 'V2' 2-6-2 No 4771 *Green Arrow* on the Settle & Carlisle
Report on the North Yorks Moors Railway
LMS No 6201 *Princess Elizabeth* on the Welsh Marches
GWR No 6024 *King Edward 1* in steam at Buckinghamshire Railway Centre.
GER 'J15' 0-6-0 No 564 on the North Norfolk Railway.
LMS 'Jubilee' 4-6-0 No 5596 *Bahamas* to Didcot

🚂 🚂 🚂 🚂 🚂

THE TRAVEL GAME (Britain 1958)

Produced by British Transport Films. As the Hook Continental express leaves Liverpool Street station, a passenger starts to guess where his fellow passengers are going. In his imagination, the journey becomes interwoven with scenes of his travelling companions at their supposed destinations; among the windmills, diamonds and cheeses of Holland; at a Rhine wine festival; on Mount Pilatus in Switzerland; in Denmark and Germany. Hubert Gregg is the guesser, and Elizabeth Lutyens composed the music.

35/16mm, Sound, Colour, 30mins, BTF

🚂 🚂 🚂

TRAVELS WITH A DUCHESS (SETTLE & CARLISLE LINE) (Britain 1987)

BBC Television. Series producers: Neil Cameron and Peter Walton. Written and presented by Miles Kington. A journey with LMS 'Princess Coronation' 4-6-2 No 6229 *Duchess of Hamilton* on the Settle & Carlisle line. (From the *Steam Days* series).

16mm, Sound, Colour, 30mins, BBC TV

🚂 🚂 🚂 🚂 🚂

THE TRAVOLATORS (Britain 1961)

Produced by British Transport Films. Approximately 40,000 people then used the Waterloo and City Underground line every day. For years they had walked to and from the platforms at the Bank by a steep passage known as the 'Drain'. But now, they can ride up and down on the first moving pavements in Europe – the Travolators. This film shows the construction of the Travolators which was achieved without disrupting normal traffic.

35/16mm, Sound, 8mins, BTF

🚂 🚂 🚂 🚂 🚂

THE TRIAL (France, Italy, West Germany 1962)

Paris Europe. Directed by Orson Welles. With Orson Welles, Jeanne Moreau and Anthony Perkins. A complex Kafka story, made up mainly of nightmares as a man is tried for a crime never revealed. A large part of the film was made in the abandoned Gare d'Orsay on SCNF, later turned into an arts centre.

35mm, Sound, 120mins, Ficit distributors

🚂 🚂

TROOP TRAIN PASSING A LEVEL CROSSING (Britain 1914-18)

A train passing over a level crossing carrying troops and equipment, probably in France.

35mm, Silent, 0.5min, NFA

🚂 🚂 🚂 🚂 🚂

TTC SUBWAY CONSTRUCTION (Canada 1957)

Toronto Transport Commission. Construction of the Toronto subway system.

16mm, Sound, Colour, 35mins, HA

🚂 🚂 🚂

THE TUNNEL (Britain 1935)

A Gaumont British Production. Directed by Maurice Elvey. With Richard Dix, Leslie Banks, Madge Evans and Aubrey Smith. Science-fiction tale of a trans-atlantic tunnel being built in the late 20th century.

35mm, Sound, 94mins, Rank

🚂

TURKSIB (USSR 1929)

Produced by Vostok Film. Directed by Victor Turin. Photography by E Slavinski and B Scrancisson.

The story of the building of the Turksib railway and the subsequent rise in the standard of living in Turkestan. It opens with shots of cotton growing and spinning and weaving. Lack of water causes the cotton to fail as the grain for food takes all the water available. If grain from Siberia could be brought to Turkestan, more cotton could be grown for all Russia. The plains and steppes are surveyed and the building of the railway commenced. When the railway is finished, civilisation breaks through bringing education, irrigation works, and new methods of farming.

The best railway scene comes when tribes of wandering nomads gather to see the first train they have ever met in their lives. Titles are used to build up the drama: 'From the farthest corner' ... (shots of tribesmen setting out on horses, camels, donkeys and even bulls) ... 'the wandering nomads' ... (details of men, women and children of the tribes) ... 'Make their way' ... (the tribesfolk on their way across the barren plains) ... 'to see' ... (the groups gather at a central spot in the distance) ... 'To see' (the empty track stretching endlessly across the arid plain) ... 'The first' ... (a locomotive is seen in the midst of the tribesmen, motionless; suddenly, it shoots steam and they leap away, men and animals alike). Then the engine moves off and the tribesmen chase it gleefully across the plain in an exciting finale to this sequence. And it's nice to see a real Russian vintage locomotive

after all those Spanish and Hollywood mock-ups.

35/16mm, Silent, 88mins, BFI/HA (rly)

🚂 🚂

TWELVE ANGRY MEN (USA 1957)

United Artists. Produced by Henry Fonda and Reginald Rose. Directed by Sidney Lumet. With Henry Fonda, Lee J Cobb, Martin Balsam, E G Marshall, Jack Warden, Ed Begley, John Fiedler and Jack Klugman. A murder case jury ready to convict an innocent man are persuaded to change their minds by one doubting member. The sounds of passing elevated electric trains become a key part of the case; as Tony Bilbow put it: 'A railway plays an important but largely offstage part.'

35mm, Sound, 95mins, United Artists

🚂

TWENTIETH CENTURY (USA 1934)

Columbia. Directed by Howard Hawks. With John Barrymore, Carole Lombard and Roscoe Kerns. A Broadway actress is lured to Hollywood in company with a Broadway producer. There is extensive use of that Hollywood favourite of the 1930s — the Atchison, Topeka and Sante Fe.

35mm, Sound, 91 mins, Columbia

🚂 🚂

TWO DUKEDOGS TO BARMOUTH (Britain 1961)

Made by Patrick Whitehouse and John Adams. Dukedogs 9004 and 9014 of the Great Western Railway on a journey from Shrewsbury to North Wales, including a visit to the Talyllyn Railway. Scenes at Barmouth and Towyn. Passing trains include Cambrian Coast Express, double-headed by BR Class '4' 4-6-0s Nos 75026 and 75005.

16mm/VID, Silent, 8mins, HA/Stirling/CV/NRM

🚂 🚂 🚂 🚂 🚂

TWO GLENS TO FORT WILLIAM (Britain 1959)

Made by P B Whitehouse and John Adams. This is almost a historic film of *Glen Loy* and *Glen Falloch* working mail between Glasgow and Fort William.

16/8mm, Silent, 7mins, CV/NRM

TWO NORWEGIAN TOWNS (Britain 1934)

Made by the Dartington Hall Film Unit. Includes railway scenes between Bergen and Oslo.

16mm, Silent, 15mins

ULSTER SHEDS (Britain 1959)

Made by P B Whitehouse and John Adams. A film made at Adelaide Shed and Queens Quay Shed at Belfast, showing many steam engines which are now withdrawn.

16/8mm, Silent, 7mins, CV/NRM

UNDER COVER (Britain 1943)

An Ealing Studios film. Directed by Sergei Nolbamdov. With John Clements and Godfrey Tearle. Wartime partisan drama. A sequence of a munitions train being blown up in Yugoslavia was shot in the now abandoned coal sidings at Ravenscourt Park (near Hammersmith).

35mm, Sound, 88mins, Weintraub

UNDER NIGHT STREETS (Britain 1958)

Produced by British Transport Films for the British Transport Commission. A commentary on the back-room boys and girls who work all night to keep London's Underground transport system on the move. The story which is told with Cockney humour and with excellent photography, shows in effect the care and thoroughness of night maintenance work that takes place during the short period when trains are not running, and must include cable, signal and shaft examination, track repairs, replacement of outdated items and dispersal of the day's accumulation of dust and litter.

35/16mm, Sound, 20mins, BTF

UNDER THE RIVER (Britain 1959)

Produced by British Transport Films. This is the story of the outstanding feat of engineering of Thomas Andrew Walker which enabled the Severn Tunnel, then the longest underwater tunnel in the world, eventually to be completed. The film provides also a record of the sight and sound of the unique group of six magnificent Cornish beam engines which kept the tunnel free of water for over 70 years before being replaced by electric pumps.

35/16mm, Sound, 27mins, BTF

UNDER THE WIRES (Britain 1965)

Produced by British Transport Films. The electrification of the London Midland Region main line between London, Manchester and Liverpool at 25kV AC, using overhead wires and drawing supply from the National Grid, was a major feat involving civil, electrical, mechanical and signal engineering of a complex and advanced nature. This film depicts some aspects of the problems involved and of the unprecedented operations which were carried out.

35/16mm, Sound, Colour, 28mins, BTF

UNDERGROUND (Britain 1928)

British Instructional Films. Produced by H Bruce Woolfe. Directed by Anthony Asquith. Script by Anthony Asquith. Photography by Stanley Rodwell. With Elissa Landi, Brian Aherne, Norah Baring and Cyril McLaglen. Bert, an electrician, and Bill, an underground porter, fight over the same girl. Eventually Bert kills the girl during a quarrel in a power house; he is pursued by Bill and finally trapped in an underground lift. There are many shots of the Underground system including a chase through Lots Road Power Station, a fight on the roof top overlooking the Thames and a lift scene shot at Covent Garden station during the night.

35mm, Silent, 109mins, NFA/Weintraub

UNDERGROUND CENTENARY (Britain 1964)

Produced by British Transport Films. London's Underground railway began with the building of the Metropolitan line in 1863. As the city expanded into the surrounding countryside, so did the railway. In 1964 with traffic congestion creating ever increasing problems, the Underground expanded again, and the film ends with work on the new Victoria line.

35/16mm, Sound, 17mins, BTF

🚂 🚂 🚂 🚂 🚂

UNDERGROUND JOURNEY (Britain 1946)

British Instructional Films. An account of a journey on the London Underground from Piccadilly.

16mm, Silent, 10mins, Pathe

🚂 🚂 🚂 🚂 🚂

UNDERGROUND RAILWAY (Britain 1946)

Pathe/British Instructional Films. An account of the London Underground.

16mm, Silent, 5mins, HA

🚂 🚂 🚂 🚂 🚂

UNDERGROUND, SUBWAY OR METRO

Underground railways have featured in many feature films. For London's Underground, there is the film Underground, Passport to Pimlico and Bulldog Jack. For the Paris Metro, look for Zazie Dans Le Metro or Metro (but called Subway for international release). For New York, see The French Connection, The Taking of Pelham 123, Practically Yours, The FBI Story, The Liquidator or The Batchelor Party. Only films which have a reasonable amount of the system are included in this book; many are just fragments, back projection scenes or, as in On The Town, only Hollywood studio reconstructions.

🚂 🚂 🚂 🚂 🚂

UNDERGROUND TRAINS REMEMBERED (Britain 1989)

Online. Produced by Wilf Watters. Commentary by David Coleman. London Underground trains from 1940 up to the present time, including World War 2 Underground scenes; LT steam locomotives (ex-GWR pannier tanks); Metropolitan Tank No 1 at the Buckinghamshire Railway Museum; the

abandoned extension to Elstree; Victoria Line; Heathrow extension; Wood Lane station (closed 1947); the Post Office Railway; the Waterloo and City line; Underground stock on the Isle of Wight; Jubilee line in 1989; Docklands Light Railway.

VID, Sound, Colour, 68min, Online

🚂 🚂 🚂 🚂 🚂

UNION PACIFIC (USA 1939)

A Paramount picture. Produced and directed by Cecil B De Mille. Script by Walter De Leon, C Gardner Smith and Jesse Lasky Jr, based on an adaptation by Jack Cunningham of a story by Ernest Haycox. Photography by Victor Milner. Process photography by Harry Lindgreen. With Joel McCrea, Barbara Stanwyck Akim Tamiroff, Robert Preston, Lynne Overman and Brian Donlevy.

The story of the building of the Union Pacific Railroad. The attempts by Burrows to sabotage the line for financial reasons, the raids on the pay train, Indian attacks, locomotives derailed, the travelling railroad frontier camps and the personal stories of a group of the engineers, drivers, surveyors and 'law and order' men who helped to construct the line are all depicted in the tradition established by The Iron Horse.

It is claimed that Cecil B De Mille thought up the idea of Union Pacific on a journey from Hollywood to New York in 1937 when film producers still travelled by train. On the section between Omaha and Chicago seeing 'the great stretches of America flash past', he thought of 'the vision, courage and hard work' of those who built the railway many years ago. From Cleveland he telegraphed the Paramount studios in Hollywood: 'Story of Building "Union Pacific" railroad to be my next work.'

In true De Mille style it was a 'big' picture. The basic 'train' used on location consisted of six locomotives and 50-car pieces of rolling stock, claimed as 'of the period of the 1860s'. 500 railwaymen were hired to run the train and build 15 miles of track on location. The locomotive J W Bowker was borrowed from the Railways and Locomotive Historical Society, re-boilered and

put back in steam for the film. Built in 1875, for the Comstock Lode line of the Virginia and Truckee Railway, it was purchased in 1896 by the Hobart Estate Company and operated at Hobart Mills, California. In 1937, the woodburning 2-4-0 engine was presented by the Hobart Estate Company to the Pacific Coast Chapter of the Railways and Locomotive Preservation Society, one of the world's oldest preservation groups. The technical adviser to the film was Lucius Beebe, New York newspaper writer on transport subjects, who wrote High Iron and other books on the history of the American Railroads.

In addition to the actuality material, extensive use was made of elaborate model work, including the derailing and almost total destruction of a train by Red Indians, who topple a water tower on top of the engine. Another good model was used for a scene of a train crashing down the snow-covered side of a mountain, shot through a haze of studio snow, with impressive sound effects. The film ends on a scene of the 'golden spike' ceremony at Promontory Point, Utah on 10 May 1869, out of which comes an enlarging insert of a 1939 diesel-hauled, transcontinental, stream-lined, aluminium-bodied express approaching rapidly. About five cars pass before the camera makes a 90° follow-through action pan; five more cars flash by and 'The End' comes up as the train disappears across the desert plain.

Here is a stock list on the final production schedule:
Baldwin 4-4-0 No 11 Reno (1872) of the Virginia & Truckee railroad.
Baldwin 2-4-0 No 21 J W Bowker (1875) of the Railway and Locomotive Historical Society.
Baldwin 4-4-0 No 22 Inyo (1875) bought by Paramount Pictures.
Central Pacific 4-4-0 No 18 Dayton (1873) bought by Paramount Pictures.

35mm, Sound, 133mins, Paramount

🚂 🚂 🚂

UNION STATION (USA 1950)

A Paramount picture. Produced by Jules Schermer. Directed by Rudolph Mate. Script by Sidney Boehm from a novel by Thomas

Walsh. Photography by Daniel L Fapp. Music by Irvin Talbot. With William Holden, Nancy Olson, Barry Fitzgerald and Jan Sterling. The blind daughter of a millionaire is seized and held to ransom by a gang who use the crowded Union Station to make a contact with the victim's family and to collect the ransom. The city and railway police co-operate to catch the criminals. The action takes place almost entirely in and about the station, with one or two good scenes of arriving and departing at Union Station, Los Angeles.

35mm, Sound, 81mins, Paramount

THE UNTOUCHABLES (USA 1987)

Paramount Pictures. Produced by Art Linson. Directed by Brian De Palma. With Kevin Costner, Sean Connery and Robert De Niro. Law enforcers go after the Al Capone gang in the 1920s. Includes a fine scene of an ambush, filmed in Chicago Union station, making visual use of the 1920s grand staircase and main cathedral-like Hall.

35mm, Sound, Colour, 119mins, Paramount

UP FOR THE CUP (Britain 1931)

British and Dominions Film Company. Produced by Herbert Wilcox. Directed by Jack Raymond. With Sydney Howard, Joan Wyndham and Moore Marriott. A Yorkshireman comes to London to see the Cup Final. Includes railway scenes on the LMS, some of which were used in the video *Steam on 35mm*.

35mm/VID, Sound, 76mins, Weintraub/125

USA TOUR OF THE CORONATION SCOT (Britain 1939)

LMS film. The tour and the visit by the 'Coronation Scot' train to the New York Worlds Fair in 1939. It was actually No 6229 *Duchess of Hamilton* disguised as No 6220 *Coronation*! (From the *Just for the record* series on video.)

35mm/VID, Sound, 12mins, BTF/RFV

VAL GARDENA, THE ITALIAN NARROW GAUGE (Britain 1961)

Made by P B Whitehouse and John Adams. Part of one of the most exhaustive film safaris of all times, as Pat Whitehouse and his team went exploring surviving steam; the resultant research formed the basis of a World Guide to Narrow Gauge.

16/8mm, Silent, Colour, 12mins, CV/NRM

THE VALE OF RHEIDOL RAILWAY (Britain 1976)

HTV Television. Produced and directed by John Mead. Presented by Wynford Vaughan-Thomas. The narrow gauge line from Aberystwyth to the waterfalls of Devils Bridge in the Cambrian Mountains features two of its locomotives GWR 2-6-2T No 7 *Owain Glyndwr* and No 8 *Llywelyn*. (From the *Great Little Trains of Wales* series).

16mm/VID, Sound, Colour, 26mins, HTV/Castle

VALLEY OF SONG (Britain 1952)

Associated British Picture Corporation. Directed by Gilbert Gunn. With Mervyn Johns, and Clifford Evans. Story of a Welsh village. Includes scenes of a GWR Welsh branch line.

35mm, Sound, 74mins, Weintraub

THE VALLEY OF THE GIANTS (USA 1938)

Warner Bros. Directed by William Keighley. With Wayne Norris, Claire Taylor and Charles Bickford. Period melodrama of lumberjacking and land grabbing in Canada. Includes a well-staged spectacular runaway steam train scene.

35mm, Sound, Colour, 79mins, Warner

VARIOUS LOCOS IN VARIOUS LOCATIONS (Britain 1987)

Railfilms. Produced by John Wildy. This video is simply a large number of recordings of preserved locomotives working on British Rail between 24 April 1982 and 26 October 1985 and edited together, including *Evening Star*, *Sir Nigel Gresley*, *Duchess of Hamilton*, *Hagley Hall*, *Earl Bathurst*, *Leander*, *Clun Castle* and *City of Truro*.

VID, Sound, Colour, 60mins, RFV

VIADUCT INSPECTION (Britain 1962)

Made by P B Whitehouse and John Adams. A rare case of taking a look at a bit of railway civil engineering on the old North Eastern system.

16/8mm, Silent, 6mins, CV/NRM

VICTORIA STATION (Britain 1919)

Topical budget. Newsreel of Lloyd George and the King leaving Victoria station.

35mm, Silent, 10secs, NFA

VICTORIA THE GREAT (Britain 1937)

Imperator Film. Produced and directed by Herbert Wilcox. With Anna Neagle and Anton Walbrook. The life of Queen Victoria. The credit titles record thanks to 'the LMS for the original train of 1841'; this consisted of a 'century-old engine and coaches used for the honeymoon of Victoria and Albert'. The locomotive in fact is Liverpool and Manchester *Lion* with the railway museum L&M replica coaches, filmed at Bricket Wood, near St Albans.

35mm, Sound, part-colour, 107mins, Imperator

VICTORIAN STEAM RAILWAYS (Britain 1987)

Video 125. Produced by Peter Middleton. Written and presented by John Huntley. A unique glimpse of railways as they were around the turn of the century, this tape covers the period from 1895 to 1901 and includes the Lumière *Train Arriving at La Ciotat station* (1895); *Train arriving at Hove station on the LBSCR* (1896); *Express Trains at Wood Green on the Great Northern Railway* (1896); *Midland Railway at Leeds* (1896); *Phantom Ride: Barnstaple to Ilfracombe* (1898); *Phantom Ride: Across the Tay Bridge* (1897); *A Kiss in the Tunnel* (1898); *South Eastern and Chatham Railway* (1899); *London and South Western 'T9s' at Southampton* (1900); *Royal Train at Portsmouth* (1901); *East Berlin station* (1896); *Berlin Elevated Railway* (1896); *The Black Diamond Express* (USA 1897); *New York Steam Elevated Railway* (USA 1896); *Steam Trams at Bradford and Leeds* (1897); *Romance of a Railway* (USA 1901). From the series: *Trains from the Ark*. Volume One.

VID, Sound, 50mins, 125

VIDEO 125

This classic video unit is run by Peter Middleton, a former Thames Television cameraman, who produces all the tapes, and photographs many himself. The mainstay of Video 125 is a series of *Driver's Eye Views* (not quite the same as Cab Rides) which include the Settle and Carlisle, the Hastings line, the Cambrian Coast, the Chilterns, the Cornish Branch Lines, HST records from London to Bristol, Exeter to Plymouth and Saltash to Penzance, Scottish runs from Dingwall to Thurso and also to Mallaig and two unusual ones: Central London Underground and Metropolitan & District. There are three archive programmes: *Victorian Steam Railways* (1895-1901); *Edwardian Scene* (1902-1912); and the *Pre-Grouping Years* (1913-1923). A speciality of the company has been to gain access to 'outtakes' and 'cut-offs' from feature and documentary films made on high-quality 35mm master film, released under the titles *Steam on 35mm* (Volumes 1 & 2) and *Diesel Electric 35mm* (Volumes 1 & 2). Two specials featured a *Day in the Severn Bridge Signal Box* and the specialised freight operation *Rolling Stone Class 59 ARC*.

VIDEO BAHNMAGAZIN EUROPA AKTUELLE BAHNBERICHTE (Britain 1988)

JC/OF. Commentary by Hans Peter Treichler. Produced and directed by John Cocking. General European railway magazine including a steam festival at Emmental; railway museum at Blonay-Chamby; 172kph record; various German, Austrian and Swiss events with steam, diesel and electric locomotives.
(Volume No 1. *Video Railway Magazine*, 1988)

VID, Sound, Colour, 60mins, JC/OF

VIDEO BAHNMAGAZIN EUROPA AKTUELLE BAHNBERICHTE (Britain, 1988)

JC/OF. Commentary by Hans Peter Treichler. Produced and directed by John Cocking. Orient Express revival with SNCF steam locomotive Class 141R; 'Venice-Simplon Orient Express'; Swiss electric locomotive class Re 4/4 II; various steam and electric locomotive events in Europe.
(Volume No 2 *Video Railway Magazine*, 1988)

VID, Sound, Colour, 60mins, JC/OF

VIDEO STEAM MEMORIES (Britain 1986)

Stirling Video. General collections of 8mm film shot between 1950 and 1968 somewhat hastily put together and covering all regions.

VID, Sound, Colour, 60mins, Stirling

VIDEO TRACK (1987-)

A video magazine issued bimonthly by the Transport Video Publishing company with over 20 issues. This 'video magazine for the railway enthusiast' has, like other projects of its type, covered a vast number of subjects over the years, of which the following are a representative sample:-
Classes of diesel locomotives: '03', '08', '20', '24', '25', '26', '27', '31', '33', '37', '42', '44', '45', '46', '47', '50', '52', '56', '58', '50' and '60'. Special Diesels: 'Warship' (green and maroon livery); 'Western' (red livery); 'Deltics', 'Prototype Deltic', Brush Type 2 and Type 4; DMUs (green livery); 'Peaks', and preserved '40' '106', 'D100', '45' '046' (green livery). Pacers, Sprinters and SuperSprinters. IC125.
Classes of Electric locomotives: include 'Wessex Electrics'; EMUs, EM1 and EM2 (Woodhead line); 'Gatwick Express'; Classes 90 and 91.
Freight in the West
Diversions round Stoke-on-Trent
Settle & Carlisle Railway
Forth Bridge Centenary
Freight in the North East
Railways in the West Midlands
The Inverness to Aberdeen line
King's Cross and Liverpool Street
Severn Valley Diesel Weekend
South Humberside Freight
Loco haulage on the Kyle line
Activity at Ely
The Era of the Diesel Hydraulics
Shrewsbury to Machynlleth
Rails Across the Fens
The Deltics on the Severn Valley
Exeter West Signalbox
The Railways of North Wales
Kings Cross in the 1960s
Weymouth to Bournemouth line
Rails North of the Capital
The Woodhead Route
First Generation Diesel Multiple Units
East Coast Electrification
Signalling Survey
Freight Today and Yesterday
Station Developments in the New World
Railways of March
Crewe Open Day
Aylesbury Open Day
Severn Tunnel Yard Closure
Weymouth Quay branch
Holyhead to Chester
Lincolnshire Somersault Signals
Wolverton Works Open Day
Warcop line closes
Redmire derailment
Coalville Open Day
Nottingham Open Day
Derby and Gloucester Open Day
Last Chinnor Freight
Flooding at Worcester
The Matlock line
Kilmarnock Works
Skegness line
Specials to Boulby Mine and Saltburn

VIDEOLINES

This video unit based on Paddock Wood has issued a mixed bag of programmes including American and Continental imports, driver's eye views (eg 'Gatwick Express') and Scottish tours. They have extended their driver's eye videos ('Reading to Leamington Spa' for example) and made available the programme on the *Flying Scotsman* Tour of Australia from Melbourne to Alice Springs in 1990.

VIDO (sic) STEAM MEMORIES (Britain 1982)

Stirling Video. An assembly of the work of Richard S Greenwood, H G Forsythe and J B Hollingsworth, taken between 1964 and 1965, featuring sundry 'Black Fives', MR 'Big Bertha' 0-10-0 No 2290 on the Lickey Incline, SDJR Fowler 2-8-0s and LNER 'A4' 4-6-2 Nos 4482 *Golden Eagle* and 4498 *Sir Nigel Gresley*.

VID, Sound, Colour, 60mins, Stirling

VIEW FROM AN ENGINE FRONT – BARNSTAPLE (Britain 1898)

A Phantom Ride taken from the buffers of an engine on the L&SW Railway crossing over a viaduct with a panorama of Barnstaple. The train then passes through an old, disused station and then through Barnstaple station and over a draw-bridge, passing a signal box on the way from the window of which a signalman waves a flag. Produced by the Warwick Trading Company.

The film starts at Barnstaple Junction, then travels out across a sharply curved iron viaduct (single line) across the River Taw. The old abandoned Quay station (renamed Town station in 1886) comes into view at the northern end of the viaduct. It had only just been abandoned when the film was made, mainly because it was in a cramped position with no room for sidings or for the brand-new Lynton to Barnstaple narrow gauge line which also opened in 1898. The new joint station for the standard gauge LSWR and the 2ft gauge Lynton and Barnstaple is clearly seen; alas, without a glimpse of the narrow gauge trains. The journey continues past

Barnstaple Town signal box and on to the single line over the swing bridge across the River Yeo, known variously as Pill Bridge and Pottington Swing Bridge. This steepest line in the West of England was opened on 20 July 1874 and closed on 5 October 1970.

35/16/VID, Silent, 7mins, NFA/HA/125

VIEW FROM AN ENGINE FRONT-ILFRACOMBE (Britain 1898)

A Phantom Ride through the country to the south of Ilfracombe, passing the town reservoirs and under numerous arches. The line plunges into a short tunnel upon leaving Morthoe and after a while the train descends the steep falling gradient towards Ilfracombe at the end of which can be seen Ilfracombe station into which the train glides. Produced by the Warwick Trading Company. The action starts on the climb from Braunton, after which the line rises 600ft in six miles, mainly at 1 in 40 with the summit reached at Morthoe Tunnel, a mere 69.5 yards in length. Then follows a 2.25 mile long bank at 1 in 36 down to Ilfracombe. The station was 225ft above sea level; it was so exposed to the wind that a protective screen was built in 1892, shortly before the film was made.

35/16/VID, Silent, 6mins, NFA/HA/125

VIEW FROM AN ENGINE FRONT – SHILLA MILL TUNNEL (Britain 1900)

A Cecil Hepworth production. *A Phantom Ride* taken at 60mph, affording a panoramic representation of some of the most beautiful of the Devonshire scenery, besides a rapid passage through the tunnel. A weird and exciting subject. By permission of the L&SWR. From the Cecil Hepworth catalogue of 1906.

35/16/VID, Silent, 1min, NFA/HA/125

VIEWS FROM A TRAIN ON A MOUNTAINSIDE (France c 1900)

Unidentified views; probably France.

35mm, Silent, 3mins, NFA

THE VIRGIN SOLDIERS (Britain 1969)

A Columbia Picture. Produced by Carl Foreman. Directed by John Dexter. With Nigel Patrick, Lynn Redgrave and Tsai Chin. Story of British national servicemen in Malaysia during the Emergency. For one scene, Stanier BR 'Black Five' 4-6-0 No 44781 was purchased by Columbia Pictures and derailed on staged track at Saffron Walden, Essex. The locomotive was purchased by Columbia at a cost of £3,500 and offered for resale after the staged crash for £1,700 to a Saffron Walden enthusiast. However, the cost of salvaging and transporting the locomotive 200 miles to the nearest preservation centre was quoted at £5,000 so No 44781 had to be sold for scrap and broken up on the spot. There was a rumour at the time that various film companies purchased 'Black Fives' and put them into cold storage for possible future film production requirements.

35mm, Sound, Colour, 96mins, Columbia

THE VIRGINIAN (USA 1929)

Paramount. Directed by Victor Fleming. With Gary Cooper, Walter Huston and Richard Arlen. Early sound Western as a ranch foreman takes on and defeats the local baddies. The first sound film to use the facilities of the Sierra Railroad, including Baldwin 2-8-0 locomotive No 29790, built in 1906.

35mm, Sound, 95mins, Paramount

A VISIT TO KING'S CROSS SHED (Britain 1959)

Made by P B Whitehouse and John Adams. Various locomotives as seen at Kings Cross Shed in 1959, including *Mallard*, *Flying Scotsman* and *Woodcock*.

16/8mm, Silent, 5mins, CV/NRM

A VISIT TO SALTLEY SHED (Britain 1960)

Made by P B Whitehouse and John Adams. This film shows a variety of engines seen on the shed one afternoon in 1960. It was part of a series of 'shed' studies made during that year.

16/8mm, Silent, 5mins, CV/NRM

VISIT TO THE GREAT WESTERN SLEEPER DEPOT AT HAYES, MIDDLESEX (Britain 1944)

GWR Unit, Paddington. Detailed record of how wooden sleepers were prepared and treated under wartime conditions. There is a self-propelled steam crane, a vast wood stock, the treatment of the wood to preserve it and coverage of the fitting of chairs, cutting of lengths and other processes. In wartime, all but the heaviest work was done by women and there is a wonderful study of the teams of ladies doing a pretty awful job but managing to keep smiling.

16mm, Silent, 9mins, HA

THE VITAL LINK (India 1951)

Indian News and Information Service. An account of the Assam railway project.

16mm, Sound, 10mins, India

VOLK'S ELECTRIC RAILWAY

The railway has been filmed on and off for some 70 years, starting with a visit by Harry Lauder in the 1920s, in many holiday films of the 1930s and 1950s, plus a definitive history in the 1980s with the film by John Payne.

VOLK'S ELECTRIC RAILWAY (Britain 1983)

John Payne/Online. Produced by John Payne and Paul Clark. Commentary by John Huntley. A film to celebrate the 100th Anniversary of the Magnus Volk Electric Railway at Brighton, including a ride from Brighton to Black Rock and back. A history of the railway; celebration led by Conrad Volk at Brighton. Details of the construction and maintenance of the line.

16mm/VID, Sound, Colour, 18mins, HA/Online

VON RYAN'S EXPRESS (USA 1965)

TCF. Produced by Saul David. Directed by Mark Robson. With Frank Sinatra, Trevor Howard, Sergio Fantoni, Edward Mulhare, Brad Dexter and John Leyton. A train load of prisoners-of-war escape from Italy to Switzerland during World War 2 under the command of an unpopular officer. 'Exhilarating action thriller with slow spots atoned for by nail-biting finale.' (Leslie Halliwell) 'Enjoy the many scrapes including one with the train doing a high wire act in the mountains.' (Tony Bilbow) Extensive use was made of steam railway facilities freely given by Italian State Railways, with a great roundup of all available locomotives.

35mm, Sound, Colour, 117mins, TCF

VOYAGE ACROSS THE IMPOSSIBLE (France 1904)

Star Films. Made by Georges Méliès. A science fiction journey including a journey and crash on the 'Paris-Righi-Sun Express', the Crazyloff line and a trip to the sun via the Jungfrau as built in the Méliès studios at Montrevil-sous-Bois.

35/16mm, Silent, 25mins, BFI/HA

W. H. SMITH VIDEOS

An important collection of transport tapes, the famous Whitehouse/Adams 'Railway Roundabout' has been released in five volumes, in association with Ian Allan SBS videos. Films from the National Railway Museum, York.

Volume 1. The 'Bristolian' in Steam Days; Trains on the Lickey Incline; Irish Narrow Gauge; Southampton Harbour; Hayling Island Branch; Cardigan Branch; Last Train from Abergavenny to Merthyr (1958).

Volume 2. GER 'E4' at Cambridge; Closing the Wye Valley Line; The Skye Line (Fort William to Mallaig); Midland Compound No 1000; A Worcestershire Branch Line; The 'Brighton Belle'; A Visit to King's Cross Shed (1959).

Volume 3. Two Dukedogs to Barmouth; 'T9' to Tavistock; Cromford & High Peak; A Visit to Perth Shed; Gordon Highlander on the Spey Valley Line; Trains at Newcastle-Upon-Tyne; Trains at York (including the old museum) (1960).

Volume 4. From Bath to Evercreech Junction; Lancashire and Yorkshire Special; Last Train from Bala to Ffestiniog; Welsh Narrow Gauge; The Severn & Wye in the Forest of Dean; Locomotives of London Transport; Swindon Locomotives Nos 3440, 2516 and 4003 (1961).

Volume 5. Isle of Wight Engines; the Cambrian Coast Express; the Bluebell Line; Southern Region Trains at Seaton Junction; A Journey from Ryde to Ventnor; the Jones Goods to Kyle of Lochalsh; Kirtley, Johnson and Company (1962).

Other titles exclusive to W H Smith are also available from time to time.

WAGONS WITH CARE (Britain 1954)

Produced by British Transport Films for the British Transport Commision. 'A million and a quarter wagons are in service on the railways of Britain, and about 90,000 of these undergo repairs each week. Much of the damage is due to wear, but the film shows how some of it could be avoided. The magnitude of the task and the organisation of repair in British Railways workshops is illustrated, together with some detail of the work itself.'

35/16mm, Sound, 23mins, BTF

WALKING WESTWARD (Britain 1978)

Westward Television. Directed by Clive Gunnell. A look around transport in Cornwall, including scenes on 'Towan's Miniature Railway', and a driver's eye view of the journey from St Erth to St Ives in a DMU, a very attractive GWR branch line that still survives.

16mm, Sound, Colour, 26mins, Westward

THE WALL (Britain 1981)

BBC Television. World War 2 story featuring scenes filmed on the Keighley and Worth Valley railway with LMS '8F' 2-8-0 No 8431.

16mm, Sound, Colour, 52mins, BBC Television

THE WARE CASE (Britain 1939)

Ealing Studios. Directed by Robert Stevenson. With Clive Brook, Jane Baxter, Barry K Barnes and Francis L Sullivan. Trial melodrama; includes a boat train Pullman scene at Waterloo and a 'King Arthur' on the front, bound for Southampton.

35mm, Sound, 79mins, Weintraub

WASH AND BRUSH UP (Britain 1953)

Produced by British Transport Films for the British Transport Commission. This is a staff instructional film showing the routine maintenance overhaul of a Standard Class 5 locomotive which had been in service 16 days. After such a period fuel is wasted through ash piling up in the firebox. In the locomotive shop a team of men, each with his special job takes over and cleans and inspects both the engine exterior and the interior working parts.

35/16mm, Sound, 26mins, BTF

WATCHING POINTS (Britain 1957)

Rank Films. From the *Look at Life* series. Some unusual railways including scenes in Switzerland, Norway and Britain are part of this survey of railways and their possible future.

35/16mm, Sound, 17mins, Rank

WATERLOO AND CLAPHAM JUNCTION IN THE 1930s (Britain 1935)

At Waterloo a Drummond 'L12' No 423 awaits departure amidst a mammoth pile of luggage. We see the 'Brighton Belle', the 'Atlantic Coast Express', various emus, a 'King Arthur' Waterloo-bound, a 'Lord Nelson' heading for Bournemouth, and we take a look at Pullman stock in the sidings. An 'Arthur' passes on truly vintage stock.

VID, Silent, 6mins, Stirling

WATERLOO ROAD (Britain 1944)

A Gainsborough picture. Directed by Sidney Gilliat. With John Mills, Stewart Granger and Alastair Sim. The film includes a chase across the tracks outside Waterloo station. There is a 'Nelson' electric unit (service No 8 Portsmouth) in the foreground and a 'Lord Nelson' class steam locomotive in the background, as John Mills leaps from the train, pursued by a Military Policeman.

35mm, Sound, 78mins, Rank

WAVERLEY STEPS (Britain 1945)

Greenpark Production for COI for Scottish Home Department. Directed by John Eldridge. A broad cross-section of life in Edinburgh; includes a run towards Edinburgh on the footplate of a Gresley Pacific and a typical day in the Edinburgh life of a railway fireman.

35/16mm, Sound, 16mins, COI

THE WAY TO THE EAST (East Africa 1955)

East African Railways and Harbours. The building of the Mombassa-Kampala line. There are scenes of the line in action, complete with Beyer-Peacock Garratt locomotives.

16mm, Sound, Colour, 35mins, EAR

THE WAY TO THE SEA (Britain 1936)

Strand Films. Directed by J B Holmes. Music by Benjamin Britten. Verse by W H Auden. An historical representation of Portsmouth and the London-to-Portsmouth road, followed by a journey on the electrified London-to-Portsmouth railway line. Imaginative use of sound, particularly Benjamin Britten's musical score, marks this out as an innovative and unusual production of its day.

35/16mm, Sound, 18mins, Strand

THE WAY TO THE WEST (East Africa 1958)

Produced by Gateway Films for the East African Railways and Harbours Board. The design and construction of an important development project in Africa. This film gives an account of the extension of the railway from Kampala, Uganda, westward to Kasese in the Ruenzori Mountains, during 1952-56. It shows something of the problems and hazards of an impressive engineering achievement accomplished over difficult terrain.

16mm, Sound, Colour, 37mins, EAR

WELLS FARGO (USA 1956-65)

With Dale Robertson. A long television series including many railway scenes using preserved American locomotives and stock on the Sierra Railroad.

Shown on BBC Television: 1957-1966

WELSH NARROW GAUGE: FFESTINIOG, TALYLLYN, VALE OF RHEIDOL (Britain 1960)

Made by P B Whitehouse and John Adams. A film made on the Talyllyn, Ffestiniog and Vale of Rheidol Railways, featuring Bill Hartley. Part of a major narrow gauge filming project which also produced a book as well as items for *Railway Roundabout*.

16/8mm, Silent, 9mins, CV/NRM

WELSHPOOL AND LLANFAIR LIGHT RAILWAY (Britain 1963)

A newsreel record of the reopening of the line after lying dormant for 18 years, with the locomotives of 1902 Beyer Peacock 0-6-0T No 1 *The Earl* and No 2 *The Countess* in action. As this coincided with the height of the Beeching cuts, a railway that was reopening was quite a story in those days.

16mm, Sound, 4mins, HA

THE WELSHPOOL AND LLANFAIR LIGHT RAILWAY (Britain 1976)

HTV Television. Produced and directed by John Mead. Presented by Wynford Vaughan-Thomas. The narrow gauge railway from Welshpool to Llanfair Caereinion in Montgomeryshire. The line has a decidedly foreign atmosphere with coaches from Austria and Africa, so it has often been used for feature films with a spy background. Two of the original 1902 locomotives are still in use: Beyer Peacock 0-6-0T No 1 *The Earl* and No 2 *The Countess*. (From the *Great Little Trains of Wales* series).

16mm/VID, Sound, Colour, 26mins, HTV/Castle

WELSHPOOL STEAM (Britain 1991)

Railfilms. Produced and directed by Nick Dodson. Research and script by Neil Wooler. Archive film by James Boyd and Roger Siviter. A complete history of the Welshpool and Llanfair, with its closure in 1956

and the reopening of the line from 1963 to 1981 in various stages.

VID, Sound, Colour, 40mins, RFV

WEST COAST MAIN LINE THROUGH THE LONDON SUBURBS (Britain 1990)

Transport Video Publishing. Various volumes and issues including:

Motive Power History of the Euston Mainline

Steam in the 20s: with 0-8-0s, 'Prince of Wales 4-6-0s, 'Claughton' 4-6-0s, 'Precursor' 4-4-0s and early electrics.

Steam in the 30s: with 'Patriots', 'Royal Scots', 'Coronation' Pacifics and a rare glimpse of the 'Turbomotive'.

Steam during the postwar years: featuring the 'Duchess' and 'Princess' Pacifics, 'Royal Scots', Jubilees, 'Britannias', Class 5s.

The Diesel Era: including 10001, EE Type 4s.

The Electric Era: comprising a detailed look at the electrification of the Euston line in the early 1960s. Includes early liveried classes in action on freight and passenger.

Study of the West Coast Route from Euston to Watford

Euston station – a history from building in 1937 to the present day. A wide range of classes, including the 'Pacifics', are shown in action in the 1930s and 1960s. Camden Bank, Willesden shed and station, Hatch End and Bushey Troughs – a detailed look at these locations in the days of steam, with a wide variety of classes in action including the 'Duchess' Pacifics. Watford station and shed.

VID, Sound, 55mins, TVP

WE'RE IN BUSINESS TOO! (Britain 1964)

Produced by British Transport Films. This film sets out to persuade the businessman who may travel from city centre to city centre by road or by air that travel by train gives him more time in which to do useful work or to relax, eat and sleep in comfort. It also shows how the railways themselves were sup-

posedly learning to sell their advantages to their customers.

35/16mm, Sound, Colour, 23mins, BTF

WESSEX STEAM IN THE SIXTIES (Britain 1987)

Rail Video. Volume One. Made from film shot by Barry Eagles during the last years of SR steam, this tape shows locations such as Winchester, Southampton, Bournemouth, Eastleigh, Portland, Ringwood Branch and Hayling Island branch. Loco classes featured include Bulleids, Standard 'Qs', Terriers, 'M7s', 'S15s' of both types, 'Ns' and 'Us'.

VID, Sound, Colour, 30mins, RVO

WESSEX STEAM IN THE SIXTIES (Britain 1987)

Rail Video production. Film by Barry Eagles. Volume Two. This is the second tape in the series made from the films of Barry Eagles depicting British Railway steam at work on the Southern Region. The majority of material in this tape is shot in the Southampton area during the period 1963-66. All major SR classes are shown including Bulleid 'Pacifics'. Standard '3s', '4s' and '5s', plus SR 'Us' and 'Ns'. Other locations include Bournemouth, Eastleigh, Southampton Terminus, Waterloo, Sway and 30096 in industrial use. USA tanks are also featured at Southampton docks and on the Lymington branch.

VID, Sound, Colour, 30mins, RVO

WEST HIGHLAND LINE (Britain 1936)

A record of the steam-hauled route from Inverness to the Kyle of Lochalsh and the run to Mallaig. There are old HR locomotives as well as LMS 'Black Fives', and a good study of the harbour terminus as it once was, as well as a busy scene at Achnasheen with HR 'Clan Goods' 4-6-0 No 17950.

16mm, Silent, 8mins, HA

WEST SOMERSET RAILWAY (Britain 1985)

West Somerset Railway. A video record of the railway offered with a slide and audio tape as a package. An interesting early experiment in promoting a preservation society. Made in association with J Associates.

VID, Sound, Colour, 40mins, West Somerset

WESTERN FINALE (Britain 1964-65)

Made by G S Holyoake. The last runs of GWR 4-6-0 locos — No 7029 *Clun Castle*; No 7808 *Cookham Manor* on 'North and West Tour' (LCGB); No 4936 *Kinlet Hall*; No 4079 *Pendennis Castle* (Ian Allan High Speed Commemorative run to Plymouth, May 1964).

16/9.5/8mm, Silent, Colour, 4mins, MFS/VID

WESTERN MAIL (USA 1947)

Directed by Robert Tansey. With Tom Keene, Frank Yaconelli and Jean Trest. A US marshal rounds up a gang of train robbers. A routine 'great train robbery' Western.

35mm, Sound, 55mins, NA

WESTERN REGION ENGINES (Britain 1960)

Made by P B Whitehouse and John Adams. This *Railway Roundabout* item features GWR 'Castle' 4-6-0 No 7023 *Penrice Castle*, BR 'Britannia' 4-6-2 No 70025 *Western Star*, GWR 0-6-0PT No 4695, GWR '6100' 2-6-2T No 6116 and something else very new at that time: Swindon/Maybach diesel-hydraulic No D823.

16/8mm, Silent, 6mins, CV/NRM/VID

WESTERN STEAM MEMORIES (Britain 1986)

Volume 1. Stirling Video. A mixed bag of 8mm material made all over the Western Region between 1950 and 1968.

VID, Sound, Colour, 60mins, Stirling

WHAT A DAY (Britain 1960)

Produced by British Transport Films. Group Travel – five typical outings by train – a ladies outing to Scotland from Newcastle; photographic and cyclists' club 'specials'; and two schoolboys' outings, one to Southampton Docks and the other to Boulogne. Cinema coaches, the TV train, and some veteran locomotives are also shown as excursion attractions.

35/16mm, Sound, Colour, 19mins, BTF

WHAT HAPPENED IN THE TUNNEL (USA 1903)

Edison. Directed by Edwin S Porter. Studio set of a moving train with photographically superimposed projection of passing scenery. A man is sitting in a train behind a pretty girl and her coloured maid. The train goes into a tunnel. When it comes out, the man finds he has kissed the coloured maid. Was this before or after *Kiss in the Tunnel* in Britain? The date suggests it was an imitation of the earlier English Film.

35mm, Silent, 1min, Lost

WHAT'S IN STORE (Britain 1954)

Produced by British Transport Films for the British Transport Commission. 'In a single year, British Railways spend £130 million on stores, materials and fuel. Outside of the main groups, such as steel for rails, timber for sleepers etc are more than 800,000 other items, ranging from watch screws to equipment for the cross-channel ferries.' The film which describes the gigantic scale was intended for staff instruction.

35/16mm, Sound, 23mins, BTF

WHAT WERE STEAM ENGINES REALLY LIKE? (Germany 1971)

Deutschen Bundesbahn production. Made by Sasse Film, Munich. As steam locomotives are being cut up for scrap and modern electrics taking over the German Federal Railways, an electric train driver goes back for a day to drive preserved HOF Pacific 01 147 on a special outing. Well assembled material.

(German title: *Wie war sie eigentlich die dampflokomotiven?*)

16mm, Sound, Colour, 21mins, HA

WHEELS A' ROLLING (USA 1949)

A record of the 'Wheels a' Rolling' pageant of the Chicago Railroad Fair of 1948 and 1949, featuring both originals and replicas of railroad motive power from its earliest days to the Burlington Zephyr of 1934 and the evolution of railways up to 1949 in the United States. It turned out more to be the Last Rites rather than the great revival of railroads intended.

16mm, Sound, Colour, 38mins, HA

THE WHEELS BEHIND THE WALLS (Britain 1947)

An LMS film. The services of the railways to the building industry just after World War 2, when the whole issue of rebuilding housing after the wartime devastation was a key issue and the roads could in no way handle the challenge before big trucks and motorways.

35mm/VID, Sound, Colour, 13mins, BTF/TVP

WHEN STEAM WAS KING (USA 1940-55)

Made by Carl Dudley. Steam on the New Haven, New York Central, Bessemer and Lake Erie, Chesapeake and Ohio, Pennsylvania, Nickel Plate, Louisville and Nashville, Erie, Great Northern, Northern Pacific, Union Pacific, Texas and New Orleans (SP) and Santa Fe.

8mm, Silent, Colour, 14mins, Blackhawk

WHEN THE DALTONS RODE (USA 1940)

Universal. Directed by George Marshall. With Randolph Scott, Kay Francis, Brian Donlevy and Andy Devine. Adventures of the Dalton Gang in a typical Western. Includes a scene of the gang leaping from a rock cliff onto the roof of a passing train and men on horseback jumping off a flat wagon whilst the train is on the move. These scenes were filmed between Jamestown and Tuolumne on the Sierra Railroad using the tall timberland scenery on that part of the line. Baldwin locomotive 2-8-0 No 29790 (1906) as well as Sierra Railroad No 24 and coaches Nos 2 and 6, plus Combine No 5, fitted with ropes on the roofs for the stunt men to grasp when jumping from the rock overhang. The actors were added later by back-projection!

35mm, Sound, 80mins, Universal

WHEN THE DEVIL DRIVES (Britain 1907)

A Charles Urban film. Whilst a taxi is taking a family to the railway station, the Devil takes the place of the driver. On arrival at the station he disappears. When the train starts, the Devil takes control of the engine and an incredible journey follows. The train flies through the air, along the sea bed, up a cliff and down an abyss. Finally the Devil's laughing face is shown in close-up.

The film starts with a number of quite unrelated railway shots obviously made for another film. They show Llandudno station on the LNWR with a train arriving, followed by a departure shot just outside Llandudno with a train hauled by a rare bird indeed – an LNWR Webb 2-2-2-2 Compound! Thereafter, all the railway effects are achieved with a German tinplate 0 gauge toy train set! The station with the family arriving at the entrance is reputed to be Pershore on the GWR.

35/16mm, Silent, 7mins, NFA/HA/125

WHERE DO THEY PLAY? (Britain 1965)

Produced by British Transport Films. Children are often unaware of the danger involved in playing near railway lines; are unaware of the damage and loss of life caused by vandalism. Driver Bill Addie visits schools to explain his responsibility to the passengers he carries, and makes children and parents more aware of their's.

16mm, Sound, 6mins, BTF

WHICKER'S WORLD ABOARD THE ORIENT EXPRESS (Britain 1983)

Yorkshire Television. Produced and directed by David Green. With Alan Whicker. More than 170 passengers celebrate the inaugural journey from London Victoria to Venice, with Alan Whicker as host and presenter. We meet Liza Minelli ('I love trains'), James Sherwood, multimillionaire, a duchess, a detective, a footballer and an arms king. Sherwood spent £11 million on restoring the Orient Express to its former glory, acquiring many Wagons Lit and Pullman carriages in the process. Restoring and running a 1920s train of great splendour proved tough going, even for a Kentucky millionaire, but the assembly has survived, in modified form, to the present time.

VID, Sound, Colour, 52mins, Yorkshire

WHITBREAD BEER COMMERCIAL (Britain 1976)

A jokey TV commerical which includes a scene of British POW's supposedly making their escape from Schwarzwald-am-See station, which was actually Wendover on the Chiltern line. Faced with Nazi soldiers and two ragged British prisioners on the usually sleepy platform at Wendover, two elderly ladies were so alarmed that they decided not to get out but went on to Aylesbury!

16mm, Sound, Colour, 1.5mins, Whitbread

WHY BOTHER? (Britain 1956)

Produced by British Transport Films. A brief story of two railway workers looking for something to do on their Winter evenings. Bob decides to attend First Aid classes, but Arthur does not. Bob goes through his course of training; Arthur goes dancing, finds a wife, and a flat. And then, after work one day...

35/16mm, Sound, 5mins, BTF

THE WILLIAM TELL EXPRESS (Britain 1987)

RV Television. A journey from Lucerne via St Gotthard to Locarno

and Lugano, joining two lakes in Switzerland. Swiss Federal Railways.

VID, Sound, Colour, 60mins, RVV

WIMBLEDON – WEST CROYDON RAILWAY (Britain 1972)

A film by Tom Martin. A detailed record of the line from Wimbledon which partly uses the bed of the horse-worked Surrey Iron Railway (opened in 1803) and goes on to Mitcham, Beddington Lane and West Croydon. There are scenes of the Merton Abbey Branch which closed to passengers in 1929 and continued to service some coal depots until final closure and track-lifting in 1974.

16mm, Silent, Colour, 21mins, TM/HA

WINDERMERE RAILWAY (Britain 1963)

A record of steam freight trains on the line from Oxenholme to Windermere via Burnside.

16mm, Silent, 9mins, HA

A WINDOW IN LONDON (Britain 1940)

Produced by Joseph Somlo. Directed by Herbert Mason. With Michael Redgrave, Sally Gray, Paul Lukas and Patricia Roc. A murder mystery set in London and first observed from an underground train. Scenes on the London Underground which include Earl's Court station; low angle shot (ground level) of passing District Railway trains; east of Barons Court station at the point where the Piccadilly tube line goes underground between the tracks of the Eastbound-Westbound District Railway; West of Earls Court, showing a District train coming out of a tunnel; West of Earls Court showing a District Railway train entering a tunnel just below Lillie Bridge Yard fly-under. Modern stock (1940 style) with automatic doors; one train with oval windows. One shot of Hammersmith cutting looking down from the abandoned high level line to Windsor.

35mm, Sound, 76mins, Rank

WINKY'S WEEKEND (Britain 1914)

Knockabout comedy of a husband on his own trying to cope. Includes a scene of a train at Holmfirth on the L&Y; there are good views of the driver and fireman but not, alas, of the locomotive!

16mm, Silent, 12mins, NFA/HA

WINTER SERVICE (Britain 1961)

Link Productions. A record of steam and diesel hauled traffic on the Barnard Castle – Kirkby Stephen line in January 1961. Ivatt '4' 2-4-0 No 43102 features prominently.

16/9.5/8mm, Silent, Colour, 4mins, MFS

WISBECH AND UPWELL TRAMWAY (Britain 1961)

Anglia Television. Produced and directed by David Kenten. A history of the famous Fenland Light Railway, running mainly alongside the public roadway. The occasion of the making of the film was the reconstruction of the journey, using a steam traction engine and a flat wagon on which was mounted the remains of an old Wisbech and Upwell carriage, which travelled the route on the public road alongside the line that was abandoned to passenger traffic in 1929. Written and presented by John Huntley.

16mm, Sound, Colour, 28mins, Anglia/HA (rly)

WITH A FINE FEELING FOR STEAM (Britain 1982)

BBC Television (Scotland). Produced by Michael Marshall. Presented by Donny B MacLeod. The story of Scottish steam railways using photographs and some early film of the 1950s. Other material was recorded on the Strathspey Railway, the Severn Valley Railway as well as an outing with LNER 'A4' 4-6-2 No 4488 *Union of South Africa*, on the 'Speyside Express'.

16mm, Sound, Colour, 25mins, BBC TV

THE WITHAM TRAIN DISASTER (Britain 1964)

Anglia Television. An account of the railway accident at Witham in 1905, involving a massive derailment on a London to Cromer express which was caused by platelayer's error. Reconstructed from stills and view of Witham station today.

16mm, Sound, 5mins, Anglia

WOMEN AT WAR (Britain 1945)

Commerical and Educational Films. Directed by John Oliver. Made with the extensive co-operation of the Great Western Railway, the film shows the work which women did during the 1939-45 period in running the railways.

16mm, Sound, 20mins, IWM/BTF

WOODSIDE LINE (Britain 1983)

A film by Ian and Stella Fagg. The last days of the line from Selsdon, Bingham Road, Woodside, and Coombe Road. It opened in 1885 and closed in May 1983.

16mm, Sound, Colour, 12mins, Fagg/HA

A WORCESTERSHIRE BRANCH LINE (Britain 1959)

Made by P B Whitehouse and John Adams. Story of one of the last official workings of a Midland Compound between Barnet Green and Ashchurch.

16/8mm, Silent, 6mins, CV/NRM/VID

WORKHORSES (Britain 1987)

BBC Television. Series producers: Neil Cameron and Peter Walton. Freight trains in the steam days, both standard and narrow gauge, filmed in a variety of sites, including a special freight makeup on the Severn Valley railway. (From the *Steam Days* series).

16mm, Sound, Colour, 30mins, BBC TV

WORKING STEAM (Britain 1983)

Lacewing production. Record of the steam engine rally at Stourpaine in 1983 including minature steam railway.

VID, Sound, Colour, 50mins, Lacewing

THE WORLD ABOUT US: THE ROMANCE OF INDIAN RAILWAYS (Britain 1975)

BBC Television. Produced by Colin Luke. Written and presented by James Cameron. Electric, diesel and steam in India in 1975. There are scenes of a primitive museum in Bombay, main line and narrow gauge trains in action and a very well filmed sequence on the Darjeeling line to the hills.

16mm, Sound, Colour, 50mins, BBC TV, Darjeeling only:HA (ref)

WORLD'S FAIR DAYLIGHT (USA 1984)

Steam Powered Video. Produced by Video Rails. A journey with 4449 from Portland to New Orleans World Fair. Footplate and lineside views. Across Arizona and New Mexico, with some aerial shots. Restoration of No 4449.

VID, Sound, Colour, 60mins, SPV

THE WRECK (USA 1914)

Produced by Vitagraph.

The story concerns a railroad president involved in a series of feuds with his son and a renegade railroad engineer. The climax comes when the westbound express, with father and son as passengers, crashes head-on into a runaway engine. The following description is taken from the *Kinematograph and Lantern Weekly* of 29 January 1914 (which claimed that this was the first time that a crash had been specially staged for a film and that the collision itself had cost £10,000):

'In the first case the final thrill of the crash of the two locomotives is most cleverly led up to. One sees a runaway engine steam out of a yard after its engineer has carelessly left the footplate. One sees its controlled course over the track: through stations, where its appearance sends the white-faced telegraphists flying to their instruments to send warning along the route; over points where the efforts of signalmen to side-track it are too late by a fraction of a second. One also follows the course of the express train proceeding towards the runaway on the same metals: sees the drunken engineer; his oblivion to warning signals and frenzied shouts from the stations he flashes through; his attack upon his fireman. The scene shows now the runaway, ever gaining momentum and now the footplate of the express engine, with the two men locked in death grips, while the calamity that is to hurl them both into eternity comes nearer with every second.

'Finally one has the stretch of track with the express and the runaway approaching from opposite directions, and the highest compliment one can pay to the art with which the preceding scenes have been presented, is to say that the comparatively few seconds which elapse before the engines clash, are filled for the onlooker with something of the horror-stricken apprehension with which one imagines the helpless spectators of a real catastrophe to experience. The attention is riveted upon the two locomotives and the imagination almost deceives one into hearing the deafening crash as they hurl together – the express engine rearing right up from the metals to be instantaneously piled with the wreckage of the carriages behind, which, their momentum checked in a second, splinter like matchboxes as they meet the wreckage of the two engines.

'Still more dramatic is the explosion of the boiler of the runaway at the very moment of impact. The whole thing passes in a few seconds, yet the dramatic quality of the scene is so intense that not a detail of the calamity is missed. One moment the locomotives are in full course – emblems of the great force under human control – and next a pile of broken wreckage, a grim reminder that the forces he evokes are sometimes too great for

man. To say that the film is powerful is hardly to do it justice – a strongly-acted studio scene may be powerful – neither would it be altogether adequate to call it simply tragic. Awe-inspiring and thrilling it certainly is and there will be few, in our opinion, among those who see the subject in the theatres who will not confess to having been affected in quite unusual degree'.

The success of *The Wreck* produced a flood of crash films and even public displays of such events. Albert E Smith, in his book *Two Reels and a Crank* (with Phil A Koury) describes what happened: 'Next, we bought the movie-film rights to a train collision staged as a public spectacle at Coney Island. A film company rented a field, laid down 500 feet of track, then sold several thousand tickets at two dollars apiece. Two retired engines were started from either end of the track and crashed head-on at the centre of the field. The public greeted the film with such enthusiasm that we immediately bought four old engines and rented an abandoned stretch of railroad track in New Jersey. Our writers prepared several scenarios, building each plot around a train smash-up as the big climax. In three pictures, we destroyed four engines, and would have kept on, except that we could not get our hands on any more retired engines.'

Both these films made use of locations and locomotives provided by the Western Pacific Railroad for the build-up to the crashes. To railway enthusiasts the scene of veteran and vintage 4-4-0 locomotives being deliberately smashed up is always alarming and present-day screenings of *The Wreck* and *The Juggernaut* are usually accompanied by a mixture of amazement and dismay which the passage of time has if anything, enhanced!

35/16mm/VID, Silent, 8mins, HA

THE WRECKER (Britain 1927)

Following the success of his play *The Ghost Train* in 1925, Arnold Ridley went on to write a play which centred on the character of a rapt old engine-driver who believes in 'rogue engines' and a spectacular

train crash created nightly on the stage. It was produced at the New Theatre St Martins Lane on 6 December 1927, and ran for 165 performances.

THE WRECKER (Britain 1929)

A Gainsborough Production. Produced by Michael Balcon. Directed by G M Bolvary. Based on a stage play by Arnold Ridley and Bernard Merivale. With Carlyle Blackwell, Joselp Striker, Benita Hume and Pauline Johnson.

A demented crook organises a series of deliberate crashes as part of a scheme to discredit the railways in favour of a rival bus company. The hero eventually tracks him down, saves an express train from disaster at the last minute and sees the crooks safely put away.

The film made extensive use of facilities offered by the Southern Railway. There are scenes at Waterloo, Sevenoaks and on the Basingstoke and Alton branch line. Motive power includes a SECR class D 4-4-0, a Maunsell LSWR 2-6-0, a LSWR H16 class 4-6-2 tank, another LSWR 4-4-0 locomotive, SR L class 4-4-0 No 756 emerging from Polchill Tunnel, Urie 4-6-0 No 452, Maunsell 'U' class 2-6-0 No A803, 'D15' class 4-4-0 No 463 and Urie-Maunsell SR King Arthur class No 773 *Sir Lavaine*. The crash was staged on the abandoned Basingstoke-Alton line at Spains Crossing, near Herriard. A Foden steam lorry with cement was driven on to the crossing and a train, consisting of Stirling SECR 4-4-0 No 148 and a set of eight-wheel coaches (re-lettered 'United Coast Lines') was allowed to run into it at speed and recorded by 22 cameras. The crash was staged on the afternoon of 19 August 1928. The coaches were the first bogie vehicle built by the SECR. If today's preservation movement had been in vogue in 1928 there would doubtless have been an outcry at the deliberate destruction of such notable relics.

The material was subsequently edited into two crashes and shots from it were later used in a sound film *Seven Sinners* (1937), also produced by Gaumont British. The main crash in *The Wrecker* breaks up into the following shots:

LS Foden lorry moving across the skyline towards the level crossing.

MS From rear of lorry, moving on to crossing.

LS (High angle) train approaches at speed towards crossing on a slight curve. The locomotive strikes the lorry, leaps off the track on its side (to screen right) and ploughs into the ground, still steaming hard.

MS Wrecked train seen through clouds of steam.

MS Locomotive on its side, furiously blowing off steam.

MS Steam swirling across the whole scene.

LS Locomotive on side; people beginning to clamber from wrecked carriages.

LS (From low angle) overturned locomotive in foreground; people leaping from overturned carriages.

MS People scrambling from carriages lying on their sides.

16mm, Silent, 59mins, HA

WREXHAM TO ELLESMERE (Britain 1963)

An 8mm record of a journey from Oswestry to Whitehurst Halt and Gobowen. Features GWR 2-6-0 No 7812 *Erlestoke Manor* and a 'Castle' and a pannier tank.

16mm, Silent, Colour, 11mins, HA

THE WRONG BOX (Britain 1966)

Columbia Pictures. Produced and directed by Bryan Forbes. With Ralph Richardson, John Mills, Michael Caine and Wilfrid Lawson. Two elderly brothers try to murder each other to get a 'tontine' lottery prize. Includes head-on train crash on the London and South Western Railway (not clearly specified) with a few real locomotive shots cut into model and studio work.

35mm, Sound, Colour, 110mins, Columbia

WYE VALLEY LINES (Britain 1958)

Made by Patrick Whitehouse and John Adams. Journey from Ross-on-Wye to Monmouth on the weekend before the line closed; GWR '14XX' class locomotive and auto-train; GWR pannier tank No 3726 from Ross-on-Wye to Chepstow.

16mm/VID, Silent, 4mins, CV/NRM/Stirling

WYOMING MAIL (USA 1950)

Universal. Directed by Reginald le Borg. With Stephen McNally and Alexis Smith. Mail train robbers and their attacks on the railroads. This film made very extensive use of the Sierra Railroad in California, with both steam locomotives Rogers 4-6-0 No 4493 (1891) and Baldwin 2-8-0 No 29790 (1906), coaches Nos 2 and 6, Combine No 5 and Caboose No 9, renamed 'UPRWRR'.

35mm, Sound, 86mins, Universal

YEAR IN REVIEW (Canada 1961)

Produced by Canadian National Railways. A review of the major advances made during the year in passenger, freight and marine services, in track construction, in hotels and in telecommunications.

16mm, Sound, Colour, 29mins, CNR

THE YELLOW BALLOON (Britain 1952)

Associated British Picture Corporation. Directed by J Lee-Thompson. With Kenneth More, William Sylvester, Kathleen Ryan and Andrew Ray. A small boy is terrorised by a murderer. The chase ends on the London Underground, with elaborate scenes shot during the night on the Northern line.

35mm, Sound, 80mins, Weintraub

YESTERDAY'S BRITAIN

Two British Transport Films including *A Day in the Peak District* (LMS 1935) and *Peak District* (BTF 1955)

VID, Sound, Part colour, 50mins, VID/BTF

YORK SIGNAL BOX (Britain 1961)

Made by P B Whitehouse and John Adams. A study of what was then a very modern, automated signalbox, controlling what had previously been done by 17 separate boxes.

16/8mm, Silent, 8mins, CV/NRM

YORKSHIRE STEAM (Britain 1985)

Yorkshire Television. Written and produced by Chris Sutton. Directed by Tony Bulley. Presented by Simon Welfare. This film combines the nostalgia of the pioneering days of steam railways in Yorkshire with some of the county's most picturesque scenery. The link is a trip behind LNER 'A1' 4-6-2 No 4472 *Flying Scotsman*. The train starts from York, calling at the Middleton Railway in Leeds and then thunders on through Bramhope Tunnel on the Leeds-Thirsk line to end the run at Harrogate. On the way, the film explores aspects of railway history, including the story of George Hudson, the 'Railway King' and the place of York in railway development.

16mm, Sound, Colour, 29mins, Yorkshire

🚂 🚂 🚂 🚂 🚂

YOUNG TOM EDISON (USA 1940)

MGM. Directed by Norman Taurog. With Mickey Rooney and Virginia Weidler. The early life of Thomas Edison, much of which takes place on an American railroad in California, including their Baldwin 2-8-0 locomotive No 29790, built in 1906 but modified with box headlight, cow catcher and large faked balloon smoke stack to look like a typical 4-4-0 of the period of the film. Use was also made of Caboose Car No 9 and the track from Oakdale via Warnerville to Hetch, Hetchy Halt and Keystone. A well edited scene shows Edison rescuing a small child from the path of a shunted box car.

35mm, Sound, 86mins, MGM

🚂

YOUNG WINSTON (Britain 1972)

Columbia. Produced by Carl Foreman. Directed by Richard Attenborough. With Simon Ward, Robert Shaw, Anne Bancroft, Jack Hawkins, John Mills and Anthony Hopkins. Early life of Winston Churchill, mainly in South Africa. The days of steam railways during the Boer War were recreated (sometimes with doubtful authenticity) on the Longmoor Military Railway, which technically had come to an end in 1969.

35mm, Sound, Colour, 157mins, Columbia/railway only: HA

🚂 🚂

YOU'RE TELLING ME (Britain 1941)

Paul Rotha productions for Ministry of Information. Irresponsible gossip

in wartime. Includes shot of GWR 'Castle' 4-6-0 No 5033 *Broughton Castle*.

35mm, Sound, 6mins, COI

🚂

YUGOSLAV NARROW GAUGE (Britain 1961)

Made by P B Woodhouse and John Adams. A most interesting film of the narrow gauge line from Sarajevo to Dubrovnik which has long since gone. The film makers were arrested as spies during the filming!

16/8mm, Silent, Colour, 18mins, CV/NRM

🚂 🚂 🚂 🚂 🚂

Z

ZAMBIA TO MANCHESTER (Britain 1979)

David Shepherd film. A record of the moving of a steam locomotive from Zambia and its shipment to Britain as part of David Shepherd's collection.

16mm, Silent, 55mins, Shepherd

🚂 🚂 🚂

ZAZIE DANS LE METRO (France 1960)

Nouvelles Editions. Directed by Louis Malle. With Catherine Demongrot, Philippe Noiret and Vittorio Caprioli. An adventurous little girl has a day out in Paris. She pays a visit to the Paris Metro, which uses quite extensive coverage of the actual railway.

35mm, Sound, Colour, 88 mins, NFA

🚂 🚂

'Mr Arnott of Waverley station
Has a very strong sense of
occasion
When the train's a non-stopper
His topper is proper.'
A scene from 'Elizabethan
Express' a British Transport Film.
British Railways

600

RA 9